# Running

Microsoft
# Windows 2000
## Professional

Built on NT Technology

Craig Stinson and Carl Siechert

PUBLISHED BY
Microsoft Press
A Division of Microsoft Corporation
One Microsoft Way
Redmond, Washington 98052-6399

Library of Congress Cataloging-in-Publication Data
Stinson, Craig, 1943-
    Running Microsoft Windows 2000 Professional / Craig Stinson, Carl Siechert.
       p. cm.
    Includes index.
    ISBN 1-57231-838-4
    1. Microsoft Windows (Computer file)   2. Operating systems (Computers)   I. Siechert,
Carl.  II. Title.

    QA76.76.O63 S755553   1999
    005.4'4769--dc21                             99-045520

Printed and bound in the United States of America.

1 2 3 4 5 6 7 8 9   QMQM   5 4 3 2 1 0

Distributed in Canada by Penguin Books Canada Limited.

A CIP catalogue record for this book is available from the British Library.

Microsoft Press books are available through booksellers and distributors worldwide. For further information about international editions, contact your local Microsoft Corporation office or contact Microsoft Press International directly at fax (425) 936-7329. Visit our Web site at mspress.microsoft.com.

**Acquisitions Editor:** Christey Bahn
**Project Editor:** Sandra Haynes
**Manuscript and Technical Editing:** Publishing.com

*Dedicated to the concept of freedom—and to
living in a country where coauthors can have
differing ideas of what that means.*

# Chapters at a Glance

## Appendixes  For Newcomers to Windows    805

## Index    863

# Table of Contents

# Acknowledgments

The development of a book like this typically goes through two phases. The first phase starts many months before the product we describe—in this case, Microsoft Windows 2000 Professional—is due to ship. Though the work is done at a relatively leisurely pace, it's a frustrating time because of the lack of accurate information, the uncertainty of schedules, the difficulty of getting motivated to work using information that is probably going to change later in the project—and the certainty that the second phase will come at the most inopportune time. The second phase, of course, is one of frenetic activity: furious rewriting and rechecking everything against the latest versions of the software, juggling tables of contents, and getting everything typeset and indexed in the shortest possible time.

Throughout both phases, we've been blessed with excellent support from our friends at Microsoft Press and Publishing.com. Acquisitions editor Christey Bahn and content manager Barbara Ellsworth got us started in the right directions. Project editor Sandra Haynes kept things on track and helped us keep pace with ever-changing schedules. Manuscript editor Chrisa Hotchkiss made sure that our subjects and verbs remained mutually agreeable. Page layout artist Lisa Bravo produced the attractive pages you are about to read, and proofreader Andrea Fox double-checked everyone's work, making sure the pages you read are free from errors. Project manager and technical editor Curt Philips admirably performed the awesome task of bringing it all together—and making sure it was right. They all gracefully tolerated the tirades of an imperious author (we won't say which one) and helped us put together a book we're proud of. For that we're grateful.

*C.S. and C.S.*

# PART I

# Introducing Windows 2000 Professional

## CHAPTER 1

# What's New in Windows 2000 Professional

S ince its first appearance in 1993, Windows NT has been Microsoft's industrial-strength operating system, the version of Windows preferred by developers, network administrators, many power users, and users running mission-critical applications. In return for enhanced reliability and security, however, Windows NT users have, until now, had to forego a certain degree of convenience and versatility. For example, because Windows NT 4 lacked support for the Plug and Play standard, many reasonably regarded it as less easy to use and administer than Windows 98. And because it supported a smaller range of multimedia hardware than Windows 98, it was perceived by many as the less exciting of Microsoft's two major operating systems.

All that changes with Windows 2000. Along with the radical name change, Microsoft has given its industrial-strength operating system a friendly user interface, the easy configurability of Windows 98, broader hardware support, superior performance, and much more. In short, Windows 2000 combines the excitement and usability of Windows 98 with the traditional strengths of Windows NT—stability and security.

This chapter provides a brief overview of the new features of Windows 2000, along with references to the chapters in which you can read a more detailed account.

# A Simpler User Interface

Windows 2000 incorporates major design changes that make the operating system easier to work with. Personalized menus reduce distraction on the Start menu. Customizable desktop toolbars and a standard folder for document storage allow users quicker access to the programs and documents they need most often. Other changes make it easier to set up network and Internet connections, install and configure printers, and use Windows on mobile computers.

## Personalized Menus

If you decide to use the optional personalized menus in Windows 2000, your Start menu displays only those items you use most frequently. The system continually monitors your menu choices, displaying the items you use and hiding those you don't. To get to a menu item that you haven't used in a while, you can either wait a moment or click an arrow at the bottom of the menu; in either case, the entire menu then unfolds. Personalized menus are discussed in Chapter 3, "Customizing the Start Menu."

Another handy improvement on the Start menu allows you to create expandable menu items for four system folders: Control Panel, My Documents, Network And Dial-Up Connections, and Printers. If you choose to make Control Panel expandable, for example, you can get to a particular section of Control Panel directly from the Start menu, without having to open the entire Control Panel folder first. These and other Start menu improvements are also discussed in Chapter 3.

## Customizable Desktop Toolbars

The Windows 2000 customizable desktop toolbars, like the system's improvements to the Start menu, are designed to provide easier access to the programs, folders, and documents that you need every day. You can add shortcuts to a toolbar by dragging them from the Start menu or another folder, and the toolbars themselves can either float anywhere on your desktop or be docked on the taskbar or any edge of your screen. Desktop toolbars are described in Chapter 4, "Customizing the Desktop."

# Easier Ways to Work with Documents

Windows 2000 provides a number of innovations that make it easier for you to open and save documents, to find documents whose storage location you have forgotten, and to locate documents on the basis of their contents.

## My Documents and My Pictures

Like Windows 98, Windows 2000 includes a system folder called My Documents, which resides on your desktop. Most of your applications will use My Documents as a default storage location for newly created files. Each user account on a computer gets its own My Documents folder, and if you're a roaming user who logs on to your account from a variety of different computers, you'll find that Windows 2000 always remembers where your own documents live. (If you don't like their current residence, you can easily change the physical location to which the My Documents folder is linked.)

Windows 2000 also includes a separate system folder called My Pictures, designed to be a default storage location for all types of image documents. If you enable Web content in your folders (an option provided by Windows Explorer), Windows 2000 supplies the My Pictures folder with a handy HTML template that includes an image previewer. The image previewer lets you see the images in the My Pictures folder without opening them in an application.

My Documents and My Pictures are described in Chapter 8, "Using Windows Explorer."

## My Network Places

Earlier versions of Windows included a system folder called Network Neighborhood that allowed you to browse the contents of network servers. Windows 2000 replaces this folder with one called My Network Places. The change has two principal benefits: It reduces distraction by removing from view (by default) servers that you seldom use. And it allows you to create shortcuts to frequently used destinations, which might be servers, shared folders, Web folders on the Internet or your company's intranet, or FTP sites. You can still browse your entire network in My Network Places, just as you could in Network Neighborhood, but My Network Places provides more direct access to the network sites you need the most. My Network Places is described in Chapter 9, "Using and Sharing Files on the Network."

### An Integrated Search Tool and Indexing Service

Searching for files on local and network storage media is easier in
Windows 2000, thanks to a search facility that is completely integrated
with Windows 2000. Clicking a Search button on Windows Explorer's
Standard Buttons toolbar opens a pane to the left of the current folder
display. Here you can type the specifications of the file or folder
you're looking for. From this search pane, you can also search for
computers on your network, people on the Internet or within your
organization, and Web pages. You access the new search facility
exactly like the corresponding feature in Microsoft Internet Explorer,
but if you're accustomed to using the Find command that is included
on the Start menu in earlier versions of Windows, you don't need to
change your habits. Search is available on the Start menu as well.

To help you find files on the basis of their content, Windows 2000
includes a powerful indexing service that operates in the background
while your computer is not otherwise occupied. Once you've created
an index, finding content on even a multigigabyte hard disk is a toler-
ably quick and painless task.

Chapter 11, "Searching for Files and Folders," describes the new search
facility and indexing service.

### Improved Dialog Boxes

The standard Open and Save As dialog boxes in Windows 2000 have
been enhanced by the addition of the places bar (a column of large
icons at the left side of the dialog box), which provides quick access
to your most recently used documents, the My Documents folder, the
Favorites folder, and My Network Places. Opening a document that's
not associated with an application (or opening it with an application
other than the one it's associated with) is easier now, thanks to a more
versatile Open With command. Once you've applied the Open With
command to a document type, the application you used to open that
document becomes available on the document's shortcut menu, in effect
allowing you to associate the document type with multiple applications.

## Easier Setup and Configuration

One of the most vital enhancements in Windows 2000 is support for
the Plug and Play standard. In most cases now, when you install a
new hardware device, the operating system automatically detects the
device, configures it, and installs the appropriate device drivers. The
Add/Remove Hardware Wizard, a component of Control Panel, is

available for those rare cases in which a device isn't correctly recognized and installed, such as older devices that don't have Plug and Play capability. Installing hardware in Windows 2000 is covered in Chapter 24, "Installing and Configuring Hardware."

Making network connections, configuring Internet service providers (ISPs), setting up virtual private networks (VPNs), setting up your system as a remote access server, and achieving direct-cable connections with other computers are all easier in Windows 2000, thanks to the new Network Connection Wizard. You can read about this wizard in Chapter 16, "Making Connections."

Further simplifying setup tasks, Windows 2000 includes an enhanced Add/Remove Programs Wizard and a sophisticated application installation and maintenance tool called Windows Installer. The refurbished wizard maintains statistics about how often you use the programs you've installed, so if and when you need to uninstall something to free up disk space, you'll know which programs you're not likely to miss. Windows Installer, if used in an Active Directory environment, allows administrators to assign or publish applications to users. Assigning and publishing are ways of making applications available to users so that they're installed automatically when they're needed. You can read more about these features in Chapter 15, "Installing and Removing Programs and System Components."

# Better Support for Mobile Computing

Support for the Advanced Configuration and Power Interface (ACPI) and an innovative offline-files feature make Windows 2000 Microsoft's strongest mobile-computing platform. ACPI provides greater control over power consumption, allowing you to extend your computer's battery life. (On systems without the requisite hardware for ACPI, Windows 2000 supports the older Advanced Power Management standard.)

Offline files, essentially a replacement for Briefcase in Windows NT, lets you work with local copies of network files and Web pages while you're disconnected from the network. (Briefcase is included in Windows 2000 because it's still useful under certain circumstances.) Synchronization Manager synchronizes changes made to the offline and online copies when you reconnect.

Power management is discussed in Chapter 26, "Power Management." And you can read more about using offline files and Synchronization Manager in Chapter 10, "Working Offline."

# Improved Support for Printers and Other Imaging Devices

A major printing innovation in Windows 2000 is support for the Internet Printing Protocol (IPP). With IPP, you can print to offsite printers via IP addresses. In addition to letting you take advantage of special service-bureau printing features that you might occasionally need, Internet printing provides a great alternative to fax and e-mail. Internet printing is discussed in Chapter 12, "Printing."

Windows 2000 also introduces support for the Imaging Color Management 2 (ICM) standard. ICM provides a communications link between the hardware devices and software programs that reproduce color. It maps colors between devices, ensuring that the original image colors are accurately interpreted by an input device (such as a scanner or digital camera), displayed on a monitor, and printed on paper or saved in electronic format. ICM is described in Chapter 6, "Making Other Customizations."

Additionally, Windows 2000 incorporates a scalable font technology called OpenType. OpenType, a superset of the TrueType technology included with Windows NT 4, handles both TrueType and Type 1 fonts (fonts designed for use with PostScript output devices) from a unified registry, allowing you to install a set of Type 1 fonts in Windows 2000 and then manage and use those Type 1 fonts the same way you manage and use the rest of your font library. Font support is described in Chapter 13, "Installing and Using Fonts."

# Faster Performance

Windows 2000 incorporates architectural changes that provide smoother multitasking and better support for large-memory and multiprocessor systems. Most users will see improved response times as a result of these changes.

In addition, the system now supports both the FAT32 file system that was popularized by Windows 98 and version 5 of the NTFS file system. (The older FAT16 file system is also supported.) FAT32 enables you to make more efficient use of large hard disks, while retaining full compatibility with Windows 98. NTFS offers numerous advantages, including advanced file security and the ability to automatically encrypt or compress individual files and folders.

As a further performance enhancement, Windows 2000 includes a disk defragmentation utility; it's no longer necessary to purchase a third-party tool for basic disk optimization. The defragmentation program, which you can use with FAT16 and FAT32 as well as NTFS volumes, reorganizes hard disk storage so that files reside on contiguous sectors, thereby improving file-access times.

Chapter 28, "Using NTFS Security," discusses file-system choices in Windows 2000, and Chapter 31, "Optimizing, Maintaining, and Troubleshooting," provides information about disk defragmentation.

## An Even More Stable Environment

Windows Installer, mentioned earlier in this chapter, not only makes it easier for system administrators to install applications on users' desktops, but it also makes Windows 2000 a more stable operating environment. Installer keeps track of dependencies among application and system components. If a critical component of an application or system utility becomes damaged, Windows Installer automatically repairs that component when you attempt to run the application or utility in question.

The stability of Windows 2000 is also enhanced via *device-driver signing*. Microsoft adds an encoded digital signature to every driver shipped with the operating system. The digital signature assures you that the driver has passed Microsoft's quality-control tests and has not been altered since it was tested. Some driver vendors might not digitally sign their drivers, but you can set up Windows 2000 to accept only signed drivers or to warn you if you're about to install an unsigned driver.

## Support for New Hardware Standards

In addition to the implementation of the ACPI power-management standard, Windows 2000 supports a variety of important new hardware standards, including:

- Universal serial bus (USB)
- IEEE 1394 (Firewire)
- DVD
- Zip drives

The operating system includes an elegant DVD player, allowing you to play back high-quality movies on your computer screen. You can read about the DVD player in Chapter 36, "Using the Multimedia Accessories."

# An Enhanced Gaming Environment

Finally, for the benefit of those who use their computers for diversion as well as business, Windows 2000 brings robust gaming and multimedia support to the Windows NT platform. The operating system's support for *DirectX*—a set of application programming interfaces (APIs) that enable faster communication between programs and hardware devices—means that Windows 2000 can run many high-performance games just as nimbly as Windows 98. And, like Windows 98, Windows 2000 allows you to divide your display across multiple monitors, giving you virtually unlimited screen space. You can read about the use of multiple displays in Chapter 4, "Customizing the Desktop."

Initially, fewer games might be available for Windows 2000 than for Windows 98, but you can expect to see a steady increase in their numbers. With Windows 2000, the NT platform is at last a place for play as well as work.

**CHAPTER 2**

# Upgrading to Windows 2000

I f you're moving from Microsoft Windows NT 4 to Windows 2000, you'll find that a number of familiar features have either been renamed or have been moved to new locations in Windows 2000. You'll also find that certain other aspects of the operating system have been either replaced or thoroughly revamped. The functionality served by My Briefcase in Windows NT 4, for example, has been largely supplanted by a new offline files feature in Windows 2000, and Windows 2000 Phone Dialer is a completely new application.

If you're upgrading from Windows 98 instead of Windows NT 4, you'll have somewhat less to relearn about the user interface. You'll already know all about the My Documents folder, for example. But some familiar tools will appear in new locations or under new names. And, of course, there will be new points to learn about the Windows 2000 user accounts and security requirements.

In this chapter, we'll enumerate some of the novelties that await you as an upgrader and point you to relevant chapters in the book.

# Renamed or Relocated Features

The following is an alphabetic list of features that have been either renamed or relocated in Windows 2000.

### Character Map (Chapter 13)

The Character Map utility appears in a new location. Open the Start menu and choose Programs, Accessories, System Tools, Character Map.

### Devices (Chapter 25)

Devices in Windows NT 4 (in Control Panel) has been replaced by Device Manager, a tool comparable to Device Manager in Windows 98. To get to Device Manager, open the Start menu, and then choose Settings, Control Panel, System. Click the Hardware tab, and then click Device Manager. Alternatively, right-click My Computer on your desktop and choose Manage from the shortcut menu. In the left pane of Computer Management, select Device Manager.

### Dial-Up Networking (Chapter 16)

The Dial-Up Networking folder in Windows NT 4 and Windows 98 is gone in Windows 2000. In its place is the Network And Dial-Up Connections folder. To get there, open the Start menu and choose Settings, Network And Dial-Up Connections.

### Favorites (Chapter 3)

The Favorites submenu doesn't appear on the Start menu by default. To add it to the Start menu, open the Start menu and choose Settings, Taskbar & Start Menu. Click the Advanced tab, and then select Display Favorites in the Start Menu Settings list.

### Find (Chapter 11)

The Find command in Windows NT 4 and Windows 98 has been renamed Search in Windows 2000. You can get to it from the Standard Buttons toolbar in Windows Explorer, as well as from the Start menu.

### Log Off (Chapter 3)

The Log Off command doesn't appear on the Start menu by default. To make it appear, open the Start menu and choose Settings, Taskbar & Start Menu. Click the Advanced tab, and then select Display Logoff from the Start Menu Settings list.

### Media Player (Chapter 36)

Media Player has been renamed Windows Media Player and moved to a new menu location. You'll find it by opening the Start menu and choosing Programs, Accessories, Entertainment.

### Modems (Chapter 24)

Modems in Windows NT 4 and Windows 98 Control Panel has a new name. In Windows 2000, it's called Phone And Modem Options—but it's still in Control Panel.

### Multimedia (Chapter 24)

Multimedia in Control Panel has also been renamed—to Sounds And Multimedia.

### Network Neighborhood (Chapter 9)

The former Network Neighborhood is called My Network Places in Windows 2000. As Chapter 9 describes, this network-browsing folder has been redesigned so that you can more easily see just the network objects you commonly use.

### Network Settings (Chapters 16 and 25)

The functionality of Network in Windows NT 4 and Windows 98 Control Panel has been distributed to several components of the Windows 2000 user interface. To configure network adapters, use Device Manager. (See Devices, earlier in this chapter.) To set up network bindings, protocols, and services, use the Network And Dial-Up Connections folder. (Open the Start menu, and choose Settings, Network And Dial-Up Connections.) To change your network identification (the name by which your computer is known to other computers on the network), open the Start menu and choose Settings, Control Panel, System. Then click the Network Identification tab.

### Passwords (Chapter 27)

Windows 2000 Control Panel doesn't include a Passwords program. To change your own password, press Ctrl+Alt+Delete. Then click Change Password. (Users And Passwords in Control Panel allows only members of the Administrator group to change passwords.)

### Power Management (Chapter 26)

Power Management in Windows NT 4 and Windows 98 Control Panel has been renamed Power Options in the Windows 2000 Control Panel.

### Printers Folder (Chapter 12)

To open the Printers folder in Windows 2000, open the Start menu and choose Settings, Printers.

### Regional Settings (Chapter 6)

Regional Settings in Windows NT 4 and Windows 98 Control Panel has been renamed Regional Options.

### Sound Recorder (Chapter 36)

In Windows 2000, the Sound Recorder program can be found on the Entertainment menu. Open the Start menu and choose Programs, Accessories, Entertainment.

### Sounds (Chapter 6)

Sounds in Windows NT 4 and Windows 98 Control Panel has been renamed Sounds And Multimedia.

### Taskbar (Chapter 4)

To customize the taskbar in Windows 2000, open the Start menu and choose Settings, Taskbar & Start Menu.

### User Manager (Chapter 27)

The functionality of User Manager in Windows NT 4 can be found under Local Users And Groups in Windows 2000. To get there, right-click My Computer and choose Manage from the shortcut menu. In the left pane of Computer Management, select Local Users And Groups.

### Users (Chapter 27)

Users in Windows NT 4 Control Panel has been renamed Users And Passwords in Windows 2000.

### Volume Control (Chapters 6 and 36)

In Windows 2000, you'll find Volume Control on the Entertainment menu. Open the Start menu and choose Programs, Accessories, Entertainment.

### Windows Explorer (Chapters 5 and 8)

Windows Explorer is located on the Accessories menu in Windows 2000. Open the Start menu and choose Programs, Accessories.

# New Features

The following is an alphabetical list of new or thoroughly revamped features in Windows 2000.

### Adding and Removing Hardware (Chapter 24)

Adding and removing hardware is easy in Windows 2000, thanks to Plug and Play and the new Add/Remove Hardware Wizard. You'll find the wizard in Control Panel. Open the Start menu and choose Settings, Control Panel, Add/Remove Hardware.

### CD Player and DVD Player (Chapter 36)

Windows 2000 includes the refurbished CD Player that was introduced with Windows 98 Second Edition, as well as DVD Player. You'll find both on the Entertainment menu. Open the Start menu and choose Programs, Accessories, Entertainment.

### DriveSpace Agent (Chapter 31)

Windows 2000 doesn't support DriveSpace or third-party disk compression programs. You can compress files and folders on NTFS volumes by means of their properties dialog boxes.

### Inbox (Chapter 19)

The Windows Messaging component of Windows NT has been completely replaced by Microsoft Outlook Express—hence, you'll find no Inbox on your desktop. Outlook Express is both an e-mail client program and an Internet newsgroup reader.

### My Briefcase (Chapter 10)

My Briefcase has been renamed Briefcase, but it's also been largely supplanted by the Windows 2000 new offline files capability.

### Phone Dialer (Chapter 22)

Windows 2000 has a completely new Phone Dialer program. To run it, open the Start menu and choose Programs, Accessories, Communications, Phone Dialer.

### Scheduled Tasks (Chapter 14)

To create, edit, or delete a scheduled task in Windows 2000, open Control Panel and choose Scheduled Tasks.

# If You're Upgrading from Windows 9x

If you're a Windows 95 or 98 veteran but Windows 2000 is your first venture onto the NT platform, you might want to start by familiarizing yourself with the system's log-on and log-off procedures (see Appendix B, "Logging On and Logging Off"). A good next stop on your orientation would be Chapter 28, "Using NTFS Security," which explains the file-system choices available to you in Windows 2000 and the special advantages conferred by the NTFS file system.

Finally, whether or not you're responsible for setting up user accounts and security parameters, you should understand how these matters are handled in Windows 2000. You'll find relevant material in Chapter 27, "Implementing Windows 2000 Security."

# PART II

# Customizing the Environment

**CHAPTER 3**

# Customizing
# the Start Menu

It all begins (and ends, as some wags are fond of pointing out) with the Start menu, which provides access to nearly everything you need to do in Microsoft Windows 2000. This invaluable command post pops up at a single click or keystroke. (On newer keyboards, press the Windows logo key; or on any keyboard, press Ctrl+Esc.) By using the Start menu, you can run programs, reopen recently used documents, visit favorite sites on the Internet, and more. In this chapter, we'll look at the various ways you can tailor the Start menu to your own needs.

If you're new to Windows (or your prior experience is with version 3.*x*), you might not be familiar with the layout and use of the Start menu, a concept first seen in Windows 95 and Windows NT version 4. Even if you've used recent versions of Windows—including Windows 98—you'll find new customization features for the Start menu in Windows 2000.

# Changing the Overall Appearance of the Start Menu

**? SEE ALSO**

For more information, see "The Start Button and Start Menu," page 835.

The left side of Figure 3-1 shows the Start menu in its default state, with large icons next to menu items and a Windows 2000 banner running up the left side of the menu. The right side of Figure 3-1 shows the same menu in an optional, more compact presentation. The icons have been reduced in size and the banner has been removed. This small-icon version of the menu is particularly useful if you have a lot of commands at the top of your Start menu—so many that the menu is threatening to become taller than your screen.

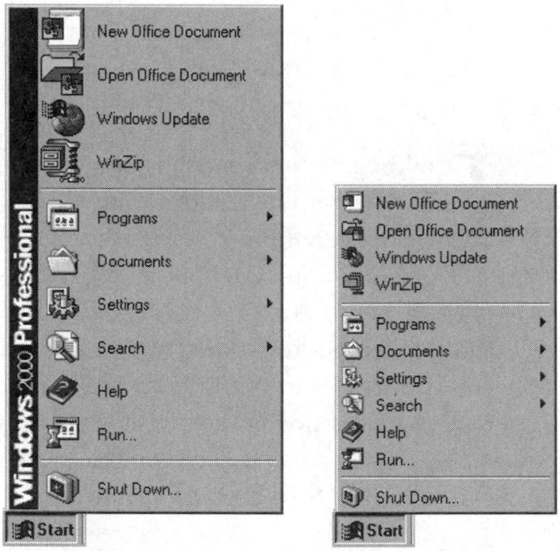

**FIGURE 3-1.**

The small-icon version of the Start menu (right) helps keep the menu from over-crowding your screen.

To switch to a small-icon Start menu:

1 Click the Start button, point to Settings, and choose Taskbar & Start Menu.

2 In the Taskbar And Start Menu Properties dialog box, select the Show Small Icons In Start Menu check box.

**TIP**

Another route to the Taskbar And Start Menu Properties dialog box is to right-click an unoccupied area of the taskbar and choose Properties from the short-cut menu.

The menus that cascade from the Start menu, such as the Programs menu or the Settings menu, are always displayed in small-icon view, and there's no option to display them with large icons. Presumably, Windows doesn't give you a choice about these submenus because some of them—Programs, in particular—grow to large proportions on many users' systems.

One other setting affects the appearance of your Start menu, however: the Menu setting. It's located on the Appearance tab in the Display Properties dialog box, shown in Figure 3-2.

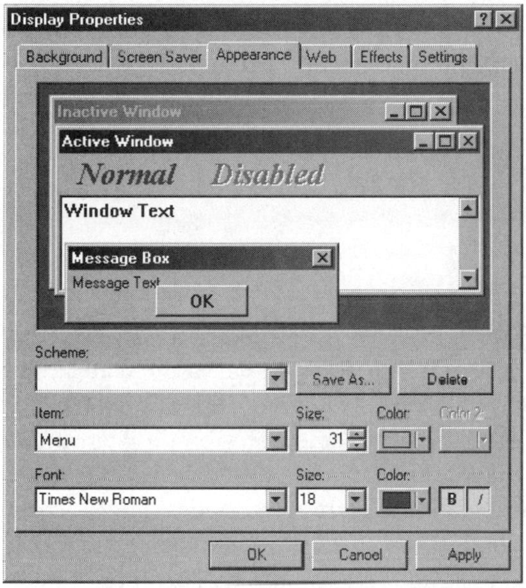

**FIGURE 3-2.**

If you want your Start menu items displayed in 18-point red Times New Roman bold italic, you can make that choice in the Display Properties dialog box. Be aware, though, that your decision here affects all menus, not just the Start menu.

To adjust the font, font size, color, style (bold, italic, bold italic, or normal), and height of *all* menus in Windows:

**1** Right-click your desktop and choose Properties from the shortcut menu.

The Display Properties dialog box appears.

**2** Click the Appearance tab.

**3** Select Menu from the Item list.

**SEE ALSO**

For more information about setting display properties, see "Changing Colors, Fonts, and Sizes," page 63.

**4** Make settings in the Font, Size, and Color boxes. You set the size and color of the font in the lower Size box and Color box, and you set the height of the menu bar and its background color in the upper Size box and Color box.

You can also change the appearance of your menus by switching from one appearance scheme to another in the Display Properties dialog box—for example, from Windows Standard to High Contrast #2 (extra large).

# Customizing the Programs Menu, the Top of the Start Menu, and the Favorites Menu

Much of the Start menu is customizable. If you don't like the arrangement of your Programs submenu, for example, you can rearrange it. If items at the top of your Start menu are getting in your way, you can delete them or put them somewhere within the Programs submenu. You can reorganize the contents of your Favorites submenu, move Favorites items onto other parts of the Start menu, or hide the Favorites submenu altogether.

> **NOTE**
>
> By default, the Start menu doesn't include a Favorites submenu. *For information about displaying Favorites, see "Displaying Optional Start Menu Items," page 31.*

## Adding an Item to the Menu

The easiest way to add an item to the Start menu is to drag it there. If you have a shortcut on your desktop, for example, that you would also like to appear somewhere on the Start menu, simply click it, hold down the mouse button, and move your mouse pointer to the Start button. When the Start menu opens, after a moment's delay, you can drag the desktop shortcut to the top of the menu or to some other location within the Programs or Favorites menus. As you move the mouse, a dark line shows where the new item will appear when you release the button.

> **NOTE**
>
> If you drag a shortcut to the Start button and release the mouse button before the Start menu opens, the new item will appear at the top of the menu.

You can use the same technique to drag items from Windows Explorer windows to the Start menu. Windows leaves the dragged item where you got it and plants a copy on the Start menu. If the dragged item isn't a shortcut to begin with, Windows creates a shortcut to it on the Start menu. Thus, for example, you can drag a folder to the Start menu without changing the folder structure of your disk in any way; Windows simply creates a pointer (a shortcut) to the folder on the menu.

If you're not sure how to get to a Windows Explorer window that displays the item you want on the Start menu, you can use the Search

**? SEE ALSO**

For more information about the Search command, see Chapter 11, "Searching for Files and Folders".

command to locate it—and then drag the item from the Search Results window to the menu. For example, suppose you want to put Notepad at the top of your Start menu, but you're not quite sure where Notepad lives. Open the Start menu, point to Search, and click For Files Or Folders. Tell Search to find Notepad, and when Notepad.exe appears in the Search Results pane, simply drag it to the Start button.

Similarly, you can drag a link from the Microsoft Internet Explorer window to the Start menu. To add to the Start menu an item that opens the currently displayed page, drag the icon at the left end of the Internet Explorer Address bar to the Start button. To add an item that opens one of the page's other link targets, drag the link to the Start button. See Figure 3-3.

**FIGURE 3-3.**

In addition to dragging shortcuts from Windows Explorer to the Start menu, you can drag links from Internet Explorer.

Drag this icon to add a shortcut to the currently displayed page.

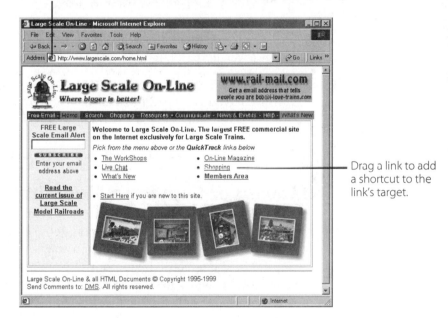

Drag a link to add a shortcut to the link's target.

In case you want to work a little harder than this, the following method is also available:

**1** Click the Start button, point to Settings, and choose Taskbar & Start Menu.

**2** In the Taskbar And Start Menu Properties dialog box, click the Advanced tab.

**3** Click the Add button.

**II**

Customizing the Environment

4 Type the path of the item you want to add to the menu, or use the Browse button to navigate to it. Then click Next.

5 Use the Select Program Folder dialog box to tell Windows where it should install the new item. Click Next.

6 Give the item a name, and then click Finish.

## Removing an Item from the Menu

To remove an item from the top of the Start menu or any part of the Programs, Favorites, or Documents submenus:

1 Click the Start button, and then release the mouse button.

2 Move the mouse pointer to the item you want to delete.

3 Right-click the item you want to delete.

4 Choose Delete from the shortcut menu.

5 Click Yes in the Confirm File Delete dialog box to send the item to the Recycle Bin.

Alternatively, you can open the Start menu, point to Settings, and click Taskbar & Start Menu. Click the Advanced tab, click Remove, and then choose what you want to remove. (This method lets you remove items only from the top of the Start menu and the Programs submenu.)

## Moving or Copying a Menu Item

To move an item from one part of the Start menu to another, simply grab it and drag it. Click the Start button, release the mouse button, move the mouse pointer to the item you want to move, and then click again and hold the mouse button down. Now move the mouse in the direction of the item's new destination. As you do, Windows draws a thick line to show where the item will land if you release the mouse button.

To copy an item to a new location, follow the same steps as for moving, but hold down the Ctrl key while you drag. A plus sign (+) next to the mouse pointer confirms that you're copying, not moving. Release the mouse button first, and then release the Ctrl key.

**? SEE ALSO**

For information about toolbars, see "Using Desktop Toolbars," page 50.

The drag-and-drop techniques that let you rearrange menu items also work for moving and copying items to off-menu locations. Thus, for example, if your menu gets crowded, you can move some items from the menu to your desktop, to a toolbar, or to a folder. In all cases, Windows creates a shortcut in the new location.

**NOTE**

> Be aware that if you move or copy a program name or folder from one part of
> the Start menu to another and subsequently uninstall that program, the unin-
> stall procedure might not be able to remove the item or folder from your Start
> menu. You might need to clean up the Start menu yourself after uninstalling.

## Sorting Menu Items

Windows lets you move or copy menu items to any location at the top
of the Start menu, on the Programs submenu, or on the Favorites
submenu, as described in the previous section. While this allows you
to place them in any order that suits you, if you prefer to revert to a
more orderly approach, you can ask Windows to re-sort a single
submenu or all submenus in its default order: folders in alphabetical
order, followed by menu items in alphabetical order.

To sort a single submenu:

**1** Click the Start button, and then release the mouse button.

**2** Move the mouse pointer to the submenu you want to sort.

**3** Right-click an item on the submenu, and choose Sort By Name
from the shortcut menu.

To sort all submenus within the Programs submenu:

**1** Click the Start button, point to Settings, and choose Taskbar &
Start Menu.

**2** Click the Advanced tab.

**3** Click Re-sort.

## Renaming a Menu Item

One gripe that many users had with earlier versions of Windows is
that it wasn't easy to rename an item on the Start menu. In Windows
2000 it is, thanks to an additional shortcut menu command. To rename
a menu item:

**1** Click the Start button, and then release the mouse button.

**2** Move the mouse pointer to the item you want to rename.

**3** Right-click the menu item you want to rename, and choose
Rename from the shortcut menu.

II

Customizing the Environment

**Rename**

New name: | sacbee Voices - Peter H. King

OK    Cancel

**4**  Edit the name (or type a new one), and click OK.

# Changing Shortcut Properties

**?  SEE ALSO**

For more information
about working with
shortcuts, see "Adding
Shortcuts to Your
Desktop," page 54, and
"Working with Folders,
Files, and Shortcuts,"
page 151. For informa-
tion about the loca-
tion of Start menu
items, see "Taking
Advantage of User
Profiles," page 33.

Items at the top of the Start menu, on the Programs submenu, and on
the Favorites submenu are ordinary shortcuts—just like the ones you'll
find on the desktop or in folders. In fact, it's only a shortcut file's location in your computer's folder hierarchy that causes it to appear on the
Start menu. Like other shortcuts, menu items have several properties
you might want to modify.

To view a menu item's properties:

**1**  Click the Start button, and then release the mouse button.

**2**  Move the mouse pointer to the item you're interested in.

**3**  Right-click the menu item, and choose Properties from the shortcut menu.

**4**  In the dialog box that appears, click the Shortcut tab.
(See Figure 3-4.)

**FIGURE 3-4.**

With this dialog box,
you can set a variety
of properties for a
Start menu item,
including its shortcut
key and the type of
window the item
should open.

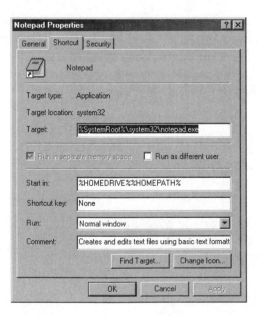

Notepad Properties

General | Shortcut | Security |

Notepad

Target type:    Application

Target location: system32

Target:    %SystemRoot%\system32\notepad.exe

☑ Run in separate memory space    ☐ Run as different user

Start in:    %HOMEDRIVE%%HOMEPATH%

Shortcut key:    None

Run:    Normal window

Comment:    Creates and edits text files using basic text formatt

Find Target...    Change Icon...

OK    Cancel    Apply

> **NOTE**

If the menu item you select is a shortcut to a Web site or Web page, you'll see a different dialog box. The properties you can change for a Web-site item are few, but for a Web page, you can assign a shortcut key or change the icon, as described in the following sections.

## Assigning a Shortcut Key

Shortcut keys are keystroke combinations that provide alternative ways to issue menu commands. For example, if you assign the shortcut Ctrl+Alt+N to the Notepad program, you can then launch Notepad by typing Ctrl+Alt+N, as an alternative to opening the Start menu, pointing to Programs, pointing to Accessories, and then locating the Notepad item on the Accessories menu.

To assign a shortcut key to an item, click the Shortcut Key box in the dialog box shown in Figure 3-4, and then press the keystroke combination you want to use. You can use any key except for Backspace, Esc, Enter, Print Screen, Spacebar, and Tab. Most keys must be combined with any combination of Ctrl, Alt, and Shift. (Letters, numbers, function keys, and other keys each have different restrictions, but the dialog box won't allow you to make an illegal shortcut key.)

> **NOTE**

Shortcut keys assigned to menu items (or to shortcuts elsewhere on your system) take precedence over any shortcut keys used by programs. For example, all Windows-based programs use Alt+F4 as a shortcut for their Exit command. If you happen to assign Alt+F4 as a shortcut for launching Notepad, you will no longer be able to quit programs by pressing this combination. Instead, no matter where you are, pressing Alt+F4 will get you another copy of Notepad. Keep this in mind as you assign shortcuts.

## Specifying the Type of Window a Menu Item Opens

The Run box in the dialog box shown in Figure 3-4 lets you indicate what kind of a window you want your menu item to open—a maximized window, a "normal" window (one that's open but not maximized), or a minimized window. To specify a window type, simply select it from the list.

## Creating a ScreenTip

If you hover the mouse pointer over a Start menu item for a few seconds, a ScreenTip appears. A *ScreenTip* is a pop-up message that explains what the menu item does. To change the ScreenTip text for any item, edit the text in the Comment box of the item's properties dialog box, shown in Figure 3-4.

## Changing a Menu Item's Icon

You can change the icons associated with programs and documents (but not folders) on the Start menu. To change an item's icon, click the Change Icon button in the item's properties dialog box, shown in Figure 3-4. A Change Icon dialog box appears and displays all the icons available for the selected item. Select the new icon you want, and then click OK twice to confirm your choice and close the properties dialog box.

If you don't find an icon you like, you can specify a different filename in the File Name box of the dialog box shown in Figure 3-5. Or you can click the Browse button and navigate to a different file. Icons are stored in files with extensions .exe, .dll, .ico, or .icl. One excellent source of icons is the file %SystemRoot%\System32\Shell32.dll, as shown in Figure 3-5.

**FIGURE 3-5.**
The Change Icon dialog box initially presents all the icons that are stored in the icon file to which your menu item points.

**NOTE**

The environment variable %SystemRoot% contains the actual path to your Windows 2000 folder. On most systems, that path is C:\Winnt. When you specify the variable, Windows goes to the right place even on systems that are set up differently. You can type environment variables almost any place where you can type an actual path, such as in Windows Explorer's Address bar.

## Using Personalized Menus

With personalized menus, Windows displays the menu items you use most frequently and hides the others. This reduces clutter and leads to shorter menus, which are easier to scan and use. A double arrow at the bottom of a submenu indicates the seldom-used items. To display these items, click the double arrow. Or if you simply wait a few seconds, Windows senses your momentary confusion and expands the menus, as shown in Figure 3-6. The newly visible items appear on a light-colored background so that they're easier to spot.

**FIGURE 3-6.**

Personalized menus hide seldom-used menu items.

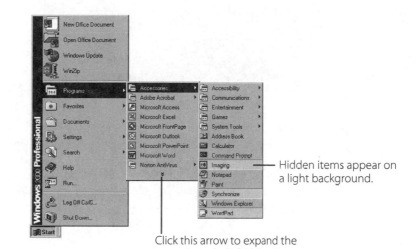

Hidden items appear on a light background.

Click this arrow to expand the menu to include hidden items.

Some will love personalized menus and others will loathe this feature. Fortunately, Windows gives you a choice. To enable or disable personalized menus:

**1** Click the Start button, point to Settings, and choose Taskbar & Start Menu.

**2** In the Taskbar And Start Menu Properties dialog box, select or clear the Use Personalized Menus check box. (See Figure 3-7, on the next page.)

> **NOTE**
>
> The personalized menu setting in the Taskbar And Start Menu Properties dialog box affects only the Start menu. To enable or disable personalized menus in other programs that use them, such as Internet Explorer or Microsoft Office 2000, set the option within that program.

Customizing the Environment

**FIGURE 3-7.**

The General tab contains a check box for turning personalized menus on and off.

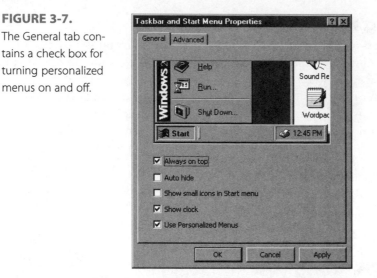

 **TIP**

Windows 2000 has another trick for dealing with an overgrown Programs menu. If your Programs menu is too tall for your screen, Windows normally displays it in multiple columns, which can quickly outgrow the screen's width. For a cleaner alternative, click the Advanced tab and select Scroll The Programs Menu in the Start Menu Settings box. This option appends an arrow at the top or bottom of a menu if it won't fit vertically; point to the arrow to scroll the menu in that direction.

# Removing Items from the Documents Menu

The Documents menu contains a shortcut to your My Documents folder, as well as shortcuts to 15 of your most recently used documents. You can prune individual items from the Documents menu in the same way that you remove items from other parts of the Start menu: right-click an item and choose Delete from the shortcut menu.

**SEE ALSO**

For information about the location of Start menu items, see "Taking Advantage of User Profiles," page 33.

Notice when you remove an item in this way, however, that the Documents menu still contains 15 items! (This is true only if you've opened more than 15 documents since you started using your computer or since you last cleared the Documents menu.) That's because the Documents menu reflects the contents of a hidden folder called Recent, which is stored as part of your user profile. Windows keeps shortcuts to all recently used documents in the Recent folder but displays only the most recent 15 on the Documents menu.

To clear the whole menu, including the backup supply of shortcuts:

**1** Click the Start button, point to Settings, and choose Taskbar & Start Menu.

**2** In the Taskbar And Start Menu Properties dialog box, click the Advanced tab.

**3** Click the Clear button.

Note that you can't add items to the Documents menu by making direct additions to the Recent folder. For the purposes of building this menu, Windows simply ignores anything in the Recent folder that it didn't put there itself. When you use the Clear command, however, *everything* in the Recent folder is deleted, no matter how it got there.

# Displaying Optional Start Menu Items

The Start menu can display two additional submenus and one additional command that are initially turned off to create a simpler and more compact menu. Use the following check boxes in the Start Menu Settings box to display or hide each of these items. (See Figure 3-8, on the next page.)

**? SEE ALSO**

For information about using Favorites in Internet Explorer, see "Keeping Track of Your Favorite Pages," page 334.

■ **Display Favorites.** Adds a submenu that presents the contents of a folder called Favorites, which is stored as part of your user profile. In addition to Internet shortcuts, you can store documents and other shortcuts in the Favorites folder, which makes it easy to return to those items. Contents of the Favorites folder are also available in Windows Explorer and Internet Explorer (on the Favorites menu and in the Favorites bar), so if you prefer to return to Favorites from those venues, you might not want the additional clutter on the Start menu.

■ **Display Administrative Tools.** Adds a submenu within the Programs menu that contains items for monitoring and controlling your computer. If you choose not to include this submenu on your Start menu, you can still reach these items by opening Administrative Tools in Control Panel.

■ **Display Logoff.** Adds a command (Log Off *username*) immediately above the Shut Down command. This doesn't save any clicks or keystrokes; whether you log off with the Log Off command or the Shut Down command, you must still confirm your intention with a click in the next dialog box that appears.

Perhaps the greatest value in adding this command to your Start menu is that you can see at a glance which user is logged on—which might be useful if you log on using different user accounts at different times.

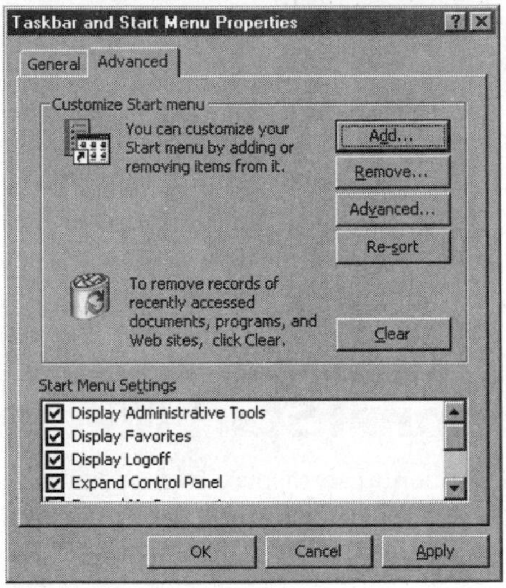

**FIGURE 3-8.**
The Start Menu Settings box contains check boxes for a variety of options that are new to Windows 2000.

## Using Cascading Menus

You can't use Windows long without seeing *cascading menus*—menus that sprout from one side of a menu item. A triangle at the right side of a menu item indicates a cascading menu, and if you point to an item that has a cascading menu, the submenu appears. The Start menu's Programs and Favorites submenus have always used cascading menus, but implementing them elsewhere was difficult (or impossible) in earlier versions of Windows. (One of the most widely used tips for Windows 95 was to create a "trick" folder—with a lengthy string of numbers and odd punctuation for its name—that resulted in a cascading Control Panel or Printers folder.)

With Windows 2000, it's easy to create a cascading Control Panel menu, a cascading My Documents menu on the Documents submenu, a cascading Network And Dial-Up Connections menu, or a cascading Printers menu on the Settings submenu. Figure 3-9 shows a cascading Printers menu, which allows you to open a printer queue directly instead of first opening the Printers folder.

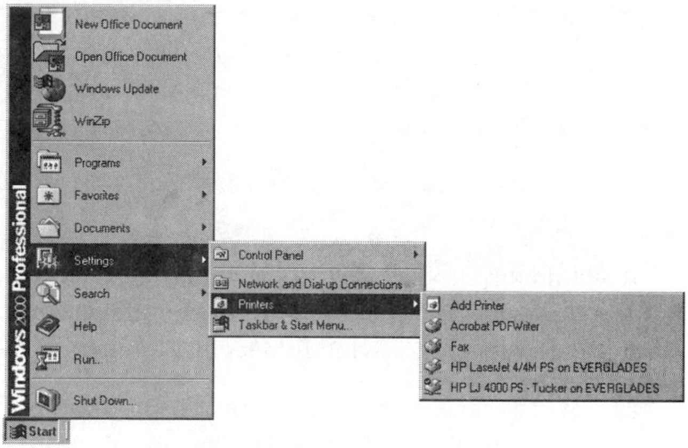

**FIGURE 3-9.**
Cascading menus allow you to open items directly instead of first opening their containing folder.

To create a cascading menu:

**1** Click the Start button, point to Settings, and choose Taskbar & Start Menu.

**2** In the Taskbar And Start Menu Properties dialog box, click the Advanced tab. (See Figure 3-8.)

**3** Select the check box for Expand Control Panel, Expand My Documents, Expand Network And Dial-Up Connections, or Expand Printers.

⭐ **TIP**

If you use cascading menus, clicking the name of a containing folder (such as Control Panel or Printers) no longer opens that folder; instead, Windows waits for you to click an item within the folder. If you want to open the folder, however, you still can: right-click the folder name and choose Open (or Explore) from the shortcut menu.

# Taking Advantage of User Profiles

If you share your computer with other users—other members of your family, for example, or colleagues at the office—you'll appreciate user profiles, which allow multiple users to share a Windows system and maintain their own preferences. Among those preferences, user profiles ensure that the Start menu is uniquely your own. Your user profile might be stored in one of three places:

■ If Windows 2000 was installed on a clean system, local user profiles are stored in the Documents And Settings folder on the same drive as your Windows system files.

II

Customizing the Environment

■ If you upgraded from an earlier version of Windows or Windows NT (and you used profiles in that version), local user profiles are stored in the Profiles folder within your Windows (or Winnt) folder.

■ If you use roaming user profiles, your profiles are also stored on a server.

Within the profiles folder, you'll find a folder for each user name that has logged on to the system. Among the folders within each user's folder are the following folders that appear on the Start menu:

■ The Start Menu folder contains all the program-launching material—the top of the Start menu and the various submenus within the Programs menu.

■ The Favorites folder contains the shortcuts that appear on the Favorites menu.

■ The My Documents folder and the Recent folder, which is hidden, contain the shortcuts that appear on the Documents menu.

You can get to the folders that generate the top and Programs components of your Start menu by simply right-clicking the Start button and choosing either Open or Explore. As Figure 3-10 shows, an Explorer window will appear, displaying shortcuts for each item at the top of your Start menu as well as a folder icon labeled Programs.

**FIGURE 3-10.**

Right-clicking the Start button and choosing Explore produces an Explorer window displaying a Programs folder and shortcuts for each item at the top of the Start menu.

The All Users profile contains items that appear on everyone's Start menu.

Note that each user's Start menu contains all of the items from the All Users profile as well as from his or her own profile. In earlier versions of Windows NT, these were called "common" program items, and they were separated from "personal" items (the ones in the user's individual profile). Windows 2000 combines the shortcuts from both areas before presenting them to you on the Start menu.

If you right-click a folder that contains items from the All Users profile and your own, you'll see that the shortcut menu has two additional commands: Open All Users and Explore All Users. These commands display the items from the All Users profile in an Explorer window.

# Customizing the Desktop

The *desktop* is the backdrop to everything you do in Microsoft Windows. It's the surface on which you run programs, a place where you can store documents and shortcuts, and, potentially, a kind of menu from which you can launch programs, open documents, and visit Web sites.

When you first install Windows, the Setup program provides a standard configuration for your desktop. You get a decent color arrangement, a serviceable screen resolution, appropriately sized buttons and icons, and so on. But because one size does not fit all, Windows gives you many choices about the appearance and behavior of your desktop. We'll explore those choices in this chapter.

# Maintaining Individual Settings with User Profiles

User profiles allow two or more users of a machine to establish individual settings that will be remembered and restored each time they log on. You're free to paint your workspace purple without offending someone else who also needs to use your machine. Nearly all the customizing steps described in this chapter, including screen resolution and color depth, are profile-specific, which means that they affect only the current profile.

# Activating the Active Desktop

Because the Windows 2000 desktop is capable of displaying Web pages and other content downloaded from the Internet, Microsoft's dialog boxes now refer to the desktop as the Active Desktop. You can choose just how "active" you want your desktop to be, however. Windows 2000 provides two mechanisms for making your desktop look and act more or less like a page on the World Wide Web:

■ You can set up your system so that you have to click an icon only once to launch or open the item represented by that icon. This makes desktop icons (and items in Windows Explorer) behave more like links on a Web page and less like icons in earlier versions of Windows, where double-clicking was required. If you place the mouse pointer on an icon in single-click mode, the pointer changes from an arrow to a hand, just as it does when you point to a link in your Web browser. And, of course, in this mode a single-click is all that's required to launch the item you're pointing at.

■ You can choose to display Web content on your Active Desktop. If you do this, your desktop can host items such as stock or news tickers that can be updated from the Internet automatically at scheduled times. An Active Desktop with Web content can also have, as its backdrop, a hypertext markup language (HTML) document, complete with links to other HTML documents. (*HTML* is the programming language used to encode Web pages.) The Show Web Content option thus makes your desktop even more fundamentally Web-like than the single-click option.

These two options are independent. You can turn on the single-click option without displaying Web content on your Active Desktop. And you can display Web content on your Active Desktop but retain the classic (double-click) mode of launching programs and opening documents.

---

**The Desktop Is a Folder**

Besides being a place to store programs, documents, shortcuts, and other folders, in most cases, a folder is also a chunk of disk space. The folder's *path* is an address that tells the operating system how to find the folder.

Windows Explorer, which we discuss more fully in Chapters 5 and 8, is the program that lets you view and manipulate the contents of folders. A few folders, such as Control Panel, Printers, and Network And Dial-Up Connections, are special and don't represent disk storage units. Although you can't put files in these "system" folders, you can still view and manipulate their contents in Windows Explorer.

The desktop is also a special folder: you don't need Windows Explorer to see and work with it. It's just there all the time, lying beneath whatever else you happen to be using. It does, however, correspond to a piece of disk real estate, and you can use Windows Explorer to work with it if you want to. The desktop's path is %UserProfile%\Desktop. (%UserProfile% is an *environment variable* that contains the actual path to your stored profile information. On a system with local user profiles, that path is typically C:\Documents And Settings\*username*, where *username* is the name of the profile that's currently in use. You can type environment variables almost anyplace where you can type an actual path, such as in Explorer's Address bar.) In addition, your Windows desktop displays the contents of a second folder—%AllUsersProfile%\Desktop—that you can use to store objects that are available to anyone who uses your system.

Because the desktop is a folder, you can store programs, documents, shortcuts, and other folders in (on) it. Also because it's a folder, certain display options that you set in Windows Explorer affect the desktop, and certain options that you set on the desktop also affect appearances within Windows Explorer.

---

# To Click or to Double-Click?

Whether you want single-clicking or double-clicking is a matter of taste. The best way to find out which mode you prefer is to try both.

## Setting the Clicking Style

To change the clicking style:

**1** Open the Start menu, point to Settings, and choose Control Panel.

**2** Open Folder Options.

II

Customizing the Environment

**3** On the General tab in the Folder Options dialog box, select Single-click To Open An Item or Double-click To Open An Item in the Click Items As Follows section. (See Figure 4-1.)

**FIGURE 4-1.**

Options at the bottom of this dialog box enable single-clicking. The Active Desktop options at the top enable the use of Web content on the desktop.

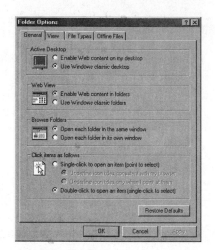

In single-click mode, the text associated with desktop icons and Windows Explorer items is normally underlined, the same way links on a Web page are underlined. In the Folder Options dialog box, you can turn off underlining by selecting Underline Icon Titles Only When I Point At Them. To turn underlining back on, select Underline Icon Titles Consistent With My Browser. Windows then honors the settings you make on the Advanced tab of the Internet Options dialog box. If you've specified in Microsoft Internet Explorer not to underline links until you point to them, the underlining will also be suppressed on your desktop and in Windows Explorer.

## Selecting Items in Single-Click and Double-Click Modes

In the default (double-click) mode, clicking an item once selects it, while clicking twice in rapid succession executes the item's default action. (An item's *default action* is the one that appears in bold type when you right-click the item; most commonly it is to open the program or document.) In single-click mode, clicking once executes the default action; to select without executing, you have to remember not to click! Simply hover the mouse pointer over the item and wait for a moment. When the item becomes highlighted, you've selected it.

To select a contiguous group of items in double-click mode, you can click the first item and then Shift-click (hold down the Shift key while clicking) the last item. To do the same in single-click mode, hover over the first item until Windows highlights it. Then hold down the Shift key while you hover over the last item.

**TIP**

> In either single-click or double-click mode, you can also select a group of adjacent items by drawing a lasso around the group. To select a group of icons, click just above and to the left of the upper left icon in the group. Then, while holding down the mouse button, drag the mouse to a point below and to the right of the lower right icon. When you release the button, the enclosed icons are all selected.

To select a noncontiguous group of items in double-click mode, hold down the Ctrl key while you click each item in turn. To do this in single-click mode, hold down the Ctrl key while you hover over each. Use the same technique to clear an item that you've already selected.

All of the foregoing applies both to items on the desktop and items in a Windows Explorer window.

**2000**  Note that choosing single-click mode also changes the behavior of dialog boxes in all programs included with Windows 2000—but not dialog boxes for many other programs. In many dialog boxes, double-clicking an item has the same effect as single-clicking it and then clicking the OK button. To bypass the OK button in a dialog box for some programs (other than those included with Windows 2000), you'll still need to double-click, even if you're single-clicking on the desktop and in Windows Explorer. If this dissonance disconcerts you, you might want to stick with double-clicking everywhere.

## To Display or Not to Display Web Content?

Enabling Web content on your Active Desktop lets the desktop host "live" items from the World Wide Web and allows it to have an HTML document as its background. If you don't need these features, there's no compelling reason to enable Web content. On the other hand, unless you notice performance degradation, there's also no particular reason not to.

If you do display live Web items on your desktop, however, you might find it convenient at times to turn off Web view. For example, suppose you have several stock-market-related items on your desktop. When the market's closed, you might find those items distracting. You can shut down each one individually, but turning off Web view closes all the items in one step. When the market reopens the next day, you can turn on Web view again to see what's happening.

To toggle Web view on or off:

**1** Right-click a blank part of the desktop.

**2** Choose Active Desktop from the shortcut menu.

If a check mark appears beside the Show Web Content command, choosing the command turns off Web view. If no check mark is there, choosing the command turns on Web view.

You can also turn on Web view by choosing Enable Web Content On My Desktop in the Folder Options dialog box, shown in Figure 4-1 on page 40. Choosing Use Windows Classic Desktop in the same dialog box turns off the feature.

## Bringing the Web to Your Active Desktop

Figure 4-2 shows a desktop with two Web items—a stock market ticker and a weather map. These items are updated periodically from the Internet.

**FIGURE 4-2.**

The stock market ticker and weather map on this desktop are Web items.

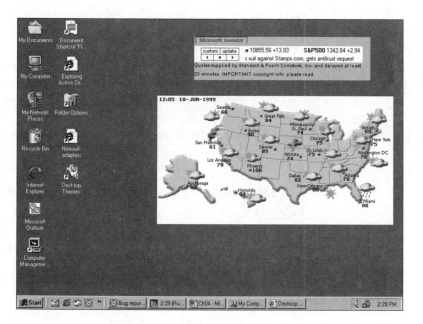

To add a Web item to your Active Desktop:

**1** Right-click the desktop.

**2** Choose Active Desktop from the shortcut menu, and then choose New Desktop Item from the submenu.

The New Active Desktop Item dialog box appears, as shown below.

From this dialog box, you have three choices:

- If you know the Uniform Resource Locator (*URL*—an item's address on the Internet or your intranet) of the item you want to add, type it in the Location box and click OK.

- If you want to display a local file (such as a picture or an HTML document) or the target of an Internet shortcut on your system, click Browse and navigate to the item you want.

**⊛ TIP**

Displaying a folder as an Active Desktop item provides convenient access to a folder's contents because it's always on the desktop. You can choose any view available in Windows Explorer, and the Active Desktop item displays any folder customization you've created. To add a folder to your Active Desktop, type the complete path of the folder you want to display in the Location text box. (This is one place where you can't use environment variables like %UserProfile%.)

- Click Visit Gallery to display the Active Desktop Gallery Web site. (When you go to this page, you might see a security warning window asking if you want to download an ActiveX control. Go ahead and click Yes if you see this message.)

**II**

**Customizing the Environment**

The Active Desktop Gallery Web site provides a list of Web sites that offer content designed expressly for display on your desktop. Figure 4-3 shows how that Web site appeared as this book was going to press. The Web sites made available via Microsoft's Active Desktop Gallery are good ones to try because their content has been tailored for desktop display. But you can subscribe to any Web site and display that site's contents on your Active Desktop.

**FIGURE 4-3.**
The Active Desktop Gallery Web site provides access to vendors who offer Web content designed for display on the desktop.

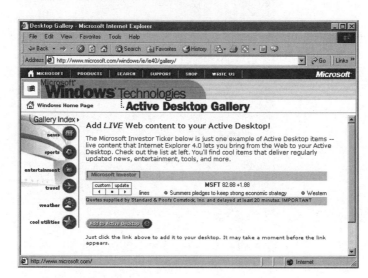

To add an item to your desktop, look for a button or link that looks like this or offers the equivalent option:

When you click that button, you'll be asked to confirm that you want to add the item to your desktop. After you confirm, you'll see a new dialog box that looks something like this.

To add the item to your Active Desktop and accept the vendor's default update schedule, simply click OK. If you want to set up your own schedule, click Customize. This launches the Offline Favorite Wizard, which lets you specify the schedule for updating the content of an Active Desktop item.

Once your Web item has arrived on your desktop, you can interact with it exactly as you would if you were working within a Web browser. When you click a link, Windows activates your browser, connects to the Internet if you're not already online, and then performs the action stipulated by that link.

⭐ **TIP**

You can also turn any Web page or link into an Active Desktop item directly from Microsoft Internet Explorer. To use the current page, drag the icon with the right mouse button (called *right-drag*) from the Address bar to the desktop, and then choose Create Active Desktop Item(s) Here from the shortcut menu. To use the target of a link, right-drag the link from your browser window to the desktop.

## Moving and Sizing Active Desktop Items

Items displayed on your Active Desktop are windows, albeit unconventional ones. You can move them around, change their sizes, and close them. You can't minimize them, however. You can lock them in place so that they can't be moved or resized.

To move one of these windows:

**1** Start by making sure the windows aren't locked in place. Right-click the desktop, and choose Active Desktop from the shortcut menu.

   If a check mark appears beside the Lock Desktop Items command, choose the command to unlock the desktop items. (If no check mark is there, click outside the menu to close it.)

**2** Hover your mouse pointer somewhere near the window's top edge.

   After a moment, a gray border pops up from the top edge.

**3** Drag this gray border to move the window.

To change a window's size, point to one of the window's borders. When your mouse pointer changes shape, drag.

**II**

**Customizing the Environment**

Icons in the gray border are similar in operation to the icons in an ordinary window's title bar.

Display the Control menu

Expand window to cover the entire desktop (or the current screen if you're using multiple monitors)

Expand window to cover the entire desktop except for a resizable area at the left side, where desktop icons appear

Restore window to normal size

Close window

## Updating an Item

Web items on your Active Desktop don't update continuously; they update only at scheduled intervals and when you request an update. To update all items immediately, right-click the desktop, choose Active Desktop from the shortcut menu, and then choose Synchronize from the submenu. To update a single item, point to the top edge of the item, click the down arrow that appears in the upper left corner to open the Control menu, and choose Synchronize.

To change an item's update schedule, visit its properties dialog box. Here are some ways to get there:

 **SEE ALSO**

For more information about changing update schedules, see "Working Offline," page 342.

■ Point to the top edge of the item, click the down arrow that appears in the upper left corner to open the Control menu, and choose Properties. (This method is available only when the Lock Desktop Items command isn't checked.)

■ Right-click the desktop, point to Active Desktop, and choose Customize My Desktop. In the Display Properties dialog box that appears, select the item whose schedule you want to change, and click the Properties button.

■ On the Start menu, point to Programs, Accessories, and then choose Synchronize. Select the item whose schedule you want to change, and click the Properties button.

 **TIP**

To see when an item was last updated, choose Synchronize from the Accessories section of the Start menu. In the Last Updated column, you'll find the date and time of the most recent update for each item.

## Eliminating an Active Desktop Item

What do you do when you're tired of looking at that news ticker, weather map, or other desktop item? You can suppress its display by simply closing it, which you can do in any of the following ways:

- Point to the top edge of the Active Desktop item, and then click the X icon that appears in the upper right corner. (This method is available only when the Lock Desktop Items command isn't checked.)

- Point to the top edge of the item, and then choose Close from the Control menu that appears when you click the down arrow in the upper left corner of the border. (This method is available only when the Lock Desktop Items command isn't checked.)

- Right-click the desktop, choose Active Desktop from the shortcut menu, and then choose the window's name from the submenu. (Choose the same command again to reopen the window.)

- In the Display Properties dialog box, click the Web tab and then clear the check box next to the window name. (Select the check box to reopen the window.)

Windows will continue to update a Web item even if it's not being displayed. To prevent further updates, right-click the desktop, point to Active Desktop, and choose Customize My Desktop. Select the item, click Properties, and then clear the Make This Page Available Offline check box on the Web Document tab.

If you want to permanently delete an item, click the Web tab in the Display Properties dialog box. (See Figure 4-4, on the next page.) Select the item you want to delete, and then click Delete.

---

### Where Is the Channel Bar?

The Channel bar was a new feature of Internet Explorer version 4 and Windows 98. Its intent was to provide easy access to *channels*—Internet sites that deliver information to your desktop in a timely fashion. The feature managed to confuse most users, and it's not included in Windows 2000. (If you upgraded a system that had Internet Explorer version 4 installed, you still have a Channel bar.) Offline viewing provides a similar capability. *For information about offline viewing, see "Working Offline," page 342.*

---

**II**

Customizing the Environment

**FIGURE 4-4.**

You can manage Active Desktop items from the Web tab of the Display Properties dialog box.

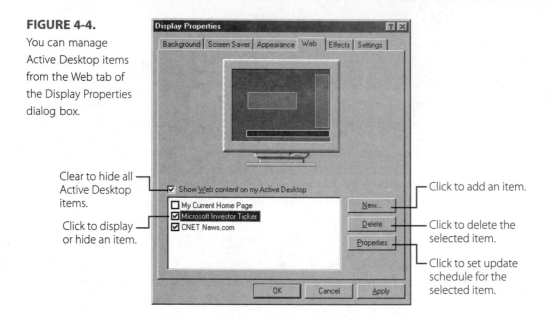

Clear to hide all Active Desktop items.

Click to display or hide an item.

Click to add an item.

Click to delete the selected item.

Click to set update schedule for the selected item.

# Personalizing the Taskbar

The taskbar houses the Start menu, the status area, and a button for each running program. You can use these task buttons to switch from one running program to another. You can also click a task button to minimize an open window or to reopen a minimized one. Your taskbar might also hold one or more *toolbars*—collections of icons that let you start programs quickly. As we'll see later in this chapter, though, toolbars can live in other desktop locations as well as on the taskbar.

The default location of the taskbar is along the bottom edge of the desktop. You can move the taskbar to any other edge of the desktop if you want to try something a little different. Point to an unoccupied area of the taskbar and drag toward another edge of the desktop.

By default, the taskbar shows one row of buttons (or one column, if your taskbar is docked against the left or right edge of the desktop). If you keep toolbars on the taskbar, you might find it convenient to expand the taskbar to two or even three rows. Simply position the mouse along the inner border of the taskbar (the edge closest to the center of the screen). When the mouse pointer becomes a two-headed arrow, drag toward the center of the screen to expand the taskbar.

# Making More Room on the Taskbar

You can also increase button space by removing the clock from the taskbar. If you don't need Windows to display the time of day, you can probably squeeze at least one more button onto the bar by unloading the clock. Right-click an unoccupied space on the taskbar and choose Properties from the shortcut menu. Then clear the Show Clock check box in the Taskbar And Start Menu Properties dialog box. (See Figure 4-5.)

**FIGURE 4-5.**

The General tab has three check boxes that affect taskbar appearance: Always On Top, Auto Hide, and Show Clock.

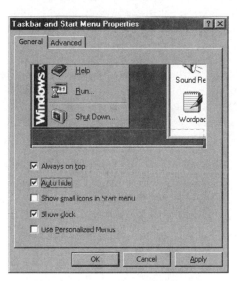

 **TIP**

You can also make room for more buttons by switching to a higher-resolution display. See "Changing Display Resolution," page 59.

**SEE ALSO**

For more information about the Appearance tab, see "Changing Colors, Fonts, and Sizes," page 63.

You can make room for more text on each taskbar button by reducing the point size of the text. You can do this by choosing a smaller size for the Inactive Title Bar item on the Appearance tab in the Display Properties dialog box. To get there, right-click the desktop, choose Properties, and click the Appearance tab.

To decode an overcrowded taskbar, rest your mouse pointer for about half a second on each button. If a button's caption is truncated, Windows displays its full text in a pop-up window (called a *ScreenTip*). If you rest your pointer on the clock, Windows displays the date in a ScreenTip.

**II**

Customizing the Environment

## Getting the Taskbar out of Your Way

By default, the taskbar is a stay-on-top window. That means it remains visible even when you're working in a maximized program. If that's inconvenient for any reason, you can tell it to get out of the way. Simply right-click any unoccupied part of the taskbar and choose Properties from the shortcut menu to open the Taskbar And Start Menu Properties dialog box, shown in Figure 4-5.

Clear the Always On Top check box and click OK. Now you'll be able to see the taskbar at all times *except* when a window is maximized or placed over the taskbar.

**⭐ TIP**

> Regardless of how you set options in the Taskbar And Start Menu Properties dialog box, you can make the taskbar visible at any time by pressing the Windows logo key or Ctrl+Esc.

Another way to make the taskbar less obtrusive is to select both the Auto Hide check box and the Always On Top check box, as shown in Figure 4-5. With these options on, Windows hides the taskbar as soon as you open any window. To get back to the taskbar, you can press the Windows logo key or Ctrl+Esc; or move the mouse pointer to the edge of the desktop where the taskbar is located.

# Using Desktop Toolbars

A toolbar is a collection of icons that simplify commonplace tasks. The standard Windows setup process installs one toolbar on your taskbar. That toolbar, called Quick Launch, includes the following icons: Show Desktop, Internet Explorer, and Outlook Express. The Show Desktop icon displays the desktop, in the process minimizing whatever windows might be open. The other icons simply launch their corresponding programs.

**⭐ TIP**

> The Show Desktop tool is particularly useful because it lets you see your desktop even when a *system-modal dialog box* (one that you must fill out before you can select another window) is blocking your view. Click this tool to reveal the desktop; click a second time to restore all of the windows that were open when you clicked the first time.

In addition to the Quick Launch toolbar, the following toolbars can be displayed on the taskbar or elsewhere on your desktop. (See Figure 4-6.)

**? SEE ALSO**

For information about the Run command, see "Running with the Run Command," page 254. For information about the Address Bar toolbar in Windows Explorer, see "Navigating Through Folders," page 143.

- **Address.** The Address toolbar provides a place where you can enter an Internet address, the name of a program or document, or the name and path of a folder. When you press Enter, Windows takes you to the Internet address, launches the program, opens the document, or displays the folder in a Windows Explorer window. The Address toolbar is functionally equivalent to the Start menu's Run command or the Address bar in Windows Explorer or Internet Explorer.

- **Links.** The Links toolbar provides a set of shortcuts to selected Internet sites. It's equivalent to the Links toolbar that you can display in Internet Explorer or Windows Explorer.

- **Desktop.** The Desktop toolbar provides copies of all the icons currently displayed on your desktop. You might find this toolbar handy if you're using an HTML page as background for your desktop and your normal desktop icons get in the way.

**FIGURE 4-6.**
You can customize these four standard toolbars and create your own new toolbars.

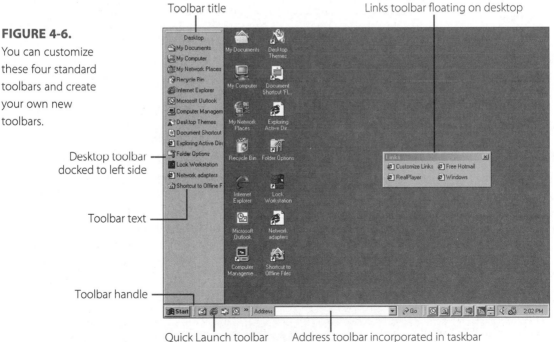

Toolbar title

Links toolbar floating on desktop

Desktop toolbar docked to left side

Toolbar text

Toolbar handle

Quick Launch toolbar       Address toolbar incorporated in taskbar

II

Customizing the Environment

⭐ **TIP**

The Desktop toolbar displays miniature versions of all the icons on your desktop. If you're covering your entire desktop with an Internet item or an HTML background, you might find it convenient to suppress the desktop display of icons and show the Desktop toolbar instead. To suppress icon display, right-click the desktop, choose Active Desktop, and then choose Show Desktop Icons.

You can customize any of the supplied toolbars except for Address. So, for example, you can add icons for your own programs or shortcuts to the Quick Launch toolbar, remove from the Links toolbar links that you don't find useful (or add links to your own favorite sites), and so on. You can also create entirely new toolbars.

Desktop toolbars appear initially on the taskbar, but you can *float* them on the desktop or *dock* them against any side of the desktop. Thus, for example, you can have your taskbar docked against the bottom edge of the desktop and line the other three edges with toolbars.

## Installing and Removing Toolbars

To install a new toolbar or remove one you're currently using, right-click any unoccupied part of the taskbar. (If you're having trouble finding an unoccupied place, first drag the inside border of the taskbar to enlarge it.) Choose Toolbars from the shortcut menu that appears, and then choose from the ensuing submenu. A check mark beside a toolbar's name means that it is already displayed. Clicking a checked toolbar name removes that toolbar.

## Sizing and Positioning Toolbars

A thin vertical bar appears at the left edge of every toolbar positioned on the taskbar. (If the taskbar is displayed vertically against the left or right edge of the desktop, the bar is horizontal and appears at the top of the toolbar.) This is the toolbar's *handle*. (See Figure 4-6.) To move a toolbar out onto the desktop, position the mouse pointer on the handle. When the pointer changes shape, drag the toolbar. To dock a toolbar against a different edge of the desktop, drag it all the way to that edge. When you release the mouse button, the toolbar will dock.

≫ **NOTE**

You can dock toolbars only against the edges of the whole desktop. If your desktop spans two or more monitors, you can't dock a toolbar against a screen edge that's adjacent to the edge of another screen. *For more information, see "Extending Your Desktop Across Two or More Monitors," page 61.*

On the desktop, the toolbar takes the form of a simple window, with a title bar and a close button.

You can move the toolbar around by dragging its title bar or close it by clicking the close button. To reposition a toolbar on the taskbar, simply drag its title bar to the taskbar. You can also use the handle to change a toolbar's size or position on the taskbar. Assuming your taskbar is horizontal, dragging the handle to the right decreases the width of the toolbar and makes more room for the toolbar on the left. Dragging to the left has the opposite effect.

To change the size of a desktop toolbar, simply drag one of its borders.

> A toolbar that's too large to fit in its taskbar space displays its remaining contents in a pop-up menu if you click the arrow that appears at its right or bottom edge.

## Customizing Toolbars

To remove a tool from a toolbar, right-click it and choose Delete from the shortcut menu. To add a tool that opens a program or document to a toolbar, drag the item's icon from the desktop or a Windows Explorer window and deposit it wherever you want it to appear on the toolbar.

Toolbars can be displayed with either large or small icons, with or without their titles, and with or without text identifying each tool. To avail yourself of any of these customizing options, right-click the toolbar you want to modify. Choose View followed by Large or Small to change the icon size; choose Show Text to suppress or display tool text; or choose Show Title to suppress or display the toolbar title.

Note that if you don't display tool text, you can still see the name of any tool simply by hovering your mouse pointer over it.

**TIP**

> When set up in a certain way, the Desktop toolbar can provide a cascading menu of all the folders and files on your system. To use this handy feature, display the Desktop toolbar somewhere on the taskbar, and be sure its toolbar title is displayed. Reduce the Desktop toolbar's size by dragging its handle (and the handles of surrounding toolbars, if necessary) until it displays only the toolbar title ("Desktop") and an arrow. Now when you click the arrow, a menu of desktop items appears. Desktop items that contain other folders and files (such as My Computer, My Documents, and My Network Places) cascade to show their contents when you point at them.

### Creating a New Toolbar

Any folder on your system can become a toolbar. This includes
Windows system folders such as Printers or Control Panel. To create a
new toolbar, right-click an existing toolbar or a spot on the taskbar,
choose Toolbars, and then choose New Toolbar. In the next dialog
box, navigate to a folder and click OK.

The folder's name will become the name of the new toolbar, and each
item within the folder will become a tool.

### Opening and Refreshing Toolbars

With the exception of the Address toolbar, every toolbar is a representation of a folder that exists somewhere on your system. To see a
toolbar's underlying folder in a Windows Explorer window, right-click
the toolbar and choose Open. If the folder is on a network server, you
can refresh it (that is, make sure it reflects the current state of the
server) by right-clicking it and choosing Refresh.

# Adding Shortcuts to Your Desktop

A shortcut is a tiny file that provides a link to a program, document,
folder, or Internet address. The file is represented by an icon that
includes a black arrow in its lower left corner, like this:

Shortcut to
Offline Files

If the shortcut is linked to a file or folder, that file or folder can be
anywhere—on a local hard disk or CD-ROM drive, on a floppy disk,
on a network server, or on the Internet. Like any other kind of file, a
shortcut can be stored in any folder, including your desktop. If you
store shortcuts for programs and documents on your desktop, you
can get to them easily at any time. For example, if you use a half
dozen or so programs nearly every day, why not simply place shortcuts for them on your desktop? Particularly if the items in question are
buried several levels deep in the Start menu, it can be easier to get to
them via desktop shortcuts.

Because a shortcut is a pointer to an object, not the object itself, you
can create and delete shortcuts without affecting the underlying object

in any way. It also means you can create a shortcut to a major program without duplicating the large file that actually runs that program. Shortcuts themselves use less than 2 KB of disk storage, so a proliferation of shortcuts isn't likely to run you out of hard disk space.

# Creating a Shortcut

There are three easy ways to create a shortcut: by dragging and dropping, by using cut and paste, and by visiting the Create Shortcut Wizard.

## Creating a Shortcut by Using Drag and Drop

If the item for which you want to create a shortcut is visible in a Windows Explorer window, right-drag that item to wherever you want the shortcut to appear. Then, from the shortcut menu, choose Create Shortcut(s) Here.

You can also right-drag an item from the Start menu to create a shortcut on the desktop:

**⊗ CAUTION**

Left-dragging *moves* the shortcut to the desktop—and it's no longer on the Start menu.

1 Click the Start button to open the menu.

2 Move your mouse pointer to the menu item you're interested in.

3 Right-drag it to your desktop.

4 Choose Create Shortcut(s) Here from the menu that appears.

All the procedures described here for creating shortcuts on the desktop work for creating shortcuts in other folders as well.

You can turn any Web link into a desktop shortcut by simply dragging the link (the underlined text) and dropping it on the desktop. Opening that shortcut later will activate your browser, connect you to the Internet (if you're not already there), and take your browser to the appropriate URL.

**★ TIP**

You can also create a shortcut by dragging an item from a Search Results window. Thus, if you want to create a shortcut to a program and you're not sure where that program resides, you can use Search to locate it. Then right-drag the found item to the desktop to create the shortcut. *For information about using the Search feature, see Chapter 11, "Searching for Files and Folders."*

**★ TIP**

> Some shortcuts can be used as targets for drag and drop. For example, if you put a shortcut for a printer on your desktop, you can print documents by dragging them from Windows Explorer windows to the printer shortcut. If you create a shortcut for a floppy disk drive or the top-level folder on a hard disk, you can copy files by dragging them from Windows Explorer windows to the shortcut. *For more information, see "Printing from Windows Explorer," page 219, and "Moving or Copying Folders, Files, and Shortcuts," page 157.*

## Creating a Shortcut by Using Copy and Paste

Right-dragging an item from a Windows Explorer window to the desktop isn't convenient when the Windows Explorer window is maximized. In that situation, the easiest way to build your shortcut is to right-click the item and choose Copy from the shortcut menu. Then display the desktop, right-click anywhere on it, and choose Paste Shortcut from the shortcut menu.

## Creating a Shortcut by Using the Create Shortcut Wizard

To use the Create Shortcut Wizard, start by right-clicking the desktop. From the shortcut menu, choose New, and then choose Shortcut. The Create Shortcut Wizard appears, as shown in Figure 4-7.

**FIGURE 4-7.**
The Create Shortcut Wizard makes it easy to populate your desktop—or any other folder—with shortcuts.

If you know the command line required to run your program or to open your document, simply type it and click the Next button. (The *command line* is whatever you would type to run your program or to open your document if you were using the Start menu's Run command.)

If you don't know the command line, or if Windows gives an error message when you click Next, click the Browse button. In the Browse For Folder dialog box, locate the item for which you want to create a shortcut. Then click the OK button. After you click OK, the wizard returns you to its initial dialog box, with the command line filled in.

Click Next, type a name for your shortcut, click Finish, and your shortcut will appear.

## Renaming a Shortcut

When you first create a shortcut, Windows gives it a default name based on the underlying object. To rename a shortcut:

**1** Right-click the shortcut.

**2** From the shortcut menu, choose Rename.

**3** Type the name you want to use.

> You can also rename any object by selecting it, pressing F2, and typing the new name.

## Assigning Other Properties to a Shortcut

**SEE ALSO**

For more information about shortcut properties, see "Changing Shortcut Properties," page 26.

You can assign a shortcut key to a shortcut, allowing you to activate the shortcut with a combination of keyboard characters. (For example, you might assign Ctrl+Alt+P to the Microsoft Paint program.) You can also change the icon displayed by a shortcut, specify what kind of window the shortcut should open (maximized, minimized, or normal), and assign an initial data folder to be used by whatever program the shortcut opens. All these customizing steps involve modifying the shortcut's properties, just as you would to customize items on the Start menu.

## Repositioning Shortcuts on the Desktop

You can change the position of your desktop shortcuts at any time. Simply drag them. You can also get Windows to help you keep your shortcuts neatly aligned. To line up desktop icons:

**1** Use the mouse to bring your shortcut icons into approximate alignment.

**2** Right-click the desktop.

**3** From the shortcut menu that appears, choose Line Up Icons.

If you want all of your desktop shortcuts organized in columns starting at the left side of the desktop, right-click the desktop, choose Arrange Icons, and then choose Auto Arrange. With Auto Arrange turned on, your icons always stay neatly aligned, even if you try to drag them out of place.

Whether you choose Line Up Icons or Auto Arrange to tidy up your desktop, Windows aligns the icons to an invisible grid that evenly spaces them. If you want the icons to be closer together or farther apart, you can adjust the grid spacing. To adjust the spacing:

**1** Right-click the desktop.

**2** From the shortcut menu, choose Properties.

**3** In the Display Properties dialog box, click the Appearance tab.

**4** Open the Item list and select Icon Spacing (Horizontal) or Icon Spacing (Vertical).

**5** Adjust the setting in the Size box. (A larger number increases the space between icons.)

> **NOTE**

In addition to controlling the desktop icons, changing the icon spacing affects the spacing of icons in folders when you use Large Icons view.

## Deleting a Shortcut

To remove a shortcut, simply select it and press the Delete key. Or right-click it and choose Delete from the shortcut menu. Note that deleting a shortcut doesn't delete the program or document that the shortcut points to; doing so deletes only the shortcut itself.

# Changing Your Desktop's Display Properties

Like just about everything else in Windows, your desktop has a properties dialog box, and that properties dialog box allows you to change many aspects of your desktop's appearance. You can modify the display resolution (so that more or less information fits on the screen), modify the color depth (the richness of color that Windows uses to display everything you see), add a background pattern or *wallpaper* (a background image, optionally displayed as a repeating pattern), change colors and fonts used for various components of the Windows user interface, install a screen saver, and change the icons assigned to standard desktop elements (such as My Computer and My Network Places). You can also use the Display Properties dialog box to get to an additional dialog box that governs your video hardware.

To see and work with the Display Properties dialog box, right-click your desktop and choose Properties. Or launch Display in Control Panel.

# Changing Display Resolution

Resolution is a measure of the amount of information that Windows can fit on your screen, expressed in pixels. A *pixel* (a contraction of the words *picture element*) is a single addressable dot on your screen. Common resolutions include 640×480 (also known as VGA resolution), 800×600 (sometimes called Super VGA or SVGA resolution), 1024×768, 1152×864, 1280×1024, and 1600×1200. The range of resolutions available to you depends on your display hardware.

The higher your resolution, the more data you can work with at once. A monitor that displays 17 rows and 9 columns of a spreadsheet at 640×480 pixels, for example, might show 33 rows and 15 columns of the same spreadsheet at 1024×768. High resolutions also allow you to keep many windows visible at once without their overlapping one another.

The tradeoff for increasing the number of pixels on the screen is that each pixel must be smaller. Smaller pixels means smaller images. A 10-point font that is easy to read at 800×600 might become illegible at 1280×1024 (depending, of course, on your visual acuity and the size of your monitor).

To change your display resolution:

1  Click the Settings tab in the Display Properties dialog box, shown in Figure 4-8, on the next page.

2  Drag the Screen Area slider to the right to increase resolution or to the left to decrease it.

3  Click OK.

4  Click OK again to answer the confirmation prompt.

5  Click Yes when Windows asks if you want to keep the new screen resolution.

**II**

Customizing the Environment

**FIGURE 4-8.**

In this dialog box, you can change the resolution and color depth of your display.

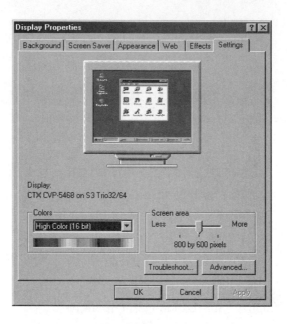

Windows asks for the confirmation in step 5 because it's possible (but unlikely) that the Display Properties dialog box will offer you a resolution choice that doesn't work on your hardware. If you happen to choose an unworkable resolution, your screen would probably go blank and you wouldn't see that final confirmation prompt. After waiting 15 seconds for your okay, Windows automatically restores your prior resolution.

If you like working with graphics programs at 1024×768 but find writing impossible at this resolution, you can make text sizes larger for all your programs. Click the Advanced button on the Settings tab and then, on the General tab of the dialog box that appears, select a larger font size.

## Changing Color Depth

The term *color depth* denotes the number of distinct colors that your system can display. The higher the color depth, the more realistic the images appear. As with display resolution, the available color depth choices depend on your hardware. The common options are 16 colors, 256 colors, 16-bit *high color* (65,536 colors), and 24-bit and 32-bit *true color* (approximately 16 million colors).

Choosing the highest possible color depth makes images look as good as they possibly can on your screen, but it might also cause images to be displayed somewhat more slowly. That's because the greater the number of colors your system can display, the more video memory it has to manage. You might want to experiment to see what color depth seems optimal on your equipment.

To change color depth, visit the Settings tab in the Display Properties dialog box. As Figure 4-8 shows, that dialog box includes a Colors list. Simply select the option you want from this list.

## Extending Your Desktop Across Two or More Monitors

If you have a computer with PCI or AGP slots, you might be able to extend your desktop across two or more monitors. You need a separate PCI or AGP display adapter for each monitor you want to use (or a single adapter that supports multiple monitor outputs). Windows 2000 supports up to 10 monitors.

> Not all display adapters supported by Windows 2000 can be used as secondary adapters. Before you try to set up multiple monitors, check the "Display Adapter" section of the Windows 2000 Hardware Compatibility List (HCL) at *www.microsoft.com/hcl/*.

Extending your desktop across multiple monitors gives you much more display real estate, allowing you, for example, to display more columns in a Microsoft Excel spreadsheet, or to have more than one maximized program visible at the same time. You can easily integrate information from different files by dragging it from one monitor to another. Or you might want a program visible on one monitor and its help files visible on another. You can assign separate resolutions and color depths to each monitor. So, for example, if you have a 19-inch monitor and a 15-inch monitor, you could run the larger display at 1024×768 and the smaller one at 800×600.

To set up and configure an additional monitor:

**1** Turn off your computer and any attached devices, and install an additional supported PCI or AGP display adapter. Connect the monitor to the new adapter.

**2** Turn on the computer. Windows detects the new hardware and installs the appropriate drivers.

**3** In Control Panel, launch Display, and then click the Settings tab.

Customizing the Environment

Once you've installed more than one supported display adapter, the Settings tab in the Display Properties dialog box changes to show the current physical arrangement of your monitors. Figure 4-9 shows an example of how that dialog box might appear. Note that a number appears on the screen of each monitor shown in the dialog box. These numbers correspond to entries in the Display list.

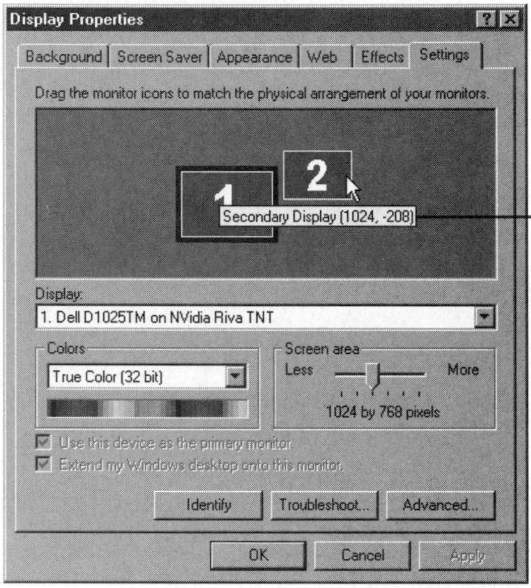

**FIGURE 4-9.**

When you have multiple display adapters installed, the Settings tab in the Display Properties dialog box lets you specify the physical arrangement of your monitors.

When you point to a secondary monitor icon, a ScreenTip shows the monitor's x-y coordinates relative to the primary monitor.

**TIP**

To see which actual monitor is represented by each monitor in the dialog box, click Identify. A large number, similar to the ones in the dialog box, appears on each monitor.

**4**  Click the icon for the new monitor, and then select Extend My Windows Desktop Onto This Monitor.

**5**  In the Screen Area box, set the resolution for the new monitor.

**6**  Drag the monitor icons so that they match the physical arrangement of your monitors.

To allow you to move display objects from one monitor to another, Windows needs to know how your monitors are physically arranged.

Once you've shown Windows the layout of your displays, you can drag icons and windows from one monitor to the other. If your secondary display is to the right of your primary display, as shown in Figure 4-9, for example, you can move an icon from primary to secondary by dragging it off the right edge of the primary display. New windows open initially on the primary monitor, which is also where the Windows logon screen appears.

If you maximize a window, it fills only the screen on which it currently resides. If a window is currently split across two or more screens, Windows maximizes it on whichever screen currently displays its largest portion.

**NOTE**

If you run Command Prompt or an MS-DOS-based program in a full-screen window, it always appears only on the primary monitor—and all other monitors are blank until you close the program or switch back to a Windows-based program.

## Changing Colors, Fonts, and Sizes

When you first install Windows 2000, it uses a combination of colors, fonts, and sizes called Windows Standard. It's a fine arrangement, but you can also choose from a number of alternative schemes or you can design your own. Once you've found a pleasing arrangement of colors, fonts, and sizes, you can name and save the arrangement. You can design as many custom appearance schemes as you want, adding each to the menu that Windows supplies. As mood or necessity dictates, you can switch from one scheme to another by choosing from a simple list.

To see what the supplied appearance schemes look like, choose Properties from the shortcut menu that appears when you right-click the desktop, and click the Appearance tab. Windows presents the dialog box shown in Figure 4-10, on the next page. The upper part of this dialog box is a preview window, showing you a sample of each screen element whose color, font, or size you can modify.

Click the Scheme box, and then use the Up arrow key and the Down arrow key to step through the list of named appearance schemes. As you highlight the name of each scheme, Windows displays a sample of that scheme in the upper part of the dialog box. You can apply any appearance scheme to your Windows environment by highlighting its name and clicking OK or Apply.

II Customizing the Environment

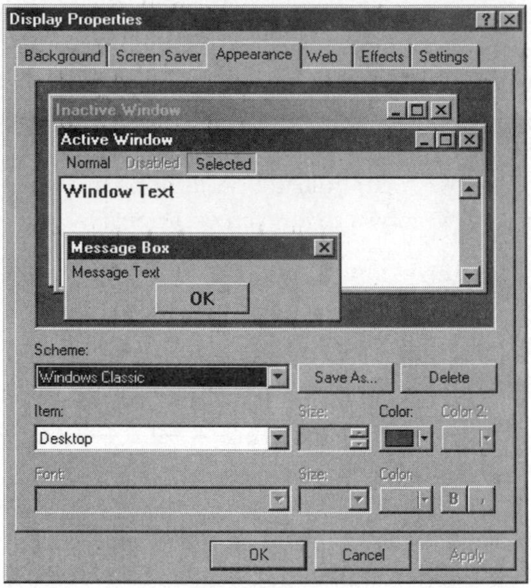

**FIGURE 4-10.**

As you select from the supplied appearance schemes or create your own, the upper part of this dialog box provides a preview of your selections.

## Modifying the Supplied Appearance Schemes

To modify one of the supplied appearance schemes, select its name in the Scheme list. In the sample window, click the screen element you want to change. Then use the list boxes and buttons at the bottom of the dialog box to make your color, font, and size selections.

For example, suppose you want to modify the Windows Standard color scheme, making the active window's title bar gradated from yellow to red, with black text in 12-point, bold, italic Verdana. To assign this admittedly garish combination:

1  Select Windows Standard in the Scheme list.

2  In the preview area of the dialog box, click the title bar labeled Active Window. (Or select Active Title Bar in the Item list.)

3  In the Font list, select Verdana.

4  In the Size list directly to the right of the Font list, select 12.

5  Click the *I* (italic) button to the right of the font-size list. (The bold button is already selected.)

6  Open the Color list to the right of the Item list and select yellow.

7  Open the Color 2 list and select red.

8  Open the Color list to the right of the Font list and select black.

## Finding a Color if You Don't See the One You Want

The Color list boxes for the item and font colors offer a selection of 20 colors. If you don't see the one you're looking for, click the button labeled Other. Windows then displays a larger menu, consisting of 48 colors. Should you fail to find exactly the shade you want in this expanded offering, you can define your own custom colors, as discussed next.

## Defining Custom Colors

To add your own colors to the ones Windows offers, open the Color list for the screen element you want to change and click the Other button. Windows opens the Color dialog box, shown in Figure 4-11.

**FIGURE 4-11.**
You can add custom colors to the Windows user interface by defining them in this dialog box.

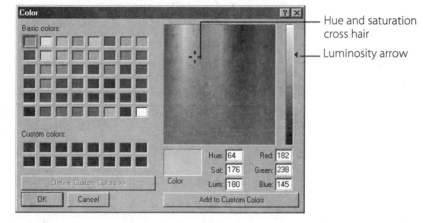

Hue and saturation cross hair

Luminosity arrow

To set a custom color with the mouse, adjust the position of two indicators—the cross hair in the big square grid and the arrow to the right of the vertical scale. As you move these indicators, Windows displays a sample of the selected color in the box near the center of the dialog box. If you prefer using your keyboard, you can precisely specify a color by entering its hue, saturation, and luminosity values, or by entering its red, green, and blue component values in the text boxes at the lower right corner of the dialog box. *For information about color parameters, see the "How Colors Are Defined" sidebar, on the next page.*

The sample color box actually comprises two halves because your system might be incapable of displaying every possible color. For colors that your system can't display directly, Windows creates a patterned mixture of two or more colors that it can display directly—a process called *dithering*. The left half of the sample box (the one marked Color) displays the dithered color; the right half (marked Solid) displays a closely related color that your system can display without dithering. However, if your system is set at a color depth that can show high color or true color, you'll see only a single box labeled Color, as in Figure 4-11.

---

### How Colors Are Defined

Colors in Windows are recorded as a combination of three parameters: hue, saturation, and luminosity. Roughly speaking, the basic quality of a color—its redness, blueness, or whatever—is defined by its *hue*. The purity of a color is defined by its *saturation*; a lower saturation value means more gray is mixed in. The brightness or dullness of a color is defined by its *luminosity*.

Hue, saturation, and luminosity are the parameters that Windows uses internally, but your video display hardware lives by a different set of numbers. Images on a color monitor are formed by a combination of pixels. To make each pixel visible, a beam of electrons is fired at three tiny spots of phosphor—one red, one green, and one blue. The result is three points of distinctly colored light so close together that they're perceived as a single light source. The apparent color of that light source is determined by the relative intensities of its red, green, and blue components.

Therefore, every combination of hue, saturation, and luminosity is translated by Windows into varying levels of energy directed at those spots of red, green, and blue phosphor. Thus, there are two sets of boxes in the lower right corner of the custom color dialog box—one for the parameters used by Windows, the other for the relative red, green, and blue intensities. You can define a custom color by modifying the numbers in either set of boxes, or by simply dragging the indicators until you see the color you're looking for.

---

## Experimenting with Color

In the Color dialog box, the vertical scale on the right controls luminosity (brightness). As you move its arrow indicator higher, the color becomes lighter. Putting the arrow at the top of the scale creates pure white, no matter where the cross hair is in the grid; putting the arrow at the bottom of the luminosity scale produces black.

The square grid controls hue and saturation. Moving the cross hair from side to side changes the hue; moving it higher increases the saturation.

To see the range of pure colors available, start by putting the luminosity arrow about halfway up the vertical scale. Then put the cross hair at the upper left corner of the square grid. This combination gives you a fully saturated red of medium luminosity. Now slowly drag the cross hair across the top of the grid; as you do so, you'll move from red through yellow, green, blue, violet, and back to red again. (Alternatively, you can enter a value in the Hue box to step the Hue parameter from 0 to 239.)

To see the effect of luminosity on color, double-click the Solid half of the sample box or press Alt+O. This moves the cross hair to the nearest position where you see a pure color in both sample boxes. Then move the luminosity arrow up and down the scale (or change the value in the Lum box).

To see the effect of saturation, put the luminosity arrow back in the middle of the scale and drag the cross hair straight up and down in the square grid (or change the value in the Sat box).

## Adding Custom Colors to Your Palette

When you find a color you like, you can add it to your Custom Colors palette by clicking Add To Custom Colors. (If you prefer to add the solid color, double-click the Solid half of the sample box or press Alt+O first.) Windows adds the color to the first available Custom Colors box. If you want to add a color to a specific box in your custom palette (for example, if you want to replace a custom color), you must select that box first, reset the custom color using any of the above methods, and then click Add To Custom Colors.

When you've filled out the Custom Colors palette to your satisfaction, click OK to return to the Appearance tab of the Display Properties dialog box. Now you can assign your custom colors to the screen elements exactly as you did the basic colors.

## Changing the Size of Particular Display Elements

You can make certain elements of the Windows user interface—such as title bars, caption (title bar) buttons, and window borders—larger or smaller by using the Size box to the right of the Item list on the Appearance tab, shown in Figure 4-10 on page 64. If a number appears in this box, the element shown in the Item list can be sized.

Windows automatically adjusts the size of elements that contain text. For example, if you increase the font size for your active title bars, Windows adjusts the height of the title bar to accommodate the larger text. But you can override Windows' judgment by manipulating the values in the Size box.

## Saving an Appearance Scheme

If you discover a pleasing new combination of colors, fonts, and sizes, it's a good idea to name and save your new scheme before leaving the Appearance tab of the Display Properties dialog box. That way, you'll be able to switch back and forth between your own custom formats and the ones supplied by Windows—or between several of your own making.

To save a scheme, simply click the Save As button and supply a name. Windows adds the name you provide to the list.

If you tire of your new scheme, you can easily remove it. Simply select its name, and then click the Delete button.

---

### Whither Desktop Themes?

Desktop themes add thematically consistent sounds and sights to your system, using wallpaper, specially designed icons, sound schemes, color schemes, fonts, animated mouse pointers, and screen savers. The Travel theme, for example, uses a train station for wallpaper, assorted propellers and clocks for mouse pointers, an airplane for a screen saver, and various toots, honks, beeps, and "a-oogas" to enliven your day.

Windows 2000 doesn't include desktop themes. However, if you installed Windows 98, Plus! for Windows 95, or Plus! for Windows 98 before you upgraded to Windows 2000, you can use desktop themes as you always have. And you'll discover a new feature: the Desktop Themes dialog box now includes an option to switch to a new theme once a month. (It uses a scheduled task to make the switch; edit the task if you want to change the interval. *For more information about scheduling tasks, see "Running Programs on Schedule," page 257.*)

Even if you didn't upgrade from Windows 98 or Plus!, you can still use desktop themes. Although Windows 2000 doesn't include any predefined themes, it does include the Desktop Themes program, an executable named %SystemRoot%\System32\Themes.exe. To use desktop themes, create a shortcut to this file. You can download predefined themes from a number of sites on the World Wide Web, or you can create your own.

To create your own theme from scratch, simply use Control Panel to set up all the elements of your theme. For example, to select wallpaper, go to the Background tab in the Display Properties dialog box. To change a mouse pointer, launch Mouse and click the Pointers tab. Then go to Desktop Themes, select Current Windows Settings, click Save As, and name your theme.

---

# Using Wallpaper

Wallpaper refers to any background image displayed on the desktop, whether a small image repeated to fill the desktop (as in conventional wallpaper), a centered image, or a large image that covers the entire desktop. If you're not using Web-content view, your wallpaper can be supplied by any graphics file with the extension .bmp, .dib, or .rle. On a desktop that has Web content enabled, you can also use GIF and JPEG files (graphics formats commonly used on Web pages), or you can drape your desktop with an HTML file stored on your computer or on a network drive, complete with live links.

To make a wallpaper choice, right-click the desktop, choose Properties from the shortcut menu, and click the Background tab. This takes you to the dialog box shown in Figure 4-12. Note that the default choice, (None), appears at the top of the list. You'll want to return to (None) if you get tired of having wallpaper.

**FIGURE 4-12.**

The Background tab in the Display Properties dialog box lets you add a pattern, picture, or HTML page to your desktop.

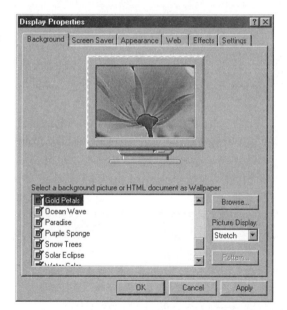

Select an image file from the Wallpaper list, or click the Browse button to find one that's not in the list. (The list initially includes image files in your My Pictures folder and the %SystemRoot% folder.) Note that if you choose a GIF image, a JPEG image, or an HTML file, Windows offers to enable Active Desktop's Show Web Content option if it's not already enabled.

After choosing a wallpaper file, you can choose either Center, Tile, or Stretch from the Display list. If you choose Tile, your image is repeated as often as needed to fill the screen. If you choose Stretch, Windows enlarges your image to fill the screen (in the process possibly distorting it beyond recognition).

# Using a Background Pattern

A *background pattern* is an 8-pixel by 8-pixel picture that can be used like tiled wallpaper. You can either fill your entire desktop with a pattern, or, if you have a centered wallpaper image, you can fill the space around that image with a pattern. Windows supplies about a dozen patterns to choose from, and you can edit any of these to create your own patterns.

To apply a pattern, first visit the Display Properties dialog box shown in Figure 4-12. Then click Pattern to open the Pattern dialog box shown in Figure 4-13. Note that the Pattern button is unavailable unless your current wallpaper is centered or you have no wallpaper.

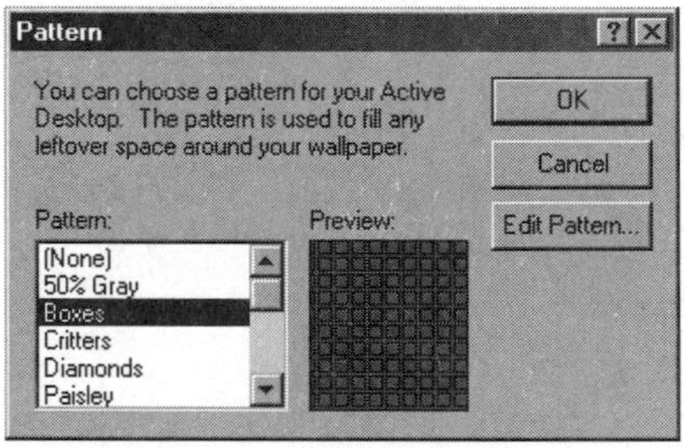

**FIGURE 4-13.**
A pattern can be used alone or with centered wallpaper.

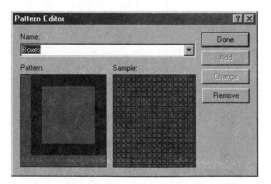

## Editing an Existing Pattern

To edit one of the Windows-supplied patterns, select its name in the Pattern list and click the Edit Pattern button. The Pattern Editor appears, as shown in Figure 4-14.

**FIGURE 4-14.**
The Pattern Editor lets you modify or create background patterns for your desktop.

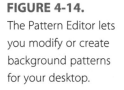

The Pattern Editor shows two boxes. The Sample box, on the right, shows a swatch of the current pattern. The Pattern box, on the left, shows a magnified image of the 8-pixel by 8-pixel cell that produces the pattern. To edit the pattern, you'll work with the Pattern box. You can see the effects of your work by watching the Sample box.

Each pixel in the Pattern box is displayed in either black or the current background color of your desktop. Clicking a pixel inverts it from black to color or vice versa. When you're satisfied with your editing, click Change to save the revised pattern. Then click OK to select it.

### Creating a New Pattern

To create a new pattern, simply edit an existing one. Then give your work a new name by replacing the text in the Name text box. Click Add, and your new pattern joins the list of existing patterns.

## Using a Screen Saver

Screen savers were originally created to prevent damage that could occur to monitors when the same picture or text remained on screen for a long period of time. With current display technology, however, the probability that you'll damage your screen with a burned-in image is remote. But screen savers have other virtues as well. They're fun to watch, and they're one way to prevent others in your vicinity from prying while you're away from your machine. As soon as you press a key or (with most savers) move the mouse, the screen saver restores the original image.

Many screen savers have a save-now option and a password option. The save-now option lets you display the saver on demand, either by pressing a certain keyboard combination or by moving the mouse to a particular corner of the screen. The password option ensures that only you are able to restore the original image. If your screen saver has these features, you can display the saver any time you walk away from your computer and be reasonably confident that no one will invade your privacy.

To install one of the Windows-supplied screen savers, right-click the desktop and choose Properties from the shortcut menu. Then click the Screen Saver tab to open the dialog box shown in Figure 4-15, on the next page.

To select a screen saver, choose it from the Screen Saver list. Then use the Wait box to specify how long a period of inactivity Windows should allow before displaying the screen saver.

Customizing the Environment

**FIGURE 4-15.**
The Screen Saver tab in the Display Properties dialog box offers a choice of customizable screen savers.

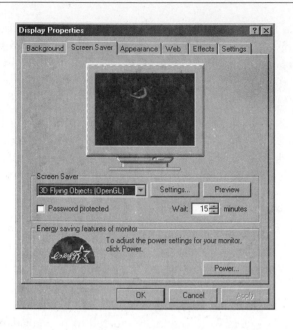

All the Windows-supplied screen savers (except for Default Screen Saver and Logon Screen Saver) include options that you can set. These options let you adjust colors, speed, and other display preferences. Figure 4-16 shows the settings dialog box for the 3D Flying Objects screen saver.

**FIGURE 4-16.**
After selecting a screen saver, you can click the Settings button to specify display options.

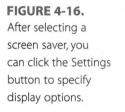

# Changing Desktop Icons

Tired of looking at the same old My Computer and Recycle Bin icons? As Figure 4-17 shows, you can go to the Effects tab in the Display Properties dialog box to change them. Simply select the icon you want to change, and then click Change Icon. You'll see a dialog box with several icons. Select a new icon from the ones displayed, or click Browse to point to a different icon file.

**FIGURE 4-17.**

The Effects tab in the Display Properties dialog box lets you change the content, size, and color depth of system icons, among other settings.

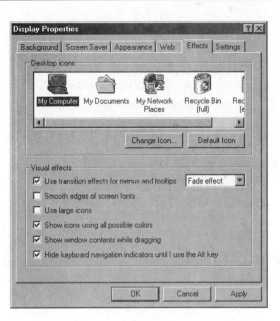

You can also use check boxes on the lower part of the Effects tab (see Figure 4-17) to enlarge your system icons and change their color depth. If you're running your system at 16-bit or higher color depth, selecting Show Icons Using All Possible Colors will get you a prettier icon display.

When you're using an HTML page as a background for your Active Desktop, some of your desktop icons might clash visually with some of your HTML links. In that case, you might want the desktop icons to disappear altogether. To perform this vanishing act, right-click the desktop, choose Active Desktop from the shortcut menu, and then choose Show Desktop Items. (If you need the icons, you can deploy them in a more compact and out-of-the-way manner by displaying the Desktop toolbar. *For details, see "Using Desktop Toolbars," page 50.*)

## Controlling Menu Appearance, Font Smoothing, and Window-Drag Display

The remaining check boxes on the Effects tab in the Display Properties dialog box, shown in Figure 4-17, control these visual effects:

- **Use Transition Effects For Menus And Tooltips.** Causes the menus (such as the Start menu and its submenus, or shortcut menus) to unfurl somewhat less than instantaneously. (The Fade Effect option causes menus to fade in from transparent to opaque. The Scroll Effect option causes menus to grow from a starting point to their full size.) Clear this check box if you want the menus to appear more quickly.

- **Smooth Edges Of Screen Fonts.** Causes Windows to fill in the jagged edges of large fonts, giving large type a more natural appearance. It also slows down your display slightly, but with a fast processor you might not notice the performance hit.

- **Show Window Contents While Dragging.** Displays the full contents of a window as you drag it. If you turn off this option, Windows displays only a ghost border while you drag and fills in the window after you release the mouse button. Turn off this option if your performance drags while you drag.

- **Hide Keyboard Navigation Indicators Until I Use The Alt Key.** Hides the underscores that identify shortcut keys on menus and in dialog boxes, in an attempt to reduce visual clutter. When you press Alt—the key you must press as part of the shortcut key combination—the underscores appear. If you prefer constant reminders of the available shortcut keys, clear this check box.

5

# Customizing Windows Explorer

W indows Explorer is the program that lets you work with the contents of folders, both ordinary disk folders where you store your programs and documents, and special folders, such as Printers or Control Panel. In this chapter, we discuss how you can customize Windows Explorer and the way it displays folder contents. *For information about how to use Windows Explorer to work with folders, files, and shortcuts, see Chapter 8, "Using Windows Explorer."*

Because the desktop itself is a folder, much of the information in Chapter 4, "Customizing the Desktop," also applies to customizing the appearance of folders in Windows Explorer.

# Customizing the Windows Explorer Window

Windows Explorer offers many ways to display the contents of a folder, and that's the subject of most of this chapter. Rather than just use Windows Explorer as it appears out of the box, you should set it up to work exactly the way you want. You start your customization by using the first three commands on the Windows Explorer View menu: Toolbars, Status Bar, and Explorer Bar.

## Customizing Toolbars

Windows Explorer has four toolbars: Standard Buttons, Address Bar, Links, and Radio. These toolbars are the same ones that are available in Microsoft Internet Explorer—because you can open any Web page in Windows Explorer. *For more information about using the Address Bar, Links, Radio, and Standard Buttons toolbars in Internet Explorer, see Chapter 18, "Using Internet Explorer."* You can display these toolbars in any combination. Open the View menu, point to Toolbars, and then choose the toolbar's name from the submenu that appears. Choose the same command again to hide a toolbar.

**⭐ TIP**

> As a quicker way to display or hide a toolbar, right-click any toolbar, which displays the same commands as the View menu's Toolbars command.

You can tailor the appearance of the Explorer toolbars in the following ways:

- To expand the toolbar area, which can be displayed on one through five lines, drag the lower boundary of the toolbar area downward. To collapse a multiline toolbar area, drag the lower boundary upward.

- To change the location or size of any of the toolbars, drag the vertical line at the left end of the toolbar. With this capability, you can combine two or more toolbars on a single line, place each on a line of its own, change their order, and change their width.

**> NOTE**

> You can also move and resize the menu bar like a toolbar, except that you can't hide it altogether.

In addition, you can customize the Standard Buttons toolbar by choosing which buttons to include, specifying their order, specifying their size, and specifying whether they include text labels.

To customize the Standard Buttons toolbar:

**1**   Open the View menu, point to Toolbars, and choose Customize.

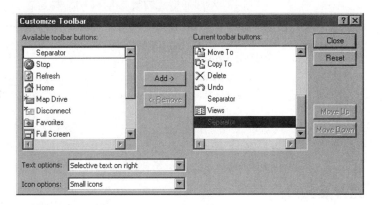

**2**   Select the buttons you want included.

To add a button, select it in the left box and click Add. To remove a button, select it in the right box and click Remove.

**3**   Set the order of the buttons.

Moving a button up in the list moves it to the left on the toolbar. Therefore, to move a button to the left, select it in the right box and click Move Up; to move it to the right, click Move Down.

**TIP**

To add or remove a button, you can drag it from one box to the other. To set the order, you can drag a button to a new position in the right box.

**4**   Select one of the following text options:

- **Show Text Labels.** Includes each button's text (as shown in the Customize Toolbar dialog box) below the button icon.

- **Selective Text On Right.** Includes the text of certain buttons (such as Back, Search, Folders, and History) to the right of the button icon.

- **No Text Labels.** Displays all buttons as unlabeled icons.

**⭐ TIP**

> To refresh your memory about a button without a text label, hover the mouse pointer over the button to display the button's text as a ScreenTip.

**5** In the Icon Options box, select Small Icons or Large Icons.

## Displaying the Status Bar

The View menu's Status Bar command displays or hides the status bar at the bottom of the Windows Explorer window. The status bar isn't an exciting display, but we mention it here because this overlooked area can provide useful information that's not immediately available anywhere else, such as the number of objects in the displayed folder and their total size, the amount of free disk space, and the target of a link you point to.

## Displaying Explorer Bars

**❓ SEE ALSO**

For information about using the Search bar, see Chapter 11, "Searching for Files and Folders." For information about the Folders bar, see Chapter 8, "Using Windows Explorer." For information about the other Explorer bars and custom bars, see Chapter 18, "Using Internet Explorer."

The View menu's Explorer Bar command branches to a submenu that lets you display one of the standard Explorer bars—Search, Favorites, History, or Folders. The Explorer bar you select opens along the left edge of the Windows Explorer window in its own pane. Figure 5-1 shows a Windows Explorer window with the History bar displayed. In addition, you can display any custom Explorer bar that you (or an application) have installed.

In previous versions of Windows, the Explorer bars (other than the Folders bar) were useful primarily for Internet exploration. But in Windows 2000, each of the Explorer bars can also be helpful in the Windows Explorer context:

- The Search bar lets you search for folders and files on your computer or on the network in addition to its traditional Web-searching role.

- Originally designed as a repository for Internet shortcuts, the Favorites bar (and the Favorites menu) can also be used for other purposes. Any folder, document, or shortcut stored in your Favorites folder appears on your Favorites bar and Favorites menu. So, for example, by creating shortcuts to disk folders that you use frequently and storing those shortcuts in your Favorites folder, you can give yourself yet another handy navigational tool.

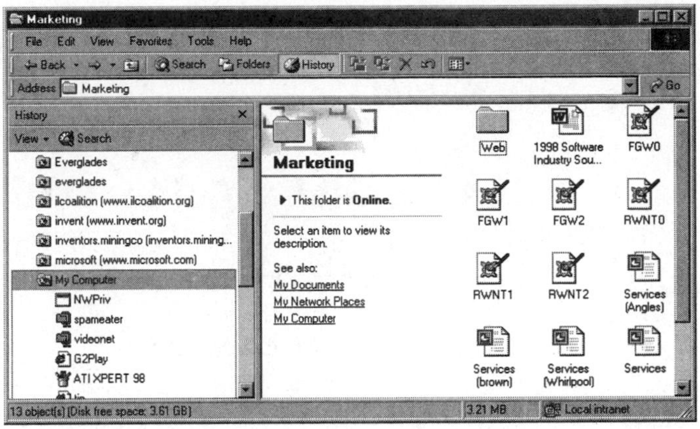

**FIGURE 5-1.**

The History pane at the left side of this Windows Explorer window is an example of an Explorer bar.

- The History bar lets you redisplay Web pages that you have recently visited. In addition, it retains links to recently used document files on your computer and on your network, allowing you to reopen them with a single click.

> By default, the Standard Buttons toolbar contains Search, Folders, and History buttons. Click one of these buttons to display an Explorer bar.

To close an Explorer bar, do any of the following:

- Open a different Explorer bar.

- Click the close button in the upper right corner of the displayed bar.

- Click the toolbar button for the displayed bar. (It appears to be indented.)

# Setting Folder Display Options

Windows Explorer gives you many ways to view the contents of your folders. You can choose from five display styles, sort folder entries in a number of ways, and decide whether to keep your folder icons in tidy columns or not. You can also choose whether filename extensions should be included with all Windows Explorer icons, decide whether the complete path of the current folder should appear in the Windows Explorer title bar, and express preferences on various other display matters.

II

Customizing the Environment

Some of the Windows Explorer display options are global options that apply to all folders you display. Others can be applied either to the current folder only or to all folders at once, and still others can be applied only to the current folder.

## Setting Global Folder Options

Many of the changes you can make to Windows Explorer are made in the Folder Options dialog box, which is shown in Figure 5-2.

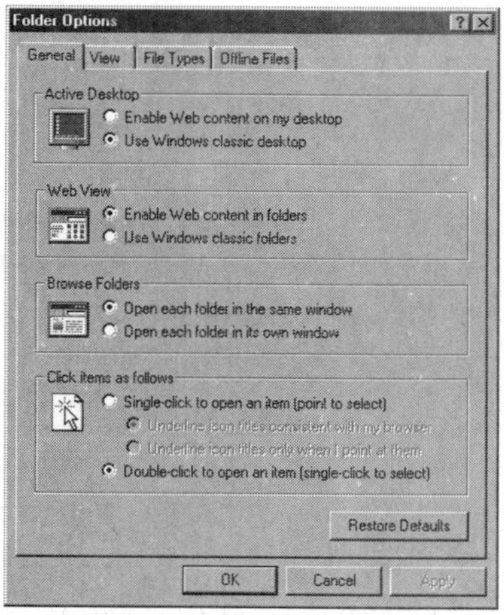

**FIGURE 5-2.**

You set many Windows Explorer options in the Folder Options dialog box.

Use either of the following methods to display the Folder Options dialog box:

- Click the Start button, point to Settings, and click Control Panel. In Control Panel, double-click the Folder Options icon.

- In Windows Explorer, open the Tools menu and choose Folder Options.

## Choosing Web View or Classic View

In the past few years, the computing world has moved rapidly toward a user interface based entirely on Internet and World Wide Web concepts. Many applications of all types—from Microsoft and from other software publishers—now sport an interface that looks just like the browser you use for exploring the Internet. (In some cases, the resemblance is more than superficial; the application actually uses your Web browser as its interface.) Because of their familiarity, Web-style interfaces can reduce the time it takes to learn a new application. And the Web's tendency toward graphically rich displays can make these interfaces visually appealing.

The trend toward Web-centric computing now extends even to the tool you use for managing your local files—Windows Explorer. Web view displays each folder as a Web page rather than as a simple directory. Figure 5-3 shows a folder in Web view and in the spartan Classic view.

**FIGURE 5-3.**

Web view enables the use of HTML templates for displaying folders. Classic view shows only the folder contents, without the accompanying graphics, links, and preview images.

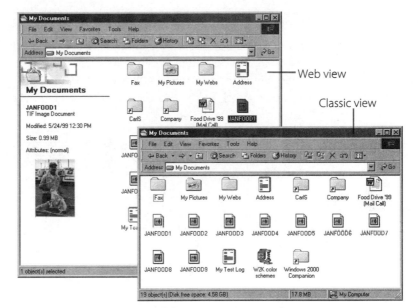

Web view

Classic view

To choose between Web view or Classic view:

**1** Open the Folder Options dialog box.

**2** Click the General tab.

**3** Under Web View, select either Enable Web Content In Folders or Use Windows Classic Folders.

What does it mean to display a folder as a Web page? The apparent difference is that Windows displays the folder using an additional frame on the left side with a pretty graphic. The frame contains links to other frequently used folders, and if you select one or more objects, it displays information (and, depending on the type of object, a preview image) about the selection.

The additional frame is part of an HTML template. Behind the scenes, Windows takes the folder contents—just as you would see them in Classic view—and pours them into the HTML template.

When you choose Web view, Windows uses an HTML template called Folder.htt, which is stored as a hidden file in %SystemRoot%\Web. Using the Customize This Folder command, described later in this chapter on page 91, you can edit Folder.htt or replace it with a different HTML template file.

The primary advantage of Classic view—other than satisfying a yearning for the good old days—is that it requires less screen space to display the same number of objects. But you might find that the file information and image preview in Web view's left frame are an adequate substitute for Details view or Thumbnails view, which means you can switch to the more compact List view. Have your cake and eat it too!

On some systems, Classic view is noticeably faster than Web view.

The folder contents are deemed more important than the graphics that grace the left side of the window. If the window is too small to display both, the graphics get the boot and the folder contents are listed just as they would be in Classic view.

## Setting Other Global Options

The View tab in the Folder Options dialog box, shown in Figure 5-4, includes a list of advanced settings that govern global display options—options that apply to all folders, including the desktop. Here's a description of those options:

- **Display Compressed Files And Folders With Alternate Color.** If you turn on this option, the names of compressed files and folders appear in blue text. Because you don't need to do anything special to use compressed files, this option is off by default; it adds visual anarchy without adding any essential information. *For information about compression, see "Compressing Files on NTFS Volumes," page 653.*

- **Display The Full Path In The Address Bar.** If you leave this option off (its default state), the Address bar shows only the name of the current folder. If you turn on the option, the Address bar shows the folder's full path. Overriding the default here can help you keep track of where your folders live within your overall folder hierarchy.

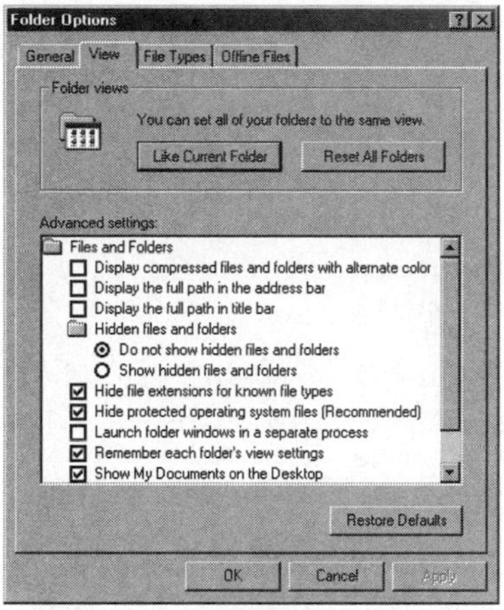

**FIGURE 5-4.**

The View tab in the Folder Options dialog box gives you choices about what to include in Windows Explorer windows.

■ **Display The Full Path In Title Bar.** Like the preceding option, this one lets you display the full path of the current folder rather than only its name. The difference is that this option places the additional information in the title bar instead of the Address bar. (Note that changing the title bar content also changes the text that appears on the window's taskbar button. You might find it either more or less useful to include the complete path in the taskbar.)

■ **Hidden Files And Folders.** By default, Windows Explorer shows all files and folders except files with the hidden attribute. Hiding these items protects them from accidental changes and deletions and reduces clutter in your folder windows.

As Figure 5-4 shows, Windows Explorer offers two options for hiding files and folders. Select the first to keep all hidden items invisible. Select the second to display files with the hidden attribute.

**TIP**

File types not shown in Windows Explorer windows are also invisible to the Search command. If you want to be able to search for particular types of files with the Search command, be sure to make those file types visible in your folders.

■ **Hide File Extensions For Known File Types.** This option, on by default, causes Windows Explorer to display the names of registered file types without their filename extensions. In most cases, you can recognize what kind of file each Windows Explorer entry represents by looking at its icon. If you're not sure what an icon signifies, you can turn off this option. Alternatively, you can switch to Details view or Web view. (Details view displays the file type for all files; Web view displays the file type for the selected file.)

When the Hide File Extensions For Known File Types option is turned off, Windows Explorer displays extensions for *all* files, not just unregistered file types. You can also display the extensions for only a particular registered file type. To do this, use the File Types tab in the Folder Options dialog box. Select the file type you're interested in, click the Advanced button, and then select the Always Show Extension check box.

### What Is a Filename Extension?

A *filename extension* is any group of characters that appears after the final period in a filename. Versions of Microsoft Windows prior to Windows 95, as well as the versions of MS-DOS on which they were built, allowed filenames to have extensions of up to three characters. Such extensions provided a means of categorizing files. All batch files, for example, had the extension .BAT; all graphics files in the Windows bitmap format had the extension .BMP, and so on.

Windows 95 did away with the three-character extension limit—as well as the onerous eight-character limit that applied to the main part of a file's name. In Windows 95, Windows 98, Windows NT, and Windows 2000, filenames can consist of up to 255 characters, including as many periods as you like and as many characters as needed after the final period.

These emancipations notwithstanding, Windows and Windows-based programs still use filename extensions to categorize files. Many programs, for example, automatically append an extension to any filename you supply, even though you might not see the extensions in the entries that appear in your Windows Explorer windows.

■ **Hide Protected Operating System Files.** Files with the hidden and system attributes are crucial to the operation of programs and to the operation of Windows itself. They're not normally included in Windows Explorer displays because accidental deletion or relocation of one of them can have serious adverse consequences—possibly requiring you to reinstall a program or even Windows itself. Therefore, unless you need to work with these types of files, it's a good idea to leave them out of sight by keeping this option turned on.

> **NOTE**

Files and folders with the hidden and system attributes are displayed only if you turn on Show Hidden Files And Folders *and* you turn off Hide Protected Operating System Files.

■ **Launch Folder Windows In A Separate Process.** Even when you don't have any Windows Explorer windows open, an Explorer.exe process is running; it controls items such as the taskbar and the desktop. When you open Windows Explorer windows with this option turned off (the default), Windows uses the already-running process. By turning on this option, you tell Windows to open a second process in a separate part of memory for controlling Windows Explorer windows. (To monitor and verify this effect, open Task Manager and click the Processes tab. *For information about Task Manager, see "Monitoring Performance with Task Manager," page 678.*)

> **TIP**

If you have trouble with Windows Explorer crashing on your system, turn on the Launch Folder Windows In A Separate Process option. Although performance might suffer slightly, your system will be more stable.

■ **Remember Each Folder's View Settings.** If you leave this option on (its default state), the display settings you assign to a folder persist. The next time you open a folder, it will look the same way it did the last time you opened it. If you turn the option off, closing a folder restores the settings that were in place when you installed Windows.

> **TIP**

You'll get faster performance if you turn off Remember Each Folder's View Settings. When it's turned on, Windows must find a folder's settings in the registry before it displays the folder.

■ **Show My Documents On The Desktop.** Leaving this option on causes the My Documents icon to appear on the desktop. If you don't use the icon, turn off this option to reduce the clutter.

■ **Show Pop-Up Description For Folder And Desktop Items.** On by default, this option causes Windows Explorer to display descriptions of certain Windows Explorer and desktop items when you hover the mouse pointer over those items.

II

Customizing the Environment

### Restoring Default Settings

If you change your mind after tinkering with the advanced settings in the Folder Options dialog box, simply click the Restore Defaults button at the bottom of the dialog box shown in Figure 5-4, on page 83.

## Setting Options That Apply to the Current Folder or All Folders

The display options described in the next several sections can be applied either to the current folder or to every folder. To apply the options to all folders, first apply them to the current folder. Then choose the Folder Options command on the View menu, click the View tab, and click the Like Current Folder button. To return all these display options to their original settings (those that were in place when you installed Windows), choose Folder Options from the View menu, click the View tab, and then click the Reset All Folders button.

---

### A Strategy for Customizing Folders

Most users have a view and sort order that they prefer for most folders—and it might not be the default Large Icons view sorted by name. You might prefer to see most folders in Details view, sorted by file type, with only a few other folders in Large Icons view. Windows provides an easy way to change the default view—but it's not intuitive, and if you don't follow this strategy from the get-go, you might need to reset options in folders you've already customized.

**1** In the Folder Options dialog box, click the View tab, and be sure that the Remember Each Folder's View Settings option is turned on.

**2** Customize a folder the way you want most folders to appear. From the View menu, select a view and a sort order. Select Auto Arrange if you like. If your preferred view is Details, select the columns you want to include.

**3** Open the Tools menu and choose Folder Options. Click the View tab, and then click Like Current Folder to set all folders the same as the current folder.

**4** As you visit other folders, customize each one as you like.

Windows remembers your settings and displays each folder the way you last customized it.

---

## Big Icons or Small?

By default, Windows Explorer displays a folder's contents as a set of large icons. Other display styles are available, and you can choose the style you prefer with commands on the View menu or by clicking the Views tool on the Standard Buttons toolbar. The alternatives to Large Icons view are Small Icons, List, Details, and Thumbnails. (See Figure 5-5.)

Views

**FIGURE 5-5.**
The View menu lets you choose between five display options.

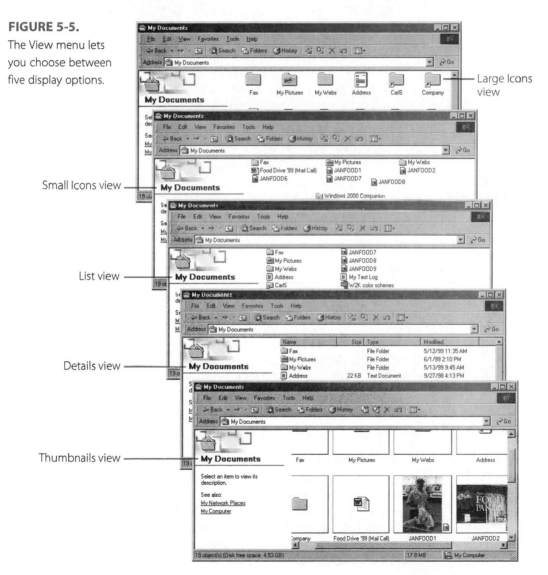

Large Icons view

Small Icons view

List view

Details view

Thumbnails view

Customizing the Environment

- **Large Icons view.** The default view for Windows folders, with easy-to-see icons.

- **Small Icons view.** Lets you see more file and subfolder names without enlarging the window.

- **List view.** Identical to Small Icons view except that the folder's contents are arranged vertically instead of horizontally, and the icons are maintained in orderly columns; you can't scatter them in hodge-podge fashion.

- **Details view.** Also arranges the folder's contents vertically, but Windows Explorer includes useful information about each entry. In most disk folders, Details view shows each entry's size, type, and the date of the most recent edit.

- **Thumbnails view.** Shows, where possible, a picture of each file's contents. You might find Thumbnails view handy for folders that contain mostly graphics files.

**TIP**

The Details view of My Computer shows the total size and available free space for each disk on your system.

**TIP**

Details view tells you when a file was last edited. To find out when it was created and when it was last accessed, right-click the filename or icon and choose Properties from the shortcut menu.

## Sorting Options

In Details view, you can sort the contents of a folder by clicking a column heading. For example, to arrange a folder's contents by file size (smallest to largest), click the Size heading. Click the column heading again to reverse the sort order (largest to smallest).

In the other views, you can sort the contents by opening the View menu, pointing to Arrange Icons, and then selecting a sort key (name, file type, file size, or date) from the submenu. You can also choose the Arrange Icons command from the shortcut menu that appears when you right-click any unoccupied area of the Windows Explorer window.

## Neatly Arranged or Casual?

In Large Icons view, Small Icons view, and Thumbnails view, you can have Windows Explorer automatically preserve an orderly arrangement of folder contents. To do this, open the View menu, point to Arrange Icons, and, if the Auto Arrange command isn't already checked, select it. With Auto Arrange turned on, any icon you add to a folder (by creating a new file, for example) automatically falls in line with the rest of the folder's contents. If you delete an icon, the remaining icons automatically close ranks. If you drag an icon out of position, Windows Explorer snaps it back into place.

If you don't like this regimentation, you can turn it off by choosing the Auto Arrange command again. With Auto Arrange turned off, you can drag your icons anywhere you please. (See Figure 5-6.)

**FIGURE 5-6.**
Turning off Auto Arrange gives you the freedom to drag icons out of their orderly rows and columns.

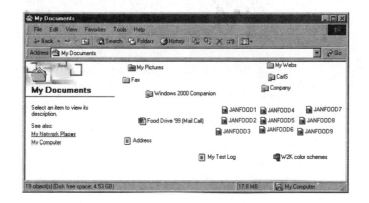

Turning off Auto Arrange has the advantage of letting you create ad hoc groupings. For example, you can put all the items that you're currently working with together at the top of the folder. But with this freedom comes some hazard: if you're too casual with your ad hoc arrangements, you can lose track of items. For example, if you drag an icon so far from its comrades that you have to scroll a long distance to see it, you might forget you have it.

**TIP**
When Auto Arrange is off, you can choose any of the sorting commands (By Name, By Type, By Size, or By Date) to return your icons to orderly rows and columns.

**TIP**
To turn Auto Arrange on or off for your desktop icons, right-click anywhere on the desktop, point to Arrange Icons, and click Auto Arrange.

Customizing the Environment

⭐ **TIP**

> If your folder icons are lined up neatly in rows and columns but they don't use the full width of the window, check to see if Auto Arrange is on. With Auto Arrange turned off, icon positions are not adjusted when a window's size changes.

## Choosing Columns in Details View

By default, Details view shows four columns: Name, Size, Type, and Modified. Windows maintains other information about folders and files, such as file attributes, creation date, access date, owner, and so on. Certain types of files contain other useful information, such as a version number, author, or number of pages. In earlier versions of Windows, this information was available only by selecting an object and displaying its properties. In Windows 2000, you can select any combination of useful columns, as shown in Figure 5-7.

To choose columns for Details view:

**1** Switch to Details view.

**2** Open the View menu and choose Choose Columns.

The Column Settings dialog box appears.

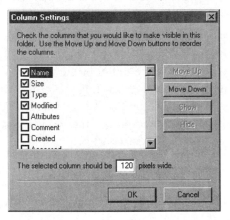

**3** Select the columns that you want to appear.

**4** Set the order of the columns.

Moving a column up in the list moves it to the left in the Windows Explorer window. Therefore, to move a column to the left, select it and click Move Up; to move it to the right, click Move Down.

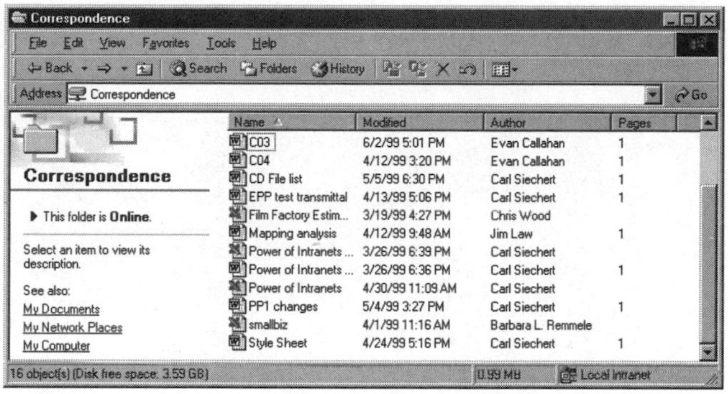

**FIGURE 5-7.**
In Details view, you can choose to display any columns that make sense for a particular folder.

**TIP**

**Adjusting Column Width in Details View**
To change the width of a column in Details view, drag the boundary between column headings. To adjust a column's width automatically so that it's just wide enough for the column's widest entry, double-click the right boundary of the column heading.

**TIP**

When you're troubleshooting problems with a program, it's sometimes important to know which version of the program and its supporting files you have. For these situations, display the Name, Modified, and Product Version columns.

# Setting Options That Apply to Only the Current Folder

Some display options can be applied to only the current folder. With these options, you can

- Apply a background picture
- Change the color of icon text
- Add a comment that describes the folder
- Apply an HTML template

The Customize This Folder Wizard leads you through the process of applying these options. To launch the wizard, choose the Customize This Folder command from Windows Explorer's View menu. Click Next on the introductory page to display the wizard page shown in Figure 5-8, on the following page.

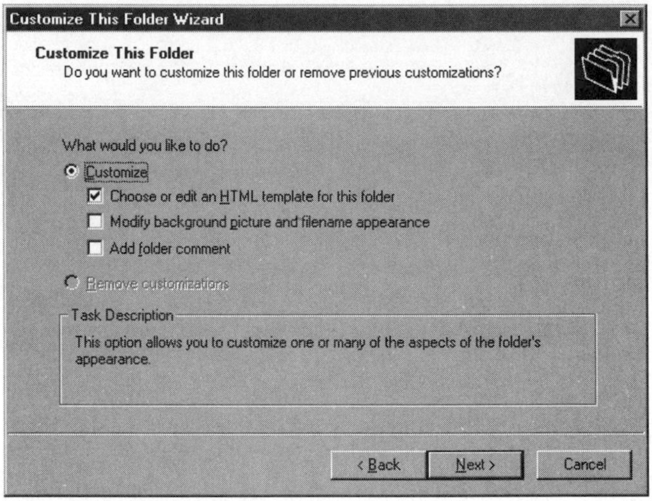

**FIGURE 5-8.**

The Customize This Folder Wizard lets you apply a background picture or an HTML page to the current folder.

> **NOTE**
>
> The Customize This Folder command is available for most folders, but you won't find it on the menu of certain special folders, including My Computer, Program Files, %SystemRoot%, and Control Panel.

## Applying a Background Image

Like the desktop, a Windows Explorer window can be decorated with a background picture.

To add a background picture to your folder:

**1** On the Customize This Folder Wizard page shown in Figure 5-8, select Modify Background Picture And Filename Appearance.

**2** Click Next.

As Figure 5-9 shows, a new page appears, on which you'll be able to choose a picture file. A preview of your selection appears at the left side of this page.

**3** Select a file from the list, or click Browse for more options. You can choose any file in the BMP, GIF, or JPEG format.

The list includes pictures in the current folder, in your My Pictures folder, and in the %SystemRoot% folder.

**4** Click Next, and then click Finish when you reach the wizard's final page.

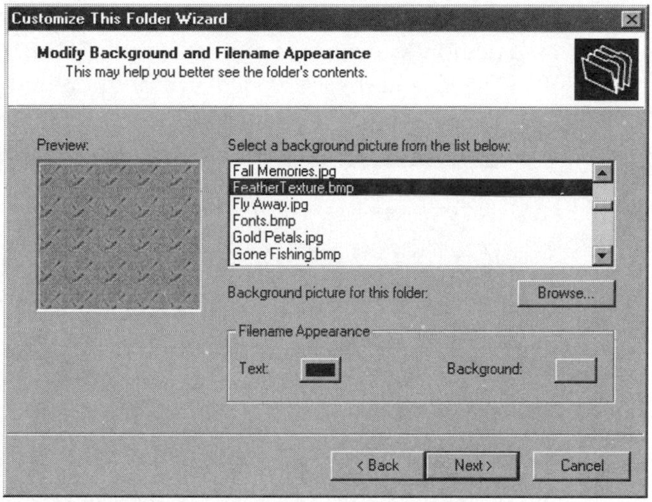
Customize This Folder Wizard
Modify Background and Filename Appearance
This may help you better see the folder's contents.
Preview:
Select a background picture from the list below:
Fall Memories.jpg
FeatherTexture.bmp
Fly Away.jpg
Fonts.bmp
Gold Petals.jpg
Gone Fishing.bmp
Background picture for this folder:
Browse...
Filename Appearance
Text:
Background:
< Back
Next >
Cancel

**FIGURE 5-9.**
A folder's background picture can be a BMP, GIF, or JPEG file. You can also use this page to change the color of a folder's text.



## Changing the Color of Icon Text

You can also use the Customize This Folder command to change the foreground and background colors of the text that appears with each folder item.

1. On the Customize This Folder Wizard page shown in Figure 5-8, select Modify Background Picture And Filename Appearance, and then click Next. (See Figure 5-9.)
2. To change the foreground color, click the Text button. To change the background color, click the Background button.
3. Click Next, and then click Finish when you reach the wizard's final page.

Figure 5-10, on the next page, shows one possible modification.

## Adding a Comment

You can add a comment to a folder that appears in the left pane when you use Web view. The comment appears there when you display the folder (as shown in Figure 5-10), or when you select the folder in its parent folder.

To add a comment to your folder:

1. On the Customize This Folder Wizard page shown in Figure 5-8, select Add Folder Comment, and then click Next.

**2** When you reach the page shown below, type your comment. In addition to plain text, you can enter HTML codes, as shown here. (The <b> and </b> codes turn bold on and off.)

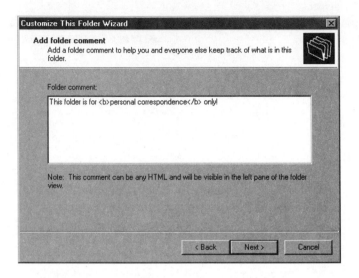

**3** Click Next, and then click Finish when you reach the wizard's final page.

**FIGURE 5-10.**

Simply applying FeatherTexture.bmp as a background image and changing icon caption text to yellow creates a distinctive, although admittedly gaudy, folder view.

Folder comment ⎯

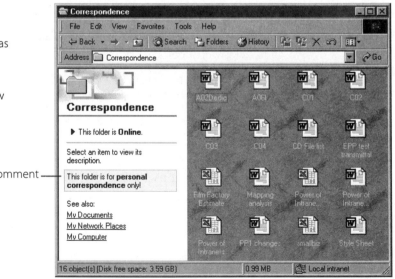

## Applying an HTML Template

When you use Web view, Windows displays folder content using an *HTML template*—essentially, a predesigned Web page with placeholders for folder items and their descriptions. In addition to the standard Web-view template, you can choose one of several others, and you can modify any of the furnished templates (including Folder.htt, the standard one).

To apply an HTML template to your folder:

**1** On the Customize This Folder Wizard page shown in Figure 5-8 on page 92, select Choose Or Edit An HTML Template For This Folder, and then click Next.

**2** When you reach the page shown below, select a template from the list.

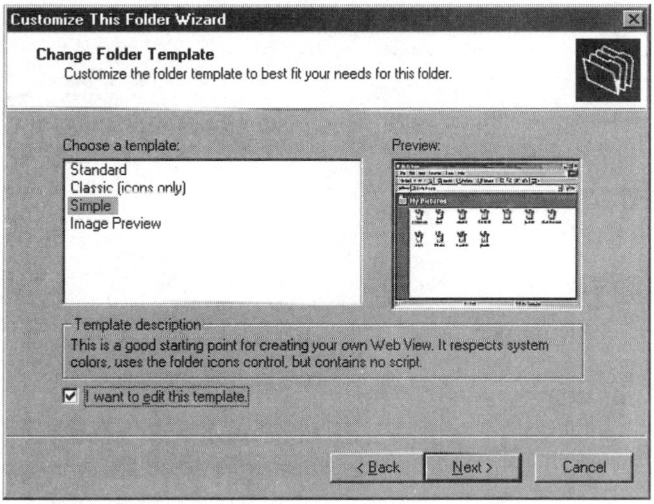

**3** If you want to edit the template before you apply it, select the I Want To Edit This Template check box.

**4** Click Next. If you selected the "edit" check box, the template opens in your HTML editor. (If you don't have a program associated with the .htt file type, the template opens in Notepad—the HTML editor for hardcore Webheads.) Make your edits, and then close your HTML editor.

**5** Back in the Customize This Folder Wizard, click Finish.

Windows copies your selected template and its accompanying graphics files to a hidden folder (named Folder Settings) within the folder you're customizing and changes the template copy's name to Folder.htt.

## Removing Your Customizations

If you change your mind about the modifications you've made via the Customize This Folder command, revisit the command and select the Remove Customizations option. Windows Explorer then reverts to its default appearance.

**CHAPTER 6**

# Making Other Customizations

The Control Panel system folder contains a variety of icons to display dialog boxes (sometimes called *property sheets*) or folders that help you customize and configure different aspects of your Windows system. We've already seen a few of these dialog boxes and folders—Display Properties and Folder Options—in earlier chapters of this book. Others will be taken up in later chapters. In the present chapter, we'll look at Control Panel itself and at most of the Control Panel items that don't fall neatly into other chapters.

Some Control Panel items are available only when you're logged on as a member of the Administrators group (or some other high-powered group). If you try to use one of these items without the proper authority, you'll be politely—but firmly—rebuffed with an "insufficient privileges" message. Some Control Panel items let ordinary users examine the properties and settings but prohibit them from making changes.

Many changes you make in Control Panel affect only the user who is currently logged on. This allows you to customize your workspace without imposing your tastes on others who share your workstation. But it also means that global changes you want to make must be made individually for each user.

# How to Get to Control Panel

Figure 6-1 shows the Control Panel folder of one of the computers used to create this book. Most of the icons in Control Panel represent generic operating system tools. But programs and hardware devices can add their own icons as well. Microsoft Office, for example, installs a Mail icon in Control Panel. Program- and hardware-specific items such as these are too numerous and variable to be covered in this book.

**FIGURE 6-1.**

The Control Panel folder contains icons to launch dialog boxes and folders that help you customize and configure your system.

You can get to Control Panel by opening the Start menu, pointing to Settings, and then choosing Control Panel. Alternatively, you can open the Control Panel icon in your My Computer folder.

## What About the Other Icons?

These Control Panel icons are described elsewhere in this book:

| | |
|---|---|
| Accessibility Options | See Chapter 7, "Using the Accessibility Features." |
| Add/Remove Hardware | See Chapter 24, "Installing and Configuring Hardware." |
| Add/Remove Programs | See "Using Add/Remove Programs," page 262. |
| Administrative Tools | See Chapter 25, "Managing Devices and Drivers"; Chapter 27, "Implementing Windows 2000 Security"; and Chapter 32, "Monitoring Your System." |
| Display | See "Changing Your Desktop's Display Properties," page 58. |
| Fax | See "Setting Up Your System," page 426. |
| Folder Options | See Chapter 5, "Customizing Windows Explorer." |
| Fonts | See Chapter 13, "Installing and Using Fonts." |
| Game Controllers | See "Installing and Configuring a Game Controller," page 526. |
| Internet Options | See Chapter 18, "Using Internet Explorer." |
| Network And Dial-Up Connections | See Chapter 16, "Making Connections." |
| Phone And Modem Options | See "Installing and Configuring a Modem," page 523. |
| Power Options | See Chapter 26, "Power Management." |
| Printers | See Chapter 12, "Printing"; and "Installing and Configuring a Printer," page 510. |
| Scanners And Cameras | See "Installing and Configuring a Scanner or Camera," page 525. |
| Scheduled Tasks | See "Running Programs on Schedule" page 257. |
| System | The System icon provides a way to see which version of Windows 2000 you have installed (including any service packs) and displays basic information about your computer. In addition, it provides shortcuts to a number of other settings that can be reached through other means. |
| Users And Passwords | See Chapter 27, "Implementing Windows 2000 Security." |

**II**

**Customizing the Environment**

As Figure 6-2 shows, you can also expand Control Panel to display its items as a submenu on your Start menu. This allows you to pick just the Control Panel item you need directly from the Start menu without having to display the entire Control Panel folder.

**FIGURE 6-2.**
You can create a Control Panel submenu for your Start menu.

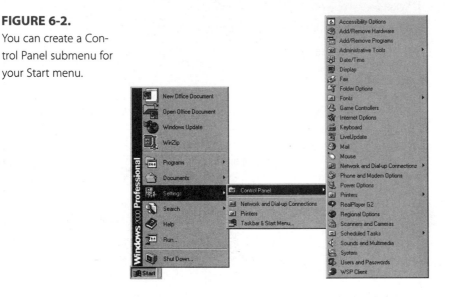

To create a Control Panel submenu:

**1** Click the Start button, point to Settings, and choose Taskbar & Start Menu.

**2** In the Taskbar And Start Menu Properties dialog box, click the Advanced tab.

**3** Select the Expand Control Panel check box.

**TIP**

If you decide to expand the Control Panel, you can still open the Control Panel folder by right-clicking Control Panel on the Start menu and choosing Open (or Explore) from the shortcut menu.

# Creating Shortcuts

You can create a shortcut for any Control Panel item, just as you would create a shortcut to a document, folder, program, or Internet site. If you find yourself using particular Control Panel items regularly, you might want to put shortcuts for those items on your desktop, on a toolbar, or on the Start menu.

To create a shortcut to a Control Panel item:

**1** In Control Panel, right-click the item and choose Create Shortcut from the shortcut menu.

**2** Windows asks whether you want to put the shortcut on the desktop. Click Yes.

**3** Leave the new shortcut on the desktop or drag it to the toolbar or folder where you want it.

You can also create a desktop or toolbar shortcut for the entire Control Panel folder by right-dragging it out of My Computer and choosing Create Shortcut(s) Here from the shortcut menu.

---

### OK, Apply, and Cancel

Once you get into a dialog box launched from a Control Panel item, you can make your selections. Most such dialog boxes have three buttons at the bottom:

- Click OK to apply your selections and close the dialog box.

- Click Apply to apply your selections without closing the dialog box. This lets you see the effect of your changes without leaving the dialog box. If you don't like what you see, you can try something else.

- Click Cancel to ignore your selections and close the dialog box without making any changes. Note that once you click Apply, you can't click Cancel to restore your old settings.

---

II

Customizing the Environment

# Resetting the Date, Time, and Time Zone

Your computer uses its system date and time to timestamp files when they are created, modified, or accessed; to schedule events; and, naturally, to show you the current date and time. The time normally appears on the taskbar. (If it's not there, right-click an unoccupied area of the taskbar, choose Properties, and then select Show Clock.) To display the date, let your mouse pointer hover for a moment on the taskbar's clock.

⭐ **TIP**

To change the display format used by the clock—for example, to change AM and PM to am and pm—use the Time tab in the Regional Options dialog box. *For more information, see "Specifying Regional Options," page 107.*

You must be logged on as a member of the Administrators group or the Power Users group to set the date and time. Changes you make here affect all users on your workstation.

To change your computer's date or time setting:

**1** Launch Date/Time in Control Panel. The Date/Time Properties dialog box appears.

In the Date/Time Properties dialog box, use the Date & Time tab to adjust your system's clock or calendar. Use the Time Zone tab if you're moving to a different time zone or to enable or disable Windows' automatic adjustment for daylight saving time.

You can also get to the Date/Time Properties dialog box by double-clicking the clock on your taskbar.

**2** On the Date & Time tab, set the correct date and time:

- To choose a different month or year, select from the month and year boxes above the calendar.

- To set the day of the month, click it on the calendar.

- To change the time of day, click the appropriate portion of the Time edit box, and then adjust the time by clicking the arrows to the right of the edit box. For example, if the clock says 2:36 P.M. but it's really only 2:31, select the 36 and then click the down arrow five times. If the clock says

A.M. but it's actually P.M., click on or beside the "AM" and then click either arrow once. Alternatively, you can double-click the hours, minutes, or seconds portion that you want to change and type in the correct value.

> While you make time-of-day adjustments, your clock stops. After you've made your changes, click Apply or OK to start the clock running again.

**3** On the Time Zone tab, select a time zone from the list above the map.

Windows uses this information to track time information for files saved on a network that operates across multiple time zones.

**4** If you want Windows to automatically adjust your system's clock when daylight saving time begins or ends, select the Automatically Adjust Clock For Daylight Saving Changes check box.

**TIP**

**Synchronizing Computers on a Network**
If your computer is part of a Windows 2000 domain, the Windows Time service periodically synchronizes your computer's clock to match the time on the domain controller. If your computer is connected to any other type of Windows network, you can manually set your computer's clock to match the time on another computer in your network. To do so, choose the Run command from the Start menu and type *net time \\computer /set /yes*, where *computer* is the name of the computer you want to synchronize with. (If your computer is a member of a Windows NT domain, you can simply type *net time /domain /set /yes* to set your clock to match the domain controller's clock.) To synchronize your clock automatically each time you start Windows, create a shortcut with this command and place it in your Startup folder.

# Adjusting Keyboard Repeat Parameters

Unless you have disabled the "typematic" behavior of your keyboard to take advantage of the accessibility features, Windows repeats a character after you have held its key down for a brief length of time. You can adjust both the repeat speed and the interval that Windows waits before beginning to repeat. To do this, launch Keyboard in Control Panel to open the dialog box shown in Figure 6-3, on the next page.

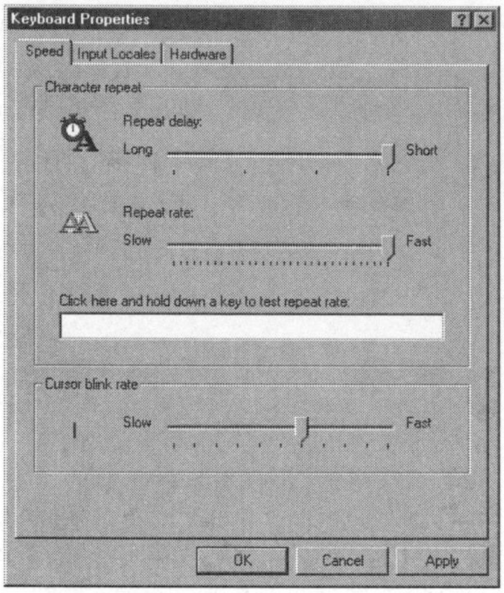

**FIGURE 6-3.**

The Keyboard Properties dialog box lets you adjust your keyboard's repeat speed and the speed at which the cursor blinks.

**❓ SEE ALSO**

For more information about controlling or disabling the keyboard repeat rate, see "Controlling the Keyboard Repeat Rate with FilterKeys (BounceKeys)," page 130.

To shorten the delay before repeating begins, drag the Repeat Delay slider to the right. To increase the repeat speed, drag the Repeat Rate slider to the right. Putting both these sliders as far as they'll go to the right makes your keyboard as responsive as Windows will allow. If you find yourself occasionally getting unwanted repeated characters, move the Repeat Delay slider, or both sliders, to the left. You can use the text box to test your settings before clicking OK.

In the lower part of the dialog box shown in Figure 6-3, you'll find another slider, for adjusting the rate at which the cursor blinks. If you're not happy with the default blink rate, you might want to experiment with moving this slider. The blinking line to the left of the slider shows your new cursor blink rate.

# Adjusting Mouse Behavior

Microsoft Windows lets you tailor the behavior of your mouse or other pointing device to suit your tastes. The options available depend on what kind of device you're using, but for most pointing devices you can adjust the pointer-movement and double-click speeds, as well as swap the functionality of the left and right mouse buttons. You might find it handy to swap mouse button functions if you're left-handed so that you can put the mouse on the left side of your keyboard and still use your index finger for most mouse commands.

To adjust mouse settings:

  **1**  Launch Mouse in Control Panel. The Mouse Properties dialog box appears, as shown in Figure 6-4.

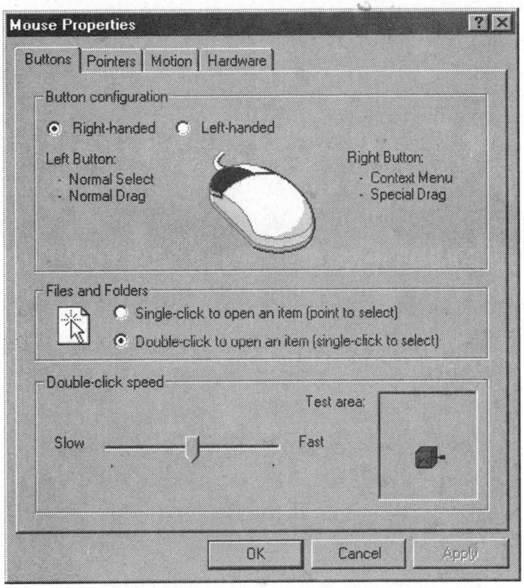

**FIGURE 6-4.**

The Mouse Properties dialog box lets you swap mouse-button functionality, adjust double-click speed, and set other mouse preferences.

**2** Set options on the Buttons tab:

- Under Button Configuration, you can swap mouse-button functionality.

- Under Files And Folders, indicate whether you want to use a click or a double-click to open files and folders on your desktop and in Windows Explorer. (This is an alternative method of setting an option available in the Folder Options dialog box. *For more information about this option, see "To Click or to Double-Click?" page 39.*)

- Under Double-Click Speed, you can adjust the time interval within which two mouse clicks in the same location are interpreted as a double-click.

**3** On the Motion tab, adjust the pointer speed and acceleration.

Pointer speed refers to the relationship between movement of the mouse on your desk and movement of the pointer on the screen. If you often find your mouse pointer overshooting its target as you select commands or objects in Windows, you might find it helpful to decrease the pointer speed. On the other hand, if you find yourself "rowing"—picking up the mouse, bringing it back through the air, and then sliding it over the mouse pad again merely to get the pointer from one side of the screen to the other—try increasing the pointer speed.

II

Customizing the Environment

Selecting the Low, Medium, or High Acceleration setting allows you to maintain precise control at slow speeds and still move the pointer across the screen quickly when you want to cover greater distances. With acceleration turned on, as you move the mouse faster, the mouse pointer moves even faster.

## Changing Mouse Pointer Shapes

Tired of the same old arrows and hourglasses? You can use the Pointers tab in the Mouse Properties dialog box to try on a different set of pointer shapes. Figure 6-5 shows a sample of what you'll find on the Pointers tab.

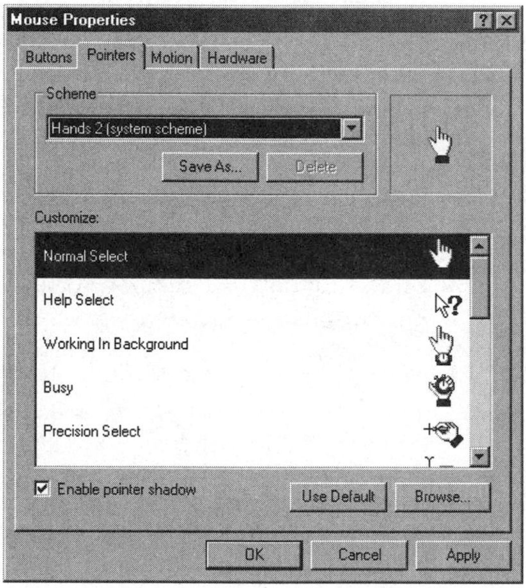

**FIGURE 6-5.**

You can select from a variety of static and animated pointer shapes.

The Customize section of the dialog box shows all the mouse actions recognized by Windows and the pointer shape currently assigned to each. To make a substitution, select an entry in this list and click the Browse button. The Browse dialog box that appears shows the available pointers, each stored in a separate file with the extension .cur or .ani. (If no files are shown, navigate to %SystemRoot%\Cursors for a nice selection.) The .cur files are static shapes, whereas the .ani files are animated. (To see only the static or animated offerings, click the Files Of Type box and select the type you're interested in.)

When you select a filename in the Browse dialog box, a Preview window shows what you've selected. Once you've selected an alternative pointer, you can return to the default by selecting it in the Customize list and clicking the Use Default button.

In the Scheme list at the top of the Pointers tab, you'll find several complete sets of pointers. You can install an entire set by selecting it from the list. Or, after you select individual pointers that you like, you can click the Save As button to create your own scheme.

To restore all the default shapes at once, choose Windows Default from the Scheme list.

 Whether you use a predefined scheme or assemble your own collection of pointers, you can add a light shadow that gives it a three-dimensional appearance. Select the Enable Pointer Shadow check box.

# Specifying Regional Options

The Regional Options icon in Control Panel allows you to adjust the way Windows displays dates, times, currency amounts, large numbers, and numbers with decimal fractions, as well as whether Windows should employ the metric or U.S. system of measurement. This Control Panel feature corresponds to what was called Regional Settings or International in earlier versions of Windows.

To modify any of Windows' regional settings, start by launching Regional Options in Control Panel. You will see the six-tabbed dialog box shown in Figure 6-6.

**FIGURE 6-6.**
You can change many regional settings at once simply by selecting a language and a country on the General tab in the Regional Options dialog box.

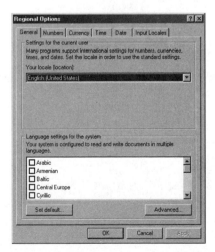

On the General tab of the Regional Options dialog box, you'll find the Your Locale box of input locales. (An *input locale* is a galaxy of settings for a specific language and geographic area, such as Canadian French or Jamaican English.) To adjust your system for a new language or country, start by selecting the new language and country from the list. (If the language you want doesn't appear in the Your Locale list, first select the region or language in the Language Settings For The System list at the bottom of the General tab. Doing so adds the associated locales to the upper list.) In response, Windows applies the default settings for all adjustable items—numbers, currency, times, and dates—all at once. In most cases, you won't need to make any further changes.

**(?) SEE ALSO**

For information about keyboard layouts, see "Installing Language Support and Using Keyboard Layouts," on the next page.

Windows installs, but doesn't change, the keyboard layout when you choose a different input locale on the General tab. To specify a different keyboard layout, use the Input Locales tab in the Regional Options dialog box or in the Keyboard Properties dialog box.

To override one or more default settings for a country, click the appropriate tab in the Regional Options dialog box and make your changes. Figure 6-7 shows the dialog box you'll see if you click the Numbers tab. Note that the Measurement System box, near the bottom of this dialog box, lets you switch between the metric and U.S. measurement systems.

**FIGURE 6-7.**

On the Numbers tab, you can choose the display formats to be used for decimal points and large numbers, as well as choose a default system of measurement.

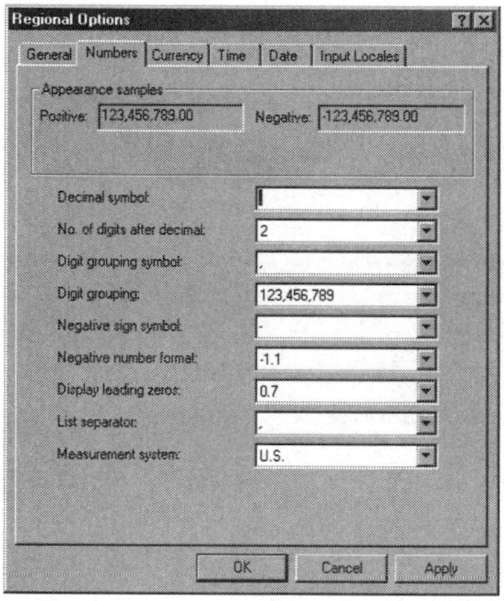

Be aware that all the settings in the Regional Options dialog box are merely defaults. Windows makes your choices available to programs, but the programs aren't required to use them. Some programs ignore the Windows default settings and instead maintain their own formatting defaults. If you ask for a particular display format style via Control Panel, but a program uses a different style, consult the documentation or Help file for that program.

Because of year 2000 (Y2K) problems and the associated frenzy, many Y2K-compliant programs ignore the date formats that you specify on the Date tab of the Regional Options dialog box, shown in Figure 6-8. Be aware that some programs *always* display four years for the date, regardless of the formatting you request. For programs that support it, Microsoft Windows 2000 provides a simpler way to keep track of which century a date belongs to. In the Calendar section of the Date tab, you can specify the end of a 100-year range. Then, in programs that recognize this setting, when you enter or view a two-digit year, it's assumed to be within this 100-year range. (Internally, of course, dates must be stored full-length to be Y2K compliant. This method merely allows you to enter dates in short form, and Windows inserts the century behind the scenes.)

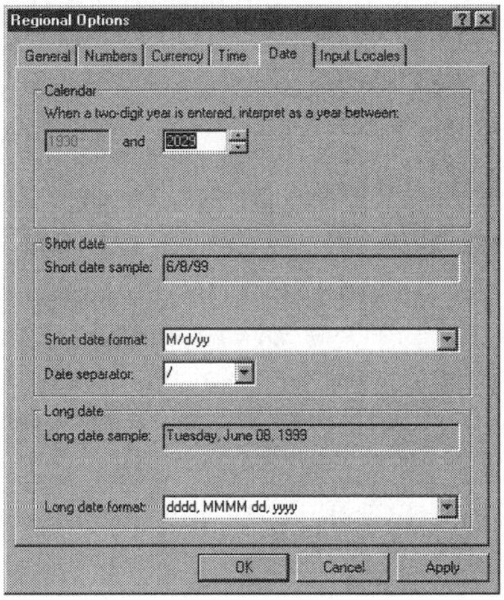

**FIGURE 6-8.**

With the Calendar setting shown here, any two-digit year from 30 through 99 is presumed to be in the 1900s, and two-digit years from 00 through 29 are presumed to be in the 2000s.

# Installing Language Support and Using Keyboard Layouts

Windows comes with support for a multitude of languages and keyboard layouts. If you work in more than one language or communicate with speakers of other languages, you might find it convenient to have two or more languages installed simultaneously. Then you can use simple mouse and keyboard procedures to switch from one language to another.

Languages and keyboard layouts are separate but related issues. When you activate another language, programs that have been written with language support in mind can provide appropriate services, such as using a different spelling checker or using special characters in TrueType fonts.

> **NOTE**
>
> Unless you have the Windows 2000 Multilanguage Version, the menus, dialog boxes, and help in Windows 2000 don't change to another language when you switch languages. If you have that version, the Menus And Dialogs box on the General tab lets you select a language for Windows elements independently of the language you specify for input.

When you switch to a different language, you get the default keyboard layout for that language, but you can choose alternative layouts. For example, for German, Windows supplies a standard layout and an IBM layout. For Russian, there's a standard layout and a typewriter layout—and so on. Some Asian languages use an input method editor (IME), a program that converts phonetic keyboard input to pictographs; you specify an IME just as you would a keyboard layout.

Even if you work only in English, you might want to investigate alternative keyboard layouts. Typing letters with accents, for example, might be simpler if you use the United States–International layout. And if the standard QWERTY system of typing isn't your preference, you can opt for the United States–Dvorak layout.

To install support for a new language:

1 Launch Regional Options (or Keyboard) in Control Panel.

   Both Control Panel items let you add an installed language to the list of input locales. If you need to install a new language, however, you must use Regional Options.

2 Click the Input Locales tab, shown in Figure 6-9.

3 Click the Add button and select the language and keyboard layout you want from the lists.

> **NOTE**
>
> If the language you're looking for isn't in the list and you launched Keyboard from Control Panel, close it and launch Regional Options instead. Click the General tab, select the language or region you want, and click OK. (You must be logged on as a member of the Administrators group to do this.) You'll need your Windows CD and you must restart your computer before you can use the new language. After you complete this process, return to the Input Locales tab.

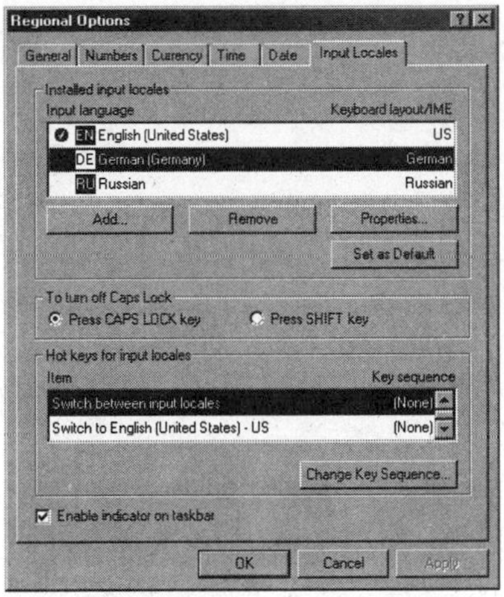

**FIGURE 6-9.**

On the Input Locales tab, you can add support for other languages or switch keyboard layouts.

**4** Select keystroke sequences (hot keys) for switching languages.

You can switch between input locales by pressing a keystroke sequence instead of returning to this dialog box. To do so, you must specify the sequence, which must include the Shift key and either the Ctrl key or the Alt key on the left side of your keyboard. Select an Item in the Hot Keys For Input Locales list, and then click Change Key Sequence to specify the key. (If you want to remove a key sequence, follow the same procedure, and clear the Enable Key Sequence check box in the Change Key Sequence dialog box that appears.)

By default, Windows displays a two-letter symbol in the status area of your taskbar whenever you have more than one language installed. You can use this symbol both as a reminder and as a switching mechanism. To switch languages, click the language symbol and then choose from the list that pops up. If, for some reason, you don't want this convenience, clear the Enable Indicator On Taskbar check box at the bottom of the Input Locales tab.

**TIP**

By right-clicking the language symbol in the status area of your taskbar and choosing Properties from the shortcut menu, you can go directly to the Regional Options dialog box without opening Control Panel.

II

Customizing the Environment

# Setting Sounds for Various Events

If your computer has a sound card, you can customize the various beeps, squeals, squeaks, and other exclamations emitted by Windows as you go about your workday. Or you can opt for golden silence instead. You can even create named sound schemes, comparable to your named appearance schemes, for easy reuse and recall.

To change the sounds used by Windows, launch Sounds And Multimedia in Control Panel. The Sounds And Multimedia Properties dialog box appears, as shown in Figure 6-10.

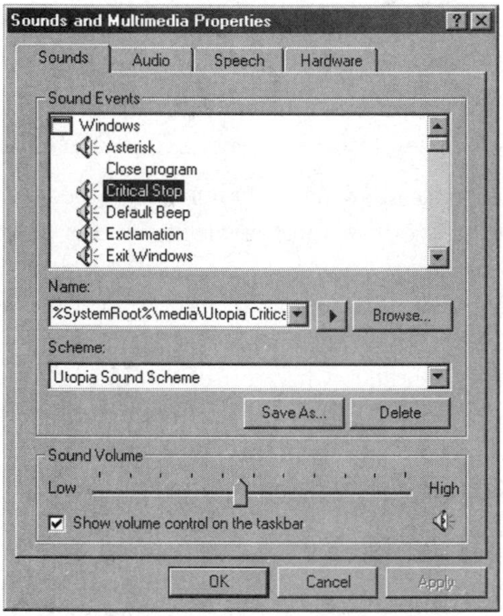

**FIGURE 6-10.**

The Sounds And Multimedia Properties dialog box lets you assign sound files to events and create named sound schemes.

The Sound Events list on the Sounds tab lists all the different system events to which you can attach (or from which you can detach) sounds. The list is structured as a two-level hierarchy. The first top-level item is Windows itself. The events subordinate to the Windows heading include events such as opening and closing programs, maximizing and minimizing windows, and starting and ending a Windows session. If you scroll downward through the Sound Events list, you will find another top-level heading for Windows Explorer and, possibly, additional headings for other applications installed on your computer.

Directly below the Sound Events list is a box labeled Name. This lists all the sound files (files with the extension .wav) that are available in the current folder.

Near the bottom of the dialog box is another box labeled Scheme. Here you will find complete sets of sounds and events that you can choose to activate. You can switch from one sound scheme to another by choosing from this list.

To hear what sound is currently assigned to an event, select the event in the Sound Events list. The name of the assigned sound appears in the Name box, and you can click the Play icon (the right-pointing arrow beside the Name box) to hear the current sound.

To assign a new sound to an event, select the event, and then choose a different item from the Name list. Click the Play button to be sure you've chosen the sound you want. If the sound you're looking for isn't listed in the Name list, click the Browse button. This takes you to the file-and-folder browser, where you can hunt for a different sound file.

To remove all sound from an event, select the event in the Sound Events list. Then choose (None) in the Name list.

Once you've hit upon a combination of sounds and events that pleases your ear, you can name it and add it to the Scheme list. Simply click the Save As button and enter a name for your new sound scheme.

## Adjusting the Volume

The slider at the bottom of the Sounds tab lets you set the volume. (You can test your new setting by selecting a sound and clicking Play.) To silence your system temporarily, click the speaker icon below the volume slider, which mutes the system.

**★ TIP**

> Select the Show Volume Control On The Taskbar check box to include an icon in the taskbar's status area that you can click to change the volume at which sounds are played or mute the system.

# Matching Colors with Color Profiles

In the past, it has been difficult—if not impossible—to reproduce colors accurately and consistently. Scanners, displays, printers, and programs each used different color management systems, and by the time an image moved from the computer screen to paper, it bore little resemblance to the scanned or digitally photographed original.

Windows remedies this problem by providing Image Color Management (ICM) 2. ICM provides a communications link between the various hardware devices and software programs that reproduce color. It maps colors between devices to ensure that the original image colors are accurately interpreted by an input device (such as a scanner or digital camera), displayed on a monitor, and printed on paper or saved in electronic format.

To set up Image Color Management:

**1** In Control Panel, open the properties dialog box for a color device:

- For a scanner or camera, launch Scanners And Cameras, select the scanner or camera in the Devices list, and click Properties.

- For a monitor, launch Display, click the Settings tab, and then click Advanced.

- For a printer, launch Printers, right-click the printer icon, and choose Properties from the shortcut menu.

**2** Click the Color Management tab to display a dialog box similar to the one shown in Figure 6-11.

**FIGURE 6-11.**
The Color Management tab lets you add and select color profiles.

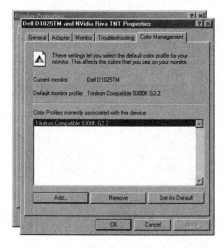

**3** If no color profiles are listed, click Add. Then select the color profile for your device.

**SEE ALSO**

For more information about the Imaging for Windows program, see Chapter 37, "Manipulating Faxes and Images with Imaging."

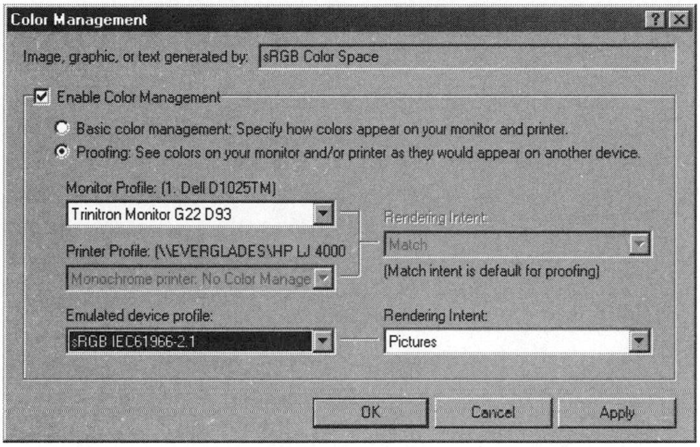

**FIGURE 6-12.**

In a program, you select installed color profiles to match colors across devices.

To display or print colors using color profiles:

**1** In your image-processing program (for example, the Imaging for Windows program included with Windows 2000 and located in the Accessories folder), open an image file.

**2** Open the File menu and choose Color Management. The Color Management dialog box appears, as shown in Figure 6-12.

**3** Select Enable Color Management.

• To match colors on your monitor and your printer, select Basic Color Management. Then select a Monitor Profile, a Printer Profile, and a Rendering Intent. (The *rendering intent* maps the colors in the image to the range of colors that the output or display device can produce. Because most devices can't produce a full range of colors, compromises must be made. Each rendering intent compromises in a way that best reproduces images of a certain type or for a certain purpose.)

• To preview colors on your monitor the way they'll appear on another output device, select Proofing. Then select a Monitor Profile, a Printer Profile, an Emulated Device Profile, and a Rendering Intent. ICM then adjusts the display and the printout to emulate the capabilities of the device you specify as the emulated device.

II

Customizing the Environment

**CHAPTER 7**

# Using the Accessibility Features

M icrosoft Windows offers a wide range of features to make computer use more accessible for people with disabilities. Whether the issue is impaired vision or hearing or an inability to use both hands for typing, Windows has a solution.

And you'll find that these features are not only for people with disabilities. If you work in a noisy environment or it's not convenient to use the mouse, for example, the accessibility features can help. Following are some of the available options. You can

- Use a special high-contrast appearance scheme throughout your Windows-based programs.

- Increase the size of icons, system text, scroll bars, and your mouse pointer.

- Use Magnifier to increase the size of everything in the current window.

- Use Narrator to read on-screen text aloud.

- Use visual cues instead of sounds to alert you to system events.

- Turn on StickyKeys, which enables you to use Ctrl, Alt, and Shift key combinations without having to hold down more than one key at a time.

- Use the keyboard instead of the mouse to click, double-click, and drag.

- Attach an alternate SerialKey input device to your serial port if you are unable to use a standard mouse or keyboard.

This chapter covers these and other accessibility features. You'll learn how to use each option, in what situations it might be appropriate, and tips for effective use.

# Getting to the Accessibility Features

Windows includes an Accessibility Wizard that simplifies your selection of accessibility features. To get to the wizard, open the Start menu and choose Programs, Accessories, Accessibility, Accessibility Wizard. You can also make accessibility-feature choices by opening Accessibility Options in Control Panel. To get to Control Panel, open the Start menu, point to Settings, and choose Control Panel.

Some options that affect the behavior of accessibility features are available only via Accessibility Options in Control Panel. For example, using Accessibility Options, you can specify that, with StickyKeys on, pressing the Shift key twice in a row turns on Shift Lock. Accessibility Options also lets you enable support for SerialKey devices, an option not provided by the wizard.

Other options that are provided by the wizard don't appear in Accessibility Options in Control Panel. For example, the wizard gives you more choices regarding visual enhancement than Accessibility Options does.

It's best, therefore, to take a walk through both the Accessibility Wizard and Accessibility Options. You might want to start with the wizard and then do any necessary fine-tuning with the help of Control Panel.

**> NOTE**

Some keyboard accessibility features can be turned on and off via special keyboard toggles. For example, pressing the Shift key five times in a row can turn on StickyKeys—or turn it off if it's already on. You'll find these shortcut keys handy if it's difficult for you to get to the wizard or Control Panel.

# Setting Options for People with Impaired Vision

Windows includes a number of features for users who are blind or have impaired vision. The Accessibility Wizard provides several options for making your display easier to read. Most of these options aren't available in Control Panel's Accessibility Options, but you can get to them via Display in Control Panel. With the wizard, you can do the following:

- Increase the size of all text.

- Increase the size of window title-bar text and menus.

- Use Magnifier to open a window that presents a magnified display of everything appearing in another part of your screen.

- Switch to a lower screen resolution (which makes text appear larger).

- Increase the size of window borders and scroll bars.

- Increase icon size.

- Choose one of four available high-contrast appearance schemes.

- Increase the size and contrast of the mouse pointer.

For users who are blind, Narrator can read on-screen text aloud. In addition, ToggleKeys provides an audible notification whenever you press the Num Lock key, the Caps Lock key, or the Scroll Lock key.

To take advantage of Windows display accessibility options:

**1**   Start the Accessibility Wizard.

**2**   Click Next (or press Enter) on the Welcome page, and on the second page, use the Up arrow key and Down arrow key to select the smallest type size you can read comfortably.

**3**   Click Next.

The Accessibility Wizard's Display Settings page appears, as shown in Figure 7-1, on the following page.

Windows proposes to select one or more of the check boxes shown in the figure, depending on which type size you selected on the previous wizard page.

II

Customizing the Environment

**FIGURE 7-1.**

The Accessibility Wizard suggests settings according to the smallest type size you say you can read, but you can override the suggestions.

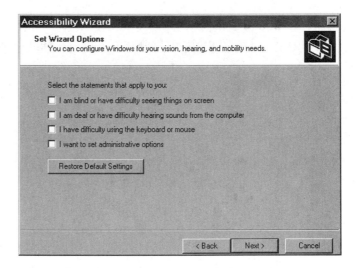

4  Make any changes to Windows' proposal that you think are appropriate, and then click Next again to open the page shown in Figure 7-2.

**FIGURE 7-2.**

The Set Wizard Options page provides a set of check boxes in which you specify the kinds of disabilities for which you want to adjust the Windows interface.

**SEE ALSO**

For information about appearance schemes, see "Changing Colors, Fonts, and Sizes," page 63.

5  On this page, select I Am Blind Or Have Difficulty Seeing Things On Screen.

6  Click Next to display the Scroll Bar And Window Border Size page, on which you can choose from four sizes of window borders and scroll bars.

Three more pages follow on which you can select enlarged icons, high-contrast color schemes, and high-visibility mouse pointers.

### Toggling Between Appearance Schemes

Because you can have one appearance scheme set in the Display Properties dialog box and another one in the Settings For High Contrast dialog box, you can easily toggle between two appearance schemes by pressing the shortcut key for High Contrast: press the left Alt key, the left Shift key, and the Print Screen key—all at the same time.

## Enlarging Screen Images with Magnifier

Magnifier initially splits your screen into two parts, with the upper part showing a magnified image of the lower part. (See Figure 7-3.) By default, you see a magnified image of your mouse pointer as well as every other screen detail. Magnifier can be sized and moved around the screen, and it can either float within the screen or be docked to any of the four edges of the screen.

**FIGURE 7-3.**

Magnifier devotes part of your screen to magnifying the rest of the screen.

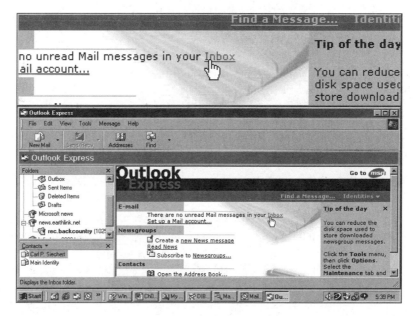

II

Customizing the Environment

**⑦ SEE ALSO**

For information about Utility Manager, see "Controlling Accessibility Settings with Utility Manager," page 138.

You can start Magnifier in either of two ways—by choosing it from the Accessibility menu of your Start menu or by using the Accessibility Wizard. In addition, users with administrator-level access can start or stop Magnifier with Utility Manager.

When you first start Magnifier, the dialog box shown in Figure 7-4 appears.

**⭐ TIP**

> You might want to assign a shortcut key to the menu command that launches Magnifier. That way you won't have to hunt for it on the menu. *For more information, see "Assigning a Shortcut Key," page 27.*

**⭐ TIP**

> With Utility Manager, users with administrator-level access can set up Magnifier to start when Windows 2000 starts.

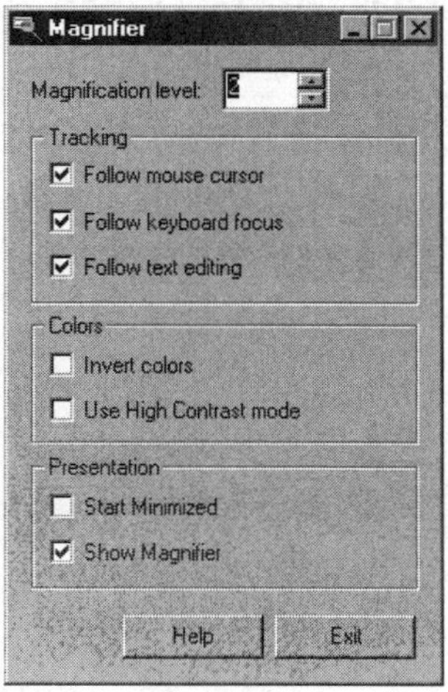

**FIGURE 7-4.**

This dialog box lets you configure Magnifier. Minimize it to get it out of the way. (Clicking Exit closes the Magnifier window.)

Use the Magnification Level box to adjust the degree of magnification—from a pointless 1 to a gigantic 9. With the check boxes, you can control other aspects of Magnifier's behavior. Chances are that you'll want to leave the first three boxes selected. That way, the image on top always stays in sync with your activity below. Try selecting the Invert Colors check box and the Use High Contrast Mode check box to see if they improve the legibility of the magnified image.

If you want, you can leave the Magnifier dialog box open on screen while you work. That way, you can adjust the magnification level up or down as situations require. If you'd prefer to get the dialog box out of the way, minimize it; it then remains on your taskbar for easy reuse.

If you don't plan to make further changes in the dialog box, select Start Minimized so that you won't be bothered with the dialog box in future Magnifier sessions.

Click Exit in the dialog box when you're ready to leave Magnifier, or right-click anywhere in the Magnifier window and choose Exit.

### Adjusting the Size and Position of the Magnifier Window

The first time you run Magnifier, the magnified image appears in a window docked at the top of the screen. You can customize the window in several ways:

- To allocate more or less space to the magnified part of the screen, drag the border that separates the two parts.

- To dock the magnified image to a different edge of the screen, place the mouse pointer in the magnified part (the pointer changes to a hand), and drag to another edge.

- To place the magnified image in a floating, resizable window, drag the magnified part toward the center of the screen.

Magnifier remembers the window size and position in effect when you exit, and uses the same position the next time you start Magnifier.

## Using Narrator to Read On-Screen Text Aloud

Narrator reads aloud text that appears in the active window. This can be useful, of course, to users who are blind or have low vision. Although Narrator's capabilities are limited and its diction far from perfect, this tool can also be useful for sighted users who want to proofread documents or who sometimes work where it's difficult to see the monitor. Narrator works well with the programs that come with Windows 2000, including WordPad, Notepad, and Microsoft Internet Explorer. You'll have varying degrees of success with other programs.

To start Narrator, choose it from the Accessibility menu of your Start menu. Users with administrator-level access can start or stop Narrator with Utility Manager.

**TIP**

With Utility Manager, users with administrator-level access can set up Narrator to start when Windows 2000 starts.

Customizing the Environment

When you first start Narrator, the dialog box shown in Figure 7-5 appears. In this dialog box, you set Narrator's few options:

■ **Announce Events On Screen.** Narrator always makes an announcement when you switch to a new window or dialog box. With this option selected, Narrator also reads the entire window or dialog box contents rather than just the title and the active item.

■ **Read Typed Characters.** With this option selected, Narrator announces each character as you type it.

■ **Move Mouse Pointer To The Active Item.** This option causes the mouse pointer to move to the active item whenever you use the keyboard to navigate in a dialog box or window. (This allows you to click with confidence, knowing that the mouse pointer is on the control that Narrator is describing.)

■ **Start Narrator Minimized.** This option causes Narrator to start as a taskbar icon, which is useful once you've configured Narrator to work the way you want.

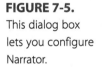

**FIGURE 7-5.**
This dialog box lets you configure Narrator.

Clicking the Voice button displays Narrator's Voice Settings dialog box, in which you can adjust its timbre to make its speech more recognizable. You can select a voice, if more than one is installed on your system, and you can adjust the speed, volume, and pitch of the selected voice. See Figure 7-6.

In general, Narrator pipes up whenever you switch to a new window, whenever a new dialog box appears, or whenever you navigate within a dialog box. With the following shortcut keys, you can request Narrator to read certain passages:

■ To read all the text in a window, select the window and press Ctrl+Shift+Spacebar.

- To read the current item (the item with the focus, such as a specific control in a dialog box), press Ctrl+Shift+Enter.

- To stop Narrator's reading, press the Ctrl key.

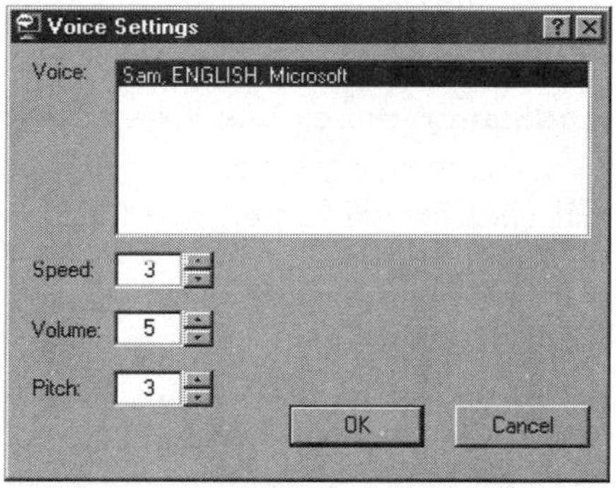

**FIGURE 7-6.**
The Voice Settings dialog box lets you choose a voice if you have more than one installed voice, and lets you set the voice's characteristics.

## Using ToggleKeys to Audibly Indicate Keyboard Status Changes

The ToggleKeys option causes Windows to sound a tone on the computer's built-in speaker each time the Caps Lock, Num Lock, or Scroll Lock key is pressed. To activate this feature using the Accessibility Wizard, step through the wizard until you come to the Set Wizard Options page shown in Figure 7-2, on page 120. Select I Have Difficulty Using The Keyboard Or Mouse, and then click Next. Keep moving through wizard pages until you come to the ToggleKeys page. Select Yes and exit the wizard.

To activate ToggleKeys using Accessibility Options in Control Panel, click the Keyboard tab, select the Use ToggleKeys check box, and then click Settings to make sure the shortcut key option is set as you want it. If you activate the shortcut key, holding down Num Lock for five seconds toggles the ToggleKeys feature on or off.

> You don't have to click Next repeatedly until you reach a Finish button to exit the wizard. After you've made the settings you want, click Cancel. The wizard then asks whether you want to save the changes you've made; click Yes.

# Setting Options for People with Impaired Hearing

The following options are designed for users who are hearing-impaired:

■ **SoundSentry** causes Windows to display a visual cue whenever your computer beeps. Separate options let you customize the visual cues for windowed and full-screen programs.

■ **ShowSounds** is the Windows equivalent of closed-captioned television. In programs that use digitized speech or other audible cues, ShowSounds instructs the program to provide visible feedback, such as text captions. Not all programs have this capability.

> **NOTE**
>
> The SoundSentry actions take place only when your system plays a sound through its internal speaker. (Most programs that beep through the internal speaker are MS-DOS-based programs.) Sounds played through external speakers via a sound card don't invoke SoundSentry.

> **TIP**
>
> The accessibility features designed for users who are hearing-impaired can also be used effectively in situations in which the computer's speakers must be turned off, or in extremely noisy workplaces.

To turn on either SoundSentry or ShowSounds via the Accessibility Wizard, on the Set Wizard Options page shown in Figure 7-2 on page 120, select I Am Deaf Or Have Difficulty Hearing Sounds From The Computer. Then proceed through the wizard to the SoundSentry and ShowSounds pages. Select Yes on the appropriate pages and then exit the wizard.

To turn on these features via Accessibility Options in Control Panel, click the Sound tab. You'll see the dialog box shown in Figure 7-7. Select the check box for either or both features, and then click Settings to specify what kind of visual cues you want.

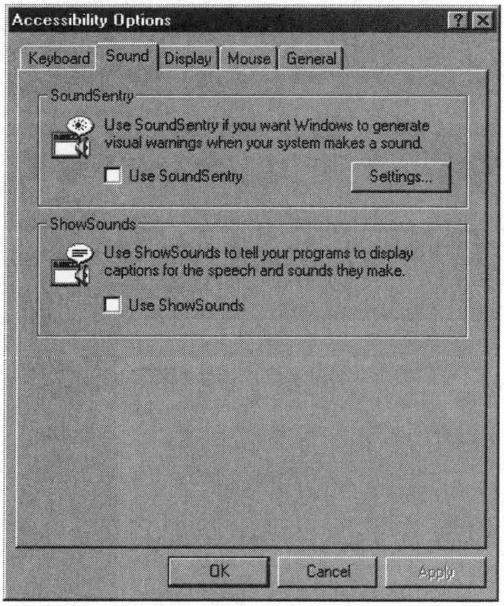

**FIGURE 7-7.**
SoundSentry and
ShowSounds
cause Windows
to augment some
of its normal sounds
with visual cues.

# Setting Options for
# People with Impaired Mobility

These options allow you to control how Windows handles keyboard
and mouse input.

- **StickyKeys.** Allows you to type keystroke combinations without
  the need to hold down one key while you press another.

- **FilterKeys.** Lets you ignore accidentally repeated keystrokes or
  brief keystrokes that are made by touching a key in error.

- **MouseKeys.** Lets you use the keyboard to simulate mouse
  movements and clicks.

- **On-Screen Keyboard.** Displays a keyboard replica on which
  you "type" by clicking its keys with a mouse or other pointing
  device.

- **SerialKey.** Enables the use of alternative input devices that connect to a serial port.

# Facilitating Entry of Keystroke Combinations with StickyKeys

Windows makes extensive use of shortcut keys, which generally require you to press more than one key at a time. For example, to use the keystroke combination Ctrl+Alt+Delete, a user must hold down the Ctrl and Alt keys while pressing the Delete key. In cases where a user is limited to one hand or a mouthstick, pressing multiple keys at the same time might not be possible.

> Depending on how your system is set up, you probably have to press Ctrl+Alt+Delete to log on. Ordinarily, accessibility settings are stored as part of your profile and aren't applied until after you log on. To get around this catch-22, open Accessibility Options in Control Panel, click the General tab, and select Apply All Settings To Logon Desktop.

StickyKeys enables users to input key combinations by pressing the applicable keys in sequence rather than simultaneously. This option causes the Ctrl, Alt, Shift, and Windows logo keys to become *sticky*—when a user presses one of these modifier keys, the key is locked down until any other key (except for Ctrl, Alt, Shift, or the Windows logo key) or a mouse button is pressed and released. Pressing the modifier key twice locks it "permanently"—until you press that modifier key a third time. While a key is locked, that key's space in the status area of the taskbar is shaded.

To turn on StickyKeys using the Accessibility Wizard, step through the wizard until you come to the page shown in Figure 7-2, on page 120. Select I Have Difficulty Using The Keyboard Or Mouse, and then click Next (or press Enter). Depending on the other options you select on this page, you'll come either immediately or eventually to the StickyKeys page, where you'll be given the option to turn on StickyKeys.

To turn on StickyKeys using Accessibility Options in Control Panel, select the first check box on the Keyboard tab in the Accessibility Options dialog box. (See Figure 7-8.) Then click Settings to make sure that options affecting the StickyKeys feature are set as you want them. Figure 7-9 shows the Settings For StickyKeys dialog box.

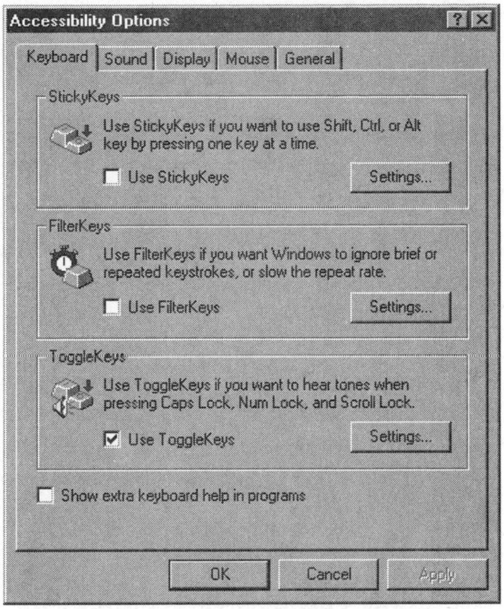

**FIGURE 7-8.**

The Keyboard tab in the Accessibility Options dialog box (accessible via Control Panel) lets you turn on or off the StickyKeys, FilterKeys, and ToggleKeys features.

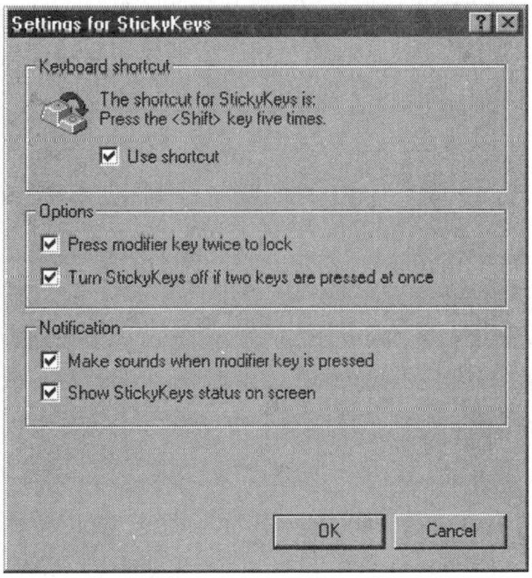

**FIGURE 7-9.**

You can customize StickyKeys behavior in the Settings for StickyKeys dialog box.

The following settings are available for StickyKeys:

■ To enable the shortcut key, select the Use Shortcut check box. Once you've done this, you can turn StickyKeys on or off by pressing the Shift key five times in succession.

- The StickyKeys feature allows users to lock a modifier key (Ctrl, Alt, Shift, or Windows) by pressing a modifier key twice. The key remains locked until you press it a third time. As a general rule, if you need the StickyKeys feature at all, you should leave this option enabled. You can, however, disable it by clearing the Press Modifier Key Twice To Lock check box.

- If several people use the same computer, keep the Turn StickyKeys Off If Two Keys Are Pressed At Once option selected (as it is by default). With this option selected, users who don't require StickyKeys can turn off the feature simply by pressing a modifier key and any other key at the same time.

- The Make Sounds When Modifier Key Is Pressed option can provide useful auditory feedback each time a Ctrl, Alt, Shift, or Windows logo key is pressed. It's a handy reminder that StickyKeys is active. If, however, you're the only user and have no need to be reminded, clear this option.

- You shouldn't need to change the default setting for Show StickyKeys Status On Screen, which displays an icon in the taskbar's status area. The icon lets you know that the feature is active and which modifier keys are currently locked.

## Controlling the Keyboard Repeat Rate with FilterKeys (BounceKeys)

The FilterKeys options provide precise control over the keyboard repeat rate. These options are particularly useful if involuntary hand movements cause accidental key presses.

**NOTE**

For reasons unknown, the feature that is called FilterKeys in the Accessibility Options dialog box is called BounceKeys in the Accessibility Wizard. FilterKeys in the Accessibility Options dialog box offers some additional settings that you can't make using the wizard.

To activate BounceKeys using the Accessibility Wizard:

1 Step through the wizard until you come to the page shown in Figure 7-2, on page 120. Select I Have Difficulty Using The Keyboard Or Mouse.

**⑦ SEE ALSO**

For information about setting the keyboard repeat rate, see "Adjusting Keyboard Repeat Parameters," page 103.

**2** Click Next. Keep moving through wizard pages until you come to the BounceKeys page.

**3** Select Yes and then click Next.

The BounceKeys Settings page allows you to set a minimum time within which repeated keystrokes will be treated as only a single keystroke; you can also test your settings on this page.

**4** When you are satisfied with your settings, exit the wizard.

To activate FilterKeys using Accessibility Options in Control Panel, click the Keyboard tab, select the Use FilterKeys check box, and then click the Settings button to make sure the options are set as you want them. Figure 7-10 shows the Settings For FilterKeys dialog box.

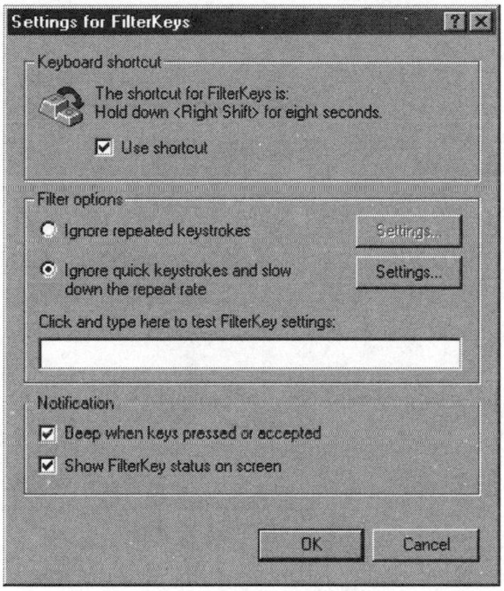

**FIGURE 7-10.**

The Settings For FilterKeys dialog box lets you ignore repeated keystrokes or brief keystrokes.

To enable the shortcut key, select the Use Shortcut check box. Once you've done this, you can turn FilterKeys on or off by holding down the right Shift key for eight seconds.

Use the Ignore Repeated Keystrokes option button to instruct Windows to ignore all but the first keystroke when a key press is rapidly repeated. The Advanced Settings For FilterKeys dialog box shown in Figure 7-11, on the next page, allows you to set a time interval within which repeated keystrokes are treated as a single keystroke. Test your settings in the test area provided before you accept them.

II

Customizing the Environment

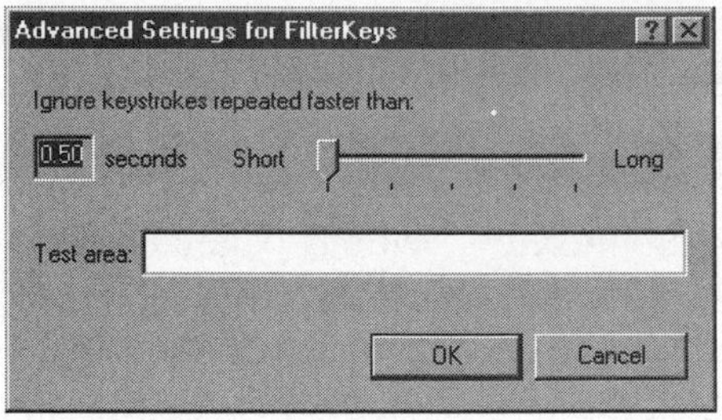

**FIGURE 7-11.**
With FilterKeys (or BounceKeys) enabled, key presses repeated more rapidly than the time shown in the Advanced Settings For FilterKeys dialog box are treated as only one keystroke.

The Ignore Quick Keystrokes And Slow Down The Repeat Rate option causes the computer to ignore keys that are tapped only briefly, as when a finger or mouthstick might slip off one key and hit another. When FilterKeys is active, these settings override Control Panel's Keyboard repeat settings. Clicking the Settings button next to this option opens the Advanced Settings For FilterKeys dialog box shown in Figure 7-12.

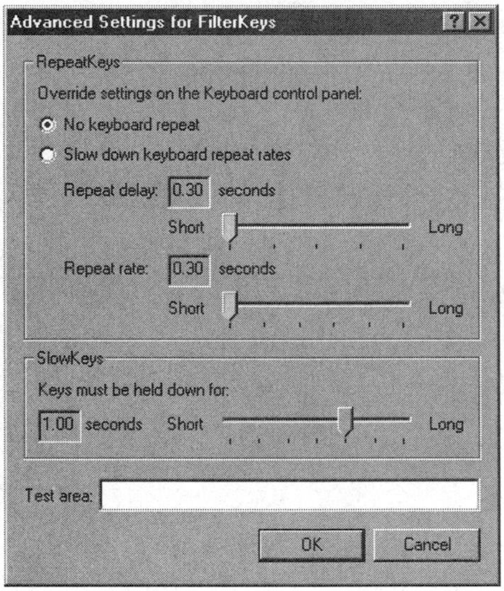

**FIGURE 7-12.**
Adjusting keyboard speed and repeat rates here overrides those set in Control Panel's Keyboard.

Select No Keyboard Repeat to turn off the keyboard repeat feature altogether. With this option selected, it doesn't matter how long you hold down a key; it won't repeat under any circumstances.

Select the Slow Down Keyboard Repeat Rates option and adjust the Repeat Delay setting and the Repeat Rate setting if you want to retain the ability to repeat keystrokes.

# Using the Keyboard Instead of the Mouse

MouseKeys lets you use Windows without a mouse. Normally, despite a program's implementation of keyboard equivalents, some tasks can be performed only by moving the mouse pointer, clicking, and dragging. But with MouseKeys on, you can use the keys on the numeric keypad to simulate mouse actions, as follows:

■ To move the mouse pointer, press any number key except 5. The arrows in Figure 7-13 show the direction in which each key moves the pointer. If you hold down a directional number key, the mouse pointer begins moving slowly and then accelerates to its maximum speed.

**FIGURE 7-13.**

Use the numeric keypad to imitate mouse actions.

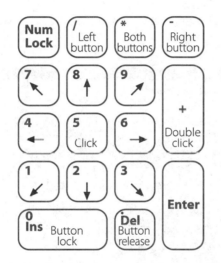

■ To select which mouse button to use for clicking and dragging, press the slash (/) key to select the left button, the minus (–) key to select the right button, or the asterisk (*) key to select both buttons. Your selection stays in effect until you select another; you don't need to select a button before each click or drag.

■ To click the selected button, press the 5 key.

■ To double-click the selected button, press the plus (+) key.

■ To drag with the selected button, position the mouse pointer on the object and press the 0 key (Ins). Then use the directional number keys to move the mouse pointer. Press the period (.) key (Del) to release the mouse button, which completes the drag operation.

■ To move the mouse pointer in larger increments, hold down the Ctrl key while you use the direction keys.

To turn on MouseKeys with the Accessibility Wizard:

**1** Select I Have Difficulty Using The Keyboard Or Mouse on the page shown in Figure 7-2, on page 120.

**2** Click Next. After several pages relating to keyboard options, you'll come to the MouseKeys page.

**3** Select Yes on the MouseKeys page and click Next again to see the MouseKeys Settings page, shown in Figure 7-14.

**4** Adjust the speed at which your mouse moves and accelerates.

**5** Decide whether you want MouseKeys to work with Num Lock on or off.

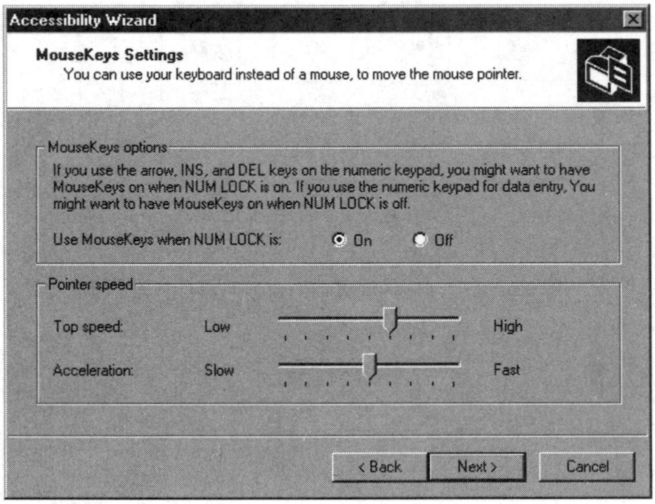

**FIGURE 7-14.**

Use this page to change the speed and acceleration characteristics of your MouseKeys mouse.

To activate MouseKeys using Accessibility Options in Control Panel, click the Mouse tab and select Use MouseKeys. Then click the Settings button to adjust the speed and acceleration of your mouse. The Settings For MouseKeys dialog box that you reach via Control Panel is organized somewhat differently than is the Accessibility Wizard's page, but it includes all the wizard's options and these three additional options:

■ The Use Shortcut option turns on the shortcut key for MouseKeys. With the shortcut key enabled, pressing the left Shift key, the left Alt key, and Num Lock at the same time toggles MouseKeys on or off.

- The Pointer Speed section activates a Ctrl+key and Shift+key throttle system. To enable this feature, select the Hold Down Ctrl To Speed Up And Shift To Slow Down check box. When enabled, if you hold down a direction key and also press Ctrl, the mouse pointer begins moving slowly and then accelerates to its maximum speed. If you hold down Shift while you hold down a direction key, the mouse pointer moves at a slow, steady rate.

- The Show MouseKey Status On Screen check box adds an icon to the taskbar status area that shows which mouse button is selected. Double-clicking the icon opens the Accessibility Options dialog box.

## Making the Mouse Pointer Easier to See and Use

**SEE ALSO**

For information about Mouse in Control Panel, see "Adjusting Mouse Behavior," page 104.

The Accessibility Wizard offers some additional options for making the mouse pointer more visible. You can change the size and color of the pointer, switch the primary and secondary mouse buttons, and change the pointer speed. These options are presented on a series of wizard pages that appear when you select I Have Difficulty Using The Keyboard Or Mouse on the Set Wizard Options page shown in Figure 7-2, on page 120. These choices don't appear in Control Panel's Accessibility Options, but you can get to them via Mouse in Control Panel.

## Using On-Screen Keyboard

MouseKeys, described earlier in this chapter, lets you use the keyboard instead of a mouse. On-Screen Keyboard, new in Windows 2000, provides the opposite functionality: it lets you use the mouse (or another pointing device) instead of a keyboard. To start On-Screen Keyboard, choose it from the Accessibility folder of your Start menu. You'll see a display similar to the one shown in Figure 7-15.

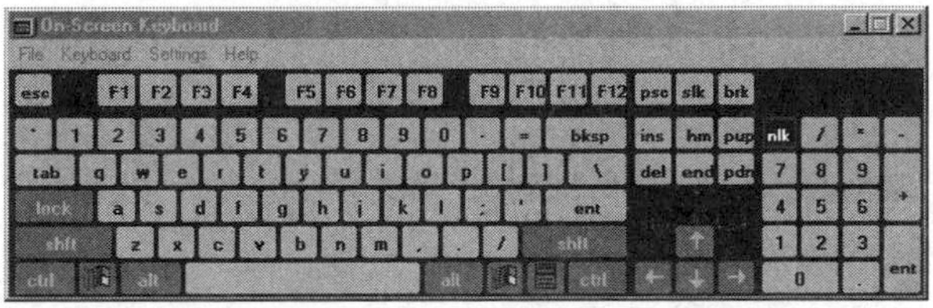

**FIGURE 7-15.**

On-Screen Keyboard lets you type by clicking "keys" in this window.

**II**

**Customizing the Environment**

To "type," you use the mouse pointer to point to a key button, and then click. To type a capital letter, click the Shift button and then click the letter button. The modifier keys (Ctrl, Alt, Shift, and Windows logo) work somewhat like StickyKeys, even if you don't have that feature enabled: when you click one of these keys, it remains locked down until you click any other key (except Ctrl, Alt, Shift, or Windows logo). If you click a modifier key by mistake, click it again to release it.

> You can't type with On-Screen Keyboard while it is the active application. Switch to the application that you want to receive the keystrokes; the On-Screen Keyboard window remains on top.

You can choose one of several keyboard arrangements by choosing commands on the Keyboard menu.

If it's difficult for you to click a mouse button, open the Settings menu and choose Typing Mode to use one of On-Screen Keyboard's alternative input methods:

- **Hover To Select.** With this method, you type a character simply by pointing at it with the mouse pointer, a head pointer, or other pointing device, and hovering for at least the number of seconds specified in the Minimum Time To Hover box.

- **Joystick Or Key To Select.** In this mode, On-Screen Keyboard continually scans the displayed keyboard, selecting it row by row, until you press a key (you can specify which key) or activate a switch connected to a serial, parallel, or game port. When you select a row, On-Screen Keyboard then selects each character in that row until you press a key or activate a switch; it then types the selected character.

**TIP**

> If you're logged on as a member of the Administrators group, you can add On-Screen Keyboard to the list of programs controlled by Utility Manager; doing so lets you easily start On-Screen Keyboard when you start Windows. To do this, open the File menu in On-Screen Keyboard and choose Add To Utility Manager.

## Installing Support for SerialKey Devices

A *SerialKey device* is a device that plugs in to one of your computer's serial ports and provides alternative access to keyboard and mouse features. To use one of these devices, you must enable its support by going to the General tab of Accessibility Options in Control Panel. Select the Support SerialKey Devices check box. Then click the Settings button and specify the serial port you'll be using and the baud rate (speed).

# Setting Administrative Options

The Accessibility Wizard also offers the following administrative settings:

- You can have StickyKeys, FilterKeys, ToggleKeys, and high-contrast display turn off automatically whenever the computer has been idle for a period of time that you specify (five minutes, by default).

- You can make your accessibility settings apply automatically to any new profiles (user accounts) created on your system. (You must be logged on as a member of the Administrators group to set this option.)

- You can save your accessibility settings in a file, and then use that file to set up another system with the same settings. (To set up another system, copy the file you create to the new system. Then simply launch the file in Windows Explorer to apply the settings.)

To avail yourself of any of these options, choose I Want To Set Administrative Options on the page shown in Figure 7-2, on page 120.

Three additional administrative settings are provided only on the General tab of Accessibility Options in Control Panel:

- **Give Warning Message When Turning A Feature On.** Causes a warning message to appear whenever an accessibility feature is turned on or off.

- **Make A Sound When Turning A Feature On Or Off.** Causes the system to make a sound whenever an accessibility feature is turned on or off.

- **Apply All Settings To Logon Desktop.** Applies the current accessibility settings to the *logon desktop*—the screen that asks for your user name and password when you first start your computer. Choosing this option makes it possible for users who need the accessibility options to log on. (You must be logged on as a member of the Administrators group to set this option.)

II

Customizing the Environment

# 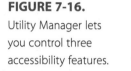 Controlling Accessibility Settings with Utility Manager

Utility Manager, shown in Figure 7-16, is a simple program that lets you start and stop three accessibility options: Magnifier, Narrator, and On-Screen Keyboard. With this tool, you can also set any of these programs to start whenever you start your computer. This makes the programs accessible at the logon desktop; programs in the Startup group on the Start menu, by contrast, start *after* you log on.

**FIGURE 7-16.**
Utility Manager lets you control three accessibility features.

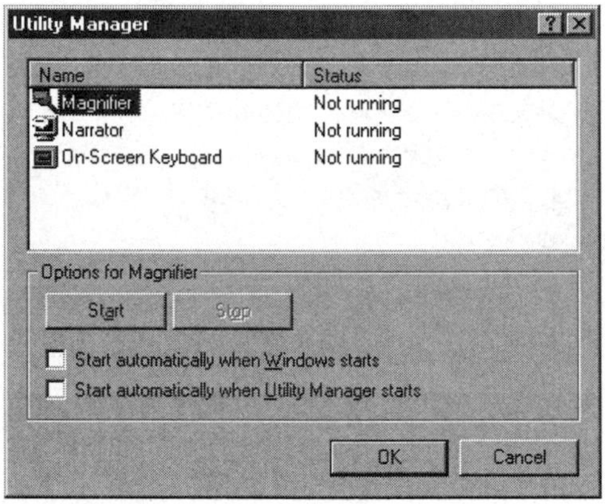

| Utility Manager | ? X |
| --- | --- |

| Name | Status |
| --- | --- |
| Magnifier | Not running |
| Narrator | Not running |
| On-Screen Keyboard | Not running |

Options for Magnifier

[ Start ] [ Stop ]

☐ Start automatically when Windows starts
☐ Start automatically when Utility Manager starts

[ OK ] [ Cancel ]

To start or stop a program, select the program name and click the appropriate button.

To set a program to start whenever you start your computer, select the program and then select Start Automatically When Windows Starts.

 **TIP**

You can open Utility Manager at any time by pressing its shortcut key, Windows logo+U.

# PART III

# Managing Documents

**CHAPTER 8**

# Using
# Windows Explorer

In this chapter, we'll look at the many ways you can use Windows Explorer to manipulate your computer's local and networked files, folders, and programs.

As you've probably discovered, you can now switch easily between Windows Explorer (the Windows *file browser* program) and Microsoft Internet Explorer (the Windows *Web browser* program), and barely notice the transition. If you type an Internet address into Windows Explorer's Address bar, for example, a Web page might appear. And if you type the path of a local folder or network share into Internet Explorer's Address bar, suddenly you're back in Windows Explorer again. For all intents and purposes, the two programs are one in Microsoft Windows 2000.

We'll save the manipulation of Internet resources via Internet Explorer for Chapter 18 and focus here on local matters—such things as navigating through your computer's folder structure, moving and copying documents, and creating and modifying associations between file types and applications. For all the details about customizing the appearance of Windows Explorer, meanwhile, please turn back to Chapter 5.

# Running Windows Explorer

**?** **SEE ALSO**

For information about clicking vs. double-clicking, see "To Click or to Double-Click?," page 39.

Any time you open a folder, Windows Explorer displays the contents of that folder. That's the simplest way to run Windows Explorer. You can also run it by opening the Start menu and choosing Programs, Accessories, Windows Explorer. (You can also open the Start menu, choose Run, and type *explorer.exe*.)

When you run Windows Explorer from the Start menu, the folder that appears initially is My Documents. This behavior represents a change from earlier versions of Windows, in which Windows Explorer opened My Computer by default. If you want, you can restore the older behavior. To make the Windows Explorer menu command open My Computer by default:

1 Open the Start menu and choose Programs, Accessories.

2 Right-click the Windows Explorer item on the Accessories menu and choose Properties.

3 Click the Shortcut tab.

4 Replace the contents of the Target field with

%SystemRoot%\explorer.exe /e,"

---

### What's in a Folder?

The basic unit of display in Windows Explorer is the folder, of which there are two kinds in Windows 2000. One kind of folder, called a *file folder*, corresponds with what, in MS-DOS days, was called a directory. Most of the folders you'll work with are of this type. If you open Command Prompt by clicking the Start menu, pointing to the Programs menu, and pointing to Accessories, and you poke about with the cd (change directory) command, you can find an MS-DOS-style directory corresponding to each file folder on your system. *To learn more about the Command Prompt, search Windows 2000 Help.*

The other kind of folder is the *system folder*. Control Panel, Printers, My Computer, My Network Places, and Scheduled Tasks are examples of system folders. These don't correspond to MS-DOS-style directories, but when displayed in Windows Explorer, they look just like ordinary folders. The reason for pointing out the distinction is that you can't perform certain tasks with system folders. You can't rename, share, or delete Control Panel, for example.

# Navigating Through Folders

Launching a folder icon from the desktop or from a Windows Explorer window causes Windows Explorer to display the contents of that folder. Thus, for example, from the Windows Explorer display of drive F shown in Figure 8-1, you could display the contents of the Documents And Settings folder by simply clicking that folder icon. By default, Windows Explorer *replaces* the current display with the display of the newly selected folder. If you prefer, you can have a new window appear instead, allowing you to see both the folder you were looking at and the one you just navigated to.

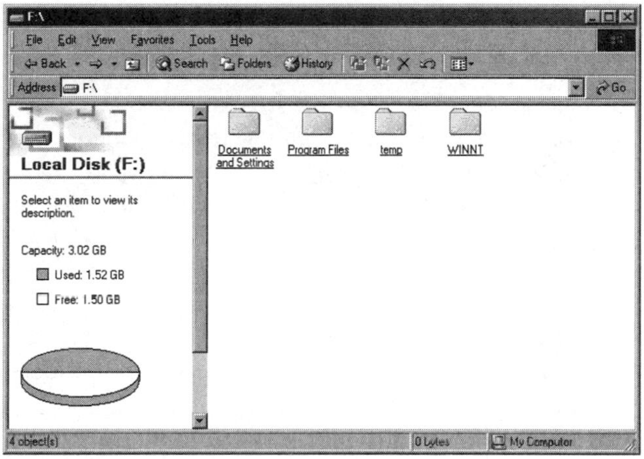

**FIGURE 8-1.**

You can move from folder to folder by clicking folder icons within Windows Explorer windows.

To have Windows Explorer open each folder in a separate window:

1  In any Windows Explorer window, choose Folder Options from the Tools menu.

2  On the General tab, select Open Each Folder In Its Own Window.

## Navigating with the Folders Bar

Figure 8-2, on the next page, shows the same folder as Figure 8-1, but includes the Folders bar—a separate pane on the left that displays the entire hierarchy of resources available to your system.

Using the Folders bar, you can navigate directly from whatever folder you're currently looking at to any other folder. To move from drive F to My Documents on the system shown in Figure 8-2, for example, you could simply click My Documents in the left pane.

III

Managing Documents

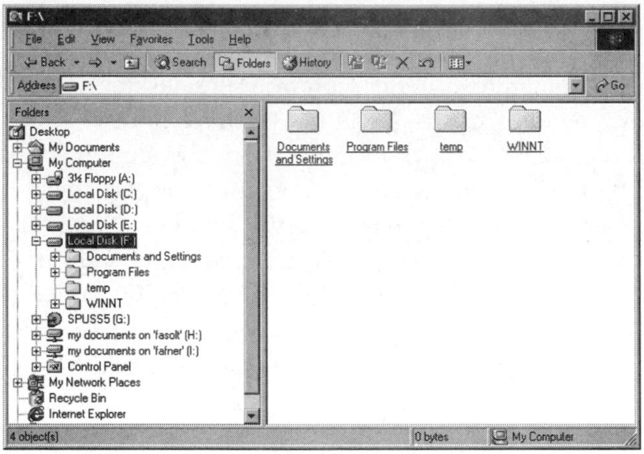

**FIGURE 8-2.**

You can often move more quickly from one folder to another by adding the Folders bar to your Windows Explorer display.

The Folders bar is an outline of your system. You can manipulate the outline entries by clicking the plus (+) symbols in the list to expand folders and clicking the minus (–) symbols in the list to close them. Note that the contents of the right pane don't change when you click a plus or minus sign—only when you click the folder name next to that plus or minus sign.

To display the Folders bar, simply click the Folders button on the Standard Buttons toolbar. To remove the Folders bar, click the Folders button again. If the Standard Buttons toolbar isn't visible, point to Toolbars on the View menu, and then choose Standard Buttons.

## Opening vs. Exploring

Although Windows remembers your preferences about some Windows Explorer display options (your choice of Large Icons, Small Icons, List, Details, or Thumbnails, for example), it remembers nothing about your choice of Explorer bar. If you right-click any folder icon, however, you will find commands named Open and Explore on the shortcut menu. Open opens the folder with no Explorer bar; Explore opens it with the Folders bar.

In most cases, one of those two commands appears in boldface type. The one that does is the default action associated with folders. (When Windows is first installed, that action is Open.) If you want your folders to always appear with the Folders bar, you can change the default action. *For details, see "Changing the Default Action Associated with a File Type," page 169.*

# Navigating with the History Bar

In Figure 8-3, we've replaced the Folders bar with the History bar. This handy pane shows an outline of all the places you've been recently—including Internet sites, as well as local and networked files and folders. If you click the View button near the top of the History bar (directly below the word *History*), you can choose to display the History bar by date, by site, by site most visited, and by order visited today. In Figure 8-3, the sites are organized by date. Within the date groupings, individual files and Web pages are collected into easily navigable categories.

**FIGURE 8-3.**

The History bar can help you find your way back to a file, folder, or Web site that you've accessed recently.

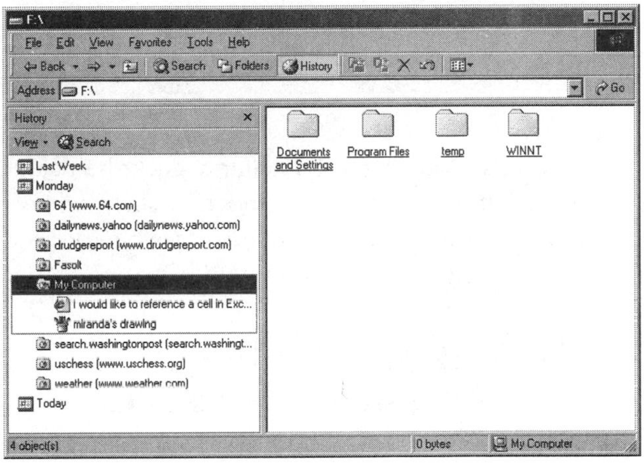

To display the History bar, simply click the History button on the Standard Buttons toolbar. To remove it, click the History button again. If the Standard Buttons toolbar isn't visible, display it by pointing to Toolbars on the View menu and clicking Standard Buttons, or you can display the History bar directly by pointing to Explorer Bar on the View menu and choosing History.

⭐ TIP

Not sure whether a file listed on the History bar is the one you want? Hover your mouse over the filename, and Windows Explorer displays the full path of the file. This might help you decide.

# Navigating with the Search Bar

If the Folders bar and the History bar aren't enough to help you locate a resource you need, try the Search bar. (See Figure 8-4, on the next page.) The Search bar lets you specify the item you want by name (full name or partial), contents, or type. This powerful tool is described in Chapter 11.

III

Managing Documents

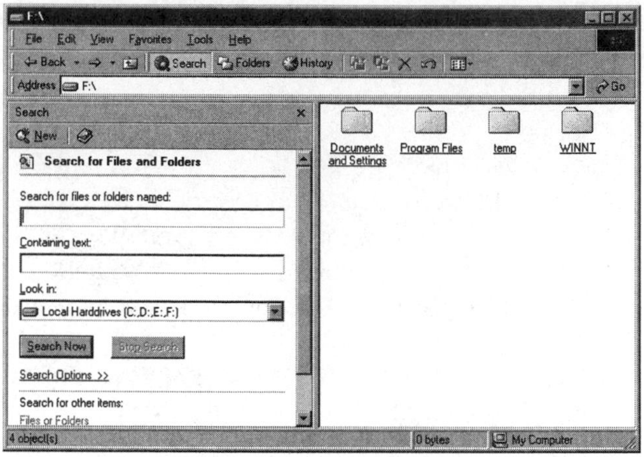

**FIGURE 8-4.**

If it exists anywhere on your computer or network, the Search bar can find it.

To display the Search bar, simply click the Search button on the Standard Buttons toolbar. To remove it, click the Search button again. If the Standard Buttons toolbar isn't visible, display it by pointing to Toolbars on the View menu and choosing Standard Buttons.

## Navigating with the Standard Buttons Toolbar

Back

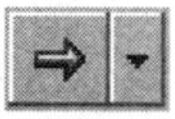

At the left side of the Windows Explorer Standard Buttons toolbar, you'll find three useful navigational tools. If you've spent any time on the Internet, the first two of these buttons, Back and Forward, will be familiar to you already. The Back button returns you to previous screens each time you click; the Forward button allows you to step forward again after you've used the Back button. Both buttons have drop-down arrows beside them. These open a menu that lets you retrace several steps with one click.

Forward

Up

To the right of the Forward button is the Up button. This one takes you up one level in your folder hierarchy.

Pressing the Backspace key is equivalent to clicking the Up button.

## Navigating with the Address Bar

The Address bar gives you yet another way to navigate. You can type the name of the folder you want to see directly into the Address bar.

Or you can click the arrow on the Address bar next to the Go button and choose from a list of possible destinations. Figure 8-5 shows an Address bar list.

**FIGURE 8-5.**
Opening the Address bar's list lets you choose from many destinations but doesn't give you an expandable outline of your entire folder structure.

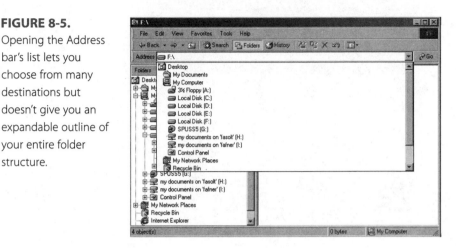

# Using the My Documents Folder

The My Documents icon on your desktop represents a special folder created automatically by Windows 2000 for every user account on the system. The My Documents folder is designed to be a default location most applications will use for document storage. It's also an absolute location. If you log on at various workstations on a Windows 2000 domain, Windows 2000 re-creates your desktop settings wherever you log on, but applications that save documents to My Documents (or any of its subfolders) will always be writing to the same physical location.

The target folder for My Documents is an ordinary file folder, which happens to be named (initially, at least) My Documents. The My Documents icon is a shortcut that points to this folder. You can see what that location is for your account by right-clicking the My Documents icon and choosing Properties from the shortcut menu. (See Figure 8-6, on the following page.) The Target folder location, shown on the Target tab of the My Documents Properties dialog box, shows the current address of the My Documents folder.

III

Managing Documents

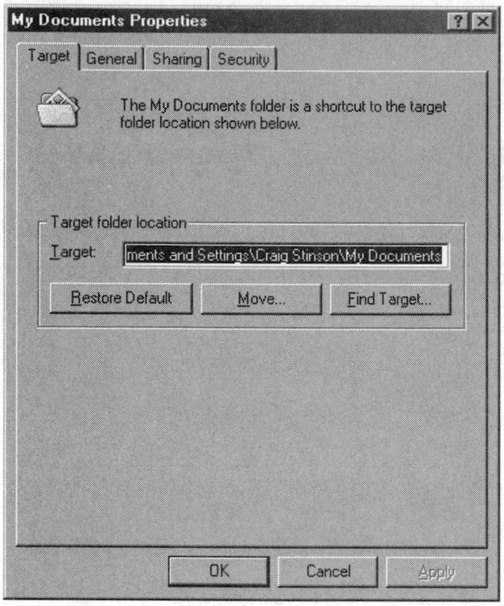

**FIGURE 8-6.**
You can change the default storage location for documents by right-clicking the My Documents icon and choosing Properties.

## Changing the Target Folder

You can change the current default location for documents on your system by changing the properties of the My Documents icon. To make My Documents point to a new location:

**1** Right-click the My Documents icon on your desktop, and choose Properties from the shortcut menu.

**2** On the Target tab, click the Move button.

**3** In the Browse For Folder dialog box, navigate to the new target location. If necessary, use the New Folder button to create a new folder.

Windows asks if you want to move all existing documents from the current My Documents target to the new one. This is an optional step. If you say no, Windows creates a new default document location but leaves all your old documents where they were.

## Using the My Pictures Folder

Windows always creates a subfolder called My Pictures in the current My Documents target. This folder is designed to be a default storage location for graphics files generated by such applications as Paint. If you've enabled Web content in Windows Explorer folders (the default state), you'll find a handy HTML template in My Pictures that previews your graphics documents without opening them. (See Figure 8-7.) Simply select an image file, and you'll see that image in the lower left corner of the window. Buttons at the top of the image previewer let you zoom in and out, display at full screen, and print the selected image.

⭐ **TIP**

> If you like the Image Preview HTML template, why not add it to other folders where you store image files? Navigate to the folder, choose Customize This Folder from the View menu, and then use the Customize This Folder Wizard to choose the Image Preview template. *For more information about HTML templates and enabling Web content in folders, see "Choosing Web View or Classic View," page 80.*

If you change the target location for My Documents, Windows creates a new My Pictures subfolder at the new location.

**FIGURE 8-7.**

The Image Preview HTML template, applied by default to your My Pictures folder, shows the contents of an image file without opening it.

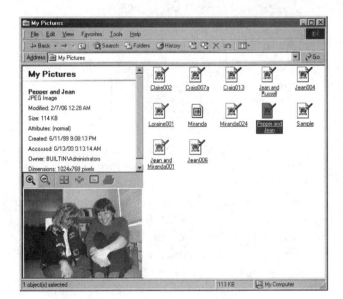

III

Managing Documents

# Running Programs and Opening Documents

Icons for programs, documents, and shortcuts in a Windows Explorer window behave exactly as they do on the desktop. Double-click or single-click them (depending on how you've set up your system), and they perform their default actions. Generally speaking, that means that programs open, documents open within their parent programs, and shortcuts activate the objects to which they're linked.

Nondefault actions are available via the shortcut menu. The choices on that menu vary depending on the kind of object you right-click. You might want to experiment with documents you use regularly to see what commands appear on their shortcut menus.

## Opening Documents in Different Programs

To open a document in a program other than the default program associated with its filename extension, choose Open With from the shortcut menu. In the Open With dialog box that appears (see Figure 8-8), select the program you want to open.

**FIGURE 8-8.**

The Open With command lets you open a document with a program other than the file type's default program. Selecting the check box makes the alternative file association permanent.

Once you've used the Open With command with a particular file type, Windows modifies the command to make it easier for you to reuse that file type with the same alternative program. For example, suppose you occasionally want to open .doc files (files that are normally associated with Microsoft Word) in WordPad. The first time you right-click a .doc file and choose Open With, you'll need to scroll through a relatively long list of program names to find WordPad. The next time you want to open a .doc file in WordPad, however, the Open With command will open a short cascading submenu, and WordPad will appear near the top of that menu.

You can use the Choose Program command from this submenu if you need to see the full list of available applications again.

## Changing the Parent Application for a File Type

As Figure 8-8 shows, the Open With command also includes a handy check box that lets you make a permanent change to a file type's association. For example, if you decide that you always want .doc files to be opened by WordPad, this is the easiest way to make the change. *For a more complicated way, see "Working with the File Types List," page 168.*

## Opening Documents That Don't Have a Parent Application

If you double-click or click a file that isn't associated with any application, Windows presents the Open With dialog box shown in Figure 8-8. Choose the application you want to open the file, and select the check box if you want to create a permanent association between the file and a particular application.

# Working with Folders, Files, and Shortcuts

Windows Explorer is a complete file-management tool. In the pages that follow, we explore the many ways in which Windows Explorer allows you to organize and reorganize your local disk resources.

## Refreshing the Contents of a Window

The Refresh command, on the Windows Explorer View menu, ensures that a Windows Explorer window's display reflects any changes to the folder's contents that might have taken place since you opened the window. For example, if you're looking at a folder on a network server, other users might be adding, deleting, or renaming files in that folder while your window is open. To be sure that what you see matches what's out there, choose Refresh from the View menu—or press F5.

## Selecting Folders and Files

The first step in many operations in Windows—opening, copying, or moving a document, for example—is to *select* the folder or file you want to use. When a folder or file is selected, its icon and title appear in a color that's different from unselected items. You can select a folder or file in a Windows Explorer window in any of the following ways:

- If you're using double-click mode, click the folder or file's icon or title; if you're using single-click mode, hover the mouse pointer over its icon or title. (Note that in Details view, you must click or hover over the icon or title to select an object—not the other parts of the description line.)

- Type the first few letters of the title.

- Use the arrow keys to move the highlight.

You'll often want to select more than one item at a time. Here are some ways to select a group of objects:

- Lasso them: hold down the mouse button while you drag a rectangle around all members of the group. (Click the mouse slightly away from the first icon so you don't select or launch it instead of drawing a box around it.)

- Hold down the Ctrl key and click (or hover over) each item in the group.

- If the items are next to one another in the window, click (or hover over) the first item. Then hold down the Shift key while you click (or hover over) the last item.

- Choose Select All from the Edit menu—or use its keyboard shortcut, Ctrl+A—to select all the items in the window.

**TIP**

**When You Want Almost Everything**

Two commands on the Windows Explorer Edit menu can be useful when you need to select nearly all the items in a folder. The first method is to select everything in the folder by pressing Ctrl+A or by choosing Select All from the Edit menu. Then hold down the Ctrl key and click (or hover over) each item you want to clear. The second method is to begin by selecting the items you don't want. Then choose Invert Selection from the Edit menu. This action clears what you've already selected and selects everything else.

## Inspecting Folder and File Properties

Windows provides you with a simple way to learn a folder or file's size, creation date, and other vital statistics. Simply right-click a folder or file and choose Properties from the shortcut menu. Figure 8-9 shows the dialog box for a folder.

**FIGURE 8-9.**

The WINNT Properties dialog box shows that the folder includes 4,264 files and 100 subfolders, occupying a total of 435 MB.

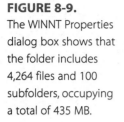

WINNT Properties

General | Sharing | Security

WINNT

| | |
|---|---|
| Type: | File Folder |
| Location: | D:\ |
| Size: | 435 MB (456,496,331 bytes) |
| Size on disk: | 427 MB (448,257,120 bytes) |
| Contains: | 4,264 Files, 100 Folders |
| Created: | Thursday, May 27, 1999, 3:02:06 PM |
| Attributes: | ☐ Read-only      Advanced... |
| | ☐ Hidden |

OK      Cancel      Apply

 **TIP**

To read the properties dialog box for an open folder, right-click anywhere within the folder's unoccupied space. Then choose the Properties command.

Notice that the folder's properties dialog box shows how many subfolders the folder contains as well as the number of files. The number of folders and files, along with their cumulative size, includes the contents of the folder and all its subfolders. (The statistics in the Windows Explorer status bar don't take into account the contents of subfolders.) The Advanced button, available only on NTFS volumes, lets you assign encryption and compression attributes, as well as archive and index the folder.

**SEE ALSO**

For information about sharing folders, see "Sharing Folders with Other Users," page 185.

If your computer is part of a network and your system has been set up to allow file sharing, the folder's properties dialog box might include a Sharing tab. By clicking it, you can make the folder available to others on your network (or make it unavailable).

Figure 8-10, on the next page, shows the properties dialog box for a file. As you can see, the properties dialog box provides information about the file's size, location, dates, parent application, and other attributes. There's even a button you can use to change the parent application, should you need to do that.

III

Managing Documents

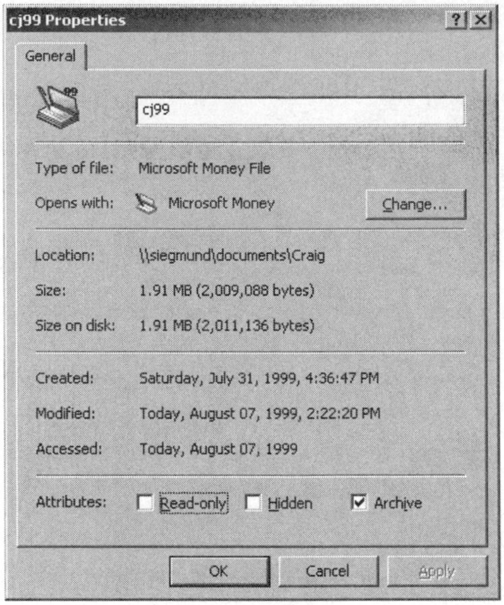

**FIGURE 8-10.**
The properties dialog box for this file provides basic information about the file's size, location, dates, and other attributes.

| cj99 Properties | ? X |
| --- | --- |

General

cj99

Type of file:   Microsoft Money File

Opens with:   Microsoft Money    Change...

Location:   \\siegmund\documents\Craig

Size:   1.91 MB (2,009,088 bytes)

Size on disk:   1.91 MB (2,011,136 bytes)

Created:   Saturday, July 31, 1999, 4:36:47 PM

Modified:   Today, August 07, 1999, 2:22:20 PM

Accessed:   Today, August 07, 1999

Attributes:   ☐ Read-only   ☐ Hidden   ☑ Archive

OK    Cancel    Apply

**? SEE ALSO**

For more information about file systems, see "Understanding File Systems," page 582.

## Additional File Properties on NTFS Volumes

The file shown in Figure 8-10 was stored on a FAT32 volume. *FAT* is a *file system*, a method of allocating space and storing files, found on systems running Windows 98 and earlier versions of Windows. *FAT32* is a newer file system introduced with the OSR2 release of Windows 95 and also found in later Windows versions. Compared to FAT, FAT32 can address larger hard disks and larger partitions of hard disks, and it also wastes less space in the way it stores files. The *NTFS file system* is the system of choice for Windows NT and Windows 2000, largely because of its additional security features.

Figure 8-11 shows the properties dialog box of a file stored on an NTFS volume. The NTFS file system records a great many additional file properties, some of which are visible in the figure. Because the properties are more numerous, the system groups them under outline headings.

Moreover, while some properties of files on an NTFS volume (the dimensions and resolution of the image file shown in Figure 8-11, for example) are read-only, others can be changed from within the properties dialog box. When you click a modifiable property, such as *Subject* in Figure 8-11, an edit field appears. You can type there, or click the arrow to choose from property values you have entered before.

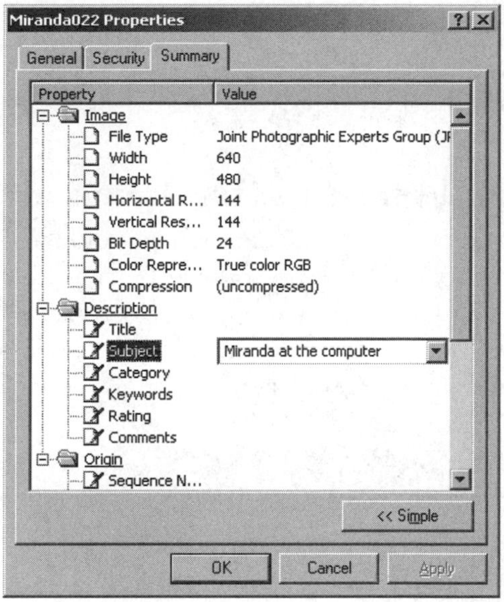

**FIGURE 8-11.**

The properties dialog box for this file on an NTFS volume includes many additional properties, some of which you can change from within the dialog box.

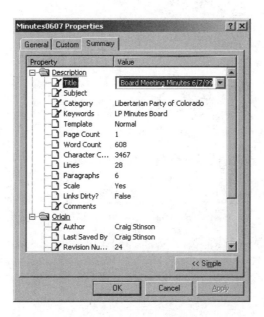

Certain other files, among them Microsoft Office documents, offer extended and modifiable properties, whether or not they are stored on NTFS volumes. Figure 8-12 shows an example of such a file—a Microsoft Word document stored on a FAT32 volume. On FAT and FAT32 volumes, the files that have these additional properties store the property values in the files themselves, not in the external file tables maintained by the file system.

**FIGURE 8-12.**

This Microsoft Word document was stored on a FAT32 volume, but, like other Microsoft Office documents, it offers the extended properties typical of files on an NTFS volume.

★ **TIP**

The Accessed line in a file's properties dialog box can help you determine whether a file might be a good candidate for deletion. If it hasn't been accessed any time during the last two years, perhaps you no longer need it.

## Inspecting Properties for Groups of Objects

By selecting two or more folders or files and then right-clicking, you can inspect properties for groups of objects. The resulting properties dialog box tells you the total size of the selected objects, whether they're all of the same type, and whether they're all located in the same folder. Figure 8-13 shows a properties dialog box for a group of files.

**FIGURE 8-13.**

This properties dialog box indicates that the 44 selected files are all Microsoft Excel worksheets, that they're stored in various folders, and that together they occupy 5.75 MB.

★ **TIP**

To select a group of folders or files that aren't all in the same folder, use the Search command. Then select each object you're interested in.

## Inspecting a Disk's Properties

The properties dialog box for a disk's top-level folder is different from all others. It uses a large pie graph to show how much of the disk is in use and how much remains available. Figure 8-14 shows an example.

To get to the top-level folder for a disk, begin by opening My Computer. Then right-click the icon for the disk you're interested in. That icon might look like a disk instead of a folder, but the object it represents is still a folder—as you can see by opening it.

**FIGURE 8-14.**

The properties dialog box for a disk's top-level folder lets you see how much space is available.

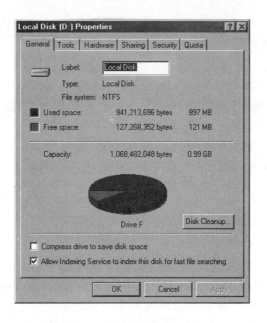

## Creating New Folders

Folders in Windows can be nested to any level. That is, you can have folders within folders within folders—to whatever degree of complexity you want.

To create a new folder, begin by displaying the folder in which you want the new folder to reside. Right-click anywhere within this parent folder's unoccupied space, and then choose New from the shortcut menu. When the submenu appears, choose Folder. (Alternatively, you can choose New from the folder window's File menu, and then choose Folder from the submenu.)

Your new folder begins with a default name, such as "New Folder" or "New Folder #2." To rename it, type the name you want and press Enter.

If you click away from the new folder before renaming it, simply right-click it and choose Rename from the shortcut menu. (Alternatively, choose Rename from the folder window's File menu.)

**? SEE ALSO**

For more information about renaming folders, see "Renaming Folders, Files, and Shortcuts," page 161.

## Moving or Copying Folders, Files, and Shortcuts

To move or copy an object in a Windows Explorer window, right-drag it from its current position to its destination. When you release the mouse button, a shortcut menu appears. From this shortcut menu, you

III

Managing Documents

can choose Copy Here, Move Here, or Create Shortcut(s) Here. Make the appropriate selection, and you're done.

To move or copy an entire folder, simply display the folder's parent folder. Then right-drag the folder icon (or the folder entry, if you're working in List view or Details view). Be aware that this action moves or replicates not only the folder, but everything within the folder as well.

If you copy an object to a new destination in the same folder, Windows gives the copy a default name, such as "Copy of Myfile." While the object is still selected, you can give it a new name by typing and pressing Enter. Later you can right-click it and choose Rename.

If you prefer to drag with the left mouse button, you can do so, but in this case you need to know the following:

- If you drag a program file from one folder to another, Windows leaves the program in its source folder and creates a shortcut to the program in the destination folder. (Note that Windows ignores this rule if more than one file is selected and at least one selected file is not a program.)

- If you drag any other file type from one folder to another on the same disk, Windows performs a move.

- If you drag from a folder on one disk to a folder on a different disk, Windows performs a copy.

- If you drag a folder or any file other than a program file from a folder to the desktop, Windows performs a move—provided the source folder resides on the disk where you installed Windows. If the source folder is on a different disk, Windows performs a copy instead of a move.

**TIP**

You can force Windows to *copy* the selected objects—regardless of file type and destination—by holding down the Ctrl key as you drag. You can force Windows to *move* objects by holding down the Shift key as you drag. And you can force Windows to *create a shortcut* by holding down the Alt key as you drag.

**TIP**

If you display the Folders bar, you can use it as a target for moves and copies. Simply drag files or folders from the right side of your Windows Explorer window and drop them in the appropriate entry on the Folders bar. You can also move entire folders by dragging them from one location on the Folders bar and dropping them in another location on the Folders bar.

## Moving or Copying Objects to Unopened Folders

In many cases, you can move or copy an object to a new folder without opening the destination folder. For example, suppose the file Rough Draft is stored in the folder PMFeature and you want to move it to the folder Outtakes, which is also stored in PMFeature. Simply grab Rough Draft with your mouse, drag it to the folder icon for Outtakes, and then release the mouse button.

> **What Will Happen When You Release the Mouse Button?**
> As you drag an object from one folder to another or to the desktop, Windows displays a ghost image of the object you're dragging. If you're dragging with the left mouse button, you can look at the lower right corner of this image to see what action Windows will perform when you release the button. If Windows is going to create a copy, you'll see a plus sign in the lower right corner. If Windows is going to create a shortcut, you'll see a shortcut arrow. If Windows is going to move the object, you won't see anything in the lower right corner. If you don't like the proposed action, click the right mouse button before you drop the object on the destination to cancel the drag operation in process.

If your destination folder is minimized on the taskbar, you can move or copy an object to it by dragging the object to the taskbar and hovering over the folder button. When the Windows Explorer window opens, you can drop the item inside it.

> If you have a shortcut for a folder on your desktop, you can move or copy items to that folder by dragging them to the shortcut.

## Moving or Copying Objects with Menu Commands

If dragging and dropping is not convenient, you can move or copy objects by using the Edit menu's Cut, Copy, and Paste commands.

- To move an object, select it and choose Cut from the Edit menu. Then select the destination folder and choose Paste from the Edit menu. (If the desktop is your destination, right-click the desktop and choose Paste from the shortcut menu.)

> When you cut an item, that item isn't removed from its source folder until you paste it somewhere. If you change your mind in midstream, simply press Esc.

III

Managing Documents

■ To copy an object, select it and choose Copy from the Edit menu. Then select the destination folder and choose Paste from the Edit menu. (If the desktop is your destination, right-click the desktop and choose Paste from the shortcut menu.)

> It's often quicker to use the keyboard shortcuts for Cut, Copy, and Paste than it is to visit the Edit menu. Press Ctrl+X to cut or Ctrl+C to copy, and then press Ctrl+V to paste.

## Moving or Copying Groups of Folders and Files

**SEE ALSO**
For more information about selecting a group of folders or files, see "Selecting Folders and Files," page 151.

To move or copy a group of folders or files, select all members of the group, and then follow the same procedure you would use to move or copy a single item. To select a group, hold down the Ctrl key while you select each member. Alternatively, if the items are located next to one another in the Windows Explorer window, you can select the first item, and then hold down the Shift key while you select the last item.

## Moving or Copying Objects with the Send To Command

When you right-click a folder or file, the shortcut menu includes a Send To command. In response to this command, Windows displays a submenu of destinations, typically including any floppy-disk drives on your system, as well as various other destinations. You can use the Send To command as a quick and easy way to copy or move a folder or file to any destination. You can also customize the Send To menu so that it includes destinations you frequently use.

**NOTE**

> When you use the Send To command with a folder destination, Windows treats the object just as if you dragged the object to the folder using the left mouse button. That is, if the destination and source folders are on the same disk, Windows performs a move; if the destination and source folders are on different disks, Windows performs a copy.

The contents of the Send To menu are determined by the contents of a hidden folder named SendTo. That folder is located within a folder identified by the name you use to log on to Windows 2000. For example, if Windows 2000 is installed on drive C and you're logged on as JoeUser, the default path of your SendTo folder will be

C:\Documents and Settings\JoeUser\SendTo

### Using Programs and Other Kinds of Destinations on the Send To Menu

Your Send To menu can include programs, printers, and other types of "destinations," as well as folders. If you right-click a document and then choose a program from the Send To menu, Windows launches the program and attempts to open the selected document. If you right-click a document and choose a printer from the Send To menu, Windows tries to print your document using that printer. In all cases, Windows does what it would have done had you dragged the selected document to a shortcut for the destination object. In other words, the Send To command is a menu alternative for a drag-and-drop operation.

### Customizing the Send To Menu

**SEE ALSO**

For more information about creating short-cuts, see "Creating a Shortcut," page 55.

To add destinations to the Send To menu, open the Send To folder and create shortcuts to additional destination items simply by dragging them into the SendTo folder. For instance, you could drag the Recycle Bin from the desktop into the Send To folder and then send an item to the Recycle Bin by right-clicking the item, pointing to Send To on the shortcut menu, and then choosing Recycle Bin.

**TIP**

If you haven't set Windows Explorer to display hidden files and folders, you won't be able to navigate to the SendTo folder. You can, however, get to the Send To folder by using the Run command. Choose Run from the Start menu, type *%UserProfile%\SendTo*, and press Enter.

# Renaming Folders, Files, and Shortcuts

The simplest way to rename an object is to right-click it, choose Rename from the shortcut menu, and then type a new name. But other methods are also available:

- Select the object and choose Rename from the Windows Explorer File menu.

- Select the object. Then click the object's name. When a rectangle appears around the object's name, type a new name or edit the current name.

  When you use this method, you need to pause a moment between selecting the object and clicking the object's name. Otherwise, Windows interprets your action as a double-click and opens the selected object. (And this method won't work at all if your computer is set up for single-click launching.)

- Select the object and press F2. Then type a new name or edit the current name.

- Display the properties dialog box for the item you want to rename. Type a new name into the dialog box.

⭐ **TIP**

If you make a mistake while changing a name, simply press Esc to cancel the process.

---

**Filename Restrictions**

Names of folders and files can include as many as 255 characters. Thus, there's no need to be cryptic or overly compact in your choice of a filename. Instead of naming that departmental budget worksheet EBUD00-1, you can call it Editorial Budget for 2000—First Draft.

Programs designed for Windows 3.*x* and not yet updated for later versions of the operating system still adhere to the old limit of eight characters plus an optional three-character extension. If a program you're using rejects long filenames, check with the vendor to see if an updated version is available.

In any filename, long or short, certain characters are prohibited. These characters are the following: * | \ < > ? / " :

Spaces and the following additional characters are prohibited in MS-DOS (short) filenames: + , . ; = [ ]

These prohibited characters are reserved for use by the operating system.

---

# Reversing Moves, Copies, and Name Changes with the Undo Command

If you change your mind after moving or copying something, you can reverse your action by choosing the Undo command from the Windows Explorer Edit menu. (If the Standard Buttons toolbar is visible, you can simply click the Undo button.) Be aware, however, that you must use the Undo command right away. As soon as you perform some other action, Undo will reverse that action, not your move or copy.

Undo

⭐ **TIP**

If you've chosen not to display extensions for registered files, be careful not to type the extension when you rename a file. For example, suppose you have a file named My Picture.bmp, and your Windows Explorer window displays that file's name as simply My Picture. If you change the name to Your Picture, be sure to type *Your Picture*, not *Your Picture.bmp*. Otherwise, the file's name will be recorded as Your Picture.bmp.bmp.

# Deleting Folders, Files, and Shortcuts

Delete

To delete an object or a group of objects, select what you want to delete and press the Delete key or click the Delete button. If you prefer a more complicated method, try one of these:

- Right-click an object and choose Delete from the shortcut menu.

- Select an object or group of objects, and choose Delete from the Windows Explorer File menu.

- Select an object (or a group of objects), and then drag it to the Recycle Bin icon on your desktop—or to a shortcut for Recycle Bin.

However you do the deed, Windows presents a prompt and asks you to confirm your intent. This protects you from accidental deletions.

> **⊛ TIP**
>
> If you don't want Windows to prompt for confirmation when you delete folders or files, clear the Display Delete Confirmation Dialog check box at the bottom of the Recycle Bin Properties dialog box.

As further protection, items you delete from hard disk folders or the desktop are automatically transferred to the Recycle Bin, whence you can retrieve them if you change your mind.

> **⊛ TIP**
>
> If you change your mind right away about a deletion, you can restore whatever you deleted by choosing the Undo Delete command from the Windows Explorer Edit menu.

# Restoring Deleted Folders, Files, and Shortcuts

Have you ever deleted one file when you really meant to delete a different one? Wiped out a whole folder by mistake? Or simply trashed a document you thought you were finished with, only to discover the following week that you desperately needed it back?

Windows provides a way to recover gracefully from accidents such as these. For a period of time after you delete an object, that object remains accessible via the Recycle Bin. If you change your mind, a simple menu command or mouse action restores selected items to the folders from which they were deleted.

The Recycle Bin is like that large trash barrel outside your house or the dumpster in the alley behind your office. Until the big truck comes to empty that container, anything you've tossed out can still be retrieved. *For information about when the big truck arrives, see "Setting Your Recycle Bin's Capacity," page 165.*

When you open the Recycle Bin, Windows displays the names of recently deleted items in an ordinary Windows Explorer window. (See Figure 8-15.) Displaying the window in Details view includes columns that show when each item was deleted and which folder it was deleted from. As in other Windows Explorer windows, you can click column headings to change the sort order, and you can use toolbar icons or commands on the View menu to switch to List view, Large Icons view, or Small Icons view.

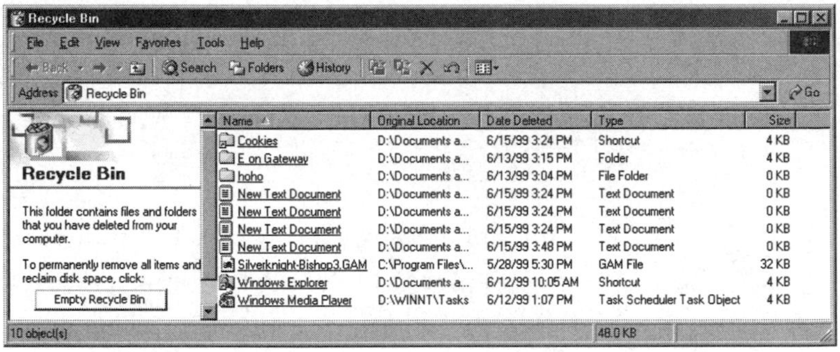

**FIGURE 8-15.**

Opening the Recycle Bin reveals an ordinary Windows Explorer window. Displaying the contents in Details view lets you see when each item was deleted.

To restore an item from the Recycle Bin, simply select it and choose Restore from the File menu (or right-click the item and choose Restore from the shortcut menu). The Restore command puts the item back in the folder from which it was deleted. If that folder doesn't currently exist, Windows asks your permission to re-create it.

You also have the option of restoring a deleted item and putting it in a different folder. To do this, select the item and do any of the following:

- Right-click the item and choose Cut from the shortcut menu. Go to the folder in which you want the item to be restored, and then choose the Paste command on that Windows Explorer window's Edit menu.

- Select the item and click the Move To button on the Standard Buttons toolbar. Then select the destination folder from the Browse For Folder dialog box.

- Drag the item directly to the destination folder, either another Windows Explorer window or to a shortcut on your desktop.

Here are three other important facts to know about the Recycle Bin:

- Items deleted from floppy disks or network servers aren't stored in the Recycle Bin. When you delete such an item, Windows asks you to confirm the deletion. Exception: Windows does provide Recycle Bin service for My Documents, even if My Documents resides on a network server.

- Some programs provide their own commands for deleting files. If you use a program's Delete command, your deleted file might not be transferred to the Recycle Bin.

- If you delete a folder, the Recycle Bin shows the deleted folder but doesn't record separate entries for the folder's files and sub-folders. If you restore the folder, however, Windows re-creates the folder and its contents.

**TIP**

The Search command can't be used to locate items in the Recycle Bin. To search for items in the Recycle Bin, sort the Recycle Bin display on the column heading of interest. For example, to find an item when you know its name, click the Name heading so that all deleted items' names appear in alphabetical order. To find items that were deleted on a particular day, click the Date Deleted column heading.

## Setting Your Recycle Bin's Capacity

Although you have only one Recycle Bin icon (plus any shortcuts to that icon that you've created), Windows actually maintains a separate recycle bin for each hard disk on your system. The default size of each recycle bin is 10 percent of the capacity of the hard disk on which it's stored. When a recycle bin exceeds that limit, Windows begins removing files permanently, starting with the files that have been in the Recycle Bin the longest.

You can make your recycle bins larger or smaller by right-clicking the Recycle Bin icon and choosing Properties. (If the Recycle Bin is already open, you can get to the shortcut menu by right-clicking the window's Control-menu icon or by right-clicking any blank area of the window.) You'll see a dialog box similar to the one shown in Figure 8-16, on the next page, with a tab for each of your system's hard disks (and a tab for My Documents, if My Documents resides on a server).

III

Managing Documents

**FIGURE 8-16.**

The Recycle Bin Properties dialog box lets you configure each hard disk's recycle bin.

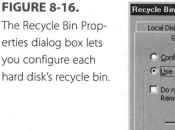

To adjust the size of all recycle bins on your system, select the Use One Setting For All Drives option, and then adjust the slider on the Global tab. To adjust the size of recycle bins individually, select the Configure Drives Independently option, and then adjust the sliders on each disk drive tab. To turn off recycle bin functionality globally, select the check box labeled Do Not Move Files To The Recycle Bin. Remove Files Immediately When Deleted. To apply this setting to only a particular hard disk, select the Configure Drives Independently option, select the tab of the drive you want to set, and then select the check box only on that tab.

**TIP**

To delete a file without moving it to the Recycle Bin, hold down the Shift key while you press Delete.

## Purging the Recycle Bin

A deleted file sitting in your Recycle Bin takes up just as much space as it did before it was deleted. If you're deleting files to free up room for new programs and documents, simply transferring them from ordinary disk folders to the Recycle Bin folder won't do you much good. You need to get the old files off your system permanently. The safest way to do this, of course, is to move the files to another storage medium, such as a floppy disk, a tape drive, or a file server. That way, you can always get your files back if you change your mind.

If you're sure you'll never need a particular file again, however, you can delete it in the normal way and then purge it from the Recycle

Bin. To delete an item from the Recycle Bin, simply display the Recycle Bin, select the item, and then press the Delete key. Be aware as you answer the confirmation prompt that this deletion removes your selection permanently.

To delete a group of items from the Recycle Bin, hold down the Ctrl key while you select each one, and then press the Delete key. (If the files are located next to one another in the Recycle Bin window, you can select the first member of the group, and then hold down the Shift key while you select the last member.)

 **TIP**

> You can check the properties of a file before deleting it by double-clicking the file's icon in the Recycle Bin window.

To empty the Recycle Bin in one fell swoop, simply right-click the Recycle Bin icon and choose Empty Recycle Bin from the shortcut menu. If you're already in the Recycle Bin window, choose this command from the File menu, or click the Empty Recycle Bin button (if you have Web content enabled and you're using the Recycle Bin's default HTML template).

## Setting Attributes for Folders, Files, and Shortcuts

*Attributes* are markers that file systems employ to identify certain characteristics of files. In Windows 2000, folders, files, and shortcuts can have no attributes or any combination of the following attributes: archive, hidden, read-only, and system. The system attribute is known only to the system—you can't even inspect its state, let alone change it. You can inspect and modify the other three attributes for a file by visiting the file's properties dialog box.

 **NOTE**

> On NTFS volumes, the archive attribute is accessible via the Advanced button on the General tab. It is identified there as "File is ready for archiving."

The archive attribute indicates that an item has been modified since it was last backed up. Each time you create a new file or change an old one, Windows sets (turns on) the archive attribute for that file. Backup programs typically clear (remove) the archive attribute when they back up a file. If you change the file after backing it up, the file again gets the archive attribute so your backup program can recognize it as needing to be backed up again.

III

Managing Documents

A few programs use the hidden attribute and system attribute (either, but usually both) to mark important files that must not be modified or deleted because they are critical components of the program or critical components of Windows.

You can open a file with the read-only attribute, but you can't save it unless you first rename it. Some programs—and many users—set this attribute to prevent accidental changes to a file.

In many contexts, the read-only attribute not only prevents an item from being altered, but also keeps it from being deleted. For example, the MS-DOS Erase and Del commands refuse to delete files that are marked read-only. (You'll get the error message "Access denied" if you try.) If you select a read-only file in a Windows Explorer window and press the Delete key, Windows presents a confirmation prompt, reminding you that the file is read-only.

⭐ **TIP**

Assigning the read-only attribute to important files prevents you from altering them and makes it less likely that you will delete them accidentally. To assign this attribute, right-click the file, choose Properties from the shortcut menu, and then select the Read-Only check box. Note, however, that you will need to remove this attribute (by clearing the check box) if you want to edit the file without changing its name.

You can assign attributes to entire folders as well as to individual files. Making a folder read-only doesn't alter the attributes of files or folders contained within the read-only folder, but it does afford some protection against accidental deletion of the folder.

▶ **NOTE**

Files stored on NTFS volumes have additional attributes dealing with indexing, compression, encryption, and permissions.

# Working with the File Types List

If you choose Folder Options on the Windows Explorer Tools menu and then click the File Types tab, Windows displays a list of all registered file types. A sample of this list is shown in Figure 8-17.

Working with this list, you can perform a number of tasks:

- Change the default action associated with a file type

- Change the application associated with a file type

■ Change a file type's icon

■ Specify whether the file type's extension should be displayed in Windows Explorer windows

■ Specify whether a file type should be opened immediately after being downloaded

■ Remove a file type from the registry

**FIGURE 8-17.**

The File Types tab in the View menu's Folder Options dialog box lists all file types known to the registry, provides details about how they're associated, and allows you to change document icons.

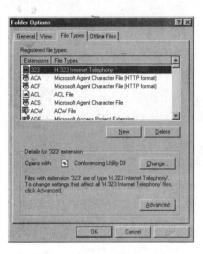

## Changing the Default Action Associated with a File Type

A file type's default action is the action that occurs when you double-click (or simply click, if you've set up your system for single-click launching) a file of that type in Windows Explorer or on your desktop. If you right-click a file in Windows Explorer or on your desktop, the file type's default action appears in boldface type on the shortcut menu. Most commonly the default action is to open a program or to open a document in its associated program.

To change a file type's default action:

1 In any Windows Explorer window, choose Folder Options from the Tools menu, and click the File Types tab.

2 In the Registered File Types list, select the file type whose default action you want to change.

3 Click the Advanced button.

4 In the list of available actions, select the action you want to be the default.

III

Managing Documents

5 Click the Set Default button, and then click OK.

> **Making Windows Explorer Always Display the Folders Bar**
> You can change the default action associated with folders from Open to Explore so that Windows Explorer always includes the Folders bar. Open the File Types list as described previously. Click the heading File Types in the Registered File Types list so that the list is sorted by type, not by extension. Select the item named Folder (*not* the one named File Folder!). Click Advanced, select Explore, and then click Set Default.

# Changing the Application Associated with a File Type

To change the application associated with a file type:

1 In any Windows Explorer window, choose Folder Options from the Tools menu, and click the File Types tab.

2 In the Registered File Types list, select the file type whose default action you want to change.

3 Click the Change button and select the program you want to associate with the file type.

# Changing a File Type's Icon

Just as you can change the icons used by your programs (see "Changing a Menu Item's Icon," page 28), you can also reassign document icons. To do this:

1 In any Windows Explorer window, choose Folder Options from the Tools menu, and click the File Types tab.

2 Find the file type of the document icon you want to change in the Registered File Types list.

3 Click the Advanced button.

4 Click the Change Icon button.

5 Choose a new icon from the Change Icon dialog box and click OK.

   If you don't see a suitable icon in the Change Icon dialog box, click the Browse button in the Change Icon dialog box and navigate to another program that might have more suitable icons. Choose the icon you want and click OK.

# Specifying Display of Extensions

**SEE ALSO**
For more information about enabling or suppressing filename extension display, see "Setting Other Global Options," page 82.

By default, Windows Explorer windows don't show extensions for registered file types. You can turn on the extension display for all file types using the Windows Explorer Folder Options command. You can also show extensions for a particular file type while suppressing the extensions for other registered file types. Here's how:

1 In any Windows Explorer window, choose Folder Options from the Tools menu, and click the File Types tab.

2 In the Registered File Types list, select the file type whose extension you want to make visible.

3 Click the Advanced button.

4 Select Always Show Extension and click OK.

# Specifying Download Behavior

To specify that files of a particular type should always be opened as soon as you have finished downloading them:

1 In any Windows Explorer window, choose Folder Options from the Tools menu, and then click the File Types tab.

2 In the Registered File Types list, select the file type you want to be opened immediately after downloading.

3 Click the Advanced button.

4 Clear the Confirm Open After Download check box, if set.

# Removing a File Type from the Registry

**SEE ALSO**
For information about the Add/Remove Programs Wizard, see "Installing New Programs," page 262.

If you use the Add/Remove Programs Wizard to uninstall Windows-based programs that you no longer need, you should not have to "unregister" the file types used by those programs. The wizard should take care of that detail for you. But if you remove a program without the wizard's assistance, you might want to visit the File Types list to clean up.

You can remove a file type from the registry as follows:

1 In any Windows Explorer window, choose Folder Options from the Tools menu, and then click the File Types tab.

2 In the Registered File Types list, select the file type you want to remove from the registry.

3 Click Delete and confirm your choice in the File Types dialog box.

# Formatting and Copying Floppy Disks

To format a floppy or other removable disk, right-click the disk's icon in Windows Explorer, and then choose Format from the shortcut menu. Windows displays a dialog box similar to the one shown in Figure 8-18.

**FIGURE 8-18.**

To format a floppy disk, right-click its icon and choose Format from the shortcut menu.

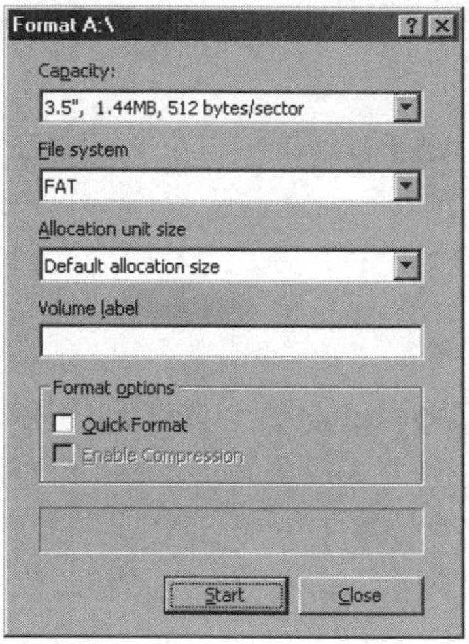

The options available in this dialog box depend on the kind of disk you're formatting. For 3.5-inch floppy disks, for example, you can choose between 1.44 MB and 720 KB in the Capacity box, but your only file-system option is FAT.

The Volume Label field is optional.

Leave the Quick Format check box cleared if you want Windows to check your disk for bad sectors as it formats. If you're in a hurry and don't mind foregoing the media check, select this check box. (You can't use this option with disks that have never been formatted.)

To copy a floppy disk, right-click its icon in Windows Explorer and choose Copy Disk from the shortcut menu. Make sure the Copy From and Copy To sections of the dialog box are correctly filled out, and then click Start. When the copy is complete, the dialog box remains on the screen. If you want to copy another disk, insert it and then click Start again.

**CHAPTER 9**

# Using and Sharing Files on the Network

With Microsoft Windows 2000, using network resources and sharing your own resources with other network users is almost as simple and straightforward as using your own local resources. Browsing a network folder is just like browsing a folder on your own hard disk. Sending a document to a network printer is just like printing at your own computer. The procedures for interacting with one kind of network computer (say, a Microsoft Windows NT server) are identical to the procedures for working with another kind (for example, a Novell NetWare server). You don't have to learn network commands to use your network's resources.

Windows provides support for networks from a number of vendors and supports the simultaneous use of multiple networking protocols. This means that, assuming your network administrator has set up your system properly, you should be able to work successfully in a heterogeneous network environment, enabling you to access computers running Windows 2000, Windows NT, Windows 98, Windows 95, Windows for Workgroups, NetWare, and other operating systems.

In this chapter, we'll look at the steps involved in working with programs and documents stored on network computers, as well as at what you need to do to share your own folders and files.

# ⟨2000⟩ Using My Network Places

**❓ SEE ALSO**

For information about setting up network connections, see Chapter 16, "Making Connections." For information about using network printers, see "Printing to a Network Printer," page 221.

My Network Places is your gateway to all available network resources, just as My Computer is the gateway to resources stored on your own system. My Network Places replaces the Network Neighborhood folder that appears in earlier versions of Windows—and you'll soon see that more than the name has changed. Launching My Network Places opens a Windows Explorer window that contains icons for network resources you use, as well as icons that let you browse the rest of your network. Figure 9-1 shows the My Network Places folder for a typical small local area network (LAN).

**FIGURE 9-1.**

The icons in the My Network Places folder represent network resources.

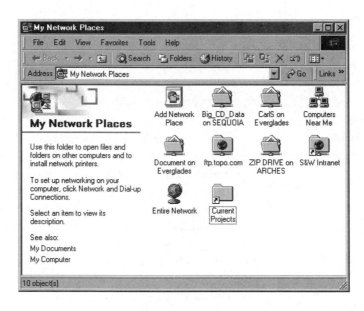

**TIP**

If you're not sure what kind of files are contained on a network computer, use Details view. You might find a comment (entered by the person who shared the resource) that describes the contents of the network computer or folder.

The Network Neighborhood folder in previous versions of Windows showed icons for each computer in your workgroup. (A *workgroup* is simply a grouping of computers defined by the network administrator.) My Network Places uses the same hierarchy, but its initial display is at

> ### Domains and Workgroups
>
> All computers in a Windows 2000 (or Windows NT) network belong to one of two functional groupings, called domains and workgroups.
>
> A *domain* is a set of computers that share a common security database and that can be administered as a group. If you enter a domain name when you log on to Windows 2000, your account participates in that domain. All security information regarding your account is stored on the special network computers known as *domain controllers,* and you have the freedom to log on to any computer in the domain (depending on how your user account is set up). Domain controllers must run Windows 2000 Server or Windows NT Server; computers running Windows 2000 Professional or Windows NT Workstation can participate in a domain only as members.
>
> A *workgroup* is a named set of computers running Windows 2000, Windows NT, Windows 98, Windows 95, or Windows for Workgroups that are grouped for browsing purposes. If your account doesn't participate in a domain, it belongs to a workgroup.

a higher level in the hierarchy, so the folder isn't cluttered with the names of computers that you seldom need to see. Furthermore, you can save additional network places at this top level. Network places can be shortcuts to network computers, shared folders, Web folders on the Internet or your intranet, or FTP sites.

 **TIP**

Don't like the name? You can rename My Network Places, Computers Near Me, and any of your network places by using the same techniques you use to rename a file on your local hard disk. The simplest way is to select the icon you want to rename, press F2, and type the new name.

## Browsing the Network

The My Network Places folder includes two icons that let you browse the network to find a particular shared resource:

Computers
Near Me

Launching Computers Near Me displays the computers in your workgroup. From here, you can expand the network objects of interest to see each computer's shared resources.

**Entire Network**

Launching Entire Network opens a folder that displays a top-level view of your entire corporate network. (If your network is particularly complex, you might find it helpful to view its structure in a Folders bar.) From here, you can expand and move through the folder hierarchy to view all the computers on your network. Figure 9-2 uses Windows Explorer to show the entire-network view of the network shown in Figure 9-1.

**FIGURE 9-2.**

The Entire Network icon displays a hierarchical view of networks, workgroups and domains, computers, and shared resources.

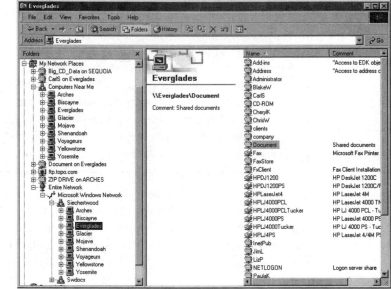

**NOTE**

If your computer is part of a domain, you won't have a Computers Near Me icon. In this case, you must use Entire Network to traverse your network hierarchy.

## Adding a Network Place

**Add Network Place**

The first icon in My Network Places launches a wizard that helps you to create a shortcut to a network resource, a Web site, or an FTP site.

To add a network place:

**1** In My Network Places, open Add Network Place.

The Add Network Place Wizard appears.

**2**  Type the location of the network place:

- Click the Browse button to navigate to a shared folder you want to add and click OK.

- Type just the name of the computer where the folder is located, preceded by two backslashes (for example, \\*server7*).

- Type the complete path to the shared folder. (For example, the path to the folder named *finance* on a shared drive named *diskd* on a computer named *server1* is \\*server1*\*diskd*\*finance*.)

- For a Web site or FTP site, type the site's address. Be sure to include the network protocol (http:// or ftp://) in the address.

**NOTE**

A shortcut to a Web site doesn't open the site in Microsoft Internet Explorer, as a shortcut in your Favorites folder does. Rather, it opens a Windows Explorer view of the folders within a Web site. Therefore, it's most useful as a shortcut to your own Web site or to Web folders on your intranet—where you might use or contribute files—rather than to a public Web site, which might not allow folder views.

**3**  Click Next, and answer the wizard's remaining questions.

- If you specified only a computer name on the first page, the wizard presents a list of shared folders on that computer. Select one and click Next.

- If you specified an FTP site, the wizard asks whether you want to log on anonymously or with a particular user name. (Obtain logon information from the site's administrator.) Select the check box or clear it and type your user name, and then click Next.

**4** On the Completing The Add Network Place Wizard page, type a name for your new network place.

The wizard suggests a name that's derived from the place's network location, but you needn't be so cryptic. Type whatever will be a useful reminder for you.

**5** Click Finish.

**⭐ TIP**

My Network Places can also hold shortcuts to folders and files within a shared folder. To create such a place, type the complete path (in the form \\*computername*\\*sharename*\\*folder*\\*filename*) on the wizard's first page. Or simply drag the folder or file from a Windows Explorer window to the My Network Places icon or window.

## Using Network Places with Applications

The real strength of My Network Places isn't that it enables you to peruse your network, but that it provides fast, easy access to network places that you use day in and day out, without forcing you to traverse a lengthy path to get to each one. Once you create a network place, as described above, it appears in the Open dialog box or the Save dialog box that appears in most applications when you choose one of those commands from the File menu. All you need to do is click My Network Places in the places bar at the left side of the dialog box, and shortcuts to all your network places appear, as shown in Figure 9-3. The Computers Near Me icon and the Entire Network icon also appear so that you can navigate to other network computers if you don't yet have a shortcut to the network place you want.

**FIGURE 9-3.**

Click My Network Places in the places bar to jump quickly to the network places you use.

Places bar ⏤

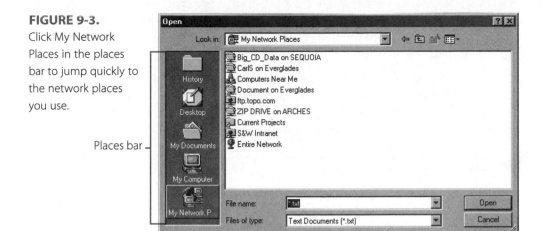

## Searching for Computers

You might know the name of a computer, but you don't know what domain it's in—or you just don't want to step through a series of folders to find it. Windows provides an easy way to get there. In the My Network Places folder, click the Search button on the toolbar. Type the name of the computer you're looking for and click Search Now. Windows searches the network and displays the matching computer names and locations in the Search Results window. Launching a computer icon there takes you to that computer's shared resources.

> If you're looking for a computer within your workgroup, you need to type only part of the name in the Search bar of My Network Places for your search to be successful. If you're looking beyond your workgroup, however, you must type the computer's complete name.

# Connecting to a Network Computer

Because the Microsoft networking services are peer-based, shared resources can reside on a traditional dedicated *server* (a computer that acts solely as a repository for shared files) or on a computer used by one of your colleagues.

In either case, to interact with another computer on your network, simply open that network computer in the My Network Places window. (If you haven't created a shortcut to the computer in My Network Places, open Computers Near Me or Entire Network to navigate to it.) This opens a Windows Explorer window where you can see all the folders and printers to which you have been granted access on the other computer. Figure 9-4 shows such a window. Opening a folder reveals all folders and files stored in that folder, and so on.

Opening Computers Near Me in the My Network Places folder also reveals an icon for your own computer. By launching this icon, you can see the names of all folders and printers on your own system that have been made available to other network users.

> **Specifying Comments**
>
> To specify a comment for your own computer, right-click My Computer and choose Manage to open the Computer Management console. Right-click Computer Management (Local) (at the top of the left pane) and choose Properties. On the Network Identification tab, type a comment in the Description box. *For information about changing the comment for one of your shared folders, see "Monitoring the Use of Shared Resources," page 188.*

**FIGURE 9-4.**
The Details view of a Windows Explorer window can include a comment for each network computer or shared resource. The person who set up the computer or shared the resource provides the comment.

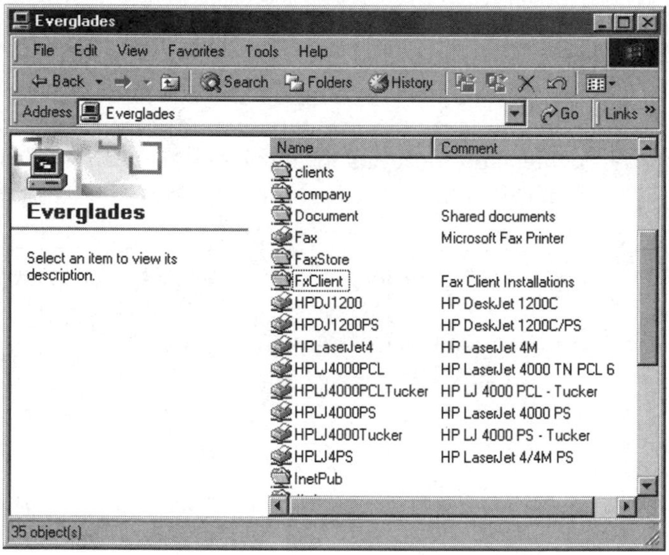

If the user account with which you logged on to the network doesn't have permission to view a network computer or resource you select, a dialog box similar to the one shown in Figure 9-5 appears. To gain access, you must provide the name of an account (and its password, of course) that has permission.

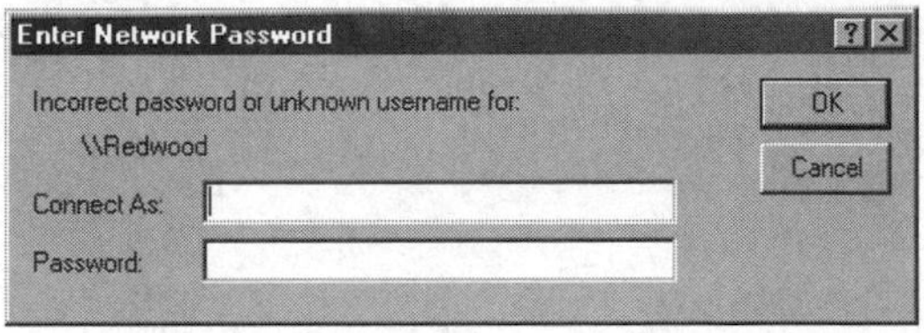

**FIGURE 9-5.**

If your own account doesn't have appropriate permissions for a shared resource, you can connect using another user account.

```
┌─────────────────────────────────────────────────────┐
│ Enter Network Password                        │?│X│  │
├─────────────────────────────────────────────────────┤
│  Incorrect password or unknown username for:    ┌──────┐ │
│     \\Redwood                                    │  OK  │ │
│                                                  └──────┘ │
│  Connect As: │                              │   ┌──────┐ │
│                                                  │Cancel│ │
│  Password:   │                              │   └──────┘ │
└─────────────────────────────────────────────────────┘
```

⭐ **TIP**

You can use the Search command to locate network computers, shared folders, and files within shared folders. *For more information, see Chapter 11, "Searching for Files and Folders."*

## Understanding Access Permissions

What you can do with a network resource depends on your access permissions to that resource. If you have *Read* permission, you can work with the folder's programs and documents, but you can't save documents to that folder. To save a document that you retrieved from a read-only network folder, specify a local folder (or a network folder for which you have Full Control permission) as the document's destination.

❓ **SEE ALSO**

For information about assigning access permissions, see "Sharing Folders with Other Users," page 185.

If you have *Full Control* permission over a network folder, you can do anything with its documents and programs that you can do with files stored in local folders. In the absence of file-specific restrictions, you can read, write, rename, delete, move, and copy files in Full Control folders, just as though they were on your own computer. (Individual files can also have access restrictions, such as more restrictive permissions or the read-only attribute.)

When you are granted *Change* permission, you can open and modify files, but you can't add new files.

▶ **NOTE**

Sharing permissions restrict access to shared network folders. If the shared folder is on an NTFS drive, its files and folders are further protected by permissions provided as part of the NTFS file system. *For more information, see Chapter 28, "Using NTFS Security."*

# Working with Mapped Network Folders

Mapping a network folder makes it appear to Windows as though the folder is part of your own computer. Windows assigns the mapped folder a drive letter, just as if it was an additional local hard disk. You

III

Managing Documents

can still access a mapped folder in the conventional manner, by navigating to it through Windows Explorer. But mapping gives the folder an alias—the assigned drive letter—that provides an alternative means of access.

Folder mapping offers the following benefits:

- It makes the network folder available to programs that don't use the Windows common dialog boxes.

  With programs that use the common dialog boxes, you can navigate to network folders just as you would with My Network Places. But to read a document from, or save a document to, a network folder using other programs (older Windows-based programs, for example, or MS-DOS-based programs), you will probably need to map the folder to a drive letter.

- It makes the network folder accessible from the My Computer icon.

  Because a mapped folder becomes a virtual disk on your local computer, an icon for the folder appears in the My Computer folder, right alongside your real local disks. If you do most of your work with files stored locally but occasionally need access to particular network folders, you might find it convenient to map them. That way, you won't have to bother opening the My Network Places icon to find the network folders you need.

- Windows can automatically reconnect to your mapped network folders at startup.

  When you navigate to a network computer using My Network Places, you might experience momentary delays while Windows locates and opens a channel to the selected computer. If you map the folder and choose the Reconnect At Logon option, any connection delays will occur at the beginning of your work session, and you'll be less likely to find them intrusive.

- Mapped folders become part of My Computer for file-search purposes.

  When you use the Search command to search for files stored on My Computer, the search encompasses not only your real local disks but also any mapped network folders. If you sometimes need to search for items that might be stored *either* locally or in a particular network folder, you can save yourself a search step by mapping the network folder.

# Mapping a Network Folder to a Drive Letter

To map a network folder to a drive letter:

**1**   Navigate to the folder in My Network Places.

Note that you can map only a shared network folder; you can't map a subfolder of a shared folder. Unlike the ordinary folder icon sported by subfolders, the icon for a network folder includes a representation of the network cable, as shown here.

**2**   Right-click the folder icon and choose Map Network Drive from the shortcut menu.

The dialog box shown in Figure 9-6 appears.

**3**   Choose a drive letter from the Drive box.

Windows proposes the first available drive letter, but you can choose any letter that's not already in use. You might want to pick one that's mnemonically related to the content of the folder—for example, *R* for Reports.

**4**   Select the Reconnect At Logon check box if you want Windows to connect to this shared folder automatically at the start of each session.

**FIGURE 9-6.**
Right-clicking a network folder icon and choosing Map Network Drive lets you turn the folder into a virtual local hard disk.

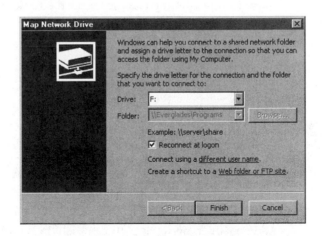

III

Managing Documents

5 If your regular logon account doesn't have permission to connect to the resource, click the Different User Name link, enter a user name and password, and click OK. (This capability is useful if you personally have multiple user accounts. For example, you might have an Administrator account that has access to some folders that are not available to your regular logon account.)

6 Click Finish.

### Unmapping a Mapped Network Folder

If you change your mind about mapping a network folder, simply right-click the folder's icon in your My Computer folder. Choose Disconnect in the resulting shortcut menu, and the tie will be severed.

# Using Path Specifications to Open Network Folders

In Windows 2000, you don't have to memorize path specifications to use network folders. Instead, you can simply navigate to the folders you need by using Windows Explorer. But every network folder does, in fact, have a path specification, and you're welcome to use path specifications whenever it's convenient.

A network folder's path consists of two backslash characters, followed by the computer name, another backslash, and a share name. The *share* name is the name assigned to the folder by the person who made it available on the network. *For more information about share names, see "Sharing Folders with Other Users."* So, for example, the network path for a folder shared as Programs on a computer named Everglades is

> \\Everglades\Programs

> **NOTE**

> If your computer is part of a Windows 2000 domain, computer names might conform to the new style, which includes the domain name. If the computer in the preceding example is part of the swdocs.com domain, the network path for the Programs folder becomes \\Everglades.swdocs.com\Programs.

Additionally, a network path can include subfolder names and file names. To get to a Microsoft Excel file on Documents, for example, you could specify

> \\Everglades\Documents\Budgets\December.xls

You can specify a shared folder's path in the Address bar of a Windows Explorer or Internet Explorer window, or via the Start menu's Run command. For example, when you want to get to a network folder quickly, without traversing a sequence of Windows Explorer windows, you can simply open the Start menu, choose Run, and type the path for the folder you need.

# Sharing Folders with Other Users

Provided you are logged on as a member of the Administrators, Power Users, or Server Operators group, you can share folders on your own system with other users on your network.

To share a folder or drive:

**1** Open Windows Explorer, and display the icon for the folder or drive you want to share.

**2** Right-click the icon, and then choose Sharing from the shortcut menu.

   This takes you to the Sharing tab of the folder's properties dialog box, as shown in Figure 9-7.

**3** Select the Share This Folder option.

**4** Accept or change the proposed share name.

**FIGURE 9-7.**
To share one of your own folders, choose the Sharing command from the folder's shortcut menu.

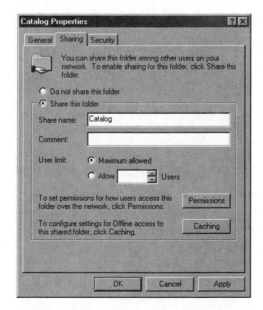

Managing Documents

> If the folder is already shared, click New Share and then type the share name. Local drives always have a default administrative share whose share name consists of the drive letter and a dollar sign (for example, C$). This share name is not visible to others, and you can't set permissions for the default share—so you'll want to create a new share.

The share name is the name that other users will see in their own My Network Places folders. Windows initially proposes to use the folder's name as its share name. That's usually a good choice, but you're not obligated to accept it. If you already have a shared folder with that name, you'll want to pick a different name.

### Hiding a Shared Folder from Casual Browsers

If you append a dollar sign to the share name (for example, *Catalog$*), the folder is not visible to users who browse the network with My Network Places or Windows Explorer. Users whom you've entrusted with the name of your shared folder can still connect to it by typing its name—including the dollar sign—into the Map Network Drive dialog box or the Run dialog box.

**5** Type a description of the folder's contents into the Comment box.

Other users will see this description when they inspect the folder's properties dialog box in their My Network Places folder (or use Details view).

**SEE ALSO**

For information about setting up caching for offline folders, see "Setting the Maximum Cache Size," page 197.

**6** To limit the number of users who can connect to the shared folder concurrently, click Allow, and then specify a number.

If network traffic seriously impacts your system's responsiveness, you might want to take advantage of this option. The default choice, Maximum Allowed, permits up to 10 concurrent users. (If you need to share a folder with more than 10 users at once, you must use Windows 2000 Server.)

## Assigning Permissions to a Shared Folder

The default permission associated with a new shared resource is Full Control to Everyone. That means that anyone on your network can do whatever they want to your files, including delete them. (If the shared folder resides on an NTFS volume, individual folders and files can

**CAUTION**

When you share a folder, you also make that folder's subfolders available on the network. If the access permissions you give for the folder aren't appropriate for any of its subfolders, either reconsider your choice of access permissions or restructure your folders to avoid the problem.

have their own access restrictions, however.) You can place limits on what particular users or groups of users can do with your shared files by clicking the Permissions button in the dialog box shown in Figure 9-7, on page 185. Then you'll see the dialog box shown in Figure 9-8.

To view or set permissions:

**1** In the Name list, select the name of the user or group you want to manage.

The shared folder permissions for the selected user or group appear in the Permissions box.

**2** Select Allow, Deny, or neither for each permission:

- **Full Control.** Allows users to read, write, rename, and delete files in the folder and its subfolders. In addition, users can take ownership of files on NTFS volumes.

- **Change.** Allows users to read, write, rename, and delete files in the folder and its subfolders, but not to create new files.

- **Read.** Allows users to read files but not write to them or delete them.

**FIGURE 9-8.**

By default, all users have Full Control over files in a new shared folder—unless access has been restricted to files individually via NTFS. You can use this dialog box to set restrictions on the entire shared folder.

III

Managing Documents

If you select neither Allow nor Deny, the user or group might inherit the permission through membership in another group that has the permission. If the user or group doesn't belong to another such group, the user or group is implicitly denied permission.

**NOTE**

To remove a name from the Name list, select it and click Remove. To add a name to the list, click Add to open the Select Users, Computers, Or Groups dialog box, where you can select the names of the users and groups you want to add. *For more information about this dialog box, see "Securing Files," page 584.*

**SEE ALSO**

For information about NTFS security, see Chapter 28, "Using NTFS Security."

Note that shared folder permissions apply only when the folder (and its files and subfolders) are accessed over a network. They don't protect files or folders when opened locally from the computer on which they reside. If the folder you're sharing is on an NTFS volume, the NTFS permissions protect the files locally, and they also apply to network users.

---

**Solutions to Common File-Sharing Problems**

To share a folder, you must be logged on as a member of the Administrators, Power Users, or Server Operators group. (Once a folder has been shared, however, the share is available to network users no matter who is logged on—or even when nobody is logged on.)

If the folder's properties dialog box doesn't have a Sharing tab, be sure your system is set up for sharing. First, check the properties dialog box for the network connection, and be sure that File And Printer Sharing For Microsoft Networks is installed and selected. *For more information, see "Configuring a Network Connection," page 272.* Then use the Services tool (right-click My Computer, choose Manage from the shortcut menu, expand Services And Applications, and click Services) and be sure the Server service is started.

---

# Monitoring the Use of Shared Resources

One potential disadvantage of sharing local resources is that if many users happen to be accessing files on your system at the same time, your system's performance might degrade significantly. At such times, you might find it helpful to know who's doing what with your shared resources. The Shared Folders tool serves this purpose. Shared Folders not only shows you who's connected to what, but it also lets you add shares, delete shares, and disconnect users. Clearly, you don't want to disconnect someone who has a valid reason to access one of your shared folders, but you might want to sever a connection that has been left open inadvertently.

To use the Shared Folders tool:

**1** On the desktop, right-click the My Computer icon, and choose Manage from the shortcut menu.

The Computer Management console appears. (Computer Management is also accessible from the Administrative Tools folder in Control Panel.)

**2** In the console tree (the left pane), expand System Tools and then expand Shared Folders.

As shown in Figure 9-9, the Shared Folders tool contains three subfolders that provide information about your shared folders: Shares, Sessions, and Open Files.

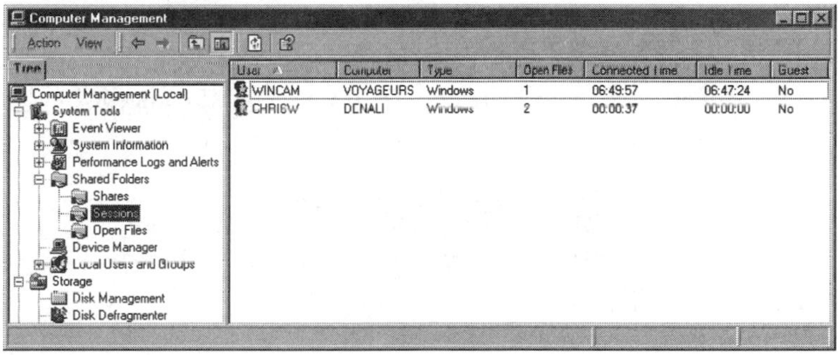

**FIGURE 9-9.**

The Shared Folders tool lets you see which of your shared resources is being used by whom. The Connected Time column shows how long a connection has been open.

- Select Shares to see a list of all your shared resources. In the # Client Redirections column, you can see how many users are connected to each folder. In this view, you can

  - View and set all properties (share name, comment, permissions, and so on) for each share. To do so, double-click a shared folder name.

  - Stop sharing a folder. To do so, right-click the shared folder name and choose Stop Sharing.

  - Create a new share. Be sure no shared folder is selected, and then choose New File Share from the Action menu. This launches the Create Shared Folder Wizard, which asks you to specify a folder, and then asks—over the course of several wizard pages—for the same type of information

**III**

**Managing Documents**

you can specify on the Sharing tab of a folder's properties dialog box, as described earlier in this chapter.

- Send an on-screen message to other Windows 2000 and Windows NT users. (If you're planning to stop sharing a folder or disconnect a user, you should first send a warning message to the affected users.) Be sure no shared folder is selected, open the Action menu, point to All Tasks, and choose Send Console Message. By default, Windows proposes to send the message to all currently connected computers, but you can add and remove computers from the list before you send your message.

■ Select Sessions to see a list of all users currently connected to your shared folders. In this view, you can disconnect a single user (right-click the user's name and choose Close Session), or you can summarily disconnect all users (right-click an unoccupied area of the right pane and choose Disconnect All Sessions).

■ Select Open Files to see a list of all files currently being used by other users. In this view, you can disconnect a single user or all users. To do so, use the methods described above for Sessions view.

### Introducing Computer Management and Microsoft Management Console

The term *console* is often applied to Computer Management because this program is the central tool for administering the computer, much as the traditional mainframe computer operator's display or console is the central location for administering the mainframe. This console is preconfigured with commonly used administrative too3ls for Windows 2000, and can be customized into various consoles to be used by those with special needs. Customization can involve adding new tools (also called *snap-ins* because they can be added, or *snapped into*, the main console) or by removing or deleting features of existing tools. Different users can be given access to particular custom consoles (known as *Microsoft Management Consoles* or *MMCs*), which makes it easier for the users to find the set of tools most relevant to their needs.

# CHAPTER 10

# Working Offline

M icrosoft Windows 2000 includes two features
designed to help you work while you're disconnected from your network or from the Internet.
If you've used Windows NT version 4 or Windows 98,
you might already be familiar with one of these features:
Briefcase. (It was called My Briefcase in these earlier
operating systems.) You might also be delighted to learn
that the other offline feature, called offline files, has largely
(but not entirely) eliminated the need for Briefcase.

Both offline files and Briefcase allow you to work with
server-based files while you're disconnected from the server.
When you reconnect, both can synchronize your files so that
you and your colleagues are always working with the current
version.

You'll need Briefcase if you copy files from a desktop computer to a portable computer via removable disk or a direct
cable connection. If you move files to a portable machine
across a network connection (LAN or dial-up), however, you
should use offline files instead of Briefcase.

# ⓶⓪⓪⓪ Using Offline Files

The general steps required to use offline files are as follows:

**1**  Set up your own computer (not the server) to allow the use of offline files.

**2**  Use the Make Available Offline command to identify folders and files that you intend to use offline.

**3**  Work offline.

**4**  Synchronize your offline files when you reconnect with the server.

## Setting Up Your System to Use Offline Files

Offline files are enabled by default on Windows 2000 Professional systems but disabled by default on Windows 2000 Server systems. To ensure that they're enabled on your system:

**1**  In any Windows Explorer window, choose Folder Options from the Tools menu.

**2**  On the Offline Files tab (see Figure 10-1), make sure the Enable Offline Files check box is selected.

The dialog box shown in Figure 10-1 also includes some other important options. We'll come back to those options later in this chapter.

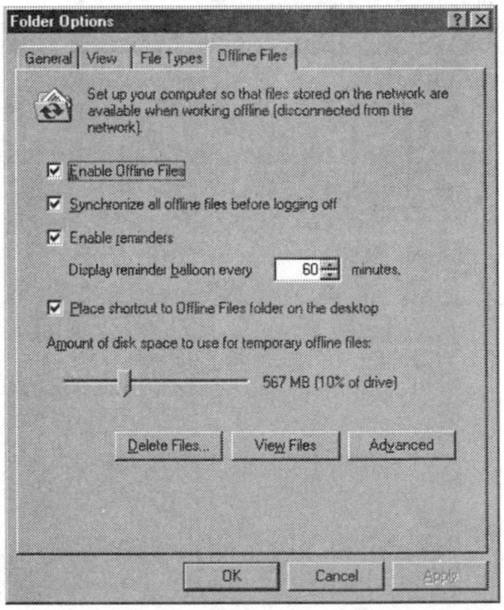

**FIGURE 10-1.**

The Offline Files tab of the Folder Options dialog box is the place to turn on or off your system's ability to work with offline files.

If you use the Make Available Offline command without first having visited the dialog box shown in Figure 10-1, the Offline Files Wizard will appear. The wizard simply steps you through some of the options shown in Figure 10-1.

# Making Files and Folders Available Offline

You can make both network files and folders (files and folders stored on a network server) and Web pages available for offline use.

To make a network file or folder available offline:

1 Open a Windows Explorer window containing the file or folder in question. For example, open My Network Places and navigate to the folder containing the file you want to use offline.

2 Select the file or folder, open the File menu, and choose Make Available Offline. Or right-click the item and choose Make Available Offline from the shortcut menu. (See Figure 10-2.)

If you apply the Make Available Offline command to a folder, all files contained in the folder become available. If the folder you select contains subfolders, a dialog box appears giving you the option to make all of the folder's subfolders available as well.

**FIGURE 10-2.**
To make a network file or folder available offline, right-click it and choose Make Available Offline from the shortcut menu.

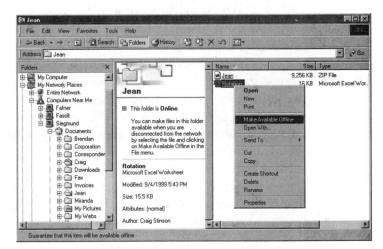

**TIP**

Don't make subfolders available offline unless you really need them. The more files you make available offline, the longer synchronization takes.

Managing Documents

When you make a file or folder available for offline use, Windows 2000 immediately copies the item from the server to your local hard disk. The local copy becomes part of your offline *cache*. You can verify that the file or folder is available offline by selecting it and reopening the File menu. A check mark appears beside the Make Available Offline command. (Windows Explorer also adds arrows to the icons of offline items.)

While you are still connected to the network, when you work with files marked for offline availability, you continue to work with the server copies. To ensure that you have the latest versions of files in your offline cache, you need to perform a synchronization before you disconnect or log off your computer. You can (and should) set up Windows 2000 to synchronize automatically at logoff. *See "Choosing Offline File Setup Options," page 196.* But if you simply disconnect your computer from the network without logging off, you must remember to synchronize manually. *See "Synchronizing," below.*

The procedure for making a Web page available offline is somewhat different because, as a first step, you need to add the page to your Favorites menu. *For information about this, see "Making Pages Available Offline," page 343.*

## Working Offline

While you're disconnected from the network (or from the Internet, in the case of offline Web pages), you can work with your offline files exactly as you would while connected. You access the files the same way, through your applications' menu commands or via Windows Explorer or Microsoft Internet Explorer. The files look exactly the same in Windows Explorer (except for the icon arrows that denote the files' offline availability), and your permissions are the same as they would be if you were connected. The only difference is that you are opening files from and saving them to your offline cache instead of a network server or the Internet. (In the case of offline Web pages, links on the pages might or might not be available, depending on the offline settings you chose for the Web pages.)

## Synchronizing

When you reconnect to the network, or just before you disconnect from the network, you'll want to *synchronize* your offline files. When you do this, Windows 2000 compares the versions in your offline cache to the versions stored in the original server locations and performs the following operations for each offline file:

- If you have changed the file while offline and the server-based copy hasn't been changed, Windows 2000 updates the server copy with your changes.

- If you haven't made changes to your offline copy but the server copy has been changed, Windows 2000 updates the copy in your offline cache.

- If both the server copy and your offline copy have been changed, a dialog box appears. You can keep your version, the server version, or both. If you choose to keep both, you need to provide a new name for your version.

- If either the offline copy or the server copy of a file is deleted, the file on the other machine will be deleted as well, as long as it wasn't changed while you were offline.

- If the server copy has been deleted and you changed your offline copy, a dialog box appears. You can save your version on the server or delete your offline copy.

- If you delete your version and the server copy has been changed, a dialog box appears asking whether you want to use your copy (in other words, delete the server copy), or use the server copy, which will copy the changed server file to your offline cache.

- If a new file has been added to a folder that you have marked for offline availability, the new file is copied to your offline cache.

Depending on how you've set up Synchronization Manager, synchronization might take place automatically when you reconnect. If it doesn't, you can synchronize all or selected offline items by running Synchronization Manager. *See "Using Synchronization Manager," page 198.*

You can synchronize an individual file or folder by selecting it in a Windows Explorer window and choosing Synchronize from the File menu, or by right-clicking it and choosing Synchronize from the shortcut menu. If you've enabled Web content in your Windows Explorer folders, you might also see a Synchronize button, similar to the one shown in Figure 10-3 on the next page. Click the button to synchronize the current folder.

III

Managing Documents

# Choosing Offline File Setup Options

Now let's return to the setup options available in the Folder Options
dialog box, shown in Figure 10-1, page 192. As a reminder, you get to
this dialog box by opening the Tools menu in any Windows Explorer
window, choosing Folder Options, and clicking the Offline Files tab.
Alternatively, you can select Folder Options in Control Panel.

## Synchronizing at Logoff

It's an excellent idea to select the Synchronize All Offline Files Before
Logging Off check box. An automatic synchronization at logoff makes
logging off take a little longer but ensures that you have the latest
versions of your offline files when you disconnect from the network.
Note, however, that you must also select the items you want synchronized automatically at logoff in Synchronization Manager. *See "Using
Synchronization Manager," page 198.*

## Enabling Synchronization Reminders

When you reconnect to your network after working offline, Windows
2000 can periodically remind you that it's time to synchronize your
files. This feature is turned on by default, and the reminders appear
(in the form of a balloon above the status area of your Windows
taskbar) at 60-minute intervals as long as your system contains any
unsynchronized files. If you turn reminders off, you can still get information about whether you need to synchronize. While you're offline, a
computer icon appears in your status area informing you that the network connection is not currently available. A moment or two after you
reconnect, a message appears above this computer icon, letting you

know that there's new information about the status of your connection. Clicking the icon brings up a dialog box, from which you can perform a synchronization.

## Creating a Shortcut to the Offline Files Folder

Windows maintains a system folder that lists all the server-based files you make available to yourself for offline use. This folder, shown in Figure 10-4, also includes information about the status of each file, the location of its server, whether the server is online or offline, and so on.

**FIGURE 10-4.**
The Offline Files folder shows the status of each offline file.

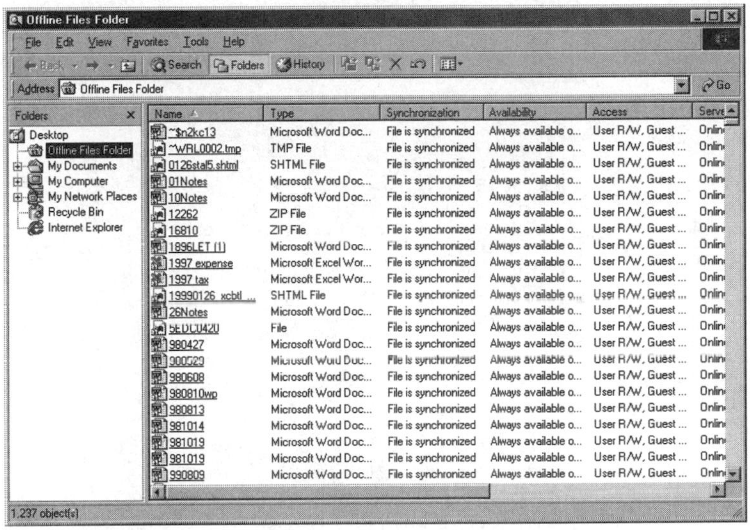

If you select the fourth check box on the Offline Files tab of the Folder Options dialog box shown in Figure 10-1 (page 192), Windows creates a desktop shortcut that simplifies access to this folder. If you prefer not to have the shortcut on your desktop, you can get to the Offline Files folder by clicking the View Files button in the Folder Options dialog box. Alternatively, you can open Synchronization Manager and click the Properties button. *See "Using Synchronization Manager," on the next page.*

## Setting the Maximum Cache Size

By default, Windows 2000 prevents the cache size from exceeding 10 percent of the size of the hard disk on which Windows 2000 is installed. You can increase or decrease that amount by dragging the slider in the Folder Options dialog box. You can't divert the cache to a different hard disk, however.

# Using Synchronization Manager

Synchronization Manager is a tool that lets you choose which share resources or Web pages you want to synchronize. You can also use it to schedule automatic synchronization. To run Synchronization Manager, either open the Tools menu in any Windows Explorer window and choose Synchronize, or open the Start menu and choose Programs, Accessories, Synchronize. Synchronization Manager is shown in Figure 10-5.

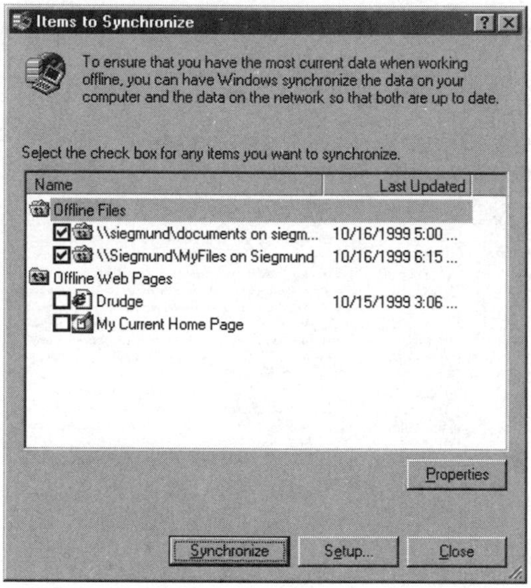

**FIGURE 10-5.**
Synchronization Manager lets you synchronize selected items or schedule automatic synchronization.

## Synchronizing Selected Shares or Web Pages

To synchronize selected network shares or Web pages, select the items you want to synchronize and click Synchronize. If you select one or more offline Web pages, Synchronization Manager activates your Internet connection and downloads the latest versions of the selected pages.

## Scheduling Automatic Synchronization

To set up scheduled synchronization, click the Setup button in Synchronization Manager. The dialog box shown in Figure 10-6 appears.

The three tabs in the Synchronization Settings dialog box shown in Figure 10-6 let you schedule synchronization at logon or logoff, during periods when your computer is idle, and at particular dates and times. Note that if you want synchronization to occur automatically whenever you log off, you must also select the Synchronize All Offline Files

Before Logging Off check box in the Folder Options dialog box shown in Figure 10-1 on page 192.

On each of these three tabs, you can specify which offline files and Web pages you want synchronized. You can click the Advanced button of the On Idle tab to stipulate how long your computer must be idle before the synchronization begins. (You can also select a check box that disables the on-idle synchronization when your computer is running on battery power.)

To schedule a date-and-time synchronization, click the Scheduled tab, and then click Add. You'll be handed off to a scheduling wizard that functions just like the one used to create scheduled program executions. *For details about using that wizard, see "Running Programs on Schedule," page 257.*

**FIGURE 10-6.**

You can schedule synchronization to occur at logon or logoff, during idle times, or at particular dates and times.

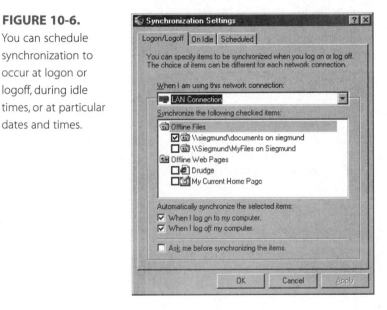

# Synchronizing Files with Briefcase

Briefcase lets you create copies of files for offline use and subsequently synchronize those files with their online originals. It's less easy to use than the offline-files feature described in the first part of this chapter. But it's the tool you need if you don't have a local-area-network connection between your portable and desktop computers. If you copy files from a desktop computer onto a floppy or other removable disk when you travel with your laptop, Briefcase is for you.

You can also use Briefcase if you have a direct cable connection between your portable and desktop machines. *For information about setting up a direct cable connection, see "Connecting Two Computers with a Direct Connection," page 294.*

## Using Briefcase with Removable Disks

The procedure for using Briefcase with removable media is as follows:

1   Put a disk (preferably a freshly formatted one) in a removable disk drive.

2   In Windows Explorer, open the folder for your removable disk.

3   From Windows Explorer's File menu, choose New, Briefcase.

4   Rename the briefcase (an optional step, but you'll want to do this if you use more than one briefcase at a time).

5   Open the briefcase. (It's a folder, almost like any other.)

    The first time you open a new briefcase, the Briefcase Wizard appears. Simply click Finish to dismiss the wizard. When you do this, the wizard sets up your new briefcase, creating the hidden files that Windows will use to track the status of your files.

6   Copy files into your new briefcase until the removable disk is somewhat less than full. Don't fill the disk, because you need to leave room for your files to grow as you work with them.

7   Insert the removable disk in your portable computer and move or copy the briefcase to your portable's hard disk (this step is optional but speeds access to your files).

8   Repeat these steps for as many removable disks as you need, but give each briefcase a unique name before moving it to your portable computer.

9   Upon returning to your desktop computer, copy each briefcase to a removable disk, and transfer the disk to your desktop computer.

10  Synchronize by opening Briefcase and choosing Update All from Windows Explorer's Briefcase menu. (The Briefcase menu appears only when a briefcase folder is selected.) If you want to synchronize only particular files, select Details view, select the files you want to synchronize, and then choose Update Selection from the Briefcase menu.

## Getting Status Information About Briefcase Files

In Large Icons view, the inside of a briefcase looks pretty much like the inside of any other folder window, except for the presence of a Briefcase menu. But if you switch to Details view, Briefcase provides useful information about the origin and status of your documents. As Figure 10-7 shows, the Status column in Details view shows you which files are current and which need updating (in other words, which files have changed since you copied them into the briefcase). The Sync Copy In column tells you where the original version of each of your files is stored.

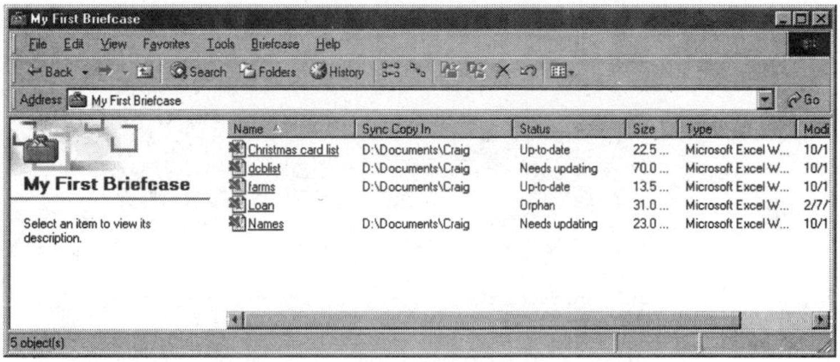

**FIGURE 10-7.**
By choosing Details view in a briefcase, you can see which of your files has changed since you copied them into the briefcase.

When your briefcase is online with the computer on which it was created (for example, when the briefcase is on a floppy disk in the desktop computer's disk drive), you can also get status information about a particular file by right-clicking it and viewing the Update Status tab of its properties dialog box. Figure 10-8, on the next page, shows the Update Status tab for a file that has been changed in the briefcase.

## Synchronizing Files

When you're ready to synchronize your briefcase files with their sync copies, you can work with either one file at a time or update the whole briefcase at once. To update a single file, select it, and then choose Update Selection from the Briefcase menu. (You can also update a group of selected files this way. Hold down the Ctrl key while you click each file you want to update. Then choose Update Selection.)

To update the entire briefcase at once, right-click the briefcase icon (in the folder where it resides) and choose Update All. You'll see a dialog box similar to the one shown in Figure 10-9, on the next page.

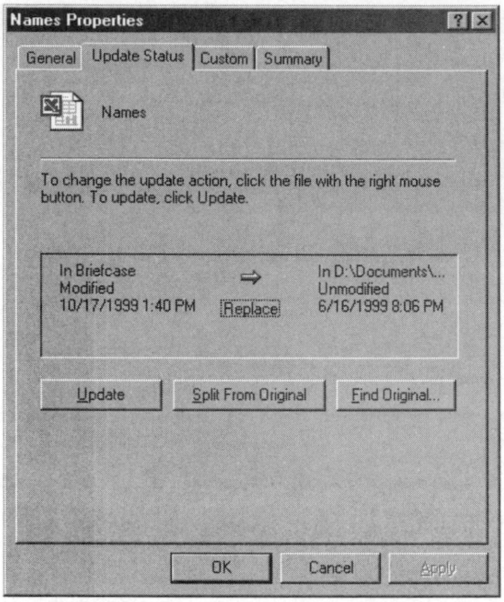

**FIGURE 10-8.**

The properties dialog box for a briefcase file can tell you where the file's sync copy resides and which version of the file is more current.

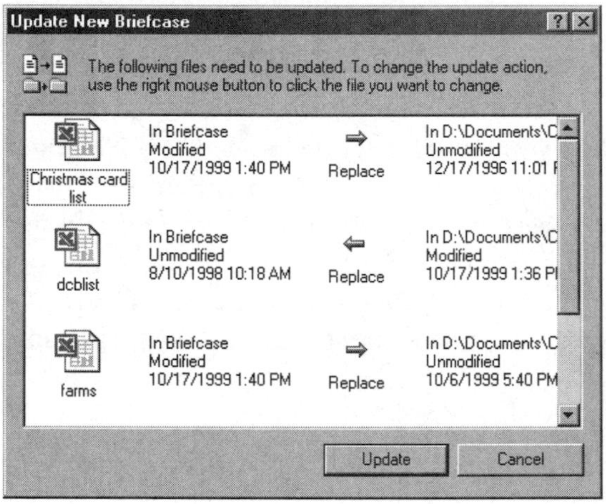

**FIGURE 10-9.**

When you choose Update All, Windows uses left-pointing and right-pointing arrows to show which copy of each changed file is newer.

Notice that the arrows in the center of the dialog box can point in either direction, depending on the target of the proposed updating. When you click the Update button, Windows copies the newer version of each file, wherever it might reside, over the unchanged version. If both files have been modified, the default action is to skip updating either file. If a file was deleted in one location, it will be copied from the other location to replace the deleted file.

If the update action that Briefcase proposes for an item isn't the action you want, right-click its entry in the Update New Briefcase dialog box. Then, from the shortcut menu, choose the action you prefer. To prevent changes to either file, choose Skip.

### Divorcing a Briefcase File from Its Sync Copy

If you move a file from a briefcase to any other folder, the link between that file and its sync copy is broken. The result is an ordinary copy. You can also sever the link between a file and its sync copy without removing it from the briefcase. To do this, select the file and choose Split From Original from the Briefcase menu. In Briefcase's Status field, your file will then be listed as an *orphan*. You can carry as many orphans as you please in your briefcase.

## Using Briefcase with a Direct Cable Connection

To use Briefcase with a direct cable connection, first connect your portable and desktop computers. On the portable, open Windows Explorer. Navigate to the folder where you want the briefcase to reside. Open Windows Explorer's File menu and choose New, Briefcase. Copy the files you want to use offline from your desktop computer to the new briefcase. Disconnect the portable computer and work offline. When you reconnect, synchronize the offline and desktop versions of your files, as described in "Using Briefcase with Removable Disks," page 200.

# CHAPTER 11

# Searching for Files and Folders

S cooting around your hard disk or network with Windows Explorer is dandy when you know where you're going. But it's not so good when all you know is "The file is out there." In that all-too-common circumstance, you'll want to use the Microsoft Windows 2000 versatile Search Assistant.

The Search Assistant can quickly locate documents, programs, and folders anywhere on your own computer or amongst the shared resources of your network. You can find what you're looking for by name, creation date, size, file type, content, or any combination of these. For example, you can ask the Search Assistant to locate all Microsoft Excel documents created within the last month that are at least 30 MB in size and contain the word *xenon*. Or you can use it to generate a list of all programs on a particular server. Or find all files that are larger than 100 KB and haven't been modified during the last six months. And so on.

> **NOTE**

The Search Assistant can do much more than find files and folders. You can also use it to find computers and printers on your network, and to find people and Web sites on the Internet. *For finding computers, see "Searching for Computers ," page 179 ; for finding printers, see "Finding Printers on the Network, " page 221; for finding people, see "Finding People," page 314; and for finding Web sites, see "Using Search to Find New Sites," page 337.*

Some of your programs might also attach themselves to the Search Assistant. If you use Microsoft Outlook, for example, you'll see an entry in the Search menu tailored for that program. You can use the Using Microsoft Outlook command to find items in one of your Outlook folders. (Be aware that program-specific entries on the Search menu invoke program-specific search engines. These might or might not work the same way as the Windows 2000 search tools described in this chapter.)

⭐ **TIP**

The Search Assistant can't locate e-mail messages stored in Outlook Express. To find such messages, use the Find tools in Outlook Express.

After you have performed a Search operation, if you leave the Search window open, Search continues rechecking the disks or folders it searched originally to see whether any new items have appeared that match your search criteria. Thus, you can use it to keep a more or less constant eye on a network server and alert you when particular files have arrived on that server. You can also take advantage of the Save Search command to make a set of search criteria easily reusable (as described in the last section of this chapter).

# Finding the Search Assistant

To launch the Search Assistant, you can do any of the following:

- Choose Search from the Start menu.

- Display the Search bar in any Windows Explorer window.

- Press F3 in any Windows Explorer window.

When you choose Search from the Start menu, a submenu appears. To search for files or folders, choose For Files Or Folders. When the Search Assistant opens, it appears with its default settings, prepared to search all of your local drives and devices. When you press F3 or

**? SEE ALSO**

For information about displaying the Search bar in Windows Explorer, see "Navigating with the Search Bar," page 145.

display the Search bar, the Search Assistant is set to search the current folder and its subfolders.

Figure 11-1 shows the Search Assistant. The window has two panes: a search pane on the left and a results pane on the right. The menu and toolbar are those of Windows Explorer—because, in fact, the Search Assistant (unlike its predecessor in Microsoft Windows NT and Microsoft Windows 98) is a component of Windows Explorer.

**FIGURE 11-1.**
The Search Assistant is a Windows Explorer component.

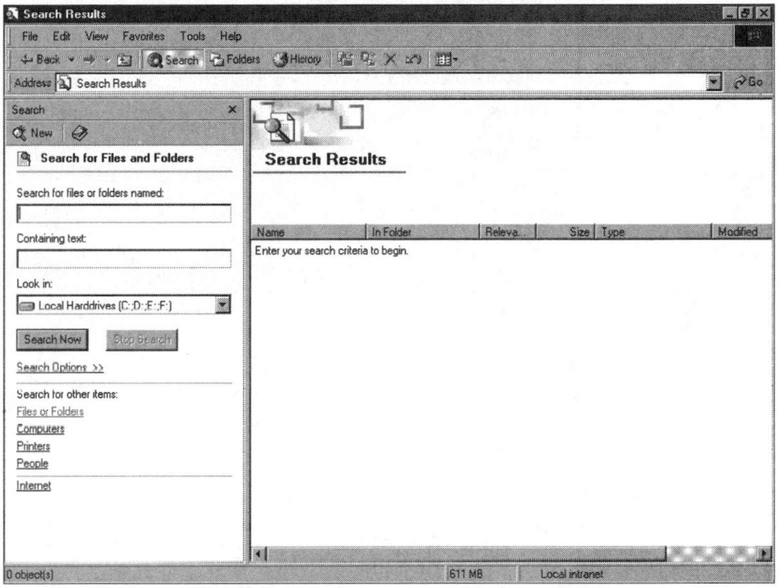

# Specifying Where to Search

**? SEE ALSO**

For information about mapping network drives, see "Mapping a Network Folder to a Drive Letter," page 183.

Use the Look In box to tell the Assistant where to search. As Figure 11-2 on the next page shows, the list includes My Documents, Desktop, all of your local storage media, and all of your mapped network shares. If what you want to search isn't included in this list, you can either type directly into the Look In box or click the Browse item at the bottom of the list.

For example, suppose you want to search Temp, a subfolder of drive D. The D:\Temp folder doesn't appear in the Look In list, so you could simply type *D:\Temp* into the Look In box. Alternatively, you could open the Look In list, click Browse, and then navigate to D:\Temp in the Browse For Folder dialog box that appears.

III

Managing Documents

**FIGURE 11-2.**

The Look In list shows all of your local media and mapped network shares, as well as My Documents and My Computer.

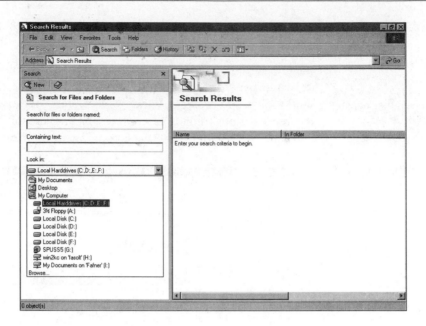

By default, Search looks for the disk or folder specified in the Look In box, plus all the subfolders of that disk or folder. If you don't want to search the subfolders:

1  Click Search Options.

2  Select the Advanced Options check box.

3  Clear the Search Subfolders check box.

# Specifying What to Search For

You can use any of the following criteria, singly or in combination, when searching for files and folders:

- File or folder name
- File content
- Creation, most recent modification, or access date
- File type
- File size

If you use a combination of criteria, Search ferrets out only those items that meet *all* criteria.

**TIP**

When you finish a search, Search retains your search criteria in case you want to perform another search based on similar criteria. If you want to start a brand new search, you should first click the New button at the top of the Search bar. That way, you won't inadvertently reuse a criterion from your previous search.

# Searching by Name

To specify a search by name, type in the first field of the Search bar. You can search by name without knowing exactly how the item you want is spelled. If you know any part of it, enter that part. The Search Assistant locates all items whose names include the letters you type. For example, if you simply type *Sales*, the Search Assistant locates items with names such as Quarter 1 Sales, Quarter 2 Sales, Sales Forecast, Salespersons, and Sales Tax.

## Using Wildcard Characters

**SEE ALSO**

For information about the search-by-file-type option, see "Searching by File Type," page 213. For information about extensions in the registry, see "Working with the File Types List," page 168.

A *wildcard character* is a character that can be used to represent one or more other characters. If you're an MS-DOS veteran, you might be accustomed to using wildcard characters in directory searches. You'll be glad to know the same wildcard characters also work with filename searches conducted by the Search command. The two wildcard characters recognized by Search are a question mark (?) and an asterisk (*).

The question mark represents any single character. For example, specifying

> 199?

returns any file or folder that includes any year from 1990 to 1999 in its name, as well as files and folders that include 199 followed by any other character (other than a space). You can use as many question-mark wildcards in a specification as you want.

The asterisk represents any single character or combination of characters. For example, searching for

> 1*4

might turn up 123r4, 1994, 1024, and so on. The most common use for the asterisk wildcard character is to find all files with a common extension. For example, to find all files with the extension .xls, you can enter

> *.xls

III

Managing Documents

---

**Interrupting a Search**

Once the item or items you're looking for appear in the Search window, you don't need to sit on your hands while Search Assistant continues searching. You can halt the search at any time by clicking the Stop Search button.

Alternatively, you can begin working with an item in the Search window while the search goes on. Simply select any item in the Search Results pane and use it however you like. You can right-click the item to get its shortcut menu, double-click it to open it (if it's a document), run it (if it's a program), drag it somewhere if you want to copy it or make a shortcut from it, and so on.

---

If you simply enter *xls* without the wildcard character and period, you get, in addition to all the files with the extension .xls, all files with *xls* anywhere else in their names. An alternative way to find all files with a certain extension is to search by the file type. But this option is useful only for file types that are recorded in your Windows registry. For extensions that aren't in the registry, the wildcard-character approach is ideal.

# Searching by File Content

To search for files containing some particular text, type the text you're looking for into the Containing Text line. Note that the text you type is treated literally—that is, you can't use wildcard characters on the Containing Text line. Also, be aware that searching for files by their content takes much longer than searching by name, modification date, type, or size. To avoid unnecessarily lengthy searches, restrict the search as much as is practical. For example, if you're looking for a Microsoft Excel spreadsheet with a particular number or phrase in it, restrict the file type to Excel documents and, if all the likely possibilities are stored in a certain folder, enter that folder name into the Look In box.

## Making a Case-Sensitive Search

Content searches ignore case by default. To make a search case sensitive:

1 Click the Search Options link. (Omit this step if Search Options is already expanded.)

2 Select the Advanced Options check box.

3 Select the Case Sensitive check box.

> Unlike the Find command in Windows NT and Windows 98, the Search Assistant doesn't retain your case-sensitive setting. If you perform a case-sensitive search and then close the Search Assistant, the next time you open the Search Assistant, the Assistant will be set to ignore case.

# Using the Indexing Service to Speed Up Content Searches

You can speed up a content search dramatically by creating an index of your local disks. The Indexing Service creates a list of all words (other than common words, such as *the*, *a*, and *an*) in all documents for which an appropriate filter is available. (The filter tells the Indexing Service how to read a document and how to distinguish the document's text from extraneous nontextual information.) This includes HTML documents, plain-text documents, and all Microsoft Office documents. Other forms of documents might be indexable as well; you'll need to experiment to determine whether the Indexing Service can work with the documents you need to search.

The Indexing Service is designed to operate unobtrusively during times when your computer is idle. Microsoft Windows estimates that an index will occupy between 15 and 30 percent of the size of the documents indexed.

To create an index of your local disks for the first time:

1 Click the Search Options link. (Omit this step if Search Options is already expanded.)

2 Click the Indexing Service link.

3 Select the option labeled Yes, Enable Indexing Service And Run When My Computer Is Idle.

# Searching by Date

To use a date or timeframe as a search criterion, click the Search Options link (unless Search Options is already expanded), and then select the Date check box. The Date section of the Search bar expands, as shown in Figure 11-3, on the next page. Use the box directly below the Date check box to search by creation date, last modification date, or most-recent-access date. (Modification date is the default.) Note that a file's most recent modification or access might

III

Managing Documents

have been performed by the operating system or a program, not directly by you. (You'd be surprised to discover how many files get accessed by the operating system in the course of a day.)

When you search for all objects created, modified, or accessed during the previous *n* days, that means the previous *n* days plus all of today. For example, if you ask the Search Assistant to locate all files modified during the previous day, it finds everything that was changed yesterday plus anything that was changed today. (To find only those files that have been created, modified, or accessed today, click Between and set both the start and end dates to today's date.)

**⭐ TIP**

> If you're trying to reuse a file created or last accessed in recent days, it might be easier to find it by opening the History bar than by using the Search Assistant. *For information about the History bar, see "Navigating with the History Bar," page 145.* You might also be able to find the file you need by opening the Start menu and choosing Documents.

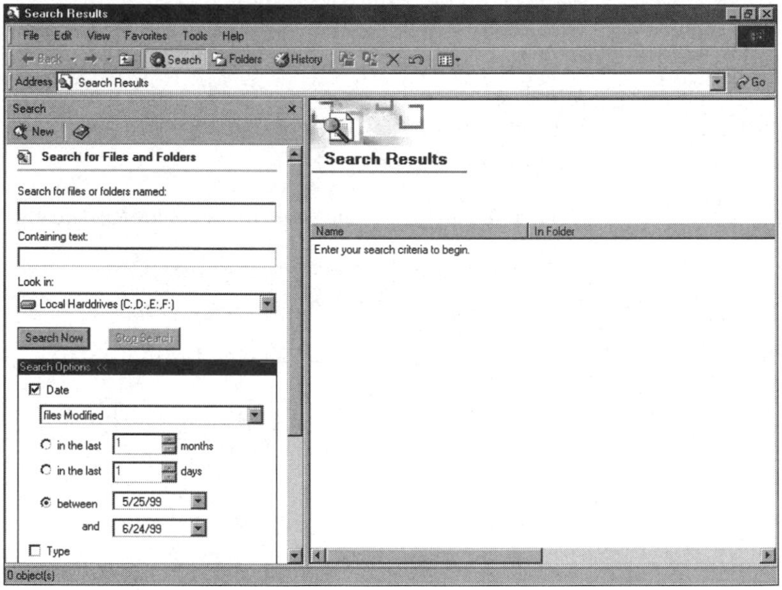

**FIGURE 11-3.**
You can search for files or folders last modified during a particular time interval.

## Searching by File Type

To search for a particular kind of file, or to restrict the search to folders only, expand the Search Options link and select the Type check box. The default type specification is All Files And Folders. To narrow the search to a particular type, select a file type from the list. Note that the list also includes some general categories, as well as the various document types known to your system's registry. For example, to search for executable programs, choose Application. To search for folders, excluding documents and programs, choose Folders, and so on.

## Searching by File Size

To search for files and folders that are larger than or smaller than a particular size, expand the Search Options link and select the Size check box. The first box lets you choose At Least or At Most, and the KB box lets you type or use the small arrows to set the threshold size you're interested in.

# Saving and Working with Search Results

To preserve the criteria that you've used in a Search operation for future use, open the File menu and choose Save Search. The Search Assistant creates a file with the extension .fnd and saves it (by default) in your My Documents folder. To perform another search using the same criteria, simply launch the search item and click Search Now.

You can work with search results in other ways besides saving them. The Search Assistant is built into Windows Explorer (and Microsoft Internet Explorer as well). Its results arrive in the right pane of the Windows Explorer window, and you can work with them there exactly as you would work with the contents of any other Windows Explorer window.

If you have your folders enabled to display Web content, a useful header appears atop the file and folder entries in the Search Results pane (see Figure 11-4, on the next page). When you select an item in

III

Managing Documents

**?** **SEE ALSO**

For information about enabling Web content in folders, see "Choosing Web View or Classic View," page 80.

the Search Results pane, the header displays a link to the item's containing folder. In some cases, depending on the type of item selected, you might also see a thumbnail of the item and a link to launch it.

An alternative way to open the folder containing a found item is to select the item in the Search Results pane and choose Open Containing Folder either from the File menu or from the item's shortcut menu.

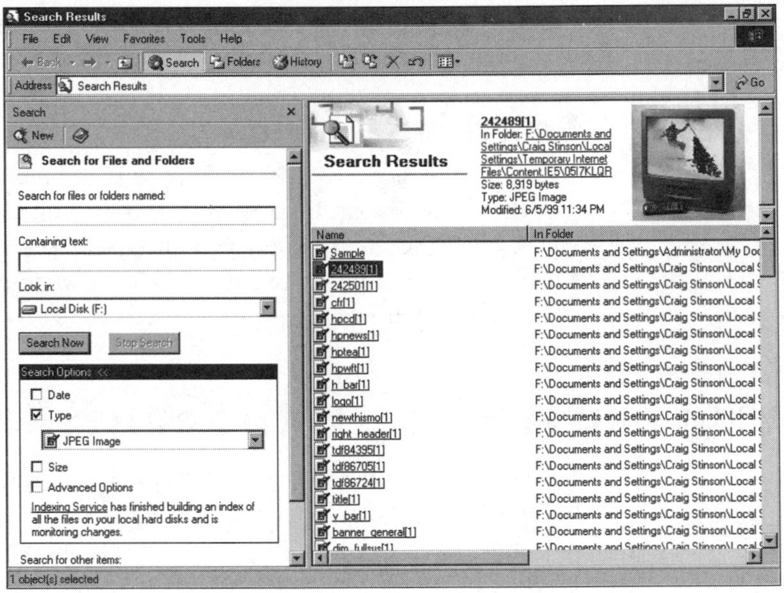

**FIGURE 11-4.**

If you have Web content in folders enabled, you'll find useful links to selected items at the top of the Search Results pane.

CHAPTER 12

# Printing

S truggles with arcane printer commands, finding printer drivers for each application, and finicky connections in the early days of personal computing are a distant memory. When it comes to translating your work from the computer screen to the printed page, Microsoft Windows provides a wealth of support, and we've reached the point where we can now take printing for granted. But you shouldn't overlook the enhancements that Microsoft Windows 2000 brings to the table:

- An improved Print dialog box makes it easier to see which of your printers has the shortest queue and to select that printer.

- If the printer you want isn't installed, you can add a printer from the Print dialog box.

- With Active Directory, you can easily find a printer with particular capabilities or one that's located in a particular place.

- Point and Print lets you start using a network printer without printer-driver setup hassles.

- Internet printing lets you print to any printer that's accessible on the Internet.

- Printed color documents match their on-screen appearance, thanks to Image Color Management (ICM) 2 support. *For information about ICM, see "Matching Colors with Color Profiles," page 113.*

- Plug and Play support and an improved Add Printer Wizard make it easier to install printers. *For information, see "Installing and Configuring a Printer," page 510.*

# Printing a Document

In Windows, there is nearly always more than one way to accomplish a task. Printing is no exception. Here are four ways to print a document:

- From a program, use the program's Print command (usually on the File menu).

- Right-click a document icon (on your desktop or in Windows Explorer) and choose Print from the shortcut menu.

- Drag a document icon to a printer icon.

- Right-click a document icon, point to Send To, and choose a printer (assuming you've added one or more printer shortcuts to your SendTo folder).

## Printing from a Program

If the document you want to print is already open, the simplest way to print it is to open the File menu and choose Print. Figure 12-1 shows the Print dialog box used by the programs included with Windows 2000. (And because this is a common dialog box, you'll see that many other programs use it too.)

⭐ **TIP**

> In many programs, you can simply click the Print button on the program's toolbar—if it has a toolbar with a Print button—to print a document. The toolbar approach typically bypasses all dialog boxes and sends your entire document to the default printer.

 The Print dialog box in Windows 2000 offers a number of improvements over its counterpart in earlier versions of Windows:

- You can point to a printer (no clicking required) in the Select Printer list on the General tab and see its status and the number of documents waiting to be printed.

- It's easier to select a printer—just one click instead of two.

- You can add a printer if the one you want isn't already installed. In the Select Printer box on the General tab, open the Add Printer icon. *For more information, see "Installing and Configuring a Printer," page 510.*

- You can find (and print to) any printer on your network by clicking Find Printer on the General tab.

- You can change printing preferences—orientation, paper source, and so on—without going to another dialog box. Simply click the Layout tab and the Paper/Quality tab.

⭐ TIP

> **Changing Settings (and Saving Paper)**
> You can select a printer, change other printing preferences, and then return to your document without printing. (This is sometimes useful because changing the layout—or even selecting a different printer—can change the way your program breaks lines and lays out pages. You might want to return to your document to check the effect before committing to paper.) To do that, make your changes in the Print dialog box, click Apply, and then click Cancel.

**FIGURE 12-1.**
The Print dialog box in most programs lets you select a printer and set options without changing system defaults.

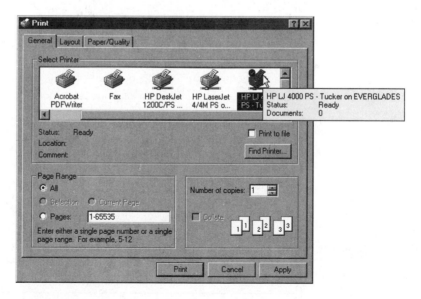

III

Managing Documents

## Selecting a Printer

The first time you open the Print dialog box (see Figure 12-1) after you start a program, the default printer is selected. (You can tell it's the default printer because its icon sports a check mark.) The *default printer*, as its name suggests, is the one that Windows uses unless you tell it to use another.

**TIP**

To make a different printer the default, right-click its icon in the Printers folder and choose Set As Default Printer from the shortcut menu. *For more information, see "Using the Printers Folder," page 225.*

If you want to print to a different printer, click its icon in the Select Printer box. When you do that, the Status line tells you how busy that printer is.

**TIP**

**Monitoring Printer Status**
While a print job that you initiate remains in a print queue, a printer icon is displayed in the taskbar status area, just to the left of the clock. When that icon disappears, you know that all your print jobs have finished. If you want to check the status of your print jobs, you can launch that printer icon to open the folder for the printer you're using and inspect that printer's queue. *For more information about print queues, see "Inspecting and Managing a Print Queue," page 227.*

## Determining How Much to Print

In addition to letting you select a printer, the Print dialog box in most programs lets you set options for that printer. For example, you can specify whether you want to print all of your document, only a range of pages, or only the portion of your document that's currently selected.

## Printing Multiple Copies

The Print dialog box also lets you indicate the number of copies you want and whether you want multiple copies collated. If you don't collate, Windows prints all copies of your first page, followed by all copies of your second, and so on. If you collate, you'll get all pages of your first copy, followed by all pages of your next copy, and so on.

**NOTE**

Some programs and drivers for some printers don't support multiple copies and collating.

**TIP**

If you commonly print more than one copy of each document on a particular printer, you can change the default number of copies. *For more information, see "Setting Printing Preferences," page 230.*

## Changing Printing Preferences

**? SEE ALSO**

For information about printing preferences, see "Setting Printing Preferences," page 230. For information about the Printers folder, see "Using the Printers Folder," page 225.

In addition to its General tab, shown in Figure 12-1, the Print dialog box might include a Layout tab and a Paper/Quality tab. Whether these tabs appear—and their content—depends on the program and on the printer you select. These tabs provide access to the same settings you can make by selecting a printer in the Printers folder and choosing the Printing Preferences command. The difference here is that the choices you make apply only to the current document in the current program; when you set printing preferences from the Printers folder, you're making default settings for all documents that you print on the selected printer.

**> NOTE**

> In most programs that do *not* use the common Print dialog box, you can still set printing preferences. In the program's Print dialog box, click Properties, and (in most cases) you'll see a document properties dialog box that includes a Layout tab and a Paper/Quality tab.

# Printing from Windows Explorer

If the document you want to print isn't open, you can launch its icon in a Windows Explorer window and then use the Print command in its parent program. But you don't need to do this.

An easier way to print that document is to right-click the document icon in Windows Explorer (or on the desktop), and choose Print from the shortcut menu. Doing so prints the document on the default printer. Alternatively, you can grab its icon and then drag it to a printer icon. This latter method is especially useful if you want to print on a printer other than the default printer.

**> NOTE**

> These methods work only with documents that are associated with their parent program in your Windows registry. You won't find a Print command on the shortcut menu of an unregistered document type. And if you try the drag-and-drop method, you'll get an error message. *For information about the registry and associating documents with programs, see "Working with the File Types List," page 168.*

You can drag a document icon to the printer icon with either mouse button. As you reach the drop zone, the printer icon darkens and your document icon sprouts a plus sign (+) to indicate that you are copying data to the printer (as opposed to moving it there permanently).

When you choose Print from the shortcut menu or drop a document onto a printer icon, Windows loads the parent program and executes its print command. Depending on the program, you might have to respond to a dialog box before printing begins. As soon as the information has been transferred to the print queue, the program closes.

★ TIP

> **Creating Targets for Drag-and-Drop Operations**
> Although you can print by dragging a document icon to a printer icon in your Printers folder, you'll probably find it more convenient to create a desktop or toolbar shortcut for each printer you plan to use this way. To create a printer shortcut, open your Printers folder and right-drag the printer's icon to your desktop or a toolbar (such as the Quick Launch toolbar, for example). From the shortcut menu, choose Create Shortcut(s) Here.

## Printing with the Send To Command

If you don't like cluttering your desktop with printer icons, or if you find it inconvenient to make those icons visible when you want to print, try using the Send To command. Simply right-click the icon or name of the document you want to print, point to Send To on the shortcut menu, and then choose the name of the printer you want from the Send To menu.

To add a printer to the Send To menu:

1   On the Start menu, point to Settings and choose Printers to open the Printers folder. (If you've set up your Start menu to include an expandable Printers folder, right-click Printers and choose Open.)

2   In a separate window, open your SendTo folder—a hidden folder with the path %userprofile%\SendTo. To do that, choose Run from the Start menu, and then type *%userprofile%\SendTo*.

 **SEE ALSO**

For more information about the SendTo folder, see "Customizing the Send To Menu," page 161.

3   Right-drag the printer's icon from the Printers folder to the SendTo folder.

4   Choose Create Shortcut(s) Here from the shortcut menu.

5   Right-click the new icon in the SendTo folder and choose Rename. Delete "Shortcut to" and then press Enter.

When you print with Send To, Windows first opens your document's parent program, just as it does when you drag the document to a printer icon.

# Printing to a Network Printer

Printing to a network printer is just like printing to a local printer, provided the network printer has been shared (your network administrator should do that for you) and you have been given access to it (also a task for your network administrator). To use such a printer, you must connect to it. If the print server (the computer that the network printer is attached to) is running Windows 2000, connecting is a one-click process that Microsoft dubs *Point and Print*. (If the print server is running another operating system, you might need to use the Add Printer Wizard to set up the connection. *For information about adding a printer, see "Installing and Configuring a Printer," page 510.*)

## Finding Printers on the Network

The first task in printing to a network printer is finding a suitable printer. How you do that—and the ease with which it's done— depends on whether or not your computer is part of a Windows 2000 Server domain that uses Active Directory.

### Browsing for Printers Without Active Directory

Using My Network Places, you can browse to each server on your network and see if it has any shared printers. The process works best if you know the location of the printer and the name of the server to which it's attached before you begin. (To connect to a printer you find in My Network Places, right-click its icon and choose Connect.)

If your computer is not part of a Windows 2000 Server domain with Active Directory, your best bet for finding a network printer is to use a program's Print dialog box (assuming the program uses the common Print dialog box). Using the Print dialog box offers two advantages over browsing with My Network Places:

- The Connect To Printer dialog box lists the shared printers in each domain, so in most cases you don't need to drill down to a particular server to find a printer.

- Once you find a printer, Windows connects to it automatically.

To find and connect to a network printer:

**1** If the program you want to print from is not already open, open Notepad (or another program included with Windows 2000).

**2** Choose Print from the File menu to display the Print dialog box. (See Figure 12-1, on page 217.)

III

Managing Documents

**3** Click Find Printer.

The Connect To Printer dialog box appears.

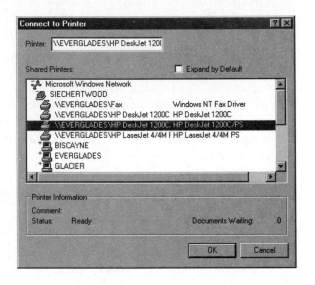

**4** Navigate through the list by double-clicking the network, domain, and server until the printer you're looking for is displayed.

**5** Select the printer and click OK.

If the print server has a suitable printer driver available, Windows 2000 installs it automatically. If a driver is not available on the server, you might be asked to provide a disk that has the printer driver files.

**6** Now back in the Print dialog box, click Print if you want to print your document on the new network printer, or click Cancel to close the dialog box without printing.

## Using Active Directory to Find a Printer

If your computer is part of a Windows 2000 Server domain that uses Active Directory, you can use Active Directory's powerful search capabilities to find a network printer that's suitable for the job you want to print.

To find a printer using Active Directory:

**1** On the Start menu, point to Search and choose For Printers. Alternatively, in the Print dialog box, click Find Printer.

Either route takes you to the Find Printers dialog box, shown in Figure 12-2.

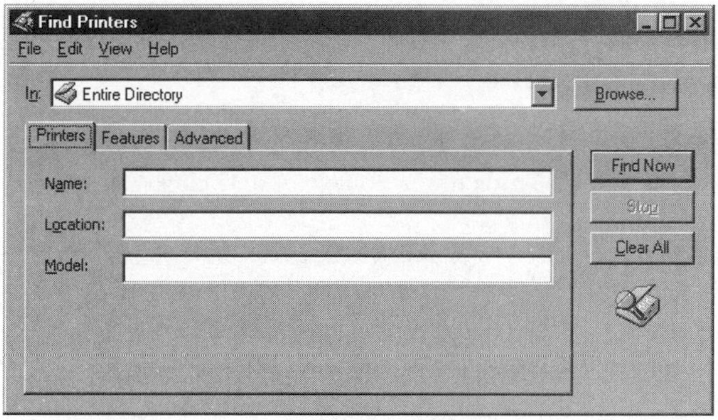

**FIGURE 12-2.**

The Find Printers dialog box lets you search Active Directory for printers of a specific model or in a specific location.

**2** Use the In box to limit the search to your domain if you don't want to search your organization's entire directory.

**3** If you know the share name, location, or model name of the printer you're looking for, type the first few letters on the Printers tab, shown in Figure 12-2. Leave these fields blank if you don't know the information or if you want to see a list of all printers.

**4** Click the Features tab, and then select the printer features you need.

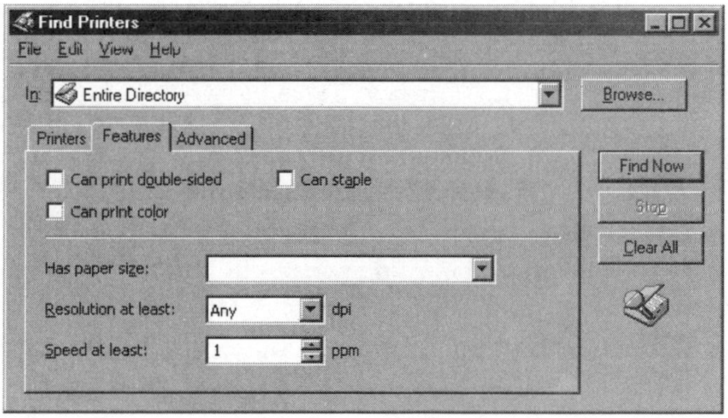

**5** If you want to narrow your search, click the Advanced tab. Click the Field list to select a field (your choices run the gamut from Asset Number to Printer Language), select a condition, enter a value, and click Add. Add as many criteria as you like; Active Directory will return only the printers that match *all* the criteria you specify.

**6** Click Find Now.

Windows returns a list of printers that match your criteria, as shown in Figure 12-3.

**7** To connect to a printer, right-click it and choose Connect. (If you got to Find Printers via the Print dialog box, simply select the printer you want and click OK.)

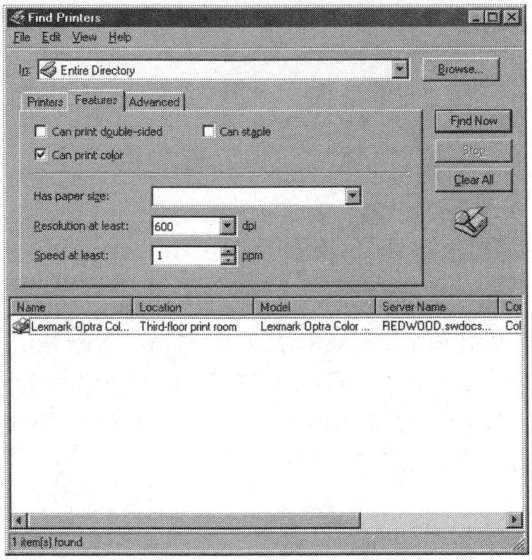

**FIGURE 12-3.**
Find Printers returns a list of printers that match all the criteria you specify.

# Printing to an Internet Printer

Windows 2000 supports a new protocol called Internet Printing Protocol (IPP). With this feature, you can connect to a printer on the Internet in the same way that you use a network printer. If your system administrator has set up printers on a Web server at work, this means you can print from home while still wearing a robe and slippers. It also means you can print to other printers that aren't on your network, such as a color printer at a nearby service bureau, or at a client's office.

Any Windows 2000 server that is accessible over the Internet (or an intranet) can be an Internet print server. (For a Windows 2000 server to be accessible over the Internet, it must have Internet Information Services [IIS] installed and running, and it must be connected to the Internet. Those topics are beyond the scope of this book.) On such a server, you simply set up and share a printer as you would for sharing over the network. Internet users can then connect to the printer, print documents, and manage print jobs. You limit access to the printer using ordinary HTTP security schemes—another topic beyond the scope of this book. Our point in mentioning this is that adding a shared printer to a Web server is incredibly simple; the hard part (which is also much easier with Windows 2000 than ever before) is setting up the Web server.

To connect to an Internet printer, use your Web browser to open *http://server/printers* (where *server* is the name of the Web server), and then simply click the printer you want from the list that appears. (Alternatively, launch Add Printer, and enter the printer's URL when the wizard asks for the printer's location.) In either case, Windows 2000 downloads the printer driver from the print server and installs it on your computer. You can then use the printer exactly like any other installed printer; in addition to printing, you can perform other printer-management tasks, as described in the following sections.

# Using the Printers Folder

Except for the actual act of printing, which you can do from programs or Windows Explorer, the locus of printing activity is a system folder called Printers. From the Printers folder you can

**? SEE ALSO**

For information about adding printers and working with printer properties, see "Installing and Configuring a Printer," page 510. For information about printing preferences and printer queues, see the following sections in this chapter.

- Add a printer. (Open the Add Printer icon.)

- Inspect and manage printer properties. (Right-click the printer's icon and choose Properties.)

- Inspect and manage printing preferences. (Right-click the printer's icon and choose Printing Preferences.)

- Set the default printer. (Right-click the printer's icon and choose Set As Default Printer.)

- Inspect and manage printer queues—the list of documents waiting to print on each printer. (Open the printer's icon.)

To get to the Printers folder, open the Start menu, point to Settings, and choose Printers. Alternatively, open the Printers icon in Control Panel. Figure 12-4, on the next page, shows a typical Printers folder.

Although Printers is a system folder, in most respects it looks and acts like an ordinary disk folder. You can choose to display or not display the toolbar and status bar, display printers as icons or list entries, select browsing and viewing options from the View menu, and use

III

Managing Documents

standard navigation techniques to move from this folder to any other folder on your system.

**FIGURE 12-4.**
Windows displays status information for the highlighted printer on the left side. You can get status information for other printers simply by pointing to them.

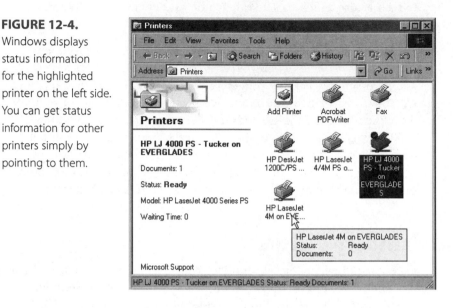

> 🌟 **TIP**
>
> **Viewing the Printers Folder in Detail**
> Display the Printers folder in Details view to see the number of queued documents and the current status of each local and network printer available to your system. Details view can also show the comment, location, and printer model for each installed printer. To select which columns you want to include, switch to Details view and choose Choose Columns from the View menu.

Within the Printers folder, you'll find entries for each printer you've installed, including local printers and printers attached to network servers. The Printers folder also includes an icon labeled Add Printer, which you can use to install new printers.

Windows uses the following icons to distinguish various kinds of printers from one another:

  A printer attached to your own computer

  A printer set as your default printer

A printer attached to a network server

A printer attached to your computer but made available (shared) to other network users

A printer attached to your computer but set up to redirect output to a disk file

**Expanding the Printers Menu**
You can bypass the Printers folder and jump right to a particular printer to view or change its properties or queue if you set up a cascading Printers menu. To do that, right-click an unoccupied area of the taskbar, choose Properties, and click the Advanced tab of the Taskbar And Start Menu Properties dialog box. In the Start Menu Settings list, select Expand Printers. Thereafter, the contents of the Printers folder sprout from the side of the Start menu's Printers command. On occasions when you do want to open the Printers folder, right-click Printers and choose Open.

# Inspecting and Managing a Print Queue

When you print a document, Windows creates a temporary file, called a *spool file,* on your hard disk (if the printer is local) or the hard disk of the computer to which your network printer is attached. After the spool file has been created, the print job enters a print queue. If no other jobs are in the queue, your document's spool file is sent to the printer. Otherwise, it waits its turn.

You can check the status of a printer's queue by launching the printer's icon in your Printers folder. Windows displays the print queue in a window similar to that shown in Figure 12-5.

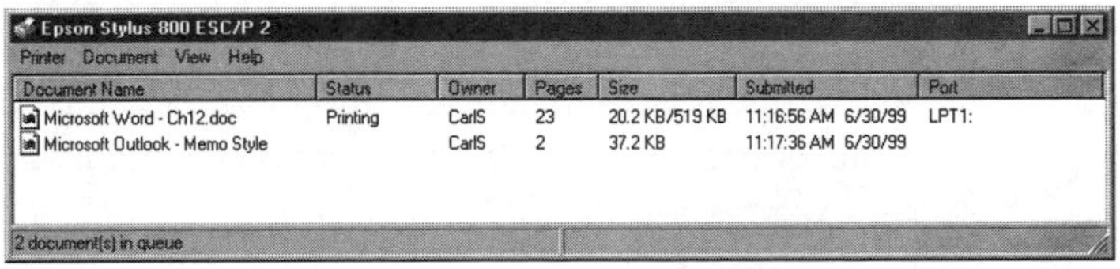

**FIGURE 12-5.**
Launching a printer icon displays the printer's queue, allowing you to manipulate the flow of jobs to the printer.

| Document Name | Status | Owner | Pages | Size | Submitted | Port |
|---|---|---|---|---|---|---|
| Microsoft Word - Ch12.doc | Printing | CarlS | 23 | 20.2 KB/519 KB | 11:16:56 AM 6/30/99 | LPT1: |
| Microsoft Outlook - Memo Style | | CarlS | 2 | 37.2 KB | 11:17:36 AM 6/30/99 | |

2 document(s) in queue

III

Managing Documents

Using commands on this window's Printer and Document menus, you can do the following:

- To pause or resume printing of a document that you own (one that you sent to be printed), select it and use the relevant commands on the Document menu. Lower-priority jobs will be printed ahead of your document as long as the document remains paused.

- To cancel printing of a document that you own, select it and press the Delete key. (Careful! There's no undo, so if you delete the wrong document, you'll need to reprint it.)

- To pause or resume the entire queue, choose Pause Printing from the Printer menu. (Your account must have Manage Documents or Full Control permission for the printer.) While the queue is paused, the window's title bar includes the word *Paused*, and a check mark appears beside the Pause Printing command.

- To delete all jobs in the queue, choose Cancel All Documents from the Printer menu. (Your account must have Manage Documents or Full Control permission for the printer.)

 **TIP**

You can pause a local printer or remove all documents from its queue without opening its queue window. Simply right-click the printer's icon in the Printers folder, and then choose Pause Printing or Cancel All Documents.

## Printer Permissions and Print Queues

**SEE ALSO**

For information about printer permissions, see "Installing and Configuring a Printer," page 510.

By default, when a printer is set up (that is, when you install and configure a local printer, or when an administrator sets up a network printer), all users are given Print permission, which allows them to print documents and to manage their own documents in the print queue. Members of the Administrators, Power Users, and Print Operators groups are also given Manage Documents permission, which allows them to manage other users' documents in the queue; and Full Control permission, which allows them to change printer properties and permissions.

## Rearranging the Queue

If you have Manage Documents or Full Control permission, you can change the order of items in a print queue. You can do this in either of two ways: by adjusting the priority assigned to selected documents, or by specifying that selected documents can be printed only during a certain time period. To use either method, right-click the document you want to modify in its queue window. Then choose Properties from the shortcut menu to arrive at the dialog box shown in Figure 12-6.

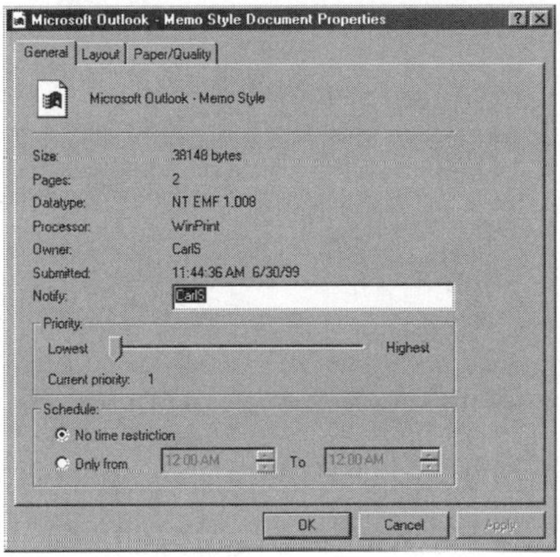

**FIGURE 12-6.**
Move the Priority slider to the right to print this document before documents with a lower priority.

If you want to print a long document while you're at home sleeping instead of tying up the printer for the rest of the day, use settings in the Schedule box to postpone the start of printing until after you leave.

## Working Offline

You can continue to "print" to your local printer, even if it's not currently available. (It's unavailable, for example, when your printer is turned off, out of paper, or when you use your computer away from its docking station.) To tell Windows to print offline, choose Use Printer Offline from the Printer menu. All your print jobs continue to join the queue, but Windows won't bother you with error messages. While the printer is offline, its icon in your Printers folder appears dimmed to provide a visual reminder of its offline status.

When you and your printer are reconnected, choose the same command again, and Windows begins printing all the jobs in the queue.

III

Managing Documents

# Setting Printing Preferences

*Printing preferences* include basic settings that you want to apply, by default, to all documents. You can override these default settings for individual documents in your program or in the Print dialog box before you print. The settings you make through printing preferences can include

- Page orientation—portrait (long edge vertical) or landscape (long edge horizontal)

- Paper size

- Paper source or tray

- Number of copies

- Page printing order—first to last or last to first

- Duplex (two-sided) printing

- Pages per sheet—some printers can print multiple reduced-size pages on each sheet of paper

- Print quality—a balance of print speed, output quality, and ink consumption

- Watermark—an image that prints on every page

Not every printer has all these options—and some printers have many, many more. To view and set the printing preferences for one of your printers, right-click its icon in the Printers folder and choose Printing Preferences from the shortcut menu. A dialog box similar to the one shown in Figure 12-7 appears. With some printers, you reach other settings by clicking Advanced; Printing Preferences dialog boxes for other printers include additional tabs with more settings.

> **NOTE**
>
> To change printing preferences for a network printer, you must have Full Control permission for the printer. *For information about permissions, see "Installing and Configuring a Printer," page 510.*

**FIGURE 12-7.**
The Printing Preferences dialog box for your printer might have different options from the ones shown here.

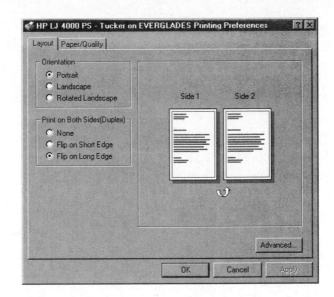

# CHAPTER 13

# Installing and Using Fonts

One of the great advantages of creating text documents in a graphical operating environment such as Windows is that you can employ a variety of fonts and typographical styles and judge their impact before committing your work to paper. Within limits and with some exceptions, what you see on the screen is what you'll get from any output device, whether it's a dot-matrix printer, a laser printer, a plotter, or a fax machine.

In this chapter, we'll look at the fonts supplied with Microsoft Windows 2000, we'll check out the procedures for adding and deleting fonts, and we'll use Character Map and Private Character Editor. Character Map is a handy utility that makes it easy to insert special characters—accented letters, commercial symbols, and so on—into your documents. Private Character Editor lets you extend the character sets of your fonts with user-defined symbols.

# Using Fonts Supplied with Windows 2000

Incorporated into Windows 2000 is a scalable font technology called OpenType. OpenType is a superset of TrueType, a technology that was introduced with Microsoft Windows 95 and included with Microsoft Windows NT 4, the immediate predecessor of Windows 2000. You can think of OpenType as a merger of TrueType technology with Adobe Systems' Type 1 technology. OpenType handles both TrueType and Type 1 fonts (fonts designed for use with PostScript output devices) from a unified registry. Among other things, this means that you can install a set of Type 1 fonts in Windows 2000 and then manage and use your Type 1 fonts the same way you manage and use the rest of your font library.

OpenType fonts, like TrueType fonts, are scalable, which means they can be used effectively in all point sizes and on all output devices. Windows 2000 comes preinstalled with several OpenType font families, including Arial, Comic Sans MS, Courier New, Georgia, Impact, Lucida Console, Lucida Sans Unicode, Microsoft Sans Serif, Palatino Linotype, Symbol, Tahoma, Times New Roman, Trebuchet MS, Verdana, Webdings, and Wingdings.

In addition to these, the operating system also provides certain vector and raster fonts for the sake of compatibility with older applications that require them. *Vector* fonts, also known as stroke fonts, are low-quality characters, like those you would draw with a pen, and are used primarily with *plotters* (special-purpose printers used for drawing charts or line graphs with pens, for example, weather maps). *Raster* fonts, also known as bitmap fonts, are stored as images in specific point sizes (as opposed to scalable outlines) and hence offer good quality, but only at the particular point sizes at which they were created.

Along with the fonts supplied by Windows 2000, you'll probably find additional fonts on your system, courtesy of particular programs or printers that you have installed. All of the major office suites, for example, provide sizeable font libraries for your use. Any font installed by a program is, of course, available not only in that program but also in any other Windows-based program you run.

## Using Your Printer's Own Font Resources

In addition to the fonts that Windows supplies and any additional fonts that you install in Windows, you can use your printer's internal fonts. Your printer driver tells Windows which fonts the printer provides, and those fonts appear in the Font dialog boxes that your programs use.

**? SEE ALSO**

For information about printer drivers, see "Specifying a Driver," page 514.

When you use your printer's internal fonts, Windows doesn't have to download font information or send each page of your document as a *bitmapped graphic* (an image represented as a series of dots). Therefore, printing is likely to be quicker. In exchange for this speed increase, however, you might have to sacrifice some degree of correspondence between the appearance of your document on the screen and its appearance on paper.

When you format a document with an internal printer font, Windows displays the same font on the screen if it can. If Windows doesn't have a screen font to match the printer font you select, it gives you the closest match that it can. For example, if you choose the Courier font that's built into your printer, Windows formats your text on the screen using its own OpenType Courier font (Courier New).

Even when the screen font used by Windows doesn't exactly match the printer font you select, Windows-based programs attempt to show you where your lines will break on the printed page. The correspondence of line endings on the screen to line endings on paper might not always be perfect, however, and some programs do a better job of this than others. If precise text positioning is critical, it's always best to avoid printer fonts that don't have equivalent screen fonts.

# Viewing and Printing Font Samples

To see samples of the fonts installed on your system, open the Start menu and choose Settings, Control Panel, Fonts. (If you've set up your Start menu to include an expandable Control Panel, right-click Fonts. From the shortcut menu, choose either Open or Explore.)

Figure 13-1, on the next page, shows an example of a Fonts folder.

The icons with an *O* represent OpenType fonts, those with two *T*s represent TrueType fonts, those with a lowercase *a* represent Type 1 fonts, and those with a capital *A* denote raster and vector fonts. The point sizes for which the nonscalable fonts were designed are usually included with the font name.

To see a sample of any font, simply launch its icon—or right-click the icon and choose Open from the shortcut menu. As Figure 13-2 on the next page shows, the ensuing window displays the font at sample point sizes.

To print the font sample, click the Print button.

III

Managing Documents

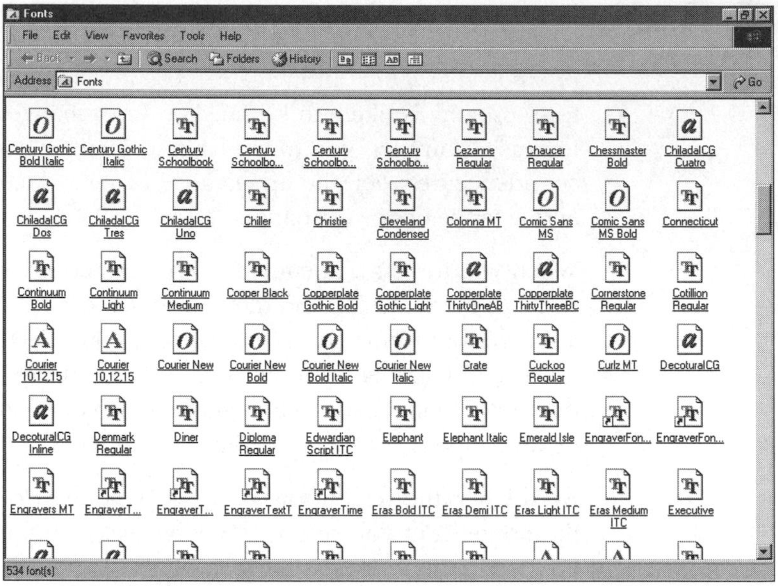

**FIGURE 13-1.**

To see samples of your fonts, install new fonts, or delete fonts, open your Fonts folder.

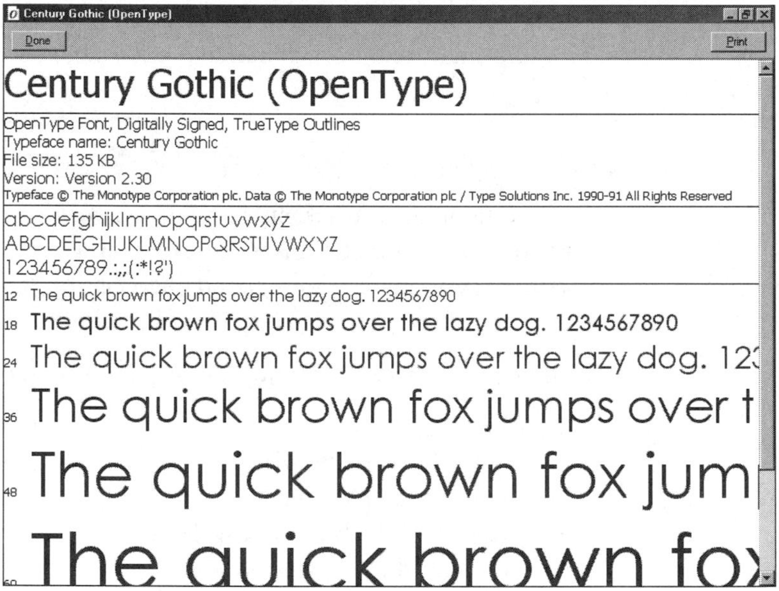

**FIGURE 13-2.**

Opening a font produces a printable sample of the font at various point sizes.

## Viewing Options in the Fonts Folder

Like any other Windows Explorer window, the Fonts folder offers a Large Icons view, a List view, and a Details view of your font library. You can choose these options from the Standard Buttons toolbar or the

View menu. In addition, the View menu of the Fonts folder offers these additional viewing options:

- **List Fonts By Similarity.** Lets you find all the fonts in your library that are similar to some other font. As Figure 13-3 shows, when you choose this option, a box containing a list of your fonts appears below the toolbar. Your font library appears in the window below the box in order of decreasing similarity to the font you select in the list, although you can click a column head to change the sort order if you want.

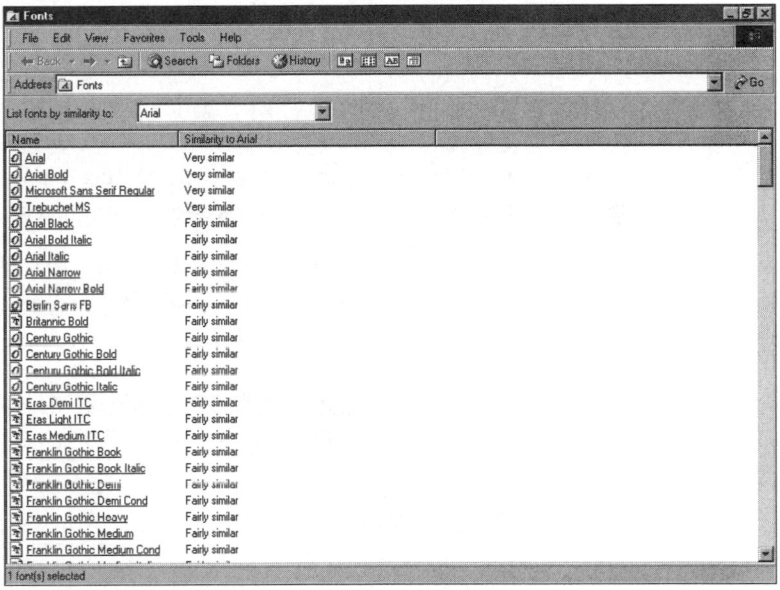

**FIGURE 13-3.**

In this "similarity" view, fonts are listed in order of decreasing similarity to Arial.

- **Hide Variations.** Displays only one font from each font family. For example, suppose your Fonts folder includes Arial, Arial Bold, Arial Italic, and Arial Bold Italic. If you choose Hide Variations, the list shows only Arial. This option, which you can use in any viewing mode, is particularly handy when you have a large font library.

- **Preview.** Sets the ScreenTip that appears when you hover over each font name or icon to display a brief phrase *in* the font itself. This gives you a quick way to see the style of the typeface without opening the sample window. (Preview is available only if you have set up Windows Explorer so that you open items with a single click.)

# Adding and Deleting Fonts

You can add and delete fonts quite easily in Windows 2000. Sometimes you don't need to do anything to make new fonts available for use other than install an application that supplies them. But sometimes you do need to install them, as described next.

## Adding Fonts

OpenType and TrueType fonts are available from other sources, including Microsoft, numerous other vendors, and Web sites. When you acquire an additional font from one of these sources, you need to install it so that Windows knows it's available.

The easiest way to install a new font is to drag it from a Windows Explorer window (a floppy disk folder, for example) and drop it into your Fonts folder. When you do this, Windows automatically updates the registry so that your system recognizes the new font.

Alternatively, you can open the Fonts folder and choose Install New Font from the File menu. You'll be greeted by the Add Fonts dialog box, as shown in Figure 13-4.

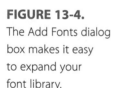

**FIGURE 13-4.**
The Add Fonts dialog box makes it easy to expand your font library.

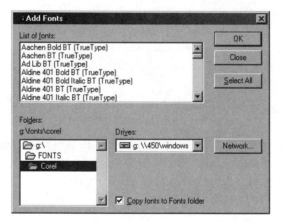

Use the Drives section and the Folders section of this dialog box to indicate where the fonts you want to install are currently stored. For example, if your new fonts are on a floppy disk in drive A, select drive A in the Drives list. The names of all fonts available for installation will then appear in the top section of the dialog box. Choose Select All if you want to install the whole lot. To install particular fonts, hold down the Ctrl key while you select the fonts you want.

When you're finished selecting fonts, click OK. In a moment your new fonts will appear in your Fonts folder and will be available for use in your programs.

---

### To Copy or Not to Copy?

If you're installing fonts from an offline medium, such as a floppy disk or a Zip disk, be sure to select the Copy Fonts To Fonts Folder check box in the Add Fonts dialog box. Windows then copies your font files into the Fonts folder. If the fonts you're installing are already stored in another folder on your hard disk, Windows duplicates the font files in the Fonts folder.

If you prefer to keep your fonts in other folders, you can do so. Simply clear the Copy Fonts To Fonts Folder check box. In the Fonts folder, Windows will create shortcuts to your font files, and, provided you don't rename or move the files, your fonts will still be available to your programs. You might want to clear the Copy Fonts To Fonts Folder check box if want to keep your PostScript (Type 1) fonts segregated from the rest of your font library (some programs expect to find PostScript fonts in a particular folder).

---

## Deleting Fonts

"Deinstalling" a font is easy: simply remove it from your Fonts folder. You can do that by deleting the font icon or by moving the icon to another folder. If you delete a font icon, Windows stores the font in your Recycle Bin, so you can restore it if you change your mind but only until your Recycle Bin deletes the font permanently.

# Embedding Fonts in Documents

If you create documents that will be read on other computers, you'd be wise to stick with fonts that all your readers are likely to have. The safest ones to use are Arial, Courier New, and Times New Roman—respectively, the sans serif, monospace, and serif faces shipped with all versions of Windows since 1992.

What happens if a reader's system doesn't have one of the fonts used by your document? For example, suppose you've formatted your entire report in Bozo Bold, but you're the only one in your company who's installed the Bozo family. In that case, Windows substitutes a closely related font on your reader's system. For example, assuming Bozo is a serif face, your reader will probably see Times New Roman on his or her computer. (You can get an idea of what fonts Windows considers "similar" by opening your Fonts folder and using the View menu's List Fonts By Similarity command.)

If it's crucial that all readers see your document in the exact fonts you've used, check to see whether the program you used to create the document supports font embedding. If the program can embed the OpenType fonts and TrueType fonts that your document uses, your document will include a copy of the font file for each font you use. Your readers will then see your document with its original fonts. And, unless the document has read-only status, they'll be able to edit with those fonts as well.

Note that embedding fonts adds greatly to the size of your document. A 5-KB report, for example, might easily grow to 50 KB with only one font embedded. If you use italic and bold, along with regular roman, your document could swell another 100 KB or so. Although most fonts can be embedded, font manufacturers can disable that capability. Therefore, even if your program can embed fonts, always check to make sure the fonts you want to use are also embeddable before you do any work that depends on this capability. (You can tell if your font is being embedded by comparing the size of the same document saved with and without embedding.)

> **Embedding Fonts in Microsoft Word Documents**
> If you're using Microsoft Word 6 or later, you can turn on embedding by choosing Options from the Tools menu, clicking the Save tab, and selecting the Embed TrueType Fonts check box. Note that this setting is file-specific—that is, changing it for one document doesn't affect other documents.

# Using Character Map

Windows 2000 uses version 2 of the Unicode character-encoding standard. *Unicode* is a 16-bit character-encoding system in which each character is stored as 16 bits, or 2 bytes, of computer data. This permits tracking 65,536 different characters. (Traditional character sets are *single-byte* and can define only 256 characters per set.) To date, about 39,000 of the Unicode character slots have been defined by the Unicode Consortium. These include all the standard Latin alphabetic characters, punctuation marks, diacritics, mathematical and technical symbols, commercial symbols, arrows, dingbats, line-drawing characters, box-drawing characters, characters from 24 non-Latin alphabets, and more.

While Unicode provides for this huge array of characters, the individual fonts on your system probably support only a subset. With the Character Map utility, you can see what's available in each font. Character Map also makes it easy to use the full range of your fonts' character support in your documents. You'll find Character Map invaluable when you need to work with a special-character font (such as Symbol or Wingdings), and when you need accented letters, commercial symbols, and other characters that aren't available on the standard typewriter keys of your keyboard. Character Map's initial display is shown in Figure 13-5.

**FIGURE 13-5.**
Character Map helps you find and use special characters in any font.

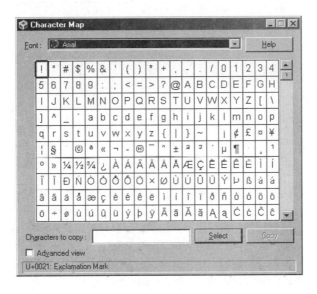

To run Character Map, open the Start menu, point to Programs, Accessories, System Tools, and choose Character Map. (You can also open the Start menu, choose Run, and then type *charmap.exe*.)

At the top of the window is a box in which you can select any font available on your system. Below the list is a table displaying all the characters available in the selected font. You can't change the size of the Character Map window (other than to minimize it), but you can get an enlarged view of any character by selecting it with the mouse or the keyboard.

To select a character with the mouse, simply click the character. To select a character with the keyboard, press Tab until the highlight is in the character grid. Then use the arrow keys to move the highlight. (Press the Spacebar to see an enlarged version of each character.) Figure 13-6, on the following page, shows how Character Map looks when the copyright symbol in Times New Roman is selected.

III

Managing Documents

**FIGURE 13-6.**

To get an enlarged view of any character, simply select it.

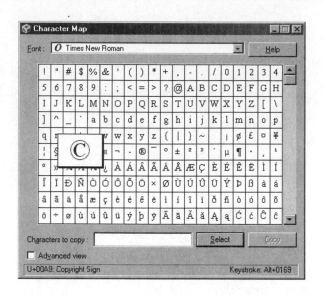

In the lower left corner of the Character Map window, you'll find the Unicode code for the selected character (00A9 in the case of the copyright symbol). In the lower right corner, you might find a keystroke combination for the selected character. If so, you can enter that character into most applications by holding down the Alt key, typing the four numbers of the keystroke combination on the numeric keypad, and then releasing the Alt key. Note that you must use the numeric keypad, and that some applications don't accept characters entered in this manner. (In Word you must turn on Num Lock before using the numeric keypad for this purpose.)

## Inserting Special Characters into Your Documents

The Alt+key method of entering characters is supported for the sake of compatibility with earlier versions of the operating system. Fortunately, you can insert special characters into your documents in much easier ways. In many applications, you can copy a character from Character Map by using drag and drop. Simply click the character once in Character Map to select it, then drag it to your document, dropping it where you want to insert it.

If your application doesn't support this drag-and-drop maneuver, you can do the following:

**1**  Select the character you want in Character Map.

**2**  Click the Select button.

**3** Click the Copy button.

**4** In your application, choose Paste or press Ctrl+V.

You can copy a whole string of characters at once using this method. Select the first character, click Select, select the next, click Select, and so on, until the entire string appears on the Characters To Copy line. Then click the Copy button.

# Searching for Characters in Character Map

Characters in Character Map are listed in order of their Unicode values. If the character you need has a relatively low Unicode value, you might be able to scroll right to it. In many cases, though, you'll need to search for it. Character Map provides a variety of ways to locate characters.

## Searching by Name

Every Unicode character has a name. For example, a lowercase *œ* ligature is called *Latin Small Ligature oe*. A capital *Œ* ligature is called *Latin Capital Ligature Oe*. (A *ligature* combines a frequently used sequence of characters into a single form.) If you know the name of the character you want, you can find it as follows:

**1** Select the Advanced View check box.

**2** Type the name of the character on the Search For line.

**3** Click the Search button.

If you don't know the entire name of the character, type some of it. For example, if you type *oe*, you'll get both the capital and lowercase œ ligatures. If you type *ligature*, you'll get all the ligatures available in the current font, and you can select the one you need.

## Searching by Unicode Value

**SEE ALSO**
To install support for multiple languages, see "Installing Language Support and Using Keyboard Layouts," page 109.

To find a character by its Unicode value:

**1** Select the Advanced View check box.

**2** Type the four-digit hexadecimal Unicode value into the Go To Unicode box.

For example, to find the Hebrew letter *Kaf* with *Dagesh*, you would type *FB3B* into the Go To Unicode box with a Hebrew font selected, such as Miriam.

### Searching by Subset

To find MS-DOS characters (characters included in the extended ASCII or OEM character set) or characters from another Unicode subset, follow these steps:

**1** Select the Advanced View check box.

**2** Select a subset from the Character Set box.

### Searching by Category

Unicode characters are grouped in categories within each font. To search for a character by its category:

**1** Select the Advanced View check box.

**2** In the Group By box, choose Unicode Subrange.

**3** In the Group By window that appears, select the category you're interested in (see Figure 13-7).

**FIGURE 13-7.**
To display a list of Unicode categories, choose Unicode Subrange in the Group By box.

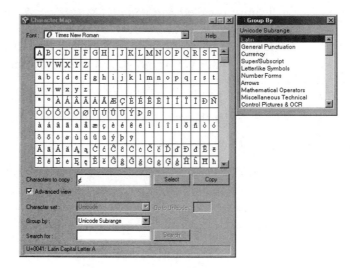

# Using Private Character Editor

Private Character Editor lets you add as many as 6,400 new characters to your fonts. You can use it to extend your fonts' character sets with new typographical designs, symbols, logos, or anything else that you're able to create with a simple black-and-white drawing program. You can add new characters to particular fonts or all fonts, and then access those characters with Character Map.

Windows 2000 doesn't automatically create a menu entry for Private Character Editor. To run the utility, choose Run from the Start menu and specify *eudcedit*.

## Selecting a Code for a New Character

Private Character Editor opens with the Select Code dialog box, as shown in Figure 13-8. The range of codes available for your characters extends from hexadecimal E000 to F8FF. Choose the code you want to use, and then click OK. To return to the Select Code dialog box later (for example, to create a new character with a different code), choose Select Code from the Edit menu (or press Ctrl+O).

**FIGURE 13-8.**
Private Character Editor uses the code range E000 to F8FF. Use this dialog box to select a code for your new character.

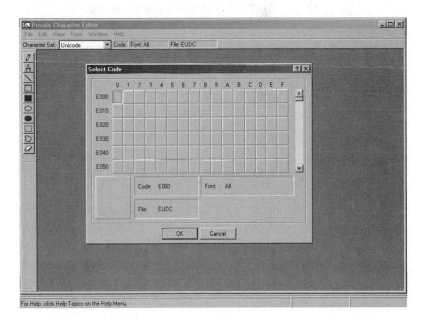

III

Managing Documents

⭐ TIP

If you change your mind about a character's code assignment after you've drawn the character, choose Save As, not Save, from the Edit menu. Save As lets you assign the character to a different code.

# Drawing Characters

Once you've selected a code for your new character, you'll find your-self in the Edit window, shown in Figure 13-9. In the grid, each square represents one pixel. Along the left side of the grid is an array of drawing tools:

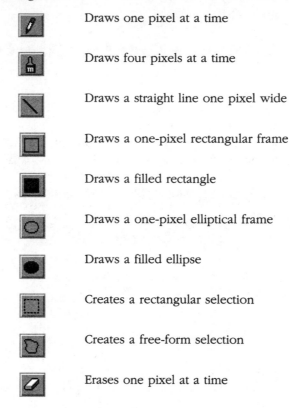

Draws one pixel at a time

Draws four pixels at a time

Draws a straight line one pixel wide

Draws a one-pixel rectangular frame

Draws a filled rectangle

Draws a one-pixel elliptical frame

Draws a filled ellipse

Creates a rectangular selection

Creates a free-form selection

Erases one pixel at a time

The tools work much like their counterparts in Paint, except that they're less powerful. You can't constrain a rectangle to square dimensions by holding down the Shift key, for example, as you can in Paint. Draw carefully, avail yourself of the eraser tool, and if you need to start over, choose Select Code from the Edit menu and answer No to the save prompt.

**FIGURE 13-9.**

Private Character Editor's drawing tools work much like those in Microsoft Paint.

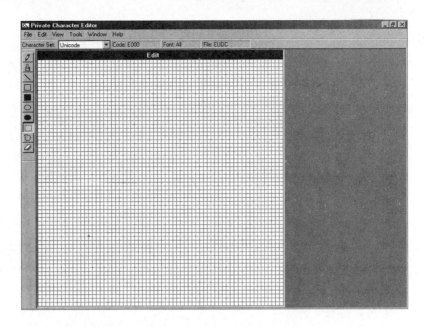

## Working from an Existing Character

You can use an existing character and modify it or use it as a reference point.

To copy an existing character into the Edit window and modify it:

**1** Choose Copy Character from the Edit menu.

**2** Select the character you want from the grid that appears, and then click OK.

> To choose a character from a specific font, click the Font button.

**3** When the character appears in the Edit window, modify it to suit your needs.

To use an existing character as a model:

**1** Choose Reference from the Window menu.

**2** Select the character you want from the grid that appears or select another font using the Font button.

**3** Click OK and the character will appear in the Reference window.

Figure 13-10 shows the Reference window with a character taken from Wingdings. You can copy parts of the character from the Reference window to your Edit window or you can use it as a visual reference while you work in the Edit window.

**FIGURE 13-10.**

The Reference window lets you use one character as a model for another.

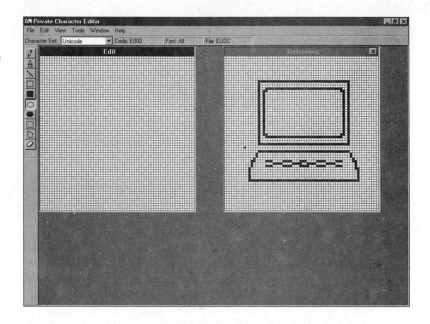

## Copying from the Reference Window

You can use the rectangular selection tool and freeform selection tool to copy portions (or all) of a character from the Reference window to the Edit window. Make your selection, choose Copy from the Edit menu, and then choose Paste from the Edit menu. The copied character appears initially in the upper left corner of the Edit window. Use your mouse to drag it into position. When it's in position, click outside the selection box to place it in your drawing.

## Reviewing a Finished Character

Eliminating the gridlines from the Edit window can facilitate a final inspection of your character. So too can drawing an outline around the character. The outline lets you see the character as it will appear in use, without the jagged edges that are inevitable in a pixel editor. You'll find the Grid command and the Show Outline command on the View menu.

## Saving a Character

To save your custom character, choose Save Character from the Edit menu. The character will be saved to the code shown on Private Character Editor's guide bar, directly below the menu bar. If that's not the code you want to use, choose Save Character As, instead of Save Character, from the Edit menu and select another available code number.

## Linking a Custom Character to a Specific Font

By default, your character becomes available in all fonts. To link the character to a specific font only:

1 Choose Font Links from the File menu.

2 In the Font Links dialog box, select Link With Selected Fonts.

3 Click Save As and specify a filename.

4 Click Save.

## Using a Custom Character

To use a custom character in a document:

1 Start Character Map.

2 If your character is linked to all fonts, choose All Fonts (Private Characters) from Character Map's Font list. If your character is linked to a specific font, choose *Fontname* (Private Characters). For example, if it's linked to Arial, look for the entry Arial (Private Characters) in the Font list.

3 Select your character and either drag it to your document or copy it to the Clipboard and paste it into your document.

## Deleting a Custom Character

Private Character Editor doesn't provide a straightforward way to remove custom characters. You can get rid of a character you no longer want, however, by creating a blank character in the unwanted character's code slot.

III

Managing Documents

# PART IV

# Managing Programs

**CHAPTER 14**

# Running Programs

Running programs from the Start menu is a process so transparent that it requires no elaboration. You can, however, get applications running in other ways, and we'll survey them briefly in this chapter.

It's useful to remember that the Programs section of the Start menu is just a collection of shortcuts—pointers to executable files located in many different parts of your local and networked storage system. Because the Programs shortcuts are all stored in a folder that the operating system recognizes as pertaining to the Start menu, those shortcuts all show up as menu items. But you can run programs from shortcuts stored anywhere—on the desktop, on a toolbar, or in any folder.

You can also run programs by launching the executables directly, wherever they might be. Most users don't populate their desktops with executable files, but you might occasionally find an executable there as the result of a download operation. (An executable on the desktop looks just like a desktop shortcut, except that it lacks the arrow in the lower left corner of the icon. If you find an executable on your desktop, it's probably a good idea to move it into an ordinary folder so that you won't inadvertently delete it.)

# Running with the Run Command

**?** **SEE ALSO**

For information about creating and using shortcuts, see "Creating a Shortcut," page 55.

The Start menu's Run command provides a way to start programs (or open documents or folders, or navigate to Web sites) by entering a command string. Apart from its accommodation of users who actually prefer typing command strings to selecting from menus, the Run command has two virtues: it allows you to specify command-line parameters along with the name of a program, and it maintains a most-recently-used (MRU) list so that you can easily reuse command strings.

Windows-based programs seldom require command-line parameters, but many accept them. For example, to run Notepad and open the file c:\autoexec.bat at the same time, you could click the Start button, choose Run, and type

> *notepad c:\autoexec.bat*

(Note that if you just typed *c:\autoexec.bat*, the program Cmd.exe, which provides MS-DOS functionality in the Microsoft Windows 2000 environment, would run the batch file instead of opening it for edit.)

If you're not sure what to put on the Run command's command line, the Browse button can help. For example, if you want to run a particular program that's not on your Start menu, but you're not sure how to enter the path to the folder where that program lives, you can choose Run, click Browse, and then use the Browse dialog box to navigate to the appropriate folder. (Alternatively, you can use the Search Assistant. *For more details, see Chapter 11, "Searching for Files and Folders."*)

# Running a Program Under a Different User Account

Sometimes a program you want to run might not be accessible to the account under which you're currently logged on. If your item is accessible to another account and you're able to log on to that account, you could log off the current account, log back on to the other account, and then run the program you want to run. But Windows 2000 offers a simpler solution. To set up a program so that you can run it under a different user account:

1 Right-click the shortcut you use to run the program. (Typically, this is a shortcut somewhere on your Start menu.)

IV

Managing Programs

2   Choose Properties from the shortcut menu, and click the Shortcut tab.

3   Select the Run As Different User check box and click OK.

When you run the program, you'll see a dialog box similar to the one shown in Figure 14-1. Enter the user name, password, and domain name for the account you want to use—just as you would if you were logging on to the operating system using that account.

The ability to run a program as a different user is of particular value to system administrators who don't want to do their nonadministrative work under an administrative account. Running a system as an administrator makes that system vulnerable to accidents and mischief. The "run as" feature makes it possible for administrators to log on with a lower level of privileges and then use their administrator privileges only when performing those tasks that require them.

**FIGURE 14-1.**

If you select the Run As Different User check box in the properties dialog box of a program's shortcut, Windows prompts you for this logon information when you run that program.

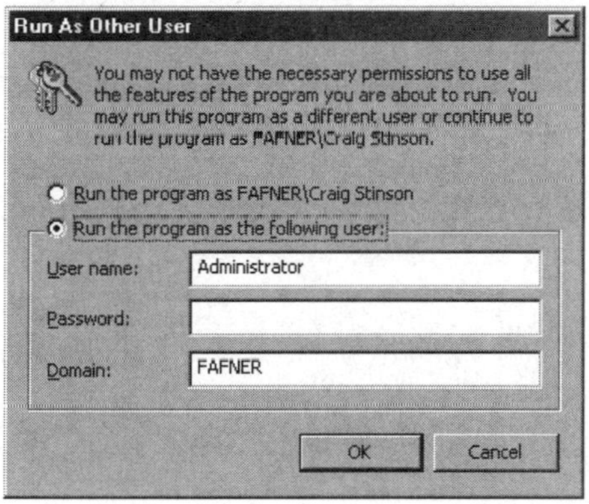

**Run As Other User**

You may not have the necessary permissions to use all the features of the program you are about to run. You may run this program as a different user or continue to run the program as FAFNER\Craig Stinson.

○ Run the program as FAFNER\Craig Stinson
● Run the program as the following user:

User name:   Administrator

Password:

Domain:   FAFNER

[ OK ]   [ Cancel ]

**Occasional or One-Time-Only Use of Run As**

You can run programs under a different account on an ad hoc basis, without modifying the programs' shortcuts. Hold down the Shift key while you right-click a program's icon (on the Start menu, a toolbar, the desktop, or in Windows Explorer) and the shortcut menu includes a Run As command. Choose that command and you'll see the Run As Other User dialog box shown in Figure 14-1.

# Running Programs at Startup

Program and document shortcuts stored in the Startup section of your Start menu are executed automatically every time you log on to Windows 2000. You can use drag-and-drop techniques to move items into or out of the Startup folder. For example, if a program is currently on your Accessories menu and you want it to run every time you log on, you can open Accessories, find the item, and then drag it over to Startup. If you want the item in both places, Accessories and Startup, copy it by holding down the Ctrl key while you drag. To delete a Startup item, right-click it and choose Delete. To move an item from Startup to some other branch of the Start menu, simply drag it where it needs to go.

If you accidentally drop an item in the wrong place, close the Start menu, right-click the desktop, and choose Undo from the shortcut menu.

> If you work with the same document every day, create a Startup shortcut to the document. Find the document in Windows Explorer (the Search Assistant can help), and then right-drag it to the Startup folder. From the menu that appears when you release the right mouse button, choose Create Shortcut(s) Here.

Using the Startup section of the Start menu is one way to get a task running automatically at logon. The Scheduled Tasks feature, which we'll look at next, is another. There are additional ways that programs can become logon tasks. For example, if you've set up your system to use offline files and have files synchronized automatically at logon, then Synchronization Manager becomes a logon task. You can see a list of your account's logon tasks as follows:

1  Right-click My Computer and choose Manage from the shortcut menu.

2  Expand System Tools, then System Information, and then Software Environment.

3  Select Startup Programs.

Choosing Manage from My Computer's shortcut menu opens Computer Management. Figure 14-2 shows an example of what you might see when you navigate to Startup Programs.

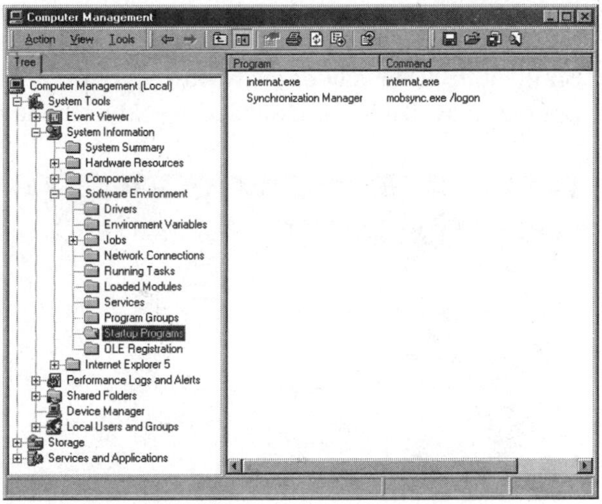

**FIGURE 14-2.**
You can find out
what's running at
startup by right-
clicking My Computer,
choosing Manage,
and navigating to
Startup Programs.

# Running Programs on Schedule

Windows 2000's Scheduled Tasks is an ideal way to set up routine
maintenance and other chores that need to be handled at scheduled
intervals. You can set up any number of programs or scripts to run at
scheduled times, and your scheduling options are extremely flexible.

Scheduled Tasks provides a user-friendly alternative to the At command, which must be run in a Command Prompt window. If you're
accustomed to using At, you can continue to do so, and tasks scheduled via At will appear in the Scheduled Tasks folder. Unlike At,
however, Scheduled Tasks lets you assign multiple schedules to
single tasks.

To set up a scheduled task:

**1** From the Start menu, choose Programs, Accessories, System
Tools, Scheduled Tasks.

**TIP**

Alternatively, you can open the Scheduled Tasks folder from Control Panel.

**2** In the Scheduled Tasks folder, click Add Scheduled Task.

**3** Complete the dialog boxes presented by the Scheduled Task
Wizard.

Figure 14-3 shows the dialog box you'll see if you choose to schedule your task monthly. Here the task has been set up to run at 5:40 P.M. on the third Thursday of every other month. A comparable range of options is available for daily and weekly schedules.

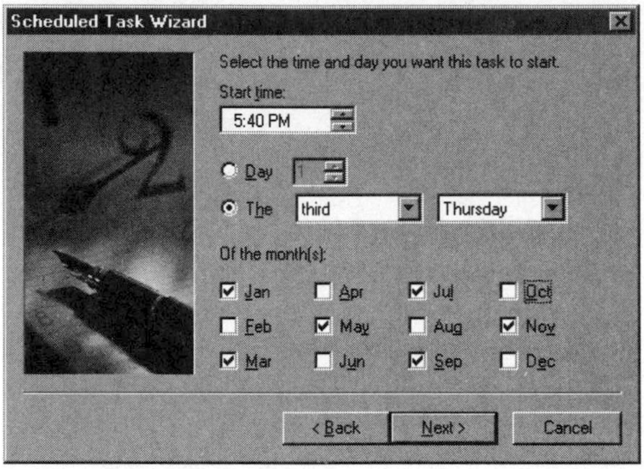

**FIGURE 14-3.**
Scheduled Tasks can
accommodate most
scheduling needs.
Here a task is being
set up to run on the
third Thursday of
alternate months.

In addition to calendar-based scheduling, you can set up tasks to run only when your computer is turned on (regardless of who logs on) and only when you log on under the current account. Scheduling a task using the latter option is equivalent to putting a shortcut for the task on your Startup menu.

## Setting Up Advanced Scheduling Options

Near the end of the sequence of pages presented by the Scheduled Task Wizard, a check box appears asking whether you want to open advanced properties for the task you're setting up. If you don't choose this option when you create the task schedule, you can go to it at any time by opening the Scheduled Tasks folder, right-clicking the task name in the list, and then choosing Properties from the shortcut menu. However you get there, the properties dialog box presents scheduling options that don't appear in the wizard. Figure 14-4 shows some of those options.

On the Schedule tab shown in the figure, you can modify the current schedule. You can also set up a multiple schedule. If you select the Show Multiple Schedules check box, the dialog box expands to accept additional scheduling parameters. You could, for example, arrange to have your task run every Friday at 5 P.M. and also at 5 P.M. on the thirtieth day of every month.

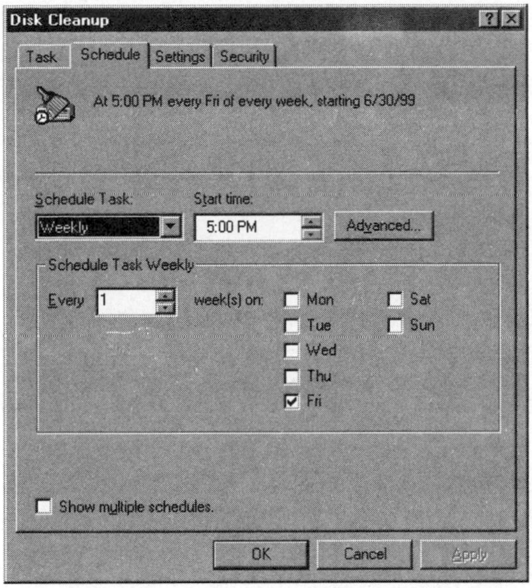

**FIGURE 14-4.**

In the task's properties dialog box, which you can access by right-clicking the task in the Scheduled Tasks folder, you can modify the current schedule or set up multiple schedules.

Clicking the Advanced button in the dialog box shown in Figure 14-4 takes you to the Advanced Schedule Options dialog box shown in Figure 14-5. Here you can set up an end date for your task as well as specify repeat parameters. You could, for example, stipulate that your task repeat every thirty minutes between the hours of 5 P.M. and 10 P.M., or run continuously for three-and-a-half hours.

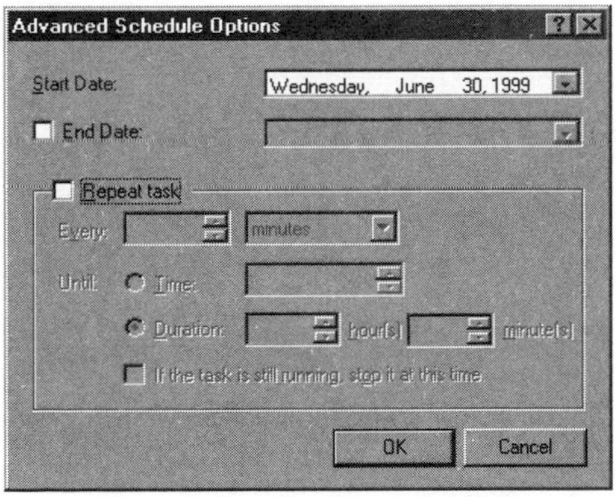

**FIGURE 14-5.**

Clicking the Advanced button in Figure 14-4 takes you to this dialog box, in which you can set up repeat parameters and an end date.

The Settings tab of the scheduled task's properties dialog box, shown in Figure 14-6 on the next page, provides additional control. Here you can provide a termination order for a task that has run too long, stipulate that a task not run if the computer is in use at the appointed hour (or stop running if someone begins using the computer), and tell the system not to run a task if the computer is running on battery power.

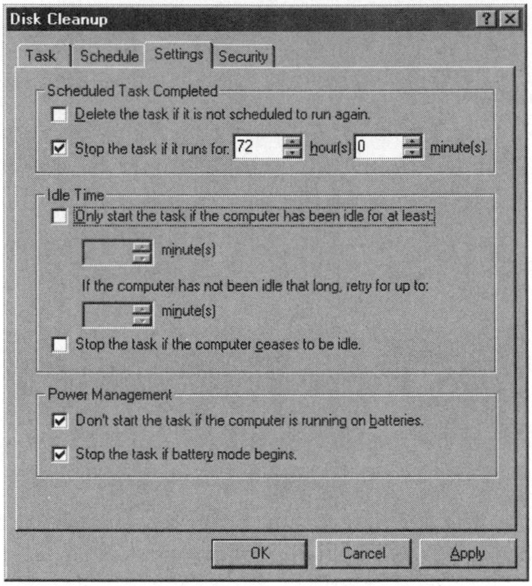

**FIGURE 14-6.**

On the Settings tab, you can control what happens if the computer is in use or running on batteries when a task is scheduled to run.

## Monitoring Scheduled Tasks

The Scheduled Tasks folder provides a way to keep track of your scheduled tasks. If you display the folder in Details view, you can see when each task is next scheduled to run, when it last ran, what the task's current status is, whether its last run was successful, and who created the scheduled task.

# Installing and Removing Programs and System Components

W indows 2000 includes a sophisticated application installation and maintenance tool called Windows Installer. This is part of Microsoft's *Zero Administration Initiative*, an attempt to reduce the amount of time spent administering computers running Microsoft Windows operating systems. Windows Installer makes it easy for administrators and end users to keep their applications running correctly, to upgrade installations and system components as newer versions become available, and to remove applications and components when they're no longer needed.

Windows Installer maintains a database of information about your applications' critical files. If a critical component of a program becomes damaged or is missing, Windows Installer automatically repairs that component when you try to run the program. (It might prompt you for a disk if the application was installed from a CD-ROM.)

Moreover, in an Active Directory environment, system administrators might assign or publish applications to users. If an application has been *assigned* to you, Windows Installer creates an item for that application on your Start menu but doesn't actually install the application on your system until the first time you run it—at which time the installation occurs automatically. If an application has been *published*, the system doesn't create a menu item, but if you try to open a file associated with the published application, Windows Installer offers to install the program on your system.

Not all applications were designed to take advantage of Windows Installer, but over time, more and more popular programs will be. Most applications, however, can be easily installed, removed, or upgraded by other means. To install a program from a CD-ROM, for example, all you typically have to do is insert the disk into your CD-ROM drive, wait a few seconds, and then follow the prompts. If nothing happens after you insert the disk, you can use Add/Remove Programs in Control Panel to install or remove your program.

# Using Add/Remove Programs

Add/Remove Programs in Control Panel makes it easy to install programs from a floppy disk or CD-ROM drive. Figure 15-1 shows the opening screen. As you can see, Add/Remove Programs provides information about the size and usage of each of your installed applications. You might find this information helpful if your disk becomes crowded and you need to remove a program or two. (To see the size and usage information for a particular program, select that program in the list.)

## Installing New Programs

To install a new program from a CD-ROM or floppy drive, click the Add New Programs button. In the new screen that appears, click the button labeled CD Or Floppy. You'll be prompted to insert your program's first installation floppy or CD-ROM. Do so, if you haven't already, and then click Next. This action launches the program's installation routine, which prompts you through the remaining steps.

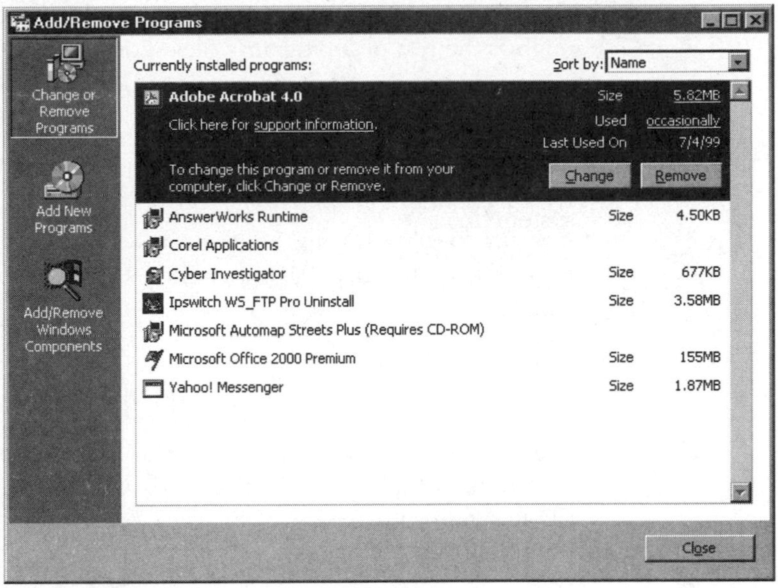

**FIGURE 15-1.**
Add/Remove Programs in Control Panel provides an easy way to install and remove applications.

IV

Managing Programs

# Uninstalling Programs

If you've ever tried to remove a Windows-based program from your system "by hand," you probably know that the task is anything but trivial. Getting rid of an unneeded program by simply deleting files is complex for the following reasons:

- Many Windows-based programs use .dll files in addition to the .exe executable program file. DLLs, *dynamic-link libraries*, are components that can be shared by two or more programs. Such components might or might not be stored in the same folder as the program's .exe files. Even if you know exactly which DLLs a program uses, deleting them all might damage another program that relies on some of the same DLLs.

- Most Windows-based programs create entries in the registry, the database in which Windows records all vital information concerning your hardware and software. Even if you safely delete all executable components of your Windows-based program, if you don't also correctly modify the registry, the registry no longer accurately describes your system.

- Some Windows-based programs (in particular, many older ones) either create their own private configuration (.ini) files or create entries in a shared Windows configuration file called Win.ini.

Private .ini files might or might not be stored in the same folder as the rest of a program's files. Completely eradicating a Windows-based program means getting rid of its .ini files (or its entries in Win.ini) as well as removing all of its other components.

For all of these reasons, but particularly because of the possibility of inadvertently deleting a DLL needed by some other program, it's best not to try removing Windows-based programs by simply going into a folder and deep-sixing its files. Instead, try the following steps (in order):

**1**  If your program is listed in Add/Remove Programs, select it there, click the Remove button, and follow the prompts.

**2**  If Add/Remove Programs doesn't list your program, check to see whether there's an uninstall utility in the folder where your program itself is stored.

It's possible that your program provides an uninstall utility, but Add/Remove Programs doesn't know about it. Look for something labeled Remove or Uninstall. With most Microsoft programs, the Setup program also serves to uninstall the program. If you don't find an obvious uninstall utility, check your program's documentation to see if it provides any useful information.

**3**  If you're still not sure how to remove the program, give the program vendor's tech-support service a call. Ask them exactly which files you should and should not delete.

## Adding or Removing Program Components

Add/Remove Programs in Control Panel includes a Change button and a Remove button (or sometimes a combined Change/Remove button) for every installed program it knows about. To add or remove components of a program, select that program in Add/Remove Programs, click Change, and then follow the prompts.

## Moving Programs

Simply packing up all of an application's files in one folder and shipping them off to some other folder might work for the most rudimentary Windows-based programs, but more often than not it will fail. If you must relocate a program, the safest way to do it is to uninstall the program first, using Add/Remove Programs in Control Panel. After you've uninstalled it, reinstall it in the appropriate folder.

# Adding or Removing Parts of Windows 2000

Windows 2000 includes both essential and optional components. When your system was first set up, chances are the person doing the setup installed many, but not all, of the optional components. As time passes you might find you need certain items that aren't currently installed. And, you might discover that some of the Windows accessories are merely taking up space on your hard disks without serving any useful purpose. In either case, it's easy to make the appropriate adjustments.

To add or remove an optional Windows 2000 component:

**1** Launch Add/Remove Programs from Control Panel.

**2** Click Add/Remove Windows Components.

The Windows Components Wizard opens.

**3** Click Next on the welcoming page to display the wizard page shown in Figure 15-2.

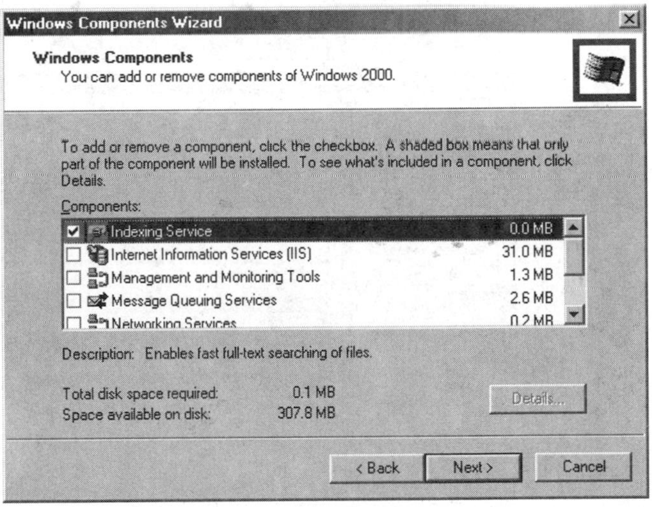

**FIGURE 15-2.**

The Windows Components Wizard lets you add or remove selected Windows 2000 components.

To install a component, select its check box. To remove a component, clear its check box. If an item itself includes subcomponents that can be installed or removed individually, the Details button becomes available when you select that item. Click Details if you want to remove or install only particular subcomponents. When you've finished making your selections, click OK. You might be prompted to insert your Windows 2000 Professional CD-ROM.

# Upgrading Your System with New Drivers and New Releases

Microsoft maintains a Web site, *http://windowsupdate.microsoft.com*, that can provide you with the latest information about new device drivers and other software components that might have become available for your system. It's an excellent idea to visit this site periodically and download from it any new items that the site recommends. To get to the Windows Update site:

1 Choose Add/Remove Programs from Control Panel.

2 Click Add New Programs.

3 Click Windows Update.

Figure 15-3 shows the Windows Update site as it appeared during the winter of 1999.

**FIGURE 15-3.**

Visiting the Windows Update site on the Internet helps ensure that your system always has the latest available drivers and other software components.

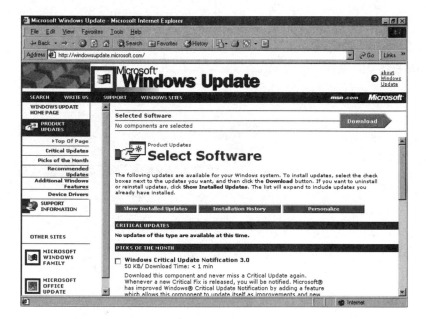

The Windows Update site checks your hardware and software (without Microsoft retaining any information), and then it checks to see if any updates are available. In addition to offering new components via download, the site also provides quick access to online support, where you can get answers to questions you might have about your system.

# PART V

# Sharing Information and Communicating

**CHAPTER 16**

# Making Connections

Microsoft Windows 2000 can help reduce the trials and complexity of making network connections to places near and far. Using networking, you can access files, folders, printers, and other devices that are connected to other computers. And you can let other people access the shared files, folders, printers, and other devices on your computer. With Windows 2000, you can make the following types of network connections:

- Connect to a private network (in most cases, a local area network, or LAN) using a network adapter.

- Connect to a private network with a dial-up connection using a modem or an ISDN adapter. Using a dial-up connection (and a suitably equipped dial-up server at your other location), you can stay current with vital data stored at the office.

- Connect to the Internet with a dial-up connection or through your local area network.

- Use a virtual private network connection to connect to your private network using your Internet connection.

■ Connect two computers via serial or parallel cables or by an infrared link.

■ Allow other users to connect to your computer via dial-up connection, virtual private network connection, or direct connection.

# Working with Network Connections

Information about all your network connections—local area network, dial-up to a private network or virtual private network using a modem or ISDN, and direct cable connection—is available in the Network And Dial-Up Connections folder. To work with your network connections, open the Start menu, point to Settings, and choose Network And Dial-Up Connections. See Figure 16-1.

**FIGURE 16-1.**

The Network And Dial-Up Connections folder contains a Make New Connection icon, an icon for each network adapter installed in your computer, and an icon for each dial-up and direct connection you have created.

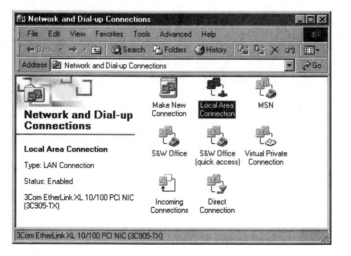

In the Network And Dial-Up Connections folder, you can

■ Create a new connection. Double-click the Make New Connection icon.

■ Open (that is, connect using) a dial-up or direct connection. Double-click its icon.

■ Check an active connection's status. (Active connections are shown in full color; icons for connections that are currently disconnected are dimmed.) Double-click its icon to display a dialog box like the one shown next.

**TIP**

You can also view a connection's status by pointing to its icon in the status area of the taskbar. To display the status-area icon, open the connection's properties dialog box and select Show Icon In Taskbar When Connected.

- Create a desktop shortcut for a connection. Right-click its icon and choose Create Shortcut.

- Copy a connection so you can make changes to the copy. Right-click its icon and choose Create Copy.

**TIP**

Sometimes it's easier to copy and modify an existing connection than to start from scratch with the Make New Connection icon.

- View or modify a connection's properties. Right-click its icon and choose Properties. (You must be logged on as a member of the Administrators group to modify connection properties.)

- Change your computer's name or join a different workgroup or domain. (You must be logged on as a member of the Administrators group to make these changes.) Choose Network Identification from the Advanced menu.

**TIP**

A cascading Network And Dial-Up Connections folder on the Start menu lets you make a connection with a single click. To set up a cascading folder, open the Start menu, point to Settings, and choose Taskbar & Start Menu. Click the Advanced tab, and then select Expand Network And Dial-Up Connections in the Start Menu Settings box.

**V**

**Sharing and Communicating**

In the rest of this chapter, we'll look at these tasks in greater detail as we explore each type of network connection.

# Working on a LAN

Configuring a computer to work on a local area network (LAN) used to be quite an ordeal. With Windows 2000, it's generally a simple matter of installing a network adapter in your computer. Windows 2000 detects your network adapter when you start your computer and then starts the local area connection automatically.

**⭐ TIP**

> If you have more than one network adapter installed, rename each local area connection to clearly identify which network it connects to. Simply right-click the icon and choose Rename.

If you need to connect to a Novell NetWare network, or your network uses a protocol other than TCP/IP (Transmission Control Protocol/ Internet Protocol), you'll need to configure your network connection.

## Configuring a Network Connection

When you install Windows 2000 (or when you install a new network adapter), Windows creates a local connection that includes the following components:

- **Client For Microsoft Networks.** A *network client* provides access to computers and resources on a network; this client works with Windows-based networks.

- **File And Printer Sharing For Microsoft Networks.** This *service* allows other computers on your Windows-based network to access shared resources on your computer.

- **Internet Protocol (TCP/IP).** A *network protocol* is the set of rules that computers on a network use to communicate. TCP/IP is the default protocol in Windows 2000 and provides easy connectivity across a wide variety of networks, including the Internet.

This default collection of clients, services, and protocols is generally all you need for working with a Microsoft network (that is, one where all computers are running Windows 2000, Windows NT, Windows 98, or Windows 95). To see the installed components, right-click the Local Area Connection icon and choose Properties. See Figure 16-2.

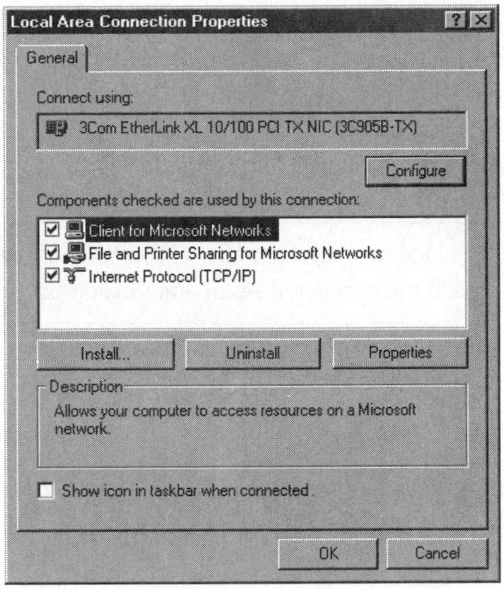

**FIGURE 16-2.**

To enable or disable an installed component, click its check box.

You can install and enable additional clients, services, and protocols, but for best performance, you should install only the ones you need. If you install and enable several protocols, for example, Windows 2000 attempts to connect using each one, which generates extra network traffic—and serves no purpose if other computers on the network don't use the same protocol.

How do you know which ones you need?

- If your computer is part of a large network, ask your system administrator. (Sorry, but too many variations exist to cover here. If you're connecting to a NetWare network, you'll probably need to add the Client Service For NetWare client; when you do that, Windows also installs two protocols: NWLink NetBIOS and NWLink IPX/SPX/NetBIOS Compatible Transport Protocol.)

- If you have a small network (where you *are* the administrator), start with the default configuration. If the other computers on your network are running Windows 2000, you don't need to make any changes. If the other computers use earlier versions of Windows or Windows NT, you'll need to see which protocol is being used on those systems; they might be using only NetBEUI. You can add the NetBEUI protocol to your Windows 2000 system, but you'll need to keep TCP/IP if you plan to connect to the Internet. If your other Windows computers use NetBEUI, a better solution is to change them to use TCP/IP. Unfortunately, TCP/IP isn't as easy to configure in other Windows versions as it is in Windows 2000; if you can't find the information you need to configure TCP/IP on the other systems, stick with NetBEUI, which doesn't require any special settings.

> **NOTE**
>
> You must be logged on as a member of the Administrators group to make any changes in the connection's properties dialog box.

To install a new component:

1 In the connection's properties dialog box, click Install.

2 In the Select Network Component Type dialog box that appears, select a component type:

- A *client* provides access to resources on a particular type of network, such as NetWare.

- A *service* provides other network features, such as network backup agents.

- A *protocol* is the language used to communicate with other computers. In addition to TCP/IP, Windows 2000 includes support for IPX/SPX (the protocol used on most NetWare networks), AppleTalk, and NetBEUI (a protocol used on some Microsoft networks).

3 Click Add.

4 Select the component you want to add, and then click OK.

After you add a component, it's available to all your network and dial-up connections. (You can confirm this fact by examining the General or Networking tab of each connection's properties dialog box.) The component isn't actually used by a connection, however, unless you enable it, which you do by selecting the check box next to the component name on the General or Networking tab.

To remove an installed component, highlight it and click Uninstall.

## Configuring TCP/IP Connections

TCP/IP, the default network protocol used by Windows 2000, is perhaps best known for the alphabet soup of acronyms that inevitably enter the discussion. Some of these—in particular DHCP (Dynamic

Host Configuration Protocol) and DNS (Domain Name System)—refer to methods for assigning and finding IP (Internet Protocol) addresses. Each network adapter has a unique IP address, which is expressed as a series of four numbers (each from 0 through 255) separated by periods, like this: 192.0.0.237

In a nutshell, DHCP is a widely used service that assigns a unique IP address to each computer as it joins the network, and DNS finds the proper IP address when you enter the name of a computer (say, by clicking a computer name in My Network Places). While this system works well, it requires somebody to set up and administer these services—usually on a Windows NT Server or Windows 2000 Server.

To the rescue comes a new feature, which includes an acronym within its acronym: APIPA (Automatic Private IP Addressing). This feature, new in Windows 2000, makes it easy to create a small private network, without any administration headaches. (A *private network* is an internal network that isn't part of a public network, such as the Internet.) When Windows 2000 starts, APIPA looks for a DHCP server. If it finds one, it obtains an IP address from the DHCP server; otherwise, APIPA assigns a unique IP address to the connection. APIPA periodically checks to make sure that the assigned IP address remains unique on the network and assigns a new address if it is not.

APIPA uses blocks of addresses that are reserved for private networks (169.254.0.1 through 169.254.255.254), so you don't need to worry about conflicts with IP addresses of Internet hosts. However, this means that your connection's IP address might not be unique on the Internet, so you can't use it to access the Internet. Not a problem. The IP address applies only to your network adapter, which connects you to your local area network. If you connect to the Internet via a dial-up connection or a different network adapter (such as one connected to a cable modem), that connection will have its own IP address. If you connect via a proxy server or a router on your network, the proxy server or the router translates your private IP address to a globally unique address provided by your ISP (Internet service provider).

All this is a long way of saying that through the miracle of DHCP, DNS, and APIPA, you'll probably never have to venture into the arcane TCP/IP settings.

If your ISP gives you a static IP address, which is common with "always-on" connections such as cable and digital subscriber line (DSL), or if you need a static IP address for any other reason, do this:

**1** In the Network And Dial-Up Connections folder, right-click the connection you want to modify and choose Properties from the shortcut menu.

**2** Highlight Internet Protocol (TCP/IP) and click the Properties button.

> The Internet Protocol (TCP/IP) Properties dialog box appears.

**3** Select Use The Following IP Address.

**4** Type the IP address, subnet mask, default gateway, and DNS server address(es).

> Your ISP or your network administrator should provide this information.

## Joining a Domain or Workgroup

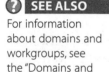
**SEE ALSO**

For information about domains and workgroups, see the "Domains and Workgroups" sidebar, page 175.

During the Windows 2000 setup process, you have the opportunity to join an existing domain or workgroup. If you bypassed that opportunity, or if you want to join a different domain or workgroup, you can—as long as you are logged on as a member of the Administrators group. Your computer can be part of only one domain or workgroup, so if you join a new one, your computer account on the old one will be disabled.

To join a domain or workgroup:

**1** In the Network And Dial-Up Connections folder, open the Advanced menu and choose Network Identification.

> The Network Identification tab of the System Properties dialog box shows your computer's current name and domain or workgroup.

**2** Click the Properties button.

> The Identification Changes dialog box appears, as shown next.

**3** Type the computer name if you want to change it.

The computer name must include only letters, numbers, and hyphens. If you are using the TCP/IP protocol, the name can be up to 63 characters long; otherwise, the maximum length is 15 characters.

> **NOTE**
>
> Do not include the domain name in the Computer Name box. (As you can see in the dialog box just shown, the full computer name in a Windows 2000 domain includes the computer name followed by a period and the domain name.)

**4** Under Member Of, select Domain or Workgroup.

**5** Type the name of the domain or workgroup you want to join.

If you're creating a new workgroup, choose a name that isn't the same as the name of any computer that will join the workgroup. The workgroup name can be up to 15 characters. Although some punctuation symbols are permitted, you can avoid problems by using only letters, numbers, and hyphens in the name. (You create a workgroup simply by using this procedure on each computer and typing the same workgroup name on all computers.)

V

Sharing and Communicating

> You can't create a domain with Windows 2000 Professional; you can only join an existing domain. Only machines running Windows 2000 Server can be set up as domain controllers.

**6** Click OK.

**7** If you're joining a domain

- Windows asks you to provide the user name and password of an account that is authorized to join the domain. Your network administrator should give you this information. Type the information and click OK.

- The domain controller sends you a welcome message.

**8** When prompted by Windows, restart your computer to effect the changes.

# Setting Up Dialing Locations

Before you can use a modem and a phone line to connect to the Internet or a remote network, you should set up a dialing location. At a minimum, a *dialing location* includes a name, a country code, and a telephone area code.

If you travel regularly to particular locations and use your modem to initiate calls from those locations, you can simplify your life considerably by letting Windows know exactly how it should place a call in each location. You can create as many dialing locations as you need. When you arrive at one of your regular destinations, you simply tell Windows where you are. Any Windows program that uses the Windows telephony interface (formally known as *TAPI*, which stands for telephony application programming interface) will then use the dialing information you've supplied.

> The first time you use any program that uses the telephony interface, Windows asks you to provide location information—your country, area code, and so on. This creates your first dialing location (called My Location), which you can then modify as described next.

To specify dialing information for a location:

**1** Open Control Panel.

**2** In Control Panel, open Phone And Modem Options.

**3** On the Dialing Rules tab in the Phone And Modem Options dialog box:

- To set up a new location, click New.

- To view or modify an existing location, select the dialing location that you want to modify and click Edit.

**4** On the General tab of the New Location dialog box (or the Edit Location dialog box shown below), specify a name for your location, the country, and the area code. Then specify the code you need to dial (if any) to use an outside line, the code to disable call waiting, and whether your phone service uses tone or pulse (rotary) dialing.

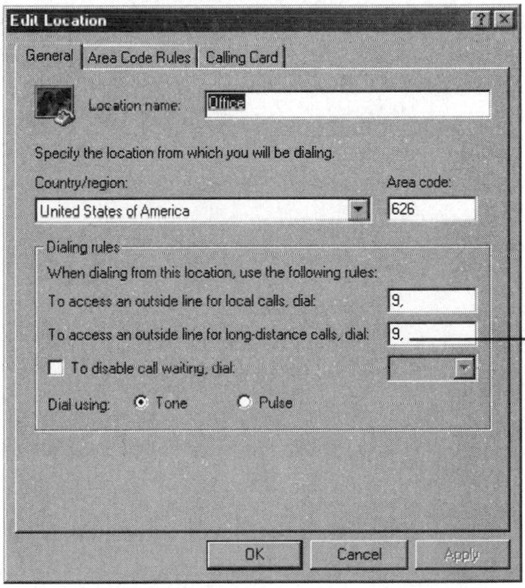

A comma in the dial string causes the modem to pause briefly.

If you subscribe to a call waiting service (a feature that makes a sound when another call comes in while you're using the phone), you should disable call waiting whenever you make a data call with your modem. Otherwise, the incoming-call signal can interrupt your modem communications. You can find the code for disabling call waiting in your phone book.

**5**  On the Area Code Rules tab, specify how phone numbers should be dialed from your area code to numbers in other area codes and to numbers within your area code.

With the proliferation of area codes has come a proliferation in dialing rules. In some areas, you must dial 1 before certain numbers but not others, for example. If you don't include any special rules on this tab, by default Windows dials 1+area code+number for all calls outside your area code, and the number alone for calls within your area code. To define different rules, click New to display the New Area Code Rule dialog box, shown below.

**6**  If you want to charge your calls to a calling card, click the Calling Card tab. Select your card from the list (or click New to define an unlisted card), and then enter your account number and PIN.

The dialing sequence of access numbers, account numbers, PINs, menu commands, and so on can be lengthy and complex—but the Edit (and New) buttons lead to a dialog box that lets you easily herd those numbers into line. You can have different dialing sequences for local, long distance, and international calls. And once it's set up, you don't have to think about it again—until you switch to another card!

# Using Dial-Up Connections

**?** **SEE ALSO**

For information about using shared resources, see Chapter 9,"Using and Sharing Files on the Network."

Dial-up connections allow you to connect to a remote computer by means of your modem and then access shared resources on the remote computer. The computer to which you connect is known as a *dial-up server*. The information that Windows requires to make the connection is stored in your Network And Dial-Up Connections folder.

Once you've connected to a dial-up server, you can browse the remote network using My Network Places. You can also access shared folders and files using Universal Naming Convention (UNC) path specifications and map shared folders to drive letters on your own computer. In other words, all the techniques you use to work with local area network resources function the same way with a dial-up connection.

## Setting Up a Dial-Up Connection

Before you can connect to a dial-up server the first time, you need to set up the connection. To set up a dial-up connection:

1 Open Make New Connection in your Network And Dial-Up Connections folder.

2 On the Network Connection Wizard's welcome page, click Next.

3 Select Dial-Up To A Private Network, and then click Next.

4 On the Phone Number To Dial page, you can type the phone number of the dial-up server, just as you want to dial it. (Include the access codes for an outside line, disabling call waiting, your long distance carrier, and so on.)

   A better alternative: Select the Use Dialing Rules check box. Then enter the area code, phone number, and country in the three boxes, and let Windows use the dialing rules you set up for your current dialing location. This makes it much easier to dial complex numbers and also allows you to travel with your computer without changing your dial-up connection.

   Click Next to continue.

 **SEE ALSO**

For information about dialing rules and dialing locations, see "Setting Up Dialing Locations," page 278.

5 Select For All Users if you want this connection to be available to anyone who logs on to your computer, or select Only For Myself to make it available only when you log on using the same account you're currently using. Click Next.

> **NOTE**
>
> This option is available only if you are logged on as a member of the Administrators group.

**6** Type a descriptive name for your new connection, and then click Finish.

The Connect dialog box appears, as shown in Figure 16-3.

**FIGURE 16-3.**
The Connect dialog box appears when you complete the Network Connection Wizard and when you double-click the connection's icon.

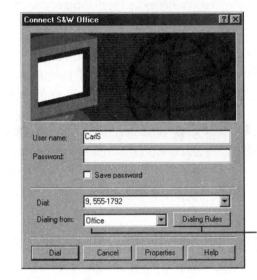

These options appear only if you select Use Dialing Rules in the connection's properties dialog box.

# Viewing and Setting Connection Properties

Once you've created your connection with the help of the Network Connection Wizard, you might need to visit the connection's properties dialog box to set additional options. To open the properties dialog box

■ If the Connect dialog box is open, click Properties. (See Figure 16-3.)

■ Otherwise, right-click the connection in your Network And Dial-Up Connections folder, and then choose Properties.

## Specifying Phone Numbers

On the General tab of the properties dialog box, you can modify the settings you made with the Network Connection Wizard. You can select a modem (if you have more than one), specify the phone number, and indicate whether you want to use the dialing rules you set up for dialing locations. In addition, you can

- Click Alternates to specify alternate phone numbers to be used if you can't get through on the first number.

- Select Show Icon In Taskbar When Connected to display an icon in the status area whenever this connection is connected. Hover the mouse pointer over the icon to see a status summary, click the icon to see status details in a dialog box, or right-click the icon to display a shortcut menu that includes a Disconnect command.

## Specifying Networking Protocols

The Networking tab of the properties dialog box works in the same manner as the Local Area Connection Properties dialog box shown in Figure 16-2 on page 273. Here you install and enable the network clients, services, and protocols that you need to communicate with the dial-up server. In the Type Of Dial-Up Server I Am Calling box, select PPP (Point-to-Point Protocol) if you're connecting to a dial-up server running any version of Windows. Select SLIP (Serial Line Internet Protocol) to connect with some UNIX servers and Internet service providers.

## Setting Dialing Options

The Options tab, shown in Figure 16-4, on the next page, allows you to bypass the Connect dialog box. (Clear the Display Progress While Connecting, Prompt For Name And Password, and Prompt For Phone Number check boxes.) The Include Windows Logon Domain check box lets you log on to a domain at the dial-up server that's different from the domain or workgroup that you're currently logged on to; when this option is selected, a Domain text box appears in the Connect dialog box.

Under Redialing Options on the Options tab, you specify what should occur if Windows can't connect the first time it dials (because of a busy line, for example). You can specify the number of times to retry and the time to wait before retrying. (If you specified alternate numbers using the General tab—and you selected If Number Fails, Try Next Number in the Alternate Phone Numbers dialog box—Windows uses a different phone number for each redial attempt.)

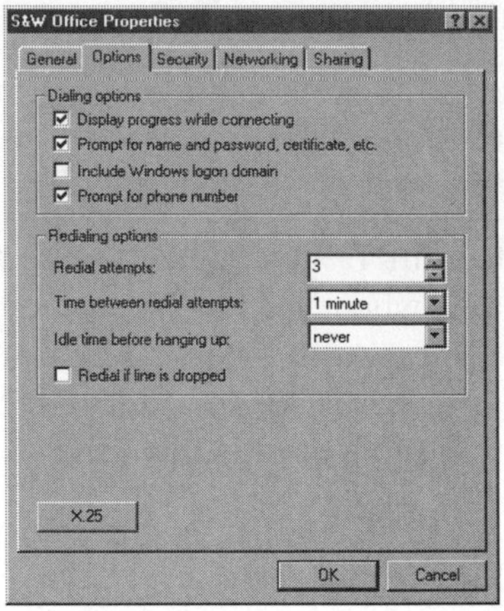

**FIGURE 16-4.**

Redialing options determine what happens if a connection isn't successful on the first attempt.

Nestled into the Redialing Options box, you'll also find the Idle Time Before Hanging Up list. Use this setting to disconnect automatically after a period of inactivity. Note that the dial-up server might also have such a setting, so the server might disconnect you before the idle time you specify is reached.

> **NOTE**

The X.25 button on the Options tab lets you configure an X.25 connection (a wide area network, or WAN, connection through a packet-switching network). Because these options require significant hardware and software setup effort by the network administrator—a topic that is beyond the scope of this book—we'll leave it to that administrator to set up the hardware and software needed on your system to make the connection. Once the system is set up, however, you'll find that using an X.25 connection is similar to using the other dial-up connections.

## Using Logon Scripts

On the Security tab of the properties dialog box, you can configure various security options. Leave this setting at Typical unless your system administrator tells you otherwise. Of more interest on the Security tab is the ability to specify a sequence of commands, encapsulated as a *script*, that will be executed automatically each time you connect. You'll need to use this option when connecting to certain Internet service providers. A script is simply a text file containing a series of instructions that will be passed to the remote computer. You can use Notepad to create such a file. To add the script to your connection, select Run Script. Then type the name of the file into the box, select the script from the list, or click the Browse button and navigate to the file.

**TIP**

Several sample scripts, which have a .scp extension, are stored in the %SystemRoot%\System32\ras folder. You can use these scripts as models for your own. The scripting language is explained in a document called Script.doc (located in the same folder), which you can read with WordPad or Microsoft Word.

## Using Multiple Device Dialing (Multilink)

If you have two or more modems and phone lines and the dial-up server that you want to connect to offers a secondary phone number (or if you and the dial-up server both have an ISDN adapter), you might be able to use multiple device dialing, also known as multilink, to achieve faster throughput. Windows combines the signals from each device, treating them as a single (relatively) high-bandwidth connection.

**NOTE**

A single ISDN adapter can act as multiple devices because ISDN comprises two 56 kbps B channels, which can be used independently or together.

To set up multiple device dialing:

**1** Click the General tab in the connection's properties dialog box. In the Connect Using box, select each of the modems (or the single ISDN modem) you plan to use.

**2** Click the Options tab. In the Multiple Devices box, select Dial All Devices if you want to always use all available lines. If you want to dynamically dial and hang up lines as needed, select Dial Devices Only As Needed; then click Configure to set the parameters for using multiple devices. If you don't want to use Multilink, select Dial Only First Available Device.

## Connecting to a Dial-Up Server

**SEE ALSO**

For information about logging on to a Windows 2000 (or Windows NT) domain using a dial-up connection, see "Setting Other Options," page 825.

Once you've set up a dial-up connection, you can access the dial-up server by simply launching the connection in your Network And Dial-Up Connections folder (or a shortcut to that connection anywhere on your system). The first time you do this, if you haven't automated the logon process by changing dialing options on the Options tab of the connection's properties dialog box, you'll be asked to identify yourself, following whatever security methods are used by the dial-up server. (See Figure 16-3 on page 282.) If the dialog box in which you do this includes a Save Password check box, you can select this check box to save yourself the trouble of retyping your password each time you connect. If you're concerned that another user will try to connect to your remote-access account without your permission, don't select this check box. Click Dial to make the connection.

**NOTE**

You must enter account information that's valid on the remote network—which might or might not be the same logon information you use to log on to your computer. (In addition to dialing your own company's network, for example, you might use dial-up connections to connect with a client's network or with an Internet service provider.)

**TIP**

You can override a connection's phone number with a command on the Advanced menu in the Network And Dial-Up Connections folder. When the Operator-Assisted Dialing command is selected, to make a connection, you click Dial, pick up the telephone handset, and use the telephone to dial the number; hang up the handset after the modem takes over the connection.

If a dialog box like the one shown below appears, you have probably enabled a protocol that isn't being used on the dial-up server. No harm will come if you click Accept, but you'll be better off if you first select the Do Not Request The Failed Protocols Next Time check box, which will disable the protocol for future calls with this connection. (And if the failed protocol isn't one that you use for other connections, you should go to the Networking tab of the connection's properties dialog box, select the protocol, and click Uninstall.)

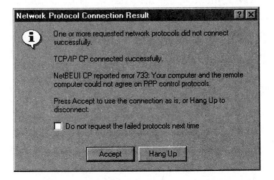

After you've connected to the dial-up server, and after the server has authenticated your logon information, a Connection Complete dialog box confirms your connection. (If you don't want to be bothered by this dialog box each time you connect, select its check box before you click OK.)

To see which resources are available while you're connected, open My Network Places. Except that it's probably not as fast, everything should work the way it does when you're connected directly to the network.

To terminate the session, right-click the connection's icon (in the taskbar status area or in the Network And Dial-Up Connections folder) and choose Disconnect.

**SEE ALSO**

For information about shortcuts, see "Creating a Shortcut," page 55. For information about mapping a folder to a drive letter, see "Mapping a Network Folder to a Drive Letter," page 183.

## Reconnecting to a Remote Folder or File

To simplify reconnection to a particular remote folder or file, create a shortcut for it *while you're connected to the dial-up server*. Then, after you disconnect, you can reconnect by launching the shortcut. Alternatively, you can map a dial-up folder to a drive letter on your own system. Then you can reopen that "drive" just as you would reopen an ordinary local drive. If Windows determines that the mapped drive isn't part of your local area network, it presents a dialog box asking if you want to use a dial-up connection.

**TIP**

You can also reconnect to a dial-up server by choosing the Start menu's Run command and typing the server's name.

# Connecting to the Internet

The Internet Connection Wizard serves several purposes: it lets you establish a new account with an ISP, reestablish a dial-up connection for an existing account, change some aspect of the way you connect to an existing account (such as the dial-up number), or connect or reconnect to an existing proxy server. If you're brand new to the Internet and need an ISP account, a visit to the wizard should be your first step. If you've just installed Windows 2000 on a new computer and need to reconnect to the account you were using on your old machine, the wizard will help with that task as well. If you want to reconfigure your connection to an existing account, you can use the wizard. (Alternatively, you can simply modify the properties of the dial-up connection you're currently using.) You might also want to use the Internet Connection Wizard if you grow dissatisfied with your current ISP and want to see what the competition has to offer.

V

Sharing and Communicating

There are three easy ways to start the Internet Connection Wizard:

- In the Network And Dial-Up Connections folder, open Make New Connection. Click Next, select Dial-Up To The Internet, and click Next again.

- Open the Start menu, and choose Programs, Accessories, Communications, Internet Connection Wizard.

- In Internet Explorer, open the Tools menu and choose Internet Options. Click the Connections tab, and then click Setup.

By whatever means you arrive, a welcome page is the first thing you'll see, as shown in Figure 16-5. Select the first option if you need a new ISP account. Select the third option if you want to reconnect to or modify an existing account, or if you need to set up a connection to a proxy server on your local area network. Select the second option if you're not sure whether you want to set up a new account or use an existing account.

**FIGURE 16-5.**

Select the wizard's first option to set up a new account, or the third option to reconnect to an existing account or to connect through your LAN.

**Creating a New ISP Account**

If you select the first option shown in Figure 16-5, the wizard makes a toll-free call over your modem to download a list of ISPs that serve your dialing location. If you make a selection from that list, you'll be asked to provide your name, address, and telephone number. Then the wizard will take you to the ISP, who will be happy to take your credit card number and open an account. Within minutes, you'll be ready to surf.

## Reconnecting to an Existing ISP Account

To reestablish your relationship with an existing ISP account, select the third option on the Internet Connection Wizard page shown in Figure 16-5. Click Next, select I Connect Through A Phone Line And A Modem, and then click Next again. On the following pages, enter the phone number, your user name and password, and a name for the connection. The wizard then offers to help you set up a mail account for this connection.

**TIP**

> The second option on the welcome page would appear to be the one to use when you want to reconnect to an existing account. However, it first dials the Microsoft Internet Referral Service and gives you the option of choosing a new ISP before leading you through the account setup steps outlined above. You can avoid that unnecessary diversion by selecting the third option instead.

## Connecting or Reconnecting to a Proxy Server

You can use the Internet Connection Wizard to establish or reestablish a connection to the Internet via a proxy server on your local area network. (A *proxy server* is a computer that serves as an intermediary between your computer and the Internet. On a local area network, this provides a single, manageable gateway that allows administrators to control all users' access to the Internet and makes each computer more secure against attack by rogue programmers.)

To establish or reestablish a connection to the Internet via a proxy server on your LAN:

1  Select the third option on the Internet Connection Wizard page shown in Figure 16-5.

2  On the page that follows, select I Connect Through A Local Area Network (LAN).

   A Local Area Network Internet Configuration page appears, as shown in Figure 16-6, on the next page.

3  Unless your system administrator instructs you otherwise, select and clear the check boxes as shown and click Next.

   Automatic discovery works best with most proxy server configurations.

V

Sharing and Communicating

**FIGURE 16-6.**

You can use the Internet Connection Wizard to set up a connection to your network's proxy server.

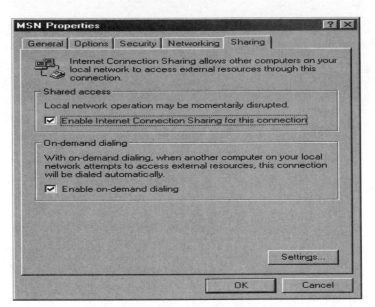

You can set up Microsoft Internet Explorer to use your LAN connection to the Internet whenever your computer is connected to the network, and to use a dial-up connection when it is not. To do so, set up both connections, right-click the desktop Internet Explorer icon and click Properties to open the Internet Properties dialog box, click the Connections tab, and select Dial Whenever A Network Connection Is Not Present.

## Modifying an Existing Dial-Up Connection

If all you need to do is change the parameters for a dial-up connection that you use to access an existing ISP account (for example, to switch to a different access number), you don't need the Internet Connection Wizard. You can open your Network And Dial-Up Connections folder, right-click the connection, choose Properties from the shortcut menu, and then make your changes. *For more information, see "Viewing and Setting Connection Properties," page 282.*

**WARNING**

To prevent rogue Internet users from accessing shared resources on your computer, be sure that file and printer sharing is disabled on your Internet connection. To check, right-click the connection, choose Properties, and click the Networking tab. If there's a check mark in the File And Printer Sharing For Microsoft Networks box, clear it.

# Sharing an Internet Connection

With Internet Connection Sharing, your home network or small office network can share a single connection to the Internet. This allows everyone on the network to access the Internet without installing a modem and phone line at each computer and without setting up a separate ISP account for each user.

To set up Internet Connection Sharing, you must be logged on as a member of the Administrators group. The computer that will serve as the Internet gateway needs two connections: one to the Internet (this can be a dial-up connection or a network adapter connected to a cable modem, for example) and one to the rest of the network (typically a network adapter).

To share an Internet connection:

1 Set up your two connections (one to the Internet, and one to the local area network) as described in the preceding sections.

2 In the Networking And Dial-Up Connections folder, right-click the Internet connection (not the network connection) and choose Properties.

3 Click the Internet Connection Sharing tab, shown below.

**4** Select Enable Internet Connection Sharing For This Connection.

Doing so makes the connection available to other users on your network.

**5** If you're using a modem and a dial-up connection, select Enable On-Demand Dialing.

With this check box selected, Windows connects to the Internet whenever anyone on the network attempts to access an Internet resource. (If you clear the check box, users at other computers can access the Internet only when you've already made a connection.)

> **NOTE**

> The Settings button on the Internet Connection Sharing tab lets you config-
> ure network applications, such as some Internet-based games.

To access a shared Internet connection on another computer, use the Internet Connection Wizard to connect through a local area network. *For more information, see "Connecting or Reconnecting to a Proxy Server," page 289.*

# Using a Virtual Private Network

A *virtual private network* (VPN) is a means of connecting to a private network (such as your office network) via a public network, such as the Internet. This combines the virtues of a dial-up connection to a dial-up server (the ability to use all your network resources and proto-cols just as if you were connected directly to the network) with the ease and flexibility of an Internet connection. By using an Internet connection, you can travel worldwide and still, in most places, connect to your office with a local call to the nearest Internet access phone number. And if you have a high-speed Internet connection (such as cable or DSL) at your computer (and at your office), you can commu-nicate with your office at full Internet speed, which is much faster than any dial-up connection using an analog modem.

VPNs use authenticated links to ensure that only authorized users can connect to your VPN, and they use encryption to ensure that data that travels over the Internet can't be intercepted and used by anyone else. Windows achieves this security using Point-to-Point Tunneling Proto-col (PPTP) or Layer Two Tunneling Protocol (L2TP).

To set up a connection to a VPN:

**1** Open Make New Connection in your Network And Dial-Up Connections folder.

**2** On the Network Connection Wizard's first page, click Next.

**3** Select Connect To A Private Network Through The Internet, and then click Next.

**4** If you need to dial to connect to the Internet, select Automatically Dial This Initial Connection and select your dial-up Internet connection from the list. If you have a full-time connection, select Do Not Dial The Initial Connection. Then click Next.

**5** Type the host name (for example, mycompany.com) or the IP address (for example, 123.45.67.89) of the computer you want to connect to. (Your system administrator should give you this information.) Click Next.

**6** Select For All Users if you want this connection to be available to anyone who logs on to your computer, or select Only For Myself to make it available only when you log on using the same account you're currently using. Click Next.

> **NOTE**

This option is available only if you are logged on as a member of the Administrators group.

**7** Type a descriptive name for your new connection, and then click Finish.

To connect to a VPN, open the VPN connection in your Network And Dial-Up Connections folder. If you don't already have a connection to the Internet open, Windows offers to connect to the Internet. Once that connection is made, the VPN server asks for your user name and password. Enter them correctly, click Connect, and your network resources should be available to you in the same way they are when you connect directly to the network.

> **TIP**

You can share a VPN connection in the same way that you share an Internet connection. *For more information, see "Sharing an Internet Connection," page 291.*

V

Sharing and Communicating

# Connecting Two Computers with a Direct Connection

Direct connections provide a simple way to connect two computers so that you can transfer files from one computer to the other. You don't need any network adapters or modems, and if your computers have infrared ports, you don't even need a cable! You can create a direct connection between the two computers' serial ports, parallel ports, or infrared ports. (You must use the same port type on each computer.)

## Selecting a Cable

Direct connection supports the following kinds of cables:

- Null-modem serial cables

- Basic four-bit parallel cables, including LapLink and Interlnk cables

- DirectParallel cables for Extended Capabilities Port (ECP)

- Universal Fast parallel cables

ECP cables provide faster performance than any of the other alternatives, but they require an ECP-enabled parallel port on both computers. A good source for parallel cables is Parallel Technologies, which you reach on the Internet at *www.lpt.com* or by phone at (800) 789-4784 (outside the United States, call 1-425-869-1119).

## Setting Up a Direct Connection

When two machines are hooked together via direct connection, one acts as host and the other acts as guest. The guest computer can access any folders shared by the host, but the host can't access shared folders on the guest.

To create or modify the host side of a direct connection, you must be logged on as a member of the Administrators group.

> **NOTE**

You must have certain networking components installed and enabled for direct connections to work properly. On both the host and guest systems, you need to have Client For Microsoft Networks and a protocol (the same one on both systems). In addition, on the host system, you must have the File And Printer Sharing For Microsoft Networks service. *For information about installing network components, see "Configuring a Network Connection," page 272.*

You should set up a direct connection first on the host computer and then on the guest computer. To set up the host computer:

1  If you're going to use a serial or parallel port, connect the cable between the two computers. If you're going to use an infrared port, be sure the infrared transceivers can "see" each other.

2  Open Make New Connection in your Network And Dial-Up Connections folder.

3  On the Network Connection Wizard's first page, click Next.

4  Select Connect Directly To Another Computer, and then click Next.

5  Select Host and click Next.

6  Select the port you plan to use, and then click Next.

   Windows lists all unused serial, parallel, and infrared ports.

7  Select which users will be allowed to connect to this computer, and then click Next.

8  Click Finish.

**?  SEE ALSO**

For more information about Incoming Connections, see "Allowing Others to Connect to Your Computer," on the next page.

If an Incoming Connections icon doesn't already exist in the Network And Dial-Up Connections folder, Windows creates one. With this icon, you set properties not only for incoming direct connections (that is, ones where your computer is the host), but also for incoming dial-up and VPN connections.

To set up the guest computer, the procedure is generally the same. The main difference is that you must specify Guest in step 5.

Once you've set up both computers, you can begin transferring files right away. To use the connection again later, simply open the connection on the guest computer.

⭐ **TIP**

Be sure to share any host computer folders that contain files you want to copy to the guest computer. *For information about sharing folders, see "Sharing Folders with Other Users," page 185.*

# Allowing Others to Connect to Your Computer

❓ **SEE ALSO**

For information about installing a network client, see "Configuring a Network Connection," page 272. For information about enabling sharing and sharing folders, see "Sharing Folders with Other Users," page 185. For information about user accounts, see "Working with Local User Accounts and Groups," page 564.

You can make your computer a remote-access server so that others can connect to it via modem, VPN, or direct connection, and then access shared files on your local drives. You must have a network client installed, with file sharing enabled, and you'll need to share the folders to which you want to give remote users access. Of course, you'll need to have the physical connection established, be it a modem (for dial-up connections); an Internet connection (for VPN connections); or a serial, parallel, or infrared port (for direct connections).

Users at the other end—the ones who want to connect to your computer—don't need to run Windows 2000; they can connect with Windows 95 or Windows 98. But they must have a local user account on your computer, or Windows 2000 security will rebuff their logon attempts.

A computer running Windows 2000 Professional can accommodate up to three simultaneous incoming connections: one dial-up, one VPN, and one direct. All three connection types are handled by the same Incoming Connections icon in the Network And Dial-Up Connections folder; if you rerun the wizard, the changes you make affect all three.

▶ **NOTE**

To create or modify incoming connections, you must be logged on as a member of the Administrators group.

To enable others to connect to your computer:

1 Open Make New Connection in your Network And Dial-Up Connections folder.

2 On the Network Connection Wizard's first page, click Next.

3 Select Accept Incoming Connections, and then click Next.

4 Select the check box next to each device where you want to permit incoming connections. (Windows lists your available modems and ports.) Click Next.

**5** If you want to allow VPN connections, select Allow Virtual Private Connections.

To receive VPN connections over the Internet, your com-puter's IP address (more precisely, the IP address of your connection to the Internet, if your computer has multiple network adapters) must be known on the Internet. This IP address should be assigned to you by your Internet service provider.

Click Next to continue.

**6** Select the check box next to the name of each user you want to allow to make an incoming connection.

Windows lists all of the local user accounts on your computer. As shown below, you can add (or delete) user accounts from this page, which can save a visit to the Computer Management console.

Callback options can be used as an additional security mea-sure for dial-up connections as well as to determine who pays for the phone call. To set callback options for a particular user, select the user name, click Properties, and then click the Callback tab. If you select an option other than Do Not Allow Callback, when your computer receives a call, it authenticates the user, dis-connects the call, and then dials the user's modem.

- Select Do Not Allow Callback if you want the remote user to make a connection with a single call to your computer.

- Select Allow The Caller To Set The Callback Number if you want the caller to be able to specify a phone number for a return call.

- Select Always Use The Following Callback Number and specify a phone number if you want your computer to call the user at a particular number. This reduces the likelihood that an intruder who has come upon a valid user name and password can access your system.

When you're finished with the Allow Users page, click Next.

**7** Select the check box next to the name of each network component you want to use for an incoming connection.

For an incoming connection to work, the calling computer and your computer have to "speak" the same network protocol. Click Install to add a new networking component. *For more information about installing network components, see "Configuring a Network Connection," page 272.*

**8** Click Next and then click Finish.

## When the Remote System Connects

If everything is set up correctly (and your modem is ready to answer the phone, if you allow incoming dial-up connections), a remote user can connect by simply dialing in, opening a VPN connection, or opening a direct connection. While someone is connected, Windows offers several indicators, as shown in Figure 16-7:

- The Incoming Connections icon in the Network And Dial-Up Connections folder changes. The icon shows the type of connection (dial-up, VPN, or direct), and the caption shows the name of the connected user.

- An icon appears in the status area of the taskbar, and if you hover the mouse pointer over the icon, a status summary appears as a ScreenTip.

- If you double-click either icon (in the Network And Dial-Up Connections folder or in the taskbar status area), a status window appears. The Details tab shows the network components in use and other information.

**FIGURE 16-7.**
When a remote system connects, Windows provides several visual indicators.

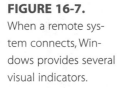

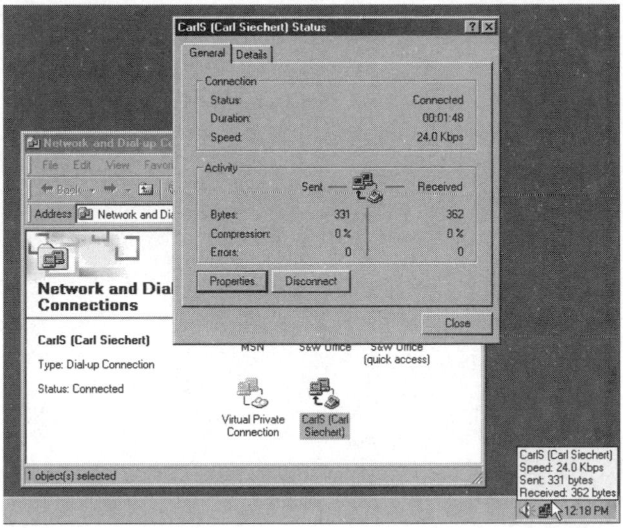

You can use the Disconnect button in the status window or the Disconnect command on the icon's shortcut menu to unceremoniously boot the remote user off your computer.

**CHAPTER 17**

# Using Address Book

A ddress Book is a versatile tool for recording contact information. You can use it to store names, addresses, personal and business telephone numbers, e-mail addresses, information about contacts' birthdays and anniversaries, NetMeeting servers and addresses, digital IDs, freeform notes, and more. You can also use it to search for people and businesses on the Internet.

An Identity feature, new in the version of Address Book included with Microsoft Windows 2000, makes it possible for multiple users to share a common Address Book file. If you share your computer with family members, for example, each of you can keep separate sets of contact information. Shared contacts can be made accessible to all users by means of a special Shared Contacts folder.

Windows 2000 makes Address Book information available to programs that request it. Microsoft Outlook Express and the Windows 2000 Fax driver, for example, are tightly integrated with Address Book. And Outlook, the personal information manager component of Microsoft Office, can easily import records from Address Book into its own contacts database.

You'll find a menu item for Address Book in the Accessories section of your Start menu. If you're running Outlook Express, you can also open Address Book by clicking the Addresses button on the toolbar. If you're creating a new message in Outlook Express, you can open Address Book by clicking the Address Book icon on the To or Cc line of the message header.

**TIP**

Regardless of how you decide to open Address Book, you can close it by simply pressing Esc.

# Choosing Display Options

Address Book shows records in Details view, by default. But, you can choose to view entries as large or small icons, or in a list format. These choices are accessible via the View menu.

In Details view, four columns are displayed. By default, those columns are Name, E-Mail Address, Business Phone, and Home Phone. You can't alter the first two columns, but you have choices about the third and fourth. To replace either of those columns with a different field from the Address Book database, right-click the column heading. Figure 17-1 shows what choices are available.

**FIGURE 17-1.**

To change one of the phone-number columns in Address Book's Details view, right-click the column heading.

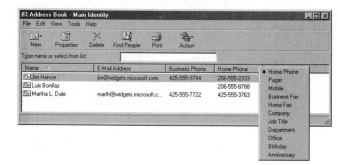

You can't add more columns to Details view, but you can change the order in which the four columns appear. To move a column, drag its heading.

You can also change the width of columns. To do so, drag the column separator at the right of the column heading. To make a column just wide enough to accommodate its widest entry, double-click the column separator at the right of the column heading.

## Sorting Options

By default, Address Book sorts entries in ascending order by first name. If that order doesn't suit you, you can make a change.

To sort by a different column field, click the field heading. Initially when you do this, you get an ascending sort. For a descending sort, click the heading again.

To sort by last name instead of first, open the View menu, point to Sort By, and choose Last Name. As Figure 17-2 shows, when you sort by last name, Address Book rearranges the names into a last name, first name format.

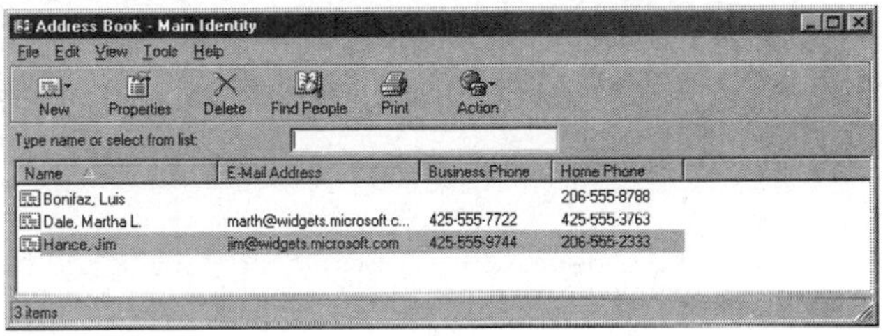

**FIGURE 17-2.**
When you sort by last name, Address Book switches to a last, first display format.

## Viewing Folders

Address Book allows you to organize your contacts into folders. You might, for example, have one folder for personal contacts and another for business contacts. Address Book also allows you to create named groups of contacts. Groups make it easy to address an e-mail message to multiple recipients. If you use folders or groups, you can see the structure of your address book more easily by choosing Folders And Groups from the View menu. This causes a folder pane to appear, comparable to the Folders bar in Windows Explorer. *For more information about using folders and groups, see "Organizing Your Address Book," page 310.*

# Entering and Editing Contact Information

Figure 17-3, on the next page, shows Address Book's data-entry form. As you can see, the form uses seven tabs to segregate various kinds of information about each of your contacts. (After you have created an Address Book record, an eighth tab—Summary—appears.) Out of all the many fields available, only one is required. You must enter some form of name for a contact; that is, your contact must have at least a first, middle, or last name. Everything else is optional.

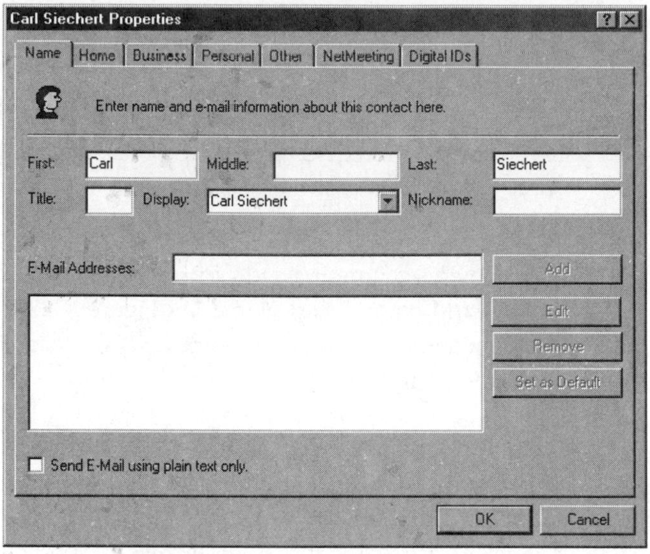

**FIGURE 17-3.**

Each entry in your Address Book has its own properties dialog box.

To create a new Address Book entry, click the New button on the toolbar and choose New Contact. To edit an existing contact, double-click it.

## E-Mail Addresses

To enter an e-mail address, click the Name tab, type the address into the E-Mail Addresses box, and then click the Add button. If you enter an invalid Internet e-mail address (by Address Book's judgment), you'll get a warning prompt. If the address is correct, prompt notwithstanding, click Yes.

You can enter as many e-mail addresses for a contact as you want. If you have more than one, select the one that you want Address Book to display in Details view, and then click the Set As Default button.

Outlook Express can send e-mail in HTML (Hypertext Markup Language), allowing you to apply rich formatting to the text of your message, include links to Web pages, and so on. If you select this option in Outlook Express, you can still opt to send messages to particular recipients in plain text. If you know that a contact can't read HTML-encoded e-mail, be sure to select the check box labeled Send E-Mail Using Plain Text Only on the Name tab of the contact's properties dialog box. Note that this check box affects all e-mail addresses for the current contact. If a contact has one e-mail address to which you want to send HTML and another to which you want to send plain text, create two separate address book records for that contact.

# Default Addresses

You can enter separate home and business addresses for a contact, using the Home and Business tabs. If you have a program that works with data from Address Book, you should specify which of the two available addresses the program should use by default. You can do that by selecting the Default check box on either the Home or Business tab. Selecting one of these check boxes clears the other.

# Web Pages

The Home and Business tabs both include Web Page fields, allowing you to associate your contact with both a personal and a professional Web site. After you've entered a URL in either of those fields, you can use the Go button to the right of the field to connect to the specified Web site.

# Finding a Contact on the Map

Below the address section on both the Home and Business tabs is a View Map button. Clicking here sends your Web browser to an Internet site that will attempt to display the associated address on a map.

# Children

To add the name of a contact's child, click the Add button on the Personal tab. An item called New Child appears in the Children window. Simply type the child's name to rename this item.

# Conferencing Servers and Addresses

On the NetMeeting tab, you can enter conferencing servers and conferencing addresses for use in NetMeeting calls. To enter server names, type into the Conferencing Server line and then click the Add button. The first server you enter is automatically used as the default by NetMeeting. To enter a conferencing address, type it into the Conferencing Address box or open the list and choose one of your existing e-mail addresses. Be aware that a person's conferencing address might not be the same as his or her e-mail address. *For more information about using NetMeeting, see Chapter 21, "Using NetMeeting."*

**V**

**Sharing and Communicating**

## Digital IDs

For more about using digital IDs, see "Using Digital Signatures and Encryption," page 412.

A digital ID, also known as a security certificate, is a statement issued by a third-party certifying authority attesting to your identity. Digital IDs enable correspondents to exchange secure (encrypted) e-mail. To associate a digital ID with an e-mail address:

1  Click the Digital IDs tab.

2  Select an e-mail address from the list.

3  Click the Import button and specify the filename of the digital ID.

# Importing Data into Address Book

Address Book provides an import facility, on the reasonable assumption that you might already have recorded contact data in another contact-management program. Even if you want to continue using that other program, you might find it helpful to import your data into Address Book so that you can use it more easily with programs such as Outlook Express that are integrated with Address Book.

Address Book can import data from a variety of sources, including other Address Book files, Netscape and Netscape Communicator address books, LDIF (LDAP Interchange Format) files, and CSV (comma separated values) files.

## Importing Windows Address Book Files

To import another Address Book file, point to Import on the Address Book File menu and choose Address Book (WAB) from the submenu. Then select the file you want to import.

Address Book imports all records in the selected file. If an imported record has the same name as a record in the current file, Address Book tries to merge the data without creating a duplicate record. But if conflicts exist between imported data and existing data—say, for example, that an existing record has one business phone number and an imported record of the same name has a different business phone number—Address Book simply creates a new record in the existing file. Folder assignments in the imported data are ignored, but group assignments are preserved. *For more about using folders and groups, see "Organizing Your Address Book," page 310.*

# Importing Data from Other Programs

To import information from another contact manager:

**1** Open the Address Book File menu, point to Import, and choose Other Address Book.

A dialog box appears, listing the supported import formats.

**2** Select a file format from the list, and then click Import:

- If you select Eudora Pro or Light, or one of the Netscape formats, Address Book will attempt to find your address book on the current disk. If it fails, you'll get the opportunity to browse to find the file.

- If you select LDIF–LDAP Data Interchange Format or Microsoft Internet Mail For Windows 3.1 Address Book, you'll be prompted to specify or browse to the file you want to import.

Text File (Comma Separated Values) is a format that most contact management programs (as well as most general-purpose database programs) can export to. Therefore, if the source of your contact data is not Eudora, LDIF–LDAP, Netscape, or Microsoft Internet Mail for Windows 3.1, you'll probably want to make your data available to Address Book by first exporting it to CSV from your other contact manager.

After you specify a CSV file for import, Address Book will ask you to map the import file's fields (columns) to Address Book fields. If the CSV file doesn't include field headings (not an unlikely circumstance), you will have to use data in the first record of the CSV file as your guide to creating this mapping. Blank fields (fields without data) in the first record of your import file can make this difficult. Either of the following strategies can help you cope with this problem.

- Before exporting the CSV file from your other contact manager, make sure that the first record is completely filled out, with no blank fields. Or

- Before importing the CSV file into Address Book, import it into a spreadsheet or database program. In your spreadsheet or database program, add field headings.

Figure 17-4 shows an example of what you might see when mapping CSV data to Address Book fields. This example uses Palm Desktop as the source program, but the CSV data was first passed through Microsoft Excel, and column headings were added in Excel.

**FIGURE 17-4.**

Before you can import CSV data, you need to map import columns to Address Book fields.

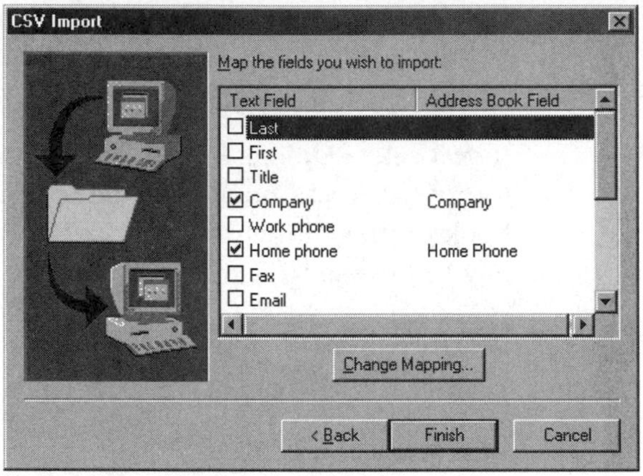

Where the import facility finds an exact match between a CSV-file column heading and an Address Book field (Company and Home phone, in the example), it selects the associated check box. These columns you don't need to map. (Clear the check box if, for some reason, you want to omit them from the import.) To map a column that doesn't exactly match an Address Book field, select its check box. You'll see a dialog box similar to the following.

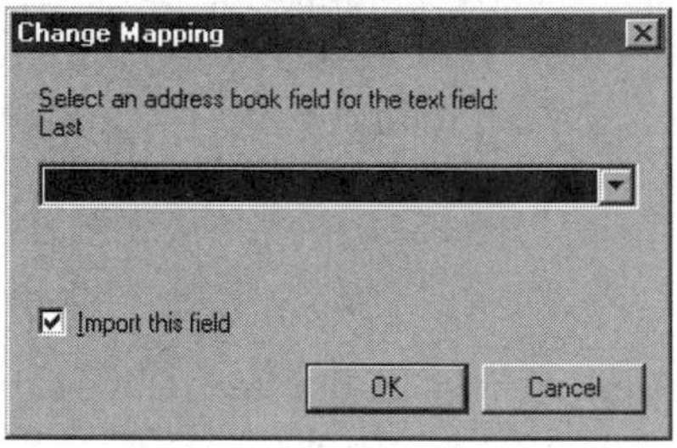

Click the small arrow to see the list of Address Book fields, select the field you want, and then click OK. Continue in this manner until you've mapped everything, and then click Finish.

If the CSV file contains records whose names match records already in your address book file, the import facility will ask if you want to replace the existing record with the imported record. If you answer No, the record won't be imported. That is, Address Book won't create a duplicate entry.

# Exchanging Electronic Business Cards

Address Book supports the vCard format, which allows you to exchange electronic business cards with other users via e-mail. To send your business card to another user:

1 Create an address book record for yourself.

2 Select your record in Address Book, choose Export from the File menu, and then choose Business Card (vCard).

3 Specify a filename and location.

4 Send your associate an e-mail message with your exported business card file as an attachment.

To store an associate's electronic business card:

1 Ask the associate to create a business card file (following the steps just listed, if your associate is using Address Book), and send you an e-mail message with that file as an attachment.

2 Save the attachment as a file, using whatever commands your e-mail client program provides.

3 Open Address Book's File menu, point to Import, choose Business Card (vCard) from the submenu, and specify the name of the attachment file.

**TIP**

If you use Outlook Express, you can automatically attach your business card to all outgoing mail and you can add business cards you receive to your Address Book by just clicking the attachment and saving it. *For details, see Chapter 19, "Using Outlook Express."*

V

Sharing and Communicating

# Organizing Your Address Book

Apart from identities (discussed in "Using Identities," page 313), Address Book provides two tools for organizing records: groups and folders.

*Groups* are collections of contacts gathered under a group name. Each contact in the group retains its individual record and can belong to any number of groups. You can continue addressing e-mail to group members individually, but you can also broadcast an e-mail to all members of the group, simply by supplying the group name as the addressee.

*Folders* can be convenient for display purposes, especially if your address book file is large. Folders allow you to view subsets of your file. A contact can belong to only one folder at a time. Note that you cannot address an e-mail to all members of a folder by specifying the folder name.

## Displaying the Folders And Groups Pane

Adding the Folders And Groups pane to Address Book's display, which you can do by choosing Folders And Groups from the View menu, lets you see your groups and folders at a glance and provides an easy way to navigate. Figure 17-5 shows Address Book with the Folders And Groups pane displayed.

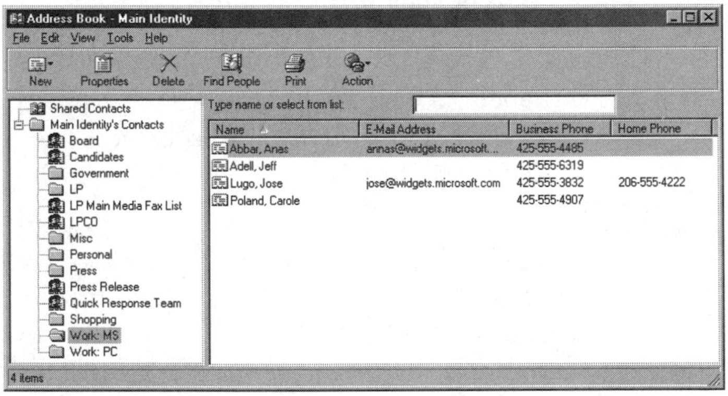

**FIGURE 17-5.**

The Folders And Groups pane lets you see the structure of your address book at a glance.

Just as you might move files between folders by using the Windows Explorer Folders bar, so can you move Address Book entries with the help of the Folders And Groups pane. For example, to move the record for Jeff Adell from the Work: MS folder (its current location) to the Personal folder, you simply drag the entry from the right pane and drop it on Personal in the left pane. Dragging a name into a folder moves it into the folder, but dragging a name to a group copies it to the group, leaving it in its original location as well. Note, however, that you cannot copy an address book record by holding down the Ctrl key as you drag.

# Creating, Populating, and Modifying a Group

To create a group, click the New button and choose New Group. You'll see the dialog box shown in Figure 17-6.

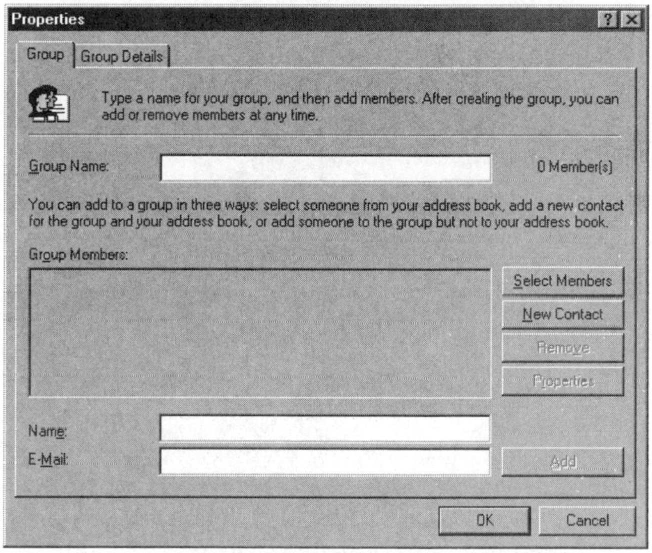

**FIGURE 17-6.**

In the properties dialog box for a new group, you can add members to the group as well as specify information that applies to the group as a whole.

On the Group tab of this dialog box, provide a name for the new group. In the fields on the Group Details tab, you can (optionally) enter information—address, telephone numbers, notes, and Web site—that applies to the group as a whole. (Note, however, that information you enter here does not get propagated to the individual group records.)

You can also use the Group tab to begin populating your group. To add a person who already has a record in your address book, click Select Members. The dialog box that appears, exemplified by Figure 17-7, on the following page, lists all of your address book's current members and groups. To add someone to a group, click his or her name in the left pane, and then click the Select button. (To select multiple names, hold down Ctrl while clicking.)

Note that you can add groups to groups. To make all members of Group A members of Group B, for example, first create Group A. Then simply add Group A to Group B the same way you would add an individual to Group B.

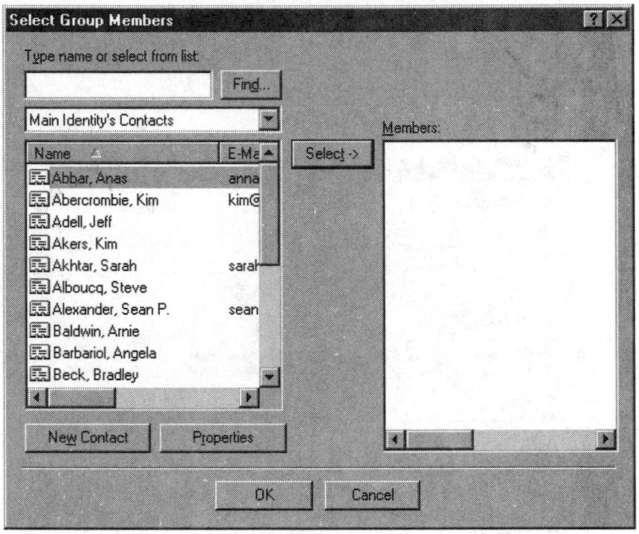

**FIGURE 17-7.**

To add someone to a group, click his or her name in the left pane, and then click Select.

If you accidentally add the wrong person to a group, simply select that person's name in the Members box (on the right in Figure 17-7) and press the Delete key. This has no effect on the person's underlying address book record.

If you're not sure whether a person belongs in a group, select that person's name and click Properties. You can then read the person's entire address book record and make up your mind.

To add a person to a group who doesn't yet have an address book record, click the New Contact button. You can do that either in the screen shown in Figure 17-6 or the one shown in Figure 17-7. Either action creates a new address book record.

To modify a group after you've created it, select its name in any Address Book view. (The Folders And Groups pane can help you do this.) Then click Properties on the toolbar.

**TIP**

An easy way to add members to an existing group is to display the Folders And Groups pane, and then drag names from the right pane to the group name in the left pane.

## Creating a Folder

To create a new folder, click New on the toolbar, select New Folder, and provide a name. Note that your new folder will be immediately subordinate to the current identity. You can't nest folders within other folders.

# 2000 Using Identities

Identities allow two or more users who share a common Windows 2000 user account to have separate Address Book files. (Note that users who share a computer but have separate Windows 2000 user accounts automatically have separate Address Book files.) Identities can share particular records by means of the Shared Contacts folder.

To create a new identity, you must run Address Book from the Start menu. If you run it from within Outlook Express or another application, the appropriate File menu commands don't appear.

To create a new identity:

**1** Open the File menu and choose Switch Identity.

**2** In the dialog box that appears, click Manage Identities.

**3** In the Manage Identities dialog box, click New.

**4** Type a name for the new identity.

**5** If you want to require a password for access to the new identity, select the check box. Then supply and confirm a password.

To switch identities, choose Switch Identities from the File menu, select the identity you want from the ensuing dialog box, and supply the correct password if prompted.

To change an identity's name or password:

**1** Choose Switch Identity from the File menu.

**2** Click Manage Identities.

**3** Select the identity you want to change and click Properties.

**V**

**Sharing and Communicating**

To share contacts among all identities:

**1**  Display the Folders And Groups pane.

**2**  Drag the appropriate records from the right pane to the Shared Contacts folder in the left pane.

# Finding People

Address Book lets you find people in your local address book, in your organization's Active Directory if you're part of a Windows 2000 domain, and worldwide on the Internet.

## Finding People Listed in Your Address Book

Address Book always displays the names of all contacts in the current folder. If you know that the contact you're looking for is in that folder, you can go straight to that contact by typing the first part of his or her name in the box directly above the window. If your contact isn't in the current folder (or you're not sure), follow these steps:

**1**  Click Find People on the toolbar.

**2**  In the Look In list of the Find People dialog box (see Figure 17-8), choose Address Book.

**3**  Fill out one or more of the remaining fields, and then click Find Now.

The records that meet your search criteria appear below the search fields.

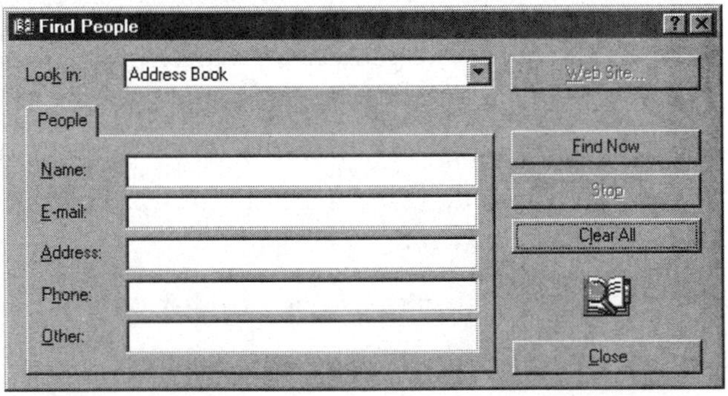

**FIGURE 17-8.**

With the Find People command, you can search your address book by name and other fields.

⭐ **TIP**

To search for people without first opening Address Book, open the Start menu and choose Search, For People.

Note the following points about searching your address book:

- If you specify more than one criterion, the Find People command displays only those records that match all criteria.

- The Find People command displays all records that include your criteria. For example, specifying 303 on the Phone line gets you all records with phone numbers in area code 303, as well as all other records with phone numbers that include the sequence 303.

- The Other line causes the Find People command to search only the Job Title and Notes fields. It won't locate records by the names of spouses or children, for example.

## Finding People in Your Organization

If you work in a Windows 2000 domain that uses Active Directory, you can use the Find People command to locate people in your organization, whether or not they're in your address book. To use Active Directory to find someone in your organization:

**1** Click Find People on the toolbar.

**2** Choose Active Directory in the Look In list.

**3** Specify a name or e-mail address on the People tab. Or click the Advanced tab and specify one or more criteria.

On the Advanced tab, you can use the first box to choose between Name, First Name, Last Name, E-Mail, and Organization. The second list offers Contains, Is, Starts With, Ends With, and Sounds Like. Then type a value into the third box. For example, to find all the Jacobsons and Jacobsens in your organization, you could specify Last Name, Sounds Like, and Jacobsen. After you specify a criterion, click the Add button. You can specify as many criteria as you like; the Find People command will return the records that match all the criteria.

## Finding People on the Internet

You can use the Find People command to look for entries in any installed LDAP directory. Address Book comes with a number of

**V**

**Sharing and Communicating**

Internet LDAP directories preinstalled. To look for someone on the Internet, choose one of the available directory services in the Look In list. In the remainder of the dialog box, specify a name or an e-mail address (or both), and then click Find Now. The Find People command activates your Internet connection if appropriate and passes your search specification to the selected directory. In a moment or two, you might be rewarded with some information about the person you seek. If the service doesn't return anything useful, you can choose a different service and try again.

It's likely that the directory you choose will turn up more than one match for your search criteria. If that happens, you might not be sure which person—if any—is the one you want. To learn more about a person whose name appears in the results section of the Find People dialog box, select that person's name and click the Properties button. You might want to do this even if only one name is returned, just to make sure you don't try to reestablish contact with someone who's never heard of you.

# Mailing, Dialing, and Initiating a NetMeeting Session

**? SEE ALSO**

For information about NetMeeting, see Chapter 21, "Using NetMeeting."

The menu that appears when you click the toolbar's Action button allows you to send e-mail to one or more contacts, dial a contact's telephone number, or initiate a NetMeeting session:

- If you choose Send Mail, Address Book activates your default e-mail client and addresses a message to the selected contact's default e-mail address. If you select a group in the Folders And Groups pane and select multiple members in the right pane (hold down the Ctrl key while you select), the Send Mail command will address the message to all those you select.

- If a selected individual has more than one e-mail address, the Send Mail To command becomes available. This command works like the Send Mail command, except that it lets you choose the e-mail address you want to use.

- If you choose Dial, the New Call dialog box that appears lets you choose numbers in the selected contact's record or enter a different number altogether. (This command activates the new Phone Dialer program, which is discussed in Chapter 22, "Using Phone Dialer.")

- If you choose Internet Call, Address Book activates NetMeeting—
provided you have entered conferencing information in the
selected contact's record.

# Printing Address Book Records

Using the Print button on the toolbar you can print all or just selected
records in your choice of three formats:

- **Memo** prints full name, company name, business and home
addresses, all phone numbers, e-mail addresses, web pages,
and notes.

- **Business Card** prints full name, job title, company name, business address, all phone numbers, and all e-mail addresses.

- **Phone List** prints full name and all phone numbers and
includes alphabetical separators.

# Exporting Address Book Data

To move the data in your Address Book to another program:

1 Open the File menu and choose Export, Other Address Book.

2 Select the export option you want and click the Export button.

3 If you selected Microsoft Exchange Personal Address Book the
data is exported. If you selected Text File (Comma Separated Values), you must supply a name for the export file. (Address Book
stores the file in My Documents by default. If you prefer a different folder, click the Browse button and navigate to that folder.)

4 In the CSV Export dialog box, select check boxes for the fields
you want to export. Then click Finish.

Most other programs that you might use to record contact information
can import Address Book's CSV file.

⭐ TIP

As an alternative to exporting from Address Book to CSV and then importing
CSV into another program, check to see whether the other program can
import an Address Book (WAB) file directly.

V

Sharing and Communicating

# Backing Up Address Book Data

One way to make a backup copy of your Address Book data is to choose Export from the File menu, and then Address Book (WAB) from the submenu. You'll be prompted for a filename. Browse to the folder or network share where you want to store your backup, supply a filename, and click Save.

Alternatively, you can simply make sure that your Address Book file is included in whatever backup procedure you routinely follow. You can find out the name and location of your Address Book file by choosing About from the Help menu.

# Using Internet Explorer

Microsoft Windows 2000 includes Microsoft Internet Explorer version 5, a tool for accessing Internet resources. You will undoubtedly use it mostly for browsing sites on the World Wide Web, but it also enables you to connect with File Transfer Protocol (FTP), Telnet, and Gopher sites. Internet Explorer is an extremely rich program with a wealth of everyday conveniences and advanced features. We explore most of those features in this chapter.

This chapter assumes that you have the means to access the Internet—that you've installed and set up a modem or that you participate in a local area network that is connected directly to the Internet—and that you've set up a connection to the Internet. *For information about setting up an Internet connection, see "Connecting to the Internet," page 287.*

## A Smattering of Internet Jargon

**Cache.** Temporary local storage of Internet sites you visit.

**Cookie.** A file containing information about you that helps a Web site customize its offerings in accordance with your preferences or buying history.

**Frame.** A rectangular area within a Web page that contains its own HTML document.

**FTP.** *File Transfer Protocol*, a protocol that lets you transfer files from one computer to another.

**Home page.** The Web page that appears automatically when you open Internet Explorer (unless you begin by launching an Internet shortcut).

**HTML.** *Hypertext Markup Language*, the language used to encode Web pages. HTML settings tell Internet Explorer (and other Web browsers) how and where to render the typography, graphics, frames, and other elements that comprise a Web page.

**HTTP.** *Hypertext Transfer Protocol*, the protocol used by the World Wide Web component of the Internet. The prefix *http://* at the beginning of an address identifies the associated site as part of the World Wide Web (or as part of an intranet).

**Internet shortcut.** An icon with an arrow in its lower left corner that looks just like any other kind of shortcut except that it represents a link to an Internet site or to an e-mail recipient.

**Intranet.** A network that uses the HTTP protocol to distribute information within an organization. An intranet might or might not be connected to the Internet.

**ISP.** *Internet service provider*, an agency that enables connections to the Internet.

**Link.** An area on a Web page that, when clicked, either takes you to another Internet site or lets you send e-mail to a particular recipient. Links can be portions of text, icons, pictures, or other graphic objects. They are often, but not always, highlighted or underlined. You can tell whether an item is a link by putting the mouse pointer over it. If the pointer changes to a hand, the item under it is a link. A link might also appear in a non-HTML document (a Microsoft Excel spreadsheet, for example, or an e-mail message) or might be encapsulated in an Internet shortcut.

**Offline Web page.** A page that is stored on your local hard disk so that you can view the last version you downloaded when your computer isn't connected to the Internet.

**Secure Web site.** A site that lets you transmit and receive encrypted data.

**Security certificate.** A statement, issued by a third-party certifying authority, that guarantees the identity of a Web site or person.

> **A Smattering of Internet Jargon**   *continued*
>
> **Telnet.** An Internet protocol that lets you log on to and issue commands to a remote computer.
>
> **URL.** *Uniform Resource Locator,* an address that uniquely identifies a World Wide Web page or other Internet resource. For example, the URL for Microsoft's Web site is *http://www.microsoft.com/.* In this book, we use the more familiar term *address* as a synonym for URL.
>
> **Web browser.** A program that, among other tasks, renders HTML documents and responds to links, allowing you to move from one Web page to another while either offline or connected to the Internet. Internet Explorer and Netscape Navigator are examples of Web browsers.
>
> **Web page.** A document encoded in HTML. Web pages are commonly made accessible from other Web pages by means of links.
>
> **Web site.** A location on the World Wide Web consisting of one or more Web pages.

# CHAPTER 18

# Starting and Ending an Internet Explorer Session

Internet
Explorer

You can open Internet Explorer by double-clicking the Internet Explorer icon on the desktop or by clicking the similar icon on the Quick Launch toolbar. You can also open the program by opening the Start menu and choosing Programs, Internet Explorer.

Provided you have not made some other product your default Web browser, the following actions also start Internet Explorer:

- In a Windows Explorer window, type an Internet address into the Address bar.

- Open the Start menu and choose Run, and then type an Internet address.

- Type an Internet address into the desktop's Address toolbar.

- Click a link to an Internet site in an e-mail message or other document.

- Click a shortcut, on your desktop or elsewhere, to an Internet site.

- Choose an Internet site on your Favorites menu (on the Start menu, in Windows Explorer, or in Internet Explorer).

V

Sharing and Communicating

**SEE ALSO**

For information about working offline, see "Working Offline," page 342. For information about dial-up connections, see "Using Dial-Up Connections," page 281.

In response to any of these actions, Internet Explorer springs to life and attempts to display the selected Internet resource. If you aren't already connected to the Internet (through a full-time network connection or through a dial-up connection) and haven't asked to work offline, Internet Explorer activates the dial-up connection with which it is associated, and that connection then dials the appointed telephone number.

To end a dial-up Internet session, close all open Internet Explorer windows, or right-click the connection's icon in the taskbar's status area and choose Disconnect from the shortcut menu. (The latter method has the advantage of leaving Internet Explorer open, allowing you to continue reading the last Web page it displayed without tying up a phone line.)

# Understanding the Internet Explorer User Interface

Figure 18-1 points out the most crucial landmarks of the Internet Explorer window.

**SEE ALSO**

For information about displaying, arranging, and customizing the toolbars, see "Customizing the Toolbars," page 370. For information about the Radio toolbar, see "Listening to Internet Radio Programs," page 353.

- **Toolbars.** Allow quick access to commands and Web pages that you use most often. Like Windows Explorer, Internet Explorer can display the Standard Buttons, Address Bar, Links, and Radio toolbars in any combination and arrangement you choose.

   The default buttons on the Standard Buttons toolbar are described in Table 18-1. The Address bar displays the address of the page you're currently viewing. You can also use the Address bar for navigation: type the address of a page you want to go to into the Address bar and press Enter. The Links toolbar provides one-click access to your most frequently used pages. The Radio toolbar makes it easy to tune to Internet radio broadcasts.

- **Explorer animation.** Indicates when Internet Explorer is waiting to receive information from a computer on the Internet; a globe icon spins around the Windows flag while Internet Explorer is waiting.

- **Document area.** Displays the Web page you are currently viewing. Any items that are highlighted (usually by underlining) are links, and clicking them takes you to the page they point to.

**SEE ALSO**

For details, see "Understanding the Status Bar," page 326.

- **Status bar.** Gives you information about what Internet Explorer is currently doing.

**FIGURE 18-1.**

The Internet Explorer window has a set of tools and controls surrounding the document viewing area.

Toolbars

Explorer animation

Document area

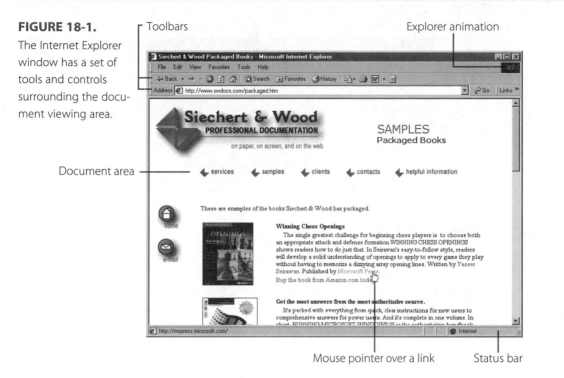

Mouse pointer over a link            Status bar

**TABLE 18-1.   Standard Buttons Toolbar**

| Toolbar Icon | Description |
|---|---|
| ⇐ Back ▾ | Displays an earlier page in the list of previously viewed pages |
| ⇒ ▾ | Displays a later page in the list of previously viewed pages |
| ⊗ | Stops downloading the current page |
| ▧ | Downloads the current page again, ensuring that the latest version is displayed |
| ⌂ | Displays your home page |
| Search | Displays (or hides) the Search bar, which provides access to Internet search providers |
| Favorites | Displays (or hides) the Favorites bar, which provides access to your favorite sites |

*(continued)*

**TABLE 18-1.** *continued*

| Toolbar Icon | Description |
|---|---|
| History | Displays (or hides) the History bar, which provides access to sites you've visited recently |
|  | Launches your mail or newsreader program (by default, Microsoft Outlook Express), and lets you send links and pages to others via e-mail |
|  | Prints the current page |

**NOTE**

Some programs add buttons to your Standard Buttons toolbar. (For example, Microsoft Office 2000 adds an Edit button, which opens the current page in your HTML editor, and a Discuss button, which lets you add discussion comments to the current page.) And Internet Explorer itself has additional buttons you can use. *For information about changing the Standard Buttons toolbar, see "Customizing Toolbars," page 76.*

## Using Full Screen View

To increase the amount of screen real estate that you can use for viewing a Web page, Internet Explorer provides a special view called Full Screen. In some instances, Internet Explorer automatically switches to Full Screen view, but you can switch to this useful view at any time. To switch to Full Screen view, press F11 or choose Full Screen from the View menu. (If you use this view frequently, you might want to add the Full Screen button to the Standard Buttons toolbar.) In Full Screen view, Internet Explorer expands to fill the screen, the title bar and window borders disappear, the menu bar merges into the toolbar, and the toolbar shrinks down to a single row, leaving the majority of the screen to display a Web page, as shown in Figure 18-2.

Full
Screen

**TIP**

**Finding the Taskbar**
Because Internet Explorer completely fills the screen in Full Screen view, the Windows taskbar isn't visible. However, it appears when you move the mouse pointer to the edge of the screen at the taskbar's usual location. Alternatively, you can use shortcut keys to switch windows: press Alt+Tab to switch to another open window, or press Ctrl+Esc to open the Start menu and display the taskbar.

**FIGURE 18-2.**

In Full Screen view, standard window elements disappear and Internet Explorer fills the screen.

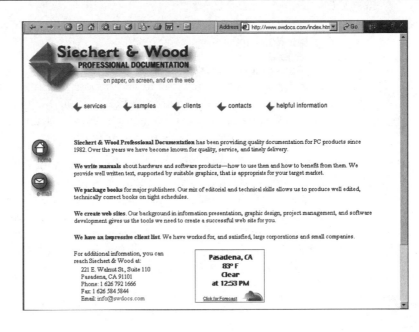

In Full Screen view, the toolbar occupies a single row at the top of the screen, but you can specify which elements you want to include on the toolbar. Right-click the toolbar and choose Menu Bar, Address Bar, Links, or Radio. A check mark in the shortcut menu identifies each element you've selected. (The Standard Buttons toolbar is always included in Full Screen view.) Within the limits of the single row, you can resize each of these elements by dragging the vertical line at the left edge of each toolbar element.

**TIP**

To completely maximize the viewing area, in Full Screen view, right-click the toolbar and choose Auto Hide. The toolbar then retracts into the top of the screen; you can redisplay it by moving the mouse pointer to the top edge of the screen.

To switch from Full Screen view back to Internet Explorer's normal window, click the Restore button, or press F11 again.

## Displaying and Hiding Explorer Bars

As we've seen in Windows Explorer, an Explorer bar is a separate pane that's displayed on the left side of the Explorer window. Three of the Explorer bars available in Windows Explorer—Search, Favorites, and History—are quite useful in Internet Explorer. (They were in fact designed for Internet Explorer and then incorporated into Windows Explorer.)

You display an Explorer bar in one of two ways: click its toolbar button, or open the View menu and choose one from the Explorer Bar submenu. To hide an Explorer bar, click its toolbar button or choose its View-menu command again. Or simply click the X (the close button) in the Explorer bar's upper right corner.

In Full Screen view, the Explorer bar retracts into the left edge of the screen. To display it, move the mouse pointer to the left edge; when you move the mouse pointer away from the Explorer bar, it again slides off the left edge. A small pushpin button appears on the Explorer bar, next to the close button. To prevent the Explorer bar from sliding away, tack it down by clicking the pushpin button. Click the pushpin button again to restore the "auto hide" behavior.

⭐ **TIP**

> You can make any Explorer bar wider or narrower by dragging its right edge.

## Understanding the Status Bar

The status bar provides information about the Web page you are viewing, as well as about the current state of the browser. The status bar is organized into sections, with each section providing a different type of information.

On the left is the current progress status. While you download a Web page, an icon and text in this area explain what the browser is currently doing. After the page has arrived, this area shows the address for any link you point to. To the right of the progress status text is the progress bar, which is active only while Internet Explorer downloads information. The bar fills up as data for the current page gets downloaded.

❓ **SEE ALSO**

For more information, see "Working Offline," page 342, and "Working with Secure Sites," page 359.

The middle section of the status bar is split into two small panes. Each pane either displays an icon or is empty. The first pane displays an icon when you are working offline. The second displays a lock icon if you have a secure connection to a Web site.

On the right end of the status bar is the security zones area. This displays the icon and name of the security zone for the current Web page.

# Getting Around the World Wide Web

Internet Explorer offers several ways to navigate the World Wide Web. You can

- Click a link to go to a page

- Enter an Internet address to go to a specific page

- Use the Forward and Back commands to revisit previously viewed pages

- Go farther back in your Web-browsing history using the History bar

- Return to a favorite page by selecting it from the Favorites menu

- Use a search provider to find a page of interest

## Using Links to Get to Other Pages

The World Wide Web works much like the HTML-based Windows Help system. In Help, you can click any word that is underlined or highlighted to get more information. The Web works the same way; on the Web these underlined items are called *links*.

---

### Shortcut Keys for Web Pages

You can use the following shortcut keys as you work with Web pages in Internet Explorer:

| Shortcut Key | Action |
| --- | --- |
| Tab | Selects the next link |
| Shift+Tab | Selects the previous link |
| Enter | Activates the selected link |
| Shift+F10 | Displays the shortcut menu for the current link |
| Ctrl+Tab | Cycles between frames (independent areas within a Web page) |
| Alt+Left arrow or Backspace | Returns to the previous page |
| Alt+Right arrow | Moves to the next page |
| Esc | Stops display of the current page |
| F5 | Refreshes display of the current page |
| Alt+Home | Displays your home page |

---

*(continued)*

Sharing and Communicating

**Shortcut Keys for Web Pages** *continued*

| Shortcut Key | Action |
|---|---|
| Ctrl+E | Opens and closes the Search bar |
| Ctrl+I | Opens and closes the Favorites bar |
| Ctrl+H | Opens and closes the History bar |
| Ctrl+O | Opens a document or Web page |
| Ctrl+N | Opens a new window |
| Ctrl+S | Saves the current page as a file |
| Ctrl+F | Finds text in the current page |
| Ctrl+P | Prints the current page |
| F11 | Switches between Full Screen and regular views |

Each page on the Web can have an unlimited number of links to other pages. You can identify a link by moving the mouse pointer over a text or graphic item on a page. If the pointer icon changes to a hand when you pass over the item, then the item is a link. Notice also that the status bar displays information about the link. (See Figure 18-1 on page 323)

To use a link, all you have to do is click it. When you do this, Internet Explorer takes you to the Web page to which the link points.

**? SEE ALSO**

For information about setting the colors for links, see "Selecting Colors," page 372.

Once you click a link and go to its linked page, Internet Explorer remembers that you used that link. To let you know that you've already used a link, Internet Explorer changes the color of the text for that link.

## Going to a Specific Web Page

If you know the address (that is, the URL) of the Web page you want, Internet Explorer's Address bar provides an easy way to get there. The Address bar always displays the address of the current Web page. However, you can also type the address of the Web page you want and press Enter, and Internet Explorer will take you there. To enter an address:

1 Press Alt+D or click the Address bar's text box to highlight the text currently in the box.

2 Type the address for the page you want to go to. The address should look something like this:

*http://www.microsoft.com/*

**3** Press Enter or click the Go button located at the right side of the Address bar.

Internet Explorer finds the page that you want. (It might take a few seconds for the Web page to respond to Internet Explorer's request for information.)

---

**Address Bar Shortcut Keys**

You can use the following shortcut keys as you work in the Address bar:

| Shortcut Key | Action |
| --- | --- |
| Alt+D | Selects all text in the Address bar |
| F4 | Displays a list of previously entered addresses |
| Ctrl+Left arrow | Moves the insertion point left to previous period or slash |
| Ctrl+Right arrow | Moves the insertion point right to next period or slash |
| Ctrl+Enter | Inserts *www.* at beginning and *.com* at end of Address bar text |

---

**⭐ TIP**

**Alternatives to the Address Bar**
If the Address bar isn't visible, you can open the File menu and choose Open. The Open dialog box that appears contains a text box where you can type the address. You have other alternatives as well: you can enter an address into the Address bar of any Windows Explorer window, into the Address toolbar that you can place on the desktop, or into the Run dialog box that appears when you choose Run from the Start menu.

**⭐ TIP**

**Reentering Addresses You've Typed Before**
Each of the address-entry boxes contains a list of its previous entries. You can click the downward-pointing arrow at the right end of the Address box to display the list. (Note, however, that each address-entry box—the Address bar and Open dialog box in Internet Explorer, the Address toolbar on the desktop, and the Run dialog box—maintains its own history of entries.)

 **Using AutoComplete and Other Keystroke Savers**

When you start typing an address, Internet Explorer attempts to complete it by displaying a list with any similar addresses that you've previously entered. If the address you want is in the list, press the

Down arrow key repeatedly until the address is highlighted, and then press Enter. (Alternatively, you can click the list item you want.) As you continue to type, Internet Explorer's AutoComplete feature narrows the list to only those entries that match what you've typed so far.

> AutoComplete also helps with Web-based forms. On a page that asks for your name and address, for example, as you begin typing into each text box, AutoComplete displays a list of similar entries you've made before.

For more information about AutoComplete, see "Setting AutoComplete Options," page 375.

Internet Explorer can eliminate keystrokes in other ways too:

- For most Internet addresses, Internet Explorer can identify the correct protocol automatically. Therefore, you can shorten your typing for these addresses by omitting the protocol—the part of the address up to and including the two slashes, such as *http://* or *ftp://*. For example, to enter the sample address in step 2 on page 328, you could type just *www.microsoft.com*.

- Pressing Ctrl+Enter adds *www.* to the beginning and *.com* to the end of the text you type into the Address bar. So the *easiest* way to get to *http://www.microsoft.com/* is to type only *microsoft* and press Ctrl+Enter.

---

### The Anatomy of an Address

Internet addresses can be cryptic. But there is logic to their structure, and understanding the logic can help you to make reasonable guesses about a company's address or about what you'll find at a particular address.

The first part of an address is the *protocol* (such as http or ftp), which is followed by a colon and two slashes. The part of the address between the two slashes after the protocol name and the next slash is the *domain name*. Domain names are typically made of two or three words separated by periods. If you read a domain name from right to left, each word more specifically identifies the site. You begin at the right with the *top-level domain*, a designation such as *.com* (for a commercial site), *.edu* (educational institution), *.gov* (government), or *.org* (organization). The next word, the *second-level domain* name, typically identifies the name of the organization, such as *microsoft*. The leftmost part tells you a little about the organization's site. For example, a domain name that begins with *www* indicates that the address is for a World Wide Web site (but not all World Wide Web sites start with *www*).

By remembering this right-to-left order of importance, you'll be able to remember, for example, that The Microsoft Network's investment advice can be found at *moneycentral.msn.com*, not *msn.moneycentral.com*.

# Using Back and Forward

Internet Explorer keeps a list of the pages you've already viewed. The Back and Forward commands—or their toolbar equivalents, shown in Table 18-1 on page 323—provide a simple way to move through that list so that you can easily return to places you have already seen. Try out the commands with this simple example:

1   On your home page, click any link to move to a new Web page.

2   When the new page appears, click the Back button on the Standard Buttons toolbar or choose the Back command from the Go To submenu on the View menu to move back to your home page.

Notice that the Forward toolbar button is now active.

3   Click the Forward button or use the Forward command on the Go To menu. You'll move forward to the page you visited in step 1.

**TIP**

### Retrace Your Steps

You can easily move two or three pages at a time by clicking the small arrow at the right edge of the Back or Forward button. Doing so displays a list of the last several pages in the back/forward list. Choose a page from this list to jump directly to that page. (You can also right-click the Back or Forward button to open its list.)

You can also return to a recently visited site by choosing it from the Go To submenu of the View menu.

# Revisiting the Past with History

The Back button provides a simple way to retrace your steps, but it only remembers where you've been during the current session. To return to a site you visited in a previous session or to a site that's many steps back from your current location, you'll want to use Internet Explorer's History feature.

To review your browsing history, display the History bar by clicking the History button (shown in Table 18-1 on page 323). A pane on the left side of the Internet Explorer window shows a list of pages you've visited, sorted by date and then by site. Figure 18-3, on the next page, shows an example of the History bar in its default view, By Date.

## Returning to Previously Viewed Sites

The top of the History bar hierarchy lists the beginning date of the past few weeks and each day in the current week. When you click a date or day, the History bar shows the sites, or domains, that you visited during that week or day, sorted alphabetically. (Internet Explorer drops the *www.* that precedes most names before sorting and displaying the list.) Clicking a site name displays a list of all the pages you visited at that site. To revisit a page that's listed on the History bar, click its title.

**TIP**

To determine precisely when you last visited a page that's listed on the History bar, right-click the page title and choose Properties. Because some pages have similar (or identical) titles, you can sometimes use the time to determine which page you want to revisit.

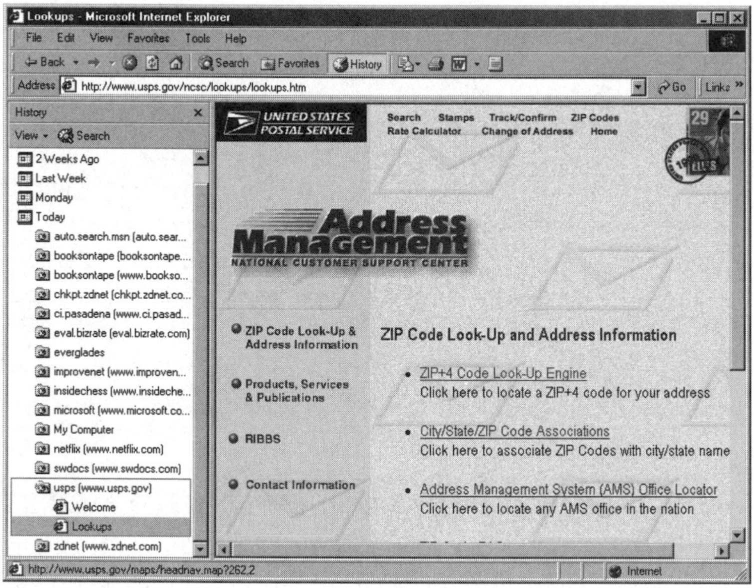

**FIGURE 18-3.**

The History bar makes it easy to return to pages you've already visited.

## Sorting the History List

The History bar's default view organizes the historical list by the date you visited each site. Clicking the View button at the top of the History bar displays a menu with four options:

- **By Date.** Displays a hierarchy of dates, sites, and pages (the default view).

- **By Site.** Displays a two-level hierarchy: sites and pages.

- **By Most Visited.** Displays the 20 pages you have visited most often.

■ **By Order Visited Today.** Displays, in reverse order, all the pages you visited today.

## Searching the History List

Often the page titles alone aren't enough to help you find a specific page you want to revisit—particularly on a site that uses the same title for all its pages. Fortunately, there's an alternative to relying on page titles and your memory for finding pages in your history.

To search your history list:

**1** Display the History bar.

**2** Click the Search button at the top of the History bar.

**3** Type a word or phrase that appears on the page you want to find.

**4** Click Search Now.

Internet Explorer searches the content of all the pages in your history list and displays matching results in the History bar. Click a result to display that page.

## Deleting Items from History

If you need to cover your tracks, you can remove any item from history. You can delete an individual page, a site (and all the pages it contains), or a date (and all the sites and pages it contains). Simply right-click the item you want to delete, and choose Delete.

You can obliterate your entire browsing history with a visit to the Internet Options dialog box. (Choose Internet Options from the Tools menu to display it.) On the General tab, shown in Figure 18-4 on the next page, click the Clear History button to do the deed.

> **NOTE**

> The History folder contains only pointers to the pages you've visited; the contents of those pages (that is, the pages' text, graphics, and media files) are stored in the Temporary Internet Files folder. Therefore, if you're intent on hiding your past, you need to delete the files in that folder. The Delete Files button on the General tab does just that.

Internet Explorer automatically deletes items from the history list after a period of time that you can specify. On the General tab in the Internet Options dialog box, use the Days To Keep Pages In History box to set the number of days' history you want to keep. The default is 20 days.

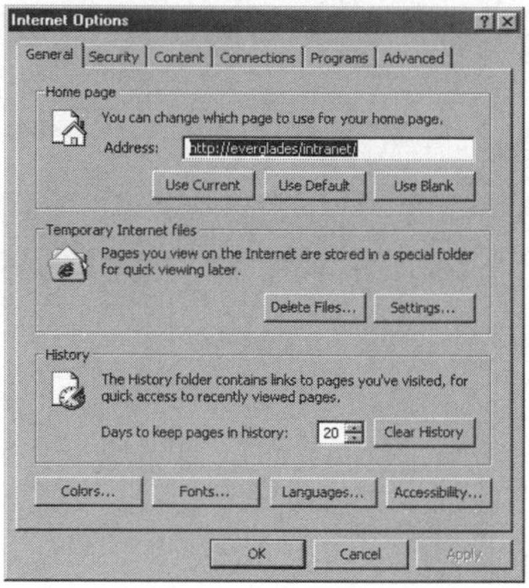

**FIGURE 18-4.**
On the General tab, you can set the number of days you want to keep pages in history. You can also delete all history items.

## Keeping Track of Your Favorite Pages

As you surf the Web and discover pages that you like, you'll probably want a way to get back to those pages easily. Internet Explorer provides a series of Favorites commands and the Favorites bar for exactly this purpose. You can have as many favorite pages as you like.

Using Favorites commands, you can create a list of your favorite pages and organize them into folders. Then, to go to a favorite page, you simply select the page you want from the Favorites menu. The Favorites menu also appears in Windows Explorer and (optionally) on your Start menu, so you can return to a favorite site easily, even if Internet Explorer isn't currently running. (You can also add file folders and document files to the Favorites menu. Choosing a file folder from the menu opens it in Windows Explorer; choosing a document file opens the file in its parent program.)

⭐ TIP

> **Show Just Your Recent Favorites**
> If your Favorites menu becomes too long, you can enable an option to make it show only the favorites you've visited recently. (You can see the rest of your favorites by clicking the arrow at the bottom of each menu.) To enable this option, open the Tools menu, choose Internet Options, and click the Advanced tab. Select Enable Personalized Favorites Menu (under Browsing).

The Favorites bar places links to your favorite pages in a pane on the left side of the Internet Explorer window for even easier access. To display the Favorites bar, click the Favorites button, shown in Table 18-1 on page 323. Figure 18-5 shows a Favorites bar.

**FIGURE 18-5.**

The Favorites bar provides a convenient way to access sites that you've marked as important to you.

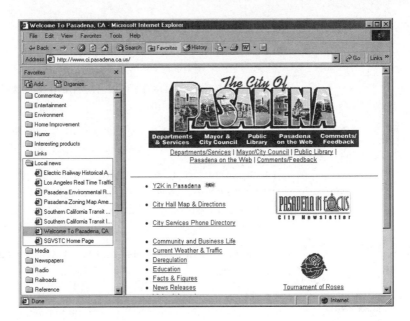

## Adding an Item to Favorites

The Add To Favorites command allows you to create a favorite-page listing for the page you're currently viewing. To add the Web page you are currently viewing to your Favorites list:

**1** Open the Add Favorite dialog box in any of these ways:

- Open the Favorites menu and choose Add To Favorites.

- Right-click the page (but not on a link) and choose Add To Favorites from the shortcut menu.

- Click the Add button at the top of the Favorites bar.

**SEE ALSO**

For more information about offline pages and synchronizing, see "Working Offline," page 342.

**2** If you want to make the page available when you're not connected to the Internet, select Make Available Offline. And if you want Internet Explorer to periodically synchronize the page (that is, download any updates), click Customize to launch the Offline Favorite Wizard.

**3** In the Name text box, make any changes you want to the name of the page.

**4** If you want to place your new favorite in a folder within Favorites

- Click the Create In button. The dialog box expands to display a folder hierarchy.

- Select an existing folder; or click the New Folder button, type a name for your new folder, and then click OK.

Organizing favorites in folders lets you group your favorite pages logically. After you create a new folder, the Favorites menu includes a cascading item with a folder icon that has the name of the folder you created.

**5** Click the OK button. This creates a favorite-page listing for the current page.

 **TIP**

Press Ctrl+D to instantly add the current page to the top level of the Favorites menu, bypassing the Add Favorite dialog box.

**TIP**

### Adding Favorites with Drag and Drop

If the Favorites bar is displayed, you can use drag and drop to add a page to your favorites. Drag the icon for the current page from the Address bar to the Favorites bar. A horizontal line indicates where the page will be added. (If you want to add the favorite to a folder, hover the mouse pointer over the folder momentarily and the folder opens.)

You can also drag a link from Internet Explorer's document area to the Favorites bar.

## Using the Organize Favorites Command

The Organize Favorites command allows you to view, organize, and modify your favorite places. Any of these steps opens the Organize Favorites dialog box:

- Open the Favorites menu and choose Organize Favorites.

- Click the Organize button at the top of the Favorites bar.

- Press Ctrl+B.

To open a folder, simply click it. When you click a folder or favorite place, information about the selected item appears in the lower left corner of the dialog box, as shown in Figure 18-6.

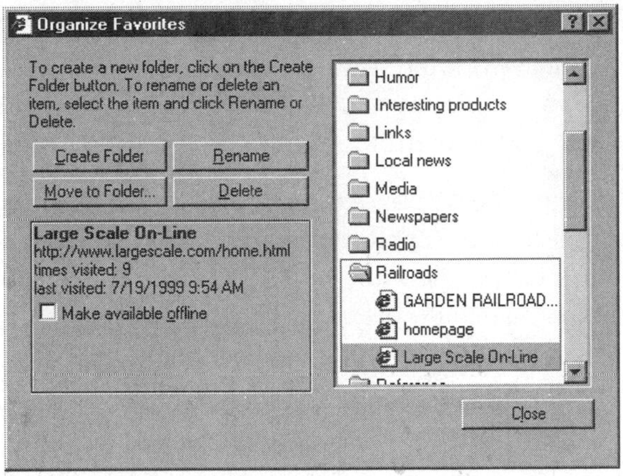

**FIGURE 18-6.**
The Organize Favorites dialog box provides a convenient way to move, rename, or delete items in your Favorites folder.

The buttons in the Organize Favorites dialog box provide an obvious and quick way to create new folders, rename or delete items, and organize items as you see fit. You might prefer these easier, but less intuitive, tricks:

- Drag favorites or folders to move them to another folder or change their order.

- Press Alt+Up arrow or Alt+Down arrow to move the selected favorite or folder up or down within the list.

- Right-click favorites or folders to see the usual shortcut menus.

**Organizing Favorites Using the Favorites Bar**
The Favorites bar provides an easy way to move, rename, or delete favorites. To move a favorite, simply drag it from one location on the Favorites bar to another. To rename or delete a favorite, right-click it and choose Rename or Delete.

## Using Search to Find New Sites

The Internet is a vast repository of information, but sometimes it's difficult to find the information you need. The Search feature in Internet Explorer provides easy access to search providers that comb the Internet for the words or topics that interest you. You can invoke the Search feature in two ways: by typing into the Address bar or by using the Search bar.

## Searching from the Address Bar

To search from the Address bar, type *go*, *find*, or *?*, followed by the words you want to search on. Then press Enter or click the Go button at the right side of the Address bar.

When you search by typing your query into the Address bar, by default Internet Explorer displays the page that most nearly matches your request, and it also opens the Search bar, where it displays a list of other matching pages.

> To change the search provider that Internet Explorer uses for Address bar searches or to change how it displays results, click the Customize button at the top of the Search bar. In the Customize Search Settings dialog box, click Autosearch Settings. Then select a search provider and an action.

## Using the Search Bar

To use the Search bar:

1   Click the Search button, shown in Table 18-1 on page 323. (If the Search bar already displays results—for example, because of a query you entered into the Address bar—click the New button at the top of the Search bar to clear the decks for a new search.)

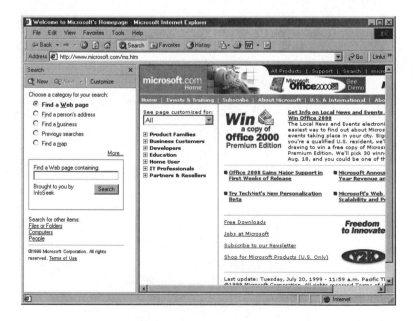

2  Select the option for the type of Internet search you want to conduct:

- **Find A Web Page.** Searches for Web pages that contain the words or phrases you type.

- **Find A Person's Address** and **Find A Business.** Search directory listings. *For more information, see "Finding People on the Internet," page 315.*

- **Previous Searches.** Repeats one of your 10 most recent searches.

- **Find A Map.** Searches for a map of a particular address or location.

- **Look Up A Word.** Searches for a dictionary, encyclopedia, or thesaurus entry.

- **Find A Picture.** Searches for an image.

- **Find In Newsgroups.** Searches for newsgroup postings that contain the words or phrases you type.

(If not all options are shown, click the More link.)

3  Enter the requested information, and then click Search.

In a moment, the results of your query appear in the Search bar.

4  Click one of the result links, and the page appears in Internet Explorer's document area.

⭐ **TIP**

For more details about a particular search result, hover the mouse pointer over the result link, and a ScreenTip appears with information about that page. Most often, this information includes the page title, the first few sentences, and the address for the page. This helps you narrow down your search without having to download another page.

If you found the page you're interested in, you can close the Search bar. But if you want to visit another page that appears in the results list, simply click the one you want to see. You can click links on the page you display or use other methods for navigating the Web, and your most recent search results remain available on the Search bar; if at any time you want to try another result, you can click its link on the Search bar.

⭐ **TIP**

If you're not satisfied with the results of the first search provider, click the Next button at the top of the Search bar to display the results from a different search provider.

## Changing Search Options

Internet Explorer provides access to most of the popular Internet search providers. Because each provider offers different features and maintains its own Web pages, you might get different results by trying the same search with different providers.

To specify the provider for each type of search:

**1** Click the Customize button at the top of the Search bar.

The Customize Search Settings dialog box appears.

**2** Select the check box for each type of search you want to include on the Search bar.

**3** For each type of search, select the check boxes for the search providers you want to use.

**4** To set the order in which search providers are used (this determines which provider's results appear first, as well as the order of the remaining providers displayed by opening the list on the Next button of the Search bar), select a provider in the list. Then click the arrows located under the list to move the selected provider up or down within the list.

> **NOTE**

> If you want to use only one search provider for all types of searches, in the Customize Search Settings dialog box, select Use One Search Service For All Searches, and then select the provider you want. Internet Explorer version 5 then updates the Search bar to show the user interface for the provider you choose, mimicking the behavior of the Search bar in Internet Explorer version 4.

## Finding Related Topics

Internet Explorer offers one more tool in its Web-search arsenal: the Show Related Links command. To display a list of links that are similar to the currently displayed page, open the Tools menu and choose Show Related Links. The Search bar appears (if it's not already displayed), populated with a list of related sites. (See Figure 18-7.)

**FIGURE 18-7.**
The Show Related Links command displays links to sites that are similar to the currently displayed page.

V

Sharing and Communicating

> **Tips for Successful Searches**
>
> Searching for information on the Internet can be a tricky task. Here are some simple tips to help you find what you're looking for much easier and faster.
>
> **Be specific.** Whenever you type a query, use as many detailed words as possible. If you're searching for recipes for chocolate chip cookies, searching for "cookies" returns many results that aren't useful. Instead, search for "chocolate chip cookie recipes." The more words you use, the more likely you'll find good results.
>
> **Use quotation marks.** Enclose phrases in quotation marks so that the search provider considers only the entire phrase—and not its component words.
>
> **Try different search providers.** Each search provider has its own algorithms and techniques for finding the best pages to match your query—and none of them indexes the entire Web. The results you get from one provider might be completely different from another. So if you're having trouble with your favorite search provider, try a different one.
>
> **Look for a tips or advanced link in the Search bar.** Some search providers include such links with the search results. Follow these links to see specific ways (such as special characters or key words) to refine your search. Special characters and other tricks you can use are different for each search provider.

# Working Offline

Most of the time, you'll use Internet Explorer while you're connected to the Internet. However, Internet Explorer is perfectly capable of displaying Web pages even when you're not connected—provided the pages themselves are available offline. Working offline allows you to browse when you don't have an Internet connection (for example, while you're traveling or when another family member is using the phone line), and it allows you to reduce the time of your Internet connection, which is particularly valuable in areas that charge for Internet use on a per-minute basis. Or if you're frustrated with the speed of your Internet connection, you can have Internet Explorer visit your favorite Web sites at night and then deliver the goods for you to read offline the following morning.

To switch Internet Explorer from online to offline mode, choose Work Offline from the File menu. This action doesn't terminate the current connection. However, the next time you take an action that would ordinarily cause Internet Explorer to create a connection to the

Internet, that connection doesn't take place. Instead, Internet Explorer searches local storage for the requested Internet resource.

**TIP**

> If you use a dial-up connection to connect to the Internet, you can begin an offline session by clicking the Work Offline button in the Dial-Up Connection dialog box.

If Internet Explorer can't find a document that you want to read offline, it displays the dialog box shown in Figure 18-8. You can then either click Connect to let the program search online, or you can click Stay Offline. Clicking the latter button is effectively the same as clicking Cancel in other dialog boxes: the dialog box closes and Internet Explorer's display remains unchanged.

**FIGURE 18-8.**
If Internet Explorer can't find your document in offline mode, you can click the Connect button to look for it online.

While reading a page offline, you can click any of its links to hop to a different document. If the document to which you hop is also available offline, everything works in this mode exactly as it would online. If not, you see the dialog box shown in Figure 18-8.

**TIP**

> If a linked document isn't available offline, the mouse pointer that appears when you point to the link changes from a hand to a hand plus a barred circle.

To switch back to online mode, simply choose Work Offline a second time. This doesn't immediately connect you to the Internet, but it clears the check mark beside the command. The next time you ask Internet Explorer to fetch a Web page, it connects rather than searching locally.

## Making Pages Available Offline

Pages become available offline in one of three ways:

**? SEE ALSO**
For more information about the cache, see "Controlling the Cache," page 373.

- Automatically, as part of the cache. Internet Explorer stores pages that you have visited recently in a *cache*. One purpose of the cache is to make it possible for you to work with documents offline; when you request a page, Internet Explorer first looks in the cache. (Another purpose of the cache is to speed up access to Web pages while you're online.)

This approach is hit-or-miss, however. As the cache fills up with newer pages, older pages are deleted—so a page you want might not be available any more. And the cached information might not be current; ordinarily, it gets updated only when you view it while you're online.

**? SEE ALSO**

For more information about saving files, see "Saving a Web Page to Disk," page 351.

- When you save a Web page. Using the Save As command on the File menu, you can save the current page in a folder. In the Save As Type box, if you select either Web Page, Complete, or Web Archive, Single File, Internet Explorer saves all the files you need to view the page offline, including graphics, frames, and style sheets. To view the page later, use the Open command on the File menu to browse to the saved file's location.

- When you make a favorite page available offline. Pages included on the Favorites menu have a Make Available Offline option. If you select this option (as described in the following sections), the page is always available offline. Optionally, you can tell Internet Explorer to connect to the Internet periodically and synchronize the stored offline version with the latest Internet version (in other words, download an updated version of the page if one exists).

The last method offers the greatest flexibility and possibilities for automation.

> **NOTE**
>
> Internet Explorer version 4 included subscriptions and channels. Although the sometimes confusing monikers and sometimes confusing procedures for using them are no longer used in version 5, the functionality of these features remains. Both names refer to a type of offline file that is periodically updated. If you upgraded from a system running Internet Explorer version 4, the channels now appear in the Favorites list rather than occupying a separate Explorer bar.

## Adding a Page to Your Offline Web Pages List

Pages that you make available offline must be in your Favorites folder. You can add the page to your offline Web pages list (that is, make it available offline) when you create the favorite or at any time later.

To add a page to your Favorites folder and make it available offline:

1  Display the page, and then choose Add To Favorites.

2  In the Add Favorite dialog box, select Make Available Offline.

**3** Change the name and location of the favorite if you like. *For more information, see "Adding an Item to Favorites," page 335.*

If you click OK at this point, your offline Web page will have the following properties:

- Internet Explorer synchronizes (updates) the page only when you use the Synchronize command—not on a predetermined schedule.

- When you synchronize the page, Internet Explorer doesn't include any pages reached by the links on the page.

- Internet Explorer assumes that you don't need to supply a name and password to access the page.

If you want to change any of these settings, click the Customize button in the Add Favorite dialog box to start the Offline Favorite Wizard.

To change other properties, go ahead and set up the favorite page and then visit the favorite's properties dialog box, as described in the following section. *For more information, see "Changing Offline Web Page Settings," on the next page.*

To make an existing favorite available offline:

**1** Open the existing favorite page's properties dialog box. (Right-click its entry on the Favorites menu or on the Favorites bar and choose Properties from the shortcut menu.)

**TIP**

Don't bother with the shortcut menu's Make Available Offline command. It launches the Offline Favorite Wizard—forcing you to step through several pages even if you don't want to change any default settings—and it doesn't offer many of the options that are available in the properties dialog box.

**2** On the Web Document tab of the page's properties dialog box, select Make This Page Available Offline.

If you click OK at this point, your offline Web page will have the same properties listed above. You can change these settings and others by visiting the Schedule and Download tabs, as described in the following section.

**TIP**

As an alternative to this procedure, choose Organize Favorites from the Favorites menu, select a favorite page, and select the Make Available Offline check box.

# Changing Offline Web Page Settings

The properties dialog box for an offline Web page is the place where you can set up a synchronization schedule, determine exactly what gets downloaded, and set up e-mail notification of changes. Do one of the following to view the properties dialog box:

- Right-click its entry on the Favorites menu or on the Favorites bar and choose Properties from the shortcut menu.

- Choose Organize Favorites from the Favorites menu, select the page, and click Properties.

## Setting Up a Synchronization Schedule

By default, Internet Explorer synchronizes your locally stored copy of an offline Web page with the original version only when you choose Synchronize from the Tools menu. Using the Schedule tab in the properties dialog box, you can set up a schedule for synchronizations. At the appointed times, Internet Explorer connects to the Internet (if you're not already connected) and updates the offline page by downloading the current version of the online page.

To set up a synchronization schedule:

**1** On the Schedule tab of the page's properties dialog box, select Use The Following Schedule(s).

**2** If the schedule you want to use isn't in the list, click Add.

The New Schedule dialog box appears.

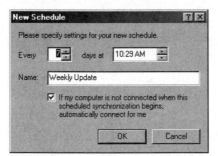

**3** Specify the number of days between updates and the time you want the updates to occur, and give the schedule a name. Select the check box if you want to connect to the Internet at the appointed time. (If you don't select the box and you're not already connected to the Internet, the connection dialog box waits for your go-ahead.) Then click OK.

**4**  Select the check box next to each named schedule you want to use for this page.

---

⭐ **TIP**

### Creating Complex Schedules

The New Schedule dialog box lets you set up schedules that update, at most, once per day. To update more frequently, you can create several schedules. But there's a better way: Set up a daily schedule, and then, on the Schedule tab, select the schedule and click Edit. In the schedule's properties dialog box that appears, click the Schedule tab. Here you can schedule updates on any of several intervals or upon certain events, on certain days of the week or month, and create multiple schedules. And by clicking the Advanced button, you can schedule updates as often as every minute and set an ending time for scheduled updates. *For more information about advanced scheduling options, see "Using Offline Files," page 192.*

---

⭐ **TIP**

### Preventing Synchronization While Traveling

It can be annoying when Internet Explorer attempts to make a dial-up connection while you're away from a phone line. To prevent such interruptions, on the Schedule tab of the properties dialog box for the offline page, select the synchronization schedule and click Edit. Then, on the Settings tab, select Don't Start The Task If The Computer Is Running On Batteries.

---

## Setting Up Download and E-Mail Notification Options

Visit the Download tab in the properties dialog box (shown in Figure 18-9, on the next page) in the following circumstances:

■ You want to change the level to which Internet Explorer downloads linked pages.

The default is zero, which means you get only the offline page—but not any pages that are reached by links on the original page. You can specify up to three levels, but be aware that the amount of material that Internet Explorer will have to download increases exponentially as you select deeper levels of links.

If you choose to include linked pages, you can limit the download to include only links to other pages at the same site (this prevents downloading pages linked to banner ads, for example) or only links to HTML pages. (Click Advanced to set the latter option.)

- You want to change the kinds of items that Internet Explorer downloads—for example, to exclude images or add sound and video. (Click the Advanced button.)

- You want to impose a maximum download size for the page.

- You want to receive e-mail notification when the page changes. (Enter your e-mail address and the name of your mail server; this feature works only with SMTP-based mail systems, which excludes many Internet mail accounts.)

- The page requires a user name and password for access. (Click the Login button.)

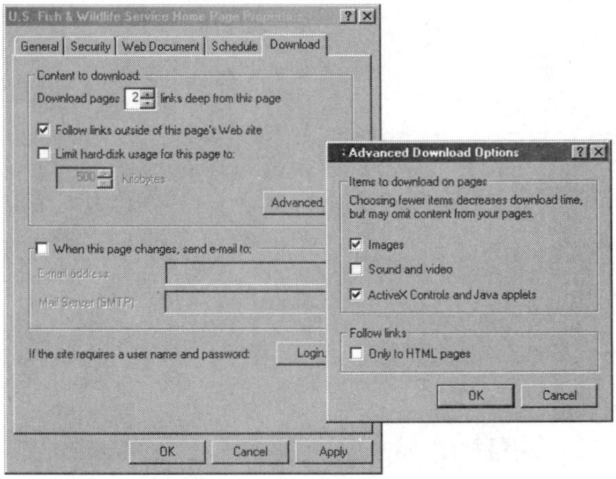

**FIGURE 18-9.**
The Download tab lets you determine what gets downloaded. Clicking Advanced displays the Advanced Download Options dialog box.

## Updating Offline Web Pages Manually

You don't have to wait for the scheduled update time to check on the status of a favorite Web page. To update it manually, right-click its entry on the Favorites menu or on the Favorites bar and choose Synchronize from the shortcut menu.

**SEE ALSO**
For more information about synchronizing offline pages and files, see "Using Offline Files," 192.

You can also perform a manual update of all your offline Web pages (and offline files) at once by choosing Synchronize from the Tools menu. Select the pages you want to update, and then click Synchronize.

## Removing Files from Your Offline List

To remove an entry from your Offline Web Pages list:

Open the Tools menu and choose Synchronize.

The Items To Synchronize dialog box appears, and it lists all your offline Web pages.

**2** Select the page you want to remove, and then click Properties.

**3** On the Web Document tab, clear the Make This Page Available Offline check box.

⭐ **TIP**

To temporarily stop synchronizing a particular offline page, clear its check box in the Items To Synchronize dialog box. Windows retains the settings you make here so that you don't need to clear the check box each time you synchronize.

# Working with Web Pages

Surfing the Web with Internet Explorer is fine, but what can you do with the information you find? This section describes how to do the following:

- Print a Web page
- Save a Web page as a document on your computer
- Create a shortcut to a page that you can reuse or share with others
- Send a Web page or a shortcut to someone else
- Use a displayed image as your desktop wallpaper
- Search for text within a page

## Printing a Web Page

❓ **SEE ALSO**

For more information about printing, see "Printing from a Program," page 216.

Internet Explorer allows you to print any Web page; simply click the Print button (see Table 18-1 on page 323) or open the File menu and choose Print. If you choose the File-menu route, you'll notice that the Print dialog box has sprouted an Options tab with features specifically for printing Web pages, as shown in Figure 18-10, on the next page.

- The Print Frames section lets you specify how you want to print a page's frames. Some Web pages are made up of multiple frames, which are much like window panes—except that you often can't see the divider between the frames. If you select Only The Selected Frame, Internet Explorer prints the frame that you last clicked. The Print Frames options aren't available if the current page doesn't use frames.

- If you select Print All Linked Documents, Internet Explorer prints the current page and also retrieves and prints all the pages that have links on the current page. Although this option can be useful in some cases, use it with care or you might end up with a lot of unneeded printouts!

- The Print Table Of Links check box lets you print a list of all the links in the current page along with their addresses.

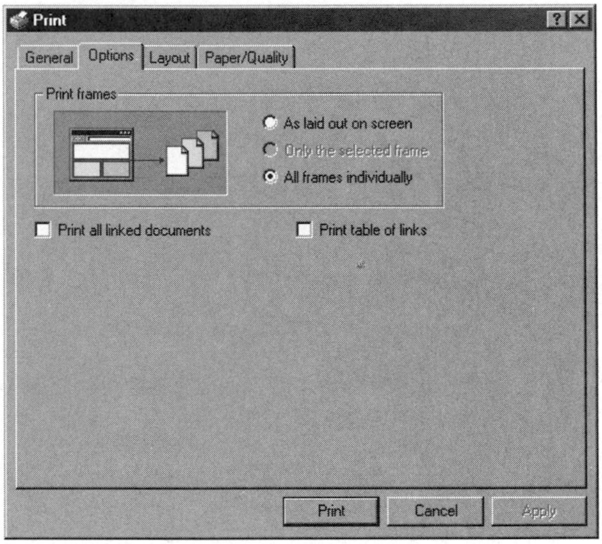

**FIGURE 18-10.**

Internet Explorer adds some unique features to the Options tab in the Print dialog box.

By default, Internet Explorer prints the title of the Web page and the page number at the top of each printed page, and the address of the Web page and the date at the bottom. You can change these default headers and footers, as well as the page margins, by opening the File menu and choosing Page Setup. (See Figure 18-11.)

⭐ TIP

You don't have to wait for a page to arrive completely before printing. If you click the Print button or choose the Print command while Internet Explorer is still downloading your page, the program waits until the entire page has arrived and then executes the command.

**FIGURE 18-11.**
To learn what the codes in the Header and Footer boxes do, click the Help button and then click the Header or Footer box.

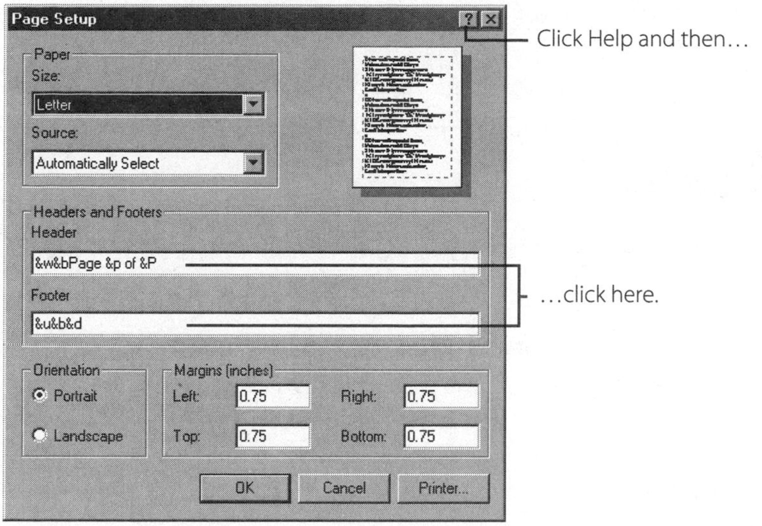

Click Help and then…

…click here.

# Saving a Web Page to Disk

With Internet Explorer you can save any Web page as a file on your computer. However, because most Web pages are created using HTML, you must consider what format to save them in. When you choose the Save As command from the File menu, you can save a Web page in any of four different formats, which you select in the Save As Type box:

- **Web Page, Complete.** Saves all files necessary to display the page, including graphics, sounds, video, frames, and style sheets, in their original format.

- **Web Archive, Single File.** New in Internet Explorer version 5; combines all information necessary to display the page in a single file. This is the most convenient option, but be aware that you might not be able to open the file with browsers other than Internet Explorer version 5 or later.

- **Web Page, HTML Only.** Saves only the current HTML page, which doesn't include any graphics, sounds, or other files.

- **Text File.** Saves only the text from the current page in an ordinary text file.

If you save the page in either Web Page format, all the HTML formatting codes remain intact, but you need a Web browser (such as Internet

Explorer), an HTML editor (such as Microsoft FrontPage), or another program capable of rendering HTML (such as Microsoft Word) to view it properly. If you save the page in text format, you lose all the HTML formatting codes, but you can load the text in almost any program.

> If you want to save only a particular graphics image, right-click the image and choose Save Picture As.

# Creating Shortcuts to Web Pages

**SEE ALSO**

For more information about shortcuts, see "Adding Shortcuts to Your Desktop," page 54.

With Internet Explorer, you can create a shortcut to any Web page. Once you create an Internet shortcut, you can keep it on the desktop, send it in an e-mail message to your friends, or embed it within a document in another program.

To create a shortcut for the currently displayed Web page, right-click the page (avoiding a graphic or a link) and choose Create Shortcut. Alternatively, open the File menu and choose Send, Shortcut To Desktop. Either method creates a shortcut on your desktop.

Once the shortcut is created, you can move it, copy it, or rename it as you see fit. To use the shortcut, simply launch it like any other shortcut, and Internet Explorer will take you to that Web page. You can use the shortcut even when Internet Explorer isn't running; like other document shortcuts, shortcuts to Internet destinations launch their associated program—in this case, Internet Explorer—if it's not already running.

**TIP**

> You can create a shortcut to the target of any link on a page by dragging the link to your desktop or to a folder.

# Sending Web Pages to Others

With Internet Explorer, you can send a Web page (or a shortcut to a Web page) to someone else via e-mail. The Send submenu on the File menu offers two commands for this purpose. Choose Page By E-Mail to send the complete page (the recipient must have an e-mail program that can display HTML files), or choose Link By E-Mail to send a shortcut. If you send a shortcut, the recipient can launch it to download the Web page. (As an alternative to the menu commands, click the Mail button, shown in Table 18-1 on page 323, and then select Send Page or Send A Link.)

Choosing either command launches your mail program's new-message window. Specify the recipient's name or address in the To box, click Send, and the page or shortcut is on its way.

## Turning a Web Image into Wallpaper

**? SEE ALSO**

For more information about wallpaper, see "Using Wallpaper," page 69.

If you see an image (or a Web page background) that you like on a Web page, Internet Explorer can save that image and install it as your desktop wallpaper. To do this, simply right-click any image in Internet Explorer. On the shortcut menu that appears, choose Set As Wallpaper to use the image as your Windows wallpaper.

## Finding Text on a Web Page

Internet Explorer's Find command helps you to find a specific word or phrase on a Web page. To find text:

1   Display the Web page on which you want to find a specific word or phrase. (The Find command works on only a single page at a time.)

2   Open the Edit menu and choose Find (On This Page).

3   Type the text you are looking for. You can type part of a word or the entire word.

4   Click the Find Next button, and Internet Explorer takes you to the first occurrence of your search text on the page.

To find additional matches, click the Find Next button repeatedly.

# Listening to Internet Radio Programs

Internet Explorer, in combination with Microsoft Windows Media Player, lets you listen to Internet radio broadcasts, even as you continue using Internet Explorer to view other pages. A wide variety of radio programs is available from locations around the globe, including simulcasts from traditional broadcast stations as well as Internet-only "radio" stations.

V

Sharing and Communicating

To listen to the radio:

**1** Display the Radio toolbar. (On the View menu, choose Toolbars, Radio.)

**2** Click the Radio Stations button and choose Radio Station Guide.

This opens Microsoft's Radio Station Guide, one of many such guides and a good starting point for your radio exploration. (See Figure 18-12.)

**3** Click a link on the Radio Station Guide page to begin listening to a station.

**FIGURE 18-12.**

The Radio toolbar and the Radio Station Guide page are your entrée to radio stations around the world.

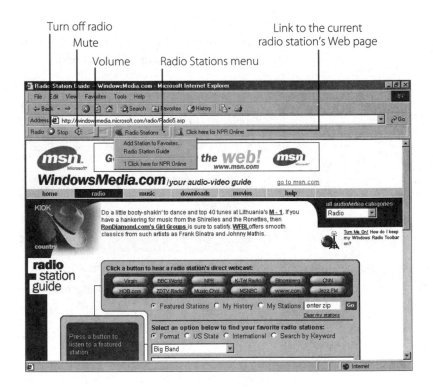

Turn off radio
Mute
Volume
Radio Stations menu
Link to the current radio station's Web page

 **NOTE**

You can browse to other pages while you continue listening, but closing Internet Explorer "turns off" the radio.

**TIP**

When you find a station you like, add it to your favorites list. On the Radio toolbar, click the Radio Stations button and then choose Add Station To Favorites. The station is thereafter available from the Favorites menu or Favorites bar.

# Downloading Files from the Internet

> **Ⓧ CAUTION**
>
> Unless you're sure of a file's provenance, you should save it to disk, close other programs you have open, and scan the file for viruses before you launch it.

On some Web sites, files are available for you to download to your computer. These files are usually shown in Internet Explorer as links. To download a file, click the link that represents the file. You will then see a dialog box like the one shown in Figure 18-13.

If the file you're downloading is a sound file or video clip that you want to play, a program that you want to run, or a document that you want to display immediately in a word processor or other program, select the first option (depending on the type of file, either Open This File . . . or Run This Program . . .). Otherwise, select Save This File (or Program) To Disk.

**FIGURE 18-13.**

When you download a file, Internet Explorer lets you launch the file immediately or save it to disk.

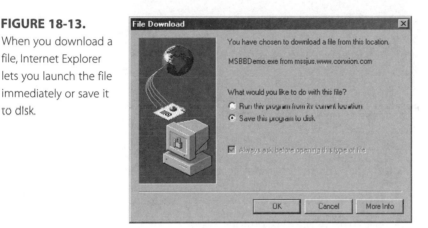

If you select the first option, Windows renders the data, just as it would if you launched an entry in a Windows Explorer window. If you select the save option, Internet Explorer presents a Save As dialog box before it begins downloading the data.

> **> NOTE**
>
> If you select the open or run option, the only copy that Internet Explorer saves on your computer is in the Temporary Internet Files folder. As its name suggests, files in this folder soon disappear as they're replaced by others—so if you want a copy of the file to use in the future, select the save option.

## Trusting Software Publishers

When you download a program or ActiveX control from a software publisher, you might see a security warning similar to the one shown in Figure 18-14. You can click Yes to go ahead with the download, No to cancel it, or More Info to read more about this publisher. If you find this kind of warning inconvenient and you trust that this publisher would never send you damaged goods, you can select the Always Trust check box at the bottom of the screen. This action adds the publisher's name to a list of trusted publishers.

**FIGURE 18-14.**

A dialog box like this appears whenever a publisher that is not on your "trusted" list tries to send an object that has a security certificate.

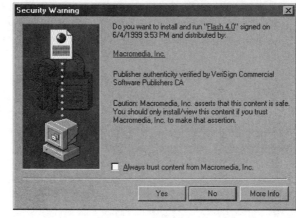

To view the list of trusted publishers:

**1** Choose Internet Options from the Tools menu.

**2** Click the Content tab.

**3** Click the Publishers button.

To revoke your trust in a publisher, select that publisher's name from the list and click the Remove button.

# Connecting to FTP, Gopher, and Telnet Sites

In addition to the ubiquitous HTTP protocol and the World Wide Web, the Internet is also home to FTP, Gopher, and Telnet sites. FTP and Gopher sites usually consist of lists of documents and files for downloading. Telnet sites allow you to interact with a host computer in much the same way you would if you were dialing up a bulletin board system (BBS). To connect to an FTP, Gopher, or Telnet site, enter the address for the site you want to connect to in the same way you would for a World Wide Web page. Just as with World Wide Web addresses, you can do this with the Address bar or with the File Open command.

What you see next depends on the type of site you're visiting.

- FTP sites look much like ordinary Windows Explorer windows. Icons represent folders and files, and you can choose your view (Large Icons, Small Icons, List, or Details) and sorting order using familiar Windows Explorer methods. You also use Windows Explorer procedures for opening, downloading (copying from the FTP site to your computer), uploading (copying in the other direction), deleting, and renaming files.

   What you can do at the FTP site depends on the permissions granted to you by the site administrator. Some sites are open to anonymous logons (that is, anybody can log on), whereas others require a user name and password. *For logon information, see the next section, "Logging On to Password-Secured FTP Sites."* On some sites, you can only view and download files; on others, you can also rename, delete, and upload files.

- For Gopher sites, Internet Explorer provides the same interface as it does for the World Wide Web. You simply click links to navigate through folders or to download files. FTP and Web sites have largely supplanted text-only Gopher sites, which are a dying breed in the rapidly evolving Internet.

- When you enter an address for a Telnet site, Internet Explorer opens a terminal program in a command prompt window, and you interact with your Telnet site using that program.

⭐ **TIP**

> Windows 2000 includes two Telnet programs. Telnet.exe is the text-based client that runs in a command prompt window, and it appears by default if you enter a Telnet address in Internet Explorer. HyperTerminal is a general-purpose communications program that you can use for Telnet sessions. *For information about HyperTerminal, see Chapter 23, "Using HyperTerminal."*

## Logging On to Password-Secured FTP Sites

The address for an FTP site that allows anonymous connections (no password required) looks much like that for a Web site. An anonymous connection to the Microsoft Corporation FTP site looks like this:

*ftp://ftp.microsoft.com*

To connect to an FTP server that requires you to provide your user name and password, use this format:

*ftp://*name:password*@ftp.microsoft.com*

(Replace *name* and *password* with the logon information assigned by the server administrator.)

⭐ **TIP**

> When you log on to an FTP site by including your name and password in the address, you can save the page as a shortcut or a favorite and you'll never need to enter the name and password again. *For information about favorites and shortcuts, see "Adding an Item to Favorites," page 335, and "Creating Shortcuts to Web Pages," page 352.* Be aware, however, that your password is saved as clear text, and anybody can glean your password by examining the properties dialog box for the favorite or shortcut—or by looking over your shoulder when the address is displayed on the Address bar.

You can also log on after you arrive at the FTP site. (If you connect to a secure FTP site without providing your credentials, you'll be rebuffed with an error message and you can't view any files.) Open the File menu (or right-click in the window) and choose Login As. Internet Explorer then displays a dialog box where you can identify yourself.

⭐ **TIP**

> To see who you're currently logged in as, look on the status bar or, if you're in Web view, look in the left side of the folder window.

# Using Security and Privacy Features

Security and privacy are related but somewhat distinct issues. *Security* means your ability to send sensitive data—your credit card numbers, for example—across the Internet without that data being intercepted by unauthorized parties. It also means your ability to screen out dangerous or objectionable content that might be coming toward you. *Privacy* means your ability to prevent Internet content providers and other parties from gathering information about you—demographic or marketing data, for example—that you'd rather they not have.

If you transact business over secure Web sites, you can be reasonably confident that third parties won't be able to intercept the information you send. In fact, thanks to encryption, you're almost certainly safer sending credit card information this way than you are sending it via fax or telephone. On the other hand, if you download a lot of material from the Internet, you probably know that there is no such thing as perfect security. There is always a chance that you might someday become the unwitting target of a malicious or incompetent programmer. The only surefire way to eliminate this hazard is not to use the Internet. If that drastic solution doesn't appeal to you, you might want to become familiar with Internet Explorer's security-zone feature.

We'll explore the concepts of security zones and secure Web sites in this section. We'll also look at how you can prevent Internet sites from gathering information about you by downloading cookies to your hard disk.

## Working with Secure Sites

Internet Explorer is a *secure browser*, which means it's capable of exchanging encrypted (secure) data with a secure Web site. A *secure Web site* is one that has been given a valid security certificate by a third-party agency such as RSA Data Security, Inc. When you're connected to a secure site, a padlock icon appears on the status bar, and whatever you upload to that site is automatically encrypted.

Internet Explorer supports three security protocols, called Secure Sockets Layer (SSL), Private Communications Technology (PCT), and Transport Layer Security (TLS). The goal of each of these protocols is to ensure privacy (no one can intercept your communications), authentication (you and the site you're visiting are not impostors), and integrity (data reaches the other end unscathed).

Internet Explorer automatically chooses the appropriate protocol for the secure site that you're using. But if you're interested in knowing what protocol a server supports or any other details about its security, you can find out as follows:

1 Log on to the secure site.

2 Open the File menu and choose Properties.

3 Click the Certificates button.

You'll see a dialog box similar to the one shown in Figure 18-15, on the following page. Here you can learn the name of the authority that issued your site's security certificate, the effective date and expiration date of that certificate, the protocol used, and so on.

**V**

Sharing and Communicating

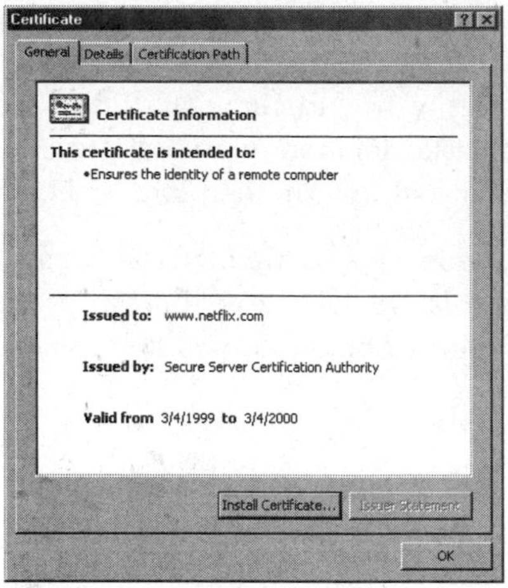

**FIGURE 18-15.**
This dialog box shows details about a secure Web site's security certificate, protocol, and other matters.

# Using Security Zones and Security Levels

Internet Explorer lets you assign any Web site to one of four categories, depending on the degree to which you trust the site. These four categories are called Trusted Sites zone, Local Intranet zone, Internet zone, and Restricted Sites zone. All sites are initially assigned to the Internet zone except sites that you access via an intranet. Internet Explorer automatically detects intranet sites and assigns them to the Local Intranet zone.

Each security zone is associated with a particular *security level*—a default configuration of defensive measures that Internet Explorer's designers consider appropriate for that zone. The Internet zone is given the medium security level, while the Local Intranet, Trusted Sites, and Restricted Sites zones are assigned the medium-low, low, and high security levels, respectively.

If you think that certain of the sites you use pose a higher than ordinary level of risk, you can move those sites to the Restricted Sites zone. On the other hand, if you find Internet Explorer's moderate safety measures intrusive with certain sites that you trust completely, you might want to assign these sites to the Trusted Sites zone.

To change a site's default zone assignment:

1 Choose Internet Options from the Tools menu and click the Security tab.

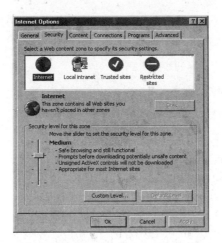

**2** Select the zone to which you want to assign the site, and then click the Sites button. (This button becomes active when you select any zone other than Internet zone.)

**3** In the ensuing dialog box, you'll see a list of sites that you've already assigned to this zone, along with a text box where you can enter the address for the new site. Enter the site's address into this text box and click the Add button.

> **★ TIP**
>
> To avoid typing errors when entering a site's address, first select the address on Internet Explorer's Address bar. Press Ctrl+C to copy the address to the Clipboard. Then use Ctrl+V to paste the address into the security-zone dialog box.

> **★ TIP**
>
> Microsoft Internet Explorer 5 Power Tweaks Web Accessories adds commands to the Tools menu that make it easier to add sites to the trusted and restricted zones. *For information about Web Accessories, see "Installing Web Accessories," page 371.*

## Redefining Security Levels

Internet Explorer has four predefined security levels, called high, medium, medium-low, and low. You can find out exactly what any of these security levels means, and, if none of the predefined security levels meets your requirements for a particular security zone, you can assign that security zone a custom security level.

To view or change settings for a security zone:

1 Choose Internet Options from the Tools menu and click the Security tab.

2 Select the zone you're interested in.

3 Click the Custom Level button.

Internet Explorer displays the dialog box shown in Figure 18-16. You can scroll through this dialog box to see exactly what potentially hazardous downloads are allowed, what kinds of downloads require you to answer a confirmation prompt, and so on. If you don't like what you see, you can change any of these settings. Internet Explorer then applies your custom settings, instead of its own predefined security level, to the selected zone. To return to the original settings, on the Security tab of the Internet Options dialog box, select the zone and click Default Level.

**FIGURE 18-16.**
You can use this dialog box to fine-tune the security level associated with a security zone.

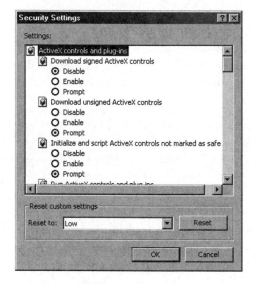

# Blocking Cookies

A *cookie*, in Internet parlance, is a bit of information about you and your preferences, deposited on your hard disk by a Web site that you've visited. Web sites use cookies to customize their offerings for particular users. If you've ever wondered, for example, how that giant bookstore in the ether knows so much about your taste in reading matter, the answer is that it reads your cookie every time you log on.

## Understanding Security Certificates

A *security certificate* is a statement issued by a third-party authority guaranteeing the identity of a Web site or person. Internet Explorer uses two kinds of certificates—site certificates and personal certificates. A personal certificate vouches for your identity. At this stage in the development of Internet commerce, a personal certificate's principal virtue is that it enables you to send encrypted e-mail. But you might at some time need to deal with a Web site that requires you to authenticate yourself by means of a personal certificate. *For information about obtaining and using a personal certificate, see "Using Digital Signatures and Encryption," page 412.*

A site certificate attests that a secure Web site is what it says it is—and not the work of an impostor. Site certificates, like personal certificates, have expiration dates. When you connect with a secure Web site, Internet Explorer makes sure that all the information on the site's certificate is valid and that the certificate hasn't expired. The program warns you if the certificate is invalid or not current by displaying a dialog box similar to the one shown below.

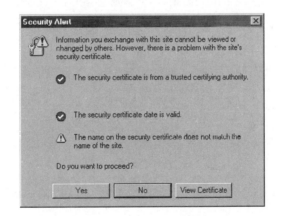

On the Content tab in the Internet Options dialog box, you'll find two buttons relating to security certificates. The Certificates button lets you inspect any personal certificates that have been installed on your computer and view a list of certifying authorities that are currently trusted by Internet Explorer. You can remove any that you don't want the program to trust.

The second button on the Content tab, Publishers, presents a list of software publishers that you have declared to be trustworthy. These publishers aren't guaranteed by a certifying authority. They are simply software sources that you, for the sake of convenience, have asked Internet Explorer to trust. *For more information about trusting publishers, see "Trusting Software Publishers," page 355.*

Cookies are stored in the %UserProfile%\Cookies folder. You can open your cookies in Notepad, but you'll find they're mostly indigestible—binary information that only a Web server can love.

In general, cookies are a convenience for end users. They make the Web sites you visit more responsive to your own needs and preferences. Cookies can contain only information that you provide; a Web site can't surreptitiously determine your e-mail address and place it in a cookie, for example. Nevertheless, some users do find them objectionable. If you want to keep Web sites from recording information about you on your own hard disk, you can either block cookies entirely or require Internet Explorer to display a confirmation prompt before downloading any cookie. To perform either of these tasks, visit the Security Settings dialog box shown in Figure 18-16 and scroll down the list of options until you come to the set labeled Cookies.

If you decide to have Internet Explorer prompt before accepting any cookies, you'll see a dialog box similar to the one shown in Figure 18-17 each time a site wants to send a cookie your way. If you tire of responding to these messages, you can return to the Internet Options dialog box or, more simply, select the check box before you click Yes.

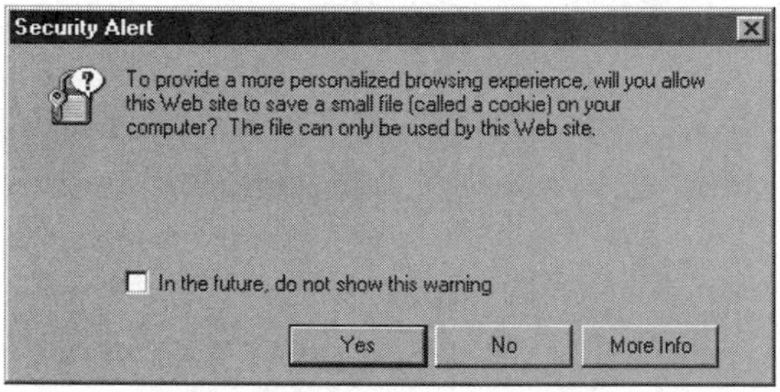

**FIGURE 18-17.**
You can ask Internet Explorer to prompt you before downloading any cookies, but you might tire of seeing messages like this.

## Blocking Pornography and Other Objectionable Content

Some Web sites provide information or pictures that you might find objectionable for you or your children. Internet Explorer provides a feature called Content Advisor to help you block the display of objectionable material. When Content Advisor is enabled, if a user tries to go to a Web page that is beyond the limits you set, Internet Explorer won't show the page, and instead displays a warning dialog box. Users who know the supervisor password can bypass the warning and view the page.

To set up Content Advisor:

**1**  Open the Tools menu, choose Internet Options, and click the Content tab.

**2**  Click Enable.

> The Content Advisor dialog box appears.

> NOTE

> After you enable Content Advisor, you can return to this dialog box by clicking Settings on the Content tab of the Internet Options dialog box, and then entering your supervisor password.

**3**  On the Ratings tab, select a category and then drag the slider to set the limits you want. As you move the slider, a description of the current setting appears below the slider. Repeat this step for each category, and then click OK.

> The Ratings tab contains a list of available rating systems and categories. By default, Internet Explorer comes with a system called RSACi, the Recreational Software Advisory Council's Internet rating system. The system has four categories: language, nudity, sex, and violence. Each category has five levels, numbered 0 through 4. A higher number indicates more explicit or intense content.

**4** If you haven't already set up a supervisor password, supply and confirm your supervisor password in the Create Supervisor Password dialog box that appears.

The supervisor password is the master key that lets you change the Content Advisor settings or bypass the Content Advisor protections. Write this password down in a safe place so that if you forget it, you won't be locked out of Internet Explorer.

The settings you make in Content Advisor apply to all users on your computer; you can't make separate settings for each user.

## Blocking Unrated Sites

Not all Internet content is rated. By default, Content Advisor blocks pages that don't have a rating, because Content Advisor has no way of knowing what types of content are on those pages. Just as when you attempt to view a site with ratings that exceed the permissible level you've defined, when you attempt to view an unrated site, you'll see a dialog box similar to the one shown in Figure 18-18.

**FIGURE 18-18.**

Content Advisor blocks pages with ratings beyond the limits you set and pages that aren't rated.

If you don't want this type of protection, you can change the default setting by clicking the General tab in the Content Advisor dialog box, shown in Figure 18-19, and selecting the Users Can See Sites That Have No Rating check box.

**FIGURE 18-19.**
The General tab lets you block unrated sites, bypass blocking, and change the supervisor password.

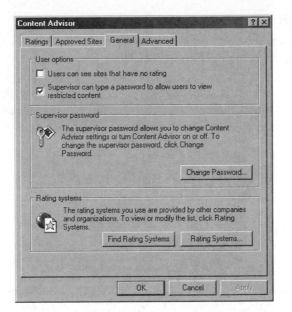

Because so many sites are unrated—including both "good" sites and "bad" sites—Content Advisor lets you create your own ratings for particular sites. To set up a list of sites that you want to allow or disallow, regardless of their claimed content rating, click the Approved Sites tab in the Content Advisor dialog box, shown in Figure 18-20. Type the site's address, and then click Always (to allow access) or Never (to prohibit access).

**FIGURE 18-20.**
The Approved Sites tab lets you effectively override a site's rating and provide a rating for unrated sites.

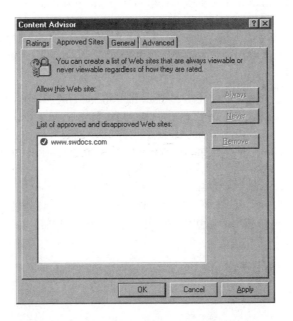

## Allowing a User to Bypass Blocking

Normally, your supervisor password is used only to turn the entire blocking mechanism on or off. If you want, however, you can allow a user to see a blocked page by supplying the password when he or she attempts to access the blocked Web page. To do this, display the Content Advisor dialog box and click the General tab. On the General tab, shown in Figure 18-19, select the Supervisor Can Type A Password To Allow Users To View Restricted Content check box.

## Turning Off Blocking

If you change your mind about blocking offensive material, simply display the Internet Options dialog box and click the Content tab. Click the Disable button and enter your supervisor password.

# Using Profile Assistant

Many Web sites request personal information, purportedly to help them deliver useful information to you. Internet Explorer provides a feature called Profile Assistant, which allows you to enter all your information once, and then control which Web sites have access to which kinds of information. Using Profile Assistant saves you from having to reenter the same information, such as your name and e-mail address, and it provides privacy safeguards.

When you visit a Web site that requests information from Profile Assistant, the request shows you the address of the requesting site, which information the site is requesting, how the information will be used, and whether the site has a secure connection. Before granting the request, you can verify that the site is legitimate, and you can choose which information you want Profile Assistant to provide, or you can refuse to give the site any information.

To configure Profile Assistant, choose Internet Options from the View menu. Click the Content tab, and then click the My Profile button. In the dialog box that appears, fill in the fields on each tab. (Remember, Web sites don't have access to this information until you explicitly give them permission.) Profile Assistant uses an Address Book record to store the information; you can select an existing record or create a new one. Click OK in the profile's properties dialog box, and then click OK in the Internet Options dialog box.

# Customizing Internet Explorer

If Internet Explorer's current setup is not to your liking, you can set a variety of options. For example, you can

- Specify a different home page (the page that appears when you start Internet Explorer)

- Select and arrange the toolbars you want

- Specify the pages that appear when you click an icon on the Links toolbar

- Add Web Accessories (program extensions that add features and functionality to Internet Explorer)

- Select colors for text, the window background, and links

- Select a font for unformatted text

- Control how much hard disk space Internet Explorer uses

- Specify when pages that you've already viewed should be updated

- Set miscellaneous options that control Internet Explorer's appearance, browsing speed, security, compatibility, and other features

To change several of these options, you use the Internet Options dialog box. To display the Internet Options dialog box, use one of the following methods:

- Choose Internet Options from Internet Explorer's Tools menu.

- Right-click the Internet Explorer icon on your desktop (not on the Quick Launch toolbar) and choose the Properties command.

- Launch Internet Options in Control Panel.

> **NOTE**
>
> Depending on how you get to it, the dialog box might be titled Internet Properties instead of Internet Options—but the content is the same.

**V**

**Sharing and Communicating**

# Changing the Home Page

The home page is the one that appears automatically when you open Internet Explorer (unless you begin by launching an Internet shortcut). You can return to the home page at any time by clicking the Home button on the Standard Buttons toolbar (see Table 18-1 on page 323), by pressing Alt+Home, or by choosing Home Page from the View menu's Go To submenu. You don't have to use the home page that Microsoft gives you; you can substitute any page you prefer.

To specify a different home page:

**1**  Display the page that you want to use as the new home page.

**2**  Display the Internet Options dialog box and click the General tab.

**3**  Click Use Current in the Home Page section, and then click OK.

Instead of displaying the page you want to use, you can type its address into the Address text box. If you use this method, don't click Use Current.

To restore Internet Explorer's original home page, return to the General tab of the Internet Options dialog box, and then click the Use Default button.

# Customizing the Toolbars

Like Windows Explorer, Internet Explorer has four toolbars: Standard Buttons, Links, Address Bar, and Radio. In addition, the menu bar is a "toolbar," and—except for the fact that you can't hide it altogether—you can move or resize it like any other toolbar.

You can display these toolbars in any combination. Open the View menu, choose Toolbars, and choose the toolbar's name from the submenu that appears. Choose the same command again to hide a toolbar.

As a quicker way to display or hide a toolbar, right-click an unoccupied area of any toolbar, which displays the same commands as the View menu's Toolbars command.

You can also tailor the appearance of the toolbars in the following ways:

- To expand the toolbar area, which can be displayed on one through five lines, drag the lower boundary of the toolbar area downward. To collapse a multiline toolbar, drag the lower boundary of the toolbar area upward.

■ To change the location or size of any of the toolbars, drag its handle (the vertical line at the left end of the toolbar). With this capability, you can combine two or more toolbars on a single line, place each on a line of its own, change their order, and change their width.

## Customizing the Links Toolbar

The Links toolbar provides convenient access to a handful of your most-favorite pages. By default, buttons on the Links toolbar take you to Microsoft-selected sites—but you can supplement or replace these with your own most-needed links. To add a link to the Links toolbar, use any of these techniques:

■ Display the page you want to add, and then drag the page icon from the Address bar to the Links toolbar.

■ Drag a link from a Web page to the Links toolbar.

■ Display the Favorites bar, and then drag a link to the Links folder on the Favorites bar.

You can also change the order of the buttons on the Links toolbar. Simply drag a button to the desired location.

To remove a Links toolbar button, right-click it and choose Delete.

## Installing Web Accessories

Internet Explorer has an extensible design, which means that new features and functionality can be added to the base program. You can find Internet Explorer Web Accessories at a number of Web sites, but a good place to start your search is at Microsoft's Web Accessories page (*www.microsoft.com/windows/ie/webaccess/*). Here you'll find

■ Explorer bars that add a separate pane with news updates, stock tickers, or links to related sites that continually update as you browse the Internet (See Figure 18-21, on the next page.)

■ Utilities that let you zoom in on images, customize your toolbars in new ways, add new menu commands, and more

To install one of the Web Accessories, follow the instructions at the Web site for downloading and installing. In most cases, you simply click a link to download and install in one step. (In others, you'll be instructed to click a link to download a file. After you complete the download, you open the file to run its setup program.) Then, in the case of Explorer bar additions, you need to stop and restart Internet

**V**

**Sharing and Communicating**

Explorer, and then choose the name of the bar from the View menu's Explorer Bar submenu.

**FIGURE 18-21.**

You can display standard Explorer bars, such as the History bar shown here, alongside Explorer bar Web Accessories, such as the New York Times Explorer bar.

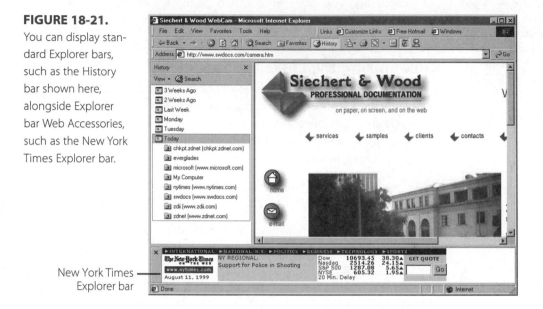

New York Times Explorer bar

## Selecting Colors

You can select the color used for ordinary text, links that you've already visited, links that you haven't visited, and the document area background. To change any of these color settings, display the Internet Options dialog box and click the General tab. Then click the Colors button to display the Colors dialog box, shown in Figure 18-22.

**FIGURE 18-22.**

You can specify colors for text, background, and links in the Colors dialog box.

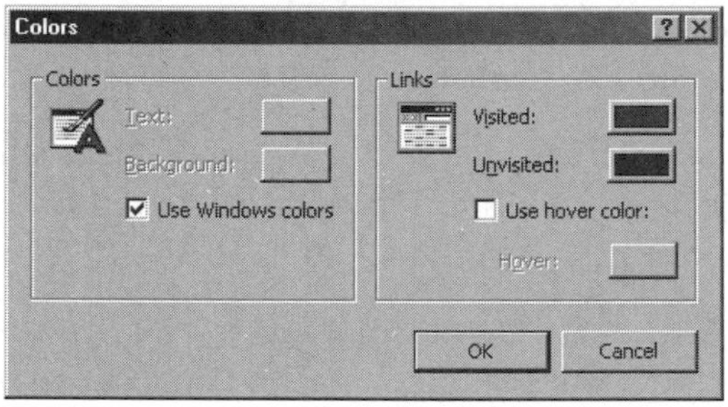

**SEE ALSO**

For information about Windows desktop colors, see "Changing Colors, Fonts, and Sizes," page 63.

By default, Internet Explorer uses the colors you specify in Control Panel's Display Properties dialog box for ordinary text and for the window background. To override these defaults, clear the Use Windows Colors check box.

Then, to specify the color for any of the four elements, click its button and then select a color in the palette that appears.

The Colors dialog box also lets you set the color to use for links that you hover the mouse pointer over. Select Use Hover Color, and then click the button and select a color in the palette that appears.

**NOTE**

> The colors you select in the Colors dialog box affect only documents that don't specify their own color settings, which override these settings.

**TIP**

> If you find it difficult to read a Web page that sets its own colors, tell Internet Explorer to ignore those color commands and use your own color settings for all text and backgrounds. On the General tab in the Internet Options dialog box, click Accessibility and then select Ignore Colors Specified On Web Pages.

## Selecting Fonts

**SEE ALSO**

For information about fonts, see Chapter 13, "Installing and Using Fonts."

Many Web pages include formatting codes that specify which fonts to use. Pages that don't include such codes display their text in one of two fonts that you can specify—one Web Page (proportionally spaced) font and one Plain Text (fixed-width or monospaced) font. To specify the fonts, click the Fonts button on the General tab in the Internet Options dialog box.

You can't specify a particular font size for text display—but you can select among five predefined sizes. To change the size of unformatted text in the Internet Explorer document area, choose the Text Size command from the View menu. A submenu offers choices from Smallest to Largest.

**TIP**

> If you find it difficult to read a Web page that sets its own fonts, tell Internet Explorer to ignore those font commands and use your own font and font size settings for all text. On the General tab in the Internet Options dialog box, click Accessibility and then select Ignore Font Styles Specified On Web Pages, Ignore Font Sizes Specified On Web Pages, or both.

## Controlling the Cache

Internet Explorer stores pages that you visit in a cache, which by default resides in the %UserProfile%\Local Settings\Temporary Internet Files folder. Internet Explorer uses these stored pages to speed the display of pages you've already visited. By default, these cached pages use as much as 3 percent of the drive on which they reside. If that's too much space (or not enough), you can change the cache size by displaying the Internet Options dialog box. On the General tab, click the Settings button to display the dialog box shown in Figure 18-23.

**FIGURE 18-23.**

You control the cache size in the Settings dialog box for temporary Internet files.

By default, if Internet Explorer finds a copy of the page you want in its cache, it uses the cached page instead of requesting another copy from the Web. Because Web pages change frequently, however, Internet Explorer checks once per session to see if the page on the Web is newer than the cached page. If the pages you're interested in never change (or you don't care if you see the latest version), you might want to override this behavior by selecting the Never option.

**Clearing the Cache Manually**

If you want to regain disk space used by the cache (or you want to eliminate all traces of the Web sites you've visited), clear the cache. To do that, display the Internet Options dialog box, click the General tab, and click Delete Files.

**Clearing the Cache Automatically**

To clear the cache every time you finish using Internet Explorer, display the Internet Options dialog box and click the Advanced tab. In the Settings list, select Empty Temporary Internet Files Folder When Browser Is Closed (near the bottom of the list, under Security).

# Setting AutoComplete Options

AutoComplete stores a list of Web sites you visit, information you enter into Web-based forms, and user names and passwords you use to gain access to password-secured sites. When you subsequently begin typing in Internet Explorer (into the Address bar, into a form, or into a password-entry box), AutoComplete displays a list of matching previous entries. To select one of these entries, click it; or press the Up arrow or Down arrow key to highlight it, and then press Enter.

To specify which entries AutoComplete saves:

1 Display the Internet Options dialog box and click the Content tab.

2 Click AutoComplete.

The AutoComplete Settings dialog box appears.

3 Select the check box for each type of entry you want AutoComplete to save. If you want AutoComplete to ask you before it saves each password, select Prompt Me To Save Passwords.

To delete previously saved entries:

- To delete the addresses of Web sites you've visited, display the Internet Options dialog box, click the General tab, and click Clear History.

- To delete entries you've made in Web-based forms, display the AutoComplete Settings dialog box and click Clear Forms.

- To delete passwords you've entered, display the AutoComplete Settings dialog box and click Clear Passwords.

> **Deleting a Single Entry**
> To delete a single entry, begin typing the entry in whatever Address bar or form field it appears. (For example, to delete a Web address, type into the Address bar.) When the offending entry appears in the list, press the Down arrow key to highlight the entry, and then press Delete.

# Moving Favorites and Cookies

Over time, you'll undoubtedly build up a sizable collection of favorites and cookies. You won't want to leave this collection behind if you purchase a new computer, or if you decide to use a Web browser other than Internet Explorer. Likewise, if you've built up a collection of bookmarks in Netscape Navigator and you decide to switch to Internet Explorer, you'll want to move those bookmarks to the Favorites menu.

Internet Explorer provides a wizard to simplify the task of moving these items. To use the wizard, open the File menu and choose Import And Export. The Import/Export Wizard appears and guides you through the process.

Use the same wizard when you want to import favorites or cookies from another computer or Web browser. If you're moving items from another computer, you must first export the items to a file on that computer, and then bring that file (via network or removable disk) to your new computer.

**CHAPTER 19**

# Using
# Outlook Express

I n today's "wired world," electronic mail (e-mail) has
become an essential communications medium. One
of the most widely used features of the Internet is the
ability it provides you to exchange messages and files with
friends, business associates, and strangers.

Another popular method that many people use to exchange
information is Internet news. Thousands of separate newsgroups on the Internet offer discussions about almost every
imaginable topic, from particle physics to ragtime music.

Microsoft Windows 2000 includes a program called Microsoft
Outlook Express that handles e-mail and Internet news in a
single "information store." Outlook Express includes a rich-
text message editor and viewer and a set of folders you can
use to organize incoming and outgoing mail and news messages. Its integration with Address Book allows you to work
with the same contacts you use for other applications that
support Address Book. Outlook Express also gives you
access to several Internet-hosted Lightweight Directory
Access Protocol (LDAP) directories that you can use to find
e-mail addresses, postal addresses, and telephone numbers.

Outlook Express can work with almost any mail or news service, including the protocols used by The Microsoft Network online service and most other Internet service providers (ISPs). It doesn't work with America Online (AOL), however; at the time of this writing, in winter 1999, AOL doesn't support third-party mail clients. If you have accounts with more than one ISP, you can use Outlook Express to manage all your mail from a single window, and you can switch between news servers to participate in more newsgroups than you might be able to access from a single ISP.

 Like Address Book, Outlook Express now supports multiple identities. This means that two or more users can easily keep their mail segregated while sharing a Microsoft Windows 2000 Professional user account. Note that if you have already used Address Book to set up more than one identity, you will automatically have the same identities in Outlook Express—and vice versa.

---

### Outlook Express vs. Outlook

As the names suggest, Outlook Express provides some of the same functions that are provided in Microsoft Outlook, the communications component of the Microsoft Office suite, which is also available as a separate stand-alone application. Outlook offers many additional e-mail, scheduling, and contact management features that aren't included in Outlook Express. If you install Outlook on your computer after you have been using Outlook Express, you can import the contents of your Outlook Express mailbox folders into Outlook.

Outlook Express is designed to provide a basic, fast, and reliable Internet mail and news client program, whereas Outlook is a more complex product with many additional features and functions. If you use your computer in a home, school, or small-business environment, Outlook Express might be adequate to do everything you need in order to send and receive mail and news messages. (Because of its simpler user interface and ability to handle newsgroups as well as e-mail, you might even find it preferable to Outlook.) On the other hand, if you want to integrate mail with other Microsoft Office applications, if you need the calendar and contact management functions in the larger program, or if you need to connect to a network mail server, you might want to consider using Outlook.

# How Outlook Express Is Organized

**?** **SEE ALSO**

For information about the optional display components, see "Changing the Appearance of Outlook Express," page 383.

Outlook Express uses an outline structure for folders, newsgroups, and messages, similar to the structure that Windows Explorer uses for folders and files. The mail component of the program gives you five default folders (Inbox, Outbox, Sent Items, Deleted Items, and Draft) and lets you create as many additional ones as you need. The news component displays each news server where you have an account as a top-level folder, with each subscribed newsgroup as a subfolder. Figure 19-1 shows the structure of a typical Outlook Express installation, with a few user-defined folders subordinate to Inbox. In this figure, the optional Outlook bar and Contacts list are visible.

**FIGURE 19-1.**

Outlook Express organizes messages and newsgroups in folders and subfolders.

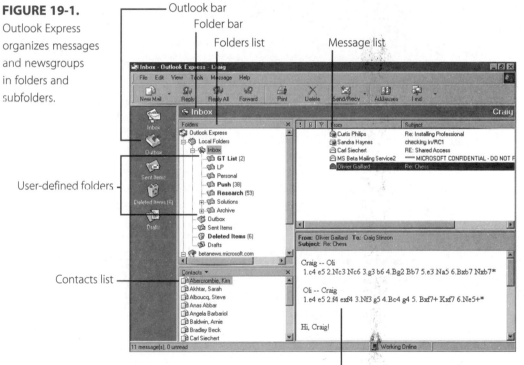

Outlook bar
Folder bar
Folders list
Message list
User-defined folders
Contacts list
Preview pane

## Getting Around in Outlook Express

If you click the Outlook Express entry at the top of the Folders list, a window similar to the one shown in Figure 19-2, on the next page, appears. This top-level window works like a Web page with graphic links to each Outlook Express function: mail, news, the address book, and other directory services. To jump directly to one of these areas, click its link.

V

Sharing and Communicating

**FIGURE 19-2.**

The top-level Outlook
Express "folder" pro-
vides links to all of
Outlook Express's
functions.

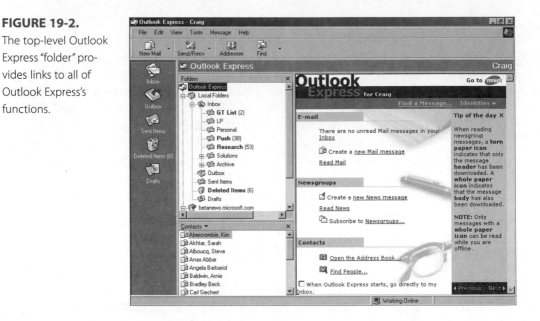

To move to any other location within Outlook Express, click its name
on the Outlook bar or the Folders list. The Outlook bar and the Folders list serve essentially equivalent functions—one with icons, the
other with an outline-style set of list entries. Initially the Outlook bar
includes only the five default mail folders, but you can add icons to it
for any folder you create. You'll probably want to make one or the
other visible but not use up screen real estate by displaying both at the
same time.

## Using Mail Folders

Although you can't rename or delete the five default mail folders, you
can create additional mail folders as either subfolders within an existing folder or as new top-level folders. Outlook Express displays message headers in each mail folder in a list like the one shown in Figure
19-3. If you display the optional preview pane (shown below the message list in Figure 19-3), you can read much of the selected message
without opening it. (You can read all of it, of course, by scrolling.) If
you want to open the message in a separate window, double-click its
header.

The following sections describe the purpose and use of the five default
mail folders.

**FIGURE 19-3.**

The message list includes a header for each message in a folder.

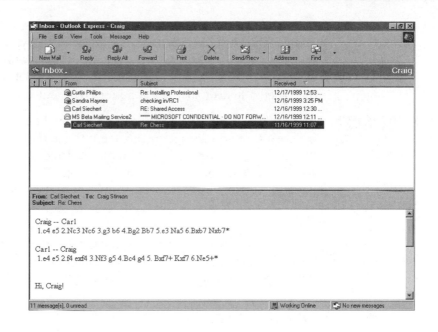

## Inbox

 **SEE ALSO**

For information about rules, see "Using Message Rules to Manage Mail," page 405.

When Outlook Express receives a new message, it places that message in the Inbox folder—unless you've created a rule to move the message to a different folder.

## Outbox

The Outbox folder contains messages that have not yet been transmitted from Outlook Express to your *mail server* (the computer dedicated to sending and receiving your mail, possibly on your local network or at an Internet service provider). After transmission is complete, Outlook Express moves the message from the Outbox folder to the Sent Items folder.

## Sent Items

After Outlook Express transmits a message, it moves it to the Sent Items folder. (If you prefer not to keep copies of the mail you send, open the Tools menu, choose Options, click the Send tab, and clear the first check box.)

## Deleted Items

When you delete a message from a folder, Outlook Express moves the message to the Deleted Items folder—the final storage place for

**V**

**Sharing and Communicating**

messages that have been deleted from other folders. You can work with messages in the Deleted Items folder just as you can with messages in other folders; you can reply, forward, or edit messages, for example. There's one key difference: when you delete a message from the Deleted Items folder, it's gone for good and you can't get it back.

**⊗ CAUTION**

If the Empty Messages From The 'Deleted Items' Folder On Exit check box (on the Maintenance tab in the Options dialog box) is selected, messages in the Deleted Items folder automatically disappear forever when you close Outlook Express.

As long as the message remains in the Deleted Items folder, you can restore a deleted message by moving it to another folder. You can do that by dragging the message from the Deleted Items folder to the name of the destination folder in the Folders list, or by selecting the message and choosing Move To Folder from the Edit menu.

## Drafts

The Drafts folder is a place to hold messages that you're not yet ready to send. When you use the Save command in the message editor, Outlook Express stores the saved message in the Drafts folder.

# Using News Folders

Internet news is another system for distributing messages, but unlike mail, *news messages* are public announcements that are posted in electronic bulletin boards devoted to a specific topic. These bulletin boards are called *newsgroups*. Along with mail, you can also use Outlook Express to send and receive news messages.

Just as Outlook Express exchanges mail with a mail server, it obtains news messages from a news server. *News servers* exchange messages with Outlook Express and other news client programs. When you set up an account with an ISP, it provides access to its news server. Most news servers handle messages posted in the thousands of public newsgroups that are available to anybody who wants to read them. In addition, some servers use the same system for *private newsgroups* that are available only to people with accounts on those servers, but which are not distributed to other servers. Therefore, you might want to configure Outlook Express to use more than one server.

As Figure 19-4 shows, Outlook Express maintains a top-level folder for each news server where you have an account. When you subscribe to an individual newsgroup, it shows up as a folder under the server where you obtain that newsgroup. When you open a newsgroup, the message list shows each message in that newsgroup.

**FIGURE 19-4.**

Newsgroups appear as subfolders within a news server folder.

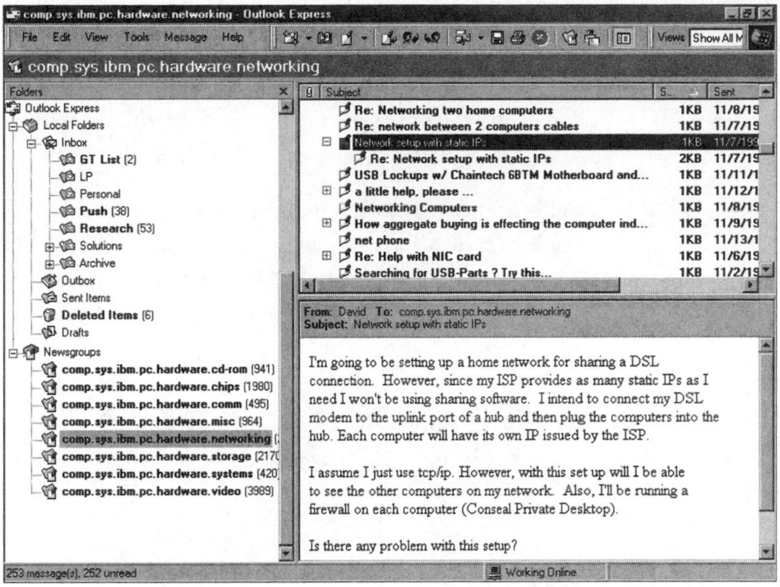

# Changing the Appearance of Outlook Express

With the single exception of the message list, all the features of the Outlook Express window are optional. You can hide or display the Contacts list, Outlook bar, Folders list, Folder bar, Views bar, status bar, toolbar, and the preview pane by choosing Layout from the View menu. Figure 19-5, on the next page, shows the Window Layout Properties dialog box that appears.

The top part of the Window Layout Properties dialog box controls the presence or absence of three different ways to display lists of Outlook Express folders:

■ The Outlook bar is a column of buttons—one for each mail folder and news server. Because the oversized buttons often necessitate scrolling the column of buttons, the Outlook bar is the most attractive and least useful of the lot.

■ The Folders list shows all mail folders, news servers, and subscribed newsgroups in outline form, much like the Folders bar in Windows Explorer.

■ The Folder bar, which displays the name of the selected folder near the top of the window, occupies the least screen space. When you click the Folder bar, the Folders list opens temporarily to let you select another folder. Once you do, the list disappears to get out of your way.

With any of these navigation tools, you simply click the name of a folder or news server and Outlook Express displays its contents in the message list. You probably won't want to make all three options visible at the same time, but you can experiment to find which ones you like best.

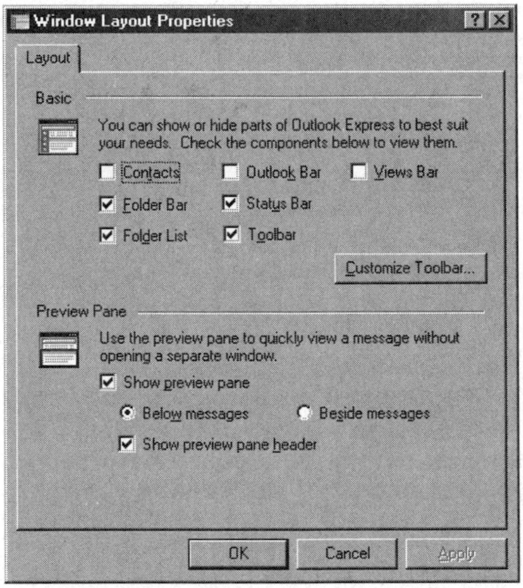

**FIGURE 19-5.**

The Window Layout Properties dialog box lets you control which elements are displayed in the Outlook Express window.

## Customizing the Toolbar

To add or remove buttons from the current toolbar, click the Customize Toolbar button in the Window Layout Properties dialog box. To add a function to the toolbar, select it in the left side of the Customize Toolbar dialog box and click the Add button. To remove a function, select it in the right side of the dialog box and click the Remove button. To change the position of an item on the toolbar, select it in the right side of the dialog box and click Move Up or Move Down. You can use the Text Options box to change the position of the text associated with toolbar buttons—or to remove the text. The Icon Options box lets you change the size of the toolbar icons.

# Viewing or Hiding the Preview Pane

The preview pane is a section of the Outlook Express window that displays the contents of the currently selected message. When you're scanning mail messages or news messages rather than taking the time to read each one entirely, you can save yourself a lot of time by selecting items from the list and reading the first few lines.

If you don't want to use the preview pane, use the Window Layout Properties dialog box to hide it, which allows more space for the message list. You can place the preview pane below the message list or arrange the message list and preview pane side-by-side.

# Customizing the Message List

Outlook Express maintains a group of display settings for each folder. These settings let you decide which columns are displayed, the order and width of the columns, and the sort order. You can customize each of these settings.

## Selecting Columns to Display

To specify which columns are displayed or to change the order in which they appear:

1  Open the View menu and choose Columns. The Columns dialog box appears, as shown in Figure 19-6.

2  To add a new column, select its check box.

3  To remove a column, clear its check box.

4  To change a column's position, select it and then click Move Up or Move Down.

**FIGURE 19-6.**

You can select which columns to display for each folder.

V

Sharing and Communicating

⭐ **TIP**

> You can change the width of any column by dragging the right border of the column heading. You can change the order of the columns by dragging a column heading to the new location; a blue line between column headings indicates where the column will go when you release the mouse button.

## Sorting Messages

The column heading that Outlook Express currently uses to sort the items in the message list has an arrowhead in it. When the arrowhead points up, the messages appear in ascending order (A to Z, or oldest to most recent); when the arrowhead points down, the messages appear in descending order (Z to A, or most recent to oldest). To use a different field to sort the message list, click that column heading. To switch between ascending order and descending order, click the column heading again.

## Organizing Mail in Conversation Threads

Outlook Express normally treats each message in a folder as a discrete entity for sorting purposes. When you have messages with replies, and particularly if the replies have replies of their own, an arrangement that treats such collections of messages as conversation threads might prove more useful. If you choose to organize your messages in conversation threads, a plus (+) sign (the common symbol for an expandable outline entry in Windows 2000) appears next to a message that has a reply. Click the plus sign to display the reply—and all additional messages in the thread.

To organize your messages in conversation threads, point to Current View on the View menu and choose Group Messages By Conversation.

Typically, your own replies to messages you receive appear initially in your Sent Items folder. To make them part of a conversation thread, you need to move them back to the Inbox folder—or move all messages in a thread to some other folder. If you move messages from various folders to a common folder, Outlook Express immediately gathers the related messages into threads.

# Setting Up Accounts

Most people are initially concerned with setting up a mail account so they can send and receive e-mail. But there's a wealth of information to explore in newsgroups, so you'll probably want to set up a news account as well. Both types of account setup are described here.

# Setting Up Mail Accounts

The standards for Internet mail specify separate servers for inbound and outbound mail, so you must have accounts on both servers to send and receive mail. Some ISPs, such as MSN (The Microsoft Network), automatically configure Outlook Express when you install their software, but many others require manual configuration. If your ISP gave you a list of account codes and passwords when you opened your account, you'll need that list now.

To set up a new Outlook Express mail account:

**1** Start Outlook Express.

**2** Open the Tools menu and choose Accounts. The Internet Accounts dialog box appears.

**3** Click the Add button and choose Mail.

   The Internet Connection Wizard starts.

**4** Use the information supplied by your ISP to fill in the blank fields in the wizard.

⭐ TIP

> You can also use Outlook Express to set up a free e-mail account using MSN's Hotmail service. You don't need an MSN account to use Hotmail. To set up a Hotmail account, point to New Account Signup on the Tools menu and choose Hotmail from the submenu.

To see a list of your mail accounts, including the ones that you set up with the Internet Connection Wizard and those that were installed automatically, click the Mail tab in the Internet Accounts dialog box. If you have accounts on more than one mail server, Outlook Express checks for new mail on each of them unless you have specifically excluded one or more accounts, as explained in the following section.

# Viewing and Changing Account Properties

To view or change a mail account's current configuration, select the name of the account on the Mail tab and click the Properties button to open the properties dialog box for the selected account, or double-click the name of the account.

Normally, Outlook Express checks all your mail accounts every time you choose the Send And Receive All command or click the corresponding toolbar button. To exclude an account, click the General tab in the properties dialog box and clear the check box at the bottom of the screen labeled Include This Account When Receiving Mail Or Synchronizing.

## Setting Up News Accounts

Most accounts you set up with an ISP also include access to their news server. To set up Outlook Express to access news messages from a news server, you'll need the information supplied by your ISP or other news provider:

1  Open Accounts from the Tools menu and choose News.

2  Click the Add button and choose News.

3  Use the information supplied by your ISP to fill in the blank fields in the wizard. You can view the names of your news accounts on the News tab in the Internet Accounts dialog box and adjust their settings by clicking the Properties button. The All tab shows your mail accounts, your news accounts, and your directory service accounts.

# Receiving and Sending Mail

Almost all electronic mail sent across the Internet and other networks uses a *store-and-forward* system: when somebody sends you a message, the message goes to a mail server, which holds it until your own computer comes looking for new mail. When Outlook Express connects to your mail server—either on a regular schedule or because you issued a specific command—it downloads all the messages that have arrived since the last connection. At the same time, it uploads any new messages from your Outbox folder to the server.

Messages you send follow a similar path. When you send a message, your mail client program (in this case, Outlook Express) transmits it to a program called a *post office server*, which reads the destination information in the message header and passes it across the Internet or some other network to the recipient's mail server, where it is held until the recipient's mail client program checks for new mail.

Before you can read a message, you must download it from your mail server. You can have Outlook Express check for new mail on a regular schedule or you can manually check for new mail at any time. If you have mail accounts with more than one service provider, Outlook Express can automatically check for new mail from the servers you specify, and you can manually check for new mail on all your accounts or from individual servers.

## Setting Up an Automatic Download Schedule

To instruct Outlook Express to check for new mail on a regular schedule:

1 Open the Tools menu and choose Options.

2 On the General tab in the Options dialog box, select the Check For New Messages Every __ Minute(s) check box.

3 Use the Minutes box to set the time between trips to the mail server.

4 If you want Outlook Express to play a sound whenever a new message arrives, select the Play Sound check box. *For information on setting sounds in Windows, see "Setting Sounds for Various Events," page 112.*

## Downloading New Mail from Your Mail Server Manually

When you want to check for new mail between scheduled downloads, or if you don't want to use a schedule at all, you can instruct Outlook Express to make an immediate connection to the server. Click the Send And Receive All button on the toolbar (its text label is *Send/Recv*), choose Send And Receive All from the Send And Receive submenu of the Tools menu, or press Ctrl+M.

If you have more than one mail account, the Send And Receive command on the Tools menu lists each of your accounts on its submenu. To check for mail everywhere, choose Send And Receive All from the submenu. To check only one account, select the name of that account from the submenu.

## Reading Messages

When Outlook Express retrieves your mail, it places each new message in the Inbox folder (unless you have set up a rule to move it to some other folder). When the Inbox folder is selected, as shown in Figure 19-7, on the next page, the message list displays a list of the messages in your Inbox. Unread messages, such as the Outlook Express welcome message in Figure 19-7, appear in boldface type, with a closed envelope icon. After you read a message, its entry changes to normal type with an open envelope icon.

**FIGURE 19-7.**

Bold text makes it easy to identify new, unread messages.

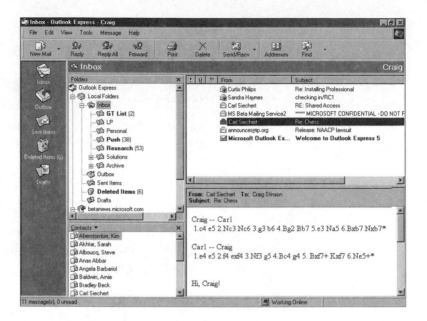

To read a message in a separate message window, either double-click its entry or select it and choose the Open command from the File menu. The message window, shown in Figure 19-8, includes a message header and the message body, in separate panes. The message header identifies the source, destination, and subject of a message and includes other useful information. The body of a message includes the text and can also include Web links and graphic images.

## Seeing Messages in the Preview Pane

The preview pane is an optional section of the main Outlook Express window that displays the contents of the currently selected message. It can be a convenient way to scan the contents of news messages without taking the time to open a separate message window. To display or hide the preview pane, choose Layout from the View menu. Select or clear the Show Preview Pane check box and click OK.

> **NOTE**

The Show Preview Pane check box is unavailable when the top-level Outlook Express folder is selected. Be sure you select another folder before choosing the Layout command.

**FIGURE 19-8.**

Double-click a message entry to display the message in a separate window.

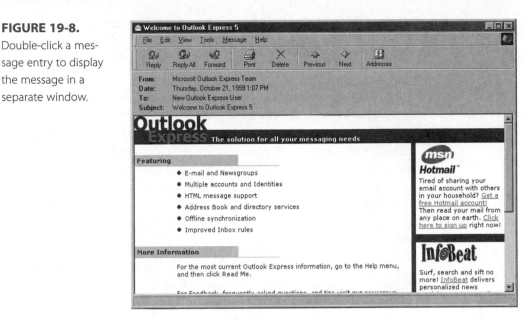

## Reading Messages Offline

It's not necessary to have an active connection between your own computer and the mail server when you want to read your mail. Because Outlook Express downloads and stores a copy of each message, you see a local copy in the message window or preview pane. Therefore, you can read your mail (and compose new messages) at any time, even if you're away from a telephone line or other network link. For example, many people who travel with a portable computer download their new mail before leaving the office and read it aboard an airplane or train.

## Viewing Attached Files

Mail messages aren't limited to text. It's also possible to send data files that are formatted for a word processor, spreadsheet, or other application; graphic images; programs; and other types of files as e-mail. A file included with a mail message is known as an *attachment*. When a message has an attached file, the Outlook Express message list includes a paper clip icon in the Attachment column next to the description of that message.

In the preview pane, a message with attached files appears with a paper clip button in the message header area. To open or save the files, click the button and choose the name of the file you want to open or save to disk. In a message window, attachments are listed in a header line below the Subject line. You can open an attachment by double-clicking its icon. If Windows recognizes the file type, it loads the file into the associated program. If the file is itself a program, double-clicking the icon runs the program.

## Replying to a Message

You will probably want to write and send replies to many of the mail messages you receive. Replies to messages can contain quotes from the original message, along with additional text. A reply includes a normally hidden line in the header that identifies the original message, so Outlook Express and other mail client programs can organize a message and its replies (and the replies to *those* replies) into a message *thread*.

To reply to a message in Outlook Express, open the original message in either the message viewer or the preview pane, open the Message menu, and choose one of the Reply To commands. Use Reply To Sender if you want your reply to go only to the person who sent the original message; use Reply To All to also send copies to all the people who received copies of the original message.

When you choose a Reply command, Outlook Express opens a new message editor window, with the To, Cc, and Subject fields already filled in, and the text of the original message quoted in the body of the message.

## Creating a New Message

Sending a mail message often involves several steps:

- Composing the text
- Changing the appearance of the message
- Attaching files to the message
- Inserting hypertext links
- Using a spelling checker
- Adding a signature
- Sending the message to your mail server

To create a new message, click the New Mail button on the toolbar, press Ctrl+N, or open the Message menu and choose New Message.

## Composing Messages

When you choose the New Message command, Outlook Express opens a message editor window. (See Figure 19-9.) Follow these steps to prepare your message:

**1** In the To field, type the e-mail address or addresses to which you want to send this message, or click the address book icon next to the field to select one or more recipients from your address book. (Use a comma or a semicolon to separate addresses if you want to include more than one.)

**2** If you want to send additional copies of the same message to other recipients, type their e-mail addresses into the Cc field or click the icon next to it to select names from your address book.

**3** If you want to send *blind copies* of this message to additional recipients, type or select the addresses in this field. The names of Bcc recipients won't appear in the copies of the message sent to other recipients. (If you don't see the Bcc line, choose All Headers from the message's View menu.)

**4** Type a brief description of the subject of this message into the Subject field.

**5** Type the text of your message into the work area at the bottom of the window.

**FIGURE 19-9.**

Start your message by filling in the address fields.

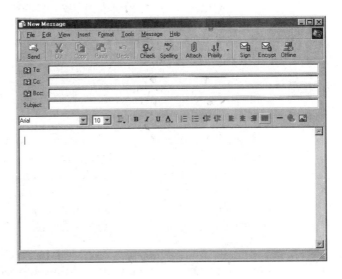

⭐ **TIP**

Press the Tab key to move from the Subject field to the message area.

## Changing the Appearance of Your Message

Outlook Express can send and receive messages that include embedded pictures, special typefaces, links to Web pages and other Internet resources, and other special features along with the text. However, you can't automatically assume that everybody who receives your messages will be able to recognize all the fancy embellishments you've added to the text. Many computer users, especially those in schools and colleges and those outside of North America and western Europe, are still using older, less sophisticated mail programs.

Outlook Express uses either of two text formats: Plain Text or Rich Text (HTML).

- **Plain Text Format.** Can be used for a message with no special typefaces, embedded graphics, or HTML codes. To select Plain Text Format for a message you are composing, open the Format menu and choose Plain Text.

- **Rich Text (HTML) Format.** Must be used for messages that include graphics, Web links, or special typefaces. To use Rich Text Format for a message you are currently composing, open the Format menu and choose Rich Text (HTML). If you select stationery when you open the message editor, the message editor automatically uses Rich Text. When Rich Text Format is active, the message editor includes the formatting toolbar shown in Figure 19-9.

**NOTE**

You can add file attachments to either Plain Text or Rich Text Format messages.

Messages that use Rich Text Format are supposed to appear as plain text in mail programs that don't recognize formatting, but in practice, many mail reading programs add formatting commands and other distractions to the text. Therefore, you should limit the number of graphic enhancements in your messages unless you know that your recipients have mail programs and newsreaders that will display them properly.

To change the default text format, in the main Outlook Express window, open the Tools menu and choose Options. Click the Send tab, and then select either HTML or Plain Text under Mail Sending Format. You can independently set the News Sending Format as well.

### Using Stationery

Outlook Express includes a folder full of special graphic backgrounds for more colorful mail messages. Just as you might use more festive paper stationery for an invitation to a birthday party than you would use in a business letter, you can use electronic stationery in your mail messages. To use stationery, either select it when you open the message editor, or choose Apply Stationery from the message editor's Format menu.

### Using a Background Color

If you prefer to use a solid color as the background of your message, choose the Background command from the message's Format menu, click Color, and then choose a color from the list.

### Using a Background Picture

If you prefer to use a picture background, open the message's Format menu and choose Background, Picture. In the Background Picture dialog box that appears, select the name of a picture file from the File list, type the name of a file directly into the File box (including its path and filename extension), or click the Browse button to find a file. You can use any .bmp, .gif, or .jpg file as your background. Whatever image you choose, Outlook Express tiles (repeats) the picture to fill the entire page.

### Using a Background Sound

You can also add sound to your e-mail message. Point to Background on the Format menu and choose Sound. Then specify the name of an audio file. You can use any .wav, .snd, .au, .aif, .aifc, or .aiff file, and you can specify that the sound be repeated continuously or a particular number of times.

### Formatting Your Text

When you use Plain Text Format, the font in which your message appears is set by the recipient's mail program. But if you use Rich Text Format, you can specify a font when you create the message, as shown in Figure 19-10, on the next page. (Note, however, that if the recipient doesn't have the same font available on his or her system, Windows—or whatever operating system the recipient uses—substitutes an available font.) To change the font in your message, select the text and use either the Font and Font Size boxes on the formatting toolbar or the Font command on the Tools menu.

**FIGURE 19-10.**

Rich Text Format lets you use different fonts in your messages.

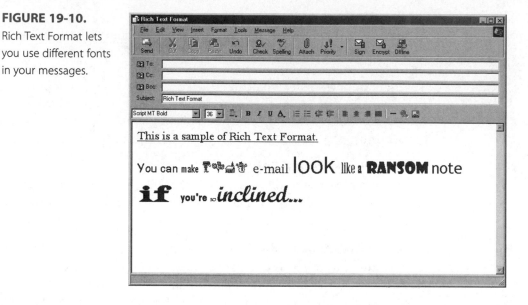

Other buttons on the formatting toolbar and commands on the Format menu control the size, color, style, and position of text in your message. (See Table 19-1.) To change the format of a block of text, select the text and then click a button on the formatting toolbar or choose a command from the Format menu.

**TABLE 19-1.   Outlook Express Formatting Toolbar**

| Toolbar Icon | Description |
| --- | --- |
| | Applies a predefined paragraph style to the selection |
| **B** | Changes the selection to boldface (or, if the selection is already boldface, changes it back to normal) |
| *I* | Changes the selection to italic (or, if the selection is already italic, changes it back to normal) |
| U | Underlines the selection (or if the selection is already underlined, removes the underline) |
| A | Changes the color of the selection |
| | Changes the selected paragraphs to a numbered list (or, if the selection is already numbered, removes the numbering) |

**TABLE 19-1.** *continued*

| Toolbar Icon | Description |
|---|---|
|  | Changes the selected paragraphs to an indented, bulleted list (or, if the selection is already bulleted, removes the bullets and indents) |
|  | Decreases the selected paragraphs' indent from the left margin |
|  | Increases the selected paragraphs' indent from the left margin |
|  | Left aligns the selected paragraphs |
|  | Centers the selected paragraphs |
|  | Right aligns the selected paragraphs |
|  | Justifies the selected paragraphs |
|  | Inserts a horizontal line (Click the line and drag its handles to change its size.) |
|  | Changes the selection to a hypertext link to an Internet address |
|  | Inserts a picture |

## Attaching Files and Pictures to Your Message

To attach a text file, data file, or program file to your message, click the Attach File button on the message editor toolbar or choose the File Attachment command from the Insert menu, and select the file you want to send from the file browser. Outlook Express opens an Attach box on the message's header and inserts the file's name and icon.

**⭐ TIP**

> Another way to insert a file is to drag it from your desktop or a Windows Explorer window to the message window.

## Adding Web Links

You can easily insert a hypertext link to a Web site or other Internet resource into your message. If you type an Internet address (one that starts with *http://* or *www*, such as *http://www.microsoft.com/* or just *www.microsoft.com*), Outlook Express automatically converts the text to a link. But you can make any text or picture in your message into a clickable link by following these steps:

**1** Select the text or picture that you want to be a link.

**2** Click the Insert Hyperlink button on the formatting toolbar or choose Hyperlink from the Insert menu.

**3** In the Hyperlink dialog box that appears, select the type of link you want (the most common types are http:, for Web destinations, and mailto:, for e-mail addresses) and the Internet address (URL).

> **NOTE**
>
> To insert hypertext links, you must use Rich Text Format.

If you want to modify a link after you create it, right-click it and choose Properties. This brings up the same Hyperlink dialog box, allowing you to change the type of link and the Internet address.

## Using a Spelling Checker

If you have installed Microsoft Office or one or more of its component programs—Microsoft Word, Microsoft Excel, or Microsoft PowerPoint—Outlook Express uses the Office spelling checker. To check the spelling in the current message in the message editor, open the Tools menu and choose Spelling. To automatically check the spelling in every message before you send it, in the main Outlook Express window, choose Options from the Tools menu, click the Spelling tab, and select the Always Check Spelling Before Sending check box.

> **NOTE**
>
> The Spelling tab appears only if you have installed a program that includes a compatible spelling checker.

## Adding a Signature to a Message

A signature is a block of text or graphics that is added to a message. Signatures normally contain the name and e-mail address of the sender, along with other information that the sender wants to include in every message, such as the name and postal address of the sender's company or organization. To create a signature in Outlook Express:

**1** Choose Options from the Tools menu, click the Signatures tab, and then click New.

**2** On the Signatures tab of the Options dialog box, shown in Figure 19-11, either type the text of your signature into the Text field, or select the File option and use the Browse button to find a text file or HTML file.

Follow the same procedure to create additional signatures.

To add your signature automatically to every message, select the Add Signatures To All Outgoing Messages check box. If you have more than one signature, use the Set As Default button to mark the one you want used automatically.

If you want your signature to appear below some, but not all, messages, leave the Add Signatures To All Outgoing Messages check box clear. Then when you want to use a signature, choose Signature from the Insert menu before sending your message. From the Signature submenu, choose the signature you want to use.

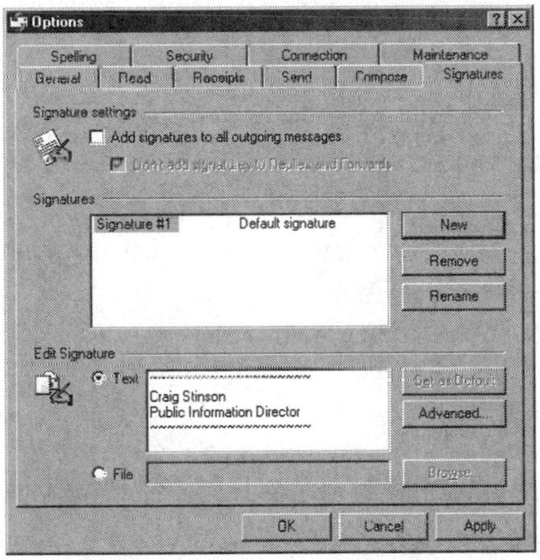

**FIGURE 19-11.**

Specify the text or file you want to appear at the end of your messages.

## Creating and Using Business Cards

Electronic business cards (using a format called vCard) are a convenient way to exchange contact information with other people and to add new names and addresses to your address book. You can attach your own vCard to outgoing messages to make it easy for the recipients of your messages to add you to their address books:

**1** Choose Options from the Tools menu.

**2** In the Business Cards section of the Compose tab, select Mail, News, or both, depending on the type of messages you want to attach your card to.

**3** Select your name in the associated list.

### Sending a Message

When you've finished composing, formatting, and checking your message, it's ready to send to the mail server. Click the Send button on the toolbar, and Outlook Express deposits the message into the Outbox to wait for the next visit to the mail server.

If you have more than one mail account set up and you want to send your message using an account other than the default account, select the account you want to use in the From box at the top of the message window. (This box does not appear if you have only one account.)

## Saving Messages and Attachments

The File menu's Save As command lets you save the selected message in an ordinary disk file, outside the Outlook Express message store. The resulting file has the extension .eml. Double-clicking an .eml file in a Windows Explorer window reopens the file in a message window in Outlook Express.

The File menu's Save Attachments command lets you store a copy of a message attachment as a separate disk file. If the file has multiple attachments, Outlook Express presents a list, so you can pick and choose the ones you want to save. When you save an attachment, you save a copy; there is no "detach" command.

# Organizing Your Mail

Outlook Express includes five standard mail folders—Inbox, Outbox, Sent Items, Deleted Items, and Drafts—but you can add as many additional folders and subfolders as you want in order to sort and store messages by topic, date, sender, or any other system. For example, you might create separate folders for sales reports, meeting agendas, and love letters.

It's easiest to work with mailbox folders when the Folders list is visible in the Outlook Express window. Use the Layout command on the View menu to display the Folders list.

# Creating and Using Folders

To create a new mail folder:

**1**  Open the File menu and choose New from the Folder menu, or right-click in the Folders list and choose New Folder.

> The Create Folder dialog box appears.

**2**  Type the name you want to assign to the new folder into the Folder Name text box.

**3**  In the folder outline, click the location where you want the new folder to appear. For a new top-level folder, select the Outlook Express folder; for a new subfolder, click the parent folder that should include the new folder.

**4**  Click OK to save your choice and close the dialog box.

You can't move, delete, or rename the five standard mail folders, but you can change any mail folder that you add to the system yourself. To move a folder (including all the messages and subfolders inside the folder) to a different location within the Outlook Express folder structure, select the folder in the Folders list and drag it to the new parent folder, or open the File menu, choose Folder, and choose Move.

To rename or delete a folder, select the folder, choose Folder from the File menu, and choose Rename or Delete; or right-click the folder and choose from the shortcut menu that appears.

**TIP**

> You can also delete a folder by selecting it and clicking the Delete button on the toolbar or by pressing the Delete key.

# Moving, Copying, and Deleting Messages

To move an individual message to a different folder, open the folder that includes the message and either drag the message to the name of the destination folder, or choose Move To Folder from the shortcut menu that appears when you right-click the message. To place a duplicate copy of the message in a new folder, hold down the Ctrl key when you drag the message, or choose Copy To Folder from the shortcut menu.

To remove a message from a folder, select the message and press the Delete key, or click the Delete button on the toolbar. Deleting a message from any folder except the Deleted Items folder actually moves the message to the Deleted Items folder. The "deleted" message resides there until you delete it from the Deleted Items folder or only until you close Outlook Express, if the Empty Messages From The 'Deleted Items' Folder On Exit check box is selected on the General tab of the Options dialog box.

# Flagging and Highlighting Messages

Flagging and highlighting are two ways of marking messages for special attention. When you flag a message, Outlook Express displays a little flag icon next to the message in the message list. When you highlight a message, the message list displays the message line in a color of your choice.

> **NOTE**

> If the Flag or Watch/Ignore columns aren't visible in your message list, you can display them by right-clicking one of the visible columns, choosing Columns from the shortcut menu, and then selecting the fields you want to add to the display.

You can flag a message "by hand" by selecting it from the message list and choosing Flag Message from the Message menu. Or you can use message rules to automatically flag all messages that meet some criterion—everything that comes down from the boss, for example. Highlighting can be done only via message rules. *For information about message rules, see "Using Message Rules to Manage Mail," page 405.*

# Watching or Ignoring Conversation Threads

If flagging isn't an adequate way to make important messages more visible, you can use the Message menu's Watch Conversation command. When you select a message and apply this command, Outlook Express displays an eyeglass icon next to the message in the message list and changes the color of the header itself. (You can specify the color by choosing Options from the Tools menu and selecting the Read tab in the Options dialog box.) If you're using conversation threads, the Watch Conversation command is applied automatically to all messages in the selected thread.

You can use another command, Ignore Conversation, to mark particularly *unimportant* message threads. Outlook Express displays a different, equally distinctive, icon in the same column as the watched messages icon—but doesn't color the header text. In fact, by repeatedly clicking in the Watch/Ignore column next to a message, you can step from a normal message, to a watched message, to an ignored message, and back to normal. As you'll see in the next section, Outlook Express also offers a way to hide ignored messages.

Figure 19-12 shows a folder with one watched and one ignored thread.

**FIGURE 19-12.**
Outlook Express uses distinctive icons to identify watched and ignored message threads. Watched threads are also high-lighted with color.

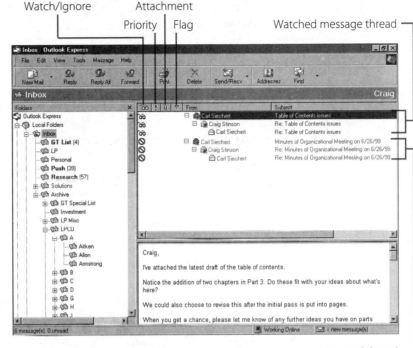

**? SEE ALSO**

For information about message rules, see "Using Message Rules to Manage Mail," page 405.

You can use message rules to apply the Watch Conversation and Ignore Conversation commands automatically to messages that meet particular criteria.

# Using Views to Hide Particular Kinds of Messages

Outlook Express comes with three standard message views:

- Show All Messages

- Hide Read Messages

- Hide Read Or Ignored Messages

The default is Show All Messages, and this view is applied by default to all folders. To apply a different view to a particular folder, open the

View menu, point to Current View, and select one of the views listed in the upper portion of the submenu. To apply a view to all your folders:

**1** Open the View menu and choose Current View.

**2** From the submenu, choose Define Views.

**3** In the Define Views dialog box, select the view you want to apply.

**4** Click Apply View.

**5** In the Apply View dialog box, choose All Of My Folders.

By creating your own custom views, you can also arrange to have particular categories of messages hidden or displayed, in either all or particular folders. To create a custom view:

**1** Open the View menu and choose Current View.

**2** From the submenu, choose Define Views.

**3** In the Define Views dialog box, click New.

**4** In the top frame of the New View dialog box (see Figure 19-13), select one or more check boxes.

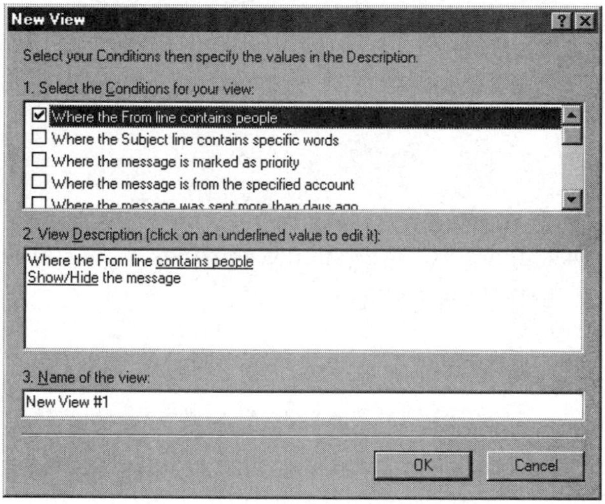

**FIGURE 19-13.**

You can use the New View dialog box to specify exactly which kinds of messages should be hidden or displayed.

**5** In the middle frame of the New View dialog box, click each blue link that appears and fill out the ensuing dialog box.

The links that appear and the dialog boxes to which they're connected depend on the choices you make in the top frame. If you enter more than one item of data for a link (for example, if you selected the Where The From Line Contains People condition and then typed *Frank*, *Saul*, and *Maria* as the specific names), you can click the Options button and choose whether to hide or show messages that match the condition, and you can choose whether all the items (names in this case) or any one of them must be present to satisfy the condition.

If you've selected more than one check box in step 4, after you define the specifics of each one as just described, you can then click the new And link that connects them, and again choose whether you want both conditions to be met (select And) or only one of the conditions (select Or). Then choose whether you want matching messages to be hidden or shown.

**6**  In the bottom frame of the New View dialog box, change the default name to a meaningful one for your new View.

Once you have created a custom view, it is listed along with the standard views and can be applied to all folders or individual folders just like the standard views.

To modify or remove a custom view, open the View menu and choose Current View, Define Views. Select a view and click Modify or Remove. To modify the view that's currently in effect, you can choose Customize Current View from the View menu.

# Using Message Rules to Manage Mail

Outlook Express lets you create message rules to manage incoming mail. You can use message rules to store messages with a particular characteristic—such as a particular sender or subject line—in a different folder, or to automatically send a reply back to the sender, forward a copy of the message to another address, or discard the message without downloading it from your mail server. Message rules can be a real time-saver if you receive a lot of routine (or junk) mail, if you want to forward your mail to another address when you're not able to receive it, or if you want to reply to all incoming mail with an out-of-the-office message while you're on vacation. Message rules are similar to Custom views, except you can do much more than simply show or hide the messages that match your rule's conditions.

You can use message rules for both e-mail and newsgroup messages.

# Creating a New Message Rule

To create a message rule for mail messages:

**1** Open the Tools menu, point to Message Rules, and choose Mail. If you've already defined at least one rule, click New in the Message Rules dialog box.

**2** In the top frame of the New Mail Rule dialog box (see Figure 19-14), select one or more check boxes.

These check boxes define the conditions under which your rule is to be carried out.

**3** In the second frame of the New Mail Rule dialog box, select one or more actions.

These check boxes tell Outlook Express what to do with mail that meets your criteria.

**4** Select each blue link that appears in the third frame of the New Mail Rule dialog box, and then fill out the ensuing dialog boxes.

The links that appear and the dialog boxes to which they're connected depend on the choices you make in the first two frames.

**5** In the fourth frame of the New Mail Rule dialog box, change the default name for your new rule to a more descriptive one.

**FIGURE 19-14.**

Message rules make your computer sort your mail for you.

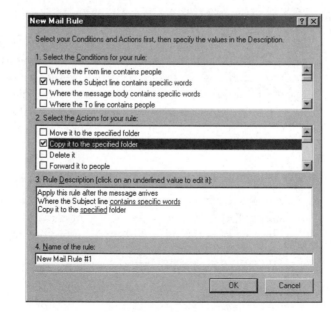

## Sending an Automatic Reply

To create a rule where the action is Reply With Message, you must first create and save the reply message. Create a message without an addressee. Then, from the File menu of the New Message dialog box, choose Save As and specify a filename and folder location. Then, in the Rule Description section of the New Mail Rule dialog box, click the message link and specify the file in which you saved your message.

## Specifying Negative Criteria

You can create a rule based on a negative criterion—for example, all messages that do *not* come from a particular sender. To do this, first set up the rule using a positive criterion. After you have finished specifying your criterion (step 4 above), you will see an Options button. Click this button to open the Rule Condition Options dialog box (Figure 19-15). In this dialog box, select the option that begins Message Does Not.

**FIGURE 19-15.**
Message rules can use negative criteria as well as positive ones.

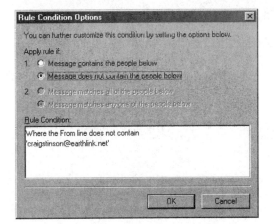

## Specifying Multiple Criteria

In rules that involve people, content, or accounts, you can specify multiple criteria. For example, if you wanted messages from either Craig Stinson or Carl Siechert deleted from the server, you could select Where The From Line Contains People in the first section of the New Mail Rule dialog box, click the Contains People link, type *Craig* and click Add, and then type *Carl* and click Add. The rule would then take effect if mail arrived from either of these senders. (Notice the names are linked by the word *or.*)

To make the rule affect only those messages that come from *both* senders, first set up the criterion in the normal way. Then click the

Options button in the Select dialog box to open the Rule Condition Options dialog box shown in Figure 19-16. In this dialog box, select the option that begins Message Matches All.

Note that the option to connect multiple criteria with Or or And is available when you enter multiple criteria for a single check box item in the Conditions section of the New Mail Rule dialog box, as well as when you select multiple conditions (multiple check boxes). When you select more than one condition in the first section of the New Mail Rule dialog box, the multiple conditions are initially linked with a blue And link. This signifies that both conditions must be met to activate the rule.

**FIGURE 19-16.**

Multiple criteria are initially joined by Or. To join them with And, use the Rule Condition Options dialog box.

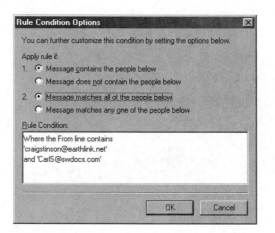

If you want any one of the conditions to be sufficient to activate the rule, click the And link and change it to Or. Note that choosing multiple actions in the second section of the New Mail Rule dialog box will always cause all the actions to take place. After all, why would you choose several actions if you want the computer to do only one of them, and which one would the computer decide to do?

# Creating a Message Rule from the Selected Message

As a handy time-saver, Outlook Express lets you create a message rule based on the sender of the current message. If you get a message from someone and you know immediately that you want all mail from that person to be handled by a rule, you can select the message and choose Create Rule From Message from the Message menu. The steps for creating the rule are the same as for creating a new rule from scratch, except that the condition is already specified.

# Blocking Obnoxious Mail

Although the purveyors of junk mail might always be able to think up new ways to reach into your Inbox, you can use Outlook Express's Block Sender command to ward off a good deal of unwanted material. When you get a message from someone from whom you never want to hear again, select the message in question and choose Block Sender from the Message menu. You'll see a dialog box similar to the following.

As soon as you click the Block Sender command, the sender's future e-mail is blocked. Clicking Yes or pressing Enter will go further and delete every message you've already received from the sender that is in the current Mail folder.

## Removing a Sender from the Blocked Senders List

If you make a mistake or change your mind about a blocked sender, you can restore him or her to your good graces as follows:

**1** Open the Tools menu, point to Message Rules, and choose Blocked Senders List from the submenu.

**2** Select the sender you want to restore.

**3** Click the Remove button to completely remove the sender from your blocked-senders list.

As an alternative, you can keep the entry in your list but clear either or both of the check boxes for blocking mail and news messages. This way you can be selective in the kinds of blocking you apply, and you can quickly reapply blocking if necessary.

## Adding a Blocked Sender by Hand

If you know the e-mail address of a junk-mail supplier, you can add that address to your blocked-senders list without waiting for the junk to arrive. Open the Tools menu, point to Message Rules, and choose Blocked Senders List. Then click the Add button and supply the e-mail address.

### Applying Rules to Existing Messages

Ordinarily, message rules are applied to new messages as they arrive. But you can also apply them to the existing messages in any folder. This can be a convenient way to clean out certain overburdened folders or send a standard reply to a large number of correspondents. To apply a rule to existing messages:

1   Choose Message Rules from the Tools menu and choose Mail or News.

2   Click the Apply Now button.

3   Select the rule or rules you want to apply. (Press Ctrl while clicking to select multiple rules.)

4   Click Browse and choose the folder to which you want the rule or rules applied. If you want to apply the rules to all your messages, choose the Local Folders folder.

# Searching for Messages

After you have been using Outlook Express for a few months or more, your mail folders will undoubtedly contain lots of messages. As a result, it might become extremely difficult to locate an old piece of mail quickly. The Edit menu's Find command provides an easy way to search for messages from or to a particular person, messages that contain a specified text string in the header or message body, messages that arrived during a specified period of time, flagged messages, or messages with attachments. To search for a message:

1   Choose Find from the Edit menu and Message from the submenu to display the Find Message dialog box, shown in Figure 19-17.

2   Specify one or more search criteria. (If you specify multiple criteria, the Find Message command locates messages that meet all criteria.)

3   Use the Browse button to specify a folder to search. Select or clear the Include Subfolders check box as appropriate.

4   Click Find Now.

   You don't need to type complete words; the Find Message dialog box reports success if the text you type appears anywhere in the specified field. Text searches aren't case sensitive.

Found messages appear in a list at the bottom of the dialog box. You can work with the messages here exactly as you do with messages in the main Outlook Express window.

**TIP**

To purge old mail messages, use the Received Before option in the Find Message dialog box. Then delete the messages that Outlook Express finds.

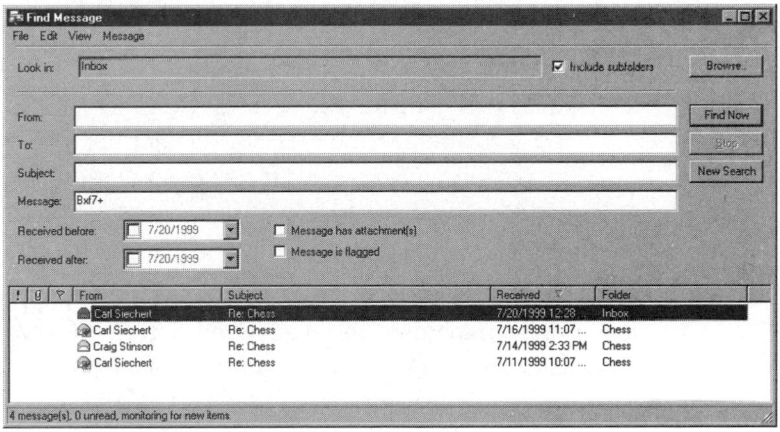

**FIGURE 19-17.**
The Find Message dialog box finds messages that contain the text you specify anywhere in a particular field.

**TIP**

**Find a Message the Moment It Arrives**
If you leave the Find Message dialog box open, the system continues to monitor incoming messages, adding appropriate ones to the list of found messages. This can be handy if you receive a large volume of mail and need to watch for mail that covers a particular topic.

# Setting Security Zones

**SEE ALSO**
For information about security zones, see "Using Security Zones and Security Levels," page 360.

Outlook Express shares the settings for the two most restrictive security zones used in Microsoft Internet Explorer, the Internet zone and the Restricted Sites zone. Therefore, for example, if you have set your Internet zone in Internet Explorer to reject Web pages with active content (such as ActiveX controls or Java applets), Outlook Express also rejects HTML messages with the same kind of active content.

**NOTE**

These security settings affect only the receipt of Rich Text (HTML) messages. Because of their limited capability, Plain Text messages can't contain any potentially harmful objects, such as Java applets.

To change your security zone settings in Outlook Express, choose Options from the Tools menu, and click the Security tab. Select either Internet Zone or Restricted Sites Zone. If you want to review or change the settings for the selected zone, select the Security tab of Internet Explorer's Options menu. Outlook Express will then use these same settings for the zone you've chosen in Outlook Express.

# Using Digital Signatures and Encryption

Digital signatures and encryption are two methods by which you can make your e-mail more secure. A digital signature assures recipients of a message that the message has not been altered since you sent it. Encryption encodes your message so that only the recipients to whom it is addressed are able to read it.

## Obtaining a Digital ID

Digital signatures and encryption both require you to obtain and use a digital ID. A *digital ID*, also known as a security certificate, is a statement issued by a third-party certifying authority attesting to your identity. Your digital ID is good only for a particular e-mail account but can be transferred from computer to computer.

To get a digital ID from a certifying authority, open the Security tab of the Outlook Express Options dialog box and click the Get Digital ID button. A Web page will open that lets you choose a digital ID. Once you have obtained your digital ID, you can digitally sign individual messages, or you can configure Outlook Express so that all your outgoing messages are digitally signed. To add your digital signature to an individual message, open the Tools menu in the New Message window and choose Digitally Sign. Alternatively, click the Digitally Sign Message button on the New Message window's toolbar.

To add your digital signature to all outgoing messages:

1 Open Outlook Express's Tools menu and choose Options.

2 Click the Security tab.

3 Select the Digitally Sign All Outgoing Messages check box.

**TIP**

After you have a digital ID, you should create a backup. This allows you to restore your digital ID if the copy on your computer is damaged or if you want to move it to a different computer. To create a backup, click the Digital IDs button on the Security tab of the Options dialog box. Select your certificate and then click the Export button. Complete the Certificate Export Wizard that opens.

## Exchanging Encrypted Messages

Outlook Express uses a public key/private key system to send and receive secure mail. To send encrypted mail to you, a correspondent must have your public key. A message sent to you is encrypted with your public key. When you receive the message, Outlook Express decodes it with your private key, which is stored on your hard disk.

When you add your digital signature to an outgoing message, you are, in effect, attaching your public key. Your private key was stored on your hard disk when you obtained your digital ID.

To enable a correspondent to send encrypted mail to you, you must first send him or her a digitally signed message. Your correspondent must then attach your public key to your address-book entry on his or her system. The procedure for doing that depends on the e-mail program that your correspondent is using. To send an encrypted message to you, your correspondent must use whatever procedure his or her e-mail program requires. On your end, Outlook Express decodes the encrypted message automatically.

To send an encrypted message to someone else, you must first obtain the recipient's public key. You do that by receiving a digitally signed message from your correspondent. When you receive the digitally signed message in Outlook Express, it will be automatically added to your Address Book and you will see a red signature icon added next to that person's name. You can also add the sender manually by right-clicking the message header in the message list and selecting Add Sender To Address Book.

To send an encrypted message to a correspondent once you have his or her public key, open the Tools menu in the New Message window and choose Encrypt. Alternatively, click Encrypt on the New Message window's toolbar.

V

Sharing and Communicating

To encrypt all outbound messages:

**1** Open Outlook Express's Tools menu and choose Options.

**2** Click the Security tab.

**3** Select the Encrypt Contents And Attachments For All Outgoing Messages check box.

## Exporting and Importing Digital IDs

Exporting a digital ID allows you to use it on a different computer. For instance, you might export the digital ID from one computer onto a floppy disk, and then carry the floppy disk to another computer and import the certificate from the floppy disk onto the computer's hard disk. To export your digital ID:

**1** Open the Tools menu and choose Options.

**2** Click the Security tab.

**3** Click Digital IDs.

**4** To export your own ID, click the Personal tab. To export someone else's, click the Other People tab.

**5** Select the digital ID that you want to export.

**6** Click Export and fill out the screens of the Certificate Export Wizard.

To import a digital ID:

**1** Open the Tools menu and choose Options.

**2** Click the Security tab.

**3** Click Digital IDs.

**4** Click Import and fill out the screens of the Certificate Import Wizard.

# Working with Internet Newsgroups

News is one of the oldest methods of distributing public information through computer networks. Newsgroups dedicated to more than 30,000 different topics carry millions of messages across the Internet every day. In addition to its mail functions, Outlook Express can also send and receive these Internet news messages.

## How Internet News Is Organized

Many of the most popular newsgroups are part of the worldwide Usenet system, which has a formal conference structure and detailed rules for creating new newsgroups. Other less formal newsgroups have fewer rules and can be limited to a geographic region, a single business, or an institution such as a college or university.

Every newsgroup has a name that describes its topic. Each name has several words or abbreviations, separated by periods. The first part of the name is usually a broad general category, such as *sci* for newsgroups related to science and technology, or *umn* for newsgroups that originate at the University of Minnesota. Each additional word describes the topic of the newsgroup in more detail, such as *sci.geo.earthquakes*.

Many of the most popular newsgroups are in one of the seven Usenet hierarchies: *comp* (computers), *news* (news about Usenet), *rec* (hobbies, arts, and recreation), *sci* (science and technology), *soc* (social issues and politics), *talk* (debates and controversies), and *misc* (topics that don't fit the other categories). Other important categories that are not part of the Usenet system include *alt* (a grab-bag category for alternative topics), *bionet* (biological science), *biz* (business topics), *clari* (news from the Associated Press and Reuters via the ClariNet service), and *k12* (topics for primary and secondary students and teachers).

Other newsgroups are operated by and for businesses and organizations and are restricted to their employees, customers, and members. These private newsgroups are usually limited to a single server, which requires a restricted password for access. For example, The Microsoft Network uses private newsgroups for conferences that are accessible only to MSN subscribers. Still other newsgroups, such as *msnews.microsoft.com*, are used by companies to provide public support for their products.

## Selecting a Newsgroup

To participate in a newsgroup through Outlook Express, you must set up an account with one or more news servers and select the individual newsgroups you want to see.

The Outlook Express Folders list shows each server where you have an account as a folder.

**? SEE ALSO**

For information about setting up an account with a news server, see "Setting Up Accounts," page 386.

After you've created a news account, the first step in reading messages in a newsgroup is to select the group from the list of newsgroups that are available from your news server. To view the list of newsgroups:

**1** Select a newsgroup server in the Folders list, and then choose Newsgroups from the Tools menu. The Newsgroup Subscriptions dialog box appears. See Figure 19-18.

**FIGURE 19-18.**

The Newsgroup Subscriptions dialog box lists all newsgroups on the selected server.

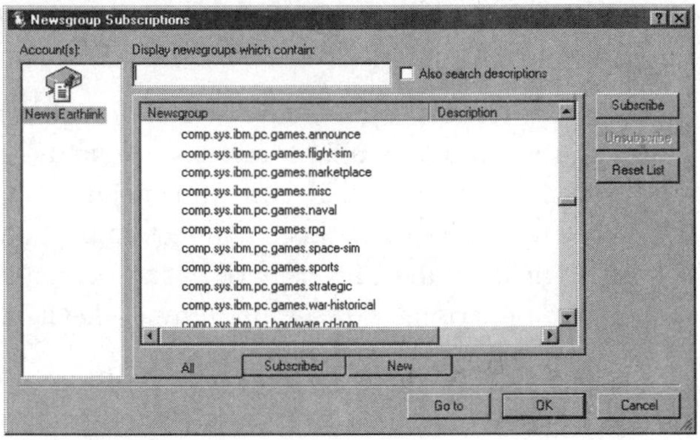

**2** If you have accounts on more than one news server, click the icon for the server you want to use.

If this is the first time you have used this server, the server transfers a list of newsgroups to Outlook Express.

**3** To see a complete list of available newsgroups, click the All tab. For a list of newsgroups that have been added since your last visit to this news server, click the New tab.

**4** Select a newsgroup from the list. If you're looking for something specific, type one or more key words into the Search field at the top of the window.

This filters the list so that it includes only newsgroup names that contain the text you type.

**5** If you expect to read the messages in a group often, double-click the name of the group, or select the name and click the Subscribe button. Outlook Express lists subscribed newsgroups under the News Server folder in the Folders list. To view a list of current messages in a newsgroup without subscribing, click the Go To button.

**TIP**

> If you have already subscribed to a newsgroup, you can go directly to a list of messages by selecting the newsgroup from the Folders list in the main Outlook Express window.

# Viewing Newsgroup Messages

When you select a newsgroup, Outlook Express connects to the server and obtains and displays a new list of messages in that group. To read a message in the Outlook Express preview pane, select the subject line in the message list. To view the message in a message window, double-click the subject line, or select it and choose Open from the File menu.

# Reading News Offline

You need a connection to the Internet to download news messages to your computer, but it's not necessary to keep that connection alive while you read them. For example, if you're using a laptop computer, it might be convenient to download a handful of newsgroups before you leave your home and read them on the train as you commute to work. Or if you use the same telephone line for both voice and data, reading news offline leaves the line free for incoming calls.

To configure your newsgroups for offline reading:

1  Select the name of the news server in your Folders list. You'll see a display comparable to Figure 19-19, on the next page.

2  Select the names of the newsgroups you want to download.

3  Click the Settings button, or right-click and choose Synchronization Settings from the shortcut menu.

4  Select one of the retrieval options:

- **All Messages.** Downloads the full text of all the messages from this newsgroup that are currently available on your news server

- **New Messages Only.** Downloads the full text (including headers) of all new messages in this newsgroup

- **Headers Only.** Downloads the headers from all new messages in this newsgroup but not the messages themselves

V

Sharing and Communicating

Once you have selected newsgroups for offline reading, you can choose Synchronize Account from the screen shown in Figure 19-19 to transfer the messages you want from the news server to your computer.

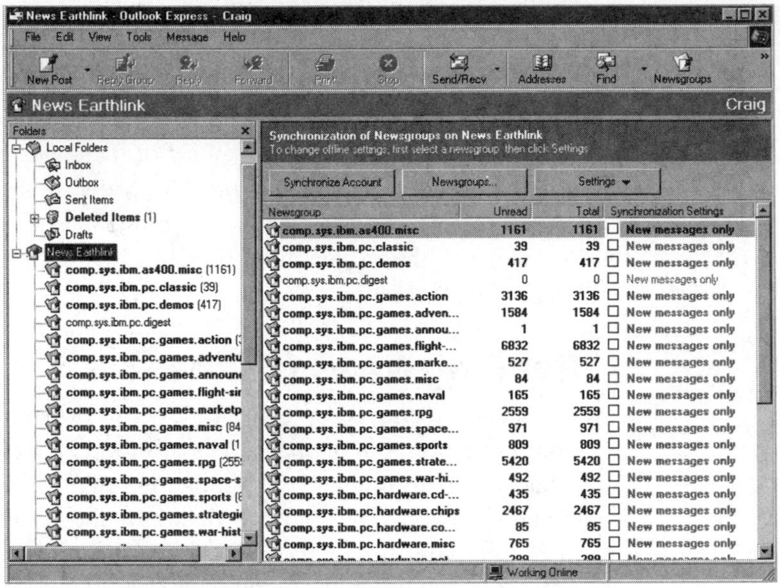

**FIGURE 19-19.**
When you select the name of a news server in your Folders list, Outlook Express displays the names of all subscribed newsgroups on that server and allows you to specify settings for offline reading.

## Marking a Message for Download

If you download only the headers of new messages rather than the full text of all messages when you connect to the server, you can mark the messages that sound like they're worth reading for later download by following these steps:

1   Open the newsgroup in Outlook Express.

2   Select the header of a message you want to read.

3   Choose one of the Mark For Offline commands from the Tools menu:

   - **Download Message Later.** Marks the currently selected message for downloading

   - **Download Conversation Later.** Marks the current message and all replies and replies-to-replies to that message

   - **Download All Messages Later.** Marks all the messages in the current newsgroup for downloading

- **Do Not Download Message.** Removes a mark from the currently selected message

**TIP**

To quickly mark message headers for later downloading, make sure the Mark For Offline column is visible in the messages list (its icon is an arrow pointing down), and click in the column next to each message you want to download. If you click a message with a plus icon next to it, all the messages in the thread are marked for download as well. Click again to remove the mark.

The next time your computer is connected to the Internet, you can retrieve the marked messages by choosing Synchronize All from the Tools menu.

**TIP**

You can use message rules to mark headers on particular topics for download. See "Using Message Rules in Newsgroups," page 422.

To read the messages you have downloaded:

**1** Open the View menu and choose Current View.

**2** Select the Show Downloaded Messages option to display a list of all the messages currently available on your system.

**3** Double-click the description of the message you want to read to load the message into a separate window, or select the header to view it in the preview pane of the main Outlook Express window.

## Forwarding a Message

If you see a message in a newsgroup that would interest somebody who might not see it in the newsgroup, you can mail that person a copy of the message. Click the Forward button on the toolbar, or choose Forward from the Message menu. The message appears in an ordinary message editor window, ready for you to address and, if you like, add any comments.

## Replying to a Message

Many people regularly read messages in newsgroups, but they never make any contributions to the ongoing conversations. These people are called *lurkers*. Almost everybody starts out as a lurker, but if you want to become an active participant in the community that grows around a good newsgroup, you will eventually want to write and post some messages of your own.

A message in a newsgroup can be either a reply to an earlier message or the start of a completely new thread. Many news readers, including Outlook Express, can list replies directly under the original message, so a reader can follow the thread easily.

To reply to a message with a new message of your own:

**1** Either select the original message in the Outlook Express window, or open the original in a separate message window.

**2** Click the Reply Group button on the toolbar, or choose Reply To Group from the Message menu.

**3** Type your reply.

**4** Click the Send button.

Sometimes it makes more sense to send a reply to a public news message back to the sender as a private mail message. Because Outlook Express is both a news program and a mail program, you can send a private reply just as you would send any other mail. To send a private reply, click the Reply button on the toolbar, or choose Reply To Sender from the Message menu.

> ⭐ **TIP**
>
> To post a reply to the newsgroup *and* copy that reply via e-mail to the sender, choose Reply To All from the Message menu.

> ⭐ **TIP**
>
> To be sure you don't miss any replies to messages that you post, display the newsgroup where you posted, open the View menu, and choose Current View, Show Replies To My Messages.

## Posting a New Message

Not every message in a newsgroup is part of an existing thread. To create and send a new message:

**1** Open the newsgroup to which you want to send a message.

**2** Click the New Post button on the toolbar, or choose New Message from the Message menu. The New Message editor window shown in Figure 19-20 appears.

**3** To simultaneously post your message to other newsgroups, click the Newsgroups icon and select the additional newsgroup names. (Note that some regard this as *spamming*, or littering groups with bulk mailings, so don't overdo it.)

**4** To simultaneously send your message to one or more mail recipients, type their e-mail addresses into the Cc line, or click the filecard icon to open your address book.

**FIGURE 19-20.**

The window for creating news messages is nearly identical to the one for creating mail messages.

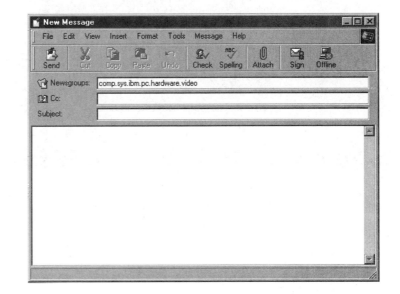

**5** Type a brief description into the Subject line.

**6** Compose the body of the message, as described in the next section.

**7** Click the Post button.

## Composing a Message

**SEE ALSO**

For information about creating and formatting mail messages, see "Creating a New Message," page 392.

Writing a news message is just like creating a mail message. The message editor window is almost identical for both services, so you can add text, formatting, and attached files to a news message just as you would for a private message.

It's possible to use Rich Text (HTML) Format in news messages, but many news reader programs won't recognize the formatting. Therefore, unless you're sending your message to a proprietary news server such as MSN, where you know that all recipients have sophisticated news readers, it's a good idea to stick with Plain Text.

### Using Message Rules in Newsgroups

Unfortunately, many newsgroups include messages from people who misuse the system by posting advertisements, abusive messages, and other irrelevancies. You can use message rules to hide messages that you don't want to view.

Message rules work in newsgroups in much the same way that they do with e-mail. The only real difference is that fewer action options are available in newsgroups, because you can't use message rules to move or copy newsgroup posts to mail folders. (You can move newsgroup posts to e-mail folders manually, however.)

To set up a newsgroup message rule, follow the steps described on page 406 for e-mail message rules—but choose News, instead of Mail, from the Message Rules submenu.

# Working with Multiple Identities

A single installation of Outlook Express can handle multiple users. Each user is known as an *identity*, and each identity maintains its own set of mail and newsgroup folders.

To create a new identity:

**1** Open the File menu and choose Identities, Add New Identity.

**2** In the dialog box that opens, type a name for the new identity.

**3** If you want to require a password for access to this identity, select the Require A Password check box. Then type and confirm the password.

To switch from one identity to another, choose Switch Identity from the File menu, select the identity you want, and type the password if required.

# Performing Maintenance in Outlook Express

Mail and news messages can quickly accumulate and consume large amounts of disk storage space. The maintenance tab on the Outlook Express Options dialog box lets you set options to regain some of that storage space.

# Reducing Wasted Disk Space

Every time Outlook Express adds a new message to a mail folder, it expands the size of the folder to make space for it. However, it doesn't automatically reduce the size of a folder if you delete a message. Therefore, your folders will eventually take up more disk space than necessary. To reclaim wasted space:

1 Open any mail folder.

2 Choose Folder from the File menu and Compact from the submenu. Or choose Compact All Folders to reduce the wasted space in all of your folders.

You can also eliminate wasted space in your news folders:

1 Choose Options from the Tools menu, and click the Maintenance tab.

2 Click Clean Up Now.

3 Click Compact to eliminate wasted space in news folders, or click Remove Messages to delete the local copies of news messages, leaving only the headers in place. (If you want to see the message bodies again, you can download a new copy from the server later.) Or click Delete to remove all messages and headers.

# Backing Up Your Message Store

Outlook Express doesn't include a command for backing up messages. You can simply include your message files in your normal file backup routine, however. Each Outlook Express folder is stored in a separate file with the extension .dbx. To find out where these files are stored, choose Options from the Tools menu and click the Maintenance tab. Then click Store Folder. If the path to the folder is too long to see, click on the path and press the keyboard's End key to scroll to the end.

**CHAPTER 20**

# Sending and Receiving Faxes

I f you have a fax device, such as a fax modem, installed on your system, Microsoft Windows 2000 automatically installs the fax service and a driver for your fax device, allowing you to send and receive faxes. The visible manifestation of the fax driver is an item in your Printers folder called Fax. (It can be renamed, of course, but that's its default name.) To fax a document, you need to do little more than open the document in its parent application, choose the application's Print command, and specify Fax as your output device.

You can make multiple copies of the fax driver and create distinct properties for each copy. For example, you could set up separate copies with separate billing codes. Or you could use one copy for immediate transmission and another for offpeak hours. Windows 2000 doesn't support shared fax devices, however.

Along with the fax driver, Windows 2000 supplies a cover page editor and four sample cover pages. You can use the samples as they are or modify them, or use the editor to build your own from scratch.

# Setting Up Your System

You'll want to take a number of setup steps before using the fax service for the first time. Among other tasks, unless someone has done this for you already, you'll need to enable the fax service to receive incoming faxes. By default, it's set up to allow outgoing faxes but to ignore incoming calls.

Many of the setup steps involve the Fax Service Management console. A few others require a visit to Fax in Control Panel.

To open the Fax Service Management console, open the Start menu and choose Programs, Accessories, Communications, Fax, Fax Service Management. The Fax Service Management console is shown in Figure 20-1.

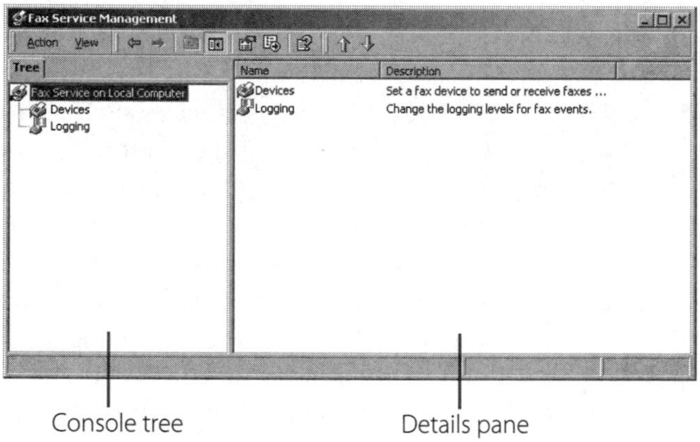

**FIGURE 20-1.**

The Fax Service Management console lets you turn send and receive capability on and off, specify your TSID and CSID, and more.

Console tree          Details pane

The Fax Service Management console has two panes, called the console tree and the details pane. The console tree should show at least two entries—Devices and Logging. If you don't see those entries, double-click the Fax Service On Local Computer entry to expand the tree.

Clicking the Devices entry produces entries in the details pane for each fax device installed on your system. Right-clicking a device entry in the details pane provides access to the device's properties dialog boxes. Clicking the Logging entry reveals, in the details pane, an item for each of the four types of logging that the fax service performs. Right-clicking each logging entry allows you to set a detail level for that kind of logging.

Right-clicking the top-level item in the console tree, Fax Service On Local Computer, provides access to a properties dialog box that governs the behavior of the fax service for all installed fax devices.

## Allowing Incoming Faxes

To enable a fax device to receive faxes:

1 Open the Fax Service Management console.

2 In the console tree, click Devices.

3 In the details pane, select the entry for your fax device. If a Yes appears in the Receive column, you're already set up to receive faxes. If a No appears in that column, right-click the entry for your fax device and choose Receive from the shortcut menu.

## Specifying Your TSID and CSID

Your TSID (transmitting station identifier) is a string of up to 20 characters that tells your fax recipients where your faxes are coming from. When you send a fax, the receiving device prints your TSID at the top of each page (unless it has been set up not to do so).

Your CSID (called station identifier) is a string of up to 20 characters that provides information to senders about who they've reached. When someone sends you a fax, the fax service on your system sends back your CSID. (You'll find CSIDs for the faxes you send in the Received By column of the Sent Faxes folder.)

To specify the TSID and CSID for a fax device:

1 Open the Fax Service Management console.

2 In the console tree, click Devices.

3 In the details pane, right-click the entry for your fax device and choose Properties from the shortcut menu.

4 On the General tab of the properties dialog box for your fax device (see Figure 20-2, on the next page), enter your TSID and CSID.

It's customary to include your fax telephone number in both the TSID and CSID.

## Specifying the Number of Rings to Wait Before Answering

On the General tab of the fax device's properties dialog box (see Figure 20-2), you can also specify the number of rings your fax device should wait before answering an incoming fax. The default is 2. If your telephone line is dedicated to fax use, you might as well reduce this value to 1.

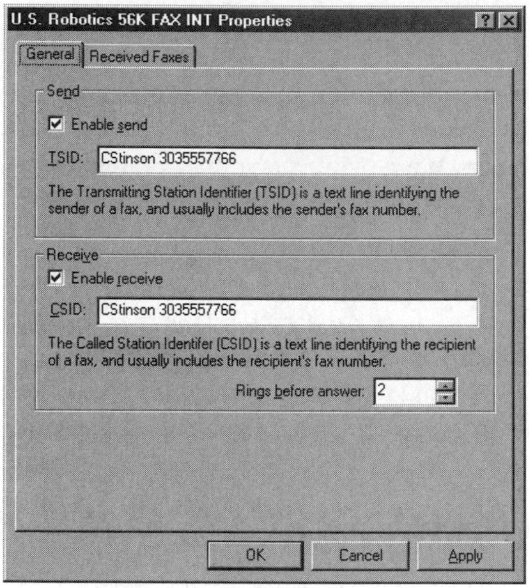

**FIGURE 20-2.**

Configure your fax device in its properties dialog box.

U.S. Robotics 56K FAX INT Properties

General | Received Faxes |

Send

☑ Enable send

TSID: CStinson 3035557766

The Transmitting Station Identifier (TSID) is a text line identifying the sender of a fax, and usually includes the sender's fax number.

Receive

☑ Enable receive

CSID: CStinson 3035557766

The Called Station Identifer (CSID) is a text line identifying the recipient of a fax, and usually includes the recipient's fax number.

Rings before answer: 2

OK    Cancel    Apply

## Telling the Fax Service Where to Store Incoming Faxes

The fax service can route incoming faxes to any or all of the following:

- A printer

- A file folder

- A local e-mail box, on a MAPI-enabled mail system.

Outlook Express is not a MAPI-enabled mail client. Microsoft Outlook, when set up in Corporate Or Workgroup mode, is an example of a MAPI-enabled client.

By default, only the second option is enabled, and incoming faxes are stored in the %AllUsersProfile%\Documents\My Faxes\Received Faxes folder. You can easily get to that folder by opening the Start menu and choosing Programs, Accessories, Communications, Fax, My Faxes. In the My Faxes folder, you'll find the Received Faxes folder; in it you'll find a .tif file for each fax you've received.

To enable either of the other routing options, or to change the folder in which a particular fax device's incoming faxes are stored, open the device's properties dialog box and click the Received Faxes tab. Figure 20-3 shows the Received Faxes tab of the fax device's properties dialog box.

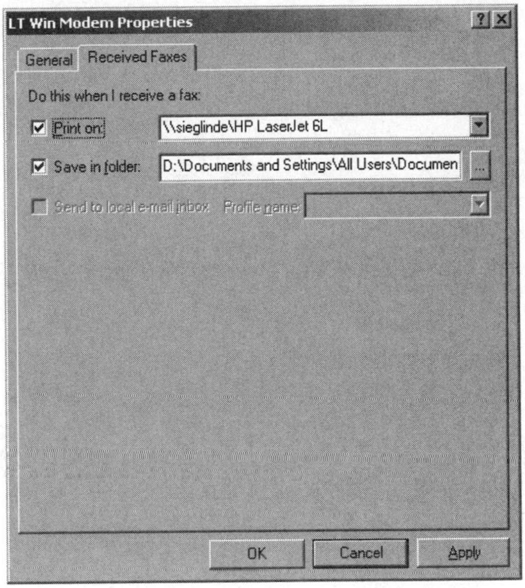

**FIGURE 20-3.**

The Received Faxes tab of the fax device's properties dialog box lets you specify where you want incoming faxes to go.

> 🌟 **TIP**
>
> If you're short of disk space and don't need disk copies of incoming faxes, you can route your faxes only to a printer. Clear the Save In Folder check box, select the Print On check box, and specify the path of a printer.

## Specifying Retry Characteristics for the Fax Service

By default, if an outbound fax fails for any reason—the line is busy, for example, or the recipient doesn't answer—the fax service tries again at 10-minute intervals until it has either succeeded or failed three times. To change the retry parameters (for all fax devices):

1  Open the Fax Service Management console.

2  In the console tree, right-click Fax Service On Local Computer, and choose Properties.

**3** In the properties dialog box (see Figure 20-4), enter values for Number Of Retries and Minutes Between Retries.

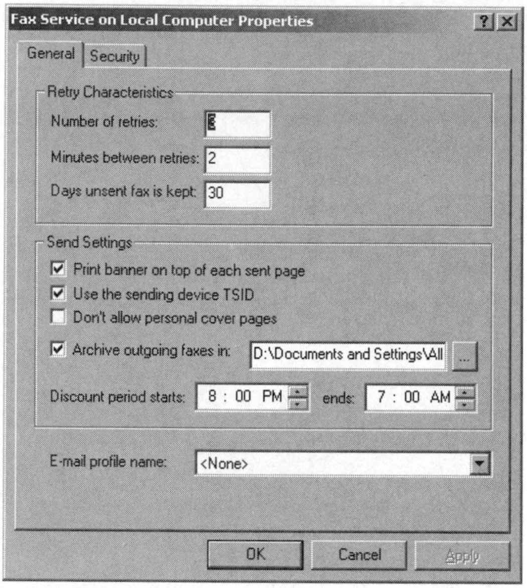

**FIGURE 20-4.**
You can specify retry characteristics for all installed fax devices in the Fax Service On Local Computer Properties dialog box.

Fax Service on Local Computer Properties

General | Security

Retry Characteristics
Number of retries: [8]
Minutes between retries: [2]
Days unsent fax is kept: [30]

Send Settings
☑ Print banner on top of each sent page
☑ Use the sending device TSID
☐ Don't allow personal cover pages
☑ Archive outgoing faxes in: [D:\Documents and Settings\All] [...]
Discount period starts: [8 : 00 PM] ends: [7 : 00 AM]

E-mail profile name: [<None>]

[OK] [Cancel] [Apply]

## Specifying Discount Hours

If your phone service costs less at particular hours of the day, you might want to indicate those hours in the Fax Service On Local Computer Properties dialog box. (See Figure 20-4.) When you send a fax, you'll have the opportunity to schedule its transmission to begin during the discount period.

## Using Other Send Settings

If Print Banner On Top Of Each Sent Page is selected (its default state), the fax service prints the following information at the top of each transmitted page:

- The date and time of transmission

- Your TSID

- Your company name (as recorded in Fax in Control Panel)

- The recipient's fax number

- The current page number

- The total number of pages in the transmission

To suppress this information, clear the first check box in the Send Settings section of the properties dialog box. (See Figure 20-4.) To suppress the TSID (and substitute your fax number), clear the second check box.

Outgoing faxes are stored by default in the %AllUsersProfile%\ Documents\My Faxes\Sent Faxes folder. To store them elsewhere, specify a new folder next to the fourth check box. To store them nowhere (and conserve disk space), clear the check box.

## Requesting E-Mail Confirmation of Sent Faxes

If you have a MAPI-enabled e-mail client installed, you can request that the fax service send you e-mail confirmation of each successful fax transmission. To do so, specify a profile name at the bottom of the Fax Service On Local Computer Properties dialog box. (See Figure 20-4.) (If you do not have a MAPI-enabled e-mail client installed, this option is not available.)

## Setting Logging Levels for Fax Events

**? SEE ALSO**

For information about using the Computer Management console to view the fax event log, see "Reviewing Fax Events," page 439.

Fax events, such as successful and unsuccessful transmissions and receipts, are recorded in the Application Log and can be reviewed via the Computer Management console. You can use the Fax Service Management console to control the amount of detail recorded. To change a logging level:

1   Open the Fax Service Management console.

2   In the console tree, click Logging. Four event-type entries appear in the details pane: Inbound, Initialization/Termination, Outbound, and Unknown.

3   Right-click one of the items in the details pane, and choose Level Of Detail from the shortcut menu. From the ensuing submenu, choose one of the four options: None, Minimum, Medium, and Maximum. The default choice for all four event types is Medium.

The inbound and outbound events relate to incoming and outgoing faxes. Initialization/Termination events occur when the fax service is started or stopped. All other fax events fall into the Unknown category.

V

**Sharing and Communicating**

# Setting Priorities for Multiple Fax Devices

If you have more than one fax device installed, an entry for each will appear in the details pane when you click Devices in the console tree. The Fax Management toolbar will also display two additional buttons: an up arrow icon (Raise The Send Priority Of This Device), and a down arrow icon (Lower The Send Priority Of This Device). By default, the device at the top of the list will be used by the fax service unless it is busy. To change the priority level of a fax device, select it in the details pane, and then click either the Raise or Lower icon.

# Specifying Information About Yourself

To make effective use of the cover pages supplied with the fax service, or cover pages that you create yourself with the help of Cover Page Editor, you'll need to record some information about yourself. To do that, open the Start menu and choose Settings, Control Panel, Fax. Figure 20-5 shows the User Information tab of Fax in Control Panel. (Depending on your hardware, your dialog box might be somewhat different.) You can use all of the fields on this form except E-Mail Address and Billing Code for your cover pages.

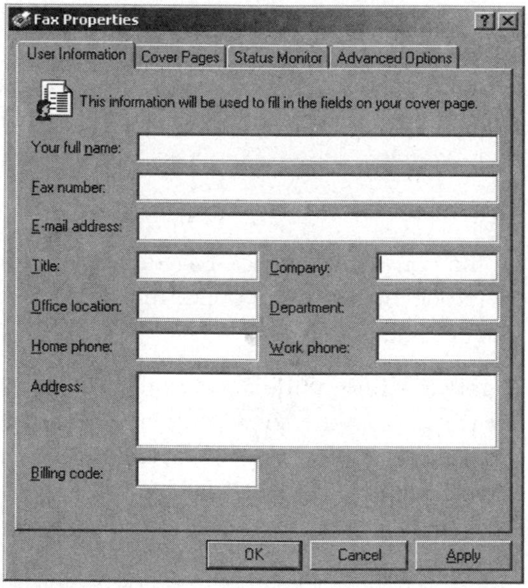

**FIGURE 20-5.**
Fax in Control Panel is where you furnish information about yourself. This information becomes available to your cover pages.

**NOTE**

If you don't supply information about yourself in Control Panel, the Send Fax Wizard will ask you for it the first time you send a fax.

If you want to associate a billing code with all faxes transmitted from your system, enter that billing code into the Billing Code field. If you use more than one billing code, leave this field blank, make separate copies of the fax driver for each code you use, and then enter the billing codes via the fax drivers' dialog boxes.

## Controlling Fax Monitor

By default, the fax service opens the Fax Monitor dialog box whenever you send or receive a fax. Fax Monitor, shown in Figure 20-6, remains visible from the time a fax event occurs until you close it. You can scroll back through the monitor's display to read about other recent fax events. You can also use Fax Monitor to abort an incoming or outgoing fax or to turn off automatic answering of the next incoming fax call.

**FIGURE 20-6.**

Fax Monitor displays information about recent fax events and the current status of your fax device.

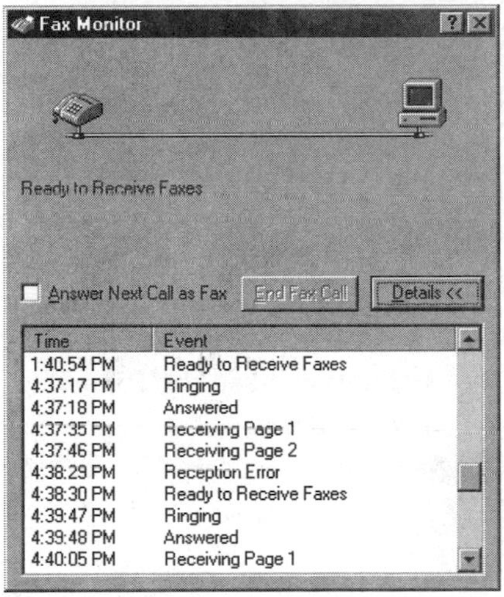

You can use the Status Monitor tab of Fax in Control Panel (see Figure 20-7, on the next page) to alter the behavior of Fax Monitor. The four check boxes in the Notification area describe your options.

**(?) SEE ALSO**

For information about associating sounds with events, see "Setting Sounds for Various Events," page 112.

If you opt to have the system play a sound when a fax event occurs, you can use Sounds And Multimedia in Control Panel to specify what sounds you'd like to hear. By default, the system plays two different telephone-ring sounds—one for an incoming fax, the other for an outbound fax.

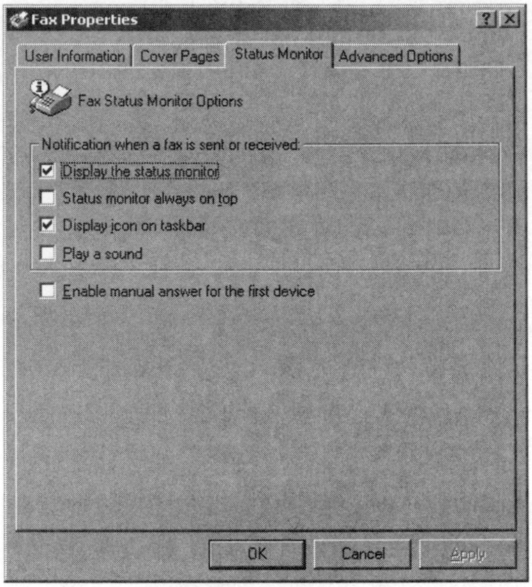

**FIGURE 20-7.**

You can use the Status
Monitor tab of Fax
in Control Panel to
control Fax Monitor's
behavior.

**FIGURE 20-7.**

You can use the Status
Monitor tab of Fax
in Control Panel to
control Fax Monitor's
behavior.

# Setting Up a Line to Be Used for Voice and Fax

If you use the same telephone line for both voice and fax calls, select
the Enable Manual Answer For The First Device check box. When
your line receives a call, you'll see the following dialog box.

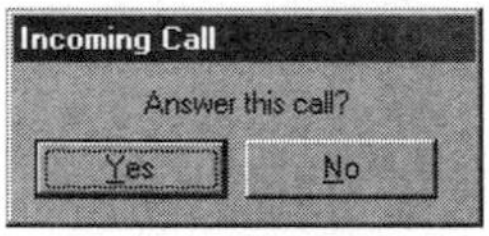

If you answer Yes, the fax service answers the call. (If you have more
than one fax device, the highest-priority device answers.)

If you know that the next incoming call will be a voice call, clear the
Answer Next Call As Fax check box in Fax Monitor. (The check box is
shown in Figure 20-6 on page 433.)

# Creating Copies of Your Fax Driver

To create one or more additional copies of your fax driver, click the
Advanced Options tab of Fax in Control Panel. Then click Add A Fax
Printer. Windows 2000 creates a copy and gives it a default name.

Creating additional copies of the driver allows you to tailor the characteristics of each copy to suit your needs. For example, you can specify a unique billing code for each driver copy or specify different image-quality settings for different copies. If you have multiple copies of your fax driver, when you print from an application, you'll see each copy in the list of available output devices and you'll be able to choose the one you want to use.

To modify any of the settings associated with a fax driver:

**1** Open the Start menu and choose Settings, Printers.

**2** Right-click the entry for your fax driver and choose Properties from the shortcut menu.

The Fax Properties dialog box that appears has four tabs: General, Sharing, Security, and User Information. The General tab includes a Printing Preferences button, which opens an additional dialog box offering choices of paper size, image quality, orientation, time to send, and billing code.

Unlike for standard printers, Windows 2000 doesn't support fax sharing, so the Sharing tab has no function. The User Information tab replicates the information you specified via Control Panel and is common to all copies of the fax driver. (If you change your title on one copy, for example, the change is transmitted to all other copies.) All other settings in the properties dialog box can be set individually for each copy of the driver.

# Faxing a Document

To fax a document from an application:

**1** Choose the application's Print command and specify a fax driver as your output device.

The Send Fax Wizard appears.

**2** Click Next to get past the welcome page and arrive at the Recipient And Dialing Information page. (See Figure 20-8, on the next page.)

**3** Use the first three lines of this page to supply the name, fax number, and country of a recipient. Then click Add. Alternatively, click Address Book and choose one or more addressees there.

**V**

**Sharing and Communicating**

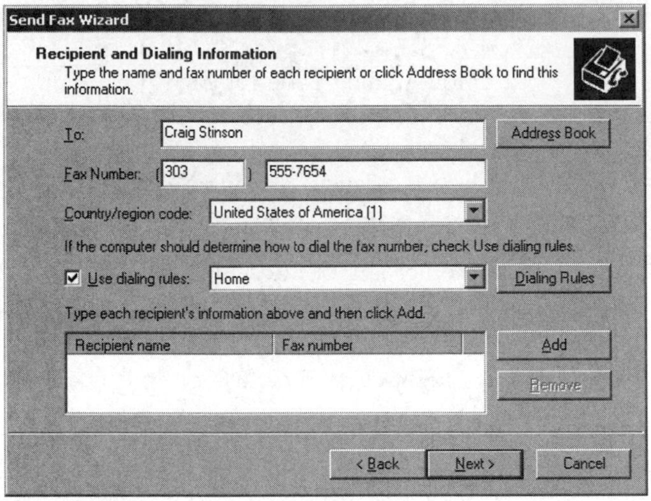

**FIGURE 20-8.**

You can type an addressee name and number or select one from the Address Book.

If you click Address Book, you'll see a window listing all the contacts in the current Address Book identity. To choose an addressee, select a name in this list, and then click the To button. You can repeat this process for as many addressees as you like. When you have finished, click OK to return to the Send Fax Wizard.

**? SEE ALSO**

For information about dialing rules, see "Setting Up Dialing Locations," page 278.

4  Unless you have a reason not to use the Windows 2000 dialing rules (which govern the way the system dials numbers in different area codes), be sure to select the Use Dialing Rules check box and choose a location from the associated list. If you need to create a new location or change the dialing rules associated with an existing location, click Dialing Rules.

5  Click Next in the wizard to go to Adding A Cover Page. (See Figure 20-9.)

6  If you want to use a cover page, select the check box and use the Cover Page Template box to choose from the available cover pages.

   The fax driver replaces fields in the cover page template with the corresponding information you entered about yourself on the User Information tab of the device's properties dialog box and the addressee information you entered in step 3. You can use the text boxes on the wizard's page to add a subject line and a note to your cover page.

7  Click Next to go to the Scheduling Transmission page, shown in Figure 20-10.

**FIGURE 20-9.**

The wizard lets you select a cover page.

**8** Tell the wizard when you want to begin sending your fax. If you specify discount hours, the system uses the discount hour setting in your fax driver's properties dialog box.

**9** Add a billing code if you want. The code you enter overrides the code specified in your fax driver's properties dialog box. If you leave the field blank, the properties dialog box setting (if any) is used.

**10** Click next to review your specifications. If everything looks right, click Finish.

**FIGURE 20-10.**

You can send your fax now, during discount hours, or at any specified time during the next 24 hours.

Address Book groups cannot be used as fax addressees. As a workaround for this limitation you can create an Address Book identity that duplicates the contents of a group. For example, if you have a group named Members, create an identity named Board and copy the members of your Members group into your Board identity. When you go to Address Book to select fax addressees, switch to the Board identity and select all members.

# Faxing a Cover Page Only

You can send a quick greeting or note to someone by faxing just a cover page, with or without a note:

1 Open the Start menu and choose Programs, Accessories, Communications, Fax, Send Cover Page Fax.

2 Complete the Recipient And Dialing Information page of the Send Fax Wizard, as described previously on page 435.

3 Select a cover page, and then type a subject and a note.

4 Tell the wizard when to transmit, click Next, and click Finish.

# Managing a Fax Queue

Outbound fax jobs awaiting transmission are displayed in a fax queue, just as pending print jobs are displayed in a print queue. The fax queue (see Figure 20-11) looks in most respects exactly like a print queue.

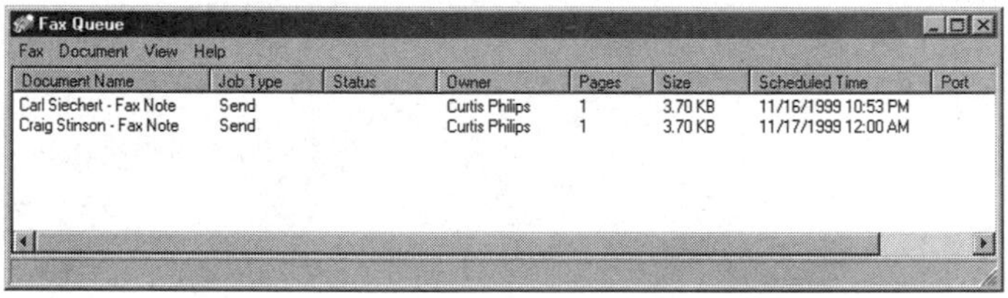

**FIGURE 20-11.**
Outbound fax jobs awaiting their turn at the modem are displayed in a fax queue.

To display a fax queue, right-click the fax icon in your taskbar status area and choose Fax Queue. Or open the Start menu and choose Settings, Printers, Fax (if Fax is the name of your fax driver).

In the Fax Queue window, you can do any of the following:

■ Cancel a fax job (Right-click it and choose Cancel from the shortcut menu.)

- Cancel all fax jobs (Choose Cancel All Faxes from the Fax menu.)

- Pause the entire queue (Choose Pause Faxing from the Fax menu.)

- Restart a paused queue (Choose Pause Faxing again from the Fax menu.)

- Inspect a fax job's properties (Right-click it and choose Properties from the shortcut menu.)

# Reviewing Sent and Received Faxes

Sent and received faxes are stored as .tif files, which are associated by default with Imaging, the application described in Chapter 37. You can use Imaging to print or annotate your faxes or to bundle two or more faxes together into a single document. Imaging's thumbnails view makes it easy to navigate multipage fax documents. *For details, see Chapter 37 "Manipulating Faxes and Images with Imaging."*

If you haven't changed the fax service's default archiving and routing parameters, you can review your sent and received faxes by opening the Start menu and choosing Programs, Accessories, Communications, Fax, My Faxes. My Faxes contains subfolders named Received Faxes and Sent Faxes, and therein you'll find your received and sent items, each with an unlovely system-provided name, such as 7a7626f800.tif.

The names might not provide much useful information, but Sent Faxes and Received Faxes have special columns that are informative: Name, Transmitted By, Sender Name, Caller ID, Routing, Recipient Name, Recipient Number, Transmission Time, and Subject. Be sure to use Details view for these folders so you can tell which fax is which. (Thumbnails view isn't available in the Sent Faxes and Received Faxes folders.)

# Reviewing Fax Events

Fax Monitor provides minimal information about fax events. To get more details, you can use the Windows 2000 Event Viewer. To open Event Viewer and view fax events only:

**1** Open the Start menu and choose Settings, Control Panel, Administrative Tools, Event Viewer.

**V**

**Sharing and Communicating**

**2** In the console tree pane, click Application Log.

**3** In the console tree pane, right-click Application Log and choose View from the shortcut menu.

**4** From the View submenu, choose Filter.

**5** On the Filter tab of the Application Log Properties dialog box, open the Event Source list and choose Fax Service. (You will need to scroll down to get to Fax Service, or type the letter *F* to scroll to its general vicinity.)

**6** Click OK.

You can filter the event log further to show only inbound, outbound, initialization/termination, or unknown events:

**1** Follow steps 1 through 5 above.

**2** From the Category list, choose the type of event you want to see.

To see the details about a particular event, double-click it in the details pane. Figure 20-12 shows a detailed view of a fax event.

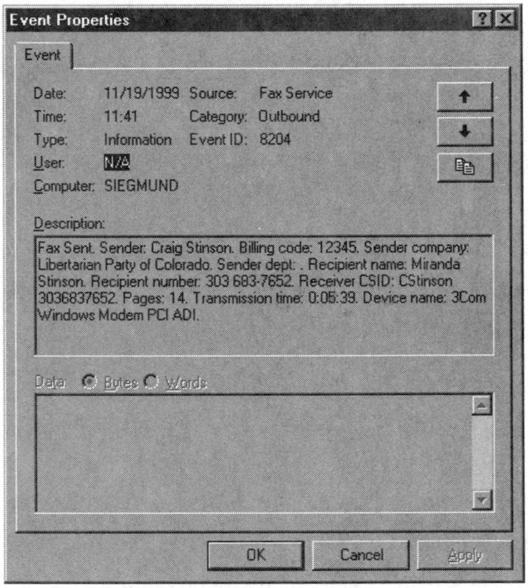

**FIGURE 20-12.**

The properties dialog box for a fax event provides details about what went where when.

---

**Retrieving Billing Code Information**

As Figure 20-12 shows, the properties dialog box for a successful fax transmission includes the billing code associated with that event. Unfortunately, this is the only place you can view billing-code information, and there's no way to filter Event Viewer by billing code. You can, however, use Event Viewer's Find command to locate items that have a particular billing code:

**1** In the console tree pane, right-click Application Log.

**2** From the shortcut menu, choose View.

**3** From the View submenu, choose Find.

**4** In the Description field of the Find dialog box, enter your billing code.

**5** Click Find Next to locate the next matching record in Event Viewer.

# Using Cover Page Editor

Cover Page Editor is a simple black-and-white graphics application that lets you design and edit cover pages. Figure 20-13 shows Cover Page Editor with one of the four cover pages supplied with Windows 2000.

**FIGURE 20-13.**

You can use Cover Page Editor to modify supplied cover pages or create your own.

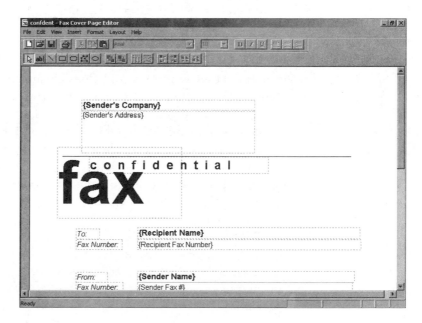

You probably won't find a Start menu item for Cover Page Editor. You can open the Start menu, choose Run, and type the name of its executable—*faxcover.exe*—or you can run it as follows:

1  From the Start menu, choose Programs, Accessories, Communications, Fax, My Faxes.

2  In the My Faxes folder, open Common Coverpages.

3  Double-click the entry for the cover page you want to work with. (To create a new cover page from scratch, open any existing cover page. Then choose New from the File menu.)

# Selecting, Sizing, and Moving Objects

Every element on a cover page that's bounded by a dotted line in Cover Page Editor is a distinct object. To size or move an object, begin by clicking it. Black handles appear around the selected object's perimeter. To change an object's size, drag one of the handles. To move an object, position the mouse along the perimeter, but not on a handle. A four-headed arrow appears beside the normal mouse pointer. Drag the object to its new location. If you change your mind, choose Undo from the Edit menu.

To move two or more objects at once, Ctrl-click each one. The objects become temporarily grouped and will move together.

## Aligning Objects

You can use the View menu's Grid Lines command to display light-blue grid lines in the editor. These might help you in positioning objects. To achieve alignment between objects, however, it's simpler to use the Layout menu's Align Objects command. First Ctrl-click each of the objects you want to align, and then choose the command. Options on the Align Objects submenu let you line up objects flush left or flush right. You can also top align and bottom align objects or center objects horizontally or vertically.

## Spacing Objects Evenly

To ensure that three or more objects have equal vertical or horizontal space between them, first Ctrl-click those objects. Then open the Layout menu, point to Space Evenly, and choose Across or Down from the submenu.

### Centering Objects on the Page

To center one or more objects on the page, vertically or horizontally, first Ctrl-click the objects. Then open the Layout menu, point to Center On Page, and choose Width or Height.

### Changing the Z Order of Stacked Objects

If two or more objects lie atop one another, the order in which they're stacked is called the *z order* (*x, y,* and *z* are the letters used in geometry to describe width, height, and depth.) To change the z order of an object relative to others, select the object, open the Layout menu, and choose either Bring To Front or Send To Back.

## Adding Fixed Text

Fixed text is text that doesn't change (as distinguished from fields, which are replaced by information about the sender, recipient, or content of a fax). To add fixed text:

Text

1   Click the Text tool on the Drawing toolbar. (If the Drawing toolbar isn't visible, choose Drawing Toolbar from the View menu.)

2   Click one corner of the place where you want the object to go. Then drag to the diagonally opposite corner. A perimeter rectangle with black handles appears as you drag.

3   Type your text within the object perimeter. Use the Format menu's Font and Align Text commands (or their toolbar equivalents) to get the text looking the way you want it.

Note that new objects don't affect the placement of existing objects. If you want to insert a line of text between two lines, you must first drag objects out of the way to make room for the incoming text.

## Inserting Fields, Images, and Graphics

Objects that begin and end with braces—such as {Recipient Name} and {Recipient Fax Number} in Figure 20-13—are fields. When your fax is sent, these fields will be replaced by data—the name and number of the person to whom you're faxing, for example. To add fields to a cover page, use the Insert menu. The available fields appear in three submenus: Recipient, Sender, and Message.

To place an image on a cover page, first open or create that image in another application (such as Paint). Copy the image to the Clipboard, and then use Cover Page Editor's Paste command. The pasted image appears in the upper left corner of the Cover Page Editor window. Use the mouse to drag it into position.

To insert lines and shapes, use the Line, Rectangle, Rounded Rectangle, Polygon, and Oval tools from the Drawing toolbar. (If you don't see the Drawing toolbar, choose the View menu's Drawing Toolbar command.)

Line       Rectangle    Rounded     Polygon      Oval
                        Rectangle

To use any of these tools other than the Polygon tool, simply click the cover page and drag. To use the Polygon tool, click each vertex of your polygon. When you have finished, double-click to close the polygon.

Holding down the Shift key while you drag constrains the Line, Rectangle, Rounded Rectangle, and Oval tools. Shift-dragging with the Line tool creates a horizontal, vertical, or 45-degree diagonal line. Shift-dragging with the Rectangle and Rounded Rectangle tools creates a square and square with rounded edges, respectively, while Shift-dragging with the Oval tool creates a circle.

## Previewing, Printing, and Saving

You can use the File menu's Print Preview command to get a bird's-eye view of your cover page. Other commands on the File menu let you send the page to the printer or store it on disk. Use the Save As command on the File menu to give your file an original name. Or use the Save command to save under the current name.

# CHAPTER 21

# Using NetMeeting

Microsoft NetMeeting is a program that lets you engage in a conference with one or many users across the Internet or a local area network. If your computer has a sound card, a microphone, and speakers, you can talk to another person in something approximating real time. If you have a video camera connected to your computer, you can exchange video images. With or without audio and video equipment, you can "chat" with others, exchange drawings and diagrams by means of a virtual whiteboard, send and receive files, and even work simultaneously in a shared program. When you're not in a meeting, you can control another computer remotely using NetMeeting's Remote Desktop Sharing.

# What You Need to Use NetMeeting

The basic requirement to run NetMeeting is simple: you need some way to reach the outside world. This can be a network connection (to meet with your coworkers), a modem (28,800 bps or faster), or some other connection to the Internet—ISDN, xDSL (any of the varieties of digital subscriber line technologies such as ADSL and SDSL), cable modem, or proxy server, for example. A network or Internet connection alone allows you to use NetMeeting's chat feature, but not much else.

As you add options, you can use more of NetMeeting's capabilities. First, the modem requirement is bumped up to at least 56,000 bps for any of the advanced features. Then add one or more of the following:

- To be able to hear others speak, add a sound card and speakers.

- To add your own voice to the fray, connect a microphone to the sound card.

- To send your picture to others, add a video capture card or camera that provides a Video for Windows capture driver.

# Getting Started with NetMeeting

To start NetMeeting, open the Start menu and choose Programs, Accessories, Communications, NetMeeting. The first time you run NetMeeting, a wizard greets you and introduces you to the program. Among other things, you'll be asked to supply your name, e-mail address, location, and comments. You need to give NetMeeting your first name, last name, and e-mail address. The other fields are optional.

**TIP**

You can change any of the entries you make in this wizard once you are in NetMeeting. Choose Options from the Tools menu and click the General tab.

Then the wizard asks whether you want to log on to a directory server whenever you start NetMeeting. If you answer in the affirmative, you'll be asked to select a directory server.

A *directory server*, also known as an *Internet location server (ILS)*, provides a listing of people available for NetMeeting calls. If you log on to such a server, you make it easy for others to reach you via NetMeeting. The server keeps track of your whereabouts (your current IP address, if you're connected to the Internet), and, while you're logged on, someone who wants to call you can simply find your name on the server and click it. A directory server can also show whether or not you have sound and video equipment, shows your physical location (city, state, and country), and provides a comments field where you can let people know a little more about you. Your e-mail address is displayed so people can contact you by e-mail if they can't reach you with NetMeeting.

You have the option of logging on to one of the public directory servers but not listing yourself there. If you do that, the directory server can still help a caller find you. But the caller will need to know your e-mail address to do this.

On the next page, the wizard asks how you plan to make NetMeeting calls: via 14,400 bps modem; 28,800 bps or faster modem; cable, xDSL, or ISDN; or local area network. And, after determining where you want NetMeeting shortcuts, this particular wizard hands you off to another wizard, which tests the volume levels of your microphone and speakers (assuming you have such equipment). Once you get past this second wizard, the program logs you on to the directory server you specified (if you did specify one), and you're ready for your first call.

> **NOTE**

NetMeeting doesn't work with IPX networks.

# The NetMeeting User Interface

Figure 21-1, on the next page, shows the most important landmarks of the NetMeeting window. At the top of the window is the Address bar. Like the Address bar in Internet Explorer, use it to type the address of the person you want to call or select from a list of previous connections. You can enter an e-mail address, a computer name, or an IP address. The three buttons down the right side of the window allow you to make and terminate calls.

The box with the NetMeeting logo is where you will see the video of the people you call, assuming they have a camera connected to their computer.

The three buttons across the middle of the window are for audio and video control. The Name box lists people to whom you are currently connected. Finally, the buttons across the bottom provide other ways to share information, including sharing programs, chat, the whiteboard, and transferring files.

V

Sharing and Communicating

**FIGURE 21-1.**

The main NetMeeting window provides the tools to make, accept, and control your calls.

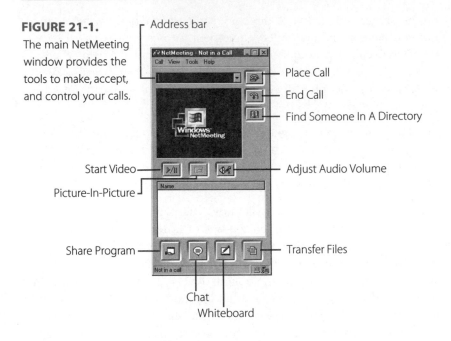

Address bar

Place Call

End Call

Find Someone In A Directory

Start Video

Picture-In-Picture

Adjust Audio Volume

Share Program

Transfer Files

Chat

Whiteboard

# Finding Someone to Call

When you click the Find Someone In A Directory button, NetMeeting displays the Find Someone window. This window provides many ways to locate people.

Initially, the Find Someone window displays either a search form (if the server you logged on to uses an HTML front end) or a list of names on the server. The names in this list are those of all users who are currently logged on to that server and have chosen to have themselves listed.

The Select A Directory list contains a number of directories from which you can find people to call:

- History shows a list of the names and addresses of people you've met with before.

- Windows Address Book displays the names of all users in your Address Book for whom you've provided conference server and conferencing address information.

- Microsoft Internet Directory provides a good way to find other NetMeeting users on the Internet. Microsoft Internet Directory is an example of an ILS server with an HTML front end. It provides a simple search that allows you to locate people you know quickly. Figure 21-2 shows both the search form and an example of the results. Simply click the name of the person you want to call.

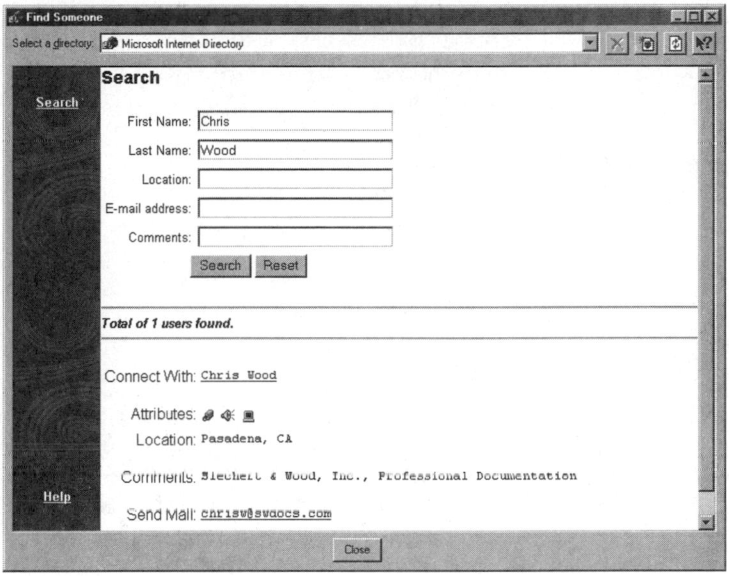

**FIGURE 21-2.**

A directory server makes it easy for people to connect to you via NetMeeting.

- The list also displays the addresses of conventional ILS servers you've previously connected to. If you haven't connected to any yet, type the name of a server such as *ils.microsoft.com* to add that server to the list of directories. The server will display the directory in the Find Someone window. You can't search a conventional ILS server, but you can sort the information on any of the columns, and then type a few letters into the Type Name Or Select From List box to move quickly in the sorted column.

**WARNING**

As you'll discover the first time you explore a directory server listing, not everyone who uses NetMeeting has business in mind, and many people who list themselves on the servers are quite forthright about the type of communication they desire. NetMeeting doesn't offer a Content Advisor for its directory listings, so you might want to discourage young family members from using this program.

V

Sharing and Communicating

If you don't find the party you're looking for, try clicking the Refresh button on the toolbar. The directory listing shows you who was logged on to the directory server when you logged on yourself—or when you last used the Refresh button. It's possible that your party logged on after you did, so it's always a good idea to click Refresh before deciding that your party isn't available.

If someone you want to call is logged on to a directory server other than the one you're currently looking at, use the Select A Directory list to switch to the directory in which your party is listed.

> **NOTE**
>
> Using Select A Directory to choose another directory server doesn't change the server that you are logged on to; it simply changes the server that's displayed.

# Placing a Call

There are several ways to place a call in NetMeeting:

- If your party is logged on to a directory server and listed on the server, you can select his or her name in the Find Someone window and click Call (or simply double-click the name).

- You can type an entry into the NetMeeting Address bar and click the Place Call button.

- You can choose New Call from the Call menu, or click the Place Call button when the Address bar is empty and use the Place A Call dialog box, shown in Figure 21-3.

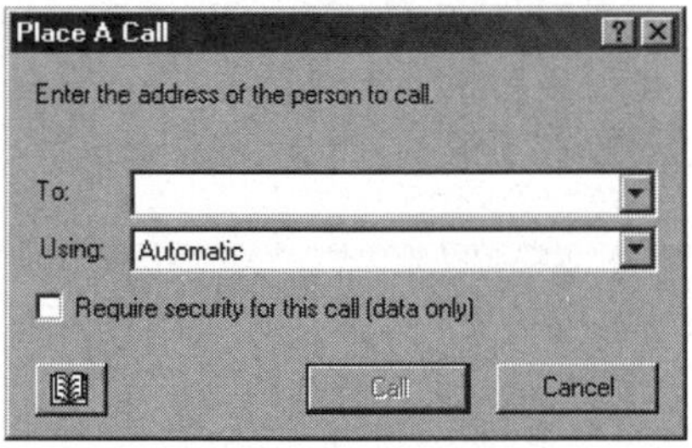

**FIGURE 21-3.**
Using the Place A Call dialog box allows you to choose to use NetMeeting's security feature on a call-by-call basis.

In either the Address bar or the Place A Call dialog box, you can enter any of the following:

- Your party's e-mail address. If your party is logged on to a different directory server from you, you can specify the server name plus your party's e-mail address using the format *servername/e-mail address.* For example, if your party is logged on to ils2.microsoft.com and his or her e-mail address is jeff@widgets.microsoft.com, you would type *ils2.microsoft.com/ jeff@widgets.microsoft.com*

- If you're calling someone on your own local area network, you can enter the network name of your party's computer. Type just the name of the computer; don't precede it with a backslash or domain name. For example, if your party is working from the computer named \\MARKETING3, simply type *marketing3*

- If your party is connected to the Internet and you know his or her IP address, you can specify the IP address. (The IP address consists of four numbers separated by periods, like this: 192.168.1.201.) Your party doesn't need to be logged on to a directory server.

⭐ TIP

The Address bar maintains a list of recently used calling addresses. If you're calling someone again, you might be able to select that person's address from the list.

When you use the Place A Call dialog box, you can usually leave Using set to Automatic. If NetMeeting has trouble finding someone and you know the address is correct, try a more specific option.

⭐ TIP

You can find your own IP address by choosing About Windows NetMeeting from the Help menu. If you have separate connections to your local area network and to the Internet, you'll see an IP address for each one at the bottom of the About Windows NetMeeting dialog box. (If you're not sure which is your IP address on the Internet, open the Start menu, choose Run, and type *cmd /k ipconfig.* The window that appears shows your IP address for each network adapter.) Be aware, though, that if you're using a dial-up connection to connect to the Internet, your IP address is probably different every time you connect.

A few moments after placing your call, if all goes well, you'll hear a sound signaling that your party has answered the call. You'll see your name, the name of the party you called, and the names of anyone else who is connected with the party you called.

If the person you call is already talking to someone else, everyone in the meeting must accept the call or you'll see the message shown on the next page.

V

Sharing and Communicating

**Problems with Internet Connections Through Proxy Server**

If you connect to the Internet through a proxy server, you might need to adjust some WinSock settings in order to be able to place and receive calls over the Internet, and to be able to send and receive audio and video over the Internet. If you're having trouble with any of these functions, search the Microsoft Knowledge Base (available on the Web at *support.microsoft.com*) for information about setting up Microsoft Proxy Server for use with NetMeeting.

# Calling by Speed Dial

NetMeeting's Speed Dial directory, shown in Figure 21-4, lets you create a list of people with whom you communicate. You can call someone from the Speed Dial list exactly as you would from a directory list—by selecting a name and clicking the Call button. The advantage of working in the Speed Dial directory is simply that the list is, presumably, much shorter than a directory server's list, so it's easier to find the party you're trying to call. Once you've added one or more names to the Speed Dial directory, you open the directory by selecting Speed Dial from the Select A Directory list in the Find Someone window.

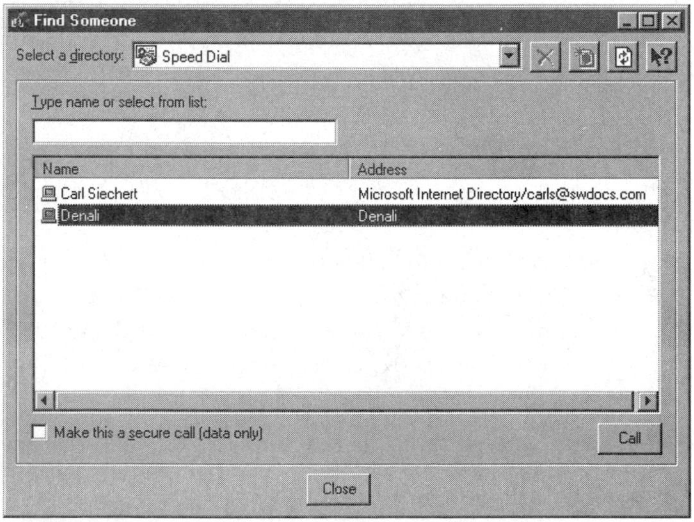

**FIGURE 21-4.**

The Speed Dial directory makes it easy to reconnect to someone you've talked to.

## Creating Speed Dial Entries

To create a Speed Dial entry, simply right-click the name you want to add to the Speed Dial directory and choose Add To SpeedDial List. You can use this method in most places where names appear in NetMeeting, including the Name list in the NetMeeting window, the Windows Address Book directory, and any conventional ILS directory. One place you can't do it is from the Microsoft Internet Directory.

## Creating Speed Dial Shortcuts

You can create a Speed Dial shortcut, suitable for storage on your desktop or elsewhere, or for e-mailing to a friend. To create a shortcut:

**1** Choose Create Speed Dial from the Call menu.

**2** In the Create Speed Dial dialog box, type the address into the Address box and choose the appropriate Call Using option.

**3** Select the Save On The Desktop option.

If you want your Speed Dial shortcut in a folder other than Desktop, you'll need to move it after it lands on the desktop.

# Calling from the History Directory

NetMeeting's History directory, shown in Figure 21-5, maintains a list of everyone you've talked to, regardless of who initiated the call. The list also includes people whose calls you have chosen not to answer.

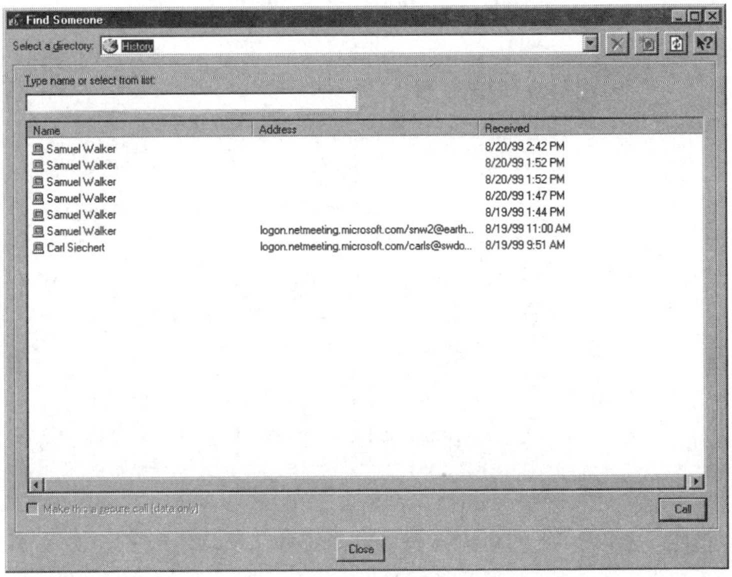

**FIGURE 21-5.**

NetMeeting's History directory keeps a log of those you've called and those who have called you.

V

Sharing and Communicating

To place another call to someone in your History list, select a name and click the Call button.

# Answering a Call

To receive a call, you must be running NetMeeting. Unless you're communicating over your own local area network, you must also be connected to the Internet. If the party calling you is planning to find you on a directory server, you must be logged on to that server. When the call comes in, you'll hear a sound like a ringing telephone—assuming you have a sound card and speakers. A message window will appear, regardless of which program you're currently working in, informing you of the caller's identity and asking whether you want to accept the call. The ringing will continue until you click Accept or Ignore, or until the caller clicks Cancel.

## Accepting Calls Automatically

You can have NetMeeting accept all incoming calls automatically. To do this, choose Automatically Accept Calls from the Call menu (when the command is selected a check mark appears next to it). If you choose this option, NetMeeting notifies you when a call arrives. It doesn't ask whether you want to accept.

## Running NetMeeting Automatically at Startup

NetMeeting also includes an option that causes the program to run automatically when you start Windows. If you exercise this option, the program watches for incoming calls and notifies you if one arrives, but it remains out of sight until then. If you want to interact with NetMeeting after starting it in this way, you can double-click the NetMeeting icon that appears in the taskbar's status area.

Note, however, that if you expect to receive calls over the Internet, your Internet connection must also be established automatically at startup for this background mode to work. Otherwise, NetMeeting reports an error when it tries to log on to your directory server.

To have NetMeeting run automatically at startup, choose Options from the Tools menu. On the General tab, select the Run NetMeeting In The Background When Windows Starts check box.

## Hanging the Do Not Disturb Sign

To have NetMeeting automatically reject all incoming calls, choose Do Not Disturb from the Call menu. After you choose this option—and until you choose it a second time—anyone trying to call you receives a message saying "The other party did not accept your call."

Note that NetMeeting always starts with Do Not Disturb turned off, even if the feature is turned on when you close NetMeeting.

# Sending and Receiving Sound

If your computer is equipped with a sound card, microphone, and speakers, you can use NetMeeting for Internet telephony. Sound communication requires the TCP/IP protocol (which means that to use it on a local area network, your network must be running on TCP/IP) and is limited to one pair of users at a time. (If you hold a conference with more than two users, you can still send and receive sound, but with only one other person at a time.)

Sound transmission can be either unidirectional or bidirectional. If you have full sound equipment, but the person you call has only a sound card and speakers (no microphone), that person can hear your voice, but there will be silence on your end.

Before you use sound for the first time, you need to run the Audio Tuning Wizard. This is a normal part of NetMeeting's initial startup procedure, so that detail has probably already been taken care of. If you change your sound card or microphone, however, you need to run the tuning wizard again. You can do that by choosing Audio Tuning Wizard from the Tools menu.

Only the first two people who connect in a meeting with three or more participants can talk to each other. The other participants must get along with the data elements of NetMeeting.

Figure 21-6, on the next page, shows the Audio tab in the Options dialog box (choose Options from the Tools menu) with default settings. The Enable Full-Duplex Audio So I Can Speak While Receiving Audio check box, selected by default, enables you to speak and listen at the same time, just as you would on a telephone. If you and the person you're calling find your sound breaking up to the point of unintelligibility, you might want to try clearing this check box. The check box is unavailable if your sound card doesn't support full duplex.

The Enable Auto-Gain Control and Automatically Adjust Microphone Volume While In A Call check boxes, both selected by default, allow NetMeeting to modify your microphone's volume level and sensitivity automatically as the volume of your voice and the level of background noise change. If there is a lot of background noise around your computer, you might want to try clearing the Enable Auto-Gain Control check box. The check box is unavailable if your sound card doesn't support auto-gain control.

The Enable DirectSound For Improved Audio Performance setting improves audio by shortening the time between when audio is sent and when you receive it. DirectSound doesn't work with all sound cards, so if it causes you problems, clear the check box.

**FIGURE 21-6.**

The default audio settings adjust your microphone's volume and sensitivity automatically as the volume of your voice and the level of background noise change.

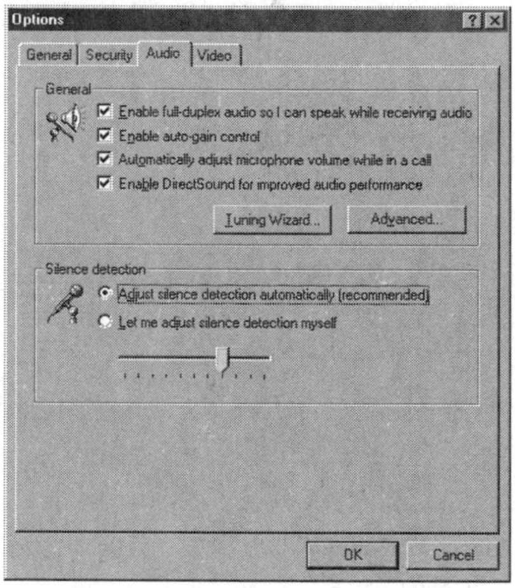

# Sending and Receiving Video

Exchange of video information works much the same way as exchange of sound. You can do this with one other party at a time, and you must be communicating via TCP/IP.

As with sound, video communication can be unidirectional or bidirectional. Video received appears in the main NetMeeting window, as shown in Figure 21-7.

**FIGURE 21-7.**

The video being received is the larger picture. The video being sent is the small picture in the lower right corner of the larger picture.

While you're sending video, you can monitor what's going out by choosing My Video from the View menu. This opens the My Video window where you can see the video you are sending. If you don't need a picture as big as the My Video window, click the Picture-In-Picture button to see a smaller version of the outgoing video in the lower right corner of the incoming video picture.

Figure 21-8, on the next page, shows the Video tab of the Options dialog box (choose Options from the Tools menu) with default settings. By default, NetMeeting receives video automatically at the start of a call if the party on the other end of the connection has a camera. By default, video is sent automatically at the start of a call if your computer has a camera.

Because video transmission uses a lot of bandwidth and can degrade the performance of some of NetMeeting's other features (particularly shared programs), sometimes you might want to clear either or both of the top two check boxes shown in Figure 21-8. You can also turn off video transmission in either direction after it has begun by clicking the Stop Video button in the NetMeeting main window.

The Send Image Size and Video Quality sections of the dialog box allow you to balance quality and performance. NetMeeting sets the size to medium and the quality to middle-of-the-road by default. If you're working with a high-bandwidth connection (for example, if you're connecting with another user on your local area network, or if your network is connected to the Internet through a high-speed T1 connection), you might want to move up to a larger image size and better quality.

**FIGURE 21-8.**

By default, NetMeeting automatically uses video whenever possible at the start of a call.

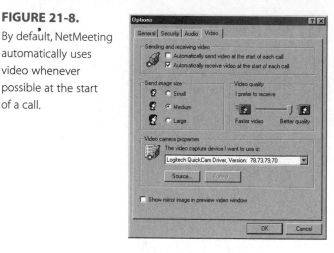

If you're using a camera attached to a video-capture card and you have more than one such card, the list at the bottom of the dialog box lets you specify the device you want to use.

If you're considering buying hardware for use with NetMeeting, you'll get better performance from a camera connected to a video-capture card than from a camera connected to your parallel port or universal serial bus (USB) port.

# Using Chat

The Chat window, shown in Figure 21-9, lets you send written messages to other call participants. You'll find this invaluable if you're not getting adequate sound quality from your connection or if you're communicating with more than one other user.

To use the Chat window, click the Chat button at the bottom of the NetMeeting window, press Ctrl+T, or choose Chat from the Tools menu. Then type whatever you want to send into the Message area of the window. When you press Enter, your message is transmitted, by default, to everyone else in the call. If you want to send it to one person only, select that person from the Send To list before you press Enter.

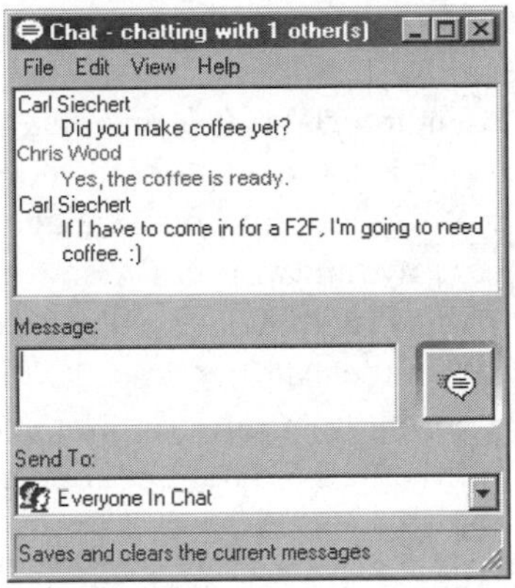

**FIGURE 21-9.**
The Chat window lets you send written messages to other call participants.

You can save or print a transcript of your chat session by choosing commands from the Chat window's File menu. Choosing Options from the View menu lets you change the way messages appear in the Chat window. See Figure 21-10.

Chat normally precedes each transmission with the sender's name. You can also display the date and time of each message. The three message formats allow you to display messages to fit various window shapes. You can change the font of messages you send and receive, which makes it easier to differentiate the messages you are sending from those you are receiving. Changing the font at your end has no effect on the appearance of chat messages on the recipient's computer.

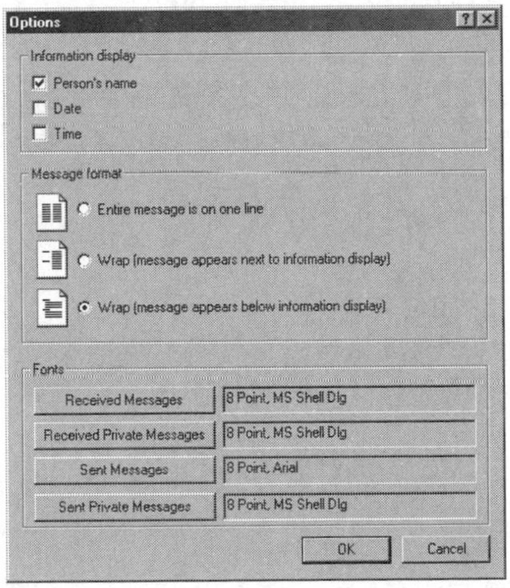

**FIGURE 21-10.**
In the Options dialog box, you control the appearance of messages in your Chat window.

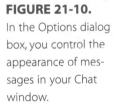

V

Sharing and Communicating

# Using Whiteboard

Whiteboard, shown in Figure 21-11, is a drawing program that functions superficially like Microsoft Paint, except that it's designed for sharing drawings, diagrams, screen shots, and other images with members of a NetMeeting conference. Anything you create in the Whiteboard window is visible to all other parties in the conversation, and any participant can modify the Whiteboard contents at any time. To run Whiteboard, click the Whiteboard button at the bottom of the NetMeeting window, press Ctrl+W, or choose Whiteboard from the Tools menu.

 **TIP**

> The Whiteboard (1.0 – 2.x) command on the NetMeeting Tools menu allows you to share a whiteboard with people using NetMeeting versions 1 through 2.11.

**? SEE ALSO**

For information about Paint, see Chapter 34, "Drawing With Paint."

Like Paint, Whiteboard includes editing and line-width tools displayed to the left of the drawing window, and a color palette displayed below. You can enlarge the available drawing space by hiding the toolbar. (Choose Tool Bar from the View menu.) With the toolbar removed, you can use commands on the Tools menu to switch between editing tools and use the Tools menu's Line Width command to change line width. Here's an overview of the available tools.

Selector

Use the Selector tool when you want to move, cut, copy, or recolor part of a drawing. Click the Selector tool, and then click anywhere on the object you want to manipulate. To select more than one object, drag a rectangle over the group of objects you want to manipulate.

**FIGURE 21-11.**
Whiteboard is a drawing program that lets you share images with other users in a NetMeeting conversation.

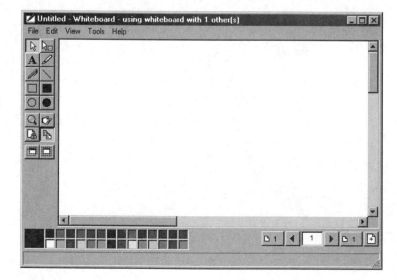

Eraser

The Eraser tool works exactly like the Selector tool except that it deletes what you select. Click an object once, and the object is gone. Fortunately, although Whiteboard has no Undo command, its Edit menu does have an Undelete command. Repair thereto if you zap the wrong object. After you have deleted something, the Undelete command stays active until you use it, even if you subsequently add new objects to your drawing. However, only the last deletion can be restored.

**TIP**

> As an alternative to using the Eraser tool, you can select an object and press the Delete key.

Text

The Text tool lets you add letters and words. Click the tool, and then click once wherever you want the text to go. Whiteboard displays a small rectangle for your text and expands the rectangle as you type. Words do not wrap. To begin a new line, press Enter. Whiteboard uses 8-point MS Sans Serif Regular in black as its default font. To change, choose Font from the Options menu or click a color in the color palette. Note that font and color changes always affect everything in the text rectangle. To emphasize part of your text, use the Highlighter tool.

Highlighter

The Highlighter tool works just like the Pen tool, except that, if you choose an appropriate color, it creates transparent lines. Thus, for example, you can use yellow highlighting to emphasize particular words in a text object without obliterating the highlighted text. Note, however, that highlighting works best with light colors. You might want to experiment with highlighting colors before you use them in a presentation with your colleagues—particularly because Whiteboard lacks an Undo command.

Pen

The Pen tool lets you add freehand elements to your drawing. Click the tool, click the line width and color you desire, click a starting point in the drawing window, and hold down the mouse button while you move the mouse.

Line

The Line tool creates straight lines in the current width and color. Note that Whiteboard's Line tool, unlike Paint's, doesn't constrain lines to particular angles when you hold down the Shift key. If you want perfect diagonals, horizontals, or verticals, you can do your work in Paint and then paste it into Whiteboard.

Unfilled
Rectangle

The Unfilled Rectangle tool creates a rectangle in the current line width and color. Note that Whiteboard lacks Paint's ability to constrain rectangles into squares. If a perfect square is what you need, it's best to create it in Paint and paste it into Whiteboard.

Filled
Rectangle

The Filled Rectangle tool creates a solid rectangle in the current color. Note that Whiteboard has no counterpart to Paint's Fill With Color tool. If you want a rectangle filled with one color and outlined with another, use Paint and paste into Whiteboard.

Unfilled
Ellipse

The Unfilled Ellipse tool creates an ellipse in the current line width and color. If you need a perfect circle, use Paint and paste.

Filled
Ellipse

The Filled Ellipse tool creates a solid ellipse in the current color.

Zoom

Clicking the Zoom tool enlarges your drawing. Clicking again returns it to normal size. If you're not displaying the toolbar, you can choose Zoom from the View menu.

Remote
Pointer

Clicking the Remote Pointer tool displays a hand with outstretched index finger. You can move the hand to draw attention to a particular part of your drawing. Click the tool a second time to make the hand disappear. Each NetMeeting participant has his or her own remote pointer that others can see but not move.

Lock
Contents

Click the Lock Contents tool to prevent others from making changes to the contents of the whiteboard. When the whiteboard is locked, click the Unlock Contents tool so other users can make changes to the whiteboard.

Synchronize

You can use the Synchronize tool to view a whiteboard page privately. (Ordinarily, when someone switches to a different page, everyone's whiteboard changes so that everyone in the meeting is, well, on the same page.) Click Unsynchronize and move to a different page, and only your whiteboard changes. When you click Synchronize, everyone's whiteboard switches to the page you're viewing.

Select
Area

The Select Area tool lets you paste a selected portion of any window into your drawing, making it easy to show the state of some program or document to your conference-mates. When you click the tool, Whiteboard displays a message telling you to select an area on the screen. Then it gets out of the way and lets you drag the area you want to paste. The area you select is pasted into the upper left corner of the whiteboard. Drag it to place it where you want it.

Select
Window

The Select Window tool works just like the Select Area tool except that it lets you paste an entire window into your drawing. When you click the tool, Whiteboard displays a message saying that the next window you click will be pasted into your drawing. Then it gets out of the way and lets you click the window you want to paste. Note that what you get is the client area of the window you click. If you click in a Microsoft Word window, for example, you get the visible part of whatever Word document you're working in, along with Word's ruler (if displayed) and toolbar. You don't get the Word menu bar or title bar. Note also that if the window you click is displaying two or more document windows, you get only the active document window. After you paste your window, the window becomes a selected object. You can drag to reposition it.

## Other Whiteboard Features

Whiteboard is object-oriented rather than pixel-oriented (as Paint is). When you create one object on top of another, they remain distinct objects. You can change the $z$ (stacking) order of objects that lie atop one another by choosing Send To Back or Bring To Front from the Edit menu.

Insert
New Page

Whiteboard lets you create multipage documents. To insert a new page after the current page, click the Insert New Page button at the lower right corner of the Whiteboard window or choose Insert Page from the Edit menu. To move between pages, click the controls next to the Insert New Page button—or press Ctrl+Page Up or Ctrl+Page Down.

To save or print the current Whiteboard document, choose commands from the File menu. When you print, the Print dialog box lets you specify whether you want all pages or a selected page range.

# Sending and Receiving Files

To send a file to all participants in your meeting, click the Transfer File button at the bottom of the window or press Ctrl+F. (Alternatively, open the Tools menu and choose File Transfer.) To send a file only to a particular person, choose that person's name from the list in the upper right corner of the File Transfer dialog box.

Files that are sent to you are stored by default in the Received Files folder, a subfolder of your NetMeeting folder. You can change that location by choosing Change Folder from the File menu in the File Transfer dialog box. You can use the View Received Files button in the File Transfer dialog box to open your Received Files folder in Windows Explorer.

# Sharing a Program

To share a program with other participants in your call, open the program you want to share. Then click the Share Program button at the bottom of the NetMeeting main window. (You can also choose Sharing from the Tools menu, or press Ctrl+S.) From the list of running programs that appears (see Figure 21-12), select the one you want to share and click Share.

To enable others to work in the shared program, click the Allow Control button in the Sharing dialog box. To allow others to take control without your permission, select the Automatically Accept Requests For Control check box.

> When a program is shared amongst users with different screen resolutions, NetMeeting uses the highest available resolution. Users of lower-resolution displays might need to scroll to see the entire program.

**FIGURE 21-12.**
You can share any of your running programs so that others can see them—or even control them.

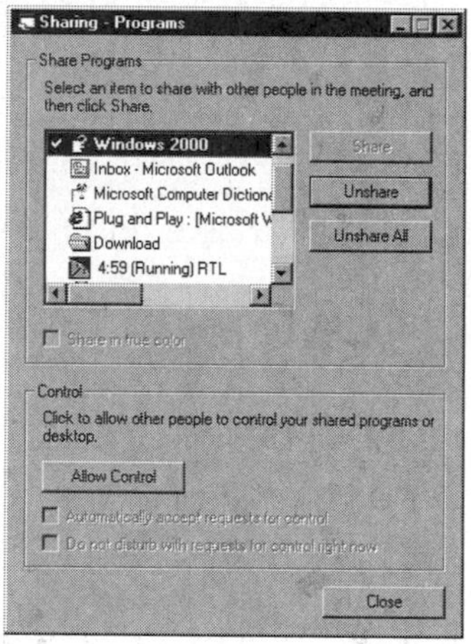

When you collaborate on a program, only one user at a time can control the program. Other users see the controlling user's mouse pointer, with the user's initials displayed beside it. When done with control, a user can use two commands on the Control menu to transfer control: Release Control transfers control back to the person sharing the program; Forward Control transfers control to another user. The person sharing the program can take control of the program away from the controlling user at any time by pressing Esc.

 **NOTE**

> If you share any Windows Explorer window, all the Windows Explorer windows you have open are shared. And once you have shared Windows Explorer, any program you start is also shared.

#  Controlling a Computer Remotely

Remote Desktop Sharing allows remote control of one computer from another. You can use Remote Desktop Sharing to control another computer on your local area network. By using an Internet connection or dial-up connection, you can control your home computer from the office, or vice versa.

**NOTE**

> While you control a computer remotely with Remote Desktop Sharing, no one else can use that computer; its mouse and keyboard are effectively locked.

To set up a computer so you can control it remotely:

**1** In NetMeeting, open the Tools menu and choose Remote Desktop Sharing.

A wizard then steps you through the process, which on a computer running Windows 2000 does little except to set up a password-protected screen saver.

**2** Once the wizard is done, close NetMeeting.

An icon will remain in the status area of the taskbar.

When you're ready to leave the computer you want to control remotely, right-click the NetMeeting Remote Desktop Sharing icon in the status area and choose Activate Remote Desktop Sharing.

**NOTE**

> If the Activate Remote Desktop Sharing command is grayed out, it is probably because NetMeeting is still running. You can use Remote Desktop Sharing only when NetMeeting isn't running on the controlled computer.

V<br>Sharing and Communicating

To remotely control a computer that you have set up as just described:

**1** At the controlling computer, start NetMeeting.

**2** Open the Call menu and choose New Call.

**3** Enter the address of the computer you want to control, be sure that Require Security For This Call is selected, and click Call.

The Password dialog box appears.

```
┌─────────────────────────────────────────────────┐
│ Remote Desktop Sharing Password          [?][X]  │
├─────────────────────────────────────────────────┤
│  You must type an administrator account name and │
│  password to gain remote access to this computer's desktop.│
│  User      ┌────────────────────────────────┐   │
│            │chrisw                          │   │
│            └────────────────────────────────┘   │
│  Password: ┌────────────────────────────────┐   │
│            │xxxxxxxxxx                      │   │
│            └────────────────────────────────┘   │
│  Domain:   ┌────────────────────────────────┐   │
│            │swdocs                          │   │
│            └────────────────────────────────┘   │
│  Host computer certificate:                      │
│  ┌────────────────────────────────────────────┐ │
│  │NetMeeting Certificate (privacy only)       │ │
│  │                                            │ │
│  │                                            │ │
│  │                                            │ │
│  │                                            │ │
│  └────────────────────────────────────────────┘ │
│            ┌────────┐      ┌────────┐            │
│            │   OK   │      │ Cancel │            │
│            └────────┘      └────────┘            │
└─────────────────────────────────────────────────┘
```

**4** If you are calling a computer that's running Windows 2000, you must enter the password for the Administrator account. If you are calling a computer running Windows 95 or Windows 98, enter the NetMeeting Remote Desktop Sharing password.

The remote computer's screen then appears in a window on your desktop, as shown in Figure 21-13.

To stop controlling the remote computer, click the End Call button in the NetMeeting window.

To temporarily disable Remote Desktop Sharing, right-click the NetMeeting Remote Desktop Sharing icon in the taskbar status area and choose Turn Off Remote Desktop Sharing. To permanently disable Remote Desktop Sharing, open NetMeeting's Tools menu and choose Remote Desktop Sharing. Clear Enable Remote Desktop Sharing On This Computer.

**FIGURE 21-13.**
The remote
computer's screen
appears in a window
on your desktop.

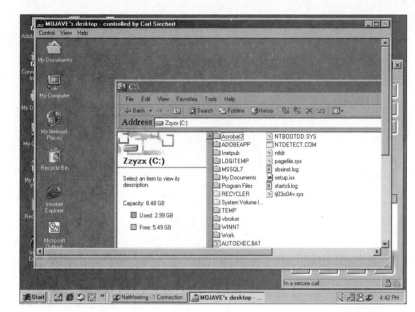

2000 **CHAPTER 22**

# Using Phone Dialer

I f you've seen the anemic Phone Dialer program that's included with earlier versions of Microsoft Windows, you'll be tempted to bypass this chapter. Don't! The old Phone Dialer was essentially a technology demonstration—proof that you could connect a phone to your computer and let the computer do the dialing. Phone Dialer in Windows 2000 is new from the ground up, and it's now a full-fledged program that allows you to:

- Make voice calls via standard telephone lines

- Make and receive voice calls via your local area network (LAN) or the Internet

- Make and receive voice conference calls via your LAN or the Internet

- Make and receive videoconference calls via your LAN or the Internet

---

**Phone Dialer vs. NetMeeting**

Phone Dialer and NetMeeting (described in Chapter 21) provide some of the same capabilities: they both allow you to make and receive voice and video calls over the Internet. In fact, you can use Phone Dialer to communicate with NetMeeting users and vice versa. Phone Dialer is essentially a picturephone; it's limited to voice and video communications. In general, NetMeeting is a better tool for business meetings because of its ancillary tools: the whiteboard, chat, file transfer, and shared applications. Phone Dialer has one advantage for meetings: it allows you to view more than one other person at a time. In addition, you might find its call history feature to be useful for tracking your phone usage.

---

The built-in directories and call-management tools make it easier to use your traditional telephone. And by using the Internet, you can bypass the long-distance telephone companies to make voice and video calls all over the world—without paying for anything beyond your normal Internet charges.

To start Phone Dialer, open the Start menu, and then choose Programs, Accessories, Communications, Phone Dialer. Phone Dialer appears, as shown in Figure 22-1. The left side of the Phone Dialer shows the available directories, and the right side shows the people in the selected directory.

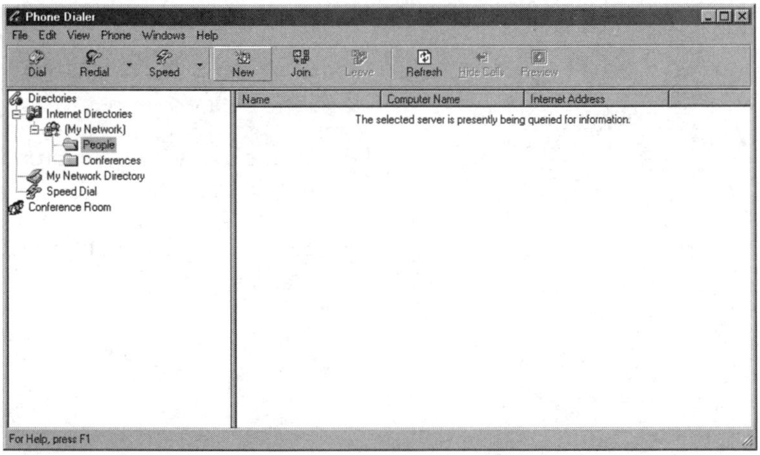

**FIGURE 22-1.**

Phone Dialer now uses Internet telephony in addition to standard phone lines.

**TIP**

**Using Phone Dialer for Ordinary Phone Calls**
Although you can use Phone Dialer to dial phone numbers by typing them into the Dial dialog box, it's usually more efficient to just dial your telephone without using Phone Dialer. However, if you must precede each phone number with a lengthy calling card code or long distance access code, you might find Phone Dialer convenient. Using Phone Dialer for manually dialed calls has other possible advantages as well: you can save as many numbers as you want in your Speed Dial directory, and your calls are included in Phone Dialer's history log.

# What You Need to Use Phone Dialer

To use Phone Dialer to place a call over ordinary telephone lines, you must have a modem installed in your computer. Unless you're using a voice modem, you must also have a telephone connected to the modem.

To communicate using a network connection (including an Internet connection), you'll need a sound card, speakers, and a microphone. You'll also need a camera if you want others to see you.

You can participate in a videoconference without a camera; you can see others, but they can't see you. Similarly, you can participate if you don't have a microphone. You can see and hear others, but you can't be heard—and what fun is that?

**SEE ALSO**
For information about NetMeeting, see Chapter 21, "Using NetMeeting."

And the people receiving your calls? To receive calls on their computer, your recipients also need to have an Internet telephony program, and the program must be running when you call. They can use Phone Dialer, Microsoft NetMeeting, or a third-party telephony program.

# Making and Receiving Voice Calls

Phone Dialer can make outgoing calls using a standard phone line and telephone, or using a connection to your network or to the Internet. You can also receive incoming network and Internet calls with Phone Dialer.

Sharing and Communicating

# Making a Call

To make a call:

**1**  Click the Dial button on the toolbar, or open the Phone menu and choose Dial.

The Dial dialog box appears.

**2**  In the Dial box, specify who you want to dial:

- If you're calling over phone lines, type their phone number.

- If you're calling over a network connection, type their computer name (for computers on your network only) or type their IP address (for computers on your network or for anyone on the Internet). To use a computer name, you must be logged on to a domain with a Domain Name System (DNS) server.

**TIP**

If you're redialing someone you've called before, click the arrow to open the list in the Dial window and select his or her number from the list of those you've recently called.

**3**  Under Dial As, select Phone Call if you're calling over phone lines, or select Internet Call if you're calling via your network or the Internet.

**4**  Click Place Call.

A call window appears in the corner of your screen (see Figure 22-2) and shows the progression of the call: Locating Remote Party, Waiting For Answer, and (if the person answers) Connected. (If the person doesn't answer, the call window reports that with a Failed message.)

**FIGURE 22-2.**

Call windows show a picture if the person at the other end has a camera.

> **NOTE**
>
> The call window initially appears below the Preview window, in which you can set your speaker volume and microphone volume. Once you've set the volume to a comfortable level, click the Close button in the Preview window to get it out of your way. (If you need to reopen the Preview window, click the Preview button on the toolbar.)

After the call is completed, you simply click the Disconnect button in the call window and hang up the handset to terminate the call.

---

**Phone Calls vs. Internet Calls**

Using the Internet to make calls has some decided advantages. You don't pay anything (other than your normal Internet charges) to make a call, no matter where you're calling. And you can send and receive video images along with your voice call, finally making reality of the picturephone concept demonstrated at the 1939 (!) and 1964 World's Fairs in New York.

The downside to Internet telephony is the speed and quality. Depending on the speed of each party's Internet connection, you might experience choppy voices and pictures, dropped voices and pictures, and delays of several seconds—as if you're making a phone call to the moon.

---

# Working in the Call Window

The call window, in addition to displaying the call status and the name, number, and (in some cases) picture of the person you're communicating with, has a handful of buttons and controls that you might find useful.

 Hide the Preview window and all call windows. To redisplay the windows, click the Show Calls button on the Phone Dialer toolbar, or simply move the mouse pointer to the edge of the screen that the windows slide into (left or right, depending on a setting on the Windows menu).

Keep the Preview window and all call windows on top of other windows. To cancel the always-on-top behavior, click the pushpin button again.

 Display a Touch-Tone keypad in a separate window. You can use this keypad to navigate through auto attendant menus ("Press 1 for sales, press 2 if you hate pressing buttons, etc.").

Add the current connection to your Speed Dial directory. You can add information from both incoming and outgoing calls.

You might want to employ one other call window trick when the person at the other end has a camera: place the mouse pointer in the picture and drag the picture to the desktop. Doing so displays the video in a separate, smaller window, allowing you to then hide the call window. Like the call windows, the desktop video window has an Always On Top button, so you can keep this smaller window on top while you continue to work in other applications. Closing this separate window returns the video to the call window from whence it came.

## Receiving a Call

To receive a network or Internet call using Phone Dialer, you must have Phone Dialer running. (You can minimize its window, but don't close it.) When someone calls you, a chime sounds, the title bar flashes, and a call window appears. The window shows the name of the caller (as he or she has defined it) and his or her network address, so you have some idea of who's calling. To stop the chimes and flashing, you must click one of the two buttons in the call window: Take Call or Reject Call. (If you reject the call, the caller sees a message that indicates what you've done.)

**TIP**

**Hiding the Taskbar Button**
To get Phone Dialer out of the way when you're waiting for a call, open the View menu and choose Hide When Minimized. Then minimize Phone Dialer. The taskbar button disappears, but an icon remains in the taskbar's status area. To restore the Phone Dialer window, double-click the icon.

# Making a Conference Call

You can use Phone Dialer to participate in conference calls—calls with more than two participants. As with other calls, conference calls in Phone Dialer can include video if one or more participants have cameras. (People without cameras can participate in any case, but only those with cameras can be seen.)

You can join a conference call that has been set up by someone else, or you can manage a conference.

## Joining a Conference

To join a conference:

**1** In the left pane, expand the directory tree to display the name of the directory server that's hosting the conference, and then click Conferences.

In the right pane, Phone Dialer displays a list of conferences on the selected server. Only the conferences that you have permission to join are displayed.

**2** Select the conference name, and then click the Join button (or choose Join Conference from the Phone menu).

Phone Dialer switches to the Conference Room display, as shown in Figure 22-3.

**FIGURE 22-3.**

When members join the conference, the Conference Room will show each video stream simultaneously.

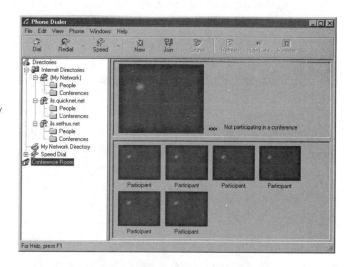

## Working in the Conference Room

You can control your view of the Conference Room in the following ways:

■ To select which picture goes in the large pane at the top, double-click one of the pictures below.

■ To enlarge all the pictures in the bottom pane to 100 percent (the default size of the picture at the top), open the View menu and choose Full Size Conference Video.

- To enlarge the picture in the top pane, right-click it, point to Selected Video Scale, and choose an enlargement percentage.

- To change the maximum number of video screens displayed, open the Edit menu and choose Options. Click the Audio/Video tab and select Internet Conferences in the Line box. Then specify a number in the Maximum Video Windows box.

## Managing a Conference Call

To set up and manage a conference call, you need to be logged on to a domain that has a conference server, and the server administrator must grant you permission to set up conference calls. If your computer is part of a Windows 2000 Server network, your network administrator can set up a local conference server, or you can use a public Internet directory.

To set up a conference call:

**1** Open the Phone menu and choose New Conference, or click the New button on the toolbar.

The Conference Properties dialog box opens.

**2** Type a name and a description for your conference.

**3** In the Conference Time boxes, set the starting and ending time for the conference.

**4** To specify who can join and manage your conference, click the Permissions tab.

By default, the person who schedules the conference has permission to join, modify, and delete the conference, and Everyone (that is, everyone who is authorized to log on to the server that hosts the conference) has permission to join. Click Add to add other users or groups. Then select each user or group and set their permissions.

To modify or delete your conference once you've scheduled it, select it in the Conferences folder of the hosting directory, open the File menu, and choose Properties.

> **NOTE**
>
> Phone Dialer doesn't notify the attendees when you set up a conference. To let them know about it, send an e-mail message.

# Using Directories

If you use Phone Dialer for making phone calls, or if you use it to make network calls to friends and associates whose computer name or IP address you know, you don't need to use a directory. But if you want to contact others, or if your regular correspondents don't have a fixed IP address (most dial-up connections get a new IP address each time they connect), an Internet location server (ILS) directory provides a good way to get in touch. *For more about ILS servers, see "Getting Started with NetMeeting," page 446.*

In Phone Dialer's left pane, under Directories, you'll find an entry for Internet Directories. Expand that entry to display the directories that have been set up on your computer. Within each directory is a People folder (which lists the people who are currently logged on to the directory server) and a Conferences folder (which lists upcoming conferences that you have permission to join).

In addition to the Internet directories that show who is currently logged on to a particular server, Phone Dialer maintains two other directories: My Network Directory and the Speed Dial directory.

To call someone listed in any directory, simply select his or her name and click the Dial button on the toolbar.

## Adding a Directory Server

If your computer is part of a Windows 2000 Server domain, the administrator might have set up a list of published ILS servers. (These can be public ILS servers on the Internet, or private ILS servers on your network.) If this is the case, the first ILS server in the list appears in the My Network directory. If your network administrator hasn't set up a list of servers (or you're not part of a domain), you can connect to public ILS servers on the Internet by adding a directory server in Phone Dialer.

To add a directory server to the list of Internet directories, open the Edit menu and choose Add Directory. Type a directory name in the Add Directory Server dialog box, as shown in Figure 22-4.

### Finding Public ILS Servers
A good source for finding public ILS servers is *www.netmeet.net*. Although its focus is on NetMeeting, you can use the same servers with Phone Dialer for connecting with a friend who uses the same server, or for meeting new people.

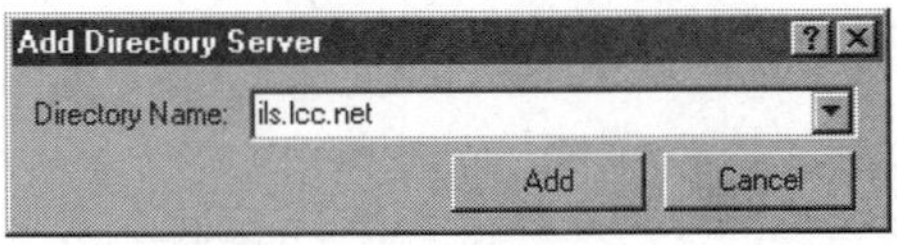

**FIGURE 22-4.**
You can connect to more than one directory server.

| Add Directory Server | ? X |
| --- | --- |
| Directory Name: | ils.lcc.net ▼ |
| | Add    Cancel |

# Adding Network Users to Your Local Directory

If your computer is part of a Windows 2000 Server network that uses Active Directory, you can add Phone Dialer directory entries for other network users with whom you frequently communicate. Names you add appear in the My Network Directory folder. To add a name:

**1** Right-click My Network Directory and choose Add User.

**2** Type the first part of the name you're looking for, and then click Search.

> Windows searches the Active Directory for matching names.

**3** After the search results appear, select a name and then click Add.

# Setting Up Speed-Dial Numbers

Phone Dialer allows you to store an unlimited number of entries in the Speed Dial directory. These entries can be for people you contact by phone, by computer name, or by IP address. To add an entry to the Speed Dial directory:

**1** Open the Edit menu and choose Add To Speed Dial List.

> The Speed Dial dialog box appears, as shown on the next page.

Click the Add To Speed Dial button in a call window to open the Speed Dial dialog box—with the fields already filled in.

**2** In the Display Name box, type the name as you want it to appear in the list.

**3** In the Number Or Address box, type the phone number, computer name, or IP address you use to dial this person.

**4** Under Dial As, select the type of connection you want to make, and then click OK

To delete a name from the directory, simply click it and press the Delete key. To reorder the names in your Speed Dial directory, or to change the information for an entry, open the Edit menu and choose Speed Dial List.

# Viewing a Log of Your Calls

To see a list of the calls you've made and received using Phone Dialer, choose Call Log from the View menu. The call log appears in a Notepad window, from which you can view, edit, and print the log.

As you'll see, Phone Dialer saves the call log as a CSV (comma separated values) file, which means you can easily import the log into a spreadsheet or database program for further analysis—or just to spruce up its appearance. Each call record has six fields:

- Call direction (incoming or outgoing)
- Date

- Time

- Duration, in minutes and seconds

- Display name

- Phone number, computer name, or IP address

Phone Dialer stores the log in the %UserProfile%\Local Settings\ Application Data\Microsoft\Dialer folder, and gives it a name like *user*_call_log.txt, where *user* is your user name. (%UserProfile% is an environment variable that contains the actual path to your profile folder. On a system with local user profiles, that path is typically C:\Documents and Settings\\*user.*)

# Configuring Phone Dialer

The default settings in Phone Dialer are generally correct, but it takes only a moment to review them, as described in the following sections.

## Setting Up Lines

You should first check to be sure that your phone and Internet connections are properly configured. To configure your connections:

**1** Open the Edit menu and choose Options.

The Options dialog box appears.

**2** If you haven't already installed and configured a modem (and you plan to make phone calls or you use a modem to connect to the Internet), click Phone And Modem Options.

In the Phone And Modem Options dialog box that appears, you can install modems and set up dialing locations (settings such as your current area code, how to dial long distance numbers, and so on). *For information about the Phone And Modem Options dialog box, see "Setting Up Dialing Locations," page 278.*

**3** Under Preferred Line For Calling, select Phone if you'll make most Phone Dialer calls via phone lines, or select Internet if you'll make most calls via your network or the Internet.

**4** In the Line Used For area, select a line for each type of call you'll make. Ordinarily, you'll leave these three items set to <Auto-Select>. But if you have more than one modem, for example, you might want to select a particular one.

# Setting Up Devices

The other area for configuration is your collection of audio and video devices. To configure your devices:

**1** Open the Edit menu, choose Options, and click the Audio/Video tab.

**2** In the Line box, select the type of calls you want to configure.

**3** In the Audio Record, Audio Playback, and Video Record boxes, select the device you want to use, if you have more than one. If you want to disable a device (for example, to mute your microphone), select <None>.

**NOTE**

**Using Preferred Devices**

If you select <Use Preferred Device>, Phone Dialer uses the preferred device as set up on the Audio and Hardware tabs of the Sounds And Multimedia Properties dialog box, which you can reach from Control Panel or, more simply, by clicking Sound Settings in the Phone Dialer Options dialog box.

**4** If you don't want to view incoming video from others, clear the Video Playback check box.

# CHAPTER 23

# Using
# HyperTerminal

HyperTerminal is a simple application that lets you connect with bulletin board systems (BBS's) and Telnet sites. Because you probably spend most of your online time using Microsoft Internet Explorer, another Web browser, or proprietary software such as that provided by America Online, you might properly think of HyperTerminal as a bit of a relic—a reminder of the days before the arrival of the Internet. Nevertheless, sometimes you might need to contact a library, a vendor's support bulletin board, or some other service that's not available on the Web. For that eventuality, Microsoft Windows 2000 provides HyperTerminal.

# A Typical HyperTerminal Session

A typical communications session using HyperTerminal goes something like this:

**1** Start HyperTerminal. *For details, see "Starting HyperTerminal," page 487.*

**2** Open or create a connection file.

Before establishing a communications link, you have to supply HyperTerminal with the phone number and some additional information about how to communicate with the service you're calling. *For details, see "Making New Connections," page 488.*

**3** Open the Call menu and choose Connect or click the Connect toolbar button, and then click the Dial button in the Dial dialog box. (Table 23-1 describes the toolbar buttons.)

**TABLE 23-1.   HyperTerminal Toolbar**

| Toolbar Icon | Description |
|---|---|
| | Creates a new connection file |
| | Opens an existing connection file |
| | Connects to a remote system (dials the modem) |
| | Disconnects from a remote system (hangs up the modem) |
| | Sends a file to the remote system |
| | Receives a file from the remote system |
| | Displays the properties dialog box for the current connection file |

HyperTerminal uses your modem's built-in dialing capabilities to establish a telephone connection with the remote computer, which is often called the *host computer* (or simply the *host*). After a connection has been established, whatever you type into

HyperTerminal's window is sent across the phone line to the host computer. If the person or computer at the other end of the line sends information back, it appears in HyperTerminal's window as though someone behind the screen were typing.

4  Log on to the host computer or service.

If you're communicating with a mainframe or information service, you'll probably be required to log on by entering a name and password.

5  Interact with the party you're connected to.

Your conversation might consist of nothing more than messages typed at the keyboard. Or you might transmit a great deal of information stored on the Clipboard by choosing Paste To Host from HyperTerminal's Edit menu. You can also exchange files with the host computer. *For details, see "Transferring Files," page 495.*

6  Log off the host computer or service.

The procedure for logging off depends on the service you use. Typically, you type *quit, exit, bye,* or a similar command at the service's command prompt or main menu.

7  Choose Disconnect from HyperTerminal's Call menu.

When you log off, the host computer might end the telephone connection itself. HyperTerminal might not recognize that, however, so it's best to use the Disconnect command regardless of what the other party does.

8  Close HyperTerminal.

If the telephone connection is still open (or if HyperTerminal thinks it is), HyperTerminal prompts you to disconnect from the host computer before quitting.

# Starting HyperTerminal

To start HyperTerminal, open the Start menu, and then choose Programs, Accessories, Communications, HyperTerminal. HyperTerminal's opening screen appears, followed by the Connection Description dialog box, as shown in Figure 23-1, on the next page.

V

Sharing and Communicating

If you've already specified connection settings—perhaps to dial up a company's support bulletin board or the local library's online research service—click the Cancel button to close the Connection Description dialog box. Otherwise, follow the instructions below to create settings for a new connection.

## Making New Connections

The first time you use HyperTerminal, or when you want to connect to a new computer service, HyperTerminal doesn't have a clue about what you want to connect to, so you'll have to supply the details it needs to get hooked up.

To create a new connection:

**1** Type a descriptive name for the connection into the Name text box.

The name doesn't have to be the actual name of the service you're connecting to, just something that will be descriptive enough for you. For example, you might call your connection to the local bicycle club BBS *Bike BBS* instead of using its official name, *UWBIKECLUB*.

**2** Select an icon to represent the new connection.

You can use the horizontal scroll bar to view the available connection icons.

**3** Click OK.

HyperTerminal displays the Connect To dialog box, as shown in Figure 23-2.

**FIGURE 23-2.**
Use the Connect To
dialog box to enter
the number for the
new connection.

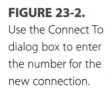

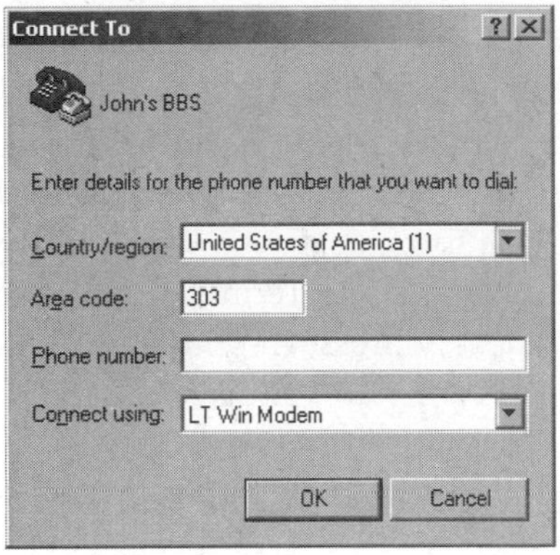

**4**  Fill in the phone number and area code.

If you have more than one modem connected to your computer, use the Connect Using list to select the modem you want to use for this connection.

If you're connecting to a Telnet site, choose TCP/IP (Winsock) from the Connect Using list. You will also then need to supply the Telnet URL (without the *Telnet://* prefix) and your port number.

**5**  Click OK.

Unless you're using the TCP/IP (Winsock) device, the Connect dialog box appears, as shown in Figure 23-3.

**6**  Click Dial to connect to the service now or Cancel if you want to connect to the service later.

**7**  After you log off or after choosing Cancel without logging on, choose Save from the File menu to retain the connection settings you just created.

**FIGURE 23-3.**
The Connect dialog
box shows the current
primary settings for
the new connection.

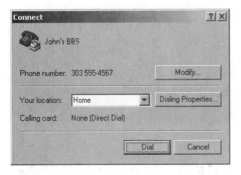

## Opening Existing Connections

To open a connection that has already been defined, use the Open command on the File menu. If you open a file for a modem connection (such as to a BBS), the Connect dialog box appears. (See Figure 23-3.) Click Dial to make the connection. If you open a file for a TCP/IP connection, HyperTerminal immediately connects to the connection's host address. (If you have a dial-up connection to the Internet, HyperTerminal first dials the connection.)

## Modifying Connection Settings

In most cases, the basic connection information you enter into the Connection Description dialog box (see Figure 23-1 on page 488) and the Connect To dialog box (Figure 23-2 on page 489) is sufficient. You can, however, customize the settings in a number of ways to suit your needs. You can do this as you create a new connection or after the connection has been defined.

To modify a dial-up connection's properties after it has been defined, open the connection, and then click the Properties button (or choose Properties from the File menu). To modify a TCP/IP connection, open it, and then select Properties from the File menu. The properties dialog box for the open connection appears, as shown in Figure 23-4.

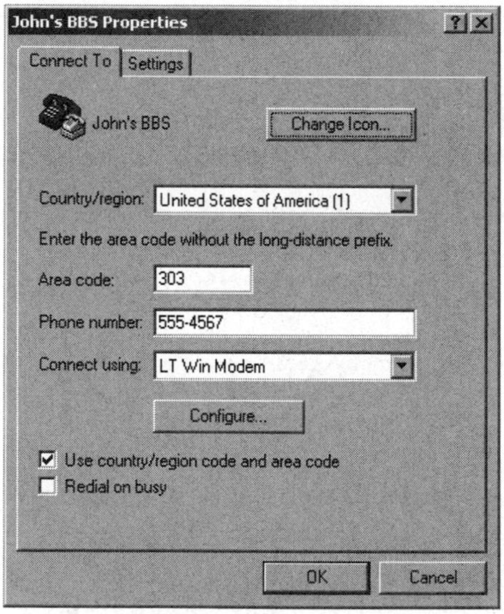

**FIGURE 23-4.**

The Connect To tab in the properties dialog box provides access to several basic settings.

The Connect To tab in the Properties dialog box includes the following controls for changing options:

- The Change Icon button lets you pick an icon from the group of icons that was presented when you created the connection. You can also change the connection name via the Change Icon button.

- Country/Region lists the part of the world where the host computer is located.

- The entries in the Area Code and Phone Number text boxes need to be changed only if the number for your connection changes or if you made a mistake when you entered them initially.

- Use the Connect Using list to specify a different modem if your computer has more than one modem attached. If you're connecting to a Telnet site, choose TCP/IP in the Connect Using list, and then specify the host address and port number. The host address should be the URL of the Telnet site.

**NOTE**
The Connect Using list also provides for direct connection to each of your computer's serial (Com) ports. Although you can use this method to connect two nearby computers with HyperTerminal (and no modems), a better solution in that case is to use Direct Connection. *For details, see "Connecting Two Computers with a Direct Connection," page 294.*

- To change the modem settings for this connection, click the Configure button. HyperTerminal displays the properties dialog box for your modem. The modem properties dialog box lets you select a port, baud rate (modem speed), and other communications parameters and dialing settings. *For details, see "Installing and Configuring a Modem," page 523.*

**TIP**
If you're connecting to a service that charges by the minute—or it's a long distance call—you can set up your modem to disconnect automatically if you don't use it for a period of time. In the properties dialog box for the connection, click Configure to display the modem properties dialog box. Click the General tab, and then select the Disconnect A Call If Idle For More Than check box. Enter a reasonably short time (perhaps 10 or 15 minutes) so you won't be paying for a lot of connect time while you're not using the system. (Unfortunately, this check box isn't available in the properties dialog box for all brands and types of modems.)

**V**
Sharing and Communicating

The Settings tab in the properties dialog box for the connection includes the following additional options, as shown in Figure 23-5.

■ Select Terminal Keys (the default) or Windows Keys to specify how function keys, arrow keys, and Ctrl-key combinations are used during connections. If you select Terminal Keys, these keystrokes are sent to the host computer; if you select Windows Keys, Windows processes these keystrokes as it does in other programs.

For example, with some services, pressing Ctrl+C stops the transmission of a file. If you have selected Windows Keys, however, pressing Ctrl+C copies the current selection (if any) to the Clipboard. It's usually best to leave this option set to Terminal Keys so these keystrokes will be passed to the host computer.

■ Under Backspace Key Sends, select what the remote computer should receive when you press Backspace. For most systems, Ctrl+H is appropriate.

■ The Emulation list is set to Auto Detect. Unless you have trouble with your connection, keep this at the default setting. If you do have trouble, contact the host computer's support staff to find out what type of terminal the remote system needs to see at your end. (A *terminal* is a simple device—consisting of a monitor, a keyboard, and a physical connection—for communicating with a host computer. HyperTerminal can act like any of several different terminal models.)

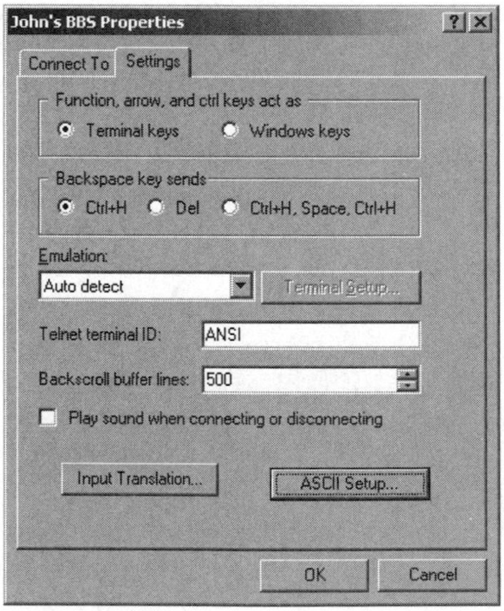

**FIGURE 23-5.**

The Settings tab in the connection's properties dialog box controls the appearance of transmitted data, among other functions.

■ ANSI is the appropriate Telnet terminal for most Telnet sites. Change this value only if required by the site you're connecting to.

■ The Backscroll Buffer Lines box lets you specify how many lines of a communication session you can review by pressing the Page Up key. (A *buffer* is an area of memory used for temporary storage.) While you're connected to another computer, everything you send and receive is stored in a buffer and displayed in HyperTerminal's window. The buffer gives you a way to review what you send and receive without capturing the "conversation" in a disk file or generating a printed transcript. As long as the buffer's capacity hasn't been exceeded, you can scroll up and down in the HyperTerminal window to reread everything that has passed back and forth over the telephone line. There is one exception: *binary files* (files containing graphics, formatted text, or executable program code) that you send or receive aren't srecorded in the buffer.

When the buffer reaches its capacity, each new line replaces the oldest line in the buffer. For example, if the buffer size is set at 500 lines, when line 501 arrives, the first line is discarded.

You can set the buffer size at anywhere from 0 to 500 lines. If you have plenty of memory, reserve a full 500 lines; if memory is scarce, choose a smaller size. If you don't have enough memory for the buffer size you request, HyperTerminal gives you as much as it can.

TIP

> The buffer is convenient because it lets you reread material that has scrolled off your screen. But if you want a complete record of your communications session, consider sending a copy of it to your printer or recording it in a text file. *For information about printing or recording to a text file, see "Creating a Transcript of Your Communications Session," page 499.*

■ If the check box labeled Play Sound When Connecting Or Disconnecting is selected, HyperTerminal plays a sound to let you know whenever a connection to a remote system is made or broken, or if the remote system sends a *bell* character (a method of ringing primitive terminals that is generated by pressing Ctrl+G on a terminal's keyboard). Unless you object to the sound, it's probably best to leave this option selected.

■ The ASCII Setup button displays a dialog box, shown in Figure 23-6, that lets you control how text is transferred between your computer and the remote computer. You might need to adjust one of these options if your display is unreadable while you're connected, for example.

The ASCII Setup dialog box offers the following options:

- The Send Line Ends With Line Feeds check box, when selected, causes HyperTerminal to add a line feed character each time you press Enter. You won't need to change this setting when communicating with most online services, but if you're communicating with a live person who complains that everything on his or her screen is displayed on one line, select this check box.

- If, after you've established connection with a remote computer, the characters you type aren't displayed on your screen, select the Echo Typed Characters Locally check box. On the other hand, if every character you type appears twice on your screen, clear this check box.

- The Append Line Feeds To Incoming Line Ends check box provides a function similar to that of the Send Line Ends With Line Feeds check box—except that it affects *your* display, not the remote system's. If everything sent by the host computer appears on a single line on your screen, select this check box. Conversely, if everything you receive is double spaced, clear this option.

- The Force Incoming Data To 7-Bit ASCII check box, when selected, ensures that you receive only standard letters, numbers, and punctuation—the original 128-character ASCII character set.

- The Wrap Lines That Exceed Terminal Width check box, when selected, causes HyperTerminal to start a new line when text you receive from the host computer reaches the right edge of the HyperTerminal window.

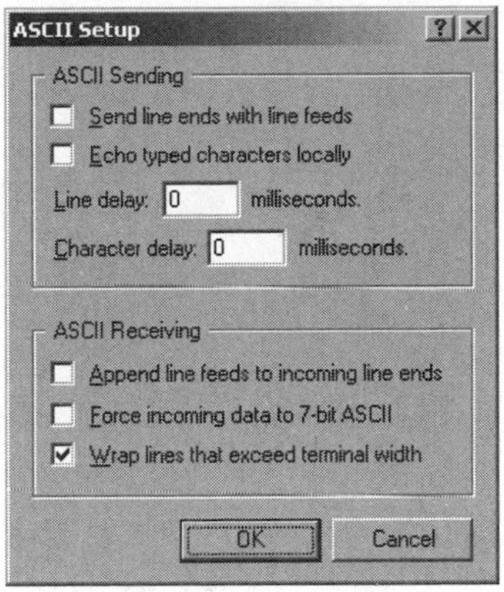

**FIGURE 23-6.**
The ASCII Setup dialog box controls the transmission of ASCII text in your HyperTerminal window.

# Transferring Files

Two common HyperTerminal tasks are sending *(uploading)* and receiving *(downloading)* files. For example, you might download new video drivers for your computer from the manufacturer's BBS, or you might need to upload an error log to a software publisher's support forum.

You can transfer two distinct types of files: text files and binary files.

*Text files*, sometimes called ASCII files, are human-readable, unformatted files that contain only letters, numbers, punctuation symbols, and basic control codes, such as line-ending codes. Text files don't require any special transfer protocols on the part of either the sending or receiving computer.

A *binary file* is any file that is not a text file. Formatted documents created in word processing, spreadsheet, or graphics programs, for example, are binary files. Programs, such as the ones to create word processing, spreadsheet, and graphics documents, are also binary files. When transferring binary files, you should use a file transfer protocol to ensure accurate transmission. A *protocol* is a method for transferring files that can provide such features as *error correction* (methods for assuring that the message received matches the one sent) and *data compression* (methods for reducing the volume of data that needs to be transmitted, mostly used for faster transmissions).

V

Sharing and Communicating

> **>) NOTE**
>
> You can also use a protocol to send or receive text files. *To do so, follow the procedure for sending or receiving binary files described in "Sending a Binary File," below.*

## Sending a Text File

To send a text file:

**1** Open the connection you'll use for the transfer.

**2** Log on to the host computer.

   Prior to sending a text file, you might need to alert the host computer to get ready for an incoming message. You can obtain the details you need from the help screens or the support staff at the remote service.

**3** Open the Transfer Menu and choose Send Text File.

   The Send Text File dialog box appears for you to enter the name and location of the text file you want to send.

**4** Enter the name of the file to send, and then click the Open button.

   The text file appears in the HyperTerminal window. If it's a large file, the beginning of the file scrolls off the screen and you'll see the end of the file.

**5** Press Enter to send the file.

> **★) TIP**
>
> When you use the method just described to send a text file, the host computer receives the file as a message incorporated in the other text of the communications session. If the text needs to be stored as a separate file, the users at the host computer will have to capture the session to a file and then edit out the unwanted portions of the session.
>
> To avoid causing the folks at the remote site these inconveniences, you can send the text file as a binary file—covered in the next section—so that it will be received as a separate file that's ready to use with no further fuss.

## Sending a Binary File

To send a binary file:

**1** Open the connection you'll use for the transfer.

**2** Log on to the host computer.

As with sending text files, you might need to alert the operators of the host computer that you're about to send a file so they can prepare their system to receive the file. If you try to send the file before the remote system is ready, HyperTerminal waits for a ready signal from the host computer.

**3** Choose Send File from the Transfer menu.

**4** In the Send File dialog box, enter the name of the file you want to send into the Filename text box. (Click the Browse button for point-and-click selection if you don't want to type the file's name and location.) Then select a file transfer protocol from the Protocol list.

The Protocol list, shown in Figure 23-7, offers a list of the available file transfer protocols. The default is Zmodem With Crash Recovery. (*Crash recovery* enables you to reconnect and continue sending from where you left off if your connection is broken before the transmission is completed.)

The host computer often displays a list of available protocols when you initiate the transfer process. Just remember, the file transfer protocol on your computer and the host computer must match.

**5** Click the Send button.

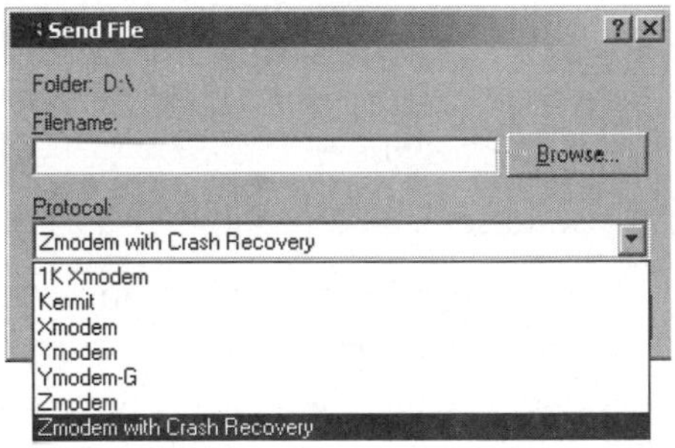

**FIGURE 23-7.**

The Send File dialog box displays the file transfer protocol options.

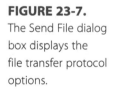

During the transfer, a dialog box similar to the one shown on the next page keeps you informed about the progress of the transfer. The Cps/bps button in the Progress dialog box lets you change the displayed throughput—how fast data is being transferred—between characters per second (cps) and bits per second (bps). If you're sending multiple files, you can click the Skip File button to skip the current file. Use the

Cancel button if you want to abort the transfer. When the transfer is completed, the dialog box disappears.

## Receiving a Binary File

To receive a binary file:

**1** Open the connection you'll use for the transfer.

**2** Log on to the host computer.

**3** Use the appropriate procedures to request the file you want to receive from the host computer.

In most remote systems, you'll need to navigate to a special download or file library area before requesting a file to download. You'll also usually need to specify a transfer protocol before receiving the file. HyperTerminal's default protocol, Zmodem With Crash Recovery, is a good choice if it's available on the host computer.

**4** Choose Receive File from the Transfer menu.

The Receive File dialog box appears, as shown in Figure 23-8. If you want the downloaded file to be stored in a folder other than the default, change the entry in the Place Received File In The Following Folder box. Change the transfer protocol in the Protocol list to match the host computer's protocol if it doesn't support the default Zmodem With Crash Recovery protocol.

**5** Click Receive and follow the on-screen directions to begin the transfer. With some protocols, such as Zmodem, the transfer begins automatically. Other protocols require you to specify a filename or otherwise signal your readiness to receive the file.

**FIGURE 23-8.**

The Receive File dialog box specifies where the received file is stored.

During the transfer, a dialog box similar to the one for sending files keeps you informed about the progress of the transfer. When the transfer is completed, the dialog box disappears.

# Creating a Transcript of Your Communications Session

You can create a transcript of any communications session in either of two ways. You can capture (save) the session information to a text file on disk, or you can send it directly to the printer. With either method you can stop and restart the process to capture only the portion of the communications session you want.

To record your session in a text file, open the Transfer menu and choose Capture Text. Enter a name for your file into the File text box of the Capture Text dialog box, and then click the Start button. Notice that the word *Capture* in the status bar is now black, indicating that capture mode is on.

You can temporarily pause capturing by choosing Pause from the Capture Text submenu. To resume capturing text, choose Resume from the Capture Text submenu. When you're finished capturing, choose Stop from the Capture Text submenu.

To create a printed transcript, choose Capture To Printer from the Transfer menu. A check mark will appear in front of the Capture To Printer command and all the session information you send or receive will be spooled to a print file in preparation for printing.

You can stop capturing to the printer—or start again—by choosing the Capture To Printer command again to toggle the check mark off and on. When you stop capturing, HyperTerminal prints the information.

As an alternative to capturing to the printer, you can print the contents of the backscroll buffer by choosing Print from the File menu. You can also print a selection of information from your online session by following this procedure:

**1**   In the HyperTerminal window, scroll to the information you want to print.

**2**   Select the information, using the standard Windows text-selection methods.

**3**   Choose Print from the File menu.

**4**   Click the Selection button and click OK.

# PART VI

# Managing Hardware

# Installing and Configuring Hardware

Many people feel that one of the greatest weaknesses of Microsoft Windows NT, the predecessor to Windows 2000, was its lack of hardware support. Only a limited number of devices was supported, which meant that you had to be very selective when you bought peripheral devices for a system running Windows NT. Support for new devices was often slow in coming, and support for some types of devices and from some manufacturers was nonexistent.

Furthermore, Windows NT didn't support Plug and Play, a technology first employed in Windows 95 that—with the right combination of hardware and software components—allowed you to simply connect a device and begin using it. Instead, once you found a device that was "supported" by Windows NT, you then faced the often-daunting task of configuring it properly.

Windows 2000 dramatically improves upon Windows NT in three key areas of hardware support:

- First, you'll find support for many more devices—and new types of devices—including:

  - **Universal serial bus (USB) devices.** This new generation of Plug and Play devices includes everything from keyboards to cameras. USB devices share a common connector, and you don't need to configure the USB port or the device manually.

  - **IEEE 1394 devices.** IEEE 1394 is a nonproprietary high-speed serial bus with roots in Apple Computer's FireWire technology. It's used by some devices that require fast data transfer, such as scanners and video cameras.

- Second, because of its use of Windows Driver Model (WDM) technology, in many cases manufacturers can develop a single driver that works for Windows 98 and Windows 2000—which should result in support for more devices sooner after they're released.

- Third, thanks to the Windows 2000 implementation of Plug and Play technology, many of the potential frustrations and bewilderments associated with hardware changes have been eliminated. In many cases, adding a new device is truly as simple as hooking up the device and getting on with your work.

This chapter explains how Plug and Play makes life easier and then offers some specific information about installing and configuring certain types of devices, including printers, modems, scanners, cameras, and game controllers.

# Letting Plug and Play Find New Hardware

Traditionally, the act of adding a new device has been an exercise in frustration for many personal computer users, as well as a heavy expense for corporate support departments.

Hardware devices typically compete for a limited number of input/output (I/O) addresses, memory addresses, interrupt request (IRQ) lines, and direct memory access (DMA) channels. For your system to work properly, all of its pieces have to dance together without stepping on each other's toes. If your new sound card wants the same interrupt request line as your existing network adapter, something's got to give.

Until recently, resolving a conflict of this kind had entailed some combination of the following: determining which resource was in contention, finding a nonconflicting alternative setting for one of the conflicting devices, making a physical adjustment to the hardware (moving a jumper, for example), and modifying some aspect of the software that used the new device.

To alleviate these difficulties, Microsoft and other computer-industry firms developed the Plug and Play specification. Plug and Play, as its name implies, is intended to make adding a new device to your computer as painless as "installing" a new toaster in your kitchen. Plug and Play has evolved considerably since its initial appearance in Windows 95 so that it's now part of a comprehensive approach to device configuration *and* power management.

The full realization of this goal requires Plug and Play support from four elements of your system:

- **The BIOS (basic input/output system).** Full Plug and Play support in Windows 2000 requires an Advanced Configuration and Power Interface (ACPI)–compliant system board and BIOS. (The BIOS, routines that manage the transfer of information between system components, is built into the computer's read-only memory, or ROM.) Most new computers (circa 1998 and later) have an ACPI BIOS.

**TIP**

**How to Tell Whether Your Computer Has an ACPI BIOS**
To find out whether your computer is ACPI compliant, right-click My Computer and choose Properties. Click the Hardware tab and then click Device Manager. In Device Manager, expand the Computer entry. If your computer has a compatible ACPI BIOS, the expanded entry reads Advanced Configuration And Power Interface (ACPI) PC.

**NOTE**

Unlike Windows 95, Windows 2000 does *not* use an Advanced Power Management (APM) BIOS or a Plug and Play BIOS for Plug and Play support. If you have one of these systems (common in 1995–98 models), you should be sure that your computer's BIOS setting for Plug and Play OS is set to No. (See your computer's documentation for information on using its system setup program for changing BIOS settings.)

- **The operating system.** Windows 2000, naturally!
- **The devices you want to install.** Most peripheral devices sold these days are also Plug and Play compliant.

Managing Hardware

■ **The drivers for those devices.** A driver is a software component that controls interaction between the operating system and the device. Drivers for many devices are included on the Windows 2000 CD. If the Windows CD doesn't have the driver you need, you should be able to get a driver from the device manufacturer—either in the box with the device or from the manufacturer's Web site. Most new drivers—even for some non–Plug and Play devices—are Plug and Play compliant. (A Plug and Play driver for a non–Plug and Play device can provide some Plug and Play capability, such as resource allocation and power management.)

**NOTE**

Windows 2000 supports legacy Windows NT drivers, but these drivers have no Plug and Play or power management capabilities.

**TIP**

**Get Updated Drivers**
Even a device that you buy today might have a newer, better driver available. Check the manufacturer's Web site and Microsoft's Windows Update site (*windowsupdate.microsoft.com*) for new versions—and look specifically for Windows 2000 (not Windows NT) drivers, which likely provide Plug and Play support. *For more information, see "Updating a Driver," page 535.*

With all four elements in place, a newly installed hardware device announces its presence and resource requirements to the operating system. If necessary, the operating system restructures resource assignments on the fly (without requiring you to turn your computer off) to eliminate conflicts. The operating system then broadcasts a message to any running programs, letting them know about the change in your hardware setup so that they can take advantage of any new features.

If a device is removed, the operating system hears about it from the BIOS and informs programs so that they can make any appropriate adjustments. Plug and Play also interacts with power management so that certain devices can be put to sleep when they're not being used and awakened as needed.

So, for example, a Plug and Play laptop computer that supports "hot-docking" can be connected to or disconnected from the docking station without first being turned off. If the docking station has access to a local or network printer, your programs will immediately be informed about any fonts or other resources offered by the printer, and you can begin printing any jobs that you have queued offline.

**⚠ WARNING**

> Even if your computer has an ACPI BIOS, always turn off the computer and any connected peripherals (monitor, printer, and so on) before adding or removing any device *inside* the system.

**❓ SEE ALSO**

For information about resolving hardware conflicts, see "Troubleshooting a Device That Isn't Working Properly," page 532.

Provided a new device doesn't present an unresolvable resource conflict, the act of adding Plug and Play hardware and drivers to an ACPI computer running Windows 2000 should indeed be toaster-transparent. And if an unresolvable conflict does arise, Windows identifies it for you so that at least you'll know what options you have.

With a *legacy* computer (one that does not use an ACPI BIOS), Plug and Play still offers significant benefits, particularly if you're installing or removing a Plug and Play device. By using the Add/Remove Hardware Wizard *(see "Installing a Legacy Device," on the next page)*, you can make Windows aware that a new device is present. If the device supports Plug and Play, Windows can determine which type of device it is and what resources it requires. By consulting the registry (where current resource assignments for all your hardware are recorded), Windows can determine whether the new device's default assignments create any conflicts. If a conflict exists, Windows can make adjustments to the new device (or another Plug and Play device already attached) to avoid the conflict.

When you attach a legacy device, Windows can't adjust the new device's chosen settings, but if some of your other devices support Plug and Play, it might be able to adjust their settings to eliminate conflicts. If not, and if conflicts exist, Windows advises you. You might then have to reset one or more jumpers on the device yourself.

# Installing a Plug and Play Device

After attaching a Plug and Play device, you might see a message indicating that Windows has recognized the new device. (If you have installed the device while your computer was turned off, this message appears at the start of your next Windows session. If your computer was on at the time you connected the device, the message simply pops up on your desktop.) If Windows needs a driver that it doesn't currently have, you might be prompted to insert a disk or the Windows CD.

**VI**

**Managing Hardware**

> **NOTE**

You must be logged on as a member of the Administrators group to install the driver files for a device, a task that Plug and Play attempts during installation of a new device. If the files already exist on your computer, any user can install a device with the assistance of Plug and Play.

If you don't see a message and your new device is working fine, assume that all is well. If you don't see a message and your device doesn't seem to be working, use Add/Remove Hardware in Control Panel to let Windows know you've installed something new.

# Installing a Legacy Device

After you install a new legacy device (one that is not Plug and Play compatible), use Add/Remove Hardware in Control Panel to let Windows know what you've done. To use Add/Remove Hardware:

**1** Open the Start menu and choose Settings, Control Panel, Add/Remove Hardware.

The Add/Remove Hardware Wizard appears.

**2** On the wizard's Welcome page, click Next.

**3** On the Choose A Hardware Task page, select Add/Troubleshoot A Device, and then click Next.

Windows then searches for new Plug and Play devices, and eventually displays the Choose A Hardware Device page, which lists all your currently installed devices.

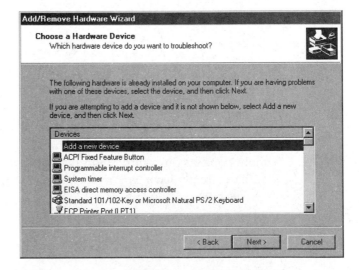

**4**  Select the first entry, Add A New Device, and then click Next.

The Find New Hardware page appears. Now you have a choice.

**5**  On the Find New Hardware page, decide whether you want Windows to search for your new hardware or whether you want to select from a list.

- If you want the wizard to try to determine what you've added, select Yes, Search For New Hardware and click Next. The wizard can detect many types of devices, even if they don't support Plug and Play. If Windows succeeds in identifying one or more new devices, it presents you with a list of all devices found. Select the first member of the list and click Next. You'll then receive instructions about what to do next. (For example, you might be asked to insert a disk or the Windows CD so that Windows can get one or more driver files.) If the wizard is unable to detect the new device, click Next after the wizard informs you of this result. You'll then see a wizard page similar to the one shown in Figure 24-1, where you can identify the device yourself.

**FIGURE 24-1.**

If you decide not to let the wizard detect your new hardware (or if it's unable to), you must tell it what type of hardware you want to install.

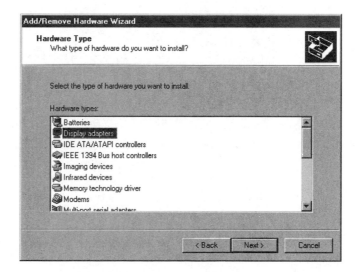

- If you prefer to skip Windows' automatic-detection services, select No, I Want To Select The Hardware From A List and then click Next. On the Hardware Type page shown in Figure 24-1, select the type of hardware you're installing and click Next. Make-and-model options appear next on the Select A Device Driver page. (See Figure 24-2.) Select the vendor of your new hardware on the left side of this page and the specific model on the right. Then click Next once more and follow the ensuing instructions.

> **NOTE**
>
> You must be logged on as a member of the Administrators group to install the driver files for a device. If the files already exist on your computer, any user can install a device with the assistance of the Add/Remove Hardware Wizard.

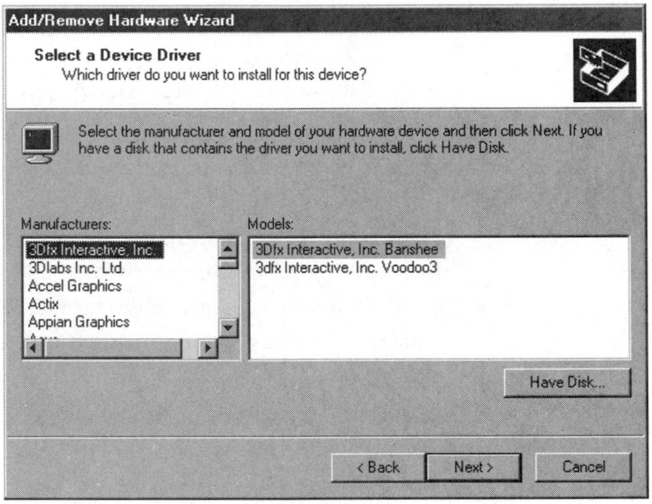

**FIGURE 24-2.**

After telling the wizard what kind of hardware you're installing, you'll be asked to identify the hardware's make and model.

## Alternative Ways to Install Certain Legacy Devices

You can use the Add/Remove Hardware Wizard to install any type of new device. For a new printer, modem, scanner, camera, or game controller, however, you can also use other Control Panel items to let Windows know what you've done. The following sections explain how to use Control Panel to install these devices, and also explain some of the device-specific settings you can make to properly configure your hardware.

# Installing and Configuring a Printer

What Windows calls a *printer* is more precisely a constellation of settings applied to an output device, referred to as the *printing device*. That device can be a traditional printer, a fax modem, a disk file, or perhaps something else altogether. Each combination of settings and output device constitutes a *logical printer*. Each logical printer is treated as a separate device and is displayed as a separate icon in your Printers folder. You can install as many logical printers as you like, and you can install multiple logical printers for the same physical printing device.

The settings that make up a logical printer include the following:

- The name of the printer

- A *share* name, if the printer is available to other network users

- For shared printers, a description that network users will see when they browse My Network Places in search of a printer (if they use Details view)

- The port to which the printing device is connected

- The driver—a software component that enables Windows to translate output into the language used by the printing device

- Various properties, including the amount of memory in the printing device, any font cartridges or soft fonts in use, and so on; the available properties vary from printer to printer

- Certain other defaults, such as the paper tray to be used, page orientation, and printing resolution

- The name of a separator-page file, if one is to be used

You might find it useful to set up several logical printers for a single printing device if you frequently switch among groups of settings. If you often switch between portrait and landscape orientations, upper and lower paper trays, or duplex and single-sided printing, for example, you can set up a logical printer for each. This way, you can simply select a different "printer" to change settings.

## Adding a Local Printer

To add a *local printer*—one that's directly attached to your computer, either by cable or by an infrared link—begin by setting up the physical printing device and attaching its cables. If the printing device you want to install conforms to the Plug and Play standard, Windows should recognize it and know automatically what kind of printing device it is, how much memory it has, what font cartridges are installed, what paper tray it's set up to use, and possibly other details.

**VI**

Managing Hardware

If you connect a Plug and Play printing device to your computer while Windows isn't running, at the beginning of your next Windows session, Plug and Play detects the device and installs the requisite driver. Depending on the device, the Add Printer Wizard may appear and ask you a few questions.

 **NOTE**

> You must be logged on as a member of the Administrators group to install the driver files for a printer.

To begin installing a non–Plug and Play printing device, or to create a new logical printer using a printing device that's already installed:

**1** Open the Start menu, point to Settings, and choose Printers to open the Printers folder.

**2** Open Add Printer to launch the Add Printer Wizard.

**3** On the wizard's Welcome page, click Next.

This brings you to the Local Or Network Printer page.

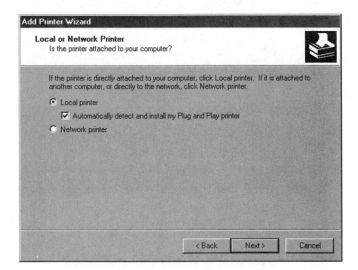

**4** If the printing device you're installing is physically connected to your own computer, select the Local Printer option.

 **NOTE**

> The term *network printer* means a printing device attached to some other computer. If the printing device is attached to the machine you're typing at, that's a local printer—even if it is to be shared with others.

**5**  Select the Automatically Detect And Install My Plug And Play Printer check box and click Next.

If Windows detects your printing device, you can skip most of the remaining steps in the following sections. And if it doesn't, you'll see a page informing you that Windows was unable to detect any Plug and Play printers. In that case, continue to the next section.

## Specifying Printer Ports

If Windows is unable to detect a Plug and Play printer in step 5 above, click Next. The wizard then displays the page shown in Figure 24-3, where you tell Windows which port to use. (The *port* provides the physical link between your computer and your printing device.)

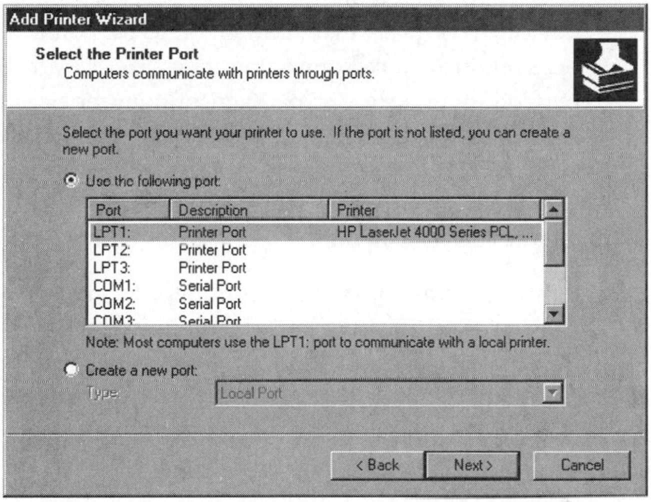

**FIGURE 24-3.**

The wizard needs to know which port your printing device is connected to.

The ports most commonly used for printing are LPT1 (or LPT with some other number) for a printing device that uses a parallel cable, and COM1 (or COM with some other number) for a printing device that uses a serial cable.

## Printing to a Disk File

To send your output to a disk file, select FILE as your printer port. Windows will prompt for a filename whenever you print. You can copy the resulting disk file to a physical printer later. For example, if you have a printing device attached to LPT1, you can copy a print file to the printing device by opening the Start menu and choosing Programs, Accessories, Command Prompt. Then, in the command prompt window, type

copy *filename* lpt1:

**VI**

Managing Hardware

where *filename* is the name of the file you want to print. The print-to-file option is also useful if the printing device on which you ultimately intend to print isn't attached to your network—for example, if you plan to use a service bureau to generate high-resolution PostScript output.

> If you sometimes want to print to a physical printer and sometimes to a file, you can change the port setting as needed by visiting the properties dialog box for your printer. *(See "Inspecting and Setting Printer Properties," page 517.)* Alternatively, you can set up two printers using the same driver. Assign one printer to a physical port and one to FILE.

## Adding a Port

In certain instances, you'll need to connect a printer to a port that doesn't yet appear in the wizard's list. For example, some printing devices have ports that allow them to be connected directly to the network instead of connecting them to a computer. These are called network-interface printers. Even printing devices that don't have a built-in network interface can be connected to an external device, such as a Hewlett-Packard JetDirect network interface, that allows a printing device to be placed anywhere on the network without being tethered to a computer.

If you're going to use your computer to manage such a printer, you must add a driver that lets your computer communicate with the printer. Doing so adds an entry to the list of available ports on your computer.

**NOTE**

> If another computer manages the network-interface printer, you don't need to add a port. Instead, click Back and then, on the Add Printer Wizard's first page, select Network Printer.

The first step in adding a port is to select Create A New Port on the Select A Printer Port page of the Add Printer Wizard. Beyond that, the details depend on the type of network-interface printer you have. You'll need to refer to the documentation for the printer or the network-interface device.

## Specifying a Driver

After you select a port and click Next, the Add Printer Wizard displays a page similar to the one shown in Figure 24-4, where you indicate the make and model of your printing device so that Windows can install the appropriate driver for it.

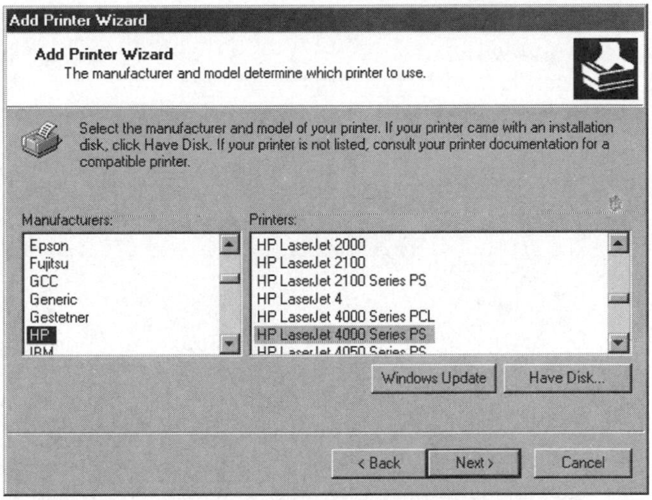

**FIGURE 24-4.**

Windows supports
hundreds of printers.
Odds are, you'll find
your make and model
in these two list boxes.

After you've made your selections in the list boxes shown in Figure
24-4, Windows might prompt you to insert the Windows CD so that it
can copy the necessary files to your system. If the required driver is
already present on your hard disk, the wizard asks your permission
to use it. (Knowing that your intention might be to install an updated
version of the driver, the wizard doesn't assume it should use the
existing driver.)

### What to Do If Your Printer Isn't on the List

If your printing device isn't on the list of supported printers shown
in Figure 24-4, you can click Windows Update (which connects to
Microsoft's Windows Update Web site) to see whether a printer driver
for Windows 2000 is available. If you received a driver disk with your
printer or can obtain one from your printer vendor (check their Web
site), click Have Disk and follow the prompts to direct the Add Printer
Wizard to your driver file.

If no driver is available, check your printer documentation to see whether
your printing device emulates another printer make and model—one for
which a Windows 2000 driver is available. If your printing device can
emulate a supported printing device, use the emulation mode and select
the supported driver on the wizard page shown in Figure 24-4.

## Naming the Printer

After you specify a driver and click Next, the wizard asks you to name
your new printer, as shown in Figure 24-5, on the next page. The
name you choose here will appear under the printer icon in your
Printers folder, as well as in your programs' Print dialog boxes.

**VI**

**Managing Hardware**

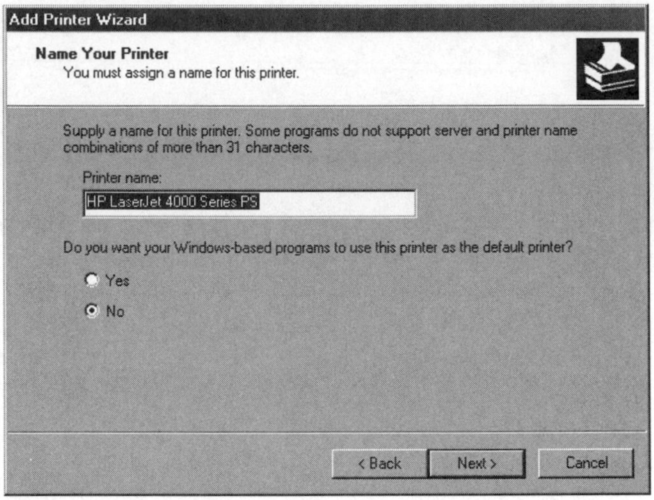

**FIGURE 24-5.**
The Add Printer Wizard proposes to use the driver name as the printer name—but you can change it to something more meaningful.

The Name Your Printer page also lets you set this printer as your default printer—the one that Windows uses unless you specify another. *For more information about the default printer, see "Selecting a Printer," page 217.*

You can easily revise the choices you make on this page at any time. To rename a printer, simply right-click it in the Printers folder and choose Rename. To make a printer the default, right-click it and choose Set As Default.

## Sharing the Printer

After naming your new printer and clicking Next, you arrive at the Add Printer Wizard's Printer Sharing page.

To share your printer with other users on the network, select Share As and then type a share name.

The share name is the name that other users will see when they connect to your printer. If you choose to share your printer, the wizard's next page asks you to supply a descriptive comment and identify the location of the printer. Users can read the comment and location information by inspecting the printer properties on their systems.

> **NOTE**
>
> If anyone using your shared printer is working with an operating system other than Windows 2000, you'll need to install the printer driver for each user's operating system. Doing so makes the necessary drivers available to these users when they connect to your printer. *For more information, see "Configuring Printer Sharing," page 519.*

### Printing a Test Page and Finishing the Installation

As the final step in the installation process, the Add Printer Wizard offers to send a test page to your new printer. This is a good idea. If you've made any incorrect choices on the wizard's pages (such as choosing the wrong port), it's better to find out now rather than when you're trying to generate some real output under a deadline.

When you've completed the test page, click Next. The final page of the Add Printer Wizard presents a summary of the options you've chosen. If any are incorrect, use the Back button to return to the relevant page of the wizard and make necessary changes. When they're correct, click Finish and the printer will be installed and will appear in your Printers folder as the wizard closes.

## Inspecting and Setting Printer Properties

The most crucial questions regarding printer setup—the printer driver and the port to be used—get resolved at the time the printer is installed. The decisions you make in these matters are recorded in your printer's properties dialog box, which you can inspect by right-clicking the printer's icon in your Printers folder and choosing Properties. They're also recorded in the Windows registry so the information is available to inquiring programs.

The properties dialog box stores many additional choices, however, that affect the behavior of your printer. You should visit the properties dialog box after installing a new printer to make sure all options are set as you want them. You might also have occasion to change properties as you work.

Property options vary from printer to printer. In the next several pages, we survey some of the most important options you're likely to find in your printer's properties dialog box.

 **NOTE**

> **Where Are the Document Settings?**
> In Windows 95 and Windows 98, the properties dialog box includes settings for selecting the default paper tray, orientation, and other document-related options. In Windows 2000 (as in Windows NT), the default document settings aren't part of the printer's properties dialog box; instead, you set those options in a separate dialog box. To get to that dialog box, right-click the printer icon and choose Printing Preferences. (You can also get there from the General tab of the printer's properties dialog box: click the Printing Preferences button.)
> *For information about document defaults, see "Setting Printing Preferences,"* page 230.

VI

Managing Hardware

## Providing a Comment

On the General tab in most printer properties dialog boxes, you can enter a comment describing the printer. This information appears in the Print dialog box and in the Printers folder (in Details view). Figure 24-6 shows an example of the General tab.

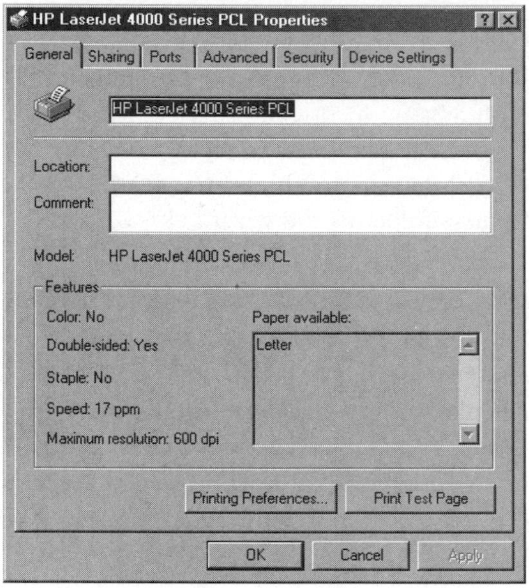

**FIGURE 24-6.**

On the General tab in a printer's properties dialog box, you can describe the printer and print a test page.

## Changing the Port

Should you ever need to change the port for a printer, you can do that on the Ports tab in the printer's properties dialog box. (See Figure 24-7.) Simply select a different port. If you want to add a new port (such as a network port), click Add Port.

## Setting Up a Printer Pool

If you have more than one printer of the same make and model attached to your computer, you can join them in a *printer pool*. Output is then directed to the first selected port that has an available printer. To set up a printer pool:

1   On the Ports tab of the printer's properties dialog box, select the Enable Printer Pooling check box.

2   Select each port that is connected to a printer of the type you're pooling.

**FIGURE 24-7.**

The Ports tab in a printer's properties dialog box lets you change ports and set up printer pools.

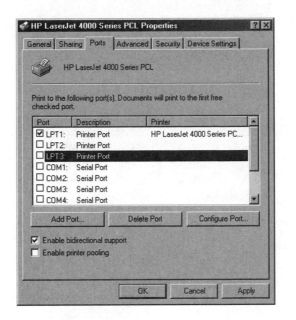

## Changing Drivers

If by any chance you've installed the wrong driver for your printer, you can fix the problem by going to the Advanced tab of the printer's properties dialog box. The Driver list includes all the drivers currently installed on your system; simply select one in the list to begin using it. If the one you want isn't on the Driver list, click the New Driver button. Windows displays the introductory page of the Add Printer Wizard and, after you click Next, displays the page listing printer manufacturers and models, as shown in Figure 24-4, on page 515.

⭐ **TIP**

Printer vendors often update their printer drivers. To get the maximum functionality from your printer, be sure you're using the latest version of the driver. If you acquire a later version, install it by going to the Advanced tab in your printer's properties dialog box. Click the New Driver button, and then click Have Disk when the list of printer manufacturers and models appears.

## Configuring Printer Sharing

The Sharing tab in a printer's properties dialog box lets you make a printer available to other network users. Simply select Shared As and provide a share name. Although Windows 2000 permits spaces and other characters in printer names, to ensure that users who are running

**VI**

**Managing Hardware**

another operating system can connect to your printer, you should be less flamboyant in your choice of a share name:

- Use only letters and numbers; don't use spaces, punctuation, or special characters.

- The entire universal naming convention (UNC) name, including the requisite backslashes and your computer name, should be 31 or fewer characters. For example, if your computer name is EVERGLADES, the share name should be 18 characters or less, which results in a UNC name something like \\EVERGLADES\HPLASERJET4000.

- If any MS-DOS users will connect to the printer, the share name must be no longer than 8 characters.

**★ TIP**

You can get directly to the Sharing tab by right-clicking the printer's icon in the Printers folder. Then choose Sharing.

**> NOTE**

You can share only printers that are connected to your computer. You can't share a network printer that you've installed.

If some of the other users on your network aren't using Windows 2000, click Additional Drivers to display the dialog box shown in Figure 24-8. Select the check box for each operating system in use by the others who will use your printer. When you do this, Windows installs appropriate drivers for the other operating systems on your computer; when another user connects to your printer for the first time, Windows provides the appropriate driver to that person's computer.

If your computer is part of a Windows 2000 domain that uses Active Directory, select List In The Directory to publish the printer in the directory, which makes it easier for others to find your printer.

**> NOTE**

If other network users can't find your shared printer, check to be sure that you've enabled printer sharing. Open the Start menu, point to Settings, and choose Network And Dial-Up Connections. Right-click the Local Area Connection icon and choose Properties. On the General tab, select File And Printer Sharing For Microsoft Networks.

**FIGURE 24-8.**
The Sharing tab lets you share your printer with other network users and include drivers for users who don't have Windows 2000.

## Setting Printer Permissions

**② SEE ALSO**

For more information about permissions, see Chapter 27,"Implementing Windows 2000 Security."

When you set up a printer, initially all users are allowed access to the printer and can manage their own documents in the print queue. (This includes users who log on to your computer as well as network users who connect to a printer you have shared.) Users who have been granted additional permissions by the system administrator can manage all documents in a queue as well as change a printer's properties. Table 24-1 shows the permissions that Windows 2000 provides for printers and their associated privileges.

**TABLE 24-1. Printer Permissions and Privileges**

| Permission | Privileges |
|---|---|
| Print | • Print documents<br>• Control properties of owned documents<br>• Pause, restart, and remove owned documents |
| Manage Printers | • Share printer<br>• Change printer properties<br>• Remove printer<br>• Change printer permissions |
| Manage Documents | • Pause, restart, move, and remove queued documents |

VI

Managing Hardware

A user account that doesn't have any of these permissions can't connect to the printer, print to it locally, or view its queue.

By default, all users have Print permission for documents they create, and members of the Administrators and Power Users groups also have Manage Printers and Manage Documents permission.

If you have Manage Printers permission for a printer, you can change other users' permissions for that printer. To do so, right-click the printer in your Printers folder, choose Properties from the shortcut menu, and click the Security tab, shown in Figure 24-9.

**FIGURE 24-9.**

The Security tab lets you control access to your printer.

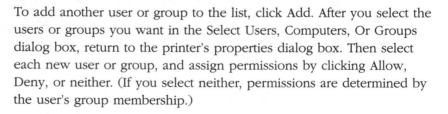

To add another user or group to the list, click Add. After you select the users or groups you want in the Select Users, Computers, Or Groups dialog box, return to the printer's properties dialog box. Then select each new user or group, and assign permissions by clicking Allow, Deny, or neither. (If you select neither, permissions are determined by the user's group membership.)

## Setting Device-Specific Options

Settings that are specific to a printer—such as the presence or absence of an envelope feeder, the amount of memory installed, and the presence of font cartridges—are recorded on the Device Settings tab of the printer's properties dialog box. Figure 24-10 shows an example, although your own printer's properties dialog box will probably differ somewhat from this one.

To see which options are available for a particular setting, click the underlined text, which allows you to set its value. Some settings accept numbers for their value; others display a list from which you can select a new value when you click the arrow.

**FIGURE 24-10.**
The Device Settings tab lets you set up paper tray assignments and specify which optional equipment your printer has.

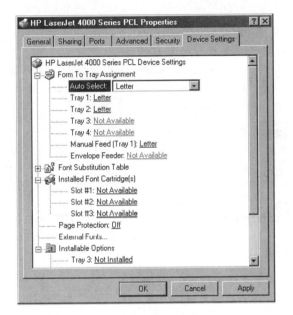

# Installing and Configuring a Modem

To install, configure, or test a modem, launch Phone And Modem Options in Control Panel. Normally, if you install a modem that conforms to the Plug and Play standard, you don't need to use the Phone And Modems Options dialog box for installation purposes. (If you do need to, click Add on the Modems tab in the Phone And Modems Options dialog box, which launches a branch of the Add/Remove Hardware Wizard that's devoted to setting up a new modem. Simply follow its prompts.)

You must be logged on as a member of the Administrators group to install the driver files for a modem.

But you might want to use Phone And Modem Options to change a modem's settings or ensure that the modem is working properly. For example, you might decide that you don't need to hear the modem's speaker every time it dials, or that you'd rather hear it at a lower volume. You can make these and other adjustments via the modem's properties dialog box. On the Modems tab of the Phone And Modem Options dialog box, select the modem and click Properties. See Figure 24-11.

To make sure your modem is connected and functioning properly, you can click the Diagnostics tab. Click the Query Modem button. Windows will commune with your modem and return a table showing the state of each of your modem's registers, along with other potentially useful information.

**?** **SEE ALSO**

For information about dialing rules, see "Setting Up Dialing Locations," page 278.

You use the Dialing Rules tab in the Phone And Modems Options dialog box to set up dialing parameters—whether to dial an area code, calling card information, and so on—for each of your dialing locations. For example, if you take your portable computer with you while traveling in New York, Denver, and Monte Carlo, you can set up dialing parameters for each locale to ensure that your modem dials the appropriate access and area codes when you're dialing in for your e-mail or holding a NetMeeting conference.

**FIGURE 24-11.**

Select a modem and click Properties to configure a modem.

# Installing and Configuring a Scanner or Camera

To install or configure a scanner or a digital camera, open Scanners And Cameras in Control Panel. The Scanners And Cameras Properties dialog box, shown in Figure 24-12, shows the scanners and cameras that are already installed on your system, including the ones that are installed by Plug and Play as well as any that you've added manually.

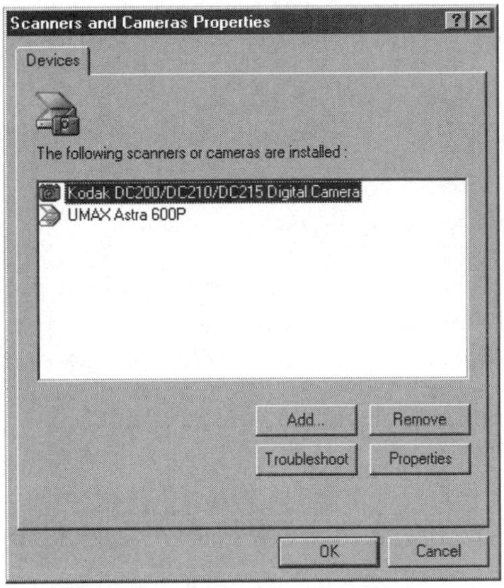

**FIGURE 24-12.**

The Scanners And Cameras Properties dialog box lets you install, configure, and remove scanners and digital cameras.

> **NOTE**
>
> You must be logged on as a member of the Administrators group to install the driver files for a scanner or camera.

To add a new scanner or camera:

1  In Control Panel, open Scanners And Cameras.

2  In the Scanners And Cameras Properties dialog box, click Add. The Scanner And Camera Installation Wizard appears.

3  Connect your scanner or camera to your computer, and then click Next.

VI

Managing Hardware

4 Select the manufacturer and model of your device, and then click Next.

If the device isn't listed but it came with a driver disk, click Have Disk. If you don't have a driver disk, check with the manufacturer or the Windows Update Web site to see if a driver is available.

5 Select the port that your device is connected to, and then click Next.

6 Accept the name that Windows suggests or provide one to your liking, click Next, and then click Finish.

To change a device's settings, select its name in the Scanners And Cameras Properties dialog box and click Properties. The settings you can make depend on the device, but might include:

■ Selecting and configuring a port

■ Associating a program (for example, a photo-editing program) that launches automatically when you use the device; you'll find these settings, if they exist for your device, on the Events tab

■ Testing the device (it must be connected)

# Installing and Configuring a Game Controller

If you have a game controller that connects to a USB port, simply plug it in and you should be ready to start shooting aliens. On the other hand, if your game controller connects to a game port or a serial port, you'll need to visit Game Controllers in Control Panel. The Game Controllers dialog box, shown in Figure 24-13, shows the game controllers that are already installed on your system, including the ones that are installed by Plug and Play as well as any that you've added manually.

 **NOTE**

You must be logged on as a member of the Administrators group to install the driver files for a game controller.

**FIGURE 24-13.**

The Game Controllers dialog box lets you install, configure, and remove joysticks, flight yokes, steering wheels, and other game controllers.

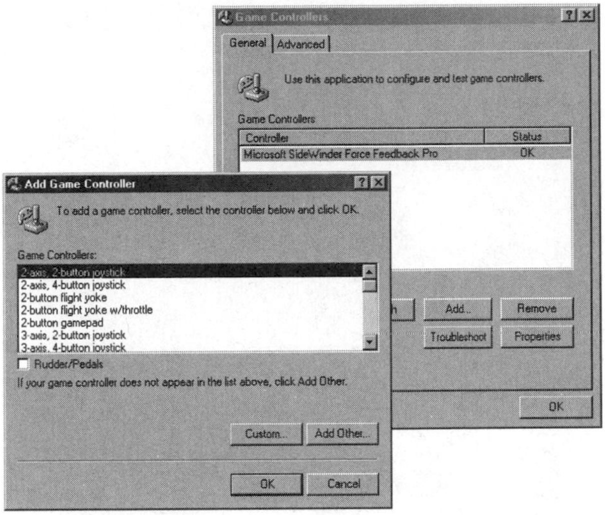

To add a new game controller:

**1** Connect your game controller to your computer.

**2** In Control Panel, open Game Controllers.

**3** In the Game Controllers dialog box, click Add.

**4** Select the type of game controller you have.

> If your game controller isn't listed, click Add Other. Doing so opens the Select A Device Driver dialog box, where you can select a manufacturer and model or use a driver disk furnished by the manufacturer. If your controller isn't listed and you don't have a driver disk (and you can't get a driver from the manufacturer or the Windows Update Web site), click Cancel to return to the Add Game Controller dialog box. Then click Custom and define the characteristics of your controller.

To change a device's settings, select its name in the Game Controllers dialog box and click Properties. The settings you can make depend on the device. (Figure 24-14, on the next page, shows an example.) In many cases, you can test the controller's buttons and other controls, and you can calibrate the controller to match your setup.

**VI**

Managing Hardware

**FIGURE 24-14.**
Clicking Properties lets
you test the selected
game controller.

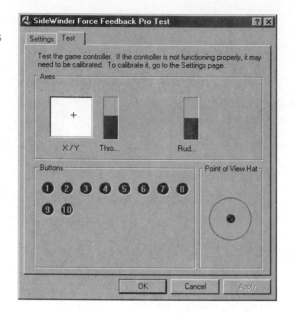

# Managing Devices and Drivers

A *device* is any piece of equipment attached to your computer—a printer, modem, monitor, or mouse, for example. A *device driver* is a program that enables Microsoft Windows 2000 to communicate with a particular device. Each of your system's devices requires one or more drivers.

Many, but not all, devices require one or more of four kinds of system resources: interrupt request (IRQ) lines, direct memory access (DMA) channels, input/output (I/O) ports, and memory addresses. For all of the elements of your system to operate harmoniously, someone or something—a user or the operating system—has to ensure that devices don't lay claim to the same resources (the same DMA channel, for example) at the same time. Fortunately, thanks to the Plug and Play standard, Windows 2000 is able to supervise resource assignments for most devices in use today, making resource-assignment conflicts rare.

Device Manager, shown in Figure 25-1, is a tool that lists all of your system's devices, shows the names of each of your device's drivers, identifies and helps you resolve any resource-assignment conflicts that might exist, provides access to other forms of troubleshooting, and provides access to the Update Device Driver Wizard, which you can use to install new versions of your drivers as they become available. If you're having trouble with a device, Device Manager should be the first place to turn. You'll also find Device Manager useful if you simply want to confirm successful installation of some new hardware item.

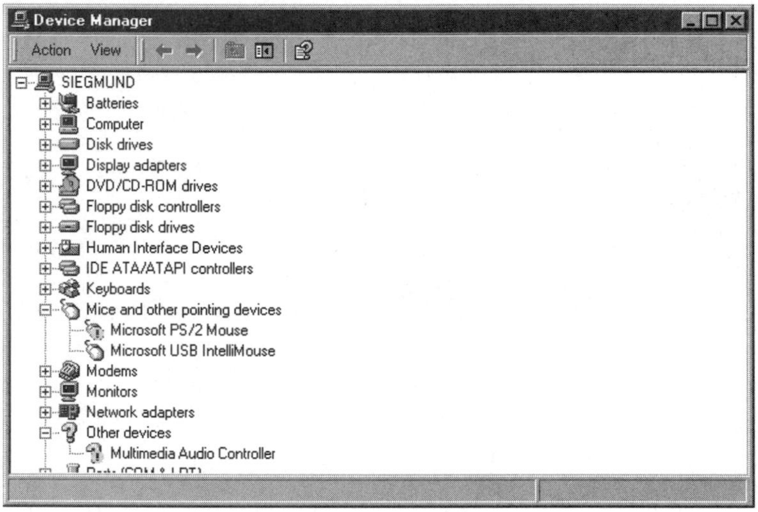

**FIGURE 25-1.**

Device Manager provides detailed information about your system's devices and drivers.

To run Device Manager:

**1** Open the Start menu and choose Settings, Control Panel, System.

**2** Click the Hardware tab.

**3** Click Device Manager.

Alternatively, right-click My Computer and choose Manage from the shortcut menu. Then click Device Manager in the console pane of Computer Management.

# Checking the Status of a Device

When you first open Device Manager, it lists each class of device as an expandable outline entry subordinate to a main entry for your computer itself, which is identified by its network name. You can expand a class entry by double-clicking it or clicking once on its associated plus sign. Expanding the class entry reveals subentries for each item in the class. So, for example, if your system has two modems, expanding the Modems entry reveals a subentry for each modem.

Devices that aren't working properly are easy to spot in Device Manager's initial display. First, their class headings are expanded. Second, the device entries themselves are marked with distinctive symbols. Device Manager uses either a yellow exclamation point or a red *X* to highlight problem devices. The exclamation point typically denotes a device that is incorrectly configured or is missing one or more device drivers. But it can also identify a device that was once working properly but isn't now physically attached to the system. (In Figure 25-1, for example, the Microsoft PS/2 Mouse has been replaced by a Microsoft USB IntelliMouse, but the user neglected to uninstall the PS/2 Mouse. Because the PS/2 mouse has been physically disconnected from the system, Device Manager flags it with an exclamation point.) A red *X* icon denotes a device that Windows 2000 has disabled because of a conflict in resource assignments.

If the entry for a device isn't flagged with an exclamation point or an *X*, you can assume that it has been installed successfully and is working properly. But you can assure yourself of its nonproblematic status by double-clicking its entry to display its properties dialog box and reading the information in the Device Status area of the General tab. Figure 25-2 shows the properties dialog box for a device that is functioning properly.

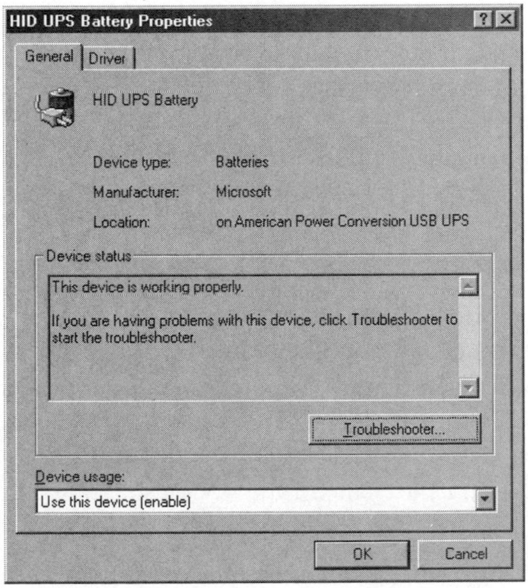

**FIGURE 25-2.**
The General tab of a device's properties dialog box tells whether the device is functioning properly.

# Troubleshooting a Device That Isn't Working Properly

If a device isn't working properly, the General tab of the device's properties dialog box will provide at least a rudimentary explanation of the problem. For example, if a driver required by a device isn't installed, you might see something like the display shown in Figure 25-3.

**FIGURE 25-3.**

If a device isn't functioning properly, the General tab provides a cursory explanation and a potentially useful command button.

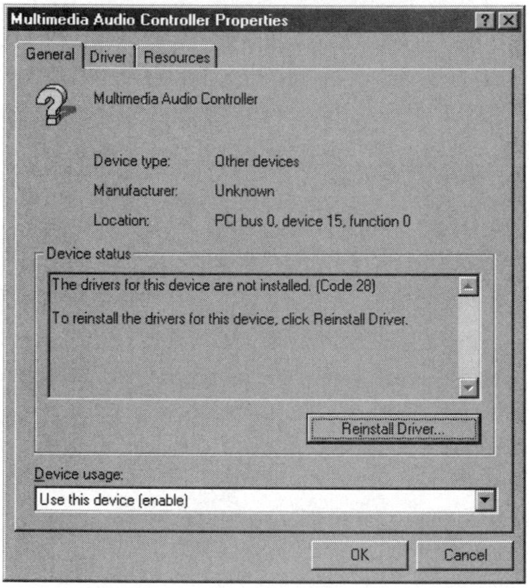

Along with the problem description, the General tab for a non-functioning device includes a command button that might help you solve the problem. In the case of a missing device driver, for example, a button labeled Reinstall Driver appears; clicking it summons the Upgrade Device Driver Wizard. This wizard, described later in this chapter (see "Updating a Driver," page 535) lets you search various places for a newer driver for your device.

If the problem is not a missing device driver, you'll probably see a button labeled Troubleshooter. (As Figure 25-2 shows, this button also appears with devices that are functioning properly—just in case you don't agree with the Windows 2000 assessment of the device's status.) Clicking this button takes you to a Help file, which might provide enlightenment. Some of the troubleshooting help files offer a diagnosis directly. (In the case of the PS/2 Mouse entry shown in Figure 25-1, for example, the Help file suggests that the device might no longer be attached to the system.) In other cases, the Help text steps you through one or more screens providing additional details about the problem—and then offers a diagnosis.

# Getting Details About a Device Driver

At times you might find it useful to know the filename or version number of a device driver. You can get this information as follows:

**1** Double-click the device entry to display its properties dialog box.

**2** Click the Driver tab.

**3** Click Driver Details.

Figure 25-4 shows the Driver File Details dialog box for a display adapter. As you can see, the dialog box displays the name and location, version number, provider, and copyright date of each driver file used by the selected device. The version number, in particular, might be good to know if you need to contact a device vendor's technical support department.

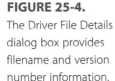

**FIGURE 25-4.**

The Driver File Details dialog box provides filename and version number information.

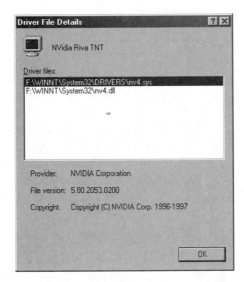

VI

Managing Hardware

# Printing Information About Devices and Drivers

To get a printed report about your system, choose Print from the View menu in Device Manager. In the Print dialog box, choose one of the following options:

- System Summary
- Selected Class Or Device
- All Devices And System Summary

If you choose the Selected Class Or Device option, Device Manager provides information about only one device or device class (depending on what you selected before you issued the Print command). If you choose System Summary, you get a report with the following headings:

- System Summary
- Disk Drive Info
- IRQ Summary
- DMA Usage Summary
- Memory Summary
- IO Port Summary

The System Summary heading indicates which version of Windows 2000 you're using, the name and type of your computer, the registered licensee of the operating system, the date and source of your computer's Basic Input/Output System (BIOS), the amount of memory installed, and assorted similar details. The disk drive section of the report provides physical details about each installed drive. The remainder of the report details resource assignments. This report can be invaluable if you're working with non–Plug and Play devices and need to manage resource assignments yourself.

The All Devices And System Summary report can easily run to 30 or more pages and provides exhaustive detail about each device on your system, along with all the information contained in the System Summary report. In addition to the driver information shown in the Driver File Details dialog box (see Figure 25-4), the report includes file size information about each driver (but not the file date).

# Updating a Driver

To keep your system running as well as it can, make sure that you're always using the most up-to-date versions of your device drivers. If you have a newer version of a device driver on a floppy disk, CD-ROM, or a local or network hard disk, you can use Device Manager to install it. You can also use Device Manager to search Microsoft's Windows Update Web site, to see whether a newer driver is available. The Windows Update site keeps track of offerings from third-party vendors as well as from Microsoft. If a driver is available that's newer than the one you're using, the Windows Update site might be able to find it, download it, and install it for you automatically.

To begin the process of updating a device driver:

1   Double-click the device in Device Manager.

2   Click the Driver tab.

3   Click Update Driver.

    The Update Device Driver Wizard appears.

4   Click Next to open the Install Hardware Device Drivers page.

Under most circumstances, you should select the recommended option, Search For A Suitable Driver For My Device. In particular, select this option if you want to check the Windows

Update site for the availability of a newer driver. You should select the second option only if you want to see a list of all the drivers Windows 2000 knows about that might be compatible with your device—including drivers for other devices of the same class (for example, CD-ROM drives other than the one that's actually installed on your system).

5 Click Next to open the Locate Driver Files page.

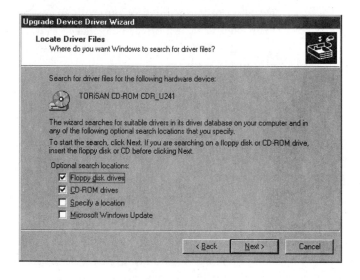

 **SEE ALSO**

For more information about Windows Update, see "Using Windows Update," page 658.

6 Select check boxes for the locations you want Windows to search. If you know the driver you want is on a CD-ROM, for example, clear everything but the CD-ROM Drives check box. If you want to search the Windows Update site, be sure to select that check box. Note that Windows will search the folder %\SystemRoot%\Inf, regardless of what you select (that is, even if you clear all the check boxes).

7 Click Next, let Windows search, and then follow the screen prompts to accept or reject what it finds.

# Uninstalling a Device

When you install a new Plug and Play device, the operating system detects the presence of the new device and takes appropriate steps to install it. When you remove such a device, however, the system might not recognize its departure. If the removed device still appears in

Device Manager (complete with yellow exclamation point), you can inform Device Manager yourself that the item is gone:

1 Right-click the Device Manager entry for the removed device.

2 Choose Uninstall from the shortcut menu.

3 Answer the confirmation prompt.

Note that uninstalling a device in Device Manager doesn't remove the driver files from your hard disk.

# Troubleshooting an Unsuccessful Plug and Play Installation

If you use Plug and Play devices exclusively, you probably won't experience an unsuccessful device installation. Occasionally, however, Plug and Play might fail to detect the presence of a new device. In that eventuality, you can try one of the following:

■ Have Plug and Play rescan your system to see whether it can detect the device.

■ Uninstall and reinstall the device.

The second option is available only if the new device appears in Device Manager but Device Manager reports that its drivers are either not present or not working properly. Also, you must be logged on with administrator privileges to uninstall and reinstall a device.

To rescan your system, open Device Manager's Action menu and choose Scan For Hardware Changes. To uninstall and reinstall a device:

1 Right-click the Device Manager entry for the device.

2 Choose Uninstall from the shortcut menu and answer the confirmation prompt.

3 If you are prompted to restart your computer, do so. Otherwise, open Device Manager's Action menu and choose Scan For Hardware Changes.

If Plug and Play fails repeatedly to detect your device, the device probably doesn't meet the Plug and Play requirements. Follow the device vendor's installation instructions. You might need to adjust the device's resource assignments manually.

# Adjusting Resource Assignments for a Non–Plug and Play Device

To work properly, devices must avoid conflicts over the assignment of IRQ lines, DMA channels, I/O ports, and memory addresses. The operating system manages resource assignments for Plug and Play devices automatically, but it can't do this for non–Plug and Play devices. Provided you are logged on with administrator privileges, you can use Device Manager to reassign resources used by non–Plug and Play devices.

> **NOTE**
>
> Changing a resource assignment in Device Manager only tells the operating system which resources the device is using. To make the device use a different resource, you might need to physically adjust the device itself—for example, by changing a switch or jumper position on the device. Consult your device's documentation for instructions.

Before you consider changing a resource assignment, you might want to make sure that a resource conflict actually exists. You can do that as follows:

**1** Double-click the Device Manager entry for the device in question.

**2** Click the Resources tab.

   The Resources tab's Conflicting Device List shows the names of any devices with which the selected device is in conflict.

To help you decide how to resolve a conflict, Device Manager can show you which resources are currently in use by which devices. To see this view of Device Manager, open Device Manager's View menu and choose Resources By Type. Figure 25-5 shows the Resources By Type view.

> **NOTE**
>
> In the case of IRQ lines, the PCI bus (and some PCI cards that plug into it) is capable of sharing an IRQ line among more than one device, as in IRQ 9 and 11 in Figure 25-5, where two devices share each line. In these cases, before you assume a conflict exists between the devices, examine each device's properties to see whether the devices are indicated as working properly or as having a conflict. The lack of an exclamation icon in the Device Manager list is your first indication that these devices might be able to share their IRQ lines.

**FIGURE 25-5.**

Device Manager's Resource By Type view can help you determine which resources are available for a non–Plug and Play device.

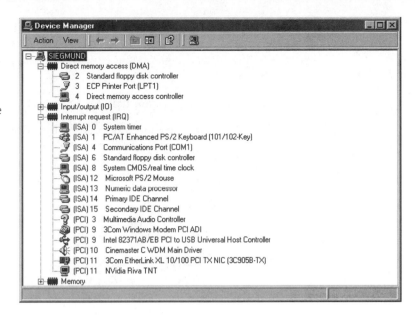

To change a resource assignment for a device:

1 Double-click the Device Manager entry for the device.

2 Click the Resources tab.

3 Clear the Use Automatic Settings check box.

4 In the Resource Settings area of the dialog box, select the resource you want to change.

5 Click the Change Setting button.

6 Select a new value for the resource.

> **⚠ WARNING**
>
> Do not change resource settings unless you thoroughly understand the hardware you're working with. Changing settings improperly can cause your computer to malfunction or become inoperable.

# Setting Driver-Signing Options

Microsoft adds a digital signature to all drivers supplied on the Windows 2000 CD-ROMs. A driver's signature assures you that the driver has passed Microsoft's reliability testing and that it hasn't been altered since it was tested. Other vendors might or might not add digital signatures to their driver files.

VI

Managing Hardware

By default, Windows 2000 warns you before installing a new, unsigned driver. You can change that default so that unsigned drivers are installed without warning. Or you can stipulate that no unsigned drivers be installed.

To change the way the system handles unsigned drivers:

1 Open the Start menu and choose Settings, Control Panel, System.

2 Click the Hardware tab.

3 Click Driver Signing.

The Driver Signing Options dialog box is shown in Figure 25-6.

4 Select one of the three options: Ignore, Warn, or Block.

5 If you want to make your setting the default for all users who log on to your computer, select the Apply Setting As System Default check box. You must have administrative privileges to use this check box.

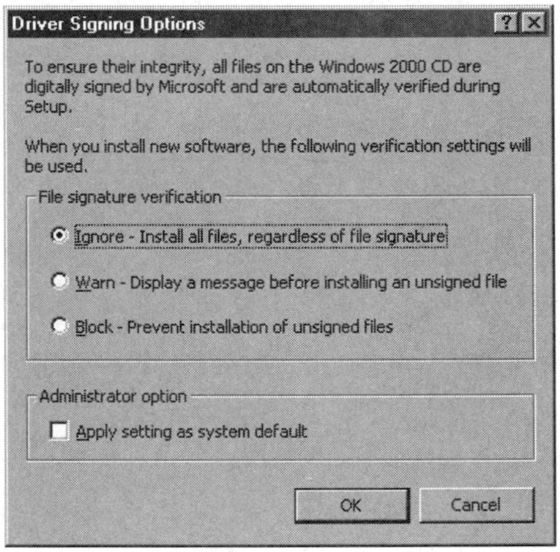

**FIGURE 25-6.**
You can specify how Windows 2000 will respond to installing a driver without a digital signature.

# Using Hardware Profiles

A *hardware profile* is a named constellation of hardware settings. Hardware profiles allow you to enable different sets of devices at different times. A typical use for this feature is to allow a portable computer to use particular devices—a CRT monitor, for example—when docked and other devices when undocked.

The Windows 2000 Setup program creates one hardware profile. You can create as many additional ones as you want. If you have more than one profile, Windows 2000 prompts you to choose a profile when you boot the operating system.

To create a hardware profile:

**1** Open the Start menu and choose Settings, Control Panel, System.

**2** Click the Hardware tab.

**3** Click Hardware Profiles.

Figure 25-7 shows the Hardware Profiles dialog box and the properties dialog box for the selected profile.

**FIGURE 25-7.**

One use for hardware profiles is to use one set of devices when your portable is docked and another when it's not.

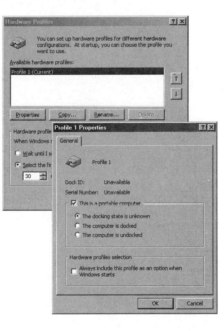

Note that the Hardware Profiles dialog box has no New button. To create a new profile, you copy an existing one, name the copy (or accept its default name), and then season to taste.

**4** Select a profile (if you have more than one), and then click Copy.

**5** Supply a name or accept the default name, and then click OK.

Once you've created one or more hardware profiles in addition to the default profile, you can disable a device for a profile as follows:

**1** Start your computer using the profile you want to modify.

**2** Start Device Manager.

**3** Double-click the entry for the device you want to disable.

**4** At the bottom of the General tab of the device's properties dialog box, open the Device Usage list.

**5** Select Do Not Use This Device In The Current Hardware Profile.

**CHAPTER 26**

# Power Management

Microsoft Windows 2000 supports the Advanced Configuration and Power Interface (ACPI) specification, which is the most sophisticated approach to power management available on today's computers. ACPI is a component of OnNow, a design initiative aimed at making computers behave more like other kinds of appliances, which spring to life more or less instantly at the press of a button, rather than having to go through a lengthy startup process.

ACPI is also the successor to an earlier power-management standard called Advanced Power Management (APM). Windows 2000 supports APM on most computers that don't meet the requirements of ACPI. The salient difference between APM and ACPI is that the former entrusts power management to your computer's BIOS (Basic Input/Output System), while power management under ACPI is a function of the operating system. With power management under software (operating system) control, ACPI-compliant systems can adjust their power states in response to applications and device drivers, as well as to user input. (Even though ACPI lets the operating system control your computer, your computer must still have ACPI support built in before it can grant such power to the operating system.)

**Make Sure Your New Computer Is ACPI-Compliant**

Most, but not all, computers manufactured after January 1, 1999, are ACPI-compliant. To take advantage of the latest power-management features offered by Microsoft operating systems, be sure that any new computers you buy meet the requirements of this specification.

In this chapter, we'll look at the procedures for implementing power schemes, displaying a battery meter, setting battery alarms, and setting up standby and hibernation parameters. All these features are available via Power Options in Control Panel. Because power-management capabilities vary considerably from one computer to the next, however, what you see on your screen might not exactly match the images shown here, and you might have more or fewer options than are described in this chapter.

**TIP**

**How to Tell If Your Computer Is ACPI-Compliant**

To confirm that your system is ACPI-compliant, right-click My Computer and choose Manage from the shortcut menu. In Computer Management, choose Device Manager. Expand the Computer entry. If the system is ACPI-compliant, the expanded entry says Advanced Configuration And Power Interface (ACPI) PC.

# Enabling or Disabling APM

If your Power Options Properties dialog box includes an APM tab, as the one shown in Figure 26-1 does, your system is not ACPI-compliant. (The APM tab doesn't appear on ACPI-compliant systems.) In that event, your first decision should be whether or not to implement APM support. Enabling APM provides the following capabilities:

- If your computer uses batteries, you can display a meter showing the amount of power remaining in each battery.

- If your system uses batteries, you can set low-battery and critical-battery alarm thresholds.

- If your system uses batteries, you can specify one set of power-down parameters for when the computer is running on battery power and another for when it is running on AC.

- Provided your computer supports a standby state, you can put it on standby, either manually (by means of the Shutdown command) or automatically (after a specified period of inactivity).

**FIGURE 26-1.**

If your computer isn't ACPI-compliant but supports APM, the APM tab appears in the Power Options Properties dialog box.

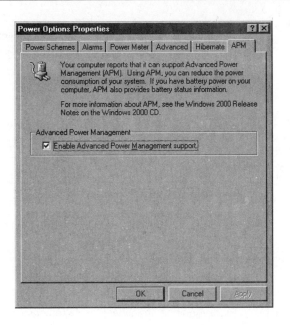

- Provided your computer supports hibernation, you can put it into hibernation, either manually (by means of the Shutdown command) or automatically (after a specified period of inactivity).

These capabilities aren't available on APM systems when APM is turned off.

With or without APM, you can do the following:

- Set power-down parameters that are effective in both battery-powered and AC-powered states.

- Put your computer into hibernation manually (provided your computer supports hibernation).

To enable or disable APM:

1  Open the Start menu and choose Settings, Control Panel, Power Options.

2  In the Power Options Properties dialog box, click the APM tab.

3  Select or clear the Enable Advanced Power Management Support check box.

**VI**

**Managing Hardware**

⭐ **TIP**

If you have a power icon in your taskbar's status area, you can open the Power Options Properties dialog box by right-clicking this icon and choosing Adjust Power Properties from the shortcut menu.

▷ **NOTE**

APM is not supported on multiprocessor computers or on computers running Windows 2000 Server.

---

### Hibernation vs. Standby

When your computer goes into hibernation, it writes the entire contents of its random access memory (RAM) to disk. On awakening, the computer restores its memory.

When your computer goes into standby mode, it simply powers down to the extent it can without writing memory contents to disk.

On awakening from either hibernation or standby, your computer appears exactly as it did before it went to sleep. Recovery from hibernation takes a little longer, since the system has to read data from disk to restore its previous state. And hibernation requires free hard disk space equivalent to the amount of your computer's random access memory.

When you're not going to be using your computer for a while, it's safer to put it into hibernation than to put it into standby. If a power interruption should occur while your computer is hibernating, you lose nothing. If a power interruption occurs during standby, you lose any unsaved work. A power interruption during standby, like a power interruption while you're working, also causes an abnormal shutdown of the operating system. On restarting after such a mishap, you must invoke the "last known good" configuration to avoid registry damage. *See "Recovering from a Damaged Registry," page 634.*

---

# Using Power Schemes

*Power schemes* are named combinations of power-down parameters. Windows 2000 provides six power schemes, each tailored for a different way of using your computer. You can apply any of the six schemes as is, or modify any of the supplied schemes. You can also create additional schemes.

To work with power schemes, open the Start menu and choose Settings, Control Panel, Power Options. In the Power Options Properties dialog box, click the Power Schemes tab. Figure 26-2 shows the Power Schemes tab for a portable computer. On a desktop system connected to an uninterruptible power supply (which provides battery backup in the event of a power outage), the Power Schemes tab looks similar to the one shown in Figure 26-2. On a system without battery power, the Running On Batteries section of the dialog box doesn't appear.

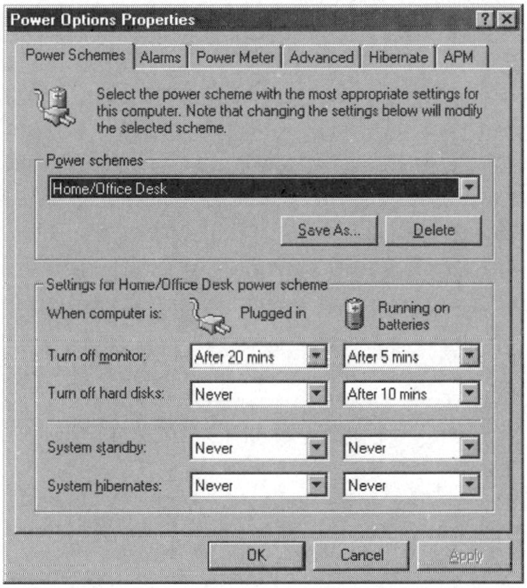

**FIGURE 26-2.**

Windows 2000 provides six power schemes.

> **⊗ CAUTION**
>
> If your system relies on APM (not ACPI) for power management and you share one or more folders with other network users, never power down your hard disks. The same is true if you use your computer as a Web server. Because APM relies on the BIOS to make power-management decisions, it can't know when someone other than you is trying to access a hard disk on your system.

To choose a different power scheme, select from the Power Schemes list. To modify the current scheme, adjust any of the parameters in the lower section of the dialog box. For example, the Home/Office Desk scheme shown in Figure 26-2 is set so that the system never goes into standby or hibernation. To have the system enter standby mode after 30 minutes of inactivity on AC power, for example, open the System Standby list under the Plugged In heading, and then choose After 30 Mins.

To make a permanent change to one of the supplied power schemes, adjust the parameters to suit your needs. Then click Save As and save the scheme under its current name. To create a new power scheme, set your parameters, click Save As, and then supply a new name.

**VI**

Managing Hardware

**⊙ NOTE**

While your computer is displaying the Windows 2000 logon screen, waiting for a user to log on, it uses whatever power scheme was in effect at the most recent logoff. Thus, if you share your computer with other users, you might find someone else's settings in effect as you log on. Once you have logged on, your own settings take effect.

# Using Hibernation and Standby

The System Hibernates options shown in Figure 26-2 appear only on computers that support hibernation and on which hibernation has been enabled. If a Hibernate tab appears in your Power Options Properties dialog box but the System Hibernates options don't appear on the Power Schemes tab, click the Hibernate tab. There you'll find an enabling check box, along with information about the amount of disk space available and the amount needed for hibernation. (See Figure 26-3.) Select the check box to enable hibernation or clear it to turn hibernation capability off.

**FIGURE 26-3.**

Select the check box to enable hibernation.

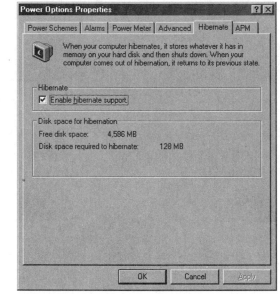

**⊙ NOTE**

On an ACPI-compliant portable computer, you might see additional options on the Hibernate tab—such as an option to hibernate whenever the computer's top is closed.

# Entering Hibernation or Standby Manually

If your system supports standby or hibernation (and hibernation has been enabled), you can put your computer in either of those states manually by choosing Shut Down from the Start menu. From the list in the Shut Down Windows dialog box, choose Standby or Hibernate.

# Awakening from Hibernation or Standby

On most computers, to awaken from standby or hibernation, you press the power button. (Check your own computer's documentation or help text to be sure.) Depending on the kind of mouse or keyboard you use, you might also be able to rouse your system from standby with a keypress or a mouse movement. But you need to enable mouse or keyboard wakeup first.

To enable your system to wake up from standby with a keypress or a mouse movement:

1  Open the Start menu and choose Settings, Control Panel, Keyboard (or Mouse).

2  Click the Hardware tab.

3  Click the Properties button.

4  Click the Power Management tab.

5  Select the check box, as shown in Figure 26-4.

**FIGURE 26-4.**

Depending on your hardware, you might be able to enable a mouse movement or keypress to rouse your system from standby.

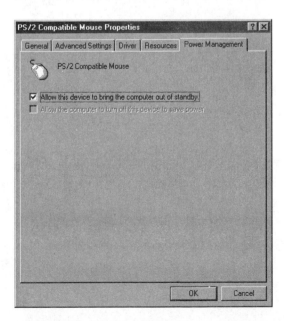

VI

Managing Hardware

## Requiring a Password to Awaken from Standby

Putting your computer into standby can be a convenient way to hide sensitive information while you're away from your desk—but only if your system requires a password to emerge from slumber. To implement this requirement:

1 Open the Start menu and choose Settings, Control Panel, Power Options.

2 Click the Advanced tab.

3 Select the Prompt For Password When Computer Goes Off Standby check box.

If you select this check box, Windows 2000 will require your logon password to emerge from standby.

# Displaying a Power Status Indicator

Windows 2000 can display a power status icon in the status area of your taskbar. On battery-powered computers that are either ACPI-compliant or have APM enabled, the icon indicates whether the computer is running on AC or battery power. On systems without battery power, the icon's only value is that it provides an easy way to get back to the Power Options Properties dialog box.

To display the power status indicator:

1 Open the Start menu and choose Settings, Control Panel, Power Options.

2 Click the Advanced tab.

3 Select the Always Show Icon On The Taskbar check box.

When your computer is running on battery power, the icon looks like a battery and shows you approximately how much power remains. When you have nearly 100 percent of your battery power left, the battery icon looks full. When you're nearly out of juice, it looks empty. The rest of the time, it appears about half full.

To get a more exact reading of your battery status, hover your mouse over the icon. Or double-click the icon to display the Power Meter dialog box, shown in Figure 26-5.

If you choose not to display the taskbar power icon, you can still display the Power Meter dialog box:

1 Open the Start menu and choose Settings, Control Panel, Power Options.

2 Click the Power Meter tab.

**FIGURE 26-5.**
Double-click the taskbar power icon to display the Power Meter dialog box.

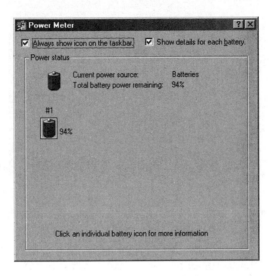

When you're not running on battery power, the taskbar icon looks like an electrical plug. If you're running on AC and recharging your battery, the icon looks like a plug with a lightning bolt running through it.

# Setting Battery Alarm Parameters

On ACPI-compliant battery-powered systems or battery-powered systems with APM enabled, Windows 2000 can display an alarm and take certain actions when your remaining battery power falls below specified thresholds. To specify the parameters governing these actions:

1 Open the Start menu and choose Settings, Control Panel, Power Options.

2 Click the Alarms tab.

Figure 26-6, on the next page, shows the default alarm settings.

VI

Managing Hardware

**FIGURE 26-6.**

Windows 2000 can sound the alarm and take appropriate action when battery power falls to dangerous depths.

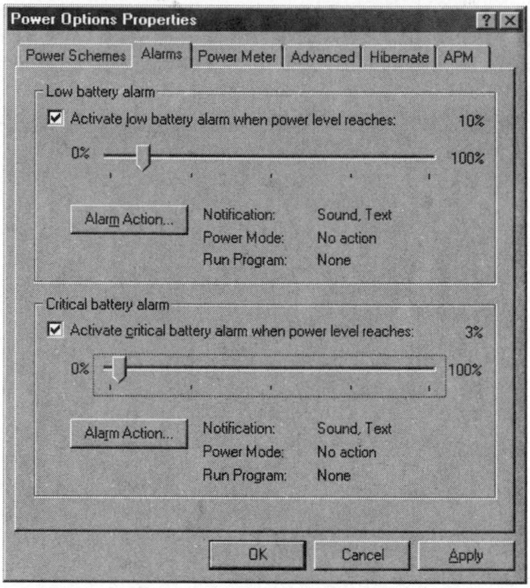

As the figure shows, you can set two different alarm thresholds. At each threshold the system, by default, produces an audible alarm and displays warning text but takes no further action. To change these defaults for either of the two alarm thresholds, click the associated Alarm Action button. Figure 26-7 shows the ensuing dialog box.

**FIGURE 26-7.**

You can customize how your computer responds to a low battery condition.

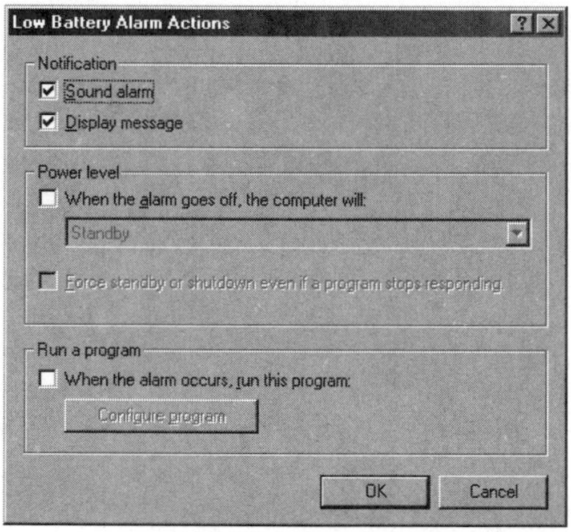

To eliminate the sound or text warning, clear the associated box. To put your computer on standby, make it hibernate, or shut it down when the alarm goes off, select the When The Alarm Goes Off, The Computer Will check box and choose an option from the list. If you select this check box, an additional check box becomes available: Force Standby Or Shutdown Even If A Program Stops Responding. Selecting this option forces the desired action to occur even if a program isn't responding (and hence cannot be shut down without potential loss of data).

**? SEE ALSO**

For more information about scheduled tasks, see "Running Programs on Schedule," page 257.

If you need to have a program run automatically when the battery hits one of your alarm thresholds, select the When The Alarm Occurs Run This Program check box, and then click the Configure Program button. The dialog box that appears next lets you specify which program you want to run, and this program then takes its place among your other scheduled tasks.

# Using an Uninterruptible Power Supply

An uninterruptible power supply (UPS) provides emergency battery power to a computer, enabling it to continue operating or perform an orderly shutdown in the event of a power interruption. If you use a UPS supported by Windows 2000, you'll probably see an additional tab in your Power Options Properties dialog box. Clicking this tab enables you to set parameters governing the behavior of your UPS.

VI

Managing Hardware

# PART VII

# Security and Administration

# Implementing Windows 2000 Security

This chapter provides an introduction to Microsoft Windows 2000 security. We'll describe basic security concepts, such as *permissions*, *rights*, *accounts*, *user accounts*, and *groups*. Then we'll take a tour of Local Users And Groups, the tool that lets system administrators create and modify user accounts.

Some of the material in this chapter is of interest primarily to system administrators. To set up accounts and modify the rights associated with those accounts, for example, you need to be logged on with an administrative account. Even if you aren't an administrator, however, a general understanding of security issues will enhance your ability to use Windows 2000 effectively. In particular, it's valuable to understand the concepts of user accounts, groups, rights, and permissions.

The Windows 2000 approach to security can be described as *discretionary*. That means that each securable system resource—each printer or file server, for example—has an owner, who has discretion over who can and cannot access the resource. Usually, a resource is owned by the user who created it. If you create a disk file, for example, you are that file's owner under ordinary circumstances. (System administrators, however, can take ownership of resources they don't create.)

**? SEE ALSO**

For more information about NTFS, see Chapter 28, "Using NTFS Security."

To exercise full discretionary control over individual files, you must store those files on an NTFS volume. Windows 2000 supports the FAT and FAT32 file systems used by Windows 98, Windows 95, and MS-DOS for the sake of compatibility, but the FAT and FAT32 systems were not designed with security in mind. To enjoy the full benefits of Windows 2000 security, you must use NTFS.

# Introducing Windows 2000 Security

The security provided by Windows 2000 is designed to meet the following requirements:

- Each user must identify himself or herself when logging on.

- The system must insulate objects assigned to processes. For example, memory used by a program must be made inaccessible to other programs, and programs must not be able to read data from deleted files.

- The owner of a resource must be able to control access to that resource.

- System administrators must be able to audit system events and restrict access to the event log.

- The system must protect itself from external tampering.

One of the ways Windows 2000 meets these requirements is by assigning each user a *security ID (SID)*. Your SID, a gigantic number guaranteed to be unique, follows you around wherever you go in Windows 2000. When you log on, the operating system first validates your user name and password. Then it creates a *security access token*. You can think of this as the electronic equivalent of an ID badge. It includes your name and SID, plus information about any user groups to which your account belongs. (User groups are described later in this chapter). Any program you start gets a copy of your security access token.

Whenever you attempt to walk through a controlled "door" in Windows 2000 (for example, when you connect to a shared printer), or any time a program attempts to do that on your behalf, the operating system examines your security access token and decides whether to let you pass. If access is permitted, you notice nothing. If access is denied, you see an unavailable menu or dialog-box control, or, in some cases, you get to hear a beep and read a noxious message.

In determining whom to pass and whom to block, Windows 2000 consults the resource's *access control list (ACL).* This is simply a list showing which SIDs have which kinds of access privileges. Every resource subject to access control has an ACL.

# Understanding Permissions and Rights

**? SEE ALSO**

For a list of Windows 2000 rights, see Table 27-2 on page 578.

Windows 2000 distinguishes two types of access privileges: permissions and rights. A *permission* is the ability to access a particular object in some defined manner—for example, to write to an NTFS file or to modify a printer queue. A *right* is the ability to perform a particular systemwide action, such as resetting the clock.

The owner of a resource (or an administrator) assigns permissions to the resource via its properties dialog box. For example, if you are the printer owner or have administrative privileges, you can restrict someone from using a particular printer by visiting the properties dialog box for that printer. Administrators set rights via Local Security Policy in Administrative Tools. For example, if you have an administrative account, you can use Local Security Policy to grant someone the right to load a device driver.

**> NOTE**

> In this book, as in many of the Windows 2000 messages and dialog boxes, *privileges* serves as an informal term encompassing both permissions and rights.

# User Accounts

The backbone of Windows 2000 security is the ability to uniquely identify each user. Windows 2000 assigns each user a user account. The *user account* is identified by a user name and password, which the user enters when logging on to the system. Windows then controls, monitors, and restricts access to system resources based on the permissions and rights associated with each user account by the resource owners and the system administrator. *For information about managing user accounts, see "Working with Local User Accounts and Groups," page 564.*

In addition to such "normal" user accounts, Windows 2000 provides two special accounts that have predefined sets of permissions and rights associated with them: the Administrator account, and the Guest account.

# Administrator Account

Every computer running Windows 2000 has a special account named Administrator. This account has full rights over the entire computer. It can create other user accounts and is generally responsible for managing the computer. Many system features and rights are off limits to accounts other than Administrator (or another account that belongs to the Administrators group). For example, most features in Computer Management, the tool used to manage user accounts and other items, are disabled when the user is not Administrator or a member of the Administrators group. *For more information about groups, see "User Groups," on the next page, and "Working with Local User Accounts and Groups," page 564.*

> To make it more difficult for intruders to use the Administrator account, you should rename it so they'll be forced to guess its user name as well as its password. *For information about renaming user accounts, see "Renaming, Deleting, and Disabling Accounts," page 571.*

# Guest Account

Most Windows 2000 systems also include an account named Guest. This account resides at the other end of the privilege spectrum. It is designed to allow an infrequent or temporary user such as a visitor to log on to the system without providing a password and use the system in a restricted manner. Choices made by the system administrator determine the level of access afforded to the Guest account. (By default, the Guest account is disabled on a clean install of Windows 2000; no one can use an account that's disabled.)

**⚠ WARNING**

> Enabling the Guest account not only allows anyone to log on to your computer using the user name *Guest* (with no password), but it allows *anyone* on your network to see your shared folders if you share them using default settings. (The other users could even be running an unsecure system such as Windows 98, which doesn't require a logon name and password.) Shared folders on a FAT32 volume are then completely open to access, and anonymous users can view, modify, create, or delete files. If your shared folders are on an NTFS volume and you use the default NTFS access permissions, they won't be able to *access* the share—but they will be able to see the shared folder name. If you must enable the Guest account, be sure you deny Guest access to shares, folders, and files that you don't want guests and other unauthenticated users to see. (A user on another computer or another domain might be authenticated on their system, but not on yours.)

# User Groups

User groups allow a system administrator to create classes of users sharing common privileges. For example, if everyone in the accounting department needs access to the Payables folder, the administrator can create a group called Accounting and grant the entire group access to that folder. If the administrator then adds all user accounts belonging to employees in the accounting department to the Accounting group, these users will automatically have access to the Payables folder. A user can belong to one group, more than one group, or no group at all.

Groups are a valuable administrative tool. They simplify the job of ensuring that all members with common access needs have an identical set of privileges. But even if you're not an administrator, you're likely to work with groups if you assign permissions to files that you own on an NTFS volume. *See "Securing Files," page 584.*

Permissions and rights are cumulative. That means that if a user belongs to more than one group, he or she enjoys all the privileges accorded to both groups. *For more information, see "How Permissions Conflicts Are Resolved," page 588.*

For convenience, Windows 2000 provides a number of predefined, standard groups: Administrators, Power Users, Users, Guests, Backup Operators, Replicator, and several special system groups. Each of these groups has various privileges associated with it by default. Administrators can use the predefined groups exactly as Windows 2000 provides them, or they can make adjustments as needed. Here is an overview of the predefined groups.

## Administrators Group

The Administrators group, which includes the Administrator account by default, has more control over the system than any other user group. (In fact, members of the Administrators group can grant to themselves any right that the group or user doesn't have by default.) All accounts in the Administrators group automatically receive the privileges reserved for the system administrator.

Although members of the Administrators group have maximum control, it is possible for a user to create a file that an Administrators group member can't access by normal means. The NTFS file system allows users to deny access to particular users or user groups, including the Administrators group. An administrator thus restrained can access the file only by assuming ownership of it, and that action generates an entry in the system event log. *See "Taking Ownership of a File or Folder," page 593.*

## Power Users Group

The Power Users group is intended for those who need many, but not all, of the privileges of the Administrators group. Power Users can't take ownership of files, back up or restore files, load or unload device drivers, or manage the security and auditing logs. Unlike ordinary users, however, Power Users can create and delete file shares; create, manage, delete, and share local printers; and create local users and groups.

## Users Group

The Users group is a catchall group. It provides base-level access to the system. Members of the Users group can't share folders or create local printers (unless they also happen to be members of the Power Users or Administrators group). Except for the special Administrator and Guest accounts, all user accounts are members of the Users group by default. Usually, the great majority of users are members of the Users group and no other.

> **NOTE**
>
> When a Windows 2000 computer participates in a domain, the Users group includes all members of the Domain Users global group. This means that anyone accessing your system over the network from another computer in your domain enjoys the same privileges as members of the Users group on your own system.

> **NOTE**
>
> Members of the Users group don't have sufficient privileges to run some older programs that don't conform to Windows 2000 standards. If you find a program that can't be run by Users but can be run by Power Users, check with the publisher to see whether they have a Windows 2000–compliant version, or add the users who need the program to the Power Users group.

## Guests Group

The built-in Guest account is automatically a member of the Guests group. Users who log on infrequently are also good candidates for the Guests group. Privileges granted to regular, well-known users of the system (who are usually members of the Users group) can be withheld from members of the Guests group. This limits these users' access and improves security.

## Backup Operators Group

Members of the Backup Operators group have the right to back up and restore folders and files—even ones that they don't otherwise have permission to access. Backup operators also have access to Windows 2000 Backup. *For information on backing up, see Chapter 29, "Protecting Your Data with Backup."*

## Replicator Group

Members of the Replicator group can manage the replication of files on the domain, workstation, or server. (File replication is beyond the scope of this book.)

## System Groups

Windows 2000 manages several special system groups for the system. Windows controls the membership of these groups; administrators can't specify who should or should not be in them. These groups aren't displayed in Local Users And Groups, but appear in certain other group lists, such as the one you see when you apply permissions to a shared folder or shared printer. You won't have occasion to use most of these, but you should be aware of two in particular:

- **Everyone.** A group containing anyone who uses the computer, including both local and remote users.

- **Authenticated Users.** A subset of Everyone that excludes the Guest user and users who anonymously access the computer across a network; by default, the Authenticated Users group is a member of the Users group.

Other system groups comprise users depending on how they connect to your system, such as Interactive (users who log on locally), Network (users who access the computer through the network), and Dialup (users who connect to your computer via a dial-up connection).

# Local vs. Domain User Accounts and Groups

The predefined users and groups we've covered in this chapter are examples of *local* users and groups. Local user accounts allow users to log on only to the computer where you create the local account. Likewise, a local account allows users to access resources only on that same computer. (This doesn't mean that you can't share your resources with other network users, even if you're not part of a domain. To do that, however, you need to create a local user account for each person who needs access to shared resources—on each computer that contains the shared resources. With more than a handful of computers and users, this gets messy.)

The alternative is to set up the network as a domain. A Windows 2000 *domain* is a network that has at least one machine running Windows 2000 Server as a domain controller. A *domain controller* is a computer that maintains the security database, including user accounts and groups, for the domain. With a *domain user account*, you can log on to any computer in the domain (subject to your privileges set at the domain level and on individual computers), and you can gain access to permitted resources anywhere on the network.

If you participate in a domain, you might come across some additional domain groups. These include the predefined groups Domain Admins, Domain Guests, and Domain Users, as well as other domain groups set up by your administrator. Domain groups can include users who access your computer from other parts of the domain. They can be set up only on a system running Windows 2000 Server.

**? SEE ALSO**

For information about logging on with a domain account vs. a local account, see Appendix B, "Logging On and Logging Off."

In general, if your computer is part of a Windows 2000 domain, you shouldn't need to concern yourself with local user accounts. Instead, all user accounts should be managed at the domain controller. But you might want to add certain domain user accounts or groups to your local groups. By default, the Domain Admins group is a member of the local Administrators group, and Domain Users is a member of the local Users group; members of those domain groups thereby assume the rights and permissions afforded to the local groups to which they belong.

# Working with Local User Accounts and Groups

Local Users And Groups is a tool in the Computer Management console that lets administrators (the built-in Administrator account plus any other members of the Administrators group) manage user accounts. If you have administrative privileges, you can use this program to do the following:

- Create, rename, disable, and delete accounts
- Change account properties

■ Create and delete groups

■ Add users to or remove users from groups

In addition, members of the Power Users group can use Local Users And Groups to create user accounts and groups, and they can modify the user accounts and groups that they have created.

**TIP**

> You can perform some basic user account management tasks in Users And Passwords, a Control Panel item. But you'll quickly run into its limitations and want to switch to Local Users And Groups. Fortunately, there's an easy way: in Users And Passwords, click the Advanced tab and then click the Advanced button.

To get to Local Users And Groups:

**1** In Control Panel, open Administrative Tools and then open Computer Management.

**TIP**

> You can also open Computer Management by right-clicking My Computer and choosing Manage.

**2** In the left pane, under Computer Management (Local), expand System Tools and then select Local Users And Groups. See Figure 27-1.

**FIGURE 27-1.**
Local Users And Groups is the tool within Computer Management where you create and maintain local user accounts and groups.

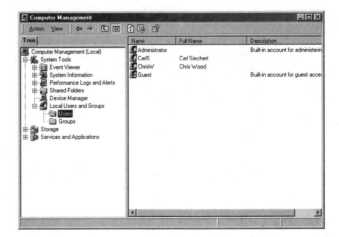

# Creating an Account

To add a new user to your system:

**1** In Local Users And Groups, select Users.

**2** Open the Action menu and choose New User.

The New User dialog box appears.

**3** In the User Name box, type the name the new user will use to log on.

This name must be unique. (That is, no other user accounts on your computer can have the same user name.) The name must be 20 characters or fewer, and can't contain any of these characters: " / \ [ ] : ; | = , + * ? < >

User names are not case sensitive (that is, a user who logs on can type the user name in uppercase, lowercase, or any mixture of the two), but Windows retains the case that you type here whenever it displays the user name.

**4** In the Full Name and Description boxes, type whatever descriptive information you want. Although Windows doesn't use this information, it appears in Local Users And Groups (among other places), which allows you, for example, to sort your user list by full name.

> **TIP**
>
> To make the Full Name useful for sorting, be sure to enter the information consistently for all users. For example, always enter *firstname lastname* or always enter *lastname, firstname*.

**5** In the Password box (and the Confirm Password box), enter the password the user will employ for his or her first logon.

> **NOTE**
>
> Passwords in Windows 2000 are case sensitive. To log on, a user must type uppercase (capital) and lowercase letters exactly the way they're entered in the New User dialog box.

The typical procedure is to supply an initial password and require the user to change it during the first logon. To set things up that way, select the User Must Change Password At Next Logon check box.

If you select the Password Never Expires check box, that setting overrides any password age that you specify via Local Security Policy. *For more information about password settings, see "Setting Password and Lockout Policies," page 574.*

**6** Click Create to create the user account. If you want to add another user (the New User dialog box remains open), repeat the above steps; otherwise, click Close if you're finishing creating user accounts.

## Modifying a User Account

After you create an account, you can modify it. In Local Users And Groups, right-click the user name and choose Properties or, more simply, double-click the user name. The user's properties dialog box appears, as shown in Figure 27-2, on the next page.

### Specifying Group Memberships

New users by default are assigned to the Users group. To change this affiliation or add a new user to one or more additional groups, click the Member Of tab in the properties dialog box. The Member Of tab lists the groups to which the user account currently belongs.

To add a new group, click Add. In the Select Groups dialog box that appears (see Figure 27-3, on the following page), select the groups you want the account to be a member of, click Add, and then click OK to return to the properties dialog box.

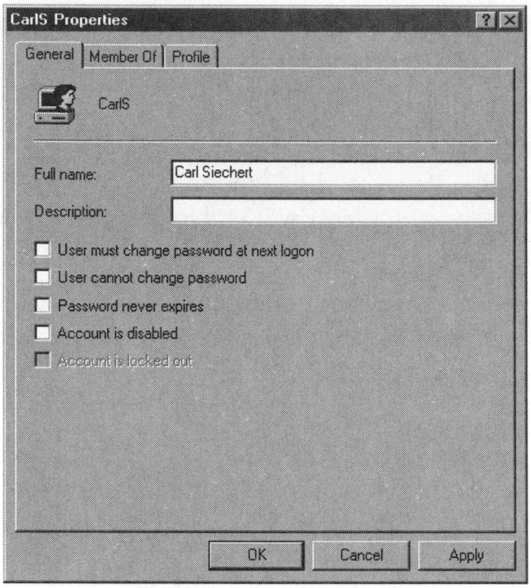

**FIGURE 27-2.**
Double-click a user
name to display its
properties dialog box,
where you can view
and modify account
settings.

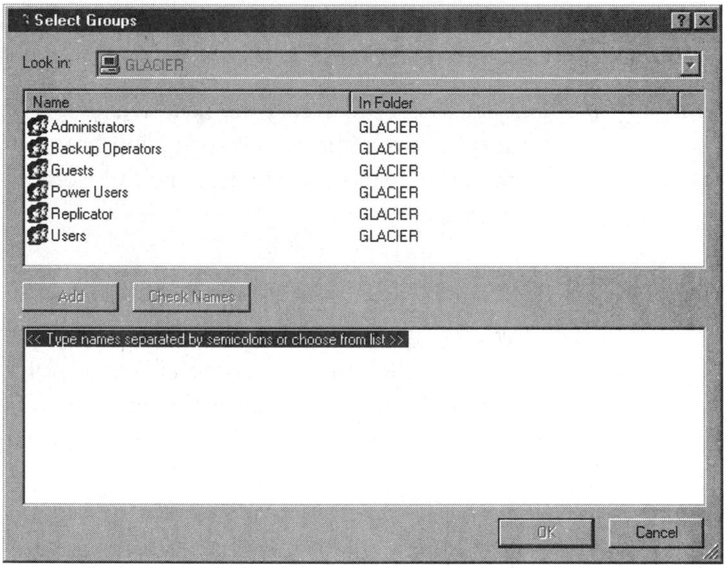

**FIGURE 27-3.**
The Select Groups
dialog box lists all the
local groups to which
you can add a user.

To remove a group from the Member Of tab, simply select it and click
Remove.

## Creating a Roaming Profile

A *user profile* is a file used by Windows 2000 to re-create a user's preferred system environment (including such items as screen colors,

desktop and Start-menu items, network connections, and so on) when that user logs on.

Windows 2000 maintains a default user profile and ordinarily makes that the starting point for any new user. When a user logs on for the first time, Windows 2000 creates a new folder to store the new user's own profile, and copies the default profile into that new folder. Changes that the user makes to the default profile are then recorded in the user's copy, not in the default profile.

For network users, administrators can create special user profiles called *roaming profiles*. A roaming profile is stored on a server (a copy is kept locally as well, for use in case the server is unavailable at logon), allowing the domain user to have the same environment settings regardless of where he or she logs on.

To create a roaming profile for a new user, click the Profile tab in the user's properties dialog box, shown in Figure 27-4. In the Profile Path box, type the location of the profile folder, in the form \\*server*\\*share*; that is, use a universal naming convention (UNC) path name rather than a drive letter.

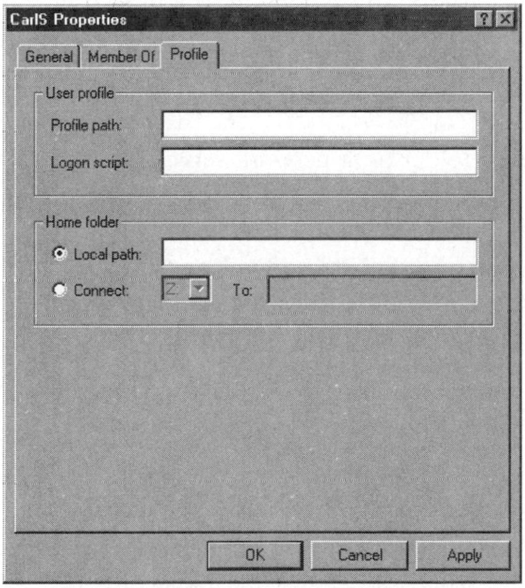

**FIGURE 27-4.**

The Profile tab lets you specify the location of profile information.

> **If you're setting up the folder on the server that contains the profile information, you must share the folder, and you must grant Full Control of the folder to the Everyone group.**

## Specifying a Logon Script

A logon script is a program file that runs whenever a user logs on. Any file with extension .bat, .cmd, or .exe can be used as a logon script.

To employ a logon script on a user's local computer, specify the path and name of the script file in the Logon Script box of the Profile tab, shown in Figure 27-4.

> **Use Environment Variables in the Path**
> A useful environment variable is %username%, which contains the user name of the current user. By using each user's user name as the name of their profile folder or file, you can then enter *%username%* in the Profile tabs af all your users to simplify administration.

## Specifying a Home Folder

A user's home folder is the default folder that appears in the File Open and File Save As dialog boxes (except for newer applications that default to the user's My Documents folder and older applications that specify their own working folder). It is also the default folder for Command Prompt sessions. The home folder can be local or on a server, and users can share a common home folder. To specify a local home folder, enter a path specification in the Local Path box of the Profile tab, shown in Figure 27-4.

To use a folder on a network server as a home folder:

1 Select Connect on the Profile tab.

2 Enter an available drive letter in the box to the right of the Connect button (or click the arrow to the right of the box to select an available drive letter from a list).

3 Enter the full network (UNC) path specification for the remote folder in the To box.

# Changing Passwords

To change a user's password, in Local Users And Groups, right-click the user name and choose Set Password. The Set Password dialog box appears, in which you can type a new password. Note that you can't ever determine a user's current password. If he or she forgets the password, you can't recover it but you can provide a new one.

**TIP**

If you don't already have Local Users And Groups open, you'll find it easier to change passwords by using Users And Passwords in Control Panel. There, you simply select a user name and click Set Password.

**Changing Your Own Logon Password**

Oddly, unless you're a member of the Administrators group, you can't use Users And Passwords to change your own password. Furthermore, Local Users And Groups won't let you change your network password if you log on to a domain. To change the password for your own local or domain user account:

1  From anywhere in Windows 2000 (you don't need to have any particular application running), press Ctrl+Alt+Delete to display the Windows Security dialog box.

2  Click Change Password.

3  Type your current password in the Old Password box. Then type your new password twice to ensure that you've typed it accurately. If the New Password and Confirm New Password lines don't match, or if your entry on the Old Password line is incorrect, Windows rejects your new password.

4  Click OK in the message box that appears, and then click Cancel or press Esc to close the Windows Security dialog box.

## Renaming, Deleting, and Disabling Accounts

To rename an account, in Local Users And Groups, right-click the user name and choose Rename. Note that changing the account's name means changing the user name—the name the person uses to log on to Windows 2000.

**? SEE ALSO**

For information about security IDs, see "Introducing Windows 2000 Security," page 558.

To delete an account, right-click it and choose Delete. Windows 2000 displays a prompt informing you that if you delete an account and then subsequently create a new account with the same user name, none of the properties, rights, or permissions of the old account will be applied automatically to the new one. Because Windows 2000 assigns a new SID to the new account, you will have to set up the reinstated user from scratch.

⭐ **TIP**

> If you're not comfortable with right-clicking and shortcut menus, you'll find the Rename and Delete commands on the Action menu.

If you are removing a user from your system with the expectation that that user will return after some period of time, you might find it more convenient to disable the account rather than delete it. You can then reenable the account (with all its properties, rights, and permissions) at the appropriate time.

To disable an account, double-click its entry to open its properties dialog box, and then select the Account Is Disabled check box. To reinstate a disabled account, visit the same dialog box and clear this check box.

⟩ **NOTE**

> You can't delete the built-in Administrator and Guest accounts. If you don't want anyone to log on using the Guest account, disable it.

## Creating a New Local Group

To add a new local group to your system:

1  In Local Users And Groups, select Groups.

2  Open the Action menu and choose New Group.

   The New Group dialog box appears.

**3** Give the group a name (use the same rules as for user accounts) and, optionally, a description.

**4** Click Add to open the Select Users Or Groups dialog box, shown below.

**5** In the Look In box, select your computer name to add local user accounts to the group, or select the name of the domain that has the users or groups you want to add. Then select the name of the user or group you want to include and click Add.

Repeat this step to add all the users and groups you want, and then click OK to return to the New Group dialog box.

**6** Click Create to create the new group; add more groups if you want (the New Group dialog box remains open), or click Close if you're finished creating groups.

## Changing the Properties of a Local Group

To change the description or membership of a local group, double-click the group name in Local Users And Groups. In the properties dialog box that appears, click Add to add members to the group. To remove one or more users, select their names and click Remove.

# Reviewing and Setting Rights

Another item in the Administrative Tools folder, Local Security Policy, lets you specify password and lockout policies for all users on a computer and assign rights to users and groups. You must be logged on as a member of the Administrators group to use Local Security Policy.

To get to Local Security Policy, open the Start menu and choose Settings, Control Panel, Administrative Tools, Local Security Policy. This opens a Microsoft Management Console window with Security Settings at its root, as shown in Figure 27-5.

**FIGURE 27-5.**
Choosing Local Security Policy opens the Security Settings tool in Microsoft Management Console.

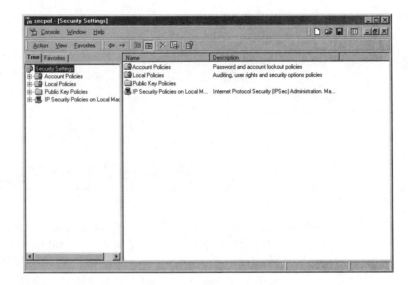

# Setting Password and Lockout Policies

Under Account Policies, you can set a variety of parameters that control password and lockout behavior for all local accounts. As shown in Figure 27-6, the right pane lists each of the policies for the item selected in the left pane. The second column in the right pane shows the local setting for each policy, which you can set by double-clicking a policy name. The third column, titled Effective Setting, shows the actual policy setting in force. This might be different from the local setting because a domain-level policy (set by an administrator on the domain controller) takes precedence over a local policy setting.

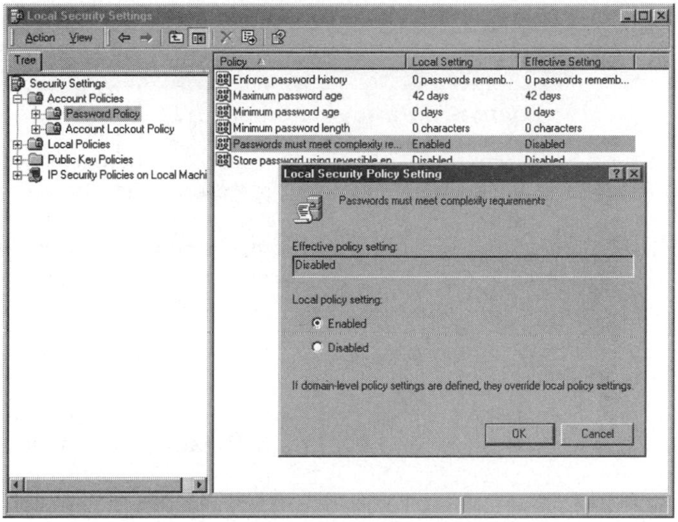

**FIGURE 27-6.**
Double-clicking
a policy opens a
Local Security Policy
Setting dialog box
that explains the
policy and lets you
set the local policy.

Password policies place restrictions on the types of passwords users can provide, and how often they can (or must) change them. Account lockout policies govern the behavior of Windows 2000 in the event that a user types the wrong password. Table 27-1 explains the most commonly used settings under Account Policies.

**TABLE 27-1.   Commonly Used Account Policies**

| Policy | Description |
| --- | --- |
| **Password Policy** | |
| Enforce password history | When a password expires, many users avoid the hassle of remembering a new password by submitting a previous password. Alternating between two passwords, thereby reusing the same passwords, compromises security. Specifying a number greater than 0 causes Windows 2000 to remember that number of previous passwords and forces users to pick a different password than any of the remembered ones. |
| Maximum password age | Specifying a number greater than 0 (the maximum is 999) dictates how long a password remains valid before it expires. (To override this setting for certain user accounts, open the account's properties dialog box in Local Users And Groups and select the Password Never Expires check box.) Selecting 0 means passwords never expire. |

*(continued)*

**TABLE 27-1.** *continued*

| Policy | Description |
|---|---|
| **Password Policy** *continued* | |
| Minimum password age | Specifying a number greater than 0 (the maximum is 999) lets a system administrator set the amount of time a password must be used before the user is allowed to change it. Selecting 0 means users can change passwords as often as they like. |
| Minimum password length | Specifying a number greater than 0 (the maximum is 14) forces passwords to be longer than a certain number of characters. (Requiring longer passwords enhances security, because longer passwords are harder to guess.) Specifying 0 permits users to have no password at all. *Note: Changes to the minimum password length setting do not apply to current passwords.* |
| **Account Lockout Policy** | |
| Account lockout duration | Specifying a number greater than 0 (the maximum is 99,999 minutes) specifies how long the user is to be locked out. If you specify 0, the user is locked out forever—or until an administrator unlocks the user, whichever comes first. |
| Account lockout threshold | Specifying a number greater than 0 (the maximum is 999) prevents a user from logging on after he or she enters a specified number of incorrect passwords within a specified time interval. |
| Reset account lockout counter after | This is where you set the time interval during which a specified number of incorrect password entries locks out the user. After this period elapses (from the time of the first incorrect password), the counter resets to 0 and starts counting again. |

**TIP**

If you use password history, you should also set a minimum password age. Otherwise, users can defeat the password history feature by simply creating a sequence of passwords at random.

If you are an administrator, you can unlock a locked-out user by double-clicking the user's name in Local Users And Groups and clearing the Account Is Locked Out check box.

# Assigning Rights to Users and Groups

To assign or change the rights for a user or group:

**1** In Local Security Policy, expand Local Policies and select User Rights Assignment.

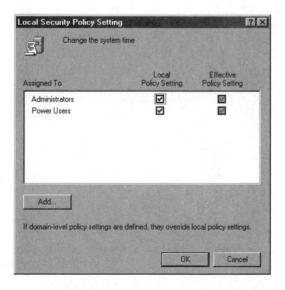

**2** Double-click the policy you want to view or modify.

The Effective Policy Setting check boxes show the actual policy setting in use. If your computer is part of a domain, domain-level settings override local settings. Unless you are a domain administrator, you can't change the domain-level settings, so the Effective Policy Setting boxes are unavailable.

**3** To add a user or group to the list, click Add.

The Select Users Or Groups dialog box appears. This dialog box functions like the one shown in Figure 27-3 on page 568, except that it shows users as well as groups.

Table 27-2 lists the default rights assigned to the built-in user groups.

**TABLE 27-2. Default Rights of Built-In User Groups**

| Group | Default Rights |
|---|---|
| Administrators | • Access this computer from the network<br>• Back up files and directories<br>• Bypass traverse checking<br>• Change the system time<br>• Create a pagefile<br>• Debug programs<br>• Force shutdown from a remote system<br>• Increase quotas<br>• Increase scheduling priority<br>• Load and unload device drivers<br>• Log on locally<br>• Manage auditing and security log<br>• Modify firmware environment values<br>• Profile single process<br>• Profile system performance<br>• Remove computer from docking station<br>• Restore files and directories<br>• Shut down the system<br>• Take ownership of files and other objects |
| Backup Operators | • Access this computer from the network<br>• Back up files and directories<br>• Bypass traverse checking<br>• Log on locally<br>• Restore files and directories<br>• Shut down the system |
| Everyone | • Access this computer from the network<br>• Bypass traverse checking |
| Guest (account) | • Log on locally |

**TABLE 27-2.** *continued*

| Group | Default Rights |
|---|---|
| Power Users | • Access this computer from the network<br>• Bypass traverse checking<br>• Change the system time<br>• Log on locally<br>• Profile single process<br>• Remove computer from docking station<br>• Shut down the system |
| Users | • Access this computer from the network<br>• Bypass traverse checking<br>• Log on locally<br>• Remove computer from docking station<br>• Shut down the system |
| (no one) | • Act as part of the operating system<br>• Add workstations to domain<br>• Create a token object<br>• Create permanent shared objects<br>• Deny access to this computer from the network<br>• Deny logon as a batch job<br>• Deny logon as a service<br>• Deny logon locally<br>• Enable computer and user accounts to be trusted for delegation<br>• Generate security audits<br>• Lock pages in memory<br>• Log on as a batch job<br>• Log on as a service<br>• Replace a process-level token<br>• Synchronize directory service data |

**CHAPTER 28**

# Using NTFS Security

Microsoft Windows 2000 provides the ability to secure access to your computer's resources. Probably your most important securable resources are your files. You can set up your Windows system so that you have complete control over any user's ability to read, write, create, or modify files and folders on your computer, but only if you use the NTFS file system. Originally created for Windows NT, the predecessor to Windows 2000, NTFS is one of three file systems you can use on your computer's hard disks.

In this chapter, we provide an overview of the various file systems. We then show you how to use security on NTFS volumes to secure your files and folders by setting access permissions, how to further protect your files by encrypting them, and how to limit the amount of each user's disk space.

# Understanding File Systems

NTFS is one of three file systems supported by Windows 2000. A *file system* is the structure in which files are organized, named, and stored on disk. The other file systems, FAT16 and FAT32, are variants of a system called FAT (file allocation table). FAT16 is the file system used by MS-DOS and all earlier versions of Windows. FAT32 is an improved file system that is available in Windows 98 and some later versions of Windows 95. Windows 2000 can read and write data to hard disk volumes formatted with any of these file systems with equal aplomb.

**NOTE**

A *volume* is a portion of a physical disk that appears as a separate disk. When a hard disk is originally set up, it can be divided into multiple *partitions*. Each partition, when formatted (*formatting* is the process of applying a file system to the partition), is referred to as a volume.

**SEE ALSO**
For information about controlling access to shared folders, see "Sharing Folders with Other Users," page 185.

With any file system, you can use shared folder permissions to control access to folders that you share over a network. You can specify which users on the network can read, write, create, or modify files and folders within each of your shared folders.

On NTFS volumes, Windows 2000 offers additional security options. In addition to managing security of folders you share over the network, you can also manage security of your files and folders for local users (that is, users who log on to your workstation). And you can apply security restrictions to any file or folder; on FAT volumes, you can set permissions only at the folder level (and only for users who connect over a network).

In addition to the security advantages described in this chapter, NTFS offers several other advantages over the FAT system:

- NTFS stores information more efficiently on very large hard disks.

- NTFS provides faster access to files in most cases.

- NTFS provides better data recovery in the event of disk problems because NTFS maintains a transaction log of disk activities.

- NTFS supports file compression. (MS-DOS-based disk compression programs—such as DriveSpace, DoubleSpace, or Stacker—don't work with Windows 2000.) *For information about file compression, see "Compressing Files on NTFS Volumes," page 653.*

VII

Security and Administration

- NTFS supports disk quotas—disk-space limits you can set for each user. *For information, see "Enforcing Disk Quotas," page 598.*

- NTFS supports file encryption for added security.

So what's wrong with NTFS? There's really only one disadvantage: NTFS volumes can't be read by other operating systems, such as Windows 9*x*, Linux, MS-DOS, or OS/2. Therefore, if you use the multiple-boot feature to run an operating system other than Windows 2000, you won't be able to access information on your NTFS volumes. (You can, however, access shared NTFS volumes over a network, even if the computer you're accessing the files with is running another operating system.)

2000 **TIP**

### Use NTFS for All Your Hard Disks

With Windows NT, many experienced users recommended setting up a small (typically about 300 MB) FAT volume for key operating system files and then formatting the rest of their disks using NTFS. In case of a hard disk problem that prevented the computer from booting, you could then boot the computer using an MS-DOS floppy disk, use MS-DOS-based tools to diagnose and solve the problems on the FAT volume (reinstalling Windows NT if necessary), and then boot the system normally. With the new Recovery Console and an improved Emergency Repair Disk in Windows 2000, this workaround is no longer necessary or recommended. Unless you plan to set up your system so that it can boot into operating systems other than Windows 2000, you should format all your hard disks using NTFS.

## Determining Which File System You're Using

Now convinced that NTFS is the way to go, you must be wondering which file system your hard disks are currently using. During setup of Windows 2000, the Setup program offers to convert your FAT disks to NTFS, so there's a good chance that your disks are already formatted as NTFS.

To see which file system you have, open My Computer, right-click the icon for your hard disk, and choose Properties. Near the top of the General tab in the properties dialog box, you'll see an entry for File System. Be sure to check each of your hard disks.

## Converting a Volume to NTFS

Windows 2000 includes a utility that lets you convert a FAT16 or FAT32 volume to NTFS. It won't convert from any other file system, and once you change to NTFS, there's no way back (short of backing up your data, reformatting your disk, and restoring your data). Unlike formatting, the Convert command does its work without destroying the existing data files on the volume.

> **⚠ WARNING**
>
> Before you convert a disk, be sure you have a current backup of the disk you're converting. The Convert command is quite reliable—but you should always back up your files before using *any* program that restructures your disk as this one does.

To convert a disk to NTFS:

1 Open the Start menu and choose Programs, Accessories, Command Prompt.

2 At the command prompt, type *convert d: /fs:ntfs*

Replace *d* with the letter of the disk you want to convert.

If you choose to convert your Windows 2000 boot partition or if Windows can't lock all users off the disk—for example, if a running program is using a file on the disk or if the disk is being shared over the network—the conversion is delayed until the next time you shut down and restart your computer.

## Securing Files

**? SEE ALSO**
For more information about ACLs, see "Introducing Windows 2000 Security," page 558.

For each file on a volume, the FAT file system stores the file's name, size, and last modification date and time. In addition to storing this information, NTFS also maintains an *access control list (ACL)*, which defines the type of access that users have to the files and folders on the system. Every file and folder stored on an NTFS volume has an ACL associated with it.

NTFS file security is managed using the Security tab of a file's properties dialog box. To get there:

1 Right-click a file in Windows Explorer.

2 Choose Properties from the shortcut menu.

**3** Click the Security tab to open a dialog box similar to the one shown in Figure 28-1.

 **NOTE**

> If the selected file isn't stored on an NTFS volume, the Security tab doesn't appear because file security is implemented only for NTFS volumes.

**FIGURE 28-1.**
The Security tab displays the users and groups that are permitted to access a file.

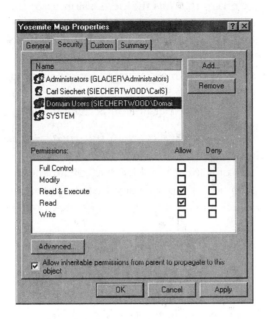

 **NOTE**

> If you're not the file's owner, you might be warned that you are allowed only to view, not change, the permissions for the file. In this case, the Add and Remove buttons in the properties dialog box are unavailable. *For information about owners, see "Taking Ownership of a File or Folder," page 593.*

You use this dialog box to view and change a user's access to a file. In this example, the dialog box shows that the selected file, Yosemite Map, has four entries in its ACL—one for the local Administrators group (the computer name is GLACIER, and it's a member of the SIECHERTWOOD domain), one for the user Carl Siechert, one for the Domain Users group, and one for a special user called SYSTEM. (SYSTEM isn't really a user; it's the Windows operating system itself.)

**? SEE ALSO**

For more information about absent or conflicting permissions, see "How Permissions Conflicts Are Resolved," page 588.

When you select a name from the Name box, the Permissions box at the bottom of the dialog box displays the type of access the selected user or group has to the file. In this example, members of the Domain Users group have Read & Execute permission and Read permission. If neither Allow nor Deny is selected for a particular permission, the user or group might still have the permission by virtue of their membership in another group that has the permission. (For example, suppose the only selected check box for the CarlS account is the Allow check box for the Read permission. Because CarlS is a member of the Domain Users group, the CarlS account also has Read & Execute permission.) If neither Allow nor Deny is selected for a particular permission *and* the user or group doesn't have the permission because of membership in a different group, the permission is denied.

**? SEE ALSO**

For more information about inherited permissions, see "Securing Folders," page 589.

A shaded check box indicates an *inherited* permission, which means the permissions have been inherited from the object's parent. The parent of a file object is the folder that contains it. A shaded check box, therefore, indicates a permission that is applied by default because the file was created in a folder with that check box selected.

**> NOTE**

In this chapter—and in the dialog boxes we discuss—*object* refers to a file or folder.

## Understanding File Permissions

The Permissions box lists the basic permissions, and you can handle most of your security needs by using these basic permissions in various combinations. But in fact, each of the permissions listed in the Permissions box represents predefined combinations of permissions. Table 28-1 shows the individual permissions represented by each permission shown in the Permissions box.

For some situations, the predefined permissions don't provide enough control over the access that a user or group has to a file. To accommodate such situations, you can assign permissions individually. To view individual permissions:

1  On the Security tab of the file's properties dialog box, click Advanced.

2  On the Permissions tab of the Access Control Settings dialog box that appears, select the user or group you want to review, and then click View/Edit.

**TABLE 28-1.** **Basic File Permissions**

| Permission | Description | Individual Permissions |
|---|---|---|
| Read | Allows the user to view the contents of a data file | • List Folder/Read Data<br>• Read Attributes<br>• Read Extended Attributes<br>• Read Permissions<br>• Synchronize |
| Read & Execute | Allows the user to run a program file | • All Read permissions listed above<br>• Traverse Folder/Execute File |
| Write | Allows the user to change the contents of the file | • Create Files/Write Data<br>• Create Folders/Append Data<br>• Write Attributes<br>• Write Extended Attributes<br>• Read Permissions<br>• Synchronize |
| Modify | Allows the user to read, change, or delete the file | • All Read & Execute permissions listed above<br>• All Write permissions listed above<br>• Delete |
| Full Control | Allows full control of the file | • All permissions listed above<br>• Delete Subfolders And Files<br>• Change Permissions<br>• Take Ownership |

As shown in Figure 28-2, a Permissions list similar to the one on the Security tab of the properties dialog box appears—but this one shows (and lets you set) individual permissions.

**FIGURE 28-2.**

Clicking Advanced and then View/Edit leads to a dialog box where you can specify any combination of permissions.

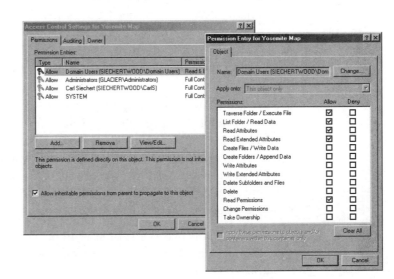

# How Permissions Conflicts Are Resolved

**? SEE ALSO**

For information about user-account groups, see "User Groups," page 561.

Using groups provides an easy way to assign and prohibit access to files and folders for many users. However, the effects of adding and removing permissions to a group are sometimes problematic. The most obvious problem involves granting access to a group when one or more members of the group shouldn't have a particular permission.

When making security changes, be aware that permissions are cumulative. Therefore, you should always review a group's membership to be sure you aren't granting a permission to someone who shouldn't have that permission.

---

### Using Groups for Setting Permissions

Because permissions are cumulative, you must devise your security management strategy with some care. Perhaps the simplest approach is to rely on groups for all security settings, rather than making settings and modifications for individual users. Instead of approaching the problem as granting access to users for particular files, think of granting access to groups. Do this only once—and then add and remove users from the groups.

For example, let's say the Accounting group should have Modify permission to the accounting files. Because Melinda works in Accounting, she is a member of the Accounting group and has all of the same permissions as her coworkers. Another group of users, called Accounting Supervisors, has Full Control permission for all accounting files. If Melinda is promoted to a management position, her new access needs can be addressed by moving her from the Accounting group to the Accounting Supervisors group. If her access is modified directly, she might not automatically receive all of the permissions she needs. Furthermore, in a large organization, explicitly managing permissions for individual users can become tedious.

---

For example, suppose Anthony, a member of the Human Resources group, is explicitly given Read permission for the January.xls file in the Payroll folder. If Write permission for the file is given to the Human Resources group, Anthony receives that permission because he is a member of the Human Resources group. Because permissions are cumulative, Anthony continues to have Read permission for the file, but he also gains Write permission.

Denying a particular permission is an exception to the cumulative rule. It overrides all other permissions, regardless of how the individual permissions are assigned. If the Human Resources group, for example, has the Deny check box selected for each permission, Anthony is denied access to the file—even if you explicitly give his user account Full Control permission.

**WARNING**

Because of the precedence given to the Deny check box, be sure you understand who is affected before you apply it—or you might lock yourself out. For example, you might have a top-secret file for which you give your user account Full Control. For extra safety, you add the Everyone group and deny each of their permissions. That would be a mistake, because your account is a member of Everyone, so you're now excluded too. (Even the file's owner— initially the user who created the file—won't be able to use the file, but the owner *can* go in and change the permissions.)

# Securing Folders

**SEE ALSO**

For information about setting permissions for shared folders, see "Sharing Folders with Other Users," page 185.

Although the effect of setting permissions for folders is mostly the same as setting permissions for files, some important differences exist.

The most obvious difference is that the Security tab of the properties dialog box for a folder includes an additional permission, List Folder Contents, as shown in Figure 28-3. List Folder Contents comprises exactly the same individual permissions as Read & Execute permission, which you can see in Table 28-1 on page 587.

**FIGURE 28-3.**

The Security tab for a folder includes the List Folder Contents permission.

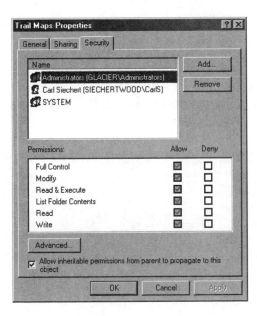

The difference between List Folder Contents and Read & Execute is the way they're inherited. (List Folder Contents is inherited by folders but not by files; Read & Execute is inherited by folders and files.) And inheritance is the most significant difference between file permissions and folder permissions.

If the Allow Inheritable Permissions From Parent To Propagate To This Object check box on the Security tab of the properties dialog box for a file or a folder is selected (the default setting), the permissions for that object are inherited from the object's parent (the folder that contains the file or folder). If the parent folder also has the check box selected, the permissions are actually inherited from *its* parent, and so on. An object can have a mix of inherited permissions and explicit permissions (those where the inherited permissions have been changed or added to). Inherited permissions are indicated by shaded check boxes for Allow and Deny; check boxes for explicit permissions are not shaded.

**⊗ CAUTION**

Any user or member of a group who has Full Control permission on a folder can delete any files in that folder, regardless of the permissions on individual files.

The advantage of this setup is that it allows you to change permissions for a single folder and have those changes propagate to its child objects without you having to go and change permissions on each individual object. When you change the permissions for users' access to a folder, you change the permissions for the files within the folder as well.

You can change or override inherited permissions in the following ways:

- Making changes to an object's parent object changes the inherited permissions for the object.

- Selecting the opposite setting (Allow or Deny) for a permission overrides the inherited permission.

- Clearing the Allow Inheritable Permissions From Parent To Propagate To This Object check box displays the dialog box shown below.

From this dialog box, you have three choices:

- Clicking Copy copies all the inherited permissions to the object, changing them to explicit permissions. In other words, the permissions remain unchanged, but they no longer change when the parent object's permissions change.

- Clicking Remove removes all the inherited permissions, leaving in place only the explicit permissions you have defined.

- Clicking Cancel closes the dialog box without making any changes.

# Changing Permissions for a File or Folder

Although it is easiest to administer file access privileges by adding users to groups that already have certain file permissions, one or more users might need access privileges not given to any group. In this case, you need to explicitly change a user's permissions. In other situations, you might want to update the permissions for an entire group.

⭐ TIP

> Before changing the access privileges of groups, you might want to first determine who is in the group.

To specify permissions for a file or folder:

**1** Right-click the file or folder in Windows Explorer and choose Properties.

**2** Click the Security tab.

**3** If you want to specify permissions for a user or group that's not shown in the Name list, click Add to display the Select Users, Computers, Or Groups dialog box (shown on the next page).

In the Look In box, select the name of the domain or computer that has the user account or group you want to add. Then select the user or group, click Add, and click OK.

4   If you want to remove a user or group from the Security tab's Name list, select it and click Remove.

That user (or members of that group) will no longer have any permissions on the object. Unless, that is, the user or members of the group are also members of another group still listed on the Security tab. Such users will have access to the file or folder. (If your intent is to positively deny access to certain users or groups, don't remove them from the Name list. Instead, change their permissions to Deny.)

**SEE ALSO**

For information about overriding inherited permissions, see the previous section, "Securing Folders."

5   For each user or group in the Name list, select the name and then click Allow or Deny for each permission you want to allow or deny.

If you want to give the user or group a special combination of permissions, click Advanced to open the dialog box shown in Figure 28-2 on page 587, and then click the View/Edit button to select individual permissions.

**NOTE**

If you select more than one file or folder in Windows Explorer before you right-click and choose Properties, the changes you make affect all of the selected files or folders. If the existing permissions are not the same for all the items in your selection, a message appears that informs you of that fact. If you click Yes in this message box, Windows changes the permissions for all selected objects to their inherited permissions, removing any explicit permissions that have been applied previously.

Remember inheritance? Here's where you can put it to good use. To change permissions for a folder and all the files and folders that it contains:

1  Display the Security tab for a folder and set the permissions for all users as described previously. Do not click OK to close the dialog box.

2  Click Advanced.

3  On the Permissions tab of the Access Control Settings dialog box that appears, select the Reset Permissions On All Child Objects And Enable Propagation Of Inheritable Permissions check box and click OK.

After you confirm your intention by clicking Yes in the message box that appears, Windows then processes each file in the folder, each subfolder in the folder, and each file in each subfolder—all the way down the path. For each object it processes, Windows removes any explicit permissions and selects the Allow Inheritable Permissions From Parent To Propagate To This Object check box. The end result is that all the files and folders end up with only inherited permissions, which are identical to the permissions you set for the folder.

# Taking Ownership of a File or Folder

Each file or folder on an NTFS volume has an *owner*, who is the person who controls permissions on the object and can assign permissions to others. The person who creates a new file is its initial owner.

To find out who owns a file or folder:

1  Right-click the file or folder in Windows Explorer and choose Properties.

2  Click the Security tab and click Advanced.

3  Click the Owner tab to open a dialog box similar to the one shown in Figure 28-4, on the next page. The Current Owner Of This Item box at the top of the dialog box shows the current owner.

It is sometimes necessary to take ownership of a file or a folder. For example, if a user who owns a file will no longer be responsible for its maintenance, a system administrator can take ownership of the file and then allow another user to take ownership, or another user can take ownership of the file directly.

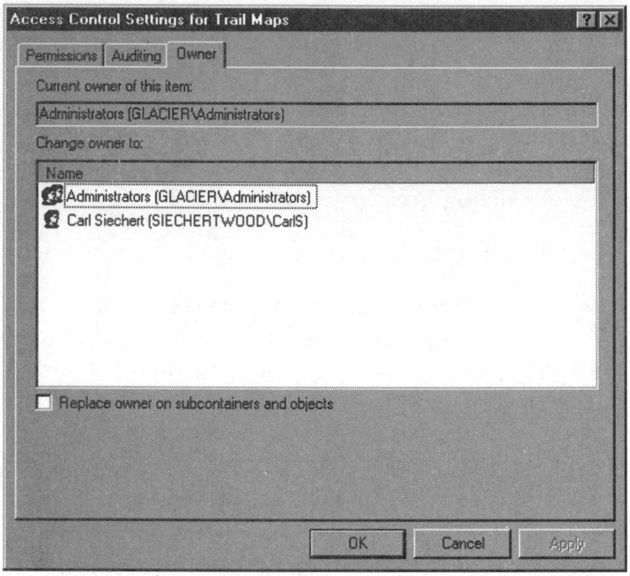

**FIGURE 28-4.**
The Owner tab shows the current owner and those who can take ownership.

To take ownership of a file or folder, you must have Take Ownership permission for the file or folder. (Take Ownership is one of the permissions included in Full Control permission.) To obtain Take Ownership permission, the current owner, another user with Full Control permission, or a member of the Administrators group must give your account Full Control permission.

To take ownership of a file or folder:

1 Display the Owner tab in the Access Control Settings dialog box, shown in Figure 28-4.

2 Select a name in the Change Owner To list, which includes your account name and the names of any groups to which you belong that have Take Ownership permission.

3 If you're taking ownership of a folder and you also want to take ownership of the folder's contents, select Replace Owner On Subcontainers And Objects.

Remember that a file can have only one owner. If you take ownership of a file, you take the ownership away from another user. However, it is also possible for a group to own a file. In that case, all members of the group have creator/owner access to the file.

Remember that the user who creates a file or folder is the owner of that file or folder (until ownership is taken by someone else). Although every member of the Administrators group has the power to take ownership of the file or folder, the owner always has the final say on who has access to the file.

---

### A User's View of Security

We've discussed the different features that are available to system administrators and file owners for setting file permissions. But how are everyday system users affected by security?

When a user attempts to perform an operation on a secured file, Windows checks the file's access control list. If the ACL allows access, the user's request is granted. However, if the user doesn't have access privileges to the file, the request is denied. The exact error message the user gets depends on which application is running, and what the user is trying to do. For example, an attempt to delete a protected file in Windows Explorer results in a dialog box message similar to the one shown below.

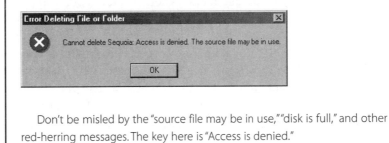

Don't be misled by the "source file may be in use," "disk is full," and other red-herring messages. The key here is "Access is denied."

---

# Setting Security on New Files and Folders

So far, our discussion of security has dealt with security settings on existing files and folders. To complete your understanding of Windows 2000 file security, you should understand how security affects newly created files and folders.

The rule is simple: new files and folders assume the permissions associated with the folder in which they are created. For example, if you create a file in a folder to which the Accounting department has

Modify permission and the Human Resources department has Full Control permission, the Accounting department has Modify permission and the Human Resources department has Full Control permission to the newly created file.

Similarly, if you *copy* existing files or folders to a different folder or *move* existing files or folders to a different volume, the copies assume the permissions associated with the destination folder because you are, in fact, creating new files or folders when you create copies or move between volumes. On the other hand, if you *move* existing files or folders to a different folder on the same volume, the files or folders keep their existing permissions; they don't inherit permissions from their new home.

# Using File Encryption

**CAUTION**

Any user who has Delete permission (one of the permissions included in Modify and Full Control access levels) can delete an encrypted file.

The Encrypting File System (EFS), new in Windows 2000, is a component that allows you to encrypt files on NTFS volumes so that only you can use them. When you encrypt a file or folder, Windows uses your encryption certificate and its private key to encrypt the data. Whenever you use the files (that is, when you're logged on with the same user account as when you originally encrypted the files), Windows uses the same certificate to decrypt the files. (It does this in the background, so you continue to use your encrypted files exactly the way you use nonencrypted files.) If anyone else attempts to open, copy, move, or rename any of your encrypted files, they'll be stopped by an access-denied message.

When you encrypt a folder, all files and subfolders in the folder are encrypted—including temporary files that some programs create while you edit a document. Therefore, for carefree automatic protection of your important files, you should encrypt folders rather than individual files. If you save most of your documents in the My Documents folder, it's a good candidate for encryption.

To encrypt a folder:

1 Right-click the folder (or file, if you want to encrypt an individual file) in Windows Explorer and choose Properties.

2 On the General tab, click Advanced to display the Advanced Attributes dialog box.

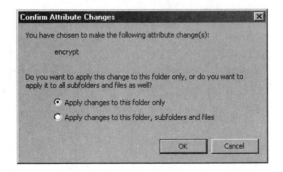

**3** Select the Encrypt Contents To Secure Data check box.

**NOTE**

> You can't encrypt compressed files. If the files you choose to encrypt are already compressed, Windows clears the Compressed attribute.

**4** Click OK to close the Advanced Attributes dialog box and click OK again to close the properties dialog box.

If you're encrypting a folder, Windows then displays a confirmation message.

**5** Select an option and click OK.

- If you select Apply Changes To This Folder Only, Windows doesn't encrypt any of the files currently in the folder. But any new files that you create in the folder (including files that you copy or move to the folder) get encrypted.

- If you select Apply Changes To This Folder, Subfolders And Files, Windows immediately encrypts all files in the folder as well as its subfolders.

Remember that only your user account (along with your encryption certificate) can use the encrypted files. You can't share encrypted files with other users over a network, or even at the same workstation.

**TIP**

**Back Up Your Encryption Certificate**

You should keep a backup copy of your encryption certificate on a floppy disk in a safe place. If you lose your encryption certificate (which could happen, for example, if one of your hard disks fails), you can restore the backup copy and still be able to decrypt your files. To back up your encryption certificate:

1 In Control Panel, open Users And Passwords.

2 Click the Advanced tab and click Certificates.

3 In the Certificates dialog box, click the Personal tab and then select the certificate with your user account name.

4 Click Export to launch the Certificate Export Wizard, and follow its instructions.

# Enforcing Disk Quotas

Another new feature in Windows 2000 is the ability to track and, optionally, limit each user's disk space on NTFS volumes. While this is probably most useful on a server that everyone on a network uses for shared storage, you might find it useful even on a single workstation that several people share.

**NOTE**

To set disk quotas, you must be logged on as a member of the Administrators group.

To enable disk quotas:

1 Right-click a disk in My Computer and choose Properties.

2 Click the Quota tab and select the Enable Quota Management check box to enable the other items on the Quota tab.

VII

Security and Administration

**3** Set the other options on the Quota tab.

- Select the Deny Disk Space To Users Exceeding Quota
  Limit check box if you want Windows to prevent users
  from saving files that would exceed their assigned space
  limit. (They'll see an "insufficient disk space" error message.) If you don't select this check box, Windows doesn't
  stop users from exceeding their limit—but it allows you to
  track disk usage by user.

- To specify a default limit for new users (that is, users
  who don't have an entry in the Quota Entries window,
  described on the next page), select Limit Disk Space To
  and set a limit and a warning level. (Exceeding the warning level doesn't trigger a warning to the user, but administrators can use this setting to more easily monitor users
  who are nearing their limit.) If you don't want to set limits
  on new users, select Do Not Limit Disk Usage.

- If you want Windows to make entries in the system log
  whenever a user exceeds his or her quota limit or warning
  level, select the appropriate check box.

## Managing Disk Quotas

When you enable quotas on a system that has existing files, Windows calculates the disk space used by each user who has created, copied, or taken ownership of the existing files. The default quota limits and warning levels are then applied to all current users and to any new user who saves a file. To view and modify the quota entries, open the disk's properties dialog box, click the Quota tab, and click Quota Entries. The Quota Entries window opens, as shown in Figure 28-5.

Quota Entries for Local Disk (D:)
Quota Edit View Help
Status | Name | Logon Name | Amount Used | Quota Limit | Warning Level | Percent Used
Above Limit | | NT AUTHORITY\SYSTEM | 1.1 KB | 1 KB | 1 KB | 110
Above Limit | [Account Info... | S-1-5-21-329068152-211... | 640.33 KB | 1 KB | 1 KB | 64033
Warning | Carl Siechert | SIECHERTWOOD\CarlS | 198.69 MB | 200 MB | 190 MB | 99
OK | | BUILTIN\Administrators | 1.98 GB | No Limit | No Limit | N/A
OK | Carl Siechert | GLACIER\CarlS | 378.4 KB | No Limit | No Limit | N/A
5 total item(s), 1 selected.

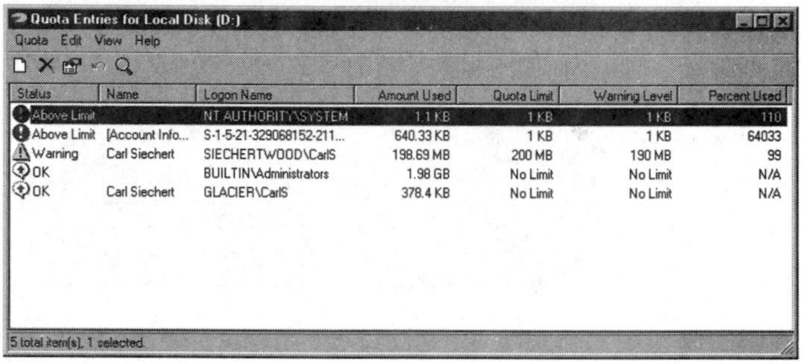

**FIGURE 28-5.**
In Quota Entries, you can review disk usage and impose limits by user.

**NOTE**

You must click OK or Apply in the disk's properties dialog box before you click Quota Entries the first time. Until you do that, the Quota Entries window shows 0 bytes as the amount used.

For each user, Quota Entries displays:

- A status indicator (OK for users who are below their warning level and quota limit, Warning for users who are above their warning level, or Above Limit for users who are above their quota limit)
- The user's name and his or her logon name
- The amount of disk space occupied by files that the user owns
- The user's quota limit and warning level
- The percentage of the quota limit currently in use

To change a user's limits, double-click his or her entry. A dialog box appears that offers choices for this user similar to the choices offered on the Quota tab for all new users.

## Creating a New Quota Entry

To specify limits for a user who doesn't yet have an entry, open the Quota Entries window, and then choose New Quota Entry from the Quota menu. A Select Users dialog box appears, in which you can select the local user accounts or domain user accounts to which you'd like to apply limits. After you select one or more user accounts, specify the limits you want to impose in the Add New Quota Entry dialog box that appears.

## Deleting a Quota Entry

If a user no longer has files on your NTFS volume, you can delete the user's quota entry by right-clicking it and choosing Delete. Because Windows insists on tracking all files if you enable disk quotas, you can't delete an entry for a user who has files on the disk.

But you can use the Delete command to find out exactly which files belong to a user and then, if you do want to delete the quota entry, you can delete, take ownership of, or move the user's files. (See Figure 28-6.) Select the files you want to act on and then click Delete, Take Ownership, or Move. When you've eliminated all of the user's files in one way or another, click Close to finish deleting the quota entry for the user.

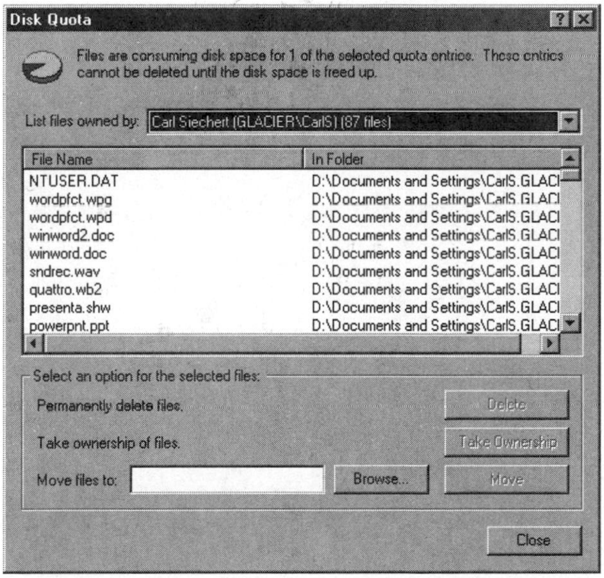

**FIGURE 28-6.**
Deleting a user's quota entry lets you see exactly which files a user owns.

# Maintenance and Optimization

# Protecting Your Data with Backup

You don't have to use computers for long to know the frustration of losing data. It happens to everyone. Although Microsoft Windows 2000 can't prevent mistakes and accidents from occurring, Microsoft Backup, the backup program included with Windows, provides a form of insurance to help you deal with such misfortunes.

With Backup, you can back up files from your own hard disks or from network drives to a tape drive attached to your computer. You can also back up to a file on a hard disk, a network drive, or removable disks (such as floppy disks or Zip disks).

You can select individual files, folders, or entire disks to back up. And you can specify whether to include all files, only those that haven't already been backed up, or only those that were changed today. You can include or exclude the Windows registry, as you choose. When you need to restore files, you can view a catalog of backup sets that includes file and folder information, so you can select the files you want to restore.

To help you automate backup routines, Backup lets you save your backup selections. You can reuse a set of backup selections by simply selecting its name. And unlike the backup programs included with previous versions of Windows, Backup in Windows 2000 includes full scheduling capabilities so that you can schedule backup jobs to run completely unattended at regular intervals. Scheduling offers the full flexibility provided by the Scheduled Tasks facility in Windows 2000.

Backup is now the place to create an Emergency Repair Disk (ERD), which helps you get your system running again if key system files become corrupted or are accidentally deleted. Armed with an ERD, a current full-system backup, and your Windows 2000 CD-ROM, you should be able to recover your system in the event of a catastrophic system failure.

# Understanding Backup Types and Strategies

The Backup program supports five common backup types: normal, incremental, differential, copy, and daily.

- A *normal* backup copies all selected files to the backup medium, regardless of when the files were last changed, and clears the archive attribute for each file to mark it as backed up.

- An *incremental* backup copies only selected files that have changed since the most recent normal or incremental backup, and clears the archive attribute for each file. Therefore, the first incremental backup after a normal backup copies all files that have changed since the normal backup, the second incremental backup copies only those files that have changed since the first incremental backup, and so on.

- A *differential* backup copies only those selected files that have changed since the most recent normal or incremental backup. Unlike incremental backups, however, a differential backup doesn't clear the archive attributes for the files it copies. There-fore, successive differential backups copy all the files that have changed since the last normal (or incremental) backup, not just the ones that have changed since the last differential backup.

- A *copy* backup copies all selected files, like a normal backup, but it doesn't clear the archive attribute. Therefore, you can use it to perform a special backup (before installing new software, for example) without affecting your normal backup routine.

- A *daily* backup copies all selected files that changed on the day the backup is done. It doesn't clear the archive attribute. You can use daily backups to save your day's work without affecting your normal backup routine.

Selecting a backup type involves evaluating tradeoffs between safety on the one hand, and time and media space on the other. If safety were your only concern, you could back up your entire hard disk every day. But the time required to do this might be burdensome, and you'd spend a fortune on backup media. If spending minimal time and money on backups were your only concern, you might back up only a few crucial files once a month. Common sense suggests there must be a happy medium.

A common strategy combines normal and differential backups as follows:

- At some regular interval, such as once a week, perform a normal backup.

- At regular intervals between normal backups—for example, at the end of each workday—perform a differential backup.

With this strategy, if the unthinkable happens and you need to restore one or more files, you need to look in only two places to find the most recent version of any file: the most recent normal backup and the most recent differential backup.

**TIP**

If the capacity of your tape drive exceeds the amount of data on all your hard disks and if you ordinarily leave your computer running all the time, you can schedule a complete normal backup to run each night while you sleep. (Just remember to insert the correct tape before you quit for the day.) Normal backups created daily provide the easiest solution when you need to restore data.

**How Does Backup Know Which Files to Back Up?**

Like most operating systems, Windows 2000 maintains an *archive attribute* for each file. Every file is either marked as needing to be archived (backed up), or it isn't marked.

Whenever a program creates or modifies a file, the operating system marks the file as needing to be archived by setting the archive attribute, which indicates that the file has changed since the last archive. When Backup sees a file with the archive attribute set, it backs up the file and, if you're performing a normal or incremental backup, clears the attribute. The next time Backup runs, the archive attribute is gone (unless you've modified the file again), and Backup knows that it doesn't need to back up the file.

You can view (and set or clear) the archive attribute for a file by viewing the file's properties dialog box.

Differential backups take longer than incremental backups (and require more tape or disk space), so some users prefer to use an incremental backup as their daily backup. If you follow this strategy, don't collect more than a half-dozen or so incremental backups between normal backups. Otherwise, you might have to search through a lot of backup sets to find particular files in the event that you need to restore them from the backup tape.

**TIP**
For extra security, you should rotate backup tapes. For example, if you do a normal backup once a week and differential backups on the intervening days, you might want to keep one week's worth of backups on one tape and then use a different tape the following week. If disaster strikes twice—your original storage medium and your backup tape are both damaged—you'll still be able to restore files from the previous time period's backup tape. Some of the files you restore probably won't be the most current versions, but you'll be better off than if you had to re-create everything from scratch.

**TIP**
If possible, store your backup tapes away from your computers. Otherwise, if you experience a fire or theft, you might lose both your originals and your backups.

# Deciding What to Back Up

Exactly what you need to back up depends on your circumstances, of course, but here's a general principle worth observing: don't make your backup routine so onerous and time-consuming that you lose the motivation to adhere to it.

In practice, what this means for many users is the following:

- Exclude program files and DLLs that you have installed from a CD, floppy disks, or a network server from your regular normal and differential backup routine. Keep programs and data in separate folders so you can easily exclude programs from backups.

**TIP**
We recommend storing all your documents in your My Documents folder or its subfolders. That way, you can easily protect your most important data by backing up that one folder.

- Include all data files (documents) in your normal and differential backups. These are the files that change the most and that would be the most difficult to replace.

- If you don't have a regular normal and differential backup routine, at least perform ad hoc backups of the files you're currently working with. If you don't have a tape drive, use Backup to back up these files to another hard disk. If you don't have another hard disk, back them up to floppy disks, Zip disks, or other removable media.

# Permissions Required for Backing Up and Restoring

Because it's designed to be a secure operating system, Windows 2000 won't let just anybody log on to a computer, back up files, and subsequently restore them somewhere else. You must have certain permissions or user rights to back up files.

**? SEE ALSO**

For more information about groups and user rights, see Chapter 27, "Implementing Windows 2000 Security." For information about permissions and ownership, see Chapter 28, "Using NTFS Security."

- If you're a member of the local Administrators group or the local Backup Operators group, you can back up all files on the local computer—even files to which NTFS security ordinarily denies you access.

- If you're a member of the domain Administrators group or the domain Backup Operators group, you can back up all files on any computer in the domain.

- If you're not a member of those groups (and your account hasn't been granted the Back Up Files And Directories user right), you can back up any files and folders that you own. In addition, you can back up any files for which you have one or more of the following permissions: Read, Read & Execute, Modify, or Full Control.

# Backing Up Files

To back up files, you must tell Backup what you want to back up, specify the backup type, and set other options. You can perform a backup job in either of two ways: by using the Backup Wizard or by

VIII

Maintenance and Optimization

making your settings manually. The wizard is easier to use and more powerful than the backup wizards in earlier versions of Windows, so it certainly deserves a second look. However, it's best suited to performing ad hoc backup jobs or scheduling a backup job to run automatically. If you want to set up a job to use repeatedly at irregular intervals, you might prefer the manual method because it's a little faster than stepping through all the wizard pages.

When you first run Backup—by opening the Start menu and choosing Programs, Accessories, System Tools, Backup—the Welcome tab appears, as shown in Figure 29-1.

**FIGURE 29-1.**

The Welcome tab is the launch point for the Backup Wizard, for the Restore Wizard, and for creating an Emergency Repair Disk.

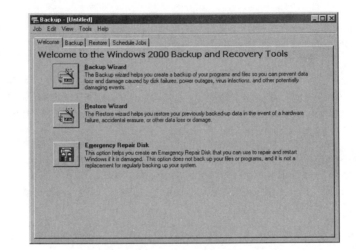

## Performing a Backup Job with the Backup Wizard

If you prefer to use the Backup Wizard, simply click the Backup Wizard button on the Welcome tab. Alternatively, open the Tools menu and choose Backup Wizard, which you can do regardless of which tab is displayed. The wizard leads you through the following steps:

- Specifying what you want to back up *(For details, see "Specifying What to Back Up," page 612.)*

- Specifying where you want to back it up *(For details, see "Specifying Where to Back Up," page 614.)*

After you complete those steps, you'll see a page similar to the one shown in Figure 29-2. On this page, you can click Finish to immediately begin backing up your files. Or you can click Advanced to let the Backup Wizard lead you through the following additional settings:

**SEE ALSO**
For information about the Advanced settings, see "Executing a Backup," page 621.

- Type of backup
- Verification
- Compression
- Append or overwrite
- Labels (names) for the media and for the backup set
- Scheduling

**TIP**

If you want to save the settings you make in the Backup Wizard as a backup job that you can reuse, you must click Advanced and set a schedule for the job. (When you set a schedule, the wizard asks you to specify a filename for the job.)

Upon completion of the Advanced track, the wizard again arrives at a page similar to the one shown in Figure 29-2. Click Finish to begin the backup process or add your backup job to the schedule.

**FIGURE 29-2.**
After you specify what you want to back up, the Backup Wizard offers to begin the backup job immediately or help you set additional options.

## Performing a Backup Job Manually

To create a backup job without the help of the Backup Wizard:

**1** Click the Backup tab.

The Backup tab provides similar functionality to the first few pages of the Backup Wizard: you specify what you want to back up and where you want to back it up.

VIII

Maintenance and Optimization

**2** Open the Job menu and choose New.

**3** Mark the items you want to back up. *For details, see "Specifying What to Back Up," below.*

**4** Specify where you want to save the backup. *For details, see "Specifying Where to Back Up," page 614.*

**5** Open the Job menu, choose Save Selections, and specify a filename for your backup selections.

Once the selections file is saved, you can reuse its settings whenever you want by clicking the Backup tab, opening the Job menu, and choosing Load Selections. You can also set up a schedule to run a backup job on a regular basis. *For details, see "Scheduling Backup Jobs to Run Automatically," page 625.*

## Specifying What to Back Up

Your first step is to tell Backup what to back up, using the two list panes on the Backup tab. The left pane is like the Folders bar in Windows Explorer; the right pane is similar to Details view in Windows Explorer.

### Marking Drives, Folders, and Files for Backup

To specify all files within a drive or folder, simply select the check box next to its name. For example, to back up all files on drive C (including all files in subfolders of drive C), click the check box to the left of *C:*. A check mark appears when you click a folder's check box. If you change your mind, click the check box a second time to remove the check mark.

If the folder you want to back up isn't at the top level of your drive hierarchy, use standard Windows Explorer techniques to reach the folder you want to back up: click the plus signs in the left pane (just like the Folders bar) or double-click folder names in the right pane.

To back up most of a drive but exclude particular subfolders, first select the check box associated with the drive. Then click the drive's plus sign to reveal its top-level subfolders. You'll find that each top-level subfolder is already selected, because selecting a drive automatically selects all of its subfolders. Now clear the check boxes next to the folders you do *not* want to back up.

To back up only particular files within a folder, first display the folder by clicking plus signs in the left pane. Next, click the folder name in the left pane, which causes the folder's filenames to appear in the right pane. Now, make your file selections by selecting the check boxes in the right pane for the files you want to back up.

To back up most of a folder but exclude particular files in that folder, first select the check box associated with the folder name in the left pane. Then click the folder name so that the folder's filenames appear in the right pane. Now clear the check boxes of the files in the right pane that you do *not* want to back up.

⭐ **TIP**

> One of the choices available via the Options command on the Tools menu lets you exclude particular files or categories of files, such as files with the extension .exe, from selected drives and folders. *For details, see "Excluding Particular Files and File Types," page 618.*

## Backing Up the System State

The last item under My Computer in the left pane is one that you won't see in Windows Explorer: System State. System State is a collection of special system files that are essential if you need to recover from a hard-disk failure, for they include all your personal settings and information that your hardware and software needs in order to run. On a computer running Windows 2000 Professional, System State includes:

- The registry, a database of configuration information about your computer and your programs

- The COM+ Class Registration database, which contains information about Component Services, a set of services that provides advanced program capabilities

- Boot files, including Ntldr and Ntdetect.com

VIII

Maintenance and Optimization

Unless you must minimize time and media use, it's a good idea to leave this option selected.

If you choose Back Up Everything On My Computer in the Backup Wizard, Backup includes all your local hard disks, System State, and everything on your desktop.

**NOTE**

You can back up the System State only for your computer. Even if you have administrative privileges on another computer on your network, you can't back up its System State across the network.

## Specifying Where to Back Up

Backup can create archives on any network drive, local hard disk, removable disks (such as floppy disks and Zip disks) to which you can save files, or tape. To indicate where you want the backup to go, select an option from the Backup Destination list. In this list you'll find the names of any tape devices attached to your system, as well as the word *File*. (If you don't have a tape drive installed, your only choice is File, so the list appears dimmed.)

### Backing Up to Tape

If you select a tape device from the Backup Destination list, Backup populates the Backup Media Or File Name list with the names of media (that is, tapes) that are in any of three *media pools*—Import, Free, or Backup. See Figure 29-3.

**FIGURE 29-3.**
Freshly prepared tapes have a name like New Media.

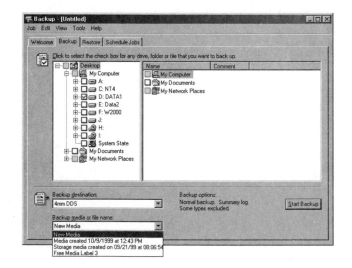

A separate program, Removable Storage, keeps track of your removable media, including tapes, and organizes the tapes into groups called media pools. Removable Storage labels each tape (that is, it places an electronic—not visible—label on the tape, much like the volume name on a hard disk). It also catalogs the contents of each tape and passes that information to programs (like Backup) that request it.

Removable Storage's forte is managing media libraries, such as automatic tape loaders and CD jukeboxes, along with the media they contain. Because Backup relies on Removable Storage to manage backup tapes—even if you have a stand-alone tape drive into which you insert tapes manually—you must use Removable Storage to prepare each new tape. Thereafter, if you have a stand-alone tape drive you'll have little occasion to visit Removable Storage because you can manage most other tape operations from within Backup.

**VIII**

Maintenance and Optimization

### Preparing New Tapes with Removable Storage

The first time you use a new blank tape, you must *prepare* it, a process in which Removable Storage erases the current contents of the tape (if any), makes the tape usable, and places it in the Free media pool. To prepare a tape:

1 Insert a new tape in the tape drive.

2 Open the Start menu, choose Run, type *ntmsmgr.msc*, and click OK.

   The Removable Storage program opens. (You can also get to Removable Storage via the Computer Management console, but the method described here eliminates much of that console's clutter.)

3 In Removable Storage, click the plus sign to expand Physical Locations.

4 Click the plus sign next to the name of your tape drive (for example, 4mm DDS), and then select Media.

5 In the right pane, right-click the tape that you inserted and choose Prepare from the shortcut menu.

6 Click Yes when Removable Storage asks you to confirm your intention to prepare the tape and write a free media label.

When you place a tape that you've previously used (for example, with an older backup program) in the tape drive, Removable Storage initially places it in the Import media pool and displays a dialog box similar to the one shown in Figure 29-4, on the next page. (A similar dialog box that contains only the check boxes appears if you insert a previously used tape *before* you start Backup.) Unless you have an unusual setup with multiple tape drives and programs other than Backup that use tape media, your best bet is to select Allocate This Media To Backup Now and also select both check boxes. That way, any such tapes you insert automatically move to the Backup media pool so they're ready to use, and you won't be bothered again with this dialog box.

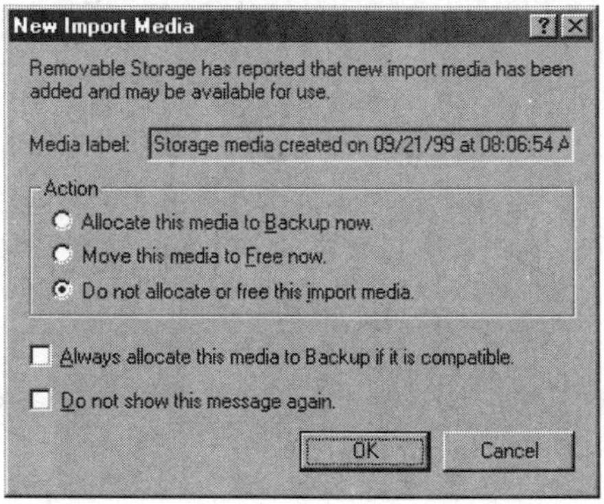

**FIGURE 29-4.**

Previously used tapes that are not in the Backup media pool go by default to the Import pool—but you can change the default.

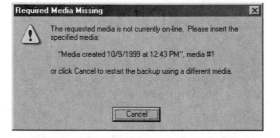

When the tape you want to use appears in the Backup Media Or File Name list—because you've prepared a new tape, because you've allocated a tape from the Import media pool to the Backup pool, or because you've used the tape with Backup before (in which case it remains in the Backup pool)—simply select the tape you want. If you have a stand-alone tape drive, you'll also need to insert the tape in the drive. If you forget to put the correct tape in the drive, Backup informs you when you execute the backup (as described later in this chapter) with a dialog box similar to the one shown in Figure 29-5.

**FIGURE 29-5.**

Identify each tape with a printed label that matches the media name. When a message like this appears, you'll know which tape to insert.

> **Required Media Missing**
>
> ⚠ The requested media is not currently on-line. Please insert the specified media:
>
> "Media created 10/9/1999 at 12:43 PM", media #1
>
> or click Cancel to restart the backup using a different media.
>
> [ Cancel ]

> **NOTE**
>
> You'll have an opportunity to change the media name ("New Media," for example, quickly loses its meaning) in the Backup Job Information dialog box. *For details, see "Executing a Backup," page 621.*

### Backing Up to a Disk File

If you select File in Backup Destination, you can specify the path and name of a disk file in the Backup Media Or File Name box.

 **TIP**

> If you type a filename in the Backup Media Or File Name box, be sure to include the .bkf extension. Unlike most other programs, Backup doesn't automatically append the extension if you type a filename.

If you're not sure how to specify the path to your backup file, click the Browse button. The Open dialog box will appear, and you can navigate to the folder of your choice. Select an existing backup file if you want to append to it or overwrite it, or type a name in the File Name box in the Open dialog box. Then click Open. When you specify a filename this way, Backup automatically appends the .bkf extension.

Note that when you back up to a file, all the disks, files, and folders you back up go into a single file—the file whose name and path you specify.

**NOTE**

> If you use removable media (such as floppy disks or Zip disks) for your backup file destination and the files you're backing up won't fit in that media's remaining free space, that's okay. When you run the backup job, Backup asks you to insert another disk when a disk becomes full; the backup can span an unlimited number of disks.

# Setting Backup Options

Before you execute your backup job, you should choose Options from the Tools menu and review the settings shown in the Options dialog box. Settings in the Options dialog box are program options; they aren't saved as part of a backup selections file. But by making appropriate default settings in the Options dialog box, you can sometimes avoid visiting the Advanced Backup Options dialog box. *For information about the Advanced Backup Options dialog box, see "Executing a Backup," page 621.*

## Choosing a Default Backup Type

On the Backup Type tab of the Options dialog box, select the type of backup you want to use by default. You can always override this setting when you execute a backup job. *For information about the five backup types, see "Understanding Backup Types and Strategies," page 606.*

VIII

Maintenance and Optimization

# Selecting a Detail Level for Reports

After every backup session, Backup creates a text file detailing its operations. You can view this report on the screen or print it. (The report is a plain text file, suitable for printing via Notepad.) You can use the Backup Log tab of the Options dialog box to tell Backup what it should and shouldn't include in the report. (See Figure 29-6.)

Choose one of three options:

- **Detailed.** Reports include all the information that appears in the Summary report, plus a list of every file backed up.

- **Summary.** Reports include a summary of the entire operation (including when it started and completed, and the number of files that were backed up), a list of all files that were scheduled to be backed up but weren't backed up (for example, scheduled files that were in use when Backup tried to copy them), and any errors and warnings encountered during the backup process.

- **None.** Backup doesn't create any report.

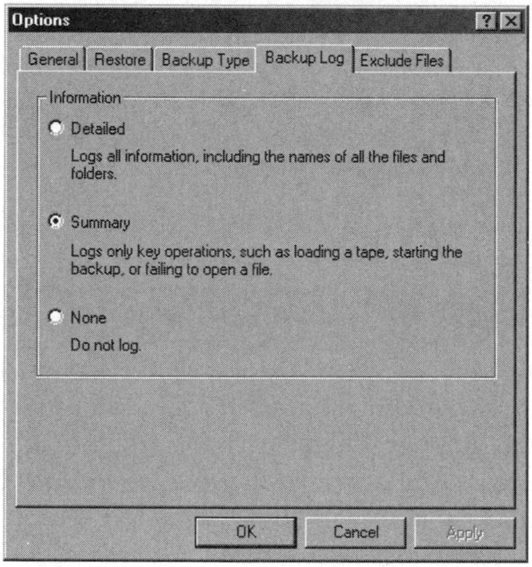

**FIGURE 29-6.**

The Backup Log tab lets you specify a level of detail for Backup reports.

# Excluding Particular Files and File Types

On the Exclude Files tab of the Options dialog box (see Figure 29-7), you can tell Backup not to back up particular types of files, even if those files are stored on selected disks or within selected folders. The top list shows files that will be excluded (that is, not backed up), regardless of who owns them. The bottom list shows files that will be excluded if you own them. *For information about file ownership, see "Taking Ownership of a File or Folder," page 593.*

**FIGURE 29-7.**

On the Exclude Files tab, you specify which files in selected folders you don't want to back up.

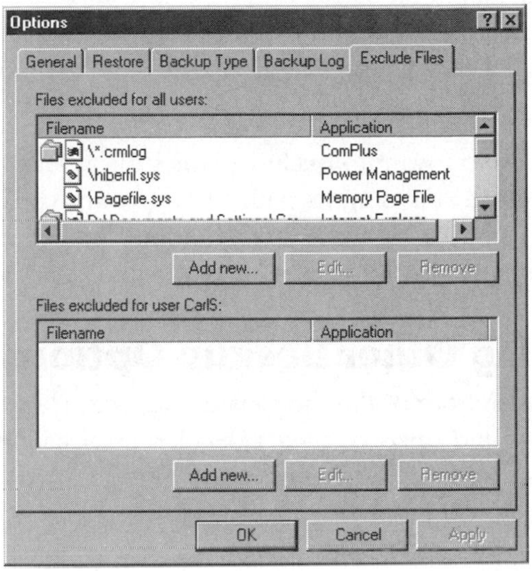

To add to either list of excluded files and file types:

**1** In the Options dialog box, click the Exclude Files tab.

**2** Click the Add New button adjacent to the list you want to change. The Add Excluded Files dialog box appears.

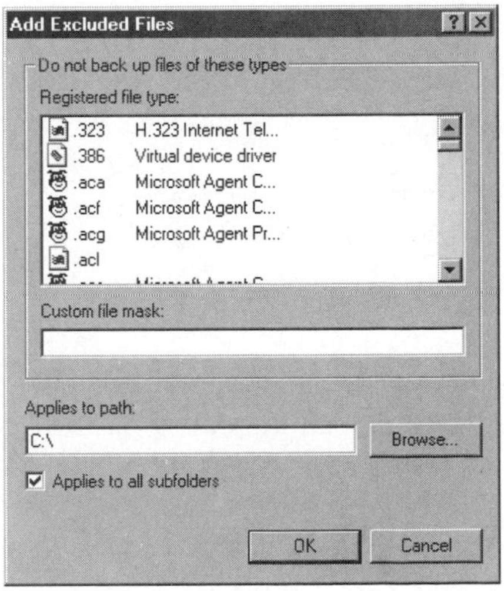

**3** To exclude all files of a certain type (that is, with a certain file-name extension), select the type in the Registered File Type list.

Alternatively, type a filename in the Custom File Mask box. To exclude a particular file, type its complete name. You can use the ? (any single character) and * (any group of characters) wildcard characters to exclude groups of similarly named files.

**4** In the Applies To Path box, specify the folder that contains the files you want to exclude. (Click Browse to navigate to the folder instead of typing its path.) If you want your selection to apply to files in the subfolders of the folder you specify in Applies To Path, select the Applies To All Subfolders check box.

## Setting Other Backup Options

The General tab of the Options dialog box, shown in Figure 29-8, contains assorted options. To get detailed information about any of these options, click the Help button (the question mark in the title bar), and then click an option.

**FIGURE 29-8.**
The General tab offers a number of choices about how Backup operates.

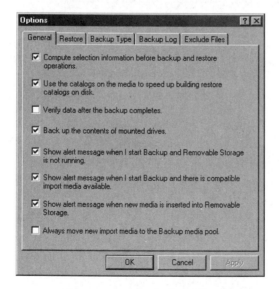

Selecting the third option, Verify Data After The Backup Completes, causes Backup to read the data it has backed up and compare it to the original files. Be aware that the verify operation effectively doubles the time required to complete a backup. If you trust your backup media, you can save a great deal of time by omitting this step by default. However, you should verify backups occasionally just to ensure that your backup device is working correctly. You can override the default behavior you set here in the Advanced Options dialog box, which is available when you execute a backup.

The last four options control Backup's interaction with Removable Storage, and they're effective only if you use tape backup devices. (Removable Storage manages the tape devices and the tape library.) If you normally back up to a file on disk, clear these check boxes.

# Executing a Backup

If you've just finished creating your backup selections, you can run the job by clicking the Start Backup button on the Backup tab.

If you're returning to Backup on another occasion, you can reopen a backup selections file by opening the Job menu and choosing Load Selections (or the name of the file you want if it appears on the Job menu). Then click Start Backup to begin the backup.

When you click Start Backup, the Backup Job Information dialog box appears, as shown in Figure 29-9.

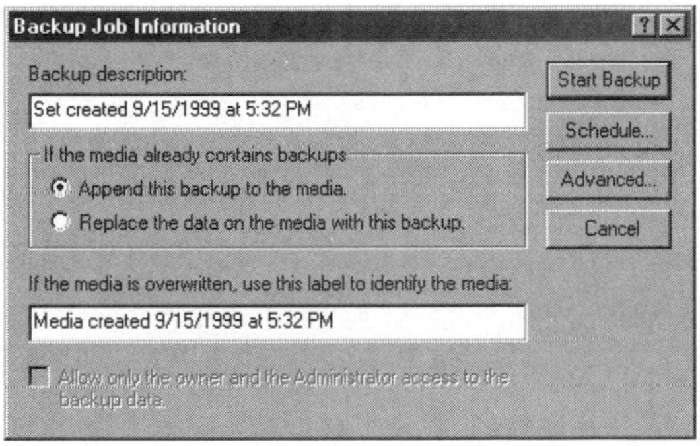

**FIGURE 29-9.**

In the Backup Job Information dialog box, you set additional backup options.

Before proceeding with the backup, you should make the following settings in the Backup Job Information dialog box:

- In the Backup Description box, type a descriptive name for the backup job. The description you place here is visible in the backup report.

- If the backup tape already contains backup data or you specified the name of an existing backup file, you can choose to add the current backup data to the existing tape or file (select Append This Backup To The Media) or overwrite the existing data (select Replace The Data On The Media With This Backup).

If you select Replace The Data On The Media With This Backup, two additional settings become available:

- In the text box near the bottom of the dialog box, you can type a label (name) for the tape or file. This name appears on the Restore tab and in Removable Storage.

- Selecting the check box at the bottom of the dialog box lets you secure the backup tape or file so that only you (as the owner) or a member of the Administrators group can read, write, or erase files from it. (When a backup tape or file is created, the account that is logged on to run Backup becomes the owner of the tape or file.) If you don't select the check box, anyone who is authorized to run Backup can restore files from the tape or file.

## Setting Advanced Options

In the Backup Job Information dialog box, click Advanced to set the following options in the Advanced Backup Options dialog box, shown in Figure 29-10.

- If you select the Verify Data After Backup check box, Backup confirms the backup by comparing the files on the drive and on the tape after the backup is complete.

**NOTE**

If you use your computer during the backup and you change any of the files that were backed up, the Verify option reports errors. Be sure to read the backup report to see whether the errors merely reflect changes that have taken place while the backup was in progress.

**TIP**

**Verify Your Backup**
Although it considerably increases the time to perform a backup, we recommend that you select the Verify Data After Backup check box. Otherwise, you'll have no assurance that *anything* is being written to tape. Discovering that you have a defective tape drive is not something you'll want to deal with while trying to restore lost files.

- Selecting the If Possible, Compress The Backup Data To Save Space check box causes your tape drive to compress files as they're backed up. Doing so typically doubles the amount of information you can store on a tape. Not all tape drives support compression; this option is unavailable if your drive doesn't support compression, or if you're backing up to a disk file.

■ Selecting the Automatically Backup System Protected Files With The System State backs up all the system files in %SystemRoot% (your Windows 2000 folder, which is normally C:\Winnt). This option, which is available only if you select System State on the Backup tab, adds over 200 MB to the size of your backup job.

■ In the Backup Type list, select a backup type. *For more information, see "Understanding Backup Types and Strategies," page 606.*

> **NOTE**

The Back Up Data That Is In Remote Storage check box relies on Remote Storage, a feature that automatically moves seldom-used files to another location, such as a network archive. Because it's a feature of Windows 2000 Server, we don't cover it in this book.

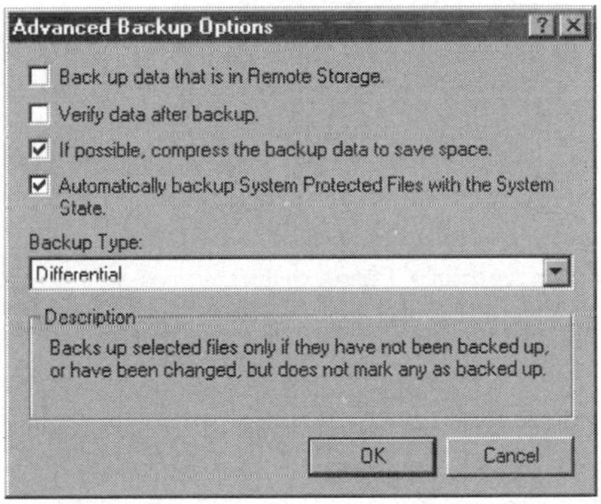

**VIII**

Maintenance and Optimization

**FIGURE 29-10.**

The Advanced Backup Options dialog box lets you select verification, compression, and backup type.

## Starting the Backup Operation

Once you have confirmed the settings in the Backup Job Information and Advanced Backup Options dialog boxes, you need to make only one more decision before you proceed: do you want to set up the job to run automatically at a scheduled time? If so, click Schedule. *For details, see "Scheduling Backup Jobs to Run Automatically," page 625.* Otherwise, click the Start Backup button in the Backup Job Information dialog box.

While the backup is under way, the program displays a progress dialog box, showing you which operation it's performing (a backup or a verify, for example), which file it's working on, how long it's been working, and how much longer it expects to be busy. (See Figure 29-11.) You can continue to work or have automated tasks run while Backup is backing up, but any files that are in use when Backup tries to copy them won't be backed up. The names of such files appear in the summary and detail versions of Backup's report.

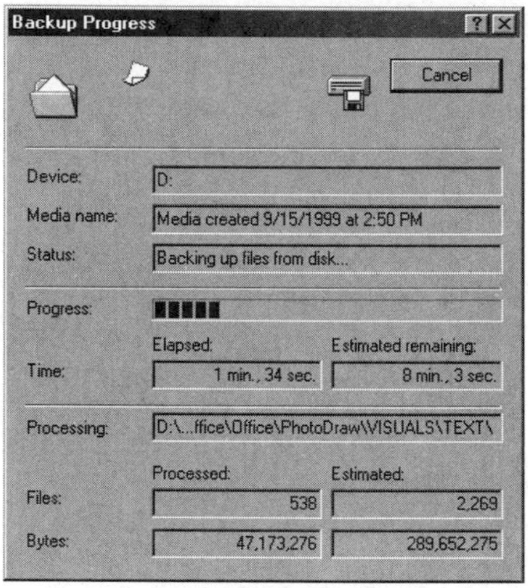

**FIGURE 29-11.**

The Backup Progress dialog box keeps you informed during the backup.

> **Backing Up to Multiple Tapes or Disks**
>
> You can back up more files than will fit on a single tape or disk. If you fill one, Backup prompts for another. Backup can also split files across tapes or disks. Backup assigns a number to each tape or disk in a media set, beginning with 1, and records the location of each backed up file. Be sure to number your tapes or disks with the same numbers! That way, if you need to restore one or more files from the set, you'll be able to find and insert the right tape or disk when Backup requests it.

## Viewing and Printing the Backup Report

When the backup job finishes—either of its own accord or because you click Cancel in the Backup Progress dialog box—a slimmer version of the Backup Progress dialog box summarizes the operation, as shown in Figure 29-12.

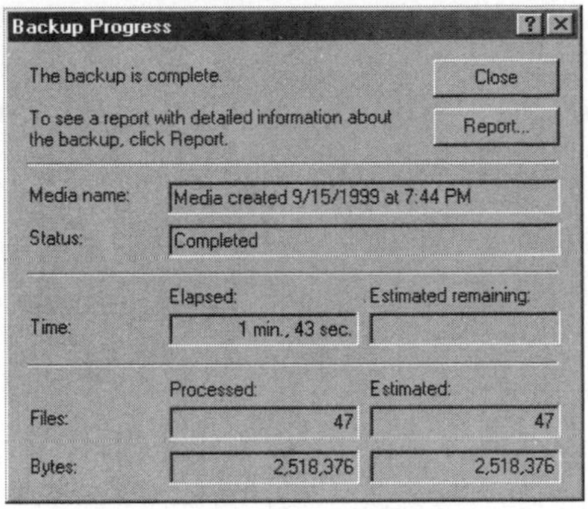

**FIGURE 29-12.**
When the backup finishes, a dialog box summarizes the operation.

**Backup Progress**

The backup is complete. — Close

To see a report with detailed information about the backup, click Report. — Report...

Media name: Media created 9/15/1999 at 7:44 PM
Status: Completed

| | Elapsed: | Estimated remaining: |
|---|---|---|
| Time: | 1 min., 43 sec. | |

| | Processed: | Estimated: |
|---|---|---|
| Files: | 47 | 47 |
| Bytes: | 2,518,376 | 2,518,376 |

Unless you selected None on the Backup Log tab of the Options dialog box, Backup creates a plain-text report that explains the backup job actions performed for each backup tape or file. You can view this report by clicking the Report button in the dialog box that Backup displays upon finishing a job. Or at any time later, you can open the Tools menu and choose Report. Backup opens the report file in Notepad. The backup report shows the ten most recent backup operations; older backup operations are deleted from the report.

To print the report after viewing it, simply use Notepad's Print command. Alternatively, you can print the report directly by choosing Report from the Tools menu, and then clicking the Print button in the Backup Reports dialog box.

# Scheduling Backup Jobs to Run Automatically

You can schedule any number of backup jobs to run at regularly scheduled intervals. If you use Backup Wizard to create a backup job, be sure you click Advanced to get to the scheduling options. To schedule a backup job without using the wizard:

1 On the Backup tab, select the files you want to back up, or open the Job menu and choose Load Selections to use previously saved selections.

2 Select a backup destination and media or filename.

3 Click Start Backup.

description of the job, such as *Full*

---

**4** Set job options in the Backup Job Information dialog box and in the Advanced Backup Options dialog box, which you reach by clicking the Advanced button. *For details, see "Executing a Backup," page 621.*

> **NOTE**
>
> Although the settings you make in these dialog boxes aren't saved as part of the selections file when you run a backup job interactively, Backup saves all these settings as part of a scheduled backup job.

**5** Click Schedule.

If you haven't already saved your backup selections, Backup prompts you to do so. (You can schedule only backup selections that have been saved in a file.) Once that detail has been taken care of, Backup displays the Set Account Information dialog box.

**6** In the Run As box, type the name of the user account you want to run the backup. In the remaining boxes, type the password for that user account, and then click OK.

The Scheduled Job Options dialog box appears.

**7** In the Job Name box, type a description of the job, such as *Full Backup* or *My Documents.*

**TIP**

To review the job options, click the Backup Details tab.

**8** Click Properties. The Schedule Job dialog box appears.

**9** Set up your schedule (or schedules), and then click OK in each dialog box.

On the Schedule tab of the Schedule Job dialog box, you can specify the interval, the start time, an ending date, and other options; and you can set up multiple schedules.

Scheduled jobs are set up as scheduled tasks that appear in your Scheduled Tasks folder. This means that you don't need to leave Backup running for the scheduled jobs to run unattended; Scheduled Tasks automatically launches Backup at the appropriate time. In fact, you don't even need to be logged on to your computer. If you're not logged on (or if someone else is logged on) at the appointed time, Scheduled Tasks launches Backup using the user account name and password that you specified in the Set Account Information dialog box; in other words, it runs that one application as if you had logged on and launched it yourself.

VIII

Maintenance and Optimization

If you're backing up to tape, before the scheduled job runs, be sure to insert the tape you specified in step 2. If you forget to put the correct tape in the drive, Backup will stop and display a dialog box similar to the one shown earlier in Figure 29-5 on page 616.

> **The Easiest Way to Schedule a One-Time Backup Job**
> You can also create a scheduled job from Backup's Schedule Jobs tab: click the Add Job button or double-click any date. Doing so launches the Backup Wizard with predefined settings (which you can modify) to create a backup job that's scheduled to run on the selected date.

## Reviewing the Schedule

The Schedule Jobs tab of the Backup window displays a monthly calendar with an icon for each scheduled job, as shown in Figure 29-13. The letter in the corner of each icon indicates the backup type: N for normal, D for differential, and so on.

To modify or delete a scheduled job, click its icon to open the Scheduled Job Options dialog box. On the Schedule Data tab, click Properties to change the schedule, or click Delete to delete the job.

**FIGURE 29-13.**
The Schedule Jobs tab shows all scheduled jobs as icons.

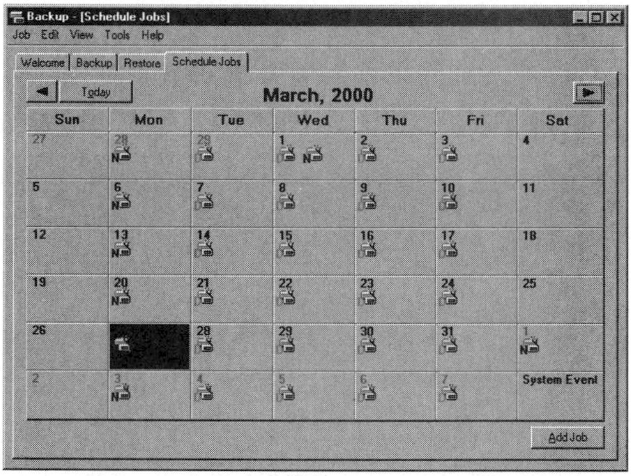

> To review the job options, click the Backup Details tab in the Scheduled Job Options dialog box. (You can't change these options here; the simplest way to do that is to create a new scheduled job.)

# Restoring Files

Like backing up, restoring is a matter of specifying what, whence, whither, and how. You can do this by invoking the Restore Wizard (click its button on the Welcome tab or choose Restore Wizard from the Tools menu) or by pointing and clicking on the Restore tab of the Backup window. There's no significant advantage to one method over the other.

To restore files by working directly on the Restore tab of the Backup window, start Backup and click the Restore tab. (See Figure 29-14.) The process of restoring files is quite similar to the process of backing up files.

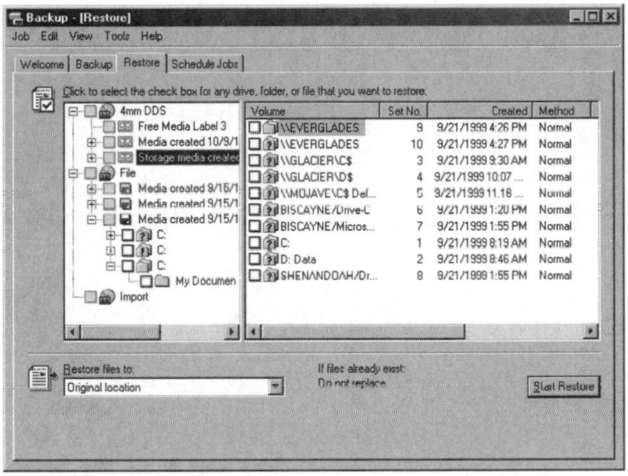

**FIGURE 29-14.**

To see the contents of a folder marked with a question mark, right-click its icon and choose Catalog.

**1** Specify the files or folders you want to restore.

The hierarchy in the left pane is organized at the highest level by media type (tape or file). Within each media type, the left pane contains an entry for each tape or each file; in either case, Backup identifies the tape or file by the media name you specified during backup. You can expand the outline until you see the drives, folders, and files that you want to restore. Mark these for restore by clicking the check box.

> **NOTE**
>
> A question mark on a folder icon indicates an item for which Backup has not yet read the catalog, or file list, from the backup media. You can force Backup to read the catalog by right-clicking a questionable folder and choosing Catalog from the shortcut menu. If you expand such an icon or mark it for restore without first cataloging its contents, Backup reads the catalog.

**2** Specify where you want the restored files to go. In the Restore Files To box, choose one of these options:

- Choose Original Location to restore the selected files to the same folder or folders they were in when they were backed up.

- Choose Alternate Location to restore the files to a different folder. The folders and files you select will be restored to subfolders within the folder you specify in the Alternate Location box, maintaining their original folder structure.

- Choose Single Location to restore all selected files from all selected folders to a single folder, which you specify in the Alternate Location box.

**3** Open the Tools menu and choose Options. On the Restore tab of the Options dialog box, select one of the three options to specify what you want Backup to do when you restore a file that already exists in the selected folder on your computer.

The default and recommended choice is not to restore any file that's already on the target disk. But you can opt to have the program restore when the backed-up copy is newer than the existing copy. Or you can have the program always restore. What you can't do is ask for a yes/no prompt every time the question arises. If you want some files always to be overwritten and some files never to be overwritten, you'll need to perform separate restore operations for each category of file. Click OK to close the Options dialog box.

**4** Click Start Restore. In the Confirm Restore dialog box, click OK.

Backup then begins restoring your files, prompting you to insert the correct media if necessary, and keeping you informed of its progress with dialog boxes similar to the ones it uses for backup operations.

> You should always restore files that you have backed up from an NTFS volume to a Windows 2000 NTFS volume. If you restore them to a FAT or FAT32 volume— or even to an NTFS volume on a computer running Windows NT 4—you'll lose some or all of the NTFS security features, including permissions, encryption, and ownership information.

# Creating an Emergency Repair Disk

Windows 2000 includes several tools that might be able to rebuild your system in the event of a catastrophic failure. One of these tools is an Emergency Repair Disk, which contains configuration information about your computer. In Windows NT 4, you needed to remember a cryptic command to create an Emergency Repair Disk; in Windows 2000, the ERD-creation process has found a home in Backup.

> Create a new Emergency Repair Disk whenever you change your hardware configuration, modify disk partitions, or install new software.

To create an Emergency Repair Disk:

**1** Insert a blank, formatted floppy disk in your computer's floppy disk drive.

**2** On the Welcome tab, click Emergency Repair Disk.

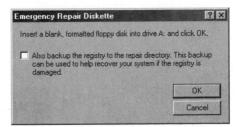

**VIII**<br>**Maintenance and Optimization**

**3** For maximum protection, select the check box in the Emergency Repair Diskette dialog box, which backs up the registry to the %SystemRoot%\Repair\RegBack folder.

In addition to creating files on the floppy disk, creating an Emergency Repair Disk also copies a number of files to the %SystemRoot%\Repair folder.

**? SEE ALSO**

For information about using the Emergency Repair Disk, see "What to Do if Windows 2000 Doesn't Start," page 663.

The next step in preparing for disaster is to make sure your Windows 2000 Professional CD is handy. The Emergency Repair Disk relies on the setup program that lives there, and even if you copied it to your hard disk, you might not be able to get to it in your time of need.

Finally, make a complete backup of your system, including the System State. Repeat this step regularly and frequently!

**CHAPTER 30**

# Working with the Registry

J ust about everything Microsoft Windows 2000 needs to know about your system—your hardware, your software, the order in which your device drivers should be loaded at startup, the resources used by your devices, the hardware profile currently in effect, the user profile currently in effect, and many application-specific settings—is stored in a database called the *registry*. This centralized information repository essentially replaces the myriad configuration files that had been used in earlier versions of Windows (prior to Windows 95). If you've used earlier versions of Windows, you might have had occasion to examine or modify files named Win.ini and System.ini. These files still exist in Windows 2000 but only to provide compatibility with older (16-bit) applications. For nearly all newer programs, as well as for the operating system itself, the registry has taken over the role once played by Win.ini and System.ini.

The registry has also eliminated the need for many of the "private" .ini files used by some programs. You might still find a handful of .ini files on your hard disk, because older programs still use them—as do newer programs that must maintain compatibility with older versions of the operating system. Windows 2000 itself still uses a few .ini files. But most of the vital stuff that makes your system run is stored in the registry.

---

**Recovering from a Damaged Registry**

Windows 2000 saves the current state of the registry every time you start the operating system successfully. If you change the registry and find your system behaving erratically, or if you change it and are subsequently unable to start the operating system, you can revert to the registry as it was the last time you started successfully, as follows:

**1** Restart your computer.

**2** After you see whatever startup messages normally appear but before your computer begins loading Windows 2000, press F8.

**3** From the menu that appears, choose Last Known Good Configuration, and then press Enter.

**4** If prompted, select the hardware profile you want to use.

You should also restore the last known good configuration after any kind of abnormal shutdown of Windows 2000. If you experience a power interruption, for example, or if someone turns off your machine without going through the normal shutdown procedure, your registry might be left in an abnormal state. If the registry is damaged but you restart successfully, the incorrect state of the registry itself becomes the last known good configuration. Then you lose the opportunity to revert to the undamaged registry. To be safe, always restart with the last known good configuration after an abnormal shutdown.

---

Although you can make changes to the registry directly, using the Registry Editor program described in this chapter, most of the time you have no need to do so. The normal, safe, and preferred way to alter the registry is by using the Windows user interface, or the user interface of an application program. When you change your wallpaper using Desktop in Control Panel, for example, Control Panel records your change in the registry; you don't have to—and shouldn't—tweak the registry directly. When you change the number of files that appear on a list of recently used files in Microsoft Excel, using the Options dialog box, Excel passes your preference on to the registry. You could accomplish the same task by changing the registry yourself, but it's not a good idea to do it that way.

The reason it's not a good idea is that making the wrong change to the registry can have serious consequences. Making the wrong changes in particular sections of the registry can even make Windows 2000 stop running, possibly forcing you to reinstall the operating system.

Nevertheless, because some useful customizations of your operating system can be made only by direct modification of the registry, it's worth getting to know how the registry is structured and how to use Registry Editor. (We'll look at two such customizations at the end of this chapter. You might read about others in computer trade magazines or on the Internet.) Just be sure that you're alert and know what you're doing any time you have Registry Editor open.

> **NOTE**

Many of the activities described in this chapter require administrative privileges.

# Exploring the Registry with Registry Editor

Windows 2000 provides two programs for reading and changing the registry. Both are called Registry Editor, and neither appears on your Start menu. The executable files are Regedit.exe and Regedt32.exe, and you can run either by opening the Start menu, choosing Run, and typing the name of the executable.

Regedt32.exe is the newer and more advanced of the two. It includes a read-only option and a Security menu, both of which Regedit.exe lack, and it's a little easier to use. Regedit.exe has two advantages over Regedt32.exe, however. Its search feature is slightly more versatile, and it provides a safer way to back up selected portions of the registry. Because of these advantages, it's important to be aware of both editors.

For the remainder of this chapter, we use the name *Registry Editor* to refer only to Regedt32.exe. We'll refer to the other editor by its executable name, Regedit.exe.

Figure 30-1, on the next page, shows Registry Editor's opening screen. In this image, Registry Editor is running in read-only mode, but you'll notice that neither the title bar nor a status bar (the program has no status bar) informs you of that fact. To determine whether you're in read-only mode, open the Options menu. If a check mark appears beside the Read-Only Mode command, you're in read-only mode. And unless you're about to make an intentional change to your registry, you should *always* use read-only mode.

VIII

Maintenance and Optimization

**FIGURE 30-1.**

Registry Editor lets you examine your registry's five pre-defined keys in separate document windows.

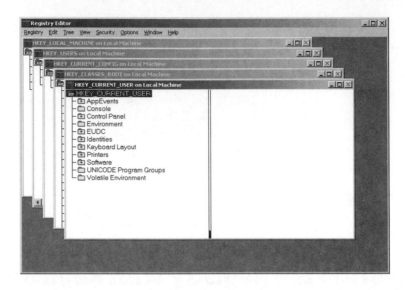

## Predefined Keys (Subtrees)

Registry Editor presents the contents of your registry in five separate document windows, each of which displays the contents of a pre-defined key. (*Predefined keys* are also sometimes called *subtrees*; the two terms are synonymous for describing subdivisions of the registry.) You can minimize, restore, and maximize these windows individually, and you can use commands on the Window menu to cascade or tile all the unminimized windows. The five predefined keys and the kinds of information they record are outlined in Table 30-1.

**TABLE 30-1.   Registry Editor's Predefined Keys**

| Key | Description |
| --- | --- |
| HKEY_CLASSES_ROOT | Contains information about file types and their associated applications |
| HKEY_CURRENT_CONFIG | Contains information about the current hardware profile |
| HKEY_CURRENT_USER | Contains the profile of the user who is currently logged on |
| HKEY_LOCAL_MACHINE | Contains information about the local computer (regardless of who is logged on) |
| HKEY_USERS | Contains the profiles of all users who log on at this computer |

The five predefined keys include some redundancy. The entire HKEY_CURRENT_USER, for example, also appears as a subkey of HKEY_USERS, and the entire HKEY_CLASSES_ROOT appears as a subkey of the HKEY_LOCAL_MACHINE subkey known as HKEY_LOCAL_MACHINE\Software\Classes. The redundancy is simply a convenience for you; it makes it easier to get to certain remote corners of the registry—the registry, while large, does not store the redundancies internally.

## Keys and Value Entries

Figure 30-2 shows HKEY_LOCAL_MACHINE in a maximized window. As you can see, Registry Editor displays information in two panes. (If you don't see two panes, open the View menu and choose Tree And Data.) On the left is an outline structure, each heading of which is called a *key*. On the right are *value entries*. The value entries in the right pane pertain to the key that's currently selected in the left pane. For example, the System key shown in Figure 30-2 has six values: Component Information, Configuration Data, Identifier, SystemBiosDate, SystemBiosVersion, and VideoBiosDate.

**FIGURE 30-2.**

Each key can have one or more value entries or none at all.

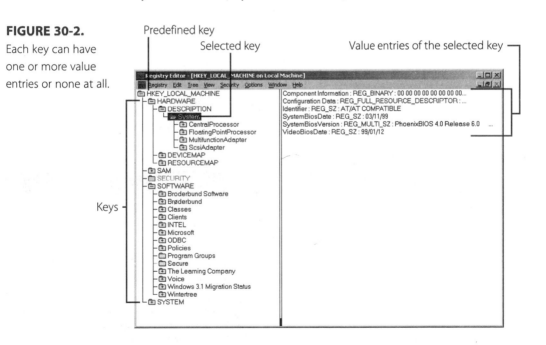

Predefined key
Selected key
Value entries of the selected key
Keys

> **⊘ NOTE**

> The particular keys and value entries on your system might vary from those shown here depending on your system's hardware, other installed software, and whether you upgraded to Windows 2000 over another operating system or installed it on a clean machine.

A key can have one value entry, multiple value entries, or none. And a key can contain other keys. The System key shown in Figure 30-2, for example, contains four keys: CentralProcessor, FloatingPointProcessor, MultifunctionAdapter, and ScsiAdapter. Keys contained within other keys are sometimes called *subkeys*. Keys without value entries are often used as placeholders for future entries or as containers for subkeys that *do* have their own value entries.

The outline that appears in the left pane looks like any other outline in Windows, but, alas, it doesn't function like any other. An item with a plus sign indicates the key contains subkeys, but to open the key and reveal its subkeys, you must double-click the key. A single-click on the plus sign won't get the job done.

## Values and Data Types

Value entries have three components separated by colons, like this:

SystemBiosDate: REG_SZ: 03/11/99

The first component is the name of the value entry, the second is the entry's data type, and the third is its value. The six data types used by Registry Editor are described in Table 30-2.

**TABLE 30-2.   Registry Data Types**

| Data Type | Description |
|---|---|
| REG_BINARY | A string of digits in hexadecimal (not binary!) notation. Digits appear in pairs, separated by spaces. Each pair represents one byte. |
| REG_DWORD | A string of 1 to 8 hexadecimal digits, preceded by 0x. No spaces appear within REG_DWORD data. |
| REG_SZ | A string of characters. |
| REG_EXPAND_SZ | A string of characters that can include a replaceable variable, such as *systemroot*. |
| REG_MULTI_SZ | One or more strings of characters. |
| REG_FULL_RESOURCE_DESCRIPTOR | A resource list for hardware components or drivers. You can't add or edit data of this type. |

When you edit the registry, it is critical that you enter data in the expected data type and observe Registry Editor's formatting conventions (the spaces between digit pairs in the binary type, for example).

# Opening a Remote Registry

Notice that the predefined keys shown in Figures 30-1 and 30-2 all end with "on Local Machine." You can use Registry Editor to inspect and edit the registries of networked computers as well, if you have the proper permissions. To open a remote registry, open the Registry menu and choose Select Computer. In the dialog box that appears, type the name of a networked computer or select it from the list of available computers.

As Figure 30-3 shows, when you open a remote computer's registry, Registry Editor simply adds more document windows, leaving the existing ones in place. Note, however, that only two predefined keys for a remote machine appear—HKEY_LOCAL_MACHINE and HKEY_USERS. These two keys contain the complete registry—the other predefined keys are for convenience only and are not made available when you access remote registries.

**FIGURE 30-3.**
You can use Registry Editor to work with a remote registry as well as a local one.

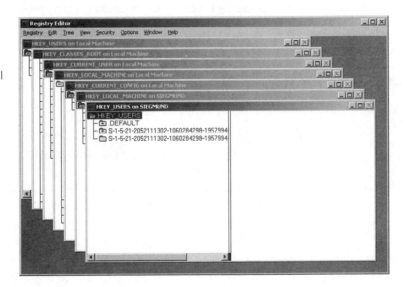

VIII

Maintenance and Optimization

# Locating Registry Data

The registry is dauntingly large and labyrinthine. A particular key that you need to see or modify can easily be nested some five or six subkeys deep within a predefined key. Whether you know the path to it or not, the quickest way to get where you want to go might be to use Registry Editor's Find Key command, a fixture of the View menu. Note that the Find Key command searches only those branches inferior to the current selection, so if you're not sure which predefined key the item you want lives in, you might need to exercise the command more than once.

Be aware, though, that because the registry is so large, a search through an entire predefined key might take a while, even on a fast computer. So don't make your searches more extensive than necessary. If you know the key you want is somewhere within HKEY_LOCAL_MACHINE\Software, for example, you can save yourself some time by starting your search at the Software key rather than at the root of HKEY_LOCAL_MACHINES.

Registry Editor's Find Key command finds only keys. You can't use it to search for values. If you need to search for a value, run Regedit.exe instead. The Find command, located on that program's Edit menu, lets you search for values as well as keys.

# Taking Precautions
# Before Editing Registry Data

In addition to being of sound mind and body, wide awake and sober, armed with accurate information, and not distracted by small children, it's smart to print or save the registry section you're about to change, before you change it. If your edits don't have the desired effect, you can then use the printout or saved file to return the registry to its former state—assuming, of course, that your changes aren't so disastrous that they keep your system from functioning at all. (If they do, restart your computer and invoke the last known good configuration. *See the sidebar "Recovering from a Damaged Registry," page 634.*)

## Saving Registry Data

You can save a portion of the registry using Registry Editor, as follows:

**1** Select a key.

**2** Open the Registry menu and choose Save Key.

Registry Editor creates a binary (not human-readable) file with (by default) no extension, encompassing the selected key and all its subkeys.

If you need to return the registry to its unedited state:

**1** Select the key from which the file was saved.

**2** Open the Registry menu and choose Restore.

**3** Select the saved file in the Restore Key dialog box, and click Open.

You will be warned that the file will overwrite and replace the contents of the currently selected key.

**4** Make sure you've selected the matching key, and then click OK.

> A section of the registry saved as a file is sometimes called a *hive*.

Be aware that if you restore a saved registry hive to the wrong part of your registry, you will almost certainly wreak havoc upon your system. A safer way to save a portion of your registry is to use Regedit.exe. With Regedit, you can back up a portion of your registry as follows:

**1** Select a key.

**2** Open the Registry Editor and choose Export Registry File.

**3** Give your export a filename with the .reg extension.

To restore the saved registry file, simply double-click it in Windows Explorer. The file contains information about the key from which it was saved and will automatically be restored to the appropriate key. Using this method you cannot inadvertently restore registry data to the wrong part of your registry.

## Printing Registry Data

To print a section of the registry, select a key, open the Registry menu, and then choose Print Subtree. Registry Editor generates a printout in Courier New font with page numbers but no other adornments. Although the command is Print Subtree, and although Registry Editor generally uses the term *subtree* to denote an entire predefined key, the printout encompasses only the current key and its subkeys.

**VIII**

Maintenance and Optimization

As a further precaution, it's a good idea to turn on Confirm On Delete before you begin editing. With Confirm On Delete on, removing a key generates a confirmation prompt. If you accidentally select the wrong registry key and hit Delete, this feature can save you from a serious mishap. Any time you plan to remove a registry key, it's a good idea to let Registry Editor serve up this confirmation prompt. Then check one more time before sending that unwanted key on its way. Remember, any changes you make in Registry Editor are effective immediately.

Confirm On Delete is a toggle on the Options menu. If a check mark appears beside the command, the feature is on; choose the command a second time to turn it off.

(Another command on the Options menu, Auto Refresh, does *not* provide additional safety. With Auto Refresh on, registry changes made by local applications while Registry Editor is running are updated immediately in Registry Editor's display.)

# Editing the Registry

Before making any changes to the registry, be sure that Read Only Mode is not selected on the Options menu.

To change the value of an existing value entry:

1 Select the window of the predefined key in which the value resides.

2 Select the appropriate key in the left pane.

3 Double-click the value entry in the right pane.

An editor window appears, appropriate for the data type of the value entry. Make your edit in this window and click OK. Note that you can't change either the name of the value entry or its data type.

To delete a value entry:

1 Select the window of the predefined key in which the value entry resides.

2 Select the appropriate key in the left pane.

3 Select the value entry in the right pane.

4 Press the Delete key.

5 Answer the confirmation prompt (if Confirm On Delete is on).

To add a value entry:

**1** Select the window of the appropriate predefined key.

**2** Select the key in which the new value entry is to reside.

**3** Open the Edit menu and choose Add Value.

The Add Value dialog box, shown below, appears.

**4** Type the name of the value entry in the Value Name box.

**5** Select the value's data type from the Data Type list.

**6** In the dialog box that appears next, type the value of the value entry.

To delete a key:

**1** Select the window of the predefined key in which the key resides.

**2** Select the key in the left pane.

**3** Press the Delete key.

**4** Answer the confirmation prompt (if Confirm On Delete is on).

Note that deleting a key deletes all its subkeys as well.

To add a key:

**1** Select the window of the appropriate predefined key.

**2** Select the key in which the new key is to reside (that is, the key that will contain the new key).

**3** Open the Edit menu and choose Add Key.

**4** In the Add Key dialog box, type the name of your new key.

VIII

Maintenance and Optimization

# Making Two Safe and Useful Registry Edits

In the remainder of this chapter, we'll look at two useful and harmless changes you can make to your registry. You might want to use these as practice to familiarize yourself with the mechanics of registry modification.

## Changing the Registered Owner and Registered Organization

If your computer came from its vendor with Windows 2000 preinstalled, you might find that certain of your programs think your name is something like Preferred Customer of XYZ, Inc. No matter how you log on and what you tell your applications, you can't seem to remove that irritating handle. You can do it with the help of Registry Editor:

1 Activate HKEY_LOCAL_MACHINE.

2 Navigate to the Software\Microsoft\Windows NT\Current Version key.

   In the right pane, you should see, among other values, RegisteredOrganization and RegisteredOwner. (See Figure 30-4.)

**FIGURE 30-4.**

You can use Registry Editor to change the name of your computer's registered owner and registered organization.

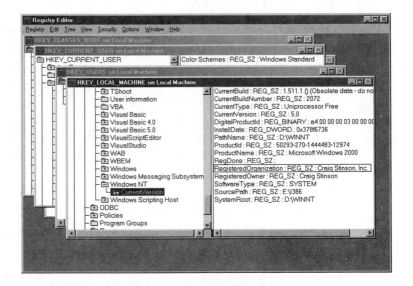

3 Double-click and edit RegisteredOrganization.

4 Double-click and edit RegisteredOwner.

5 If you have Auto Refresh turned off, open the View menu and choose Refresh Active.

3

# Changing or Pruning the Run MRU

The Start menu's Run command maintains a most-recently-used (MRU) list of your past Run commands. You can change the order in which these commands appear or delete particular commands:

**1** Activate HKEY_CURRENT_USER.

**2** Navigate to Software\Microsoft\Windows\CurrentVersion\ Explorer\RunMRU.

Note that the third subkey is Windows, not Windows NT. As Figure 30-5 shows, the RunMRU key includes a value for each item on the most-recently-used list. The values are given alphabetical names, beginning with the letter *a*. The MRUList value entry stipulates the order in which the commands appear. In the figure, for example, the MRUList value entry has the value ijhgfedcba, which means that the first item to be displayed on the Run menu will be item *i* (regedt32). The second will be item *j*, (regedit), and so on.

**3** To change the MRU order, double-click and edit the MRUList value. To delete an item, select it and press Delete. (Answer the confirmation prompt if necessary.) Then edit the MRUList value to remove the deleted letter.

**4** If you have Auto Refresh turned off, open the View menu and choose Refresh Active.

**FIGURE 30-5.**

You can use Registry Editor to prune or alter the Run command's most-recently-used list.

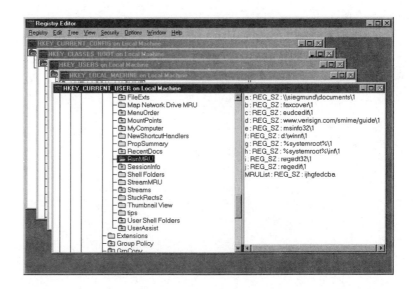

**CHAPTER 31**

# Optimizing, Maintaining, and Troubleshooting

This chapter takes up three interrelated topics: how to get your system running as well as it can, how to perform routine maintenance on your system so that it always hums along happily, and what to do when things go awry. Microsoft Windows 2000 provides tools to help you keep your system in good order. If you have adequate hardware to begin with and you use these maintenance tools regularly, the odds are good that you'll never have serious problems. In case you do run into trouble, however, Windows 2000 also provides direct links to Microsoft's Internet-based support services, as well as improved diagnostic information to assist support personnel.

# Getting Optimal Performance from Windows 2000

Aside from the speed of your microprocessor, the elements of your system that have the most bearing on Windows' performance are *physical memory* (that provided by random-access memory chips and often called *RAM*) and available hard disk space. Windows loves memory. No matter what you run—but particularly if you run large, computation-intensive programs such as graphics editors and computer-aided design programs—you can scarcely have too much RAM. In any event, you shouldn't even try to run Windows 2000 with less than 32 MB, and if you're getting unsatisfactory performance on a system with less than 64 MB, one of the first solutions to consider is plugging in some additional memory.

## Virtual Memory

Windows uses part of your hard disk as *virtual memory*—that is, as an extension of main memory. When physical memory gets overloaded, Windows writes some data from memory to a hidden file on your disk. When Windows needs that information again, it reads it back from the paging ("swap") file, at the same time (if necessary) swapping something else out, a process called *demand paging*.

Because disk access is far slower than memory access, paging impedes performance. Increasing the amount of physical memory on your system improves performance by minimizing paging. You might also be able to improve performance by increasing the size of your system's paging file, by moving the paging file to a faster hard disk, or by letting your system use more than one disk for paging.

To adjust your system's virtual memory parameters:

1 Open the Start menu and choose Settings, Control Panel, System.

2 Click the Advanced Tab.

3 Click the Performance Options button, and then click the Change button in the Performance Options dialog box.

Windows displays the Virtual Memory dialog box, shown in Figure 31-1.

The top part of this dialog box lists each local hard disk and shows the size of that disk's paging file, if any. The system shown in the figure, for example, has two local disks, C and D, and a paging file on D.

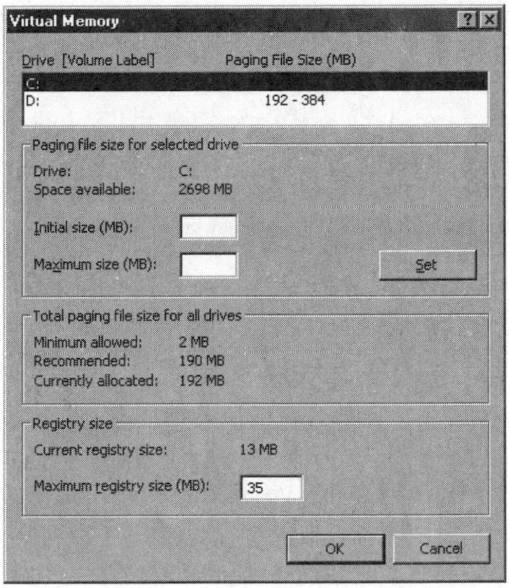

**FIGURE 31-1.**

You can use this dialog box to change the Windows default paging parameters.

VIII

Maintenance and Optimization

Paging files have a minimum size and a maximum size. They never shrink below the minimum size. Under heavy demand, they might increase to the maximum.

You might be able to improve your system's performance by changing the virtual memory parameters in the following ways:

- Create a paging file on each disk.

- Increase the size of your paging files.

- Make the paging files' minimum sizes equal to their maximum sizes.

Having multiple paging files can improve performance because your disk controller can access multiple disks simultaneously. Making the minimum size equal to the maximum size increases the amount of disk space that is permanently allocated to the paging file but eliminates the time required to increase the size of the file.

To change your virtual memory parameters:

**1** In the dialog box shown in Figure 31-1, select the disk you want to adjust.

**2** Enter values in the Initial Size and Maximum Size boxes.

**3** Click Set.

You must be logged on with administrative privileges to change virtual memory settings. Repeat the preceding steps for each disk on which you want to set or change virtual memory. When finished, click OK. In some cases, you'll see a message that Windows needs to restart to effect your changes.

## Application Response

By default, a Windows 2000 Professional system is set up to allocate more processor resources to the foreground process than to any background processes. (The *foreground* process is the program that you're currently interacting with in your active window. A *background* process is any other program that might be doing calculation or other work in inactive windows) The alternative is to allocate equal time to all processes. If you use your computer for applications (as opposed to using it strictly as a server), you should leave the default setting in place. To check the setting on your system, open the Start menu and choose Settings, Control Panel, System. Click the Advanced tab, and then click Performance Options.

# Performing Routine Maintenance

Just as you perform regularly scheduled maintenance on your car, so should you take some simple maintenance steps at regular intervals to keep your Windows system running smoothly. In particular, it's wise to do the following:

- Remove unneeded files from your hard disk so that you always have enough room on disk.

- Defragment your hard disks occasionally to optimize file access times.

- Periodically check your disks for file-system and media errors.

- Visit the Windows Update Web site from time to time, to make sure you're using the latest versions of your device drivers and system files.

- Update your Emergency Repair Disk (ERD) regularly.

## Freeing Up Hard Disk Space

If available hard-disk space falls too low, you will begin seeing error messages from programs and from Windows itself. You might see these even when you have 100 MB or so of free space, simply because Windows is running out of room to page memory. Here are some ways to free up space on your hard disk:

- Uninstall programs that you don't need.

- Uninstall Windows components that you don't need.

- Delete or move documents that you don't need.

- Use file compression on NTFS volumes.

## Cleaning Up with Disk Cleanup

The easiest way to take most of these steps is to run Disk Cleanup, a utility program supplied with Windows. Figure 31-2 shows a sample of the work that Disk Cleanup can do. The program lists several categories of potentially expendable disk files and shows you how much space you could recover by deleting each category. The More Options tab, meanwhile, provides access to the Windows Setup program (so you can delete unneeded components of Windows) and Add/Remove Programs (so you can get rid of programs you aren't using).

**FIGURE 31-2.**

The easiest way to recover disk space is to use Disk Cleanup.

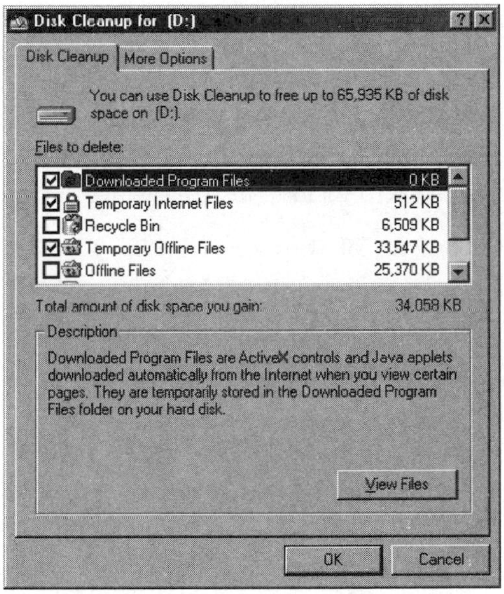

To run Disk Cleanup, open the Start menu and choose Programs, Accessories, System Tools, Disk Cleanup. Disk Cleanup begins by asking which drive you want to clean up. Select a drive and click OK.

⭐ **TIP**

> In a Windows Explorer window, right-click the icon for the drive you want to clean up and choose Properties. On the General tab in the properties dialog box, click Disk Cleanup.

## Uninstalling Programs and Windows Components You Don't Need

To see a list of programs that can easily be uninstalled, open Add/Remove Programs in Control Panel. To uninstall a program, select its name and click the Add/Remove button. To uninstall Windows components that you don't need, open Add/Remove Programs and click the Windows Setup tab.

You might also want to consider uninstalling unneeded components of some of your programs. Perhaps you don't need 3,000 clip-art images, a French dictionary (assuming you don't write in French), or the Help files for a programming language in which you don't program. Try opening Add/Remove Programs in Control Panel and running the uninstall routine for your largest programs. Many uninstall programs let you remove particular components without getting rid of the entire program. If your program doesn't have this capability, you can simply back out of the uninstaller without removing anything.

## Deleting or Moving Unneeded Documents

When looking around for document files that are good candidates for deletion, be sure to include the following:

- The contents of your Recycle Bin

- Old files with the extension .tmp

- Files with the extension .chk

- Files with the extension .bak or that begin with the words *Backup of*.

❓ **SEE ALSO**

For more information about the Recycle Bin, see "Restoring Deleted Folders, Files, and Shortcuts," page 163.

To empty your Recycle Bin, select it in the Disk Cleanup list, or right-click the Recycle Bin icon on your desktop and choose Empty Recycle Bin. To remove items selectively, open Recycle Bin. If necessary, choose Details from the Windows Explorer View menu to see the date on which each file was deleted. Click the Date Deleted column heading so the arrow on the heading points upward, indicating that the files are sorted by deletion date, with the oldest files at the top. These oldest files are probably your best candidates for removal.

**NOTE**

When you delete files from your Recycle Bin, they're gone for good.

Many programs create temporary files while you work. These files, which commonly have the extension .tmp, are normally deleted when you quit the program. If you have any kind of irregular shutdown, however (for example, if the program crashes, the power fails, or you turn off your computer without going through the normal shutdown procedure), the temporary files linger until you ferret them out and remove them by hand.

After deleting unneeded Recycle Bin contents and .tmp files, wander through your hard disk and see whether you can find ordinary documents that can safely be archived onto removable media or a server. This will give your system a little room to breathe, allowing more efficient paging and forestalling the day when you have to face those low-disk-space error messages again.

VIII

Maintenance and Optimization

## Compressing Files on NTFS Volumes

If you choose, Windows 2000 can automatically compress files stored on NTFS volumes. All you need to do is set a property for a file, a folder, or an entire NTFS volume, and the operating system compresses your files for you. When you open a compressed file, the file is decompressed, and when you save it again, it's recompressed. The process requires no intervention from you once you've set it in motion.

 **TIP**

Open files (files that are in use by an application or operating system process) can't be compressed. Therefore, before compressing an entire NTFS volume, you should close as many applications as possible.

To compress a file, group of files, or folder:

1 Select the item in question.

2 Right-click, and choose Properties from the shortcut menu.

3 On the General tab of the properties dialog box, click Advanced.

4 In the Advanced Attributes dialog box, select Compress Contents To Save Disk Space. Click OK in both dialog boxes.

5 If you have selected a folder, indicate in the ensuing dialog box whether you want to compress only that folder or that folder plus all of its subfolders.

To compress an entire NTFS volume:

**1**  Open My Computer.

**2**  Right-click the disk and choose Properties from the Shortcut menu.

**3**  On the General tab of the properties dialog box, select Compress Drive To Save Disk Space.

When you click OK to leave the properties dialog box, the operating system begins compressing the selected folders and files. During this process, you might see a dialog box similar to the following.

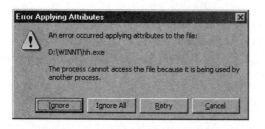

If you can close the item that Windows is trying to compress, do so, and then click Retry. Otherwise, click either Ignore or Ignore All. If you click Ignore All, Windows goes on compressing all the files it can, ignoring those it can't. If you click Ignore, a new Error dialog box appears each time the system encounters an open file.

You can have Windows Explorer display compressed files and folders in a contrasting color. To do this, open the Windows Explorer Tools menu, choose Folder Options, and click the View tab. Under Advanced Settings, select Display Compressed Files And Folders With Alternate Color.

Here are some other points to note about NTFS file compression:

■  Compressed files can't be encrypted.

■  If you create a new file in a compressed folder, the file is compressed.

■  If you copy a file into a compressed folder, the file is compressed.

■  If you move a file from a different NTFS volume into a compressed folder, the file is compressed.

- If you move a file from the same NTFS volume into a compressed folder, the file retains its current compression state. That is, if it's already compressed, it remains compressed. If not, it remains uncompressed.

- The degree of compression Windows achieves depends on the contents of the file. On the whole, however, NTFS compression provides rather modest gains. If you have a third-party compression utility, you might want to continue applying that program to certain files, particularly those you seldom use.

> **NOTE**
>
> Windows 2000 doesn't support the DriveSpace compression program used by Microsoft Windows 95 and Windows 98.

## Optimizing Disk Performance with Disk Defragmenter

When you store files on a freshly formatted disk, Windows writes each file's data in a set of adjacent disk clusters (*clusters* are units of storage space on disks). One file might use clusters 3 through 24, for example, the next 25 through 31, a third 32 through 34, and so on. As soon as you begin deleting files, however, this neat pattern is likely to be broken.

For example, if you delete the file that occupies clusters 25 through 31, and then you create a new file 20 clusters in length, Windows stores the new file's first 7 clusters in 25 through 31 and the remaining 13 somewhere else. This new file, in other words, will be *fragmented*; that is, it will occupy at least two noncontiguous blocks of clusters. As time goes on and you add and delete more files, the odds are good that more and more of your files will become fragmented.

Fragmentation doesn't affect data integrity, but it does reduce the efficiency of your hard disk. Fragmented files take longer to read and write than contiguous ones.

You can eliminate disk fragmentation and enhance performance by using the Windows 2000 Disk Defragmenter program. This program rearranges files, storing each file in a block of contiguous sectors.

To run Disk Defragmenter, open the Start menu, and then choose Programs, Accessories, System Tools, Disk Defragmenter. Alternatively, right-click the icon for any local hard disk in a Windows Explorer window and choose Properties. Then select the Tools tab and click Defragment Now.

In the initial display, you'll see a list of your local hard disks, showing their file systems, capacities, and free space statistics. To determine whether a disk is sufficiently fragmented to warrant defragmentation, select that disk and click Analyze. (See Figure 31-3.)

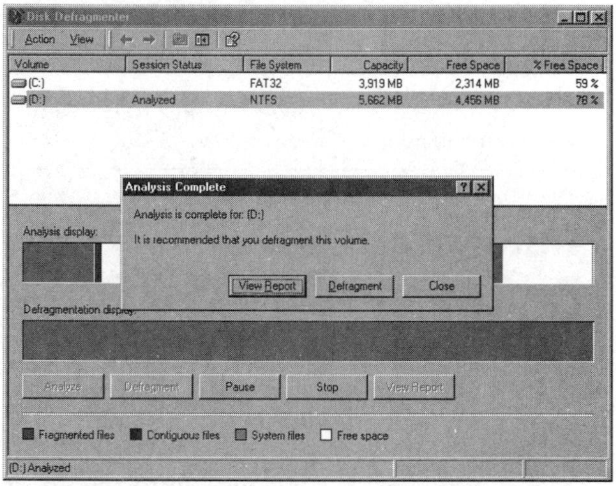

**FIGURE 31-3.**

Disk Defragmenter can analyze a disk and report the degree to which files are currently fragmented.

Whether or not Disk Defragmenter recommends defragmentation, you can click View Report to see the details about what its analysis has found. (See Figure 31-4.) From the Analysis Report dialog box, you can print, save the report as a file, or go ahead and start the defragmentation process.

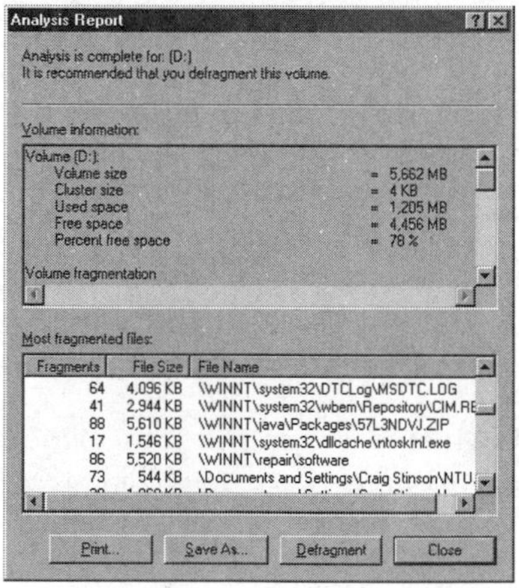

**FIGURE 31-4.**

With several large files broken up into 60 or more disjunct pieces, this disk is a good candidate for defragmentation.

While your disk is being defragmented, you can continue working with your computer normally, but because of the intense background activity, you might find that your applications don't respond as quickly as usual.

**NOTE**

Windows 2000 Disk Defragmenter is supplied by Executive Software and is a scaled-down version of Executive Software's Diskeeper 5. To learn more about the full product, you can visit *www.execsoft.com.*

# Checking Your Disks for File-System and Media Errors

Windows 2000 includes a tool that checks your disks for *logical errors* in the file system (invalid entries in the tables that keep track of file locations) and problems involving the physical disk media. To check a disk for either kind of error:

**1** Right-click the disk in a Windows Explorer window.

**2** Choose Properties from the shortcut menu.

**3** In the properties dialog box, click the Tools tab.

**4** Click Check Now.

**5** Fill out the following dialog box, and then click Start.

- If you select neither check box, Windows checks the disk only for file-system errors and reports any that it finds.

- If you select the first check box, Windows checks only for file-system errors and attempts to fix any that it finds. The system requires exclusive access to the disk to complete this process. If any disk files are in use, an error message appears, asking if you would like to reschedule the task to occur automatically the next time you start your computer.

- If you select the second check box, Windows checks the disk for media errors. If it finds any bad sectors, it recovers readable information from those sectors and then marks the sectors as unusable.

## Using Windows Update

Windows Update, shown in Figure 31-5 as it appears as of this writing, is a Web site maintained by Microsoft to help users keep their systems equipped with the latest versions of device drivers and system files. If you have an Internet connection, you can get to Windows Update by opening the Start menu and choosing Windows Update from the top of the menu (above the Programs command). Alternatively, direct your Web browser to *http://windowsupdate.microsoft.com*. It's a good idea to visit this site regularly.

**FIGURE 31-5.**

The Windows Update site can inform you when new device drivers or system files are available.

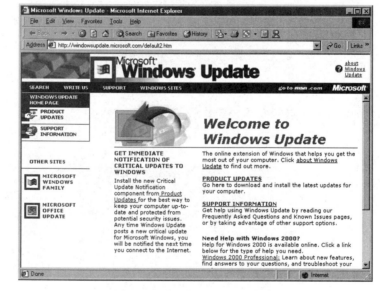

If you click Product Updates, Windows Update can (with your permission) determine which devices you're using and check to see whether newer versions are available. The system will advise you that no information is sent to Microsoft when you do this—but, of course, it *is* Microsoft that's reading your hardware. What the message means is that the information isn't passed along to the marketing folks in Redmond. In any case, if newer driver versions are available, Windows Update can download and install them for you automatically.

On the home page of the Update site, you'll also be able to download a Critical Update Notification component. If you elect to do this, whenever Microsoft posts a critical update to your operating system, you'll be notified as soon as you connect to the Internet.

The Update site also provides access to online Help support regarding Windows 2000.

## Updating Your Emergency Repair Disk

An *Emergency Repair Disk (ERD)* is a floppy disk that, under some circumstances, can help you repair a damaged operating system. If system files or a disk partition's boot sector become corrupted, you might be able to correct the problem with an ERD. You should re-create your ERD regularly, to ensure that it always has relatively current information about your system.

To create or re-create an ERD:

**1** Open the Start menu and choose Programs, Accessories, System Tools, Backup.

**2** Open Backup's Tools menu and choose Create An Emergency Repair Disk.

**3** When prompted, insert a blank, formatted, 1.44 MB disk in your floppy disk drive.

For information about using the ERD, see "Repairing a Damaged Installation with an Emergency Repair Disk," page 665.

# What to Do When Things Go Awry

Given the complexity of Windows, the ambitious scope of current programs, and the multitude of potentially conflicting hardware devices that Windows has to support, it's almost inevitable that some component of your system, at some time, will not work exactly the way you expect or intend. When that moment of perplexity arrives, you'll need to know a few basic troubleshooting procedures.

## Using the Help File's Troubleshooters

The Help text supplied with Windows 2000 includes troubleshooters for a number of common problems, including problems with networks, modems, printers, and displays. To see which troubleshooters are available, choose Help from the Start menu. Click the Contents tab in the main Help document that appears, click the Troubleshooting And Maintenance topic, and then click Windows 2000 Troubleshooters.

The Help text for this topic includes a link to each of the available troubleshooters. (You'll also find troubleshooting buttons in many of the Windows 2000 dialog boxes.)

Each of the Help file's troubleshooters presents a branching series of questions about your current problem. At each step in the process, the troubleshooter suggests a remedy you can try. If the suggested remedy doesn't solve your problem, the troubleshooter asks another question or offers another suggestion.

The troubleshooters won't solve every problem that might arise, but they provide a good, interactive way to start your search for help.

## Using Microsoft's Online Help Resources

If your cry for help isn't answered by the Help file's troubleshooters or other local Help documents, the next place to shout is online. Choose Help from the Start menu and then click the Web Help button on the Help application's toolbar. From the list of links that appears, click Contact Product Support. On the next page that appears, click Microsoft Web Site. These actions take you to the home page of Microsoft's Product Support Services (PSS), shown in Figure 31-6. To get help on Windows, point to the All Products heading, and then choose Windows Family from the list that appears.

From the PSS home page, you can also get to Microsoft's Knowledge Base (see Figure 31-7), a database of help articles that have been compiled by PSS. You can search the Knowledge Base for useful information, either by entering a specific article number (if you know it) or by typing plain-English questions. To get to the Knowledge Base from the PSS home page, click Where Is The Knowledge Base (or another similar link, if the PSS home page has changed by the time you read this).

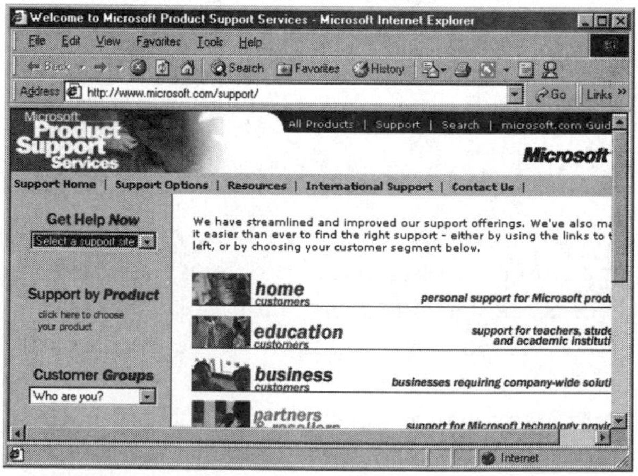

**FIGURE 31-6.**

The Help application's Web Help button takes you here—to the home page of Microsoft's Product Support Services.

**FIGURE 31-7.**
The Knowledge
Base provides a
wealth of technical
help information.

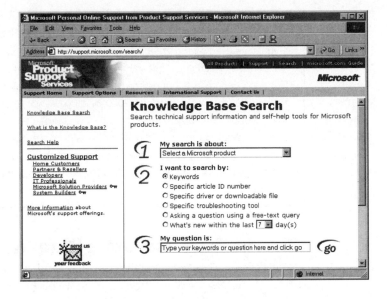

# What to Do if a Program Stops Running

If your immediate problem is that a program stops responding, or *hangs,* you'll want to close the program so that you can either try running it again or get on with something else. Windows provides a mechanism that lets you terminate an errant program without affecting other running programs or Windows itself. To remove a hung program, hold down the Ctrl and Left Shift keys and then press Esc. On the Applications tab of the Windows Task Manager window that appears, select the name of the program that has hung, and then click End Task.

# Using Device Manager to Track Hardware Conflicts

If two hardware devices are both trying to make use of the same I/O address, direct memory access (DMA) channel, or interrupt request (IRQ) level, odds are one or both of those devices aren't going to work optimally. If you suspect that a resource conflict of this kind is causing some component of your system to malfunction, you can follow up on your suspicion with the help of Device Manager. *For information about using Device Manager, see Chapter 25, "Managing Devices and Drivers."*

VIII

Maintenance and Optimization

> **Where Is System File Checker?**
>
> If you have used Windows 98, you might be familiar with a tool called System File Checker, which could inform you if any of the operating system's critical files had been changed or deleted since they were installed. You won't find System File Checker in Windows 2000, because Windows 2000 performs this maintenance duty for you automatically. If any protected system file is changed, deleted, or overwritten, the operating system checks the current version's digital signature to determine whether the current version is correct. If it isn't, Windows restores the original file, prompting you for the Windows 2000 CD if necessary.

## What to Do if You Get a Blue-Screen Crash

It's unlikely in Windows 2000 that you'll see the fabled "blue screen of death" (a message screen appearing on a solid blue background that informs you Windows has stopped running and must be restarted), but it's by no means impossible. Under certain conditions—such as when an errant device driver tries to write into an improper memory address—Windows 2000 might simply quit, after displaying a screen full of apparently inscrutable information.

If that happens, resist the temptation to turn off the power and throw the box in the river. Before you do anything else, read the blue screen. Look for an error number and some descriptive text. Write that information down. Then get out the *Windows 2000 Professional Getting Started* booklet that came with your Windows 2000 CD. In Appendix B, "Troubleshooting Specific Stop Errors," look for information about the error number your system reported. You'll find troubleshooting information there, as well as information about where to look for further help on the Microsoft Product Support Services Web site.

If you can't find a printed copy of *Windows 2000 Professional Getting Started*, look for an online copy of it, assuming you can restart your system. Open the Start menu, choose Help, and click the Contents tab. Open Introducing Windows 2000 Professional and click Getting Started Online Book. Finally, click the Windows 2000 Professional Getting Started link.

# What to Do if Windows 2000 Doesn't Start

If Windows 2000 doesn't start at all, you can try the following remedies:

- Start the system in safe mode.

- Use the Windows 2000 Recovery Console.

- Repair your installation with an ERD.

- Reinstall Windows 2000.

## Starting Windows in Safe Mode

Some circumstances—a resource conflict between peripherals, a problem with network settings, or a problem with display settings—might prevent Windows from starting in its normal mode. You might, however, be able to start Windows in safe mode. In safe mode, the operating system loads only the most essential drivers—for keyboard, mouse (but not a serial mouse), basic video, disk drives, and certain system services. Everything else is disabled. Once the system restarts in this scaled-down manner, you can open Control Panel, change display settings, check Device Manager for resource conflicts, and so on. After making changes of this sort, you can try again to start Windows normally.

To start Windows in safe mode, press F8 while Windows is starting. From the menu that appears, choose Safe Mode.

### Safe Mode Options

In addition to the basic safe mode just described, the menu that appears when you press F8 offers the following options:

- **Safe Mode With Networking.** Adds networking drivers to the basic set of drivers enabled by safe mode.

- **Safe Mode With Command Prompt.** Works like safe mode, except that you end up at a command prompt instead of in Windows 2000.

- **Enable Boot Logging.** Creates a log file %windir%\ntbtlog.txt listing successful and failed driver initializations. Opening this file in any plain-text editor (Notepad, for example) might help you determine whether a specific driver is malfunctioning.

- **Enable VGA Mode.** Works like safe mode, except that a default VGA driver is installed instead of your own video card's basic driver. This mode is particularly useful if your system fails immediately after you have installed a new video adapter.

■ **Last Known Good Configuration.** Doesn't start your computer in safe mode, although this option appears on the menu with the safe mode options. Instead, it starts Windows 2000 with the registry as it existed the last time you successfully started your system. Use this option if your registry appears to be corrupted. Also use it after a power failure or if someone turns your computer off without going through the normal shutdown procedure.

■ **Debugging Mode.** Works like safe mode, except that Windows 2000 sends debugging information through a serial computer to another computer.

## Using Recovery Console

The Windows 2000 Recovery Console program is a command-line program that you can start if Windows itself fails to start. Recovery Console requires that you log on with an administrator's password, and its use requires a high level of expertise. But it might be your best option in the event that Windows refuses to start even in safe mode.

You can perform a variety of administrative tasks from Recovery Console, including the following:

■ Start and stop Windows 2000 services

■ Enable or disable device drivers

■ Format drives

■ Create or delete partitions

■ Read and write data on local drives (including NTFS volumes)

■ Repair the system partition's boot sector

■ Repair the master boot record

■ Change file attributes

■ Execute batch files

■ Copy files (including compressed files) to your system from floppy disks or CD-ROMs

You can start Recovery Console by running it from the Windows 2000 setup disks. Alternatively, you can install Recovery Console on your system in advance.

To run Recovery Console from the Windows 2000 setup disks:

**1** Insert the Windows 2000 Professional Setup Disk 1 (a 3.5-inch floppy disk) in drive A. Or, if your system can boot from a CD-ROM drive, insert the Windows 2000 Professional CD in your CD-ROM drive.

**2** Turn on the computer and follow the screen prompts.

**3** Choose the option to repair your Windows 2000 installation.

**4** Choose the option to use Recovery Console.

To install Recovery Console in advance:

**1** Be sure you're logged on as an administrator.

**2** Insert the Windows 2000 CD.

**3** Say No when the Setup program asks whether you want to upgrade to Windows 2000.

**4** Open the Start menu, choose Run, and type

$d$:\i386\winnt32.exe /cmdcons

(where $d$ is the drive letter of your CD-ROM drive).

**5** Follow the instructions that appear.

To run Recovery Console if you have installed it in advance, restart your computer. Then choose Recovery Console from the list of available operating systems that appears.

## Repairing a Damaged Installation with an Emergency Repair Disk

If you have created an Emergency Repair Disk, the Windows Setup program might be able to use the information on that disk to repair a damaged installation. Follow these steps:

**1** Insert the Windows 2000 Professional Setup Disk 1 (a 3.5-inch floppy disk) in drive A. Or, if your system can boot from a CD-ROM drive, insert the Windows 2000 Professional CD in your CD-ROM drive.

**2** Turn on the computer and follow the screen prompts.

**3** Choose the options to repair your Windows 2000 installation.

**4** When prompted, insert your ERD and follow the on-screen instructions.

VIII

Maintenance and Optimization

## Reinstalling Windows 2000

If all else fails, you can reinstall Windows 2000. Note that if you have installed one or more service packs since your original installation of Windows 2000, you will need to reinstall those as well. And you will need to reinstall your applications once Windows 2000 is running again.

# Monitoring Your System

W hether you're in charge of a single workstation or an entire network, it's always possible that the imps of electronics will suddenly start gobbling memory, blocking communication lines, causing gridlock on a hard disk, or producing pandemonium on the data bus. At those times, you might wish you could dive into the system to take an up-close and personal look at what's going on. Well, you can't; but with Microsoft Windows 2000, you can check on what the computer system is doing. You can then put aside a lot of guesswork and base corrective actions on fact.

In this chapter we'll look at Event Viewer and Task Manager. Event Viewer is the Windows 2000 tool for tracking noteworthy occurrences on your system. Task Manager is a simple utility that can give you an overview of your system's performance. Windows 2000 includes a third program, System Monitor, that charts and records performance statistics in exhaustive detail. But System Monitor is beyond the scope of this book. For a detailed treatment of System Monitor, see *Microsoft Windows 2000 Professional Expert Companion*, published by Microsoft Press.

# What Do You Monitor?

System monitoring is one of those subjects you can look at from several perspectives, seeing different pieces of the whole from each. Basically, however, system monitoring boils down to looking at the system from two related but separate points of view:

■ First, there's the issue of "What's going on in there?" For this, Windows 2000 provides Event Viewer. Event Viewer lets you monitor a whole slew of happenings, known collectively as *events*, that are stored continually in a set of files called *event logs*. Events can range from innocuous and expected occurrences, such as logon/logoff activities and print jobs, to serious and unexpected errors, such as driver problems or a disk on which storage space is becoming scarce. With Event Viewer, you can record and monitor significant incidents related to the computer, its security, and its applications.

■ Second, there's the issue of how the computer itself is performing. Here, you are concerned not so much with *what* is happening (that is, with events), as you are with *how well* the computer is making things happen. If you're a programmer, for example, you might be interested in how quickly and effectively your program is running under Windows 2000. This area of monitoring focuses on matters such as processor time, memory use, disk access, cache effectiveness, and the behavior of threads and processes.

When you need to know how well your computer is functioning, turn to Task Manager, which provides information about a few key indicators of performance and system usage. For more a more comprehensive look, use System Monitor, which allows you to view, chart, record, and analyze system efficiency. System Monitor also lets you monitor another Windows 2000 computer on your network.

# Monitoring System Activities with Event Viewer

To Windows 2000, an event is any occurrence that's potentially noteworthy—to you, to other users, to the operating system, or to an application. Event Viewer is the operating system's means of telling you about these events. It functions as a combination report card and status report by storing lists of events in log files that you can review, archive, or transfer to a database or spreadsheet for analysis.

Windows 2000 recognizes three broad categories of events: system events, security events, and application events. Events of each type are recorded in separate log files.

System events are generated by Windows 2000 itself and by installed components, such as services and devices. They are recorded in a file called the *system log*. Windows 2000 classifies system events according to their severity as either errors, warnings, or information events, as follows:

- Errors are system events that represent possible loss of data or functionality. Examples of errors include events related to network contention or a malfunctioning network card, and loss of functionality caused by a device or service that doesn't load at startup.

- Warnings are system events that represent less significant or less immediate problems than errors. Examples of warning events include a nearly full disk, a timeout by the network redirector, and data errors on a backup tape.

- Information events are all other system events that Windows 2000 logs. Examples of information events include someone using a printer connected to your computer, or the successful loading of a database program.

Security events are generated by Windows 2000 when an activity you choose to audit succeeds (a *success audit*) or fails (a *failure audit*). Security events are recorded in a file called the *security log*. They include file-related events, such as attempts to access files or change permissions (NTFS volumes only), and other security-related events, such as logon/logoff events and changes to security policies. By default, Windows 2000 auditing is turned off, so you will likely see no events in the security log. To enable event auditing, open Local Security Policy from Administrative Tools in Control Panel. In the left pane, open Local Policies and select Audit Policy. In the right pane, right-click each event type you want to audit, and then select Success, Failure, or both Success and Failure in the ensuing dialog box.

Application events are generated by applications and are recorded in a file called the *application log*. The application developer determines which events to monitor, and how those events will be recorded in the application log. Windows 2000 Backup, for example, records an application event whenever you erase a tape or run a backup.

The importance of a Windows 2000 log depends on your situation. If you work in a security-conscious environment, or one in which users freely access resources on each other's machines, you'll find the event logs useful in helping you keep track of who, what, when, and where. If you don't care about such details, the security log will probably be of little interest to you, but the system log can still be helpful in diagnosing performance problems and hardware errors, and the application log can give you insight into how certain applications are working. Only applications designed to record their "thoughts" in the application log will appear there, but those that are so designed provide an obvious benefit—to you, your technical support person, and even the developer—for identifying and resolving problems that may arise.

If your computer is set up to share files or a printer with other users, checking the system log for print jobs and the security log for logon/logoff access will give you a feel for how and when your computer's resources are being used. Although the information might simply make you feel more in control of your system, you might also find patterns that help you determine better ways to manage it.

## Viewing a Log

You can easily see what a log looks like even if you never before thought of monitoring your system. To view a log, open Event Viewer:

1 Open the Start menu and choose Settings, Control Panel.

2 In Control Panel, open Administrative Tools.

3 In Administrative Tools, open Event Viewer.

4 Select a log to view.

Figure 32-1 shows Event Viewer's System Log.

**NOTE**

> To view audit events, you must be logged on as a member of the Administrators group.

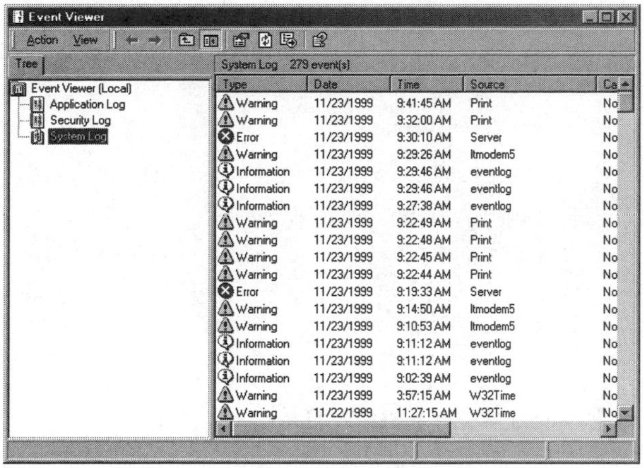

**FIGURE 32-1.**

The System Log records events generated by the operating system itself and its installed components.

Each event occupies one line in the details pane (the right pane). In addition to the Date, Time, and Computer columns, each event also includes the following categories of information (you might have to scroll the display to see all the columns):

- The Type column at the far left of each line identifies the event type. You might see any of the following icons in an event log:

    ❌ Indicates an error event, such as a loss of data or functionality

    ⚠️ Indicates a warning event, such as a nearly full disk

    ⓘ Indicates an information event, such as someone using a printer attached to your computer

    🔑 Indicates a success audit event, such as someone successfully logging on to the system

    🔒 Indicates a failure audit event, such as an unsuccessful attempt to log on to the system

- The Source column shows the name of the application software or system component that logged the event.

- The Category column tells you how the event is classified by the source. Although many events simply have None in this column, categories can be descriptive. The security log, for example, shows categories such as Logon/Logoff and Object Access (for file and folder access).

- The Event column shows the number used to identify each particular type of event. This number is associated with a text description that appears when you view an event's details.

VIII

Maintenance and Optimization

■ The User column identifies the user account involved in generating the event. Many events, particularly system events, aren't generated by a particular user, so these events show N/A in the User column.

### Sorting Entries in Event Viewer

To sort entries in Event Viewer, click the heading of the column on which you want to sort. Each time you click, an arrow in the heading will switch from pointing up to indicate ascending order, to pointing down for descending order.

## Examining Event Details

To get a closer look at an event in the Event Viewer window, select the event you want to see. Then use one of these methods to open the Event Properties dialog box:

■ Double-click the event.

■ Select the event and press Enter.

■ Right-click the event and choose Properties from the shortcut menu.

All methods lead to a dialog box similar to the one shown in Figure 32-2.

**FIGURE 32-2.**
An event's properties dialog box provides details about the event.

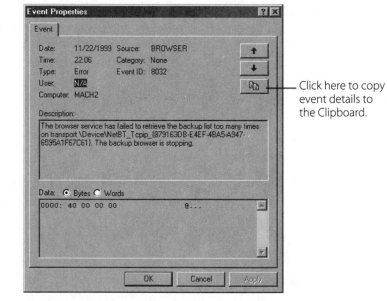

Click here to copy event details to the Clipboard.

The Event Properties dialog box provides a verbal description of the event in the Description box, along with the same summary information that appeared in the Event Viewer log. For some events, additional information is available in the Data area. This information might be useful to programmers or support technicians who are familiar with the product that generated the event.

If you want to view details for other events, you can do so without first returning to the main window: click the arrow buttons to display the event above or below the currently displayed event. When you've finished viewing event details, click OK to return to Event Viewer's main window.

## Filtering Events

As you can see from even a cursory look at your system log, events can pile up quickly, obscuring those of a particular type (such as print jobs) or those that occurred at a particular date and time (such as repeated, failed logon attempts). You can use Event Viewer to pinpoint clusters of events, or those that occur cyclically, by filtering the log to display only the events that interest you:

**1** In the Event Viewer window, select the log you want to filter—system, security, or application.

**2** Choose Filter from the View menu. The Filter tab of the log's properties dialog box appears, as shown in Figure 32-3.

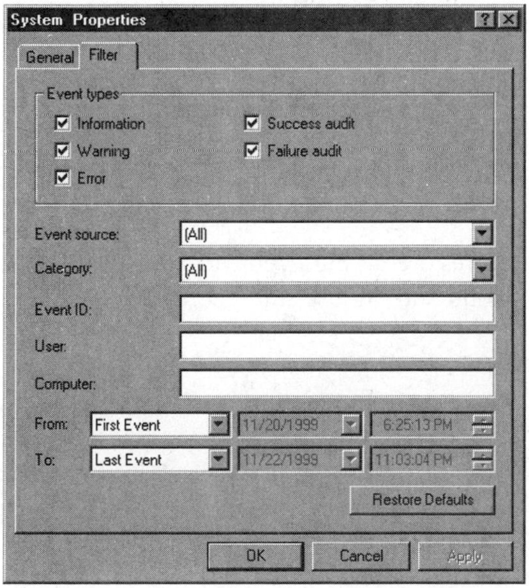

**FIGURE 32-3.**
You can filter a log to show only particular events.

VIII

Maintenance and Optimization

**3** Choose any combination of the following filtering criteria:

- Under Event Types, specify the types of events you want to include.

- Select a source program and a category from the Event Source and Category lists.

- In the next fields of the dialog box, type an Event ID, a User account name, and a Computer name, if you want to refine your filter request further.

- In the From and To boxes, specify the range of dates and times you want to include.

**4** Click OK to activate the filter.

In a few seconds, a list of events matching your specifications appears on the screen. Figure 32-4, for example, shows the results of filtering a system log to include only error events.

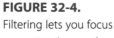
**FIGURE 32-4.**
Filtering lets you focus your attention on the events that matter.

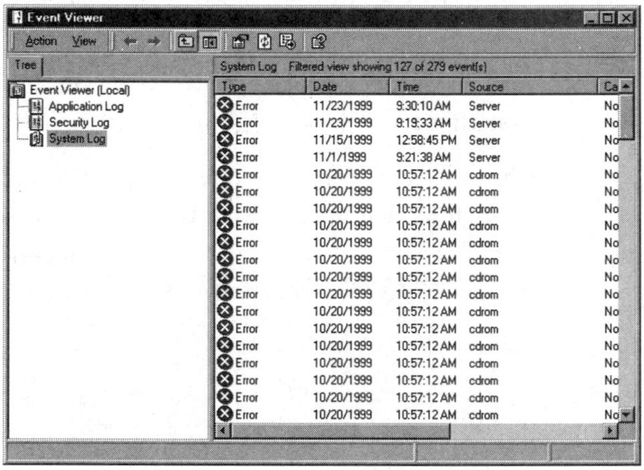

To restore all the events to your Event Viewer window, open the View menu and choose All Records.

## Searching for an Event

The Find command on the View menu provides another way to search a log. Find is exactly what you need when you want to find a single needle in an event haystack. When you choose Find, a dialog box similar to the one shown in Figure 32-5 appears.

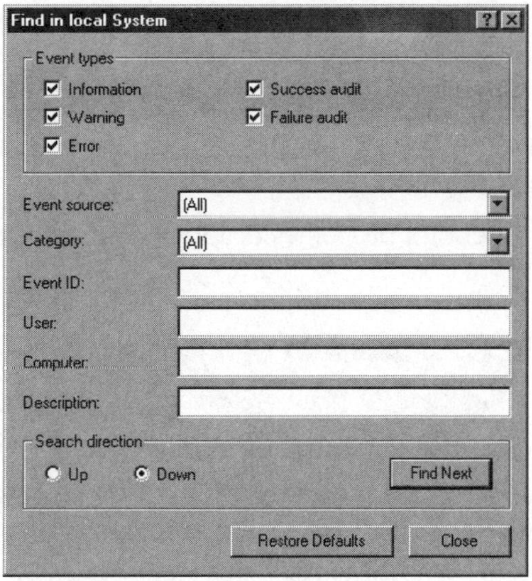

**FIGURE 32-5.**
Use Find to locate
particular events with-
out filtering the log.

Much of this dialog box is similar to the Filter dialog box, but some elements are different:

- The Description box allows you to type a portion of the text description you see when you view the event details. If you specify text here, you can zero in on exactly the event or events you seek. However, the Find command doesn't search for binary data; you can't type a set of hexadecimal numbers and expect Find to show you the event that produced those numbers in the Detail dialog box.

- The Search Direction buttons let you specify the direction of the search. Select Down to search through the event log from the current position to the end, or select Up to search from the current position back to the beginning. When Find reaches the end of the log, it asks if you want to continue searching from the other end.

- The Find Next button is the Find command's version of OK, meaning "go and do it." Click the Find Next button repeatedly to search until you find the matching event you want.

## Managing Logs

By default, the system, security, and application logs each hold 512 KB of information. If the log becomes full, another default tells Windows 2000 to begin overwriting the oldest information, but only if it is at

VIII

Maintenance and Optimization

least seven days old. (If the log becomes full before seven days have passed, new events aren't recorded.) To adjust either or both of these default settings:

1 Right-click the log in the console tree and choose Properties from the shortcut menu.

The log's properties dialog box appears, as shown in Figure 32-6.

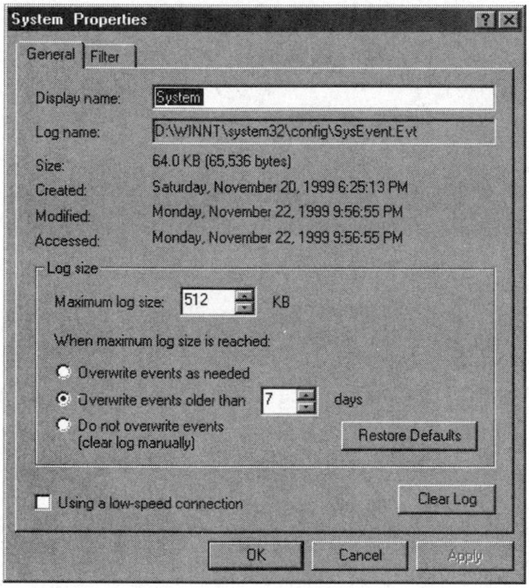

**FIGURE 32-6.**

A log's properties dialog box specifies such information as the capacity of the log.

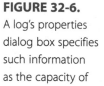

System Properties dialog box with General and Filter tabs. Display name: System. Log name: D:\WINNT\system32\config\SysEvent.Evt. Size: 64.0 KB (65,536 bytes). Created: Saturday, November 20, 1999 6:25:13 PM. Modified: Monday, November 22, 1999 9:56:55 PM. Accessed: Monday, November 22, 1999 9:56:55 PM. Log size — Maximum log size: 512 KB. When maximum log size is reached: Overwrite events as needed; Overwrite events older than 7 days; Do not overwrite events (clear log manually). Restore Defaults button. Using a low-speed connection checkbox. Clear Log button. OK, Cancel, Apply buttons.

2 Under Log Size, choose the option you want to use when the log reaches its maximum size.

> **NOTE**

If you specify a size smaller than the current size of the log, you must clear the log before the new size takes effect. This extra step prevents you from destroying existing records by inadvertently making the log too small to hold all of the currently recorded events.

- If you select Overwrite Events As Needed, all events are recorded, but old events might be discarded before you have a chance to review them.

- The second option ensures that events aren't deleted until a certain time has elapsed (you can specify 1 through 365 days). This is a good choice if you archive logs on a regular schedule. If the log reaches its maximum size before the specified time has passed, however, the system stops recording events until you clear the log or the requisite time has passed so that old events can be overwritten.

- The last option, which requires you to clear the log manually, means that when the log is full, the system stops recording events until you clear the log.

> **NOTE**
>
> If the system stops recording events because the log is full, a warning message appears on the screen.

## Restoring the Default Settings

To restore a log's default properties, redisplay its properties dialog box. Then click Restore Defaults.

## Clearing and Archiving Logs

You can clear a log by clicking Clear Log in the log's properties dialog box. (See Figure 32-6.) Alternatively, select the log in the console tree, and then choose Clear All Events from the Action menu.

To archive a log, select it in the console tree, and then choose Save Log File As from the Action menu. Event Viewer saves the log as an .evt file, which you can subsequently reopen in Event Viewer. The .evt file includes the binary data as well as the text associated with each event.

Alternatively, you can export a log to a text file that you can subsequently read in another application, such as a spreadsheet. An exported log includes the text associated with events, but not the binary data. To export a log, select it in the console tree, choose Export List from the Action menu, and then choose a file format. Your options include comma-delimited and tab-delimited formats in Unicode and ANSI character systems. All major spreadsheet programs can read archived logs in any of these formats, but if your Windows installation uses a non-Latin alphabet, you might need to pick one of the Unicode options.

## Reopening an Archived Log

To reopen an archived log, open the Action menu, and then choose New Log View. The archived log appears as a new subentry in the Event Viewer console tree.

# Monitoring Performance with Task Manager

Task Manager provides an easy way to monitor a few key indicators of your system's performance. In particular, Task Manager focuses on these three indicators:

- CPU (processor) usage

- Virtual memory usage

- Processes (roughly equivalent to programs)

Although it can be a useful tool, Task Manager provides information about only a handful of indicators. And, except for a graph that shows the last few minutes' activity, Task Manager doesn't track these indicators over time, so you can't use it for identifying chronic or sporadic conditions; it only shows what is happening here and now. When Task Manager doesn't provide the information you need, however, you can turn to a more sophisticated tool for monitoring and tracking performance: System Monitor.

## Starting Task Manager

Unlike most applications included with Windows 2000, Task Manager doesn't have a shortcut on the Start menu. To start Task Manager, do any of the following:

- Right-click an unoccupied area of the taskbar and choose Task Manager from the shortcut menu.

- Press Ctrl+Left Shift+Esc.

- Press Ctrl+Alt+Delete and then click the Task Manager button. (When you press Ctrl+Alt+Delete, all your windows disappear, and only the Windows 2000 Security dialog box is visible. Don't worry. As soon as you click Task Manager, your windows reappear along with the newly opened Task Manager window.)

The first time you start Task Manager, the Applications tab is displayed, as shown in Figure 32-7.

**FIGURE 32-7.**
Task Manager's Applications tab shows the status of each running program.

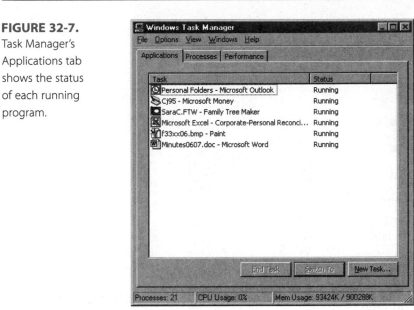

The main part of the window displays the names of all applications you've started, along with their status. You can use Task Manager as a task switcher, by selecting a program name and clicking Switch To. Or you can use it as a terminator, by selecting an application and clicking End Task. You can even use it as a launcher. If you click New Task, a dialog box functionally equivalent to the Start menu's Run dialog box appears.

## Understanding the Processes Tab

The Processes tab, shown in Figure 32-8, on the following page, lists all the currently running processes. Click the Processes tab to display it.

A *process* is an executable program (such as Windows 2000 Explorer or Microsoft Word), a service (a function controlled by Services in Control Panel, such as Event Log or Messenger), or a subsystem (such as the one for Windows 3.*x* applications). You can use the Processes tab to see which processes are running, and which ones are dominating processor and virtual memory usage.

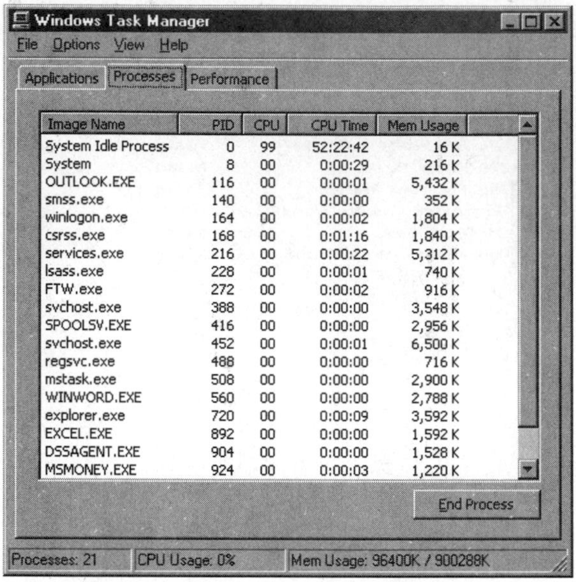

**FIGURE 32-8.**

The Processes tab provides a complete list of everything running on your system.

By default, the Processes tab displays for each process:

- **Image Name.** The process name

- **PID.** The process ID, a number that uniquely identifies a process while it runs

- **CPU.** The percentage of elapsed time that the process used the processor (CPU) to execute instructions

- **CPU Time.** The elapsed time (in hours, minutes, and seconds) that the process has been running

- **Mem Usage.** The number of kilobytes of virtual memory used by the process

Other process-related columns are also available for display. To make your selections, choose Select Columns from the View menu while the Processes tab is displayed.

## Understanding the Performance Tab

Click the Performance tab and you'll find lots of charts and numbers that tell you how your system is doing, as the example in Figure 32-9 shows.

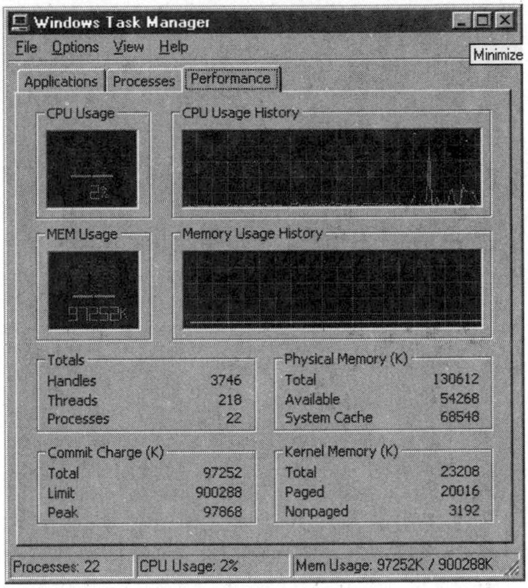

**FIGURE 32-9.**

The Performance tab provides a picture of your system's activity.

The Performance tab depicts the state of your system with four graphical images, as well as providing a great deal of textual information. The CPU Usage image shows the amount of current processor usage, expressed as a percentage of its total capacity. The CPU Usage History image charts CPU usage over time. The MEM Usage image shows the amount of virtual memory that has been "committed," or used, and the Memory Usage History image charts virtual memory usage over time.

In the textual area of the dialog box, perhaps the most important section is Commit Charge (K), which tells you the current, maximum allowable, and maximum committed virtual memory.

Task Manager displays an icon in the taskbar's status area. This icon is a miniature representation of the CPU Usage box, so you can monitor processor usage at a glance—even when Task Manager is minimized. Hover the mouse over the icon and a ScreenTip will tell you the percent of total CPU usage at the moment.

**TIP**

**Avoiding Taskbar Clutter**
Choose Hide When Minimized from Task Manager's Options menu. Then when you minimize Task Manager, it doesn't display a button on the taskbar. You can restore Task Manager by double-clicking its icon in the status area.

# PART IX

# Using Accessory Programs

# Writing with Notepad and WordPad

This chapter introduces the two text-processing programs supplied with Microsoft Windows 2000. Notepad is a plain-text editor suitable for working with files—such as HTML documents—that must be absolutely free of word-processor formatting data. WordPad is what's sometimes called an executive word processor—a program that's easy to learn and easy to use but lacks the sophistication of Microsoft Word and other full-featured word processors. To find shortcuts to both Notepad and WordPad, open the Start menu and choose Programs, Accessories.

# Using Notepad

Notepad's *raison d'être* is the fact that certain kinds of files must include nothing but text. These include source-code files for programming languages, HTML documents, and .ini files—the files containing configuration information that are used by certain applications (and by some components of the operating system). Notepad is ideal for working with files such as these, because, unlike WordPad or another word processing program, it generates absolutely nothing but a stream of text characters.

 The version of Notepad supplied with Windows 2000 offers a few improvements over its predecessors. Most notable is increased capacity. If you've used earlier versions, you might have noticed that the program wasn't capable of editing large text files. If you tried to open a file that was beyond the old Notepad's capacity, a dialog box gave you the choice of opening it in WordPad instead, or of not opening it at all. You'll be glad to know the Windows 2000 version of Notepad has essentially unlimited capacity. Opening a 12 MB text file saved from Registry Editor, for example, is no problem.

You'll also be pleased to see that the new Notepad supports such standard shortcuts as Ctrl+O (Open), Ctrl+S (Save), Ctrl+N (New), Ctrl+P (Print), Ctrl+F (Find), and Ctrl+H (Replace). The inclusion of a Replace command is itself a new feature, as previous versions could search but not replace. The current version's menus also have been rearranged slightly to conform better with Windows standards. The Font command, for example, now resides on a Format menu, as it does in most word processors.

Here's a quick rundown of Notepad's improved, but still modest, feature set.

## Using Notepad as a Time Log

Like every version of Notepad from the beginning of Windows, the current version has a hidden feature (that is, one that appears nowhere on the menus) that enables you to use the program as a time log. To use this feature, type *.LOG* on a line by itself at the top of a new file. (Be sure to include the period at the beginning and type *LOG* in capital letters.) Save the file and close it.

Each time you reopen this file, Windows appends the current date and time at the end of the file. Thus, to log a work activity:

**1**  Open the file.

The current time and date appear at the bottom of the file. You can add some brief text to its right as a notation, such as *Start Project*.

**2** Save the file and close it, or leave it open or minimized.

**3** After completing the work you want to log, reopen the file. If you left the file open, choose Open from the File menu to reopen it anyway (answer yes when prompted to save) so that a new time and date will be appended to the file.

**4** Add a notation to the right of the new date if you want—such as *Stop for Lunch*—save it, and close it.

Alternatively, you can add the current date and time to a file manually by opening the Edit menu and choosing Time/Date. (F5 is the shortcut key for this command.) The date and time appear at the current cursor location.

## 2000 Understanding Encoding Options

As Figure 33-1 shows, Notepad's Save As dialog box now includes an Encoding list, offering four options: ANSI, Unicode, Unicode Big Endian, and UTF-8. ANSI is the default and is suitable for English and other languages that use the Latin alphabet. Unicode, a superset of ANSI, allows for a great many additional characters. If you work with Hebrew, Russian, Arabic, Japanese, or another language that doesn't use the Latin alphabet, you will probably need to save your files in Unicode.

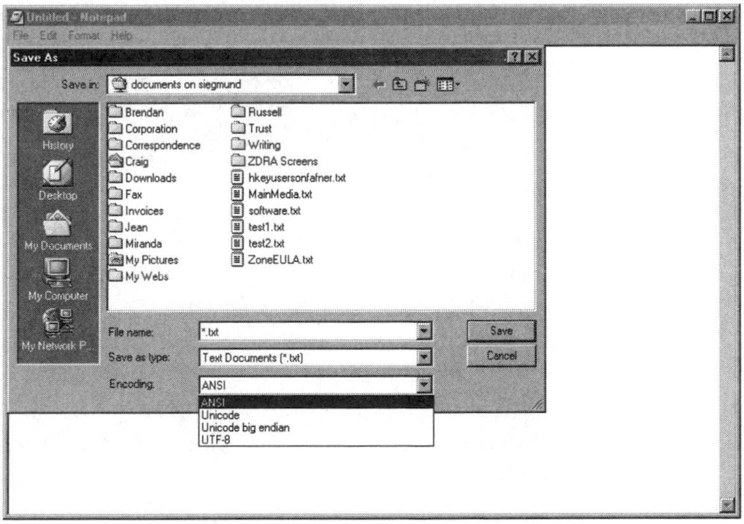

**FIGURE 33-1.**

You can save Notepad documents in any of four encoding schemes.

IX

Using Accessory Programs

Use Unicode Big Endian if you need to transport your documents to a Macintosh or other computer that doesn't use an Intel microprocessor. (The term *big endian* refers to the order in which the two bytes of a data word are stored.) UTF-8 (8-bit Universal Character Set Transmission Format) is an 8-bit reduction of Unicode. You might need to use this encoding option if you must transmit Unicode data across a medium that supports only 8 bits of significant data.

## Setting Page Setup and Printing Options

Notepad's Page Setup dialog box (shown in Figure 33-2) offers paper selection, print orientation, margin, and header/footer options. Your settings here remain in effect only for the current session. If you switch from portrait orientation to landscape, for example, the Landscape setting will remain in place for all files you work with in the current session. The next time you open Notepad with any file, however, the Orientation setting will revert to the setting you make in the printer's printing preferences dialog box.

**FIGURE 33-2.**

Notepad always reverts to these margin, header, and footer settings at the beginning of a session.

By default, Notepad prints the filename as the page *header* (the text at the top of each page). It prints the word *Page* followed by the page number as the page *footer* (the text at the bottom of each page). Header and footer are both centered by default. You can put any literal text you want in the header or footer (literal text is printed as is on every page). Notepad also recognizes the following codes, which either format the text or act as variables to be replaced with text at print time.

| Type This | Notepad Prints |
|-----------|----------------|
| &f | The current filename (or *(Untitled)* if you haven't saved the file) |
| &d | The current date |
| &t | The current time |
| &p | The page number |
| && | A literal ampersand |
| &l | The header or footer left aligned |
| &c | The header or footer centered |
| &r | The header or footer right aligned |

Notepad now uses the common Windows Print dialog box—the same one used by WordPad. See Figure 33-14 on page 710. With this dialog box, you can now choose which printer you want to use and specify the page range that you want to print.

# Searching, Replacing, and Navigating

The Edit menu includes the aforementioned Find and Replace commands. Once you've searched for something, you can search for it again by using the Edit menu's Find Next command—or, more simply, by pressing F3.

The Edit menu's new Goto command (the shortcut is Ctrl+G) lets you move directly to a particular line number. You might find this useful if your file consists of information arranged in lines, such as the records of a database file or the numbered lines of a programming language like Basic. It's less useful for files containing text in paragraphs.

 **TIP**

> **Counting the Number of Lines in a File**
> Want to know the number of lines in your file? Press Ctrl+G to open the Goto Line dialog box and type a very large number in it. Notepad will beep and tell you there's no such line number. Acknowledge by clicking OK, and the Goto Line dialog box will then replace your large number with the number of the last line in the file. Use that number to estimate the length of the file, the number of records in a database file, the number of lines in a computer program, or perhaps divide the number in half to move to the middle of the file. If you want to count only entire lines (no matter how long each line—or paragraph—might be), make sure the Word Wrap feature on the Format menu is turned off.

To get to the end of a file, press Ctrl+End. To get to the beginning, use Ctrl+Home. To select everything in the file, press Ctrl+A, or choose Select All from the Edit menu.

**IX**

**Using Accessory Programs**

## Choosing Display Options

The Format menu includes two commands that affect the display, but not the content, of your file: Word Wrap and Font.

The Word Wrap command, a toggle that's on by default, causes text to wrap at the right edge of the window, just as it wraps at the right margin in a word processing program. If you're using Notepad as a program source-code editor, you might want to turn this feature off to prevent lines from wrapping.

The Font command summons a common font dialog box. Note that your choice of font affects the entire document. You can't apply it to individual selections, and the font is not recorded in the file, because that would defeat the purpose of producing files that are text-only—that is, files with no formatting codes. However, Notepad will remember the font you select and continue to use it as its default display font until you change it again.

# Using WordPad

WordPad is the successor to Write, the mini-word processor that was included with Windows versions 3.1 and earlier. In the past, many programs have used Write documents for documentation, for licensing information, and as last-minute "read me" files. You can still read those files in Windows 2000, even though Write no longer exists. Simply launch a Write document to read it in WordPad.

WordPad can also read and save documents in any of five other file formats: Microsoft Word, Rich Text Format (RTF), Text, Text (MS-DOS format), and Unicode text. The Word format can be read by all recent versions of Microsoft Word as well as by many other popular word processors. Rich Text Format was designed as a universal interchange format so that a file in one format could be converted to any other proprietary format. The first program saves its file as RTF and then the second program imports the RTF into its format. RTF is WordPad's default file format.

> **NOTE**
>
> The version of WordPad included with Windows 2000 can *read* files created in the native format of Word 97 and Word 2000. But the Word format it uses for *saving* is that of Word 6.

WordPad's opening screen looks like the one shown in Figure 33-3.

**FIGURE 33-3.**

WordPad opens with a blank editing area.

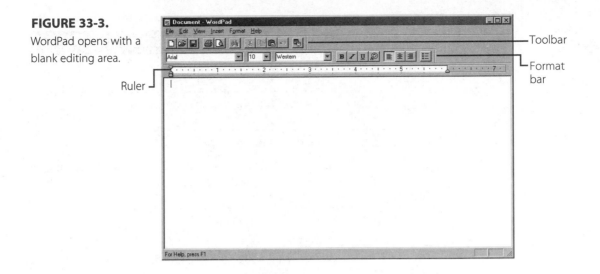

The following elements make up the WordPad window:

- **Toolbar.** WordPad's toolbar, like the toolbar in most other programs, contains buttons for issuing commonly used commands. To see what a particular button does, simply hover your mouse pointer over the button. A short description appears just below the mouse pointer, and a more detailed description appears on the status bar. Table 33-1 describes the buttons on the toolbar.

- **Format bar.** Like the toolbar, the format bar provides one-click access to commands. Most of WordPad's formatting options are available on the format bar. Table 33-2, on the following page, describes the buttons on the format bar.

- **Ruler.** The ruler provides an easy way to change tab and margin settings.

**TABLE 33-1.  WordPad Toolbar**

| Toolbar Icon | Description |
|---|---|
|  | Creates a new, blank document |
|  | Opens an existing document |
|  | Saves the current document to disk |

*(continued)*

IX

Using Accessory Programs

**TABLE 33-1.** *continued*

| Toolbar Icon | Description |
|---|---|
| | Prints the current document |
| | Displays a preview of the printed page |
| | Finds text that you specify |
| | Cuts (deletes) the selection and places it on the Clipboard |
| | Copies the selection to the Clipboard |
| | Pastes (inserts) the Clipboard's contents at the insertion point |
| | Steps back through your previous editing or formatting actions, undoing each one |
| | Inserts the date and time in your document |

**TABLE 33-2. WordPad Format Bar**

| Format Bar Icon | Description |
|---|---|
| Arial | Changes the font (typeface) of the selection |
| 10 | Changes the font size of the selection |
| Western | Makes available the character set for the language selected when working with Unicode fonts |
| **B** | Changes the selection to boldface (or, if the selection is already boldface, changes it back to normal) |
| *I* | Changes the selection to italic (or, if the selection is already italic, changes it back to normal) |
| U | Underlines the selection (or, if the selection is already underlined, removes the underline) |
| | Changes the color of the selection |
| | Left aligns the selected paragraphs |

**TABLE 33-2.**  *continued*

| Format Bar Icon | Description |
|---|---|
|   | Centers the selected paragraphs |
|  | Right aligns the selected paragraphs |
|  | Changes the selected paragraphs to an indented, bulleted list (or, if the selection is already bulleted, removes the bullets and indents) |

# Creating a WordPad Document

Creating a basic WordPad document couldn't be easier. Follow these two essential steps:

**1** Type.

**2** Save.

When you start WordPad, all you have to do is type the text you want, pressing Enter twice when you want a blank line between paragraphs. To save a document for the first time, click the Save button on the toolbar (or choose Save from the File menu). Give the document a name, and choose a document type from the Save As Type list.

## Inserting the Date or Time

You can easily add the date or time to a WordPad document. Just click the Date/Time toolbar button, select a format from the Date And Time dialog box shown in Figure 33-4, and choose OK. The current date or time appears at the insertion point in the format you selected.

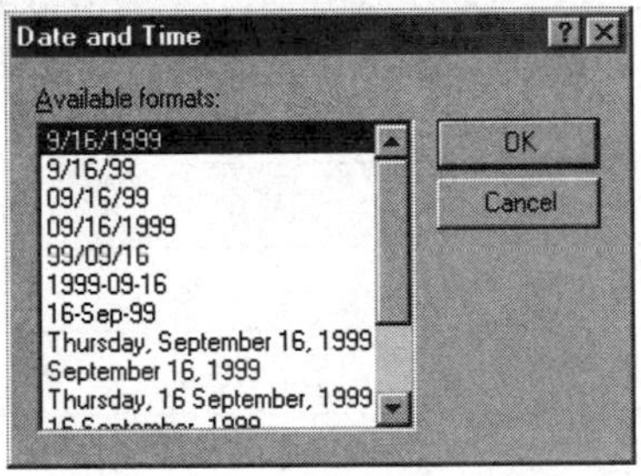

**FIGURE 33-4.**

WordPad allows you to choose from many date and time formats.

Date and Time

Available formats:

9/16/1999
9/16/99
09/16/99
09/16/1999
99/09/16
1999-09-16
16-Sep-99
Thursday, September 16, 1999
September 16, 1999
Thursday, 16 September, 1999
16 September, 1999

OK
Cancel

**IX**

**Using Accessory Programs**

## Starting a New Document

When you click the New button on the toolbar or choose New from the File menu, WordPad opens the New dialog box shown in Figure 33-5.

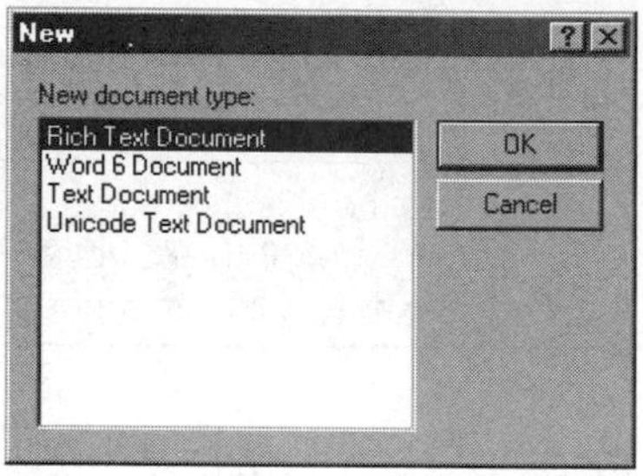

**FIGURE 33-5.**
The New dialog box lets you specify a document type.

When you select a document type and choose OK, WordPad closes the current document (prompting you to save if necessary) and presents a blank document window. The document window uses the view options for the document type you selected.

 **SEE ALSO**

For information about view options, see "Changing View Options," page 708.

## Navigating in a Document

You can use the mouse or the keyboard to move around in WordPad documents. The keystrokes you use in WordPad for moving the insertion point are listed in Table 33-3.

▶ **NOTE**

> Don't use Tab, Spacebar, or Backspace when all you want to do is move the insertion point. The Tab key and Spacebar add blank space to your document, and the Backspace key erases the character to the left of the insertion point.

**TABLE 33-3.   Navigating in WordPad**

| Pressing These Keys | Moves the Insertion Point |
| --- | --- |
| Right arrow | To the next character |
| Left arrow | To the previous character |
| Down arrow | To the next line |
| Up arrow | To the previous line |
| Ctrl+Right arrow | To the beginning of the next word |
| Ctrl+Left arrow | To the beginning of the previous word if the insertion point is between words, or to the beginning of the current word if the insertion point is in a word |

**TABLE 33-3.** *continued*

| Pressing These Keys | Moves the Insertion Point |
| --- | --- |
| Ctrl+Down arrow | To the beginning of the next paragraph |
| Ctrl+Up arrow | To the beginning of the current paragraph or to the beginning of the previous paragraph if the insertion point is at the beginning of a paragraph |
| Page Down | To the next screen of text |
| Page Up | To the previous screen of text |
| Ctrl+Page Down | To the end of the last line currently visible on the screen |
| Ctrl+Page Up | To the beginning of the first line currently visible on the screen |
| Home | To the first character in the current line |
| End | To the last character in the current line |
| Ctrl+Home | To the beginning of the document |
| Ctrl+End | To the end of the document |

## Selecting Text

WordPad uses the same methods for selecting text as virtually all other Windows-based word processors and text editors. You can do any of the following:

- Position the mouse pointer at one end of the area you want to select, press and hold down the mouse button as you drag the mouse to the other end of the area to be selected, and then release the mouse button.

- Place the insertion point at one end of the area you want to select, move the mouse pointer to the other end of the area to be selected (without clicking), and then hold down the Shift key while you click.

- Hold down the Shift key while you press any of the arrow keys or other navigation keys to extend the selection in the direction of the arrows. You can also select text by using the Shift key with any of the navigation keystroke combinations described in Table 33-3. For example, to select text one word at a time, hold down the Shift key while you press Ctrl+Right arrow for each word you want to select (including the space that follows it).

**NOTE**

If you extend the selection so that it includes more than one word, WordPad extends the selection by whole words, so you needn't be so precise in cursor positioning. If you prefer to control the selections character by character, choose Options from the View menu, click the Options tab, and turn off Automatic Word Selection.

These additional techniques are common to WordPad and Word, and they allow mouse users to quickly select the current word, the current line, the current paragraph, or the entire document:

- Double-click to select the current word.

- Triple-click to select the current paragraph.

To use the following techniques, start by positioning the mouse pointer in the margin area to the left of your text. You can tell you're in the correct place when the mouse pointer changes from an I-beam to a northeast-pointing arrow.

Now you can do any of the following:

- Click once to select the current line.

- Double-click to select the current paragraph.

- Triple-click or hold down the Ctrl key and click once to select the entire document.

**TIP**

Press Ctrl+A to quickly select the entire document. For this shortcut, it makes no difference where the insertion point or mouse pointer is located.

## Editing Text

The insertion point in Windows documents always lies *between* characters. To insert text into an existing document, simply position the insertion point where you want the new material to go. Whatever you type is inserted to the left of the insertion point, and the existing text moves to the right to accommodate the new text.

To replace existing text, start by selecting the text you want to replace. When a block of text is selected, whatever you type replaces the text in the selection.

To erase a small amount of text, position the insertion point either before or after the text you want to erase. Then press Backspace or

Delete. Backspace erases the character to the left of the insertion point; Delete erases text to the right of the insertion point. Careful! The Backspace and Delete keys both repeat—if you hold down either key, it continues to erase text until you release the key.

To erase a large amount of text, start by selecting the text. Then press Delete.

## Undoing Mistakes

WordPad's Edit menu includes a valuable Undo command that enables you to recover from many mishaps—unwanted deletions, formatting changes that don't produce the desired effect, and even search-and-replace operations that you immediately regret.

As a shortcut for the Undo command, press Ctrl+Z.

The Undo command can reverse more than one editing action. The first time you use it, it undoes your most recent action. The second time, it reverses your next-to-most-recent action, and so on. Note, however, that the command doesn't tell you what it's about to undo, and that, unlike more sophisticated word processors, WordPad doesn't offer a Redo command to reverse your last Undo action.

## Copying and Moving Text

You can use the standard Clipboard procedures to copy or move text from one place to another within a WordPad document, from one WordPad document to another WordPad document, or from a WordPad document to a document created in a different program. After selecting the text, choose Cut or Copy from the Edit menu to move or copy the text block, or use the respective shortcut keys, Ctrl+X or Ctrl+C. Then move the insertion point to the location you want to paste the text block, and choose Paste from the Edit menu or press Ctrl+V.

# Finding Text

WordPad's Find command helps you locate a particular combination of text (letters, numbers, or words and spaces).

To open the Find dialog box shown in Figure 33-6, on the next page, choose Find from the Edit menu or click the Find button on the toolbar. See Table 33-1 on page 691. As a shortcut for the Find command, press Ctrl+F. Type the text you're looking for in the Find What text box.

IX

Using Accessory Programs

**FIGURE 33-6.**

Enter the text you want to search for in this dialog box.

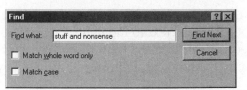

Select Match Whole Word Only if you want WordPad to find the search text only if it's a whole word. With this option selected, a search for *and* would find only the word *and*, but not *band, android,* or *salamander.* Select Match Case if you want WordPad to find instances of the search text only if the capitalization is an exact match. With this option checked, a search for *Microsoft* would not find *MICROSOFT*.

## Starting a Search

After you have filled out the Find What text box and chosen your search options, you can start the search by clicking the Find Next button or pressing Enter. WordPad searches from the insertion point forward; if it reaches the end of your document without finding your search text, it continues the search starting at the top of the document.

As soon as WordPad finds an occurrence of your search text, it selects the text and stops searching, but the dialog box remains on the screen. At this point, you have several options:

- If you have found what you're looking for and don't want to do any more searching, close the dialog box by pressing Esc or by clicking Cancel or the dialog box's Close button.

- If you want to search for the next occurrence of the same search text, click Find Next again.

- If you want to search for different text, replace the text that's currently in the Find What text box with the new text, and then click Find Next.

## Repeating a Search

If you want to resume working on your document but you think you might need to search for the same text again, you can do either of the following:

- Move the Find dialog box to a position on your screen where it won't be in your way. Then click outside the dialog box (or press Alt+F6) to return to the document. When you're ready to repeat the search, simply click the Find Next button again, or press Alt+F6 to return to the Find dialog box and then press Alt+F to choose the Find Next button.

- Close the dialog box. When you want to repeat the search, press F3 (or choose Find Next from the Edit menu).

# Replacing Text

The Edit menu's Replace command lets you replace one set of characters or words with another. As a shortcut for Replace, press Ctrl+H. The Replace dialog box appears, as shown in Figure 33-7. You can confirm each replacement, or you can have WordPad replace every occurrence of the search text automatically.

**FIGURE 33-7.**

When you choose the Replace command, this dialog box opens.

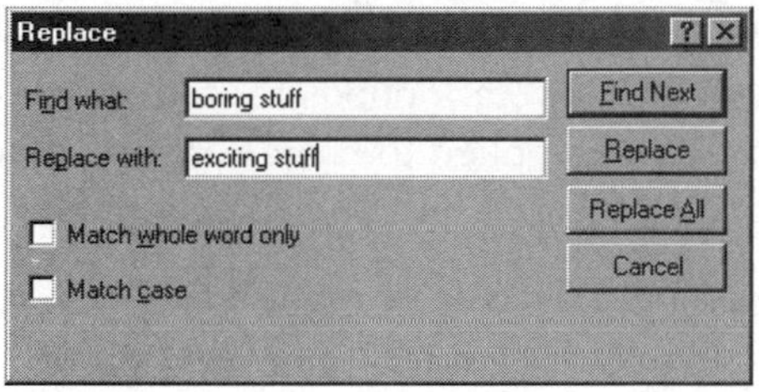

## Telling WordPad What to Replace

To specify the text you want to replace, fill out the Find What text box. (This box works exactly the same way as the Find What text box in the Find dialog box.) Enter the new text in the Replace With text box.

## Replacing What You Want to Replace

When you've filled out the Replace dialog box, you can start the Replace operation in either of two ways:

- To replace all occurrences of the search text automatically, click Replace All.

- To have WordPad pause for confirmation before making each replacement, click Find Next.

If you click the Find Next button, WordPad stops as soon as it finds an occurrence of your search text. At that point, you can do any of the following:

- If you do *not* want WordPad to replace this occurrence of the search text, click Find Next.

- If you want WordPad to replace this occurrence and continue searching for further occurrences, click Replace.

- If you want WordPad to replace this and all other occurrences of the search text, click Replace All.

- To stop the Replace operation without making any further replacements, press Esc or Alt+F4, click the dialog box's Close button, press Alt+F6, or click anywhere outside the dialog box.

If you press Alt+F6 or click outside the dialog box, the dialog box remains on the screen. You can use it at any time by pressing Alt+F6 again or clicking within the dialog box.

## Formatting Your Document

WordPad provides several options for formatting documents, including options that can be applied to characters, to paragraphs, or to the entire document.

The following options can be applied either to a selection of existing text or to new text that you're about to enter. If you select a character or group of characters before choosing one of these options, the option is applied to the selection only. If you don't select text before choosing the option, the option is applied to everything new that you type at the current insertion point position, but not to existing text. You can

- Choose fonts and point sizes

- Apply boldface, italics, strikeout, or underlining

- Change text color

The following options apply to individual paragraphs or selections of consecutive paragraphs. You can

- Create bulleted lists (such as the one you're looking at right now)

- Apply indents

- Set a paragraph alignment style (flush left, flush right, or centered)

- Define tab stops

The File menu's Page Setup command contains several more formatting options that apply to the entire document. You can

- Specify paper size

- Specify left, right, top, and bottom margins

**TIP**

> You can use the ruler to apply left and right margin settings to selected paragraphs (or to all paragraphs from the insertion point onward, if the insertion point is at the end of the document).

- Select a page orientation: *portrait* (vertical, like a portrait painting) or *landscape* (sideways, like a landscape painting).

## Changing Fonts

The easiest way to choose a font or point size is by making selections from the format bar. Simply click the small arrow to open the Font list and select a new font. Open the Font Size list to select a new size or type a number directly into the box.

### Adding Font Attributes

WordPad's font attribute options include bold, italic, underline, color, and strikeout. Buttons for all of these except strikeout are located on the format bar, as shown in Table 33-2 on page 692. (You must access Strikeout in the Font dialog box, as described on the next page.) You can use all of these options singly or in combination with one another.

 **TIP**

> You can press Ctrl+B, Ctrl+I, or Ctrl+U as shortcuts for bold, italic, or underline.

### Changing Text Color

To change the color of your text, click the Color button (shown in Table 33-2 on page 692) on the format bar and pick the color you want. (See Figure 33-8.)

**FIGURE 33-8.**

You can open the Color list by clicking its format bar button.

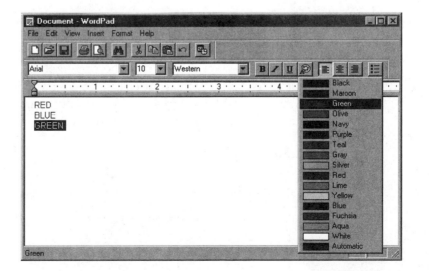

IX

Using Accessory Programs

You might have noticed the color named Automatic at the bottom of Figure 33-8. Automatic applies no color attribute at all. Instead, text formatted as Automatic is displayed in the Windows font color defined in the Display Properties dialog box. For most color schemes, the Windows font color (and, therefore, the Automatic color in WordPad) is black. If you select any color other than Automatic, WordPad uses it regardless of the settings in the Display Properties dialog box.

### Using the Font Dialog Box

You can access all of the character formatting options just discussed from the Font dialog box shown in Figure 33-9. (Choose Font from the Format menu.) If you plan to make several changes at once, it can be easier to use the Font dialog box than to click several buttons on the format bar.

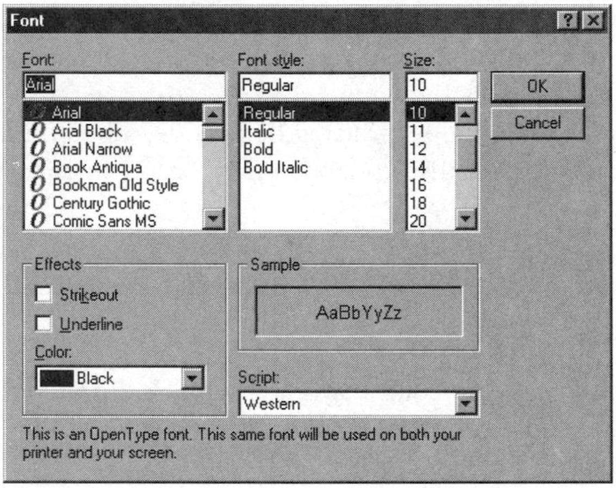

**FIGURE 33-9.**

The Font dialog box presents all the character formatting options in one place.

## Adding Bullets

With WordPad, it's easy to add a bullet in front of a paragraph. With the insertion point anywhere in the paragraph, simply click the Bullets button on the format bar (or choose Bullet Style from the Format menu.) To add bullets to several consecutive paragraphs, select the paragraphs before choosing the bullet style.

## Indenting Text

You can use three kinds of indents in WordPad paragraphs, singly or in combination:

- An indent from the left margin that applies to all lines in a paragraph

- An indent from the right margin that applies to all lines in a paragraph

- An indent from the left margin that applies to only the first line in a paragraph

You can use the last of these options to set up automatic paragraph indenting or to create a paragraph with hanging indentation (described in the next section).

Choose Paragraph from the Format menu to open the dialog box shown in Figure 33-10.

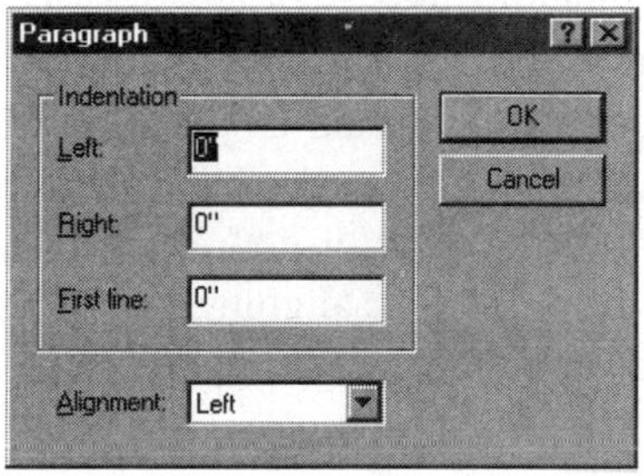

**FIGURE 33-10.**

The Paragraph dialog box lets you set indents and alignment.

Left and right indents are measured from the left and right margins, respectively. The first-line indent is measured from the left indent. Simply fill out the appropriate boxes and click OK.

You can also set indents by dragging the ruler's indent markers. *For details, see "Using the Ruler to Format Your Documents," page 705.*

### Using Hanging Indents

A paragraph is said to have *hanging indentation* when all of its lines except the first are indented. This style is useful for such documents as bibliographies and bulleted or numbered lists. To set up a hanging indent, simply specify a positive left indent and a negative first-line indent.

With a left indent of 2 inches and a first-line indent of –2 inches, for example, all lines except the first will appear two inches from the left margins. The first line will start at the left margin.

### Aligning Text

WordPad offers three paragraph-alignment styles:

- Flush left (left margin straight, right margin *ragged*, or uneven, with lines breaking at the whole word nearest to the margin)

IX

Using Accessory Programs

- Centered (both margins ragged, each line centered between the margins)

- Flush right (left margin ragged, right margin straight)

To specify the alignment for the paragraph that contains the insertion point, select an option from the list in the Paragraph dialog box (see Figure 33-10), or click one of the three alignment buttons on the format bar (see Table 33-2, page 692).

## Setting and Using Tab Stops

By default, WordPad documents have tab stops every 0.5 inch. You can replace those default stops with tab stops of your own wherever you like. You can do this by filling out a dialog box or by using the ruler. When you set your own tab stops by either method, WordPad removes its 0.5-inch tab stops to the left of your tab stops. All of the WordPad tab stops to the right of your rightmost tab stop remain in place. WordPad offers only left-aligning tab stops. For tabs that align right, centered, or on decimal points, you'll need a full-featured word processor like Word.

Tab stops apply to the entire paragraph in which the insertion point is positioned when you set them. If you continue typing beyond the current paragraph by pressing the Enter key, the new paragraphs you type will also have the same tab settings. You can set different tab stops in each paragraph if you like.

To set tab stops with a dialog box (shown in Figure 33-11), choose Tabs from the Format menu. In the text box, type the distance from the left margin to where you want a tab stop to be, and then click Set to add the setting to the Tab Stop Position list. Repeat this procedure for each tab stop you want to add. When you're finished adding tab stops, click OK.

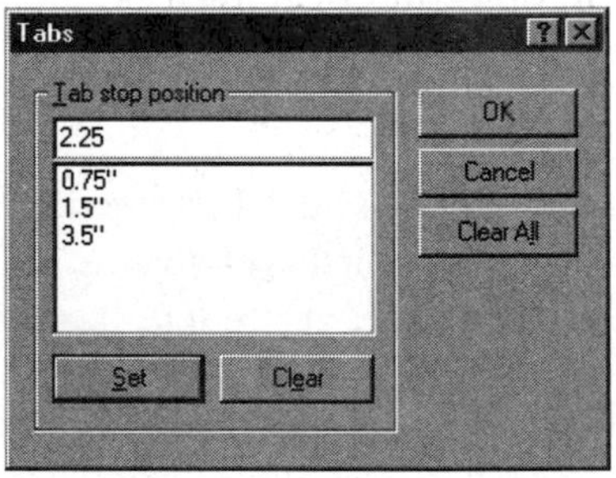

**FIGURE 33-11.**

Use the Tabs dialog box to set tab stops.

To remove a tab stop from the Tabs dialog box, select the tab stop you want to remove and click Clear. To remove all tab stops at once, click Clear All.

## Setting Margins

WordPad's default top and bottom margins are 1 inch. The default left and right margins are 1.25 inches. To override any of these settings, choose Page Setup from the File menu and make changes in the appropriate margin text boxes.

Note that the margin settings in the Page Setup dialog box apply to the entire document. If you want to change left or right margins for particular paragraphs, set indents instead, as just described.

## Using the Ruler to Format Your Document

The ruler (shown in Figure 33-12) provides an easy way to set tabs and indents. If the ruler isn't displayed, choose Ruler from the View menu to display it.

**FIGURE 33-12.**

WordPad's ruler shows the space between a document's margins, as well as the indents and tab stops for a paragraph.

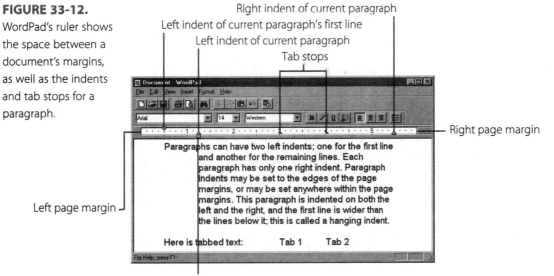

The white area of the ruler indicates the space between the left and right margins of the page. Markers on the ruler indicate the indent and tab-stop settings for the paragraph that contains the insertion point.

IX

Using Accessory Programs

> You can change the units used by the ruler. To do so, choose Options from the View menu, and then click the Options tab. In the Measurement Units section, select Inches, Centimeters, Points, or Picas.

### Setting Indents with the Ruler

To set left or right indents with the ruler, simply drag the left or right indent marker to a new location. Note that if you drag the upward pointing triangular marker, only the left indent changes. If you instead drag the rectangular box below the left indent marker, the left indent and the first-line indent markers move in unison.

### Setting Tab Stops with the Ruler

You can use the ruler interactively to manage tab stops for the currently selected paragraph (the paragraph that contains the insertion point):

- To set tab stops with the ruler, just position the mouse pointer over the ruler where you want the tab stop and then click.

- To adjust the position of any tab stop, drag the tab-stop marker along the ruler.

- To remove a tab stop, simply drag the tab-stop marker off the ruler and release the mouse button.

## Putting Pictures and Other Objects in WordPad Documents

**? SEE ALSO**
For information about OLE Linking and Embedding, see Appendix D, "Cutting, Pasting, Embedding, and Linking."

WordPad is capable of acting as destination and source program for OLE Linking and Embedding. This means that you can store links to or embed the following kinds of data, among others, in your WordPad documents:

- Graphical images copied to the Clipboard from OLE source programs, such as Paint or Microsoft Word

- Charts or worksheet ranges copied from Microsoft Excel

- Sound annotations copied from Sound Recorder

## Saving and Retrieving Documents

WordPad uses the same procedures for saving and retrieving documents as most other Windows-based programs. Use the following File menu commands:

- Save, to save the current document

- Save As, to save the current document under a new name or to choose different file-saving options

- New, to remove the current document from memory and begin creating a new one

- Open, to load an existing document from disk into memory

By default, WordPad is set up to save new documents in Rich Text Format with an extension of .rtf. To save a file as a different type, choose Save As, open the Save As Type list, and choose the type you want. If you don't specify an extension, WordPad automatically uses .doc for Word for Windows 6.0 files, .txt for text files, and .rtf for Rich Text Format files.

## Choosing a File Type

When you save a document with Save As or begin a new document, WordPad gives you the opportunity to choose a different file format. The following file format descriptions will help you make an informed choice:

- **Word for Windows 6.0.** This is the same file format used in Microsoft Word for Windows 6.0. If you use a document saved in this format with any recent version of Word, or with another word processor that accepts Word for Windows 6.0 documents, all of your formatting will remain intact.

- **Rich Text Format (RTF).** RTF is a compromise between the Word for Windows 6.0 and Text Document formats. It's a format that was designed for transferring formatted text between diverse programs. Most word processors have an option for saving documents in Rich Text Format. If you want to use a WordPad document in a word processor that doesn't support the Word 6.0 format, try RTF.

- **Text Document.** This option saves documents as plain (unformatted) text. WordPad saves the words in your document but removes all character, paragraph, and document formatting. Your document also loses any embedded or linked data and any pictures pasted in as static objects. The main reason to use the Text Document format is to create or edit MS-DOS batch files, Windows configuration files, and HTML code.

- **Text Document–MS-DOS Format.** This option is like Text Document in every respect except one: it saves documents using the extended ASCII character set instead of the Windows-standard ANSI character set. Use this format if you plan to reopen the document in an MS-DOS-based program.

- **Unicode Text Document.** This option is like Text Document in every respect, except that it saves documents using the Unicode character set instead of the Windows-standard ANSI character set.

## Changing View Options

Each document type has its own default options that determine whether the ruler, toolbars, and status bar are displayed and how word wrap behaves when you open or start a new document in that format. You can choose separate settings for regular and embedded text.

To look at or change the view options, choose Options from the View menu. The Options dialog box appears, as shown in Figure 33-13.

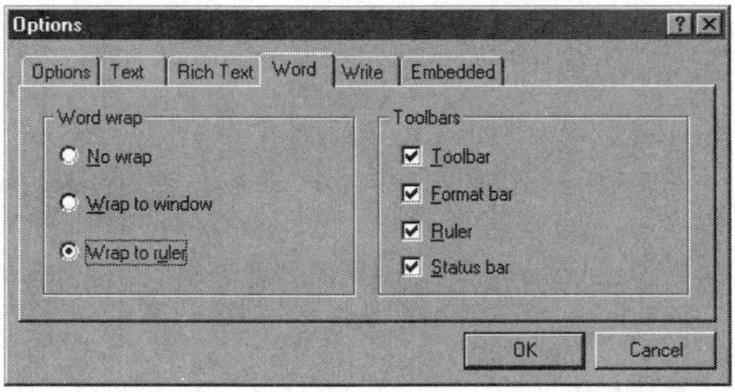

**FIGURE 33-13.**

Change text viewing options here.

Click the tab for the document format you want and make the changes you want.

*Word wrap*, which is the default action in most word processors, means that when the text you type reaches the right margin, the rest of the text automatically moves to the next line. Here's what the different options mean:

- The No Wrap option disables word wrap altogether. By default, word wrap is turned off (No Wrap is selected) for text files. That's because text format is often used for entering program code, for which you don't want text to move around on you.

- If you select Wrap To Window, when the text you type reaches the right edge of the document window, the text wraps to the next line. This setting affects only the screen display, not the printed pages. This is the default setting for RTF.

- If you select Wrap To Ruler, when the text you type reaches the right margin as defined on the ruler, the text wraps to the next line, just like it will when you print the pages. This is the default setting for Word 6 and Write documents.

In the Toolbars section of the Options dialog box, you can select which options you want displayed; clear the ones you don't want displayed. You can always override these selections by choosing View menu commands.

## Putting It on Paper

To print your document, choose Print from the File menu. As a shortcut, press Ctrl+P. The Print dialog box appears, as shown in Figure 33-14, on the next page.

- To switch to a different printer, choose one from the Select Printer box.

- To change the settings for your selected printer, right-click the Printer and choose Properties.

- To print more than one copy, change the number in the Number Of Copies box.

- To print a range of pages instead of the entire document, select the Pages option and enter the page range in the Pages box.

When you've made all your selections in the Print dialog box, choose Print to send your document to the printer.

**TIP**

**Use the Toolbar for One-Click Printing**
If you want to print your document and don't plan to change any options in the Print dialog box, simply click the Print toolbar button. This sends the document directly to the printer, bypassing the Print dialog box. If you choose Print from the File menu or press Ctrl+P, the Print dialog box opens.

IX

Using Accessory Programs

**FIGURE 33-14.**

The Print dialog box allows you to choose printing options and send your document to the printer.

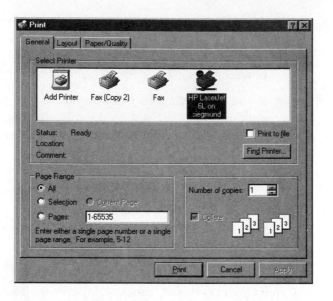

## Saving Paper with Print Preview

If you want to see what your document looks like before you print it, click the Print Preview button shown in Table 33-1 on page 691, or choose Print Preview from the File menu.

Print Preview, shown in Figure 33-15, allows you to perform the following tasks:

- Move from page to page to see where WordPad has placed page breaks. To do this, click Next Page or Prev Page.

- View two pages of your document at once by clicking Two Page.

- Zoom in to get a closer look at the document, or zoom out to get back to the default full-page view. Click Zoom In or Zoom Out.

- Open the Print dialog box by clicking Print. You can easily preview a document and then print it in one procedure.

**TIP**

**Zooming in Preview Mode**

In preview mode, shown in Figure 33-15, the mouse pointer changes to a magnifying glass. When the magnifying glass is visible, click anywhere in the document to zoom in one level, and then click again to zoom in to the second level. When the mouse pointer turns back to an arrow, clicking zooms you back out to full-page view (or two-page view if previously selected).

**FIGURE 33-15.**

Use the Print Preview window to preview your printed output.

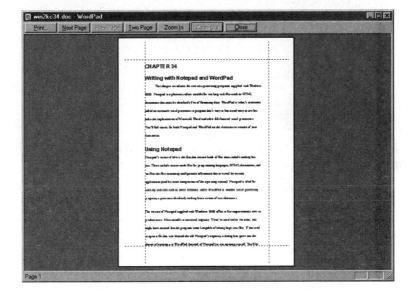

## CHAPTER 34

# Drawing with Paint

This chapter introduces Microsoft Paint, the drawing program included with Microsoft Windows 2000 that lets you create and edit graphics images. You can use Paint to produce anything from simple text-oriented flyers and line diagrams to complex works of art. You can start from scratch on a blank canvas, or you can modify existing images. Any graphics information that you can copy to the Clipboard, you can paste into Paint and modify—everything from clip art images to images created in other Windows-based programs (like Microsoft Excel charts) to scanned images.

As installed with Windows 2000, Paint reads and writes standard Windows .bmp files. Other programs you install might include additional graphics filters that work with Paint. For example, with Microsoft Office 2000 installed, Paint also supports JPEG and GIF file formats. You'll find the GIF and JPEG options useful if you use Paint to prepare or edit images for use in Web pages.

# Introducing Paint

To get Paint running, open the Start menu and choose Programs, Accessories, Paint. The opening screen looks like the one shown in Figure 34-1.

**FIGURE 34-1.**

When you start Paint, you get a blank drawing area.

Mouse pointer

Toolbox

Drawing area

Foreground color

Background color

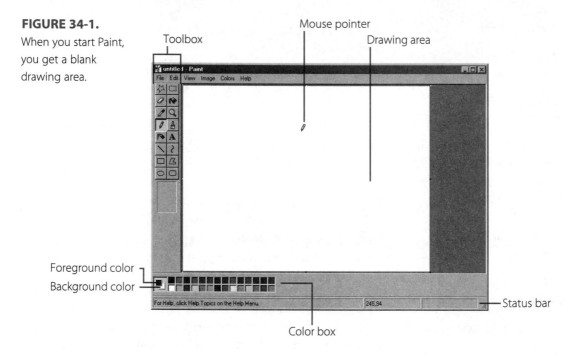

Status bar

Color box

The blank area that makes up most of Paint's window is the *drawing area*. The icons to the left of the drawing area make up the *toolbox*. These icons represent the drawing and editing tools that you use to draw and edit images in the drawing area.

At the left side of the *color box*, Paint displays the current foreground and background color selections. When you start Paint, the foreground color is black and the background color is white.

In Figure 34-1, notice that the Pencil tool in the toolbox appears indented and the mouse pointer in the drawing area is in the shape of a pencil. The pointer changes shape depending on which tool is active. Like the insertion point in a word processing program, the pointer indicates where your next drawing action will take place.

When you use Paint to create a picture, you use tools to apply various elements to the drawing area—your canvas in Paint. This works much like painting in real life. If you were creating a real painting on a real canvas, you might use a variety of paintbrushes. If you were painting a house, you might use rollers, spray cans, and so on. The Paint program provides the tools to make it easy to create exactly what you have in mind.

The general steps for creating a picture are:

1 Select a drawing tool.

> To select a tool, just click it.

> Each drawing tool is specialized for a particular kind of object. To draw a straight line, for example, select the Line tool; to draw a rectangle, select the Rectangle tool—and so on.

> It's easy to figure out what many of the tools do just by looking at their icons. If that doesn't give you enough of a clue, remember that you can position the mouse pointer over a tool to display a ScreenTip that tells you what the tool is. *For information about each of the tools and its properties, see "Exploring the Toolbox," page 724.*

2 Select a line width, brush shape, or rectangle type from the group of choices below the toolbox. (Notice that the choices change depending on which tool you have selected.)

> You can draw lines from one pixel to five pixels wide, and you can select from several different brush shapes and rectangle types.

3 Select a foreground color.

> To select a foreground color, click a color or pattern in the color box.

> If you don't find the color or pattern you want in the color box, you can create it with the Edit Colors command on the Colors menu. *For more information, see "Editing Colors," page 740.*

4 Select a background color.

> Some tools, such as Rectangle and Ellipse, can use the current background color to fill the shape they draw in the foreground color. Other tools, such as Line, use the foreground color if you draw with the left mouse button and the background color if you use the right button. You need to concern yourself with this step only if you're using a tool that uses the background color.

> To select a background color, right-click the color or pattern you want to use in the color box.

**5** Draw.

> After drawing the new object on the canvas, it's not too late to change your mind, thanks to the Undo command. *For more information, see "Making Quick Fixes with Undo and Repeat," on the next page.*

# Saving and Opening Paint Documents

To save a Paint document for the first time, choose Save or Save As from the File menu. The Save As dialog box appears.

You can select from several bitmap formats. To pick one, open the Save As Type list, as shown in Figure 34-2. Click the format of your choice and then click the Save button.

- Select Monochrome Bitmap to store the picture as a black-and-white image.

- Select 16 Color Bitmap to store the picture in color but without the full spectrum of colors. This is an efficient way to store images in which you haven't used more than 16 colors because it uses less disk space than the 256-color and 24-bit color options.

- Select 256 Color Bitmap to include more of the color spectrum. This takes more disk space and is usually a good compromise.

- Select 24-Bit Bitmap to save the picture with the full spectrum of colors. You'll generally want to use this option for photographic quality images, such as scanned images or those imported from a high quality clip art collection. The 24-bit format takes the largest amount of disk space, but it retains the highest degree of picture accuracy.

> **NOTE**

There's usually no reason to save an image using more colors than your system can display (unless you're going to use the image on a system that can display more colors or print it on a color printer). If you use a 256-color display driver, for example, you'll never see the additional colors stored by a 24-bit color image. By default, Paint proposes to save the image using the maximum number of colors your system can display. *To find out how many colors are in your system's palette, or for information about changing this setting, see "Changing Color Depth," page 60.*

**FIGURE 34-2.**
The Save As dialog box lets you specify the name, format, and location of the file.

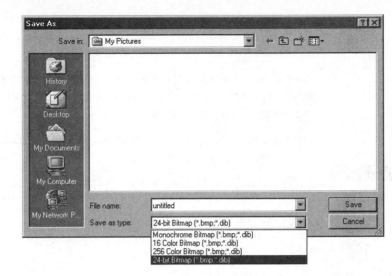

### Previewing Your Saved Pictures in Windows Explorer

You might find it convenient to save all your picture files in a single folder, such as the My Pictures folder within My Documents. Whatever folder you choose, you'll be able to easily preview your pictures if you apply the Image Preview template to the folder. When you select a picture file in such a folder, you can see its dimensions and other attributes, view it, and print it—all without opening Paint. *For information about setting up a folder with the Image Preview template, see "Setting Options That Apply to Only the Current Folder," page 91.*

To open a saved Paint document when the Paint program is already running, choose Open from the File menu and double-click the name of the file you want.

### Opening Recently Used Documents

Paint lists the last four documents you used at the bottom of the File menu. To open one of these recent documents, just select the name of the file you want to open from the File menu.

# Making Quick Fixes with Undo and Repeat

Mistakes happen. When you draw something you didn't mean to or change your mind after an editing procedure, Paint lets you gracefully take one, two, or even three steps back.

To undo your last action in Paint, choose Undo from the Edit menu. To undo your second-to-last action, choose Undo again. Choose Undo a third time to undo your third-to-last action.

Paint is so forgiving, it even lets you change your mind after you use Undo. You can restore any actions you changed with Undo by choosing Repeat from the Edit menu.

Just as with Undo, you can repeat up to three actions.

> **⭐ TIP**
>
> The keyboard shortcut for Undo is Ctrl+Z. Just like choosing Undo from the Edit menu, you can press Ctrl+Z up to three times to undo up to three actions. The keyboard shortcut for Repeat is Ctrl+Y.

# Setting Up for a New Picture

Although you can start a new picture without any planning, taking a few minutes to prepare your "canvas" can save time later. You should consider these items when setting up for a new picture:

- The background color or pattern that will be used for your picture

- The dimensions of the picture

- Whether you want to work in color or black and white

## Choosing a Background Color or Pattern

A new Paint document always uses white as its background color. To make the background anything other than white, click your selection in the color palette. Then click the Fill With Color tool and click the canvas.

## Establishing the Size and Shape of Your Picture

Just as a word processing document can extend beyond a single screen, the actual size of your picture might be larger or smaller than what you see in Paint's drawing area.

To specify the dimensions of your picture, choose Attributes from the Image menu. You'll see a dialog box like the one shown in Figure 34-3.

**FIGURE 34-3.**

The Attributes dialog box sets the size and colors for your picture.

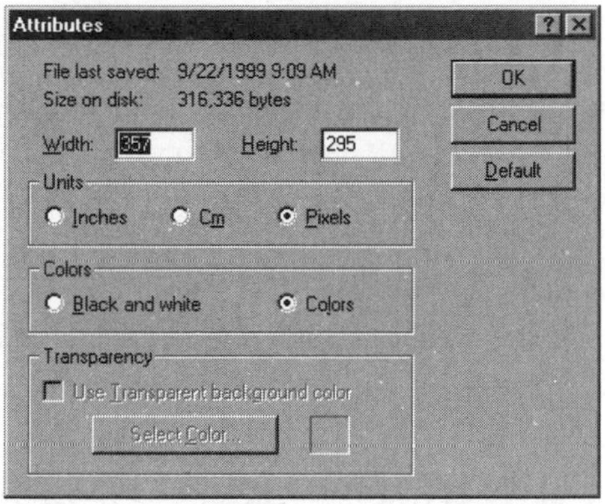

Specify the width and height you want for your picture, in whatever units you find most convenient to work with. You can use inches, centimeters, or pixels. (A *pixel* is a single dot of information on your display.)

To revert to the default size for your screen's resolution, click the Default button.

> **NOTE**
>
> Paint allows you to change the image size at any time—even after you've begun painting. However, if you reduce the picture size so that part of the image gets cropped, that part of the image won't be restored if you later enlarge the picture. (You can recover it by using the Undo command. *See "Making Quick Fixes with Undo and Repeat," page 717.*)

## Choosing Color or Black and White

The Attributes dialog box is also the place where you decide whether your image will be in black and white or color.

When making this choice, you should consider the medium in which you're most likely to generate your new image. Color is unquestionably more interesting to work with than black and white, but if you're going to print your image on a black-and-white printer, you'll get better control of the final product by working in black and white.

> **NOTE**
>
> You can change the setting of the Colors section of the Attributes dialog box at any time—even after you've begun painting. If you switch from Colors to Black And White, all colors in your image change to black or white. Be sure this is what you want before you proceed, for the Undo command does *not* restore colors that have been converted this way.

# Seeing the Larger Picture

Figure 34-4 shows a picture that's considerably larger than the drawing area of Paint's window. Paint offers three ways to see more of a large picture. You can

- Use the View Bitmap command.

- Remove the toolbox, color box, and status bar.

- Use the scroll bars to bring other parts of the picture into view.

**FIGURE 34-4.**

Paint can create and edit a picture that's larger than the drawing area.

## Using the View Bitmap Command

The View Bitmap command, on the View menu, temporarily removes all elements from the screen except your picture, giving it the maximum possible space, as you can see in Figure 34-5. If your picture is smaller than your screen, Paint centers the picture on the screen. If your picture is larger than the screen, Paint places the upper left corner of the image from the drawing area in the upper left corner of the screen.

> **NOTE**
>
> If you have more than one monitor *(for details, see "Extending Your Desktop Across Two or More Monitors," page 61)*, the View Bitmap command always displays your picture (or the portion of it that fits) only on the primary display, regardless of where the Paint window appears. You can continue to work in other windows on displays other than the primary display.

**FIGURE 34-5.**
The View Bitmap command removes all extraneous screen clutter.

After you use this command, your very next keystroke or mouse click returns the display to its previous state (unless you're working in another window on a different display), so you can't do any work with your picture in this mode. It's a useful command, though, when you want to see those parts of your picture that lie just off the screen.

 **TIP**

The keyboard shortcut to the View Bitmap command is Ctrl+F. After pressing Ctrl+F, press any key to return to the normal display.

## Removing the Toolbox, Color Box, and Status Bar

To give your picture as much breathing room as possible and still be able to work with it, use the Tool Box, Color Box, and Status Bar commands on the View menu. Removing the toolbox extends the drawing area to the left edge of Paint's program window. Removing the color box extends the drawing area to just above the status bar. Removing the status bar extends the drawing area to the bottom of Paint's program window.

All three commands are toggles. Choose Tool Box once, for example, to make the toolbox go away. Choose it again to make it reappear.

 **TIP**

The keyboard shortcut for toggling the toolbox on or off is Ctrl+T. To toggle the color box on or off, press Ctrl+L.

**IX**

**Using Accessory Programs**

## Moving Around on a Large Canvas

Paint displays scroll bars whenever the entire picture won't fit in the drawing area. Use the scroll bars to move to a different part of a large picture. For example, the right side of a large picture comes into view with just a couple of clicks on the horizontal scroll bar, as you can see in Figure 34-6.

**FIGURE 34-6.**

By scrolling to the right, you can see that this picture has more people than at first appeared.

# Precise Pointer Positioning

For certain kinds of work in Paint, it's helpful to know precisely where the mouse pointer is or how large an object is as you're drawing it. This information could be useful if, for example, you're trying to draw two vertical lines of exactly the same length. The numbers that are displayed toward the right side of Paint's status bar whenever the mouse pointer is in the drawing area give you pointer position information, which you can use for that purpose.

In Figure 34-7, the numbers on the far right end of the status bar indicate the size of the object being drawn. The first of the two size numbers shows how much horizontal space the object occupies. The second number shows the vertical space.

While you're drawing an object, the numbers just to the left of the size numbers (the pointer position numbers) indicate the mouse pointer position where you began. After you release the mouse button, those numbers show the location of the pointer.

**FIGURE 34-7.**
The size and position of the rectangle are shown on the right side of the status bar.

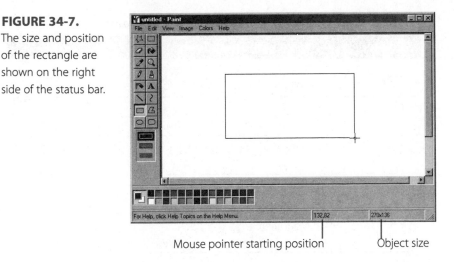

Mouse pointer starting position          Object size

These numbers are expressed in pixels. A pixel is the smallest increment by which you can move the mouse pointer. So if the size numbers are, for example, 270×136, the object occupies 270 horizontal pixels and 136 vertical pixels.

The pointer position numbers to the left of the size numbers represent the offset from the upper left edge of the picture. For example, the number pair 132, 82 means 132 pixels from the left and 82 pixels from the top edge of the picture.

> **NOTE**
>
> The position numbers are always visible on the status bar as you move the mouse pointer over the drawing area. The size numbers, however, are visible only while you're drawing an object.

# Understanding the Pointer Shapes

The drawing or editing tool you use determines the mouse pointer's shape. Paint's default tool is the Pencil, and the pointer shape corresponding to that tool is the pencil shape. At other times during your work in Paint, it won't be quite so clear from the pointer shape which tool you've selected. Table 34-1, on the next page, shows the variety of pointer shapes Paint uses.

**TABLE 34-1. Mouse Pointer Shapes Used in Paint**

| Pointer | Used with These Tools |
|---|---|
| | Free-Form Select, Select, Text, Line, Curve, Rectangle, Polygon, Ellipse, Rounded Rectangle |
| | Eraser |
| | Fill With Color |
| | Pick Color |
| | Magnifier |
| | Pencil |
| | Brush |
| | Airbrush |

When you work with text in Paint, the mouse pointer is replaced by an insertion point and an I-beam. These look and function exactly like the insertion point and I-beam in WordPad and other text-processing programs.

# Exploring the Toolbox

To use a tool in Paint, you simply click its icon in the toolbox. Paint's toolbox includes the sixteen tools shown in Table 34-2.

**TABLE 34-2. Paint Tools**

| Tool | Description |
|---|---|
| | The Free-Form Select tool selects an irregularly shaped cutout. (A *cutout* is a selection that can be cut, copied, moved, and manipulated in a variety of other ways. *See "Working with Cutouts," page 733*.) |
| | The Select tool selects a rectangular cutout. |

**TABLE 34-2.** *continued*

| Tool | Description |
|------|-------------|
| | The Eraser tool erases portions of an object from a picture. |
| | The Fill With Color tool fills enclosed shapes with the foreground or background color. |
| | The Pick Color tool changes the foreground or background color to match the color in another part of the picture. |
| | The Magnifier tool zooms in on portions of the picture. |
| | The Pencil tool draws free-form lines. |
| | The Brush tool draws free-form lines using a variety of brush shapes. |
| | The Airbrush tool creates "spray paint" effects. |
| | The Text tool adds text to a picture. |
| | The Line tool draws straight lines. |
| | The Curve tool draws smooth curves. |
| | The Rectangle tool draws rectangles and squares. |
| | The Polygon tool draws irregular closed shapes. |
| | The Ellipse tool draws ellipses and circles. |
| | The Rounded Rectangle tool draws rectangles and squares with rounded corners. |

You might think of the Free-Form Select, Select, Eraser, Pick Color, and Magnifier tools as editing tools and the rest as drawing tools. We'll look at the drawing tools first and then examine the editing tools.

# Using Paint's Drawing Tools

Paint provides 11 drawing tools that let you apply paint to your canvas.

## Free-Form Drawing with the Pencil Tool

The Pencil tool is the default drawing tool when you start Paint. To draw using the foreground color with the Pencil, move the mouse pointer into the drawing area, press the left mouse button, and drag. (To draw using the background color, use the right mouse button.)

### Drawing Straight Lines

If you want to draw perfectly straight vertical, horizontal, or 45-degree diagonal lines with the Pencil tool, hold down the Shift key while you draw. *For more information about drawing straight lines, see "Drawing Straight Lines with the Line Tool," on the next page.*

## Free-Form Drawing with the Brush Tool

The Brush tool works like the Pencil tool except that you can choose from a variety of brush shapes.

When you select the Brush tool, the available brush shapes appear in the box just below the toolbox. Click the brush shape you want to select it. The mouse pointer shape changes to reflect the brush shape you choose.

If you're adept at calligraphy, try one of the diagonal shapes. They allow you to paint with thick and thin brush strokes.

To draw with the Brush, hold down the left mouse button (to draw using the foreground color) or the right mouse button (to draw using the background color) and drag.

The Brush tool is primarily intended for free-form drawing. If you want to draw straight lines, it's best to use the Line or Pencil tool.

## Spray Painting with the Airbrush Tool

The Airbrush tool deposits a circular pattern of dots. To use it, click the Airbrush tool and then click one of the three spray sizes that appear below the toolbox. Move the mouse pointer to the drawing area, hold down the left mouse button (to draw using the foreground color) or the right mouse button (to draw using the background color) and drag.

Like a real can of spray paint, the slower you drag the mouse, the denser the spray; the faster you drag, the lighter the spray.

## Drawing Straight Lines with the Line Tool

The Line tool creates straight lines. To draw a line, click the Line tool and then choose the line width from the choices that appear below the toolbox. Move the mouse pointer to the drawing area and hold down the left mouse button (to draw using the foreground color) or the right mouse button (to draw using the background color) and drag.

> **Drawing at 90-Degree or 45-Degree Angles**
> To draw perfectly straight vertical, horizontal, or diagonal lines, hold down the Shift key while you drag. Using the Shift key to create lines will eliminate—or at least reduce—the jagged edges that lines at other angles sometimes have.

## Drawing Curved Lines with the Curve Tool

The Curve tool lets you create a line with two curves in it. To draw a curved line:

**1**  Click the Curve tool.

**2**  Click one of the line width choices that appear below the toolbox.

**3**  Position the mouse pointer in the drawing area at the place where you want the curve to begin, hold down either mouse button and drag to where you want the curved line to end, and then release the mouse button.

   At this point you have a straight line.

**4**  Move the mouse pointer near the part of the line you want to bend. Hold down either mouse button and drag in the direction you want the line to curve.

   Now you have a line with one curve.

**5**  To add a second bend, repeat step 4. Use the left mouse button if you want the curve to appear in the foreground color or the right mouse button if you want it to appear in the background color.

It might take some practice to get used to the behavior of the Curve tool. If your curve isn't shaping up the way you want, click both mouse buttons (or the Curve tool in the toolbox) any time before finishing the second bend to delete the line, and then start over.

IX

Using Accessory Programs

## Drawing Rectangles and Squares with the Rectangle Tool

To create rectangles and squares, use the Rectangle tool. Click the Rectangle tool, and then choose the rectangle type from the three choices below the toolbox:

- The first rectangle type lets you draw the outline of the rectangle using the foreground or background color.

- The second type lets you draw the outline in either the foreground or background color with the interior filled in with the other color.

- The third type lets you draw a solid rectangle filled with the background or foreground color, without a border.

> **Setting the Border Width**
> To set the line width for the border of a rectangle, rounded rectangle, ellipse, or polygon, click the Line tool and select a line width before you click the Rectangle, Rounded Rectangle, Ellipse, or Polygon tool.

After choosing the rectangle type, move to the drawing area, and then hold down the left mouse button (to use the foreground color for the rectangle's outline) or the right button (to use the background color) and drag diagonally to create the rectangle.

**TIP**

> You can create a perfect square by holding down the Shift key while you drag.

## Drawing Rectangles with Rounded Corners

To draw rectangles with rounded corners, use the Rounded Rectangle tool. The Rounded Rectangle tool works exactly the same as the regular Rectangle tool except that it produces rounded corners.

## Drawing Ellipses and Circles with the Ellipse Tool

To create ellipses (ovals) or circles, use the Ellipse tool. The Ellipse tool works much like the Rectangle tool described above. After selecting the tool, you choose a type—outline only, filled outline, or solid, just as with the rectangles. Then put the mouse pointer where you want the corner of an imaginary rectangle that will contain your figure.

Hold down the left mouse button (to use the foreground color for the ellipse's outline) or the right mouse button (to use the background color) and drag to expand the figure. When the figure reaches the desired size, release the mouse button.

⭐ **TIP**

> To create a perfect circle, hold down the Shift key while dragging.

## Drawing Irregular Closed Shapes with the Polygon Tool

To create any kind of closed shape other than a rectangle, square, ellipse, or circle, use the Polygon tool. With this tool, you can draw as many straight-line segments as you want. Each segment begins where the last one ended. When you double-click, Paint closes the polygon by connecting the end of your last line segment with the beginning of your first.

You can create anything from simple triangles to complex shapes with overlapping lines. To create a polygon:

1 Click the Polygon tool.

2 Choose the polygon type from the three choices below the toolbox: outline only, filled outline, or solid.

3 Move the mouse pointer to the beginning of the first line segment. Hold down the left mouse button (to use the foreground color for the polygon's outline) or the right mouse button (to use the background color) and drag to the end of the first line segment.

4 Move the mouse pointer to the place where you want the next line segment to end and click using the same mouse button.

   Paint draws a new line segment from the end of the first line.

5 Repeat step 4 until the mouse pointer is at the end of the next-to-last line segment you want, and then double-click.

⭐ **TIP**

> To create perfect vertical, horizontal, or diagonal line segments, hold down the Shift key while creating each segment.

## Using the Fill With Color Tool to Fill an Enclosed Shape

The Fill With Color tool allows you to fill any enclosed portion of your picture with the current foreground or background color.

To use the Fill With Color tool, click it in the toolbox, and then position the mouse pointer over the area in the picture you want to fill. Click the left mouse button to fill the area with the foreground color, or click the right mouse button to fill the area with the background color.

Note that if the area you want to fill has any gaps—even a gap of a single pixel—the color will leak through the gap. If that happens, use the Undo command, and then patch the leak and try again. To patch a very small leak, you might want to use the Zoom command. *For information about the Zoom command, see "Fine-Tuning Your Image with Zoom," page 739.*

## Adding Text with the Text Tool

Paint's Text tool is a special kind of implement. You don't really *draw* with this tool; instead, you choose a typeface, style, and point size, and then type characters from the keyboard (or paste them from the Clipboard). Nevertheless, after you've completed your text entry, the text behaves just like any other part of your picture.

The general procedure for adding text is as follows:

1 Select the Text tool.

2 Drag diagonally to create a rectangular text frame about the size you want for your text.

 An insertion point—like the one in a word processing program—appears inside the frame to let you know where your text will appear.

⭐ **TIP**

> **Placing Text Over an Opaque Background**
> By default, text frames are transparent—text appears in the foreground color and the frame's background is "clear," allowing the image underneath to show through. This can be a problem if you're adding text on top of a colored background. Black text on a black background, for example, isn't legible. To use the color box's background color for your text frame's background color, click the icon for the opaque option (just below the toolbox). The text frame is filled with the selected background color.

**3** Type your text or choose Paste from the Edit menu.

For more information about formatting text, see Chapter 13, "Installing and Using Fonts."

**4** Change text attributes using the Fonts toolbar, shown below, which appears when you create a text frame. (If the Fonts toolbar isn't visible, choose Text Toolbar from the View menu.) You can select a font, size, and style (bold, italic, underlined, or a combination).

**5** Click outside the text frame or select another tool from the toolbox to confirm the text entry.

Until you confirm the text entry by clicking outside the frame or by choosing another tool, you can edit the text or change the font, size, or style of the text. However, once you confirm the text entry, you can't do any text editing other than erasing or using the Undo command and starting over.

**Moving the Text Frame**
Before you confirm the text entry, you can move the text frame. To do so, move the mouse pointer to any edge of the frame; the pointer changes to a standard pointer arrow. Then drag the frame where you want it. You can also make the frame larger if you run out of text space. Point to one of the resizing handles (the solid boxes along each side of the frame) and drag outward.

# Using Paint's Editing Tools

The editing tools in Paint's toolbox let you clean up your drawing as well as select or view part of it for further manipulation.

## Using the Eraser Tool to Clean Up Mistakes

For information about erasing a large area of your drawing, see "Erasing a Cutout," page 738.

The Eraser tool lets you "erase" anything in the drawing area by simply dragging the mouse over the portion of the object you want to remove. What the eraser is really doing, however, is painting with the current background color. So, if you have a black object—text, rectangle, whatever—on a white background, dragging the Eraser tool over any of the black portions of the object appears to erase them, but it's really just "whitewashing" them to match the white background.

**IX**

**Using Accessory Programs**

To use the Eraser tool, click the Eraser icon in the toolbox, and then select from one of the four eraser sizes that appear below the toolbox. Finally, position the mouse pointer where you want to start erasing, hold down the left mouse button, and drag.

> **Erasing a Single Color**
> Right-dragging the Eraser tool erases (applies the current background color to) only the portions of the drawing area that are in the current foreground color. Set the foreground color to match the color of the object you want to erase, and nothing else in the drawing will be disturbed.

## Selecting a Color with the Pick Color Tool

The Pick Color tool lets you change the foreground or background in the color box to the color of any object in your drawing. To change the foreground color, click the Pick Color tool, and then click the object or area in your drawing that's drawn in the color you want to use as your new foreground color. To change the background color, click the Pick Color tool, and then right-click the object or area in your drawing that's drawn in the color you want to use as your new background color.

## Using the Magnifier Tool

For more information about magnified views, see "Fine-Tuning Your Image with Zoom," page 739.

Using the Magnifier tool, you can zoom in to a specific portion of your drawing or magnify the entire image. To magnify a particular area of the drawing, click the Magnifier tool. Move the pointer—which assumes the shape of a large rectangle—over the portion of the drawing you want to enlarge, and then click. Paint magnifies the drawing and places the portion of the drawing area that the rectangle pointer was over at the center of the drawing area. To return to normal, unmagnified view, click the Magnifier tool again, and then click anywhere in the drawing area.

If you want to enlarge the image by a factor of 2, 6, or 8, click the Magnifier tool, and then click 2×, 6×, or 8× just below the toolbox. You can return the drawing area to normal size by clicking the Magnifier tool, and then clicking the 1× choice just below the toolbox.

Paint remembers the last magnification you used and uses that factor as its default the next time you use the Magnifier tool to select an area to be enlarged.

### Defining Cutouts with the
### Free-Form Select Tool and the Select Tool

The Free-Form Select and Select tools at the top of the toolbox are used for specifying *cutouts*—selected areas of the drawing that can be manipulated in various ways. *See "Working with Cutouts," below.*

Using the Free-Form Select tool, you can define any portion of any shape in the drawing area as a cutout. The Free-Form Select tool is particularly useful when you want to select an irregularly shaped object and don't want to include any of the surrounding canvas. Using the Select tool, you can define a rectangular-shaped cutout.

To use the Free-Form Select tool, start by clicking the Free-Form Select tool icon. Then position the mouse pointer somewhere along the edge of the object you want to select. Hold down the left mouse button and then drag around the object. You draw a solid line as you drag the mouse. When you have the object completely surrounded, release the mouse button. (You don't actually have to close the selection. When you release the mouse button, Paint connects the current pointer position to the place where you started.) When you release the mouse button, Paint displays a dotted rectangular line around the object you've selected.

When the object you want to select is rectangular, or when it doesn't matter whether you select a bit of background canvas along with the object, the Select tool is the best way to go.

To use the Select tool, position the mouse pointer at one corner of the object you want to select, and then drag to the opposite corner.

# Working with Cutouts

**? SEE ALSO**

For information about defining a cutout, see "Defining Cutouts with the Free-Form Select Tool and the Select Tool," above.

After you've defined a cutout, you can do any of the following with it:

- Cut it to the Clipboard
- Copy it to the Clipboard
- Copy it to a separate disk file
- Move it to another place within the current picture
- Copy it to another place within the current picture

- Sweep it across your picture, leaving a trail of copies in its wake

- Change its size or shape

- Stretch (distort) or skew (slant) it

- Flip or rotate it

- Reverse its colors

- Erase it

**⭐ TIP**

> The easiest way to perform most cutout operations is to select a command from the cutout's shortcut menu. After you define a cutout, right-click it to display its shortcut menu.

## Cutting or Copying a Cutout to the Clipboard

To put your cutout on the Clipboard, choose Cut or Copy from the Edit menu (or from the shortcut menu that appears when you right-click the selection). If you choose Cut, Paint removes it from the current picture and transfers it to the Clipboard. If you choose Copy, Paint puts a copy of the cutout on the Clipboard and leaves the current picture unchanged.

---

### Linking and Embedding Cutouts

The Paint program can be a source for linked objects. That means that pictures created or edited in Paint can be linked or embedded in documents created by programs that can create compound documents, such as WordPad, Microsoft Excel, or Microsoft Word. *For information about linking and embedding, see Appendix D, "Cutting, Pasting, Embedding, and Linking."*

---

When you use the Cut command to put the cutout on the Clipboard, the area of the picture that was occupied by the cutout assumes the current background color. If you want the area to look like the blank canvas after the cutout is removed, be sure the current background matches your initial background color.

## Copying a Cutout to a Disk File

**? SEE ALSO**

For information about the Save As dialog box, see "Saving and Opening Paint Documents," page 716.

You can copy a cutout to a separate disk file, thereby creating a new Paint document. It's a good idea to do this if you want to use the cutout in different pictures.

To save the cutout to a new document, choose Copy To from the Edit menu or the cutout's shortcut menu and fill out the Save As dialog box that appears.

# Pasting a Cutout from the Clipboard

To paste a cutout from the Clipboard, choose Paste from the Edit menu. Your cutout appears in the upper left corner of the drawing area surrounded by a dotted line. At this point, you can drag it to any part of the drawing area, or you can manipulate it in any of the other ways described in the following sections.

Note that pasting in Paint is a bit different from pasting in other programs. In a word processor, for example, you first position the insertion point where you want the contents of the Clipboard pasted, and then choose Paste. In Paint, you paste first, and then you position the pasted object.

**> NOTE**

> Paint handles Clipboard text differently from graphics. When you paste text from the Clipboard, you must position the insertion point first, and then choose the Paste command.

# Pasting from a Disk File

To paste a cutout that was saved as a separate disk file, open the Edit menu, choose Paste From, and then choose the file you want from the Open dialog box that appears. This dialog box is the same as the one that appears when you choose Open from the File menu.

When you choose Paste From, the cutout appears in the upper left corner of the drawing area, just as when you paste from the Clipboard.

**★ TIP**

> If you want to place the contents of a saved cutout somewhere other than the drawing area's upper left corner, you can drag it after you choose Paste From. But there's an easier way: use the Select tool to define a cutout *before* you choose Paste From, and the saved cutout is then pasted into the upper left corner of the selected cutout.

## Moving a Cutout

To move a cutout from one place to another, position the mouse pointer anywhere within the dotted line (the pointer changes to a four-headed arrow), and then drag. When you move a cutout, the portion of the picture you move the cutout onto is obscured by the cutout object.

## Copying a Cutout Within a Picture

To make a duplicate of a cutout, position the cursor within the dotted area surrounding the cutout and hold down the Ctrl key while dragging the mouse. The original cutout remains where it was and a duplicate appears where you release the mouse button.

## Sweeping a Cutout

To *sweep* a cutout means to create a trail of copies with it as you pass the mouse across the canvas. Figure 34-8 shows an object that has been swept across the canvas.

**FIGURE 34-8.**

Sweeping can be useful, or it can just make a mess.

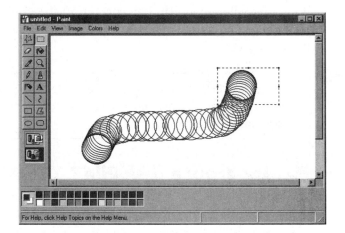

To sweep a cutout, first move the cutout where you want to begin the sweep. Then position the cursor within the dotted area and hold down the Shift key while dragging.

The speed at which you drag the mouse determines the number of copies that result from the sweep.

⭐ **TIP**

Most often you will want to select the icon for transparent drawing below the toolbox. Otherwise, each new image in the sweep obscures part of the image that preceded it.

> **This Ought to Clear Things Up**
>
> Cutouts can be moved, copied, or swept either opaquely or transparently. When you move, copy, or sweep a cutout opaquely (the default), any background portions of the cutout are moved, copied, or swept along with the foreground material and can obscure another object that the cutout lands on. If you move, copy, or sweep a cutout transparently, any parts of the cutout that are in the current background color disappear, allowing the underlying image to show through. To select transparent operations so the background won't obscure other parts of the drawing, clear the check mark from the Draw Opaque command on the Options menu, or click the draw transparent icon below the toolbox (the bottom icon).
>
> The opaque and transparent options also control the background of a text box when you use the Text tool.

## Resizing a Cutout

You can change the size of a cutout horizontally, vertically, or both. To change the size of a cutout, position the mouse pointer over one of the handles in the dotted rectangle surrounding the cutout. There are eight handles—one in each corner and one in the middle of each side.

When the mouse pointer is correctly positioned, it assumes the shape of a double-headed arrow. If it's on a corner handle, the arrow is diagonal and you can size vertically and horizontally at the same time.

## Stretching and Skewing a Cutout

To adjust a cutout with absolute precision, choose Stretch/Skew from the Image menu to display the Stretch And Skew dialog box, as shown in Figure 34-9, on the next page. Using this dialog box, you can alter the size of the cutout either horizontally or vertically by specifying a percentage greater or smaller than its original 100 percent. You can skew the cutout horizontally or vertically by specifying the number of degrees to skew.

To change the size of a cutout, enter the percentage in the appropriate text box. For example, to double the vertical size of a cutout, enter 200 in the Vertical text box.

To skew the cutout, enter the number of degrees to skew. Use a positive number to skew the cutout in the direction of the icon in the dialog box, or a negative number to skew the cutout in the opposite direction.

**IX**

**Using Accessory Programs**

## Flipping or Rotating a Cutout

Using the Image menu's Flip/Rotate command, you can flip any image vertically or horizontally, or rotate it 90, 180, or 270 degrees. To flip or rotate a cutout, choose Flip/Rotate from the Image menu; the Flip And Rotate dialog box appears. Select the Flip Horizontal, Flip Vertical, or Rotate By Angle option. If you select Rotate By Angle, you must also select one of the angle options. Finally, click OK.

## Reversing the Colors of a Cutout

The Image menu's Invert Colors command reverses the colors of your cutout. Black becomes white, white becomes black, and colors switch to their complementary color on the red-green-blue color wheel.

Inverting color can give unexpected, and sometimes unwanted, results. Just remember that you can use the Undo command if the new colors aren't what you had in mind.

## Erasing a Cutout

You can erase a large area by defining it as a cutout and then choosing the Clear Selection command from the Edit menu or the cutout's short-cut menu. Like the Cut command *(see "Cutting or Copying a Cutout to the Clipboard," page 734)*, this command removes the cutout and re-places it with the current background color. However, it doesn't move the cutout to the Clipboard, so if you want to leave the Clipboard contents unchanged, use the Clear Selection command.

# Fine-Tuning Your Image with Zoom

Paint stores images you create as *bitmaps*, which record the position and color of each pixel in the picture.

You might not normally be aware of separate pixels as you create and modify your Paint images. But, when you want to see and edit the image pixel by pixel, Paint can accommodate you.

Simply choose Zoom from the View menu, and then choose Large Size from the Zoom submenu. The image appears enlarged with a small section of the picture shown in "real size" in a small window in the upper left corner of the drawing area, as shown in Figure 34-10. The small window is called a *thumbnail*. (If the thumbnail doesn't appear, choose Show Thumbnail from the Zoom submenu.)

**FIGURE 34-10.**

In Zoom view, every pixel is visible.

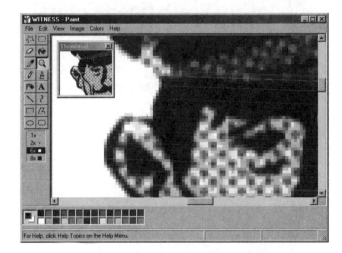

**TIP**

To make it easier to edit in the zoomed-in view, choose Show Grid from the Zoom submenu. This shows each pixel in its own square.

To specify a zoom percentage, choose Zoom from the View menu, and then choose Custom to display the Custom Zoom dialog box. The dialog box lets you choose zoom percentages of 100%, 200%, 400%, 600%, or 800%.

You can also specify a zoom percentage using the Magnifier tool. Click the Magnifier tool in the toolbox, and then click 1×, 2×, 6×, or 8× just below the toolbox.

You can perform any of the normal picture creation and editing maneuvers while you're zoomed in. One of the more useful tools is the Pencil because you can manipulate one pixel at a time. You can click to paint a single pixel, or drag to draw in the usual way.

# Editing Colors

For most of your day-to-day painting needs, the standard set of 28 colors or patterns that appear in the default color box are more than adequate. However, when the creative need arises, Paint lets you replace any of the standard colors by choosing from a group of 48 predefined colors or by creating almost any custom colors you can imagine.

## Choosing Predefined Colors

To replace one of the colors in the color box with any of the 48 pre-defined colors, click the color you want to replace, and then choose Edit Colors from the Colors menu to display the Edit Colors dialog box shown in Figure 34-11. Alternatively, just double-click the color.

**FIGURE 34-11.**

The Edit Colors dialog box gives you additional colors to splash on your palette.

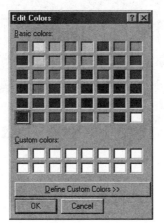

In the Basic Colors group, click the color you want to use as the selected color's replacement, and then click OK. The color you originally selected is replaced in the color box with the new color. Repeat the process to replace as many of the default colors as you want.

The default color set will reappear the next time you start Paint.

# Adding Custom Colors

**? SEE ALSO**

For more information about using the Edit Colors dialog box, see "Defining Custom Colors," page 65.

When none of the 48 predefined colors will do, you can create virtually any color in the rainbow and add it to your color palette. To create a custom color, click the color in the color box that you want to replace with the custom color, and then choose Edit Colors from the Colors menu. When the Edit Colors dialog box appears, click the Define Custom Colors button to expand the dialog box, as shown in Figure 34-12.

**FIGURE 34-12.**

The expanded Edit Colors dialog box lets you create custom colors.

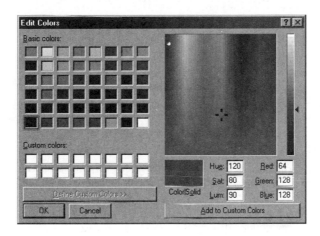

Drag the cross-hair pointer in the large color box and the luminosity pointer along the vertical color swatch at the right until the color you want to use as a new color appears in the Color|Solid box. (Or you can enter numeric values in the Hue, Sat, and Lum, or Red, Green, and Blue text boxes.) Then click the Add To Custom Colors button. The new color is added to the first empty square in the Custom Colors portion of the dialog box. The new color replaces the original color you selected in the color box when you click the OK button.

**> NOTE**

Before leaving the Edit Colors dialog box, you can create as many as 16 custom colors, which you can use to replace colors in the color box, as described in the previous section.

IX

Using Accessory Programs

# Ⓑ Scanning Images

If you have a scanner installed, you can scan images directly into Paint instead of drawing from scratch. You can then use Paint to touch up your scanned images before saving them.

To scan an image:

**1** Open the File menu and choose Select Source to display a dialog box similar to the one shown below.

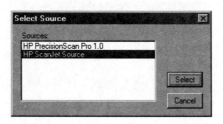

The Select Source dialog box lists all the scanners you have installed. *For information about installing a scanner, see "Installing and Configuring a Scanner or Camera," page 525.*

**2** Select the scanner device you want and click Select.

**3** Open the File menu and choose Scan New.

A dialog box specific to your scanner appears.

**4** From the scanner dialog box that appears, set your scan options and use its controls to scan the image.

**5** Close the dialog box to return to Paint, where you'll see your newly scanned image.

# Making Wallpaper

Printing your pictures on paper isn't the only way to use your Paint creations. You can also use them as Windows wallpaper—the background for your desktop. If you already have a Paint image saved on your computer's hard disk, you can use the Display Properties dialog box to choose it as your wallpaper. However, there's an easier way to use the current Paint image as wallpaper without using the Display Properties dialog box at all.

**NOTE**

You can use a Paint image as your desktop wallpaper only if you're *not* displaying Web content on your desktop. To disable Web content so you can display wallpaper, right-click the desktop, point to Active Desktop, and clear the check mark from Show Web Content. If there's no check mark next to Show Web Content, simply click anywhere else to close the shortcut menu; your desktop is ready to be wallpapered.

**SEE ALSO**

For information about using the Display Properties dialog box to apply wallpaper, see "Using Wallpaper," page 69.

Before you can use a Paint image as wallpaper, you must save it. Once the image is saved, choose Set As Wallpaper (Tiled) or Set As Wallpaper (Centered) from the File menu. The Tiled option displays as many copies of the picture as required to fill the screen. Centered uses one copy of the image—centered on the screen.

As soon as you choose one of the Set As Wallpaper commands, the image immediately becomes your wallpaper, although you won't be able to see it if Paint is maximized or if your desktop is covered with other programs.

**TIP**

Before you use a Set As Wallpaper command, you might want to move the wallpaper file to the folder in which your other wallpaper files are stored. This makes the file easier to find in case you ever change to another wallpaper file and then want to switch back. The default folder for wallpaper files is %SystemRoot%, which is C:\Winnt on most systems.

# Crunching Numbers

A mong its accessories, Microsoft Windows 2000 includes Calculator. This oft-overlooked tool won't replace your favorite spreadsheet program. But Calculator can replace the four-function handheld calculator that too frequently gets lost amidst the shuffle of papers on your desk—and then some. In addition to its convenience, Calculator offers other advantages over an inexpensive handheld calculator:

- Calculator offers 32-digit precision, which allows you to work with extremely large and extremely small numbers. Most inexpensive calculators can handle only 8 digits.

- Calculator can perform many scientific and statistical functions, which are usually available only in specialized handheld calculators.

- Calculator can work in binary, octal, and hexadecimal in addition to decimal, a feature that's usually available only in specialized calculators for programmers.

- You can copy results from Calculator to the Clipboard and then paste them in another application, saving time and reducing the likelihood of errors.

We don't mean to suggest that Calculator will be your most-used program, but if you haven't used it in awhile, it deserves another look.

# CHAPTER 35

# Switching Between Standard View and Scientific View

To start Calculator, open the Start menu and choose Programs, Accessories, Calculator. Calculator has two operating modes. You can use it as a standard arithmetic calculator with memory buttons, in which case it looks like this:

Or you can use it as a scientific calculator, in which case it looks like this:

To switch from one mode to the other, open the View menu and choose Standard or Scientific.

Calculator clears the display when you switch from one mode to the other, but it retains any value in its memory register.

In both standard and scientific modes, Calculator can operate precisely on numbers with up to 32 digits. With less accuracy, it can handle much larger (and smaller) numbers, which Calculator displays using scientific notation. (*Scientific notation* expresses numbers as the product of a number times a power of 10, with the letter *e* separating the two numbers. For example, 3.32e6 is scientific notation for 3,320,000— or 3.32 times $10^6$.)

# Entering Numbers and Symbols into Calculator

You can enter numbers and symbols either by clicking them with the mouse or by typing them at the keyboard. For example, to have Calculator compute the sum of two and two, you could:

**1**  Click 2.

**2**  Click the plus sign (in the lower right corner of the standard-mode window).

**3**  Click 2.

**4**  Click the equal sign (right next to the plus sign).

Or you could type:

    2+2=

Try experimenting with both methods to see what works best for you.

If you're adept at typing numbers, you'll probably find it quicker to enter numbers at the keyboard. To get the result of a calculation, you can press either the Enter key or =. You'll find the mouse convenient for entering such things as sqrt and 1/x. If you prefer to use the keyboard all the time, you can do so; the Calculator buttons all have keyboard equivalents. (Online help includes a handy table of keyboard equivalents.)

## Grouping Digits

Calculator normally displays large numbers as a simple string of digits. You can make the display more readable by choosing Digit Grouping from the View menu. This breaks up large numbers with commas when you use the decimal number system or spaces when you use the hexadecimal number system.

## Copying and Pasting with Calculator

Calculator can exchange numbers with other programs by way of the Windows Clipboard. If you choose the Copy command (on the Edit menu) in Calculator, whatever number Calculator is currently displaying is transferred to the Clipboard. If you choose the Edit menu's Paste command while in Calculator, the current contents of the Clipboard are transferred into Calculator character by character, as if you typed the characters at the keyboard.

# Using the Standard Calculator

The standard arithmetic calculator functions almost exactly like an inexpensive pocket calculator, except that you don't have to fumble around looking for it on your desk.

## Clearing and Correcting

If you make a mistake while entering a number, press Backspace or click the Backspace button. This will erase the last digit from the display; you can continue erasing a character at a time until you correct the error.

To clear the last entry in a sequence of numbers and arithmetic symbols, press Delete or click CE (clear entry). For example, if you're adding up a list of numbers and you make a mistake, simply click the CE button and reenter the last number; you don't have to start over.

To clear the current calculation entirely and return the display to a 0, press Esc or click C.

## Entering Numbers and Operators

The heart of Calculator's standard window is the ten-key pad. To the right and below the pad are all the basic arithmetic operators. Note that for division, you use the slash button (/), and for multiplication, you use the asterisk (*).

The sqrt button produces the square root of whatever number is in the display. To get the square root of 796.5, for example, enter *796.5* and click sqrt. You don't have to click the = button.

The % button lets you figure percentages. Let's say you wanted to figure the 8.75 percent sales tax on a $56.50 purchase. You would do the following:

**1** Enter *56.5* (with or without the trailing 0; it doesn't matter).

**2** Click the multiplication button (*).

**3** Enter *8.75*.

**4** Click the percentage operator (%).

Your sales tax will be 4.94375, or $4.94.

The 1/x button produces the reciprocal of whatever number Calculator is currently displaying. Entering *10* and then clicking 1/x, for example, will give you 0.1.

The +/- button changes the sign of the number currently on display. The typical use for this button is to enter a negative number in the middle of an arithmetic operation. For example, to multiply 52 times –23, you would:

**1** Enter *52*.

**2** Click the multiplication button.

**3** Enter *23*.

**4** Click the +/- button.

**5** Click =.

You'll get the result –1196.

Note that if you enter *52*, click the multiplication button, and then enter *–23* followed by =, you get a different result. Calculator treats the minus sign as a replacement for the multiplication operator and simply subtracts 23 from 52.

IX

Using Accessory Programs

# Using Calculator's Memory Feature

In both standard and scientific modes, Calculator has four memory buttons, marked MC, MR, MS, and M+. These provide a storage bin from which you can use a value repeatedly.

For example, suppose you want to divide each of a dozen numbers by the same factor—say, 0.01375. To spare yourself the drudgery of entering that factor in a dozen separate calculations, you could do this:

**1** Enter *.01375*.

**2** Click the MS (store in memory) button.

   Calculator stores the current value (0.01375) in its memory register and displays an M in a box directly above the memory buttons.

**3** Enter the first of your dozen numbers.

**4** Click the / button.

**5** Click the MR (recall from memory) button.

**6** Click =.

**7** Repeat steps 3 through 6 for each remaining number.

Here's what each memory button does:

- MS *stores* the currently displayed value in the memory register, replacing any value that might have been there before.

- M+ *adds* the value currently displayed to the value in the memory register.

- MR *recalls* the value currently in memory and enters it into the current calculation. The value remains in memory.

- MC *clears* the memory register. The M displayed above the memory buttons disappears.

# Using the Scientific Calculator

Calculator's scientific mode provides all the features of the standard calculator plus the following:

- Additional arithmetic operations

- Exponential and logarithmic operations

- Calculations in the binary, octal, and hexadecimal number systems

- Bitwise operations

- Trigonometric calculations

- The ability to open a statistics window, enter a sequence of numbers in that window, and calculate the numbers' sum, average, and standard deviation

## Order of Evaluation in the Scientific Calculator

In Calculator's standard mode, calculations are always performed in the order in which they're entered. If you type 4+5*6=, for example, Calculator displays 54, the result of adding 4 to 5 and multiplying the sum by 6.

This is not the case in Calculator's scientific mode. Here, the order in which an expression is evaluated depends on the operations involved. Multiplication and division, for example, are always performed before addition or subtraction. In the scientific calculator, therefore, the expression 4+5*6 returns 34, the result of adding 4 to the product of 5 times 6.

Fortunately, it isn't necessary to memorize Calculator's rules about operator precedence. You can simply watch Calculator's display as you enter your calculation. Whenever you type an operator (for example, +, *, or /), Calculator checks to see whether the operator you just entered has a higher precedence than the previous operator you entered. If it doesn't have a higher precedence, Calculator evaluates the last operation and displays an intermediate result. If it does have a higher precedence, no intermediate result is displayed.

For example, suppose you type the following in Calculator's scientific mode:

    4*5+

After you type the plus sign, Calculator, recognizing that addition has a lower precedence than multiplication, evaluates 4*5 and displays the intermediate result—20. If, on the other hand, you type

    4+5*

Calculator sees that your last operation, multiplication, has *higher* precedence than the previous one, addition. So, it *does not* display an intermediate result. Instead, it waits for your next number or numbers. If you follow the asterisk with

    6=

Calculator goes ahead and multiplies 5*6. Then it adds 4 to the result.

What if you need to override Calculator's normal order of operations? You can do that in either of two ways. In the case of 4+5*6, for example, you can simply click the = button after entering the 5. That forces Calculator to carry out the addition and display the intermediate result—9. Now you can complete the calculation by entering *6=.

Alternatively, you can enter parentheses before and after the operation you want Calculator to perform first. Expressions within parentheses are always evaluated immediately, regardless of what follows the closing parenthesis.

With that discussion of precedence out of the way, let's now take a tour of the scientific calculator's capabilities.

## Additional Arithmetic Operations

The scientific calculator offers these additional arithmetic operations not available in the standard calculator:

- The Mod button is a *modulus* operator. It returns the remainder of a division. For example, 65 mod 7 is 2 (because 65 divided by 7 equals 9, with a remainder of 2). To perform this calculation, you enter *65*, click the Mod button, enter 7, and then click the = button.

- The n! button returns the *factorial* of the currently displayed number. For example, if you enter 6 and then click the n! button, Calculator returns 720 (6 × 5 × 4 × 3 × 2 × 1).

- The ( (left parenthesis) and ) (right parenthesis) buttons allow you to nest calculations within calculations, in effect changing the order in which expressions are evaluated. You can nest up to 25 levels.

- The Int button (short for *integer*) strips the fractional component from the currently displayed number. For example, if you click Int when 456.789 is displayed, the display changes to 456. To strip the integer portion of a number, first select the Inv (inverse function) check box, and then click Int. The Int button works only when Calculator is using the decimal number system.

- The Exp (exponent) button lets you enter numbers in scientific notation. For example, to enter $6.4 \times 10^{-14}$ (which is displayed as 6.4e-14), you would enter *6.4*, click Exp, enter *14*, and then click +/-. The Exp button works only when Calculator is using the decimal number system.

- F-E toggles the display between normal (fixed) and scientific (exponential) notation. The F-E button works only when Calculator is using the decimal number system.

## Exponential and Logarithmic Operations

The scientific calculator offers these exponential and logarithmic functions:

- The x^y button lets you raise a number to any power. For example, to find the seventh power of 2, enter *2*, click x^y, enter *7*, and then click the = button.

- The x^3 button returns the cube of the currently displayed number.

- The x^2 button returns the square of the currently displayed number.

- The log button returns the common (base 10) logarithm of the currently displayed number.

- The ln button returns the natural (base $e$) logarithm of the currently displayed number.

The Inv check box, located along the left edge of the window, provides the inverse function of the above operations. First select Inv, and then click the function you want to use. After you use an inverse function, the Inv box clears automatically.

When the Inv check box is selected, x^y returns the yth root. For example, to find the seventh root of a number, enter the number, select Inv, click x^y, and then click 7. Similarly, the inverse of x^3 and x^2 return the cube root and square root, respectively, of a number. And the inverse of log and ln return 10 and $e$, respectively, raised to the power of a number.

# Hexadecimal, Octal, and Binary Number Systems

The Hex, Dec, Oct, and Bin options let you switch between the hexadecimal, decimal, octal, and binary number systems. If Calculator is displaying a number when you switch, it converts that number to the system you switch to. So, for example, if you want to know the octal equivalent of 123456 decimal, you can simply enter that number (be sure you're in decimal mode when you do), and then select Oct.

> **NOTE**
>
> In all number systems except decimal, Calculator works only with positive integers. When you switch from decimal to one of the other number systems, Calculator discards the fractional portion of the number, if any.

You can enter only those digits that are appropriate for the current number system. If you're in binary, for example, Calculator accepts only 0 and 1. If you're in hexadecimal, you can use the A through F buttons, as well as the numerals 0 through 9.

When you use the binary, octal, or hexadecimal number systems, you can select one of the options at the right side of the Calculator window to change the size of the value currently displayed. If the Qword option is selected, Calculator displays the full value of the current number, which can be up to 64 bits (16 digits in hexadecimal). If you switch to Dword, Calculator displays only the least significant 32 bits. Selecting Word displays only the least significant 16 bits, and selecting Byte displays only the least significant 8 bits.

# Bitwise Operations

The And, Or, Xor, and Not buttons perform logical bitwise operations on numbers in any number system, by internally converting the numbers to binary, performing the bitwise operation, and then displaying the answer in the selected number system.

The Lsh button shifts numbers left by the number of bits you specify. (For example, to shift the displayed number left by 4 bits, click Lsh, enter 4, and click =.) When the Inv check box is selected, Lsh shifts numbers the specified number of bits to the right.

# Trigonometric Functions

The sin, cos, and tan buttons return sine, cosine, and tangent, respectively. When the Inv check box is selected, they return arcsine, arccosine, and arctangent. For hyperbolic functions, first select the Hyp check box, and then the button for the function you want. The trigonometric functions are available only when you use the decimal number system.

The options on the right side of Calculator's window govern the way Calculator expects to see angles expressed. The default setting is Degrees, but you can switch to Radians or Grads.

To switch the displayed number from normal decimal format to degree-minute-second format, click dms. In degree-minute-second format, the degrees are to the left of the decimal point. The minutes are the first two digits to the right of the decimal point, and the seconds are to the right of the minutes. To switch back, select Inv, and then click dms.

Pressing the pi button enters the constant pi. A shortcut for entering $2\pi$ is to select Inv and then click pi.

# Statistical Functions

To calculate sums, averages, and standard deviations of groups of numbers, first click the Sta button. That opens a separate window in which you can enter as many numbers as you like. See Figure 35-1.

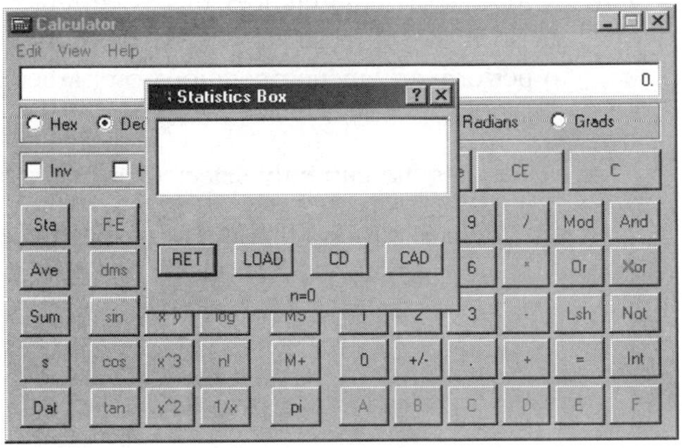

**FIGURE 35-1.**

The Statistics Box window collects values on which you can perform statistical calculations.

After the Statistics Box window opens, you'll want to move it to another part of the screen so that it doesn't overlap the main Calculator window. You'll be moving back and forth between the two windows, so it's helpful to be able to see both at once.

To enter numbers into the statistics box, enter the number in the main Calculator window, and then click the Dat button to move the displayed value to the statistics box.

When you have entered all the numbers you need to work with, you can perform the following calculations. The result will be displayed in the main Calculator window.

- **Sum.** Click the Sum button.

- **Sum of squares.** Select Inv and then click Sum.

- **Mean.** Click Ave.

- **Mean of squares.** Select Inv and then click Ave.

- **Sample standard deviation.** Click the s button. Calculator uses $n-1$ for the population parameter.

- **Population standard deviation.** Select Inv and then click s. Calculator uses $n$ for the population parameter.

The four buttons in the Statistics Box window do the following:

- RET activates the main Calculator window.

- LOAD displays the number that is currently highlighted in the statistics box in the main Calculator window. This makes it easy to perform arithmetic operations on particular values in the statistics box.

- CD deletes the currently selected number from the statistics box.

- CAD deletes all the numbers from the statistics box.

# Using the Multimedia Accessories

S ound and video can greatly enhance your computing experience. Some programs use multimedia to demonstrate concepts that aren't easily explained by using words alone. Others use multimedia to provide realistic simulations of faraway places. And multimedia has more mundane uses too. You can have your computer chirp to let you know that a new e-mail message has arrived, or you can watch full-length movies on your computer screen, for starters.

Most recent computers include at least the basic equipment necessary to take advantage of the multimedia capabilities in Microsoft Windows 2000. With the cost of multimedia hardware plummeting, it makes sense for most people to explore what multimedia can do for them.

Here are some things you can do with the multimedia tools provided by Windows:

- Add sounds to documents. For example, you can record spoken instructions for the users of a spreadsheet or a word processing document.

- Play DVD movies, games, or reference works on your DVD drive.

- Play audio CDs on your computer. You can certainly be more productive while listening to Beethoven or Pearl Jam. (Or, at any rate, you can have a better time.)

- Attach custom sounds to various Windows events.

- See an electronic encyclopedia come to life with movies of Neil Armstrong stepping onto the moon or Martin Luther King giving his "I Have a Dream" speech. Or watch an animation of the workings of a CD player.

- Play interactive multimedia games with lifelike sound, video, and animation.

---

### Multimedia Sound

When it comes to multimedia sound, there are two main varieties: wave (.wav) and MIDI (.mid) files. The primary advantage of wave files is that they can be faithfully reproduced on any multimedia computer system. Like an audio CD, a *wave file* is a recording of the sound. Of course the quality of the playback depends on the quality of the equipment, but a voice sounds pretty much like a voice and a piano like a piano, regardless of the equipment.

*MIDI files* are more like sheet music. Sheet music describes how the music should be played and which instruments should play which parts. If you give a piece of sheet music to two bands or orchestras, you'll get two different renditions. Because MIDI files only describe the music, they can be stored in a small fraction of the size of wave files. For this reason, many multimedia programs provide sounds in the MIDI format.

Fortunately, Windows supports the General MIDI standard that at least ensures that the correct instruments are used for playback of each part of the sound file. However, there is no guarantee that a voice or a piano will sound anything like a voice or a piano. That is determined by the MIDI capabilities on your computer's sound card.

MIDI files can be translated into real sounds by simulating the sounds with a process called FM (frequency modulation) synthesis, or by using samples of actual instruments (wave table synthesis).

FM synthesis produces sounds that are, at best, low-quality facsimiles of what the creators of the sounds intended. The route to realistic MIDI sounds is a sound card (or an add-on card) with wave-table synthesis, which uses samples of actual musical instruments to play sounds. The results are much closer to recordings of real music and can greatly enhance the listening experience.

# Playing Audio CDs with CD Player

Windows 2000 includes Microsoft CD Player, a deluxe CD player application that lets you play audio discs through your computer's sound card and speakers. As Figure 36-1 shows, this CD player has controls that look and work just like those of a traditional CD player. But the Windows player is a little smarter than most, because it can record and display disc titles, performers' names, and track titles along with the customary track-timing information.

**FIGURE 36-1.**

The Windows 2000 deluxe CD Player works just like the player on your stereo rack, but it's smarter.

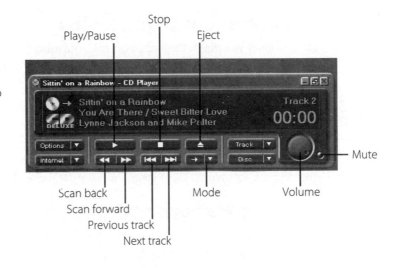

To play a disc, simply pop it into your CD or DVD drive. In a moment or two, CD Player will spring to life and go to work. To play a disc that's already in the drive, you can find and launch CD Player by opening the Start menu and choosing Programs, Accessories, Entertainment. (You can also choose Run from the Start menu and type *cdplayer.exe*.)

## The Internet Connection

When you first insert a CD, CD Player offers to download track names from the Internet for you. If you accept this offer, the system activates your Internet connection and polls a Web site such as Tunes.com to see if it has information about the disc you just loaded. If your disc is among the ones that this Web sites knows about, the site downloads title, artist, and track information, and this information becomes part of the album database maintained by CD Player. The title and artist then appear in CD Player's window, and you can see your disc's playlist by clicking the Track button.

IX

Using Accessory Programs

If the Web site doesn't have information about your disc, you can try a different Web site. To download CD information from a different Web site:

1 Click the Options button.

2 Choose Preferences.

3 Click the Album Options tab.

4 Choose a site from the Primary Provider list.

# Creating Your Own Playlist

If you can't get playlist information for your disc from the Internet (or if that information is incorrect), you can create or edit your own playlist:

1 Click the Options button.

2 Choose Playlist.

Choosing Playlist takes you to the Playlists tab of the Preferences dialog box. Here you'll find a hierarchical listing of all discs known to CD Player's album database. (See Figure 36-2.)

**FIGURE 36-2.**
CD Player's album database records title, performer, and track data for the discs you play.

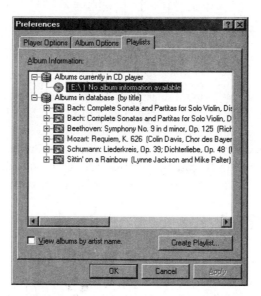

3 Select the entry subordinate to Albums Currently In CD Player.

4  Click Create Playlist. (This will say Edit Playlist if a playlist already exists for this disc.)

5  Type the disc's artist (or artists) and title on the Artist and Title lines.

6  In the Available Tracks box, select a track number and type its title. Continue in this manner until you've completed the playlist to your satisfaction.

   If you'd like to upload the information to the Internet so that music Web sites can consider adding it to their database, click the Internet Upload button when you're done.

However you create the playlist for this CD—by downloading it from the Internet or typing it in yourself—CD Player maintains it permanently in the album database. The next time you insert this disc in your player, the program fetches the playlist from your hard disk.

## Modifying the Playlist

CD Player can play your CD's tracks in random order (click the Mode button), but if you favor a particular nonstandard order, you can establish that playback order by rearranging the playlist. If the list contains tracks you never want to hear, you can remove them from the playlist. And if it contains tracks you want to hear more than once, you can create multiple playlist entries for them.

To reorder the playlist:

1  Click the Options button.

2  Choose Playlist.

3  Select the album whose playlist you want to reorder. (If the album isn't currently in your CD drive but is in the album database, expand the Albums In Database entry and select the album in the list that appears.)

4  Click the Edit Playlist button.

   The Playlist Editor appears.

**5** In the Playlist window, move track titles up or down by clicking the music symbols and dragging.

To remove a track from the playlist, select its name in the Playlist Editor and click the Remove button.

To add a second or subsequent instance of a track to the playlist:

**1** In the Playlist Editor's Available Tracks box (*not* in the Playlist box below it), choose the track you want to add.

**2** Click Add To Playlist.

**3** In the Playlist box, drag the new entry from the bottom of the list to the position you want.

⭐ **TIP**

> To restore the default playback order and any tracks you might have removed, click the Reset button in the Playlist Editor window.

## Playback Modes

To select a playback mode, click the Mode button (see Figure 36-1, page 759) and choose from the list. CD Player offers five modes: Standard, Random, Repeat Track, Repeat All, and Preview. In Standard mode, CD Player follows the order specified in your Playlist. In Preview mode, CD Player plays a sample—five seconds in length, by default—of each track in turn; when you get to one you want to hear, simply click the Play button. To increase or decrease the default preview Time, click Options, choose Preferences, and drag the Preview Time slider.

## Timing Display Options

CD Player offers four timing display options: track time elapsed (the default), track time remaining, CD time elapsed, and CD time remaining. To change the current timing display option, click Options, and then choose Preferences.

## Tiny View vs. Normal View

CD Player includes a *tiny view* option that shrinks the program's window to about a fifth of its normal size. You can still get to the program's most important controls in tiny view. To switch between tiny and normal views, click the button next to the Close button, in the upper right corner of the window (where the Maximize button appears in most application windows). Or click Options and choose from the ensuing menu.

You can also operate CD Player entirely from an icon in your taskbar status area. To use CD Player this way, first click Options and choose Preferences. On the Player Options tab, select the Show Control On Taskbar check box. Once the icon appears in your status area, you can simply click it to start or pause playback. To exercise other playback controls and options, right-click the icon.

# Playing DVD Movies

If your system is equipped with a supported DVD drive and decoder, the Windows 2000 Setup program automatically installs DVD Player. To play a DVD movie, simply insert the disc in your DVD drive. Your disc will start playing automatically. To play a disc that's already in the drive, open the Start menu and choose Programs, Accessories, Entertainment, DVD Player. (Or choose Run from the Start menu and type *dvdplayer.exe*.)

Figure 36-3, on the next page, shows an example of DVD Player's initial display. The readout on the left shows you what part of your disc is currently in play. To the right of this display is a set of controls that operate much like the controls on a standalone DVD player. At the far right are some useful command buttons.

**IX**

*Using Accessory Programs*

★ TIP

If you're unsure which button to click for a particular function, right-click any button. You can then choose from the menu that appears.

**FIGURE 36-3.**

DVD Player looks like a stand-alone DVD player with a few extra controls.

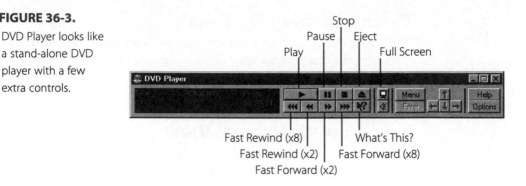

To make DVD Player use the full screen, click the Full Screen button. Once the player is using the full screen, you can right-click anywhere on the screen to get a menu of playback options. From this menu, you can return to a windowed display.

To see a menu of content options available on your DVD disc, click the Menu button. Once the menu appears, you can move between options by clicking the arrows to the right of the Menu button. To make a selection, click Enter.

## Playback and Subtitle Language Options

To choose a playback language, click the Options button, choose Language, and then select from the available languages. To choose a subtitle language, click Options, choose Subtitles from the Options menu, and then select from the available languages. You can use one language for sound and a different language for subtitles.

## Playback Speed Options

DVD Player can play movies at normal speed, double speed, and half speed. To exercise one of these options, right-click any control button and choose Play Speed from the ensuing menu.

## Setting Parental Controls

DVD Player allows you to control which movies particular users can see, based on the standard movie rating system. To put controls in place:

1   Click Options and choose Show Logon.

2   Type and confirm an administrator password.

This administrator password has nothing to do with any administrator passwords associated with Windows 2000 itself. The first person who visits DVD Player's Show Logon dialog box becomes the de facto administrator for the application and gets to apply the controls.

**3** Click OK to leave the Show Logon dialog box.

**4** Click Options again and choose Set Ratings.

**5** Enter your password.

**6** In the User Name field, type the name of a user.

**7** From the Rating box, choose the highest rating you want to allow for this user.

**8** In the Password field, type the password required to change the rating level for this user. Then click Save.

# Using Windows Media Player

Windows Media Player is an application that can render a wide variety of sound and video formats, including streaming sound and video downloaded from Web sites. Chances are, if you've ever downloaded a sound or video clip from the Internet, you've seen (or heard) Media Player in action, because Media Player is the application associated by default with many Internet media formats.

When you download a media clip from the Internet, Media Player starts automatically. To run Media Player and play a locally stored media file, open the Start menu and choose Programs, Accessories, Entertainment, Windows Media Player, and then use the File menu to open your clip. (Or choose Run from the Start menu and type *mplayer2.exe*.)

Figure 36-4, on the next page, shows Media Player's standard display, and Table 36-1 describes the functions of the various components of that display. Two smaller alternatives to the standard display, called Compact and Minimal, are available via commands on the View menu.

**FIGURE 36-4.**

Media Player's standard view includes the usual controls, information about the current clip, and more.

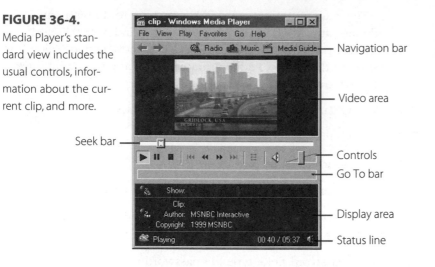

Navigation bar

Video area

Seek bar

Controls

Go To bar

Display area

Status line

You can control which display elements appear in these alternative views by choosing Options from the View menu and clicking the Custom Views tab.

**TABLE 36-1.  Media Player Standard Display**

| Component | Description |
|---|---|
| Navigation bar | Arrows let you move between clips played during the current session; Radio, Music, and Media Guide buttons connect you to Microsoft Web sites, from which you can find radio broadcasts, music, and video clips. |
| Video area | Displays contents of current video clip. |
| Seek bar | Shows progress of the current clip; drag the bar to move forward or back within the clip. |
| Controls | Includes the standard play, pause, stop, rewind, and fast forward buttons, a control for previewing items in a playlist, and a volume control. |
| Go To bar | Lets you move between markers in the current clip. (Not all clips include markers.) |
| Display area | Shows information about the current clip. |
| Status line | Displays status information about the current clip—whether it's being downloaded, buffered, played, or paused, for example. |

## Viewing Closed Captions

Some video clips come with optional closed captioning. To see the captions, choose Captions from the View menu. To turn captioning off again, execute the Captions command a second time.

## Playing a Clip Repeatedly

Windows Media Player gives you the option of playing a video or sound clip repeatedly—something that might prove useful if you're setting up a demo application. To play a clip more than once:

**1** Choose Options from the View menu.

**2** Click the Playback tab.

**3** Enter the number of times you want your clip to repeat, or select the Repeat Forever option.

The Playback tab also lets you adjust the sound volume and balance between your left and right speakers.

## Keeping Up with Enhancements to Media Player

Microsoft expects to issue enhanced versions of Windows Media Player from time to time. Whenever you're connected to the Internet, you can find out if a newer version is available by choosing Check For Player Upgrade from the Help menu. If you're not using the latest and greatest, an Upgrade Now button appears, allowing you to download the update.

# Controlling Sound Volume

The Volume Control program allows you to control the loudness of your computer's various sound sources. To run Volume Control, open the Start menu and choose Programs, Accessories, Entertainment, Volume Control. (Or choose Run from the Start menu and type *sndvol32.exe*.) The Volume Control window is shown in Figure 36-5, on the next page.

**TIP**

You can also open Volume Control by double-clicking the volume icon in the taskbar's status area.

IX

Using Accessory Programs

**NOTE**

The sound sources available on your computer depend on which type of sound card you have and whether you have an internal modem. Your Volume Control window might have controls for sources different from the ones shown in Figure 36-5.

**FIGURE 36-5.**

The Volume Control window displays sliders for each sound source.

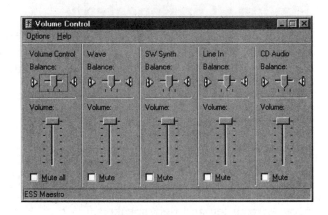

Drag the balance and volume controls for each audio source. For example, use the CD balance and volume controls to change the balance and volume of your CD-drive output.

The balance and volume controls marked Volume Control let you adjust the overall balance and volume. If the master volume is at its lowest level, it won't matter what the other levels are, you won't hear anything.

**TIP**

Clicking the taskbar's volume icon brings up a control that serves the same function as the master volume control of the Volume Control window—without opening the Volume Control program.

The Mute check boxes let you turn off the volume for any of the audio sources. As with the master volume controls, be careful with the Mute All check box. If Mute All is selected, all sound is turned off for that device.

The Wave controls adjust the volume and balance of wave (.wav) files that are used in a number of multimedia applications. The Line-In controls adjust the balance and volume of a device you might have connected to the line input of your sound card.

You can choose to display controls for only the devices you have installed or want to control by choosing Properties from the Options menu. In the Properties dialog box, shown in Figure 36-6, clear the boxes for the devices you don't want to control.

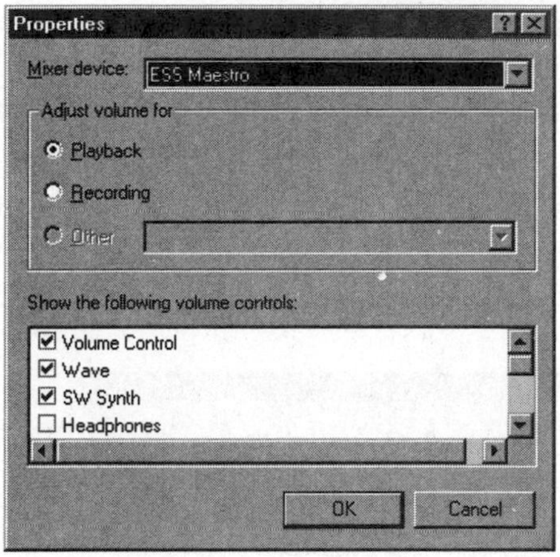

**FIGURE 36-6.**
The Properties dialog box lets you select which sound sources you want to control.

# Recording Sounds with Sound Recorder

If you have a microphone attached to your sound card, you can use Microsoft Sound Recorder to make your own voice recordings, which you can then add to other documents. And if your sound card has a Line In connector, you can connect a stereo receiver or other sound source to it and use Sound Recorder to make recordings from that source.

You can use voice recordings to annotate documents. For example, suppose you want to provide explicit instructions about how to interpret a particular portion of a spreadsheet—how you arrived at your assumptions, and so on. You could add those instructions to the spreadsheet so the person using it could hear the instructions in your own words—and in your own voice.

To make a sound recording:

**1** Open Sound Recorder by clicking the Start menu and choosing Programs, Accessories, Entertainment, Sound Recorder. (Or from the Start menu, choose Run and type *sndrec32.exe*.)

IX

Using Accessory Programs

The Sound Recorder window appears, as shown in Figure 36-7.

2  Choose Properties from the File menu. In the properties dialog box that appears, click Convert Now to display the Sound Selection dialog box shown in Figure 36-8.

3  Choose the file format and attributes you want.

Higher sampling rates require more disk space but provide better quality. (Expressed in hertz, the sampling rate measures the number of times that a sound is recorded in each second.) If you find the sound quality unacceptably low, use the Attributes box to choose a higher sampling rate or 16-bit sound.

4  Turn on the microphone, if it has an on/off switch, and then click the Record button (the big red dot) and start talking.

As you record, the green line expands and contracts like an oscilloscope to indicate sound levels. You can see how much time has elapsed. The maximum recording length is 60 seconds.

5  When you finish the recording, click the Stop button.

6  Choose Save from the File menu, and then name the file if you haven't already.

Sound Recorder saves its documents as wave files and gives them the filename extension .wav.

To embed a sound file into any application that supports OLE linking and embedding:

**1**   Open or record the file you want to embed.

**2**   Use Sound Recorder's Copy command to put the sound data on the Clipboard.

**3**   Activate the application into which you want to embed the sound (the destination application).

**4**   Put the cursor where you want the sound file to be embedded. Then use the destination program's Paste command.

In the destination document, the embedded sound file is displayed as a small speaker icon. To play the sound, double-click the icon.

## Controlling Input Levels for Recording

**SEE ALSO**
For more information about the Volume Control program, see "Controlling Sound Volume," page 767.

You can control the input volume level for the sounds that you record. To adjust volume, use the Volume Control program. With the Volume Control program running, choose Properties from the Options menu to display the Properties dialog box. Click the Recording option and click OK. Balance and volume controls let you adjust the recording volume level for each sound source.

## Editing Sound Files

Sound Recorder's Edit menu has six editing commands, in addition to the Copy command.

- The Insert File and Mix With File commands allow you to combine two or more sound files. To use either command, first position the slider at the point in the current file where you want the incoming file to appear. The Position indicator to the left of the oscilloscope display will help you find the appropriate spot.

   The Insert File command adds a sound file at the current location and moves the remainder of the file forward. The Mix With File command superimposes the incoming sound file on whatever sound data is already at the current location.

- The Paste Insert and Paste Mix commands combine sounds in a similar manner, except that they use the Clipboard as their source instead of a sound file.

IX

Using Accessory Programs

- The two Delete commands on the Edit menu simply delete data from the current location to the beginning or the end of the file.

You can also edit a sound file with commands on the Effects menu. These commands actually change the sound data that makes up your file, not merely the playback mode. For example, if you increase the speed of a file and then use the Save command, the file plays at the increased speed each time you open it.

# Manipulating Faxes and Images with Imaging

Imaging for Windows is a program that lets you view and annotate fax transmissions and other graphics images. (We'll be referring to Imaging for Windows in this chapter simply as *Imaging*, as the program's name appears on its title bar.) With Imaging, you can create multipage "scrapbook" files of images and faxes and use thumbnails to navigate between pages. You can also use the product to convert documents from one supported graphics file type to another. With three file types—.tif, .jpg, and .bmp—you can add annotations, such as text boxes or freehand drawings, to your images. Imaging can also manage any TWAIN-compliant scanner, allowing you to scan photographs and other documents and save the resulting images in one of the program's native file formats. (*TWAIN* is the name of a standard interface that enables any capture device, like a scanner, to work with any graphics software, as long as both are designed to be TWAIN-compliant.)

The Imaging for Windows program is supplied by Eastman Software and is a scaled-down version of another Eastman product called Imaging for Windows Professional Edition. Imaging Professional adds such advanced features as optical character recognition (allowing you to turn faxes into editable documents) and the ability to create hyperlinks that connect your local documents with documents on the World Wide Web. If you have an Internet connection, you can read about Imaging Professional by choosing the About command from the Imaging Help menu, clicking Contact Info, and then clicking Visit Web Site.

Imaging includes Imaging Preview, a separate program that lets you preview, rotate, size, and print images—but not annotate them or assemble them into multipage documents. By default, when you double-click a supported image file type in a Windows Explorer window, your file appears in Imaging Preview. If you want to annotate the image, you can then open the full program by choosing Open Image For Editing from the preview program's File menu. (You can also change the program's default behavior so that images open in the full program by default.)

# File Types Supported by Imaging

Imaging supports three file types: .tif, .jpg, and .bmp. When you work with any of these file types, Imaging can manage an annotation layer in addition to the underlying bitmap graphics data. You can add free-hand drawing, *rubber stamps* (preset messages such as "approved" or "rejected," along with the current date), and make other assorted changes to the annotation layer. When you're satisfied with the result, you can merge the annotations into the underlying bitmap, making the annotations a permanent part of the document.

Imaging can save files in any of its three native file types. It can open files from the following additional formats: .pcx, .dcx, .xif, .gif, and .wif. When you open one of these types of files, Imaging's title bar displays the legend Read-Only. If you want to annotate one of these files, first save it in one of the three native formats.

# Basic Options

On Imaging's Tools menu, you'll find a command called General Options. The dialog box for this command, shown in Figure 37-1, lets you specify four settings that govern basic aspects of Imaging's behavior. You can tell the program how you want images to be sized initially (the default behavior enlarges or reduces image size so that their width fits the width of the main window), whether you want scroll bars, which folder you want Imaging to use by default, and whether you want image files associated with the full Imaging program or the preview program.

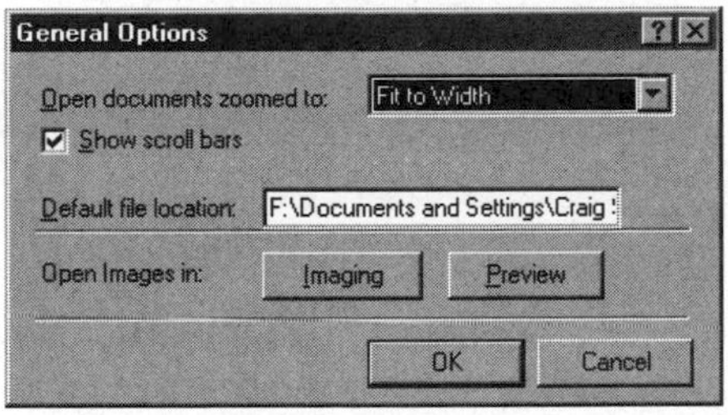

**FIGURE 37-1.**
Here you can specify whether files you launch should open in the full Imaging program or in Imaging Preview.

⭐ **TIP**

If you choose to forego scroll bars, you can still move around a large image by using the Drag button on the Imaging toolbar. Click the hand (or choose Drag from the Edit menu), and then drag any part of the image.

# Toolbar Options

❓ **SEE ALSO**

For information about the Annotation toolbar, see "Annotating Images," page 784.

Imaging offers four toolbars to simplify command selection. You can use the View menu's Toolbars command to tell the program which of these toolbars you want to see. Table 37-1 describes the toolbars that appear at the top of the Imaging window. Standard, Imaging, and Scanning.

⭐ **TIP**

You can dock any toolbar at either the top or bottom of your window. You can also float any toolbar. To relocate a toolbar, click a space that isn't occupied by a tool, and then drag.

**TABLE 37-1.   Imaging Toolbars**

| Toolbar Icon | Description |
|---|---|
| **Standard Toolbar** | |
|  🗋 | Creates a new, blank document |
|  📂 | Opens an existing document |
|  💾 | Saves the current document to disk |
|  🖨 | Prints the current document |

*(continued)*

**TABLE 37-1.** *continued*

| Toolbar Icon | Description |
|---|---|
| **Standard Toolbar** *continued* | |
| ✂ | Cuts (deletes) the selection and places it on the Clipboard |
| 📋 | Copies the selection to the Clipboard |
| 📋 | Pastes (inserts) the Clipboard's contents in the upper left corner; drag to the location you want and then click outside the selection |
| ↺ | Undoes your most recent change |
| ↻ | Redoes the last action canceled by Undo |
| 🔍+ | Zooms in; doubles the current magnification level |
| 🔍− | Zooms out; halves the current magnification level |
| ⊡→ | Fits the selection in the window |
| ⊕ | Zooms to the best fit, fitting either the image height or width in the window |
| ↔ | Fits the image width in the window width |
| 200% ▾ | Changes the magnification (zoom) level to a pre-defined percentage or any value you type from 2 percent through 6500 percent |
| **Imaging Toolbar** | |
| ✋ | Allows you to drag the image within the window instead of using scroll bars |
| ▢+ | Allows you to select a rectangular area of the image |
| ▷ | Allows you to select annotations |
| ✎ | Hides or displays the Annotations toolbar |

**TABLE 37-1.** *continued*

| Toolbar Icon | Description |
|---|---|
| **Imaging Toolbar** *continued* | |
| | Rotates the page 90 degrees to the left (counterclockwise) |
| | Rotates the page 90 degrees to the right (clockwise) |
| | Displays the previous page, the next page, or the page corresponding to the number you type |
| | Changes to one-page view |
| | Changes to thumbnails view |
| | Changes to page-and-thumbnails view |
| **Scanning Toolbar** | |
| | Scans an image and creates a new document |
| | Scans an image and inserts it before the current page |
| | Scans an image and places it after the last page of the current document |
| | Scans an image and replaces the current page |

# Opening and Scanning Files

To open a document in Imaging, simply use the File menu's Open command. You can do this from either the preview program or the full program. The only point to note here is that the Files Of Type list, at the bottom of the File Open dialog box, always defaults to the last file type you used. If the file you opened or saved most recently used the .tif format, for example, the File Open dialog box initially shows only .tif files. To see another file type—or all supported file types—make your selection from the Files Of Type list.

To acquire an image from your scanner, you must be in the full program, and you must have a TWAIN-compliant scanner installed. If you have more than one such scanner, use the File menu's Select Device command to choose the one you want to use. Then choose Acquire Image from the File menu. This command activates your scanner driver, which might ask you for further information—such as the nature of the source image and the resolution at which you want to scan. Once your scanner has finished its work, the image you scanned appears in Imaging's main window.

**NOTE**

The Acquire Image command creates a new document from the scanned image. You can also append or insert a scanned image as a new page in an existing document. *See "Adding Pages to a Document," page 782.*

## Setting Compression Options

The Tools menu's Scan Options command, depicted in Figure 37-2, lets you specify the kind of compression that Imaging will apply to your scanned data. The default option, Best Display Quality, applies *loss-less compression*, which means that your scanned image retains as much color and resolution detail as the scanning operation supplies. The resulting file can be quite large, however. The Smallest File Size option performs a *lossy* compression, which generates a dramatically smaller file, but one that may lack perfect fidelity to the source image. The Good Display Quality And Small File Size option is a compromise between these two extremes.

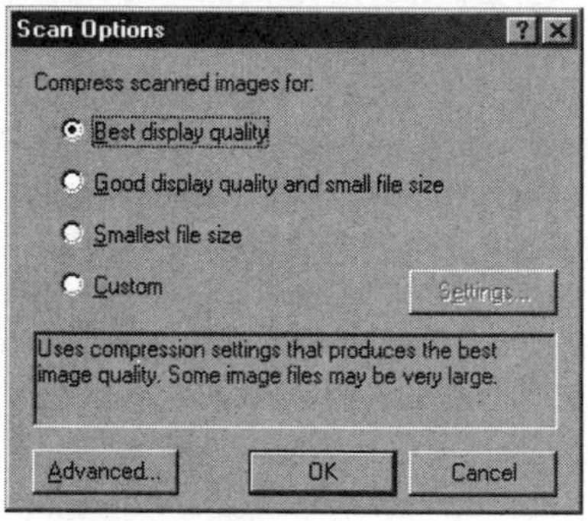

**FIGURE 37-2.**

The Scan Options dialog box lets you change the mode of compression that Imaging applies to data supplied by your scanner.

If you select Custom and click the Settings button, Imaging displays a second dialog box, shown in Figure 37-3. The various tabs in this dialog box show the method of compression that Imaging is currently set to apply to each of six document types—black and white, 16 shades of gray, 256 shades of gray, 16 colors, 256 colors, and true color. You can select alternative compression methods from the Compression boxes on each of these tabs.

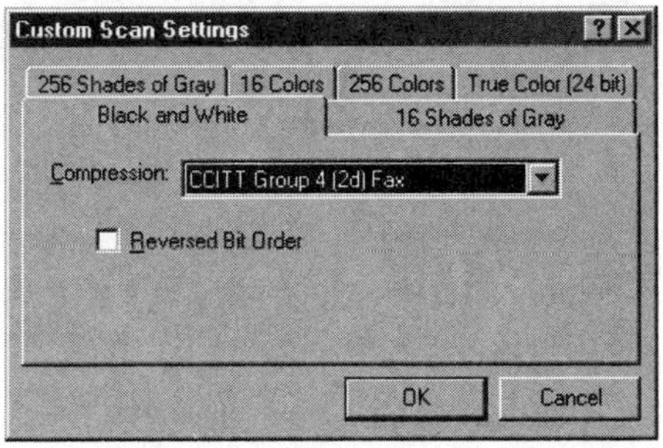

**FIGURE 37-3.**
In the Custom Scan Settings dialog box, you can change the default compression method used for any of six document types.

## Transfer Mode Options

By clicking the Advanced button in the Scan Options dialog box (see Figure 37-2), you can specify the manner in which Imaging allocates memory to a scan operation. In the default mode, called Memory, Imaging allocates one block of memory at a time. In the alternative mode, called Native, Imaging allocates one large block of memory at the beginning of the scan. Native makes for a quicker scan but can cause Imaging to allocate more memory than is actually needed. If memory isn't abundant on your system, you'll probably want to stick with the Memory option.

# Selecting a View

The full Imaging program offers three views: One Page, Thumbnails, and Page And Thumbnails. You can switch between these via commands on the View menu. Figure 37-4, on the next page, shows a multipage document in Imaging's Page And Thumbnails view.

**TIP**

In Page And Thumbnails view, you can change the width of the thumbnails pane by dragging the border between the two panes. Widening the thumbnails pane lets Imaging display two or more columns of thumbnails.

In any of these three modes, you can also switch to a Full Screen view, in which the title bar, toolbars, status bar, and window borders

IX

Using Accessory Programs

**FIGURE 37-4.**

In Page And Thumbnails view, a thumbnail pane appears to the left of the main window. You can move between pages by clicking thumbnails.

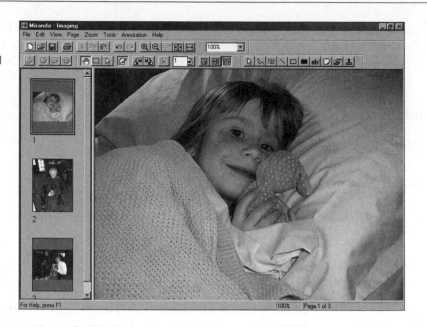

are all removed. To do this, choose Full Screen from the View menu or press Ctrl+F. In Full Screen view, a Full Screen button appears. Click this button to return to a normal windowed presentation, or press Ctrl+F again.

**TIP**

To display toolbars while working in Full Screen view, right-click the Full Screen button, and then choose the toolbar you want from the shortcut menu. You can select several (or all) toolbars at once by choosing Toolbars from the shortcut menu.

## Changing Thumbnail Dimensions

To change the size of the thumbnails used by Imaging, choose Thumbnail Size from the Tools menu. As Figure 37-5 shows, a large black handle appears at the lower right corner of a sample thumbnail in the Thumbnail Size dialog box. You can drag that handle to change the dimensions of your thumbnails. Alternatively, you can select a different shape from the Aspect Ratio list, or type numbers directly into the Width and Height boxes. Those boxes display the current dimensions, in pixels, of your thumbnails.

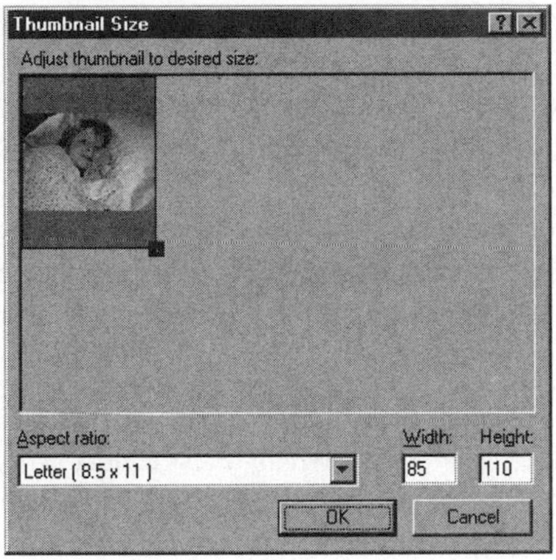

**FIGURE 37-5.**
You can drag the
handle in the
Thumbnail Size
dialog box to change
the dimensions of
your thumbnails.

# Navigating in a Multipage Document

Page And Thumbnails view and Thumbnails view are handy because they offer a simple way to navigate from one page to another in a multipage document. Clicking a thumbnail in Page And Thumbnails view changes the current page to that of the selected image. Double-clicking an image in Thumbnails view presents the selected image in One Page view.

You can also get around without the thumbnails, however, by choosing commands from the Page menu. Next and Previous let you move forward or back a page at a time, First and Last take you to the first page and last page, respectively, and Go To lets you hop to a specific page. Go Back takes you to the page you were looking at last.

**TIP**

Ctrl+Page Down and Ctrl+Page Up are shortcut keys for the Page menu's Next and Previous commands.

# Rotating and Zooming

If you scan a picture taken in portrait orientation and it arrives in Imaging in landscape orientation, you can set matters aright by choosing the Rotate Page command from the Page menu. The submenu that appears lets you rotate the image 90 degrees to the left or right, or a full 180 degrees.

Commands on the Zoom menu let you change the magnification of your image, from 2 percent of actual size to 6500 percent. (Actual size means the size the image would have if displayed as a bitmap on your desktop.) The Zoom In and Zoom Out commands (and their respective shortcut keys, Ctrl+Up arrow and Ctrl+Down arrow) double and halve the current magnification. The commands at the bottom of the menu let you select a specific magnification value. Choose Custom to enter a value that doesn't have its own menu entry.

> **TIP**
>
> The Zoom list on the Standard toolbar shows you the current magnification. You can click the arrow to the right of this figure to choose a different magnification, or you can simply type in a different percentage.

Fit To Height and Fit To Width, in the middle of the Zoom menu, adjust the magnification of your image to fit the current dimensions of Imaging's main window. Best Fit sizes the image to either the width or height of the window, whichever results in less unused space in the window.

### Zooming to a Selected Area

To focus on a particular portion of an image:

1 Click the Select Image button on the Imaging toolbar. (Alternatively, you can press Ctrl+Spacebar or choose Select Image from the Edit menu.)

2 Drag your mouse pointer across the area of the image that you're interested in.

3 Choose Zoom To Selection from the Zoom menu.

Imaging magnifies the selected portion of the image so that it fills the main window.

# Adding Pages to a Document

To add a new page at the end of the current document, choose Append from the Page menu. To add a new page before the current page, choose Insert from the Page menu. In either case, a submenu appears, allowing you to specify whether the new page is to be scanned or read from an existing disk file. If you choose Existing Page, Imaging presents the equivalent of the File Open dialog box. If you choose Acquire Image, Imaging awakens your scanner.

You can append pages only to files with the .tif extension.

Be aware that while Imaging lets you assemble related source files into an image "scrapbook," the program lacks a convenient way to disassemble the resulting document. If you subsequently decide to extract a particular page, you're limited to copying that page to the Clipboard and then pasting it into another graphics program. If you want to delete a page, right-click it in Page And Thumbnails view and select Delete Page from the shortcut menu.

# Getting and Setting Page Properties

The Page menu's Properties command, shown in Figure 37-6, lets you see and change several properties of the current page. The dialog box has four tabs.

The Color tab lists the six color-depth options available in Imaging, in order of increasing depth. You can use this tab to switch to a lower color depth—for example, to change an image from true color to 256 shades of gray. You might want to reduce the color depth of an image if you plan to fax it or print it on a black-and-white printer.

**FIGURE 37-6.**

The Page Properties dialog box lets you change the color depth, compression, and other properties of the current page.

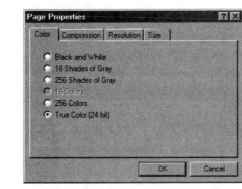

Note the following points about color depth:

- You can decrease, but not increase, the color depth of an image. Once you have reduced an image, for example, from True Color to 256 Colors, you can choose True Color but you will still have a maximum of only 256 different colors.

- Black And White means literally that. To get the familiar look of a black-and-white photograph, select 256 Shades Of Gray.

IX

Using Accessory Programs

■ Certain color depths are not available with certain document types. For example, .tif documents can't be displayed at 16 colors.

The Compression tab lets you change the method that Imaging uses to reduce the amount of data required to store your image. The available options vary with the file type and color depth of your document. No compression is available for .bmp documents.

The Resolution tab provides another way to reduce the disk storage requirements for the current page. Switching to a lower resolution produces a smaller file, at the expense of image quality. You can use the Resolution box to select from the available resolutions, or you can enter values (expressed in dots per inch) directly into the X and Y boxes.

The Size tab lets you change the overall height and width of your page. Reducing the size of your page is the only method of cropping available in Imaging, and it can be used only to crop from the right or lower edge. Increasing the size of your page adds white space to the right of or below the image. If you reduce page size and don't like the result, click Undo immediately, or the change will be irreversible.

# Annotating Images

You can add nine types of annotations to documents saved in the .tif, .jpg, or .bmp format. These annotations are available via the Annotation toolbar or the Annotation menu. Be aware that when you select an annotation tool by clicking an Annotation toolbar button or choosing an Annotation menu command, your selection remains in effect until you deactivate it. For example, if you select the Attach-A-Note tool, each time you click your image, you get a new Attach-A-Note annotation. To deactivate an annotation tool, choose Select Annotations from the Annotation menu or click the Annotation Selection button (the arrow) on the Annotation toolbar. You can also deactivate an annotation tool by clicking the Drag button or the Select Image button (both on the Imaging toolbar), or by choosing their Edit-menu equivalents.

Annotation
Selection

After you create an annotation, you can change its appearance by right-clicking it and choosing Properties from the shortcut menu. The options vary with the kind of annotation involved. With lines, for example, you can change thickness and color. With text, you can change font and color, and so on.

The annotation tools, and the Annotation toolbar buttons you use to select them, are described in Table 37-2.

**TABLE 37-2.   Imaging Annotation Tools**

| Toolbar Icon | Description |
|---|---|
| | The Freehand Line tool draws squiggly lines. Click where you want the line to begin, drag at will, and release the mouse button where you want the line to end. |
| | The Highlighter tool creates a filled rectangle that is, by default, yellow and transparent, providing a way to call attention to a particular block of text. Click where you want a corner of the rectangle to appear, drag to the opposite corner, and release the mouse button. You can highlight graphics as well as text, but the Highlighter tool affects the color of the underlying graphics. |
| | The Straight Line tool adds straight lines. Click at one end point, drag to the other, and release the mouse button. |
| | The Hollow Rectangle tool lets you create a box around an area of interest. Click where you want a corner to appear, drag to the opposite corner, and release the mouse button. |
| | The Filled Rectangle tool works like the Hollow Rectangle tool, except that the resulting box is filled with an opaque background color. (You can use the Properties command to make the background transparent—but if that's what you want, you might as well use the Highlighter tool instead.) |
| abl | The Text tool allows you to add any amount of text to your document. Click and type. |
| | The Attach-A-Note tool creates a solid rectangle on which you can type. Click and drag to make the rectangle, and then type. |
| | The Text From File tool allows you to import the textual contents of a specified file. Click the image, and then specify the file you want to import. |
| | The Rubber Stamp tool adds a preset text block or image, including (optionally) the current date or time. Supplied stamps include Approved, DRAFT, Received, and Rejected. You can create your own as well; see the following section. Click where you want the stamp to appear, and then choose the stamp you want to use from the Rubber Stamp Properties menu. |

IX

Using Accessory Programs

⭐ TIP

If you don't like the annotation you just created, select it by clicking a portion of it, and press the Delete key.

# Creating and Changing Rubber Stamps

Choosing Rubber Stamps from the Annotation menu generates the Rubber Stamp Properties dialog box, shown in Figure 37-7. Here you can select one of the supplied stamps or click the Create Text or Create Image button to make your own rubber stamp. To create a text stamp, click Create Text. In the ensuing dialog box, you can specify the name and content of the stamp. Click the Date or Time button to add the current date or time to the content of your stamp. (Imaging adds the codes %x and %X to generate the current date and time, respectively.) To create a graphic stamp, click the Create Image button. In the dialog box that appears next, specify the name of your stamp and the graphics file that you want to use as an image. If you don't know the name and path of your graphics file, click the Browse button to find it.

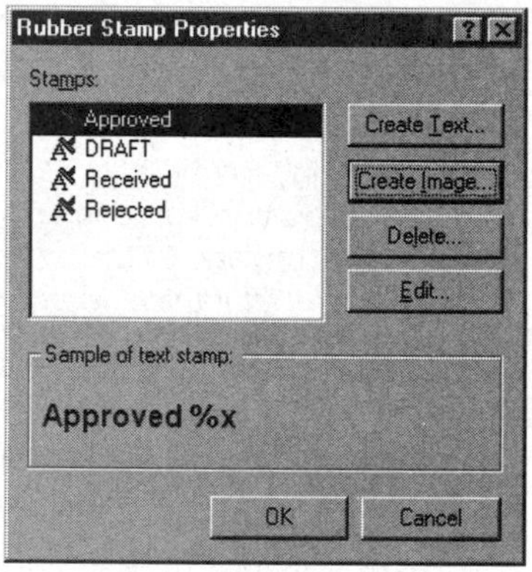

**FIGURE 37-7.**
Open the Annotation menu and choose Rubber Stamps to display this dialog box.

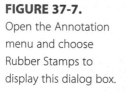

Back in the Rubber Stamp Properties dialog box, select the stamp you want from the list, and then click OK. Imaging then applies the selected stamp wherever you click the image.

If you click the Rubber Stamp button on the Annotation toolbar rather than using the Annotation menu, Imaging bypasses the Rubber Stamp Properties dialog box. Instead, you get a pop-up menu of predefined stamps. (You can't create new stamps using this method.) Choose a rubber stamp from the menu, and then click the image to apply the stamp.

**NOTE**

Rubber stamps that include the date and time use the short date style and the time style from the Regional Options dialog box. Visit Control Panel if you want to change these styles.

## Working with Annotations

Annotations live initially in a separate layer of your document. Here they can be manipulated at will. You can copy and paste them, modify their properties, or delete them. To perform any of these actions with an annotation, first choose Select Annotations from the Annotation menu, or click the Annotation Selection tool on the Annotation toolbar or the Imaging toolbar. Then click the annotation you want to manipulate. (To select more than one annotation, hold down the Ctrl key as you click each one, or drag your mouse across the set of annotations you want to select.) To change an annotation's properties, right-click and choose Properties from the shortcut menu. To cut, copy, or clear (delete), choose from the shortcut menu or the Edit menu.

Once you have annotated your document to your satisfaction, you can use the Annotation menu's Make Annotations Permanent command to merge the annotation layer with the rest of your document. After you do that, you will not be able to manipulate the annotations.

# Creating a New Document

You can use the New command on the File menu to create a new Imaging document from scratch. When you do this, Imaging displays a dialog box similar to the Page Properties dialog box shown in Figure 37-6, on page 783. The only difference is that the New Blank Document dialog box adds a File Type tab. Here you can specify whether you want your document to be in the .tif, .jpg, or .bmp format.

**? SEE ALSO**

For information about Paint, see Chapter 34, "Drawing with Paint."

Note that while you can use Imaging's annotations tools to build a new document, if the document you're creating consists primarily of graphics objects (lines, boxes, and other shapes), you will probably have an easier time working in Microsoft Paint and then importing the resulting .bmp file into Imaging. Paint's tools are considerably more versatile than Imaging's.

IX

Using Accessory Programs

# Printing, Faxing, and Mailing

Once you've assembled and annotated your Imaging document, you can use the Print command on the File menu to print it or send it to a fax program. To print or fax, open the File menu and choose Print, and then select the printer or fax driver you want to use from the Select Printer list in the Print dialog box.

To send your Imaging document via e-mail, choose Send from the File menu. Imaging responds by opening a message form in your default e-mail client program, with your document as an attachment.

# CHAPTER 38

# Playing Games

C hances are you chose Microsoft Windows 2000 Professional for some set of reasons other than its suitability as a gaming platform. Because Windows 2000, like its predecessor Microsoft Windows NT 4, prevents applications from making direct access to your computer's hardware, this operating system disallows some of the programming methods that many older games written for the MS-DOS and Windows 9*x* platforms have employed.

But if you've dismissed the potential of Windows 2000 as a gaming platform, you might be in for a pleasant surprise. Thanks to Windows 2000 support for *DirectX*, a set of application programming interfaces (APIs) that facilitates faster communication between programs and hardware devices, you can expect software vendors to provide more and more high-performance multimedia games that run under your operating system.

# Windows 2000 as a Gaming Platform

The advanced hardware support in Windows 2000 also enhances the system's potential as a gaming platform:

- Built-in joystick support lets you just plug in a joystick, follow Windows through the calibration routine, and play. (Your computer must have a game port, which typically is included on a sound card or a multifunction I/O card.) Windows 2000 Professional also supports force feedback joysticks and universal serial bus (USB) game controllers.

- Plug and Play makes the installation and setup of the requisite gaming hardware—sound cards, joysticks, CD-ROM drives, and so on—nearly painless.

- Support for multiple monitors provides additional opportunities for game developers.

To underscore the point that Windows 2000 is a system suitable for running quality games, Microsoft included a visually and sonically exciting pinball game with your operating system. This game, 3D Pinball for Windows, made its debut as part of the Plus! accessory package for Microsoft Windows 95. It makes its first appearance on the NT platform with Windows 2000.

In this chapter, we'll look at Microsoft 3D Pinball for Windows—Space Cadet, along with the three other games supplied with Windows 2000 Professional—Solitaire, Minesweeper, and FreeCell. You'll find menu items for all four games by opening the Start menu and choosing Programs, Accessories, Games.

# Playing 3D Pinball

Microsoft 3D Pinball is an electronic realization of an old-fashioned pinball machine, with a twenty-first century space-travel theme. You start out as a Cadet and try to work your way through the game's nine playing levels until you reach the rank of Fleet Admiral. The ring of yellow lights near the center of the table (see Figure 38-1) indicates your current rank.

**FIGURE 38-1**

Player 1 is ready to launch the first ball by holding down Spacebar and then releasing.

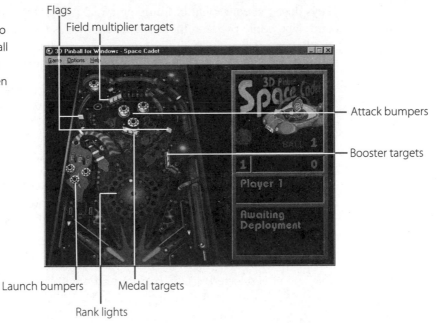

Flags

Field multiplier targets

Attack bumpers

Booster targets

Launch bumpers

Medal targets

Rank lights

In 3D Pinball, you can have from one to four players. To specify the number of players for a game, choose Select Players from the Options menu.

## Starting a Game

Before you begin a game, you might want to put 3D Pinball into full-screen display. To do that, press F4. (The game doesn't have a conventional Maximize button.) In full-screen display, the window borders, title bar, and menu bar all disappear. Your entire screen becomes a pinball machine. Press F4 again to return to a windowed display.

To start a game, press F2 (or choose New Game from the Game menu, if you're playing in windowed display). If you need to pause at any time, simply press F3. Press F3 again to resume.

## Keyboard Controls

By default, the left and right flippers are controlled by the z and slash (/) keys on your keyboard, respectively. Pressing the x and period (.)

IX

**Using Accessory Programs**

keys does the equivalent of bumping a real pinball table from the left and right, while pressing the Up arrow key gives the table a bump from the bottom. Be careful with the bump keys; overuse will cause a *tilt*, disabling the pinball controls until the current ball drains.

You can change the keyboard characters assigned to the flippers and bump functions. To do so, press F8 or choose Player Controls from the Options menu.

## Sound Effects

By default, 3D Pinball is a rather noisy game, perhaps better suited for home than office. But you can play it silently if you need or prefer to. Choose Sounds from the Options menu to turn off the standard sound effects. Select the option again to turn them back on.

On the same menu, you'll also find a Music option. Off by default, when this option is selected, a little background tune plays while *you* play.

## Strategy Tips

Figure 38-1 shows some of the more important landmarks on the 3D Pinball table. Your score increases any time your ball hits any of the targets, bumpers, or flags (as well as in many other ways). It's a particularly good idea to try to knock down all three targets in any of the target banks. Knocking out the entire field multiplier target bank, for example, multiplies the scores you receive by hitting any of the other landmarks on the table. Each time you knock out a complete target bank, the bank resets, and the bonus you receive by knocking out that target bank again increases.

There's so much going on in 3D Pinball that you probably won't be able to take it all in without a little study. One good way to figure the game out is to watch its self-running demo. You can do that by choosing Demo from the Game menu. While the demo plays, you can read the text messages that appear at the lower right corner of the screen—something that's difficult to do while you're playing the game yourself.

While the game might be complex, the basic strategy is simple enough: have a good time and keep the ball in play.

# Playing Solitaire

The Solitaire game that comes with Windows 2000 Professional is the same popular item that has been distracting Windows users since Windows 3 was introduced in 1990. It's a computerized version of the classic Klondike game; if you've played solitaire with a deck of cards, you'll be right at home with this program.

When the game is started, the deck appears in the upper left corner of the playing area with its contents face down, and placeholders for four suit stacks appear in the upper right corner. Below the deck and the suit stack placeholders are seven row stacks, as shown below.

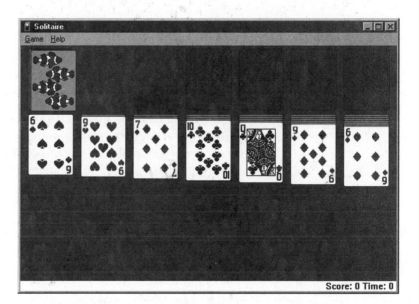

The seven row stacks below the deck and suit stacks have one face-up card each. The row stack on the left end has only one card. The number of cards in each row stack increases by one, so the row stack on the right has seven cards.

The objective of the game is to build four complete suit stacks, each containing all the cards of one suit from ace through king. If you accomplish this, an entertaining *Winner* graphic sequence plays on your display.

# Rules of the Game

You can add cards to the row stacks from the deck or from other row stacks in decreasing order and alternating color. For example, you can move a black three onto a red four.

You can add cards to the four suit stacks only in consecutive, ascending order. You can move cards to the suit stack from the top of the deck or from the last card in a row stack.

To move cards from one place to another, drag them. As a shortcut for moving a card to the suit stacks, you can double-click the card. For example, if you double-click an ace, it automatically jumps to an empty suit stack.

If you create an empty row stack by moving some cards, you must use a king to start that row stack.

When you move cards in the row stacks, you'll eventually uncover a face-down card. You can turn over a face-down card by clicking it.

After exhausting all the available moves, you can deal more cards from the deck by clicking the deck. By default, three cards are dealt when you click the deck, but you must use the top card first. If the top card is an ace, double-click it to move it to an empty suit stack. It the card is not an ace, but it can be used in a row stack or an existing suit stack, drag it there. If you can't move the card anywhere, click the deck again to deal another three cards. If you run through all the cards in the deck, you can turn over the dealt cards by clicking the circle that appears when the last card has been dealt.

When you get to the point that you can run through all the cards in the deck without being able to make any additional moves, the game is over.

Figure 38-2 shows a Solitaire game in progress with all four suit stacks under construction.

# Changing Game Options

To change the game's options, choose Options from the Game menu. The Options dialog box appears, as shown in Figure 38-3.

The Draw Three option specifies that three cards are dealt when you click the deck. You can select the Draw One option to have only one card presented each time you click the deck, which makes the game less challenging—purists might even call it cheating. (If you select Draw One while using Vegas scoring, however, you're allowed only one pass through the deck.)

**FIGURE 38-2.**

Click the circle to turn over the dealt cards so you can go through the deck again.

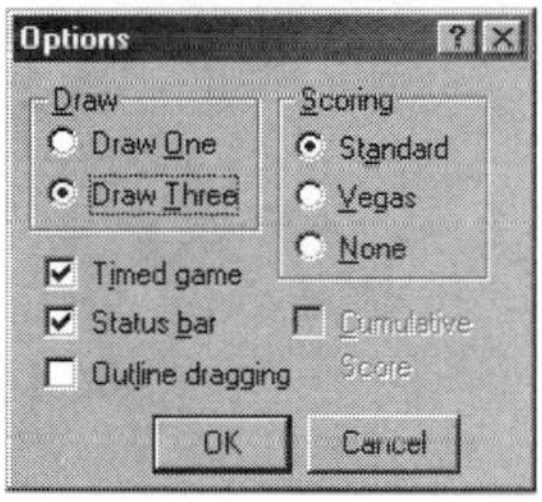

**FIGURE 38-3.**

The Options dialog box lets you select dealing and scoring options.

The Timed Game option lets you choose whether to time the game or not. If you clear the Status Bar check box, you won't be able to see your score or time.

⭐ **TIP**

> If you find that cards move in a jerky fashion when you drag them, select the Outline Dragging option. With this check box selected, you'll drag only an outline of the card, which puts less stress on your computer's processing power.

The scoring options, Standard, Vegas, and None, are described in the next section.

## Scoring

Solitaire lets you choose one of two methods for scoring your games. Or you can choose not to keep score. You select scoring options in the Options dialog box, shown in Figure 38-3. (To display this dialog

IX

Using Accessory Programs

box, choose Options from the Game menu.) By default, Solitaire uses Standard scoring and game timing, which awards points for various moves and deducts points for other moves and for playing too slowly.

When using Standard scoring, you receive 10 points for every card you move to a suit stack, 5 points for every card you move to a row stack, and 5 points if you turn over a card in a row stack. You lose 15 points if you move a card from a suit stack back to a row stack, 20 points each time you turn the deck after the third pass through the deck (if you're using the default Draw Three option), and 100 points each time you turn over the deck (if you're using the Draw One option).

When the Timed Game option is on, you lose 2 points for every 10 seconds of play, but you'll receive bonus points at the end of a fast game. The faster your game, the more bonus points you'll receive.

If you select Vegas scoring, you start the game by betting $52 and are awarded $5 for every card you move to a suit stack. The objective of the game when playing with Vegas scoring is to win back your $52 and more. Solitaire tracks your cumulative winnings if you also select the Cumulative Score check box.

With Vegas scoring, you're limited to three passes through the deck if you select the Draw Three option, or only one pass if you select Draw One.

## Selecting Card Backs

In addition to making functional changes to the game with the Options dialog box, you can change the design that appears on your face-down cards by choosing Deck from the Game menu to display the Select Card Back dialog box. Just click the design that strikes your fancy, and then click the OK button.

## Strategy Tips

Try these tips to improve your solitaire game:

- Even though the objective of the game is to build up your suit stacks, you might find it useful to move a card from a suit stack to a row stack to make additional moves possible.

- You can move a group of cards from one row stack to another by dragging the highest number card that you want to move and dropping it on the other row stack.

- Pay attention to all the possible moves as you play. It's easy to be lulled into ignoring some possible moves as you focus on the most obvious. For example, after using one of the cards you were dealt, you might find that additional moves become possible between row stacks, or from row stacks to suit stacks.

**TIP**

You can undo any card move by choosing Undo from the Game menu. You can't undo more than your last move.

# Playing Minesweeper

Minesweeper is a game of logic and deduction. The objective is to uncover all the squares in a minefield (presented as a grid of squares) that don't contain mines, and mark the squares that do, as quickly as possible—while avoiding the sudden death of "stepping on" a mine.

When you start Minesweeper, a gridlike minefield appears, as shown in Figure 38-4.

**FIGURE 38-4.**

Minesweeper depicts a "minefield," where each square in the grid might be concealing a mine.

The game starts when you make your first move by clicking a square to uncover it. Each square contains a number or a mine, or is blank. If the square contains a number, the number indicates how many of the directly adjoining squares contain mines. If the square you reveal is blank, there are no mines in the adjacent squares, so the surrounding squares are uncovered automatically. If you click a square that contains a mine, you lose and all the mines are displayed.

If you win a game (no small feat), the smiley face between the counters appears with sunglasses. If you lose, the smiley face frowns. Figure 38-5, on the next page, shows a winning game and a losing game.

To start a new game, choose New from the Game menu, or click the smiley face.

**FIGURE 38-5.**

A winner and a loser. Notice that all the mines are displayed in the losing game.

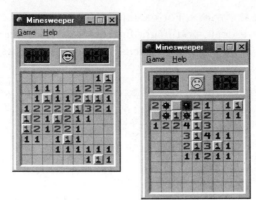

The counter in the upper left portion of the Minesweeper window indicates the number of unmarked mines in the minefield. The counter in the upper right portion of the Minesweeper window displays the elapsed game time from the instant you uncover the first square. The clock stops when you finish the game—or when it finishes you.

You can mark squares that you think contain mines by right-clicking them. When you mark a square, a flag marker appears in the square and the number in the counter displaying the total number of mines is decreased even if the square doesn't actually contain a mine. This can be misleading.

If you're not certain that a square contains a mine, right-click twice to mark it with a question mark. If you mark a square with a question mark, you can clear the question mark by right-clicking. You can then uncover the square by clicking the square or mark it as a mine square by right-clicking again. If you lose a game, any squares you incorrectly marked are displayed as crossed-out mines. You can disable the feature that lets you mark squares with question marks by choosing Marks (?) from the Game menu to clear its check mark.

## Customizing Minesweeper's Levels of Play

Minesweeper offers three levels of play—Beginner, Intermediate, and Expert. You can also specify custom levels. To specify the degree of difficulty, choose the level from the Game menu.

The Beginner level is the default and presents a grid of 8 rows by 8 columns with 10 mines. Intermediate uses a 16 by 16 grid with 40 mines. Expert uses a 16 by 30 grid with 99 mines.

You can set a custom level by choosing Custom from the Game menu. The Custom Field dialog box appears, as shown in Figure 38-6.

Enter the number of rows you want (up to a maximum of 24) in the Height box, the number of columns (up to 30) in the Width box, and the number of mines (from 10 to 667, depending on grid size). Then click the OK button.

**FIGURE 38-6.**
The Custom Field dialog box lets you control the size and difficulty of the game.

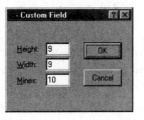

 **NOTE**

Whichever level you choose becomes the new default.

## Keeping Score

You're playing against the clock, so you improve your score by winning as quickly as possible. As soon as you win (or lose), the timing counter stops so you can see how long the game lasted.

Minesweeper keeps track of the best winning times for each of the three predefined levels, but not for custom levels. To display your best times, choose Best Times from the Game menu.

 ## Sound Effects

Minesweeper operates silently by default. To hear the clock tick and the bombs explode, choose Sound from the Game menu.

## Strategy Tips

Your first click in a new game is a safe one. You won't blow up with this first move, no matter where you make it. Your second click is another matter.

Once you've uncovered a few squares, you can start to deduce which squares are the most likely to be concealing mines. The following tips might help:

- Remember that the number that is revealed in a square you click indicates the number of mines in the eight surrounding squares (or fewer if the square is along an edge of the playing board).

- If you uncover a square labeled 1, and there is only one covered square next to it, that square must contain a mine. Mark the uncovered square by right-clicking it.

- If you're not sure about the contents of a square, mark it with a question mark (two right-clicks), and then clear it or mark it as a mine square later.

- If you point at an uncovered square that contains a number and press both mouse buttons, Minesweeper flashes the surrounding squares. If you have already marked the requisite number, Minesweeper uncovers the remaining surrounding squares, saving you the time and effort of clicking each one individually.

# Playing FreeCell

If you're looking for a form of solitaire that you can win more times than you lose, FreeCell is your game—unlike the traditional Solitaire, which it superficially resembles. FreeCell is a puzzle that can usually be solved. Once you get the hang of it, you might find that the challenge of the game is to put together long winning streaks, rather than to win an individual encounter. (FreeCell keeps track of your winning and losing streaks; press F4 to see your statistics.)

The objective of FreeCell, like traditional Solitaire, is to stack all of the cards in their respective suits, beginning with the ace. Unlike Solitaire, however, FreeCell deals all the cards face up; nothing is hidden. Figure 38-7 shows a FreeCell game in progress.

**FIGURE 38-7.**
The objective of FreeCell is to move cards to the four home cells in the upper right corner.

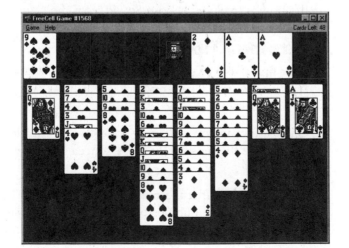

The four rectangles in the upper left are the free cells. During play, you move cards from the layout stacks to the free cells to get them out of the way temporarily. Each free cell can hold only one card; you can't stack cards in free cells. In Figure 38-7, one free cell is occupied—by the nine of spades.

The four rectangles in the upper right are the home cells. That's where you build stacks for each suit, beginning with the ace. In Figure 38-7, beginning stacks for three suits appear in the home cells.

To move a card, click to select it, and then click where you want the card moved. You can cancel a move by clicking the card a second time before completing the move. As a shortcut, you can double-click a card in the columns to move it directly to an open free cell.

## Rules of the Game

You win FreeCell by moving all the cards to the home cells. Following are the legal moves in FreeCell:

- Only the bottom card in each layout column and cards in the free cells can be moved.

- The bottom card in any column can be moved to any empty free cell.

- Cards can be moved to a home cell from the bottom of any layout column or from a free cell. You can move a card to a home cell, however, only if the card is the next highest in a suit. The bottom card on each home cell must be an ace. The next card must be the two of that same suit, and so on.

- Cards can be stacked within the layout as in a traditional solitaire game (cards of opposite colors in descending order). Using Figure 38-7 as an example, you could move the jack of clubs from the eighth column onto the queen of diamonds in the first column. This action would uncover the ace of spades, which could then take its place in the fourth home cell. (And, in fact, FreeCell would move that ace to the home cell for you automatically.) You can move cards back and forth between the layout and the free cells.

- Any card can be moved to an empty column.

IX

Using Accessory Programs

# Visual Feedback

Changes in the mouse pointer help you find legal moves. In Figure 38-7, for example, if you click the jack of clubs and then hover over the queen of diamonds, the mouse cursor changes from its normal shape to an open downward-pointing arrow. If you click the jack of clubs and then hover over a free cell, the cursor becomes a solid upward-pointing arrow.

These cues become particularly useful when you want to move a set of cards through free cells onto another layout stack. For example, in Figure 38-7, you could move four of diamonds, five of clubs, six of diamonds, and seven of clubs from the sixth column onto the eight of hearts in the fourth column. You would do this by moving the four, five, and six to free cells, moving the seven to the eight of hearts, and then moving the six, five, and four (in that order) from free cells onto column 4. Visual feedback from FreeCell would let you know that the complex move is legal. If you clicked on the four of diamonds and then hovered over the eight of hearts, the cursor shape would become an open downward arrow. And, in fact, if you then clicked the eight of hearts, FreeCell would carry out the complex move for you automatically.

FreeCell also provides a visual alert—a flashing title bar—if you should reach a state where you have only one legal move available. If you're fortunate, that legal move might open additional moves for you.

> When you can't tell the suit of a partially covered card, right-click it. While you
> hold the mouse button down, FreeCell shows you the entire card.

# Strategy Tips

You'll do best in FreeCell if you consider your task to be organizing cards in the layout stacks, rather than moving them to home cells. If you get the cards organized down below, the home cells will take care of themselves.

Remember that once you've played a card to a home cell, you can't move it back to the layout. Sometimes a card is more useful to you on the layout than it is on its home stack. Some cards move automatically to the home row as they become available, but only if they have no possible strategic value on the layout stacks. For example, if you have three home rows with cards through three stacked on them, and the fourth row has a two, the three will be automatically moved when it becomes available, because a three is of no value on the layout stacks when there are no more twos to play on it. When you begin a game, your first goal should be to get at least one ace of each color to the home stacks.

Try to keep at least one free cell open. Don't move a card to a free cell just because you can—if you do, you might not have an empty free cell when you really need it.

Two cards of the same rank lying atop one another in a layout stack represent a potential hazard. When you see cards doubled in this manner, it's often a good idea to "undouble" them as quickly as you can.

## Changing Game Options

You can play 32,000 different hands of FreeCell. When you press F2 or choose New Game from the Game menu, FreeCell selects a game at random. To select a specific game, press F3 or choose Select Game from the Game menu, and enter the number of the game you want to play. If you want to play the same hand over, choose Restart Game.

FreeCell normally beeps and displays an error message when you try to make an illegal move. You can turn that action off by choosing Options from the Game menu and clearing the Display Messages On Illegal Moves check box. You can also turn off animation for faster play and you can turn off the double-click action of moving a card to a free cell.

# For Newcomers to Windows

# Setting Up
# Windows 2000

Microsoft Windows 2000 offers many exotic installation methods. For example, you can use automated installation scripts that include predefined answers to questions asked by the Setup program, use disk imaging (cloning), or use remote network installation. These methods are designed for deploying Windows 2000 Professional to a large number of computers (for example, in large corporations), and you'll find details about their use in the *Microsoft Windows 2000 Professional Resource Kit*.

This appendix describes the simplest method: installing Windows 2000 Professional on a single computer.

Windows 2000 is much easier to install than earlier versions of Windows, and on-screen information does a pretty good job of guiding you through the process. In this appendix, we show how to start the process and provide assistance with some of the minor stumbling blocks you might encounter along the way.

# Preparing for Installation

Before you rip into the Windows 2000 package and insert the CD-ROM into your computer's CD drive, take a few minutes to prepare for installation.

- Be sure your computer meets the system requirements for Windows 2000 Professional.

- Get information about your network from your network administrator.

- If your computer already has an earlier version of Windows installed:

  - Print a copy of the computer's configuration.

  - Back up your computer's hard disk.

  - Uncompress your hard disk if it's compressed.

  - Decide whether you want to upgrade your existing Windows installation or install a new copy.

## Checking System Requirements

Windows 2000 isn't for every computer; for best performance, you'll need a fast computer with plenty of memory and hard disk space. At a minimum, you'll need

- Pentium or higher processor (or compatible), 166 MHz or faster

- 32 MB of random access memory (RAM)

- VGA or higher resolution monitor

- Keyboard

- Microsoft Mouse or compatible pointing device

**NOTE**

> The Setup program doesn't actually enforce the minimum requirement for processor speed. That is, it will allow you to install Windows 2000 on any Pentium-class computer, regardless of the processor speed. (It refuses to install if you don't meet the other requirements.) But you probably won't be satisfied with the results on slower systems.

To install from the CD-ROM, you'll also need

- CD-ROM or DVD drive

For Newcomers to Windows

- 1.44-MB 3.5-inch floppy disk drive (unless your CD-ROM drive is bootable and supports running the Setup program from the CD)

To install from a shared network folder, you'll also need

- A network adapter card compatible with Windows 2000

- A working network connection

- Permission to access the shared network folder that contains the setup files

### If Possible, Add Memory

The optimum balance between price and performance for you depends on your budget, the type of work you do, and your degree of impatience waiting for the computer to complete a task. If your funds are limited, you'll get the most bang for your buck by adding memory; 96 MB to 256 MB provides excellent performance for most purposes.

If you're unsure about whether your computer meets these requirements, you can learn a lot about it by printing a configuration report, as explained later in this chapter. To determine whether your computer and its devices are compatible with Windows 2000, check the Hardware Compatibility List (HCL). You can find a copy of the HCL (saved as a text file that you can view with Notepad or WordPad) in the Support folder on the Windows 2000 Professional CD. An updated version of the HCL is available on the Internet at *www.microsoft.com/hcl*.

### Check Other Compatibility Issues Before You Install

The Windows 2000 Professional CD includes a program that lets you check your system for hardware or software that might not be compatible with Windows 2000, and it produces a report listing these items along with notes and other information about using your existing hardware and software. To use this program, your computer must already have Windows 95, Windows 98, or Windows NT installed. To run it, insert the Windows 2000 Professional CD into your CD-ROM drive. (If an invitation to set up Windows 2000 appears, ignore it for now.) Open the Start menu and choose Run. In the Run dialog box, type *d:\i386\winnt32 /checkupgradeonly* (substitute the letter of your CD-ROM drive for *d*), and click OK. The program displays its results on the screen and also saves the report in the Windows (or Winnt) folder as a text file named Upgrade.txt (on systems running Windows 95 or Windows 98) or Winnt32.log (on systems running Windows NT).

# Gathering Network Information

During installation, the Setup program asks about your network configuration, and you'll need to be prepared to provide

- **The name of your computer.** Each computer on a network must have a unique name. (For greatest compatibility, the name should contain only letters, numbers, and hyphens, and it should be no longer than 15 characters.)

- **The name of your domain or workgroup.** A domain requires that at least one computer on the network is a domain controller, and it must be running one of the server versions of Windows NT or Windows 2000 (Windows 2000 Server or Windows 2000 Advanced Server, for example). If your networked computer won't be part of a domain, it will be in a workgroup; to enable computers to easily "see" each other on the network, use the same workgroup name for every computer.

- **The IP address of your computer.** Each computer on a network must have a unique numeric address. You need to provide an IP address only if your network requires you to use a static IP address (that is, one that doesn't change, as opposed to one that's assigned to your computer automatically). If you're setting up a small network in which all computers will run Windows 2000, you don't need to assign an IP address.

Your network administrator should be able to provide all of this information.

**TIP**

> If your computer is already connected to a network and you're running an earlier version of Windows NT, a configuration report (described in the following section) includes all the information you need.

If your computer will be part of a domain, the network administrator must set up a domain account for your computer before you can join the domain (or you must have an account with domain administrative privileges to add the computer during setup). To configure your network connection during setup, your computer must be connected to the network before you begin the installation.

> **NOTE**
>
> You can change any of the network settings after you install Windows 2000—so if you don't have the information yet, don't let that stop you. But you will need to properly configure your network connection before you can interact with other computers on your local area network (LAN). *For more information, see "Working on a LAN," page 272.*

## Printing Configuration Information

The Setup program normally does a first-rate job of identifying and configuring all the devices attached to your computer. In some cases, however, it's unable to detect certain settings—such as the interrupt request (IRQ) used by an old adapter—and you'll need to enter those settings yourself as you configure the device. But it's also difficult for *you* to determine the correct settings unless you open up your computer—or you have a configuration report in hand. Therefore, if your computer and its devices are working properly and you're running an earlier version of Windows, it's an excellent idea to print a configuration report before you begin installing Windows 2000.

To print a configuration report from Windows NT 4:

1 Open the Start menu and choose Programs, Administrative Tools (Common), Windows NT Diagnostics.

2 Click Print.

3 In the Create Report dialog box, make the settings shown below, and then click OK.

To print a configuration report from Windows 95 or Windows 98:

**1** Right-click the My Computer icon on the desktop and choose Properties from the shortcut menu.

**2** Click the Device Manager tab.

**3** Click Print.

**4** In the Print dialog box, select System Summary and click OK.

## Backing Up Your Hard Disk

If your computer already has an earlier version of Windows installed, you should back up all the files on the hard disk where you plan to install Windows 2000 before you begin the installation. The Microsoft Backup program included with Windows NT allows you to back up your files to tape. The Backup program included with Windows 95 and Windows 98 also allows you to back up your files to a file on a hard disk, a network drive, or removable disks (such as floppy disks or Zip disks).

To start the Backup program in Windows NT, open the Start menu and choose Programs, Administrative Tools (Common), Backup.

To start the Backup program in Windows 95 or Windows 98, open the Start menu and choose Programs, Accessories, System Tools, Backup. (If Backup doesn't appear on the menu, use Add/Remove Programs in Control Panel to install Backup.)

You should also export data files that you want to reuse or import into equivalent Windows 2000 programs, such as e-mail messages, Web browser bookmarks, and so on.

## Uncompressing Your Hard Disk

Windows 2000 is incompatible with DriveSpace and DoubleSpace—disk compression programs that came with Windows 98, Windows 95, and MS-DOS 6—as well as third-party compression programs. Therefore, unless you're planning to start fresh and format your hard disk (a task that the Setup program can perform for you), you need to uncompress any compressed drives.

To uncompress a drive using Windows 95 or Windows 98:

**1** Open the Start menu and choose Programs, Accessories, System Tools, DriveSpace.

For Newcomers to Windows

**2** In the DriveSpace dialog box, select the compressed drive.

**3** Open the Drive menu and choose Uncompress.

To uncompress a drive using MS-DOS:

**1** At the command prompt, type *drvspace* (if you have MS-DOS 6.22) or *dblspace* (if you have an earlier version).

**2** Select the drive you want to uncompress.

**3** Open the Tools menu and choose Uncompress.

# Upgrading vs. Installing a New Copy

The Setup program can *upgrade* your computer to Windows 2000 Professional if your computer has one of the following operating systems installed:

- Windows 95 (all versions)
- Windows 98 (all versions)
- Windows NT Workstation 3.51
- Windows NT Workstation 4

With any of these operating systems, you have a choice: you can upgrade to Windows 2000 Professional, or you can install a new copy of Windows 2000 Professional (sometimes called a *clean install*). (If you have a different operating system, if you already have more than one operating system installed, or if you're installing onto a new, blank hard disk, your only choice is to install a new copy.)

If you choose to upgrade, Setup replaces your existing Windows files but it preserves your settings, such as desktop appearance, color schemes, network connections, and so on. More important, it retains the programs you have installed and all of their settings. So, after you complete the upgrade installation, you're ready to pick up right where you left off before installing—with the added features of Windows 2000. (Some programs that work in earlier versions of Windows don't work with Windows 2000, however. The upgrade report described earlier in this chapter identifies many such programs. *For details, see "Checking System Requirements," page 808.*)

If you choose to install a new copy, Setup installs Windows 2000 in a new folder. When Setup completes, all Windows preferences and options will be set to their default settings. And you'll need to install the programs you use—even if you already installed them under an earlier version of Windows.

In summary, upgrading provides the simplest, fastest method for moving a computer running Windows to the latest version, with minimal interruption. On the other hand, installing a new copy discards (or at the very least, ignores) the arcane registry entries, files, and other detritus that accumulate over time, giving you an opportunity to start fresh. A clean install allows you to free up disk space and it might improve performance.

# Beginning the Installation

The Setup program manages the entire installation process: requesting information from you, detecting your computer's hardware configuration, copying files, and restarting the computer as needed. On-screen messages explain what Setup is doing, and (for the most part) explain your options at each step along the way.

How you start the Setup program depends on whether you're installing from the CD or from a shared network folder, and whether your computer already has an earlier version of Windows installed. (To install from a network folder, the folder must contain the contents of the i386 folder from the CD. You must have a working network connection, and you must have Read access to the shared folder.) The following sections explain how to start Setup in each of these scenarios.

## Installing from the Windows 2000 Professional CD

To start an installation from an earlier version of Windows:

1 After Windows starts, insert the Windows 2000 Professional CD into your CD-ROM drive.

2 If a message appears that asks whether you want to upgrade your computer to Windows 2000 Professional, click Yes—even if you plan to install a new copy.

If no such message appears, open the Start menu and choose Run. (If you're running Windows 3.1 or Windows NT 3.*x*, in Program Manager, open the File menu and choose Run.) In the Run dialog box, type *d:\i386\winnt32* (replace *d* with the letter of your CD-ROM drive) and click OK. (If you're running Windows 3.1, type *d:\i386\winnt* instead.)

**3** When the Welcome page of the Windows 2000 Setup Wizard appears, select the appropriate option: Upgrade, or Install A New Copy. *For information about this choice, see "Upgrading vs. Installing a New Copy," page 813.*

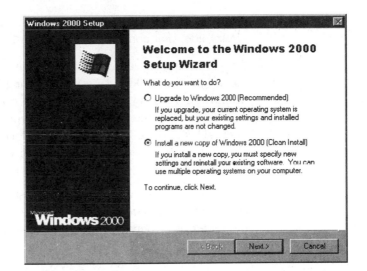

You can't upgrade from Windows NT Server (any version), Windows NT Workstation versions earlier than 3.51, or Windows 3.1. If you're running one of those operating systems, the Upgrade option is unavailable.

**4** Click Next and follow the on-screen instructions.

To start an installation if you don't have an earlier version of Windows installed:

**1** With your computer turned off, insert Windows 2000 Setup Boot Disk 1 into your computer's floppy disk drive.

**> NOTE**

If your computer is able to boot from the CD-ROM drive, you can insert the Windows 2000 Professional CD into the CD-ROM drive instead of inserting the Setup Boot Disk into your floppy drive.

**2**  Turn on the computer.

**3**  Follow the on-screen instructions.

## Installing from a Shared Network Folder

To start an upgrade installation from a shared network folder:

**1**  Use your existing operating system to connect to the shared network folder that contains the Windows 2000 setup files.

**2**  If you're using an earlier version of Windows, open the Start menu and choose Run. (If you're running Windows 3.1 or Windows NT 3.*x*, in Program Manager, open the File menu and choose Run.) In the Run dialog box, type *path*\*winnt32* (replace *path* with the drive letter to the folder or its network path— information your network administrator can provide) and click OK. (If you're running Windows 3.1, type *path*\*winnt* instead.)

If you're using another operating system, at the command prompt, type *path*\*winnt* (replace *path* with the drive letter to the folder or its network path) and press Enter.

**3**  Follow the on-screen instructions.

# Completing the Installation

This section is intended to guide you through the trickier areas of the Setup program. Fortunately, those areas are few and far between. And except for the first two choices described in the following sections— selection of an installation partition and a file system for the system drive—the other settings you make during setup can be changed at any time later. If you're unsure how to proceed at some point, accept the default setting proposed by Setup. After you complete the installation, refer to other sections of this book for information on changing particular settings and options.

# Selecting a Partition

A hard disk can be divided into one or more logical partitions; when you run Windows 2000 (or another operating system), each partition appears to be an independent hard drive. During Setup, if you don't choose to upgrade an existing version of Windows, you might see a screen similar to the one shown in Figure A-1. Setup needs you to select the partition on which you want to install Windows 2000. You can install Windows 2000 on any partition that has enough free space. If you want to continue using another operating system that's already installed, you must install Windows 2000 on a different partition from the one used by the other operating system.

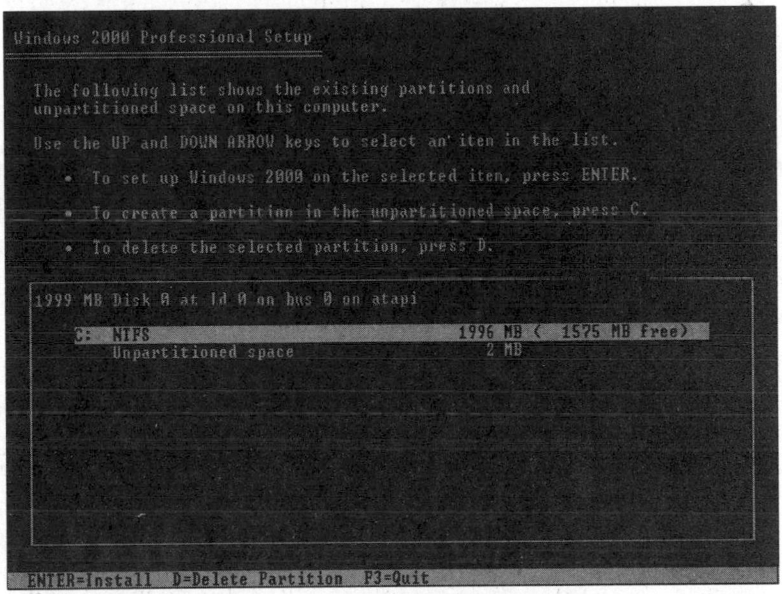

**FIGURE A-1.**

Select a partition for Windows 2000—or clear the decks and create a new partition.

At this point, you have the opportunity to completely remove all data from your hard drive and start with a clean slate. If you really want to start fresh—and you have backups of any files you want to save—select a partition and press D to delete the partition. Confirm your decision on the next two screens, and then repeat the process for each remaining partition. Then select Unpartitioned Space, press C to create a partition, and specify the size. Repeat this step to create more than one partition on your hard disk.

**⊘ WARNING**

*Be sure* you have backups of any data you want before you delete a partition. Once you do that, any data previously on the hard disk is irretrievable.

When the partitions are set up the way you want them, select the one on which you want to install Windows 2000 and press Enter. If the partition hasn't been formatted, the Setup program then formats it. (If you created other new partitions, you can format them after you finish installing Windows 2000.)

## Selecting a File System

The Setup program might ask you whether you want to format (or convert) your hard disk to the NTFS file system, either during the character-based portion of Setup (see Figure A-2) or during the graphical portion (see Figure A-3).

**FIGURE A-2.**

If you select an unformatted partition, Setup must format it.

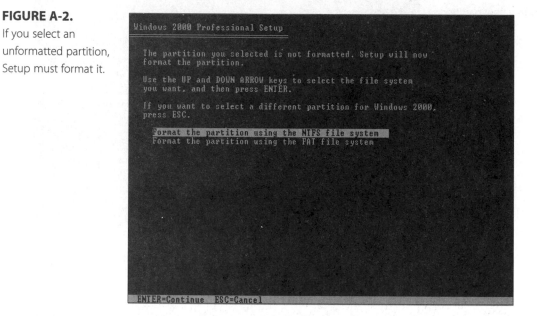

**? SEE ALSO**

For information about file systems, see "Understanding File Systems," page 582.

If you're going to use another operating system on your computer in addition to Windows 2000 (in a multiple-boot configuration), you probably want to use the FAT file system. (In other words, you do *not* want Setup to convert the disk to NTFS.) If Windows 2000 will be your only operating system, you'll be better off with NTFS.

**FIGURE A-3.**
Allow Setup to convert your partition to NTFS unless you're going to set up a computer that also boots another operating system.

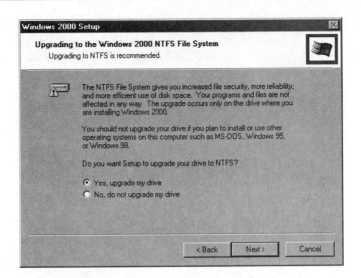

## Specifying the Computer Name and Administrator Password

When the screen shown in Figure A-4 on the next page first appears, you'll see that Setup proposes a cryptic name for your computer based on your name, with various characters appended to it. This is one place where you should feel free to override the default proposed by Setup and enter a name that's easier to remember and easier to type. If your network administrator has assigned a computer name for you, use it. Otherwise, create a name that's unique on your network (that is, it's not the same as the name of any other computer, workgroup, or domain), that's 15 characters or less, and that contains only letters and numbers. (The actual rules aren't this strict, but you might encounter problems if the name is longer or if it includes spaces or punctuation.)

**? SEE ALSO**
For information about user accounts, see Chapter 27, "Implementing Windows 2000 Security."

This same screen is the place where you create the password for the Administrator user account. This user account has complete control of the computer, and you shouldn't use it as your everyday account. Be sure to write down the Administrator password you create and store it in a safe place; if you can't find it when you need to perform administrative tasks (such as adding new hardware, creating user accounts, or taking ownership of files created on your computer by someone else), you're sunk. (You might need to reinstall Windows to regain your administrative privileges.)

For Newcomers to Windows

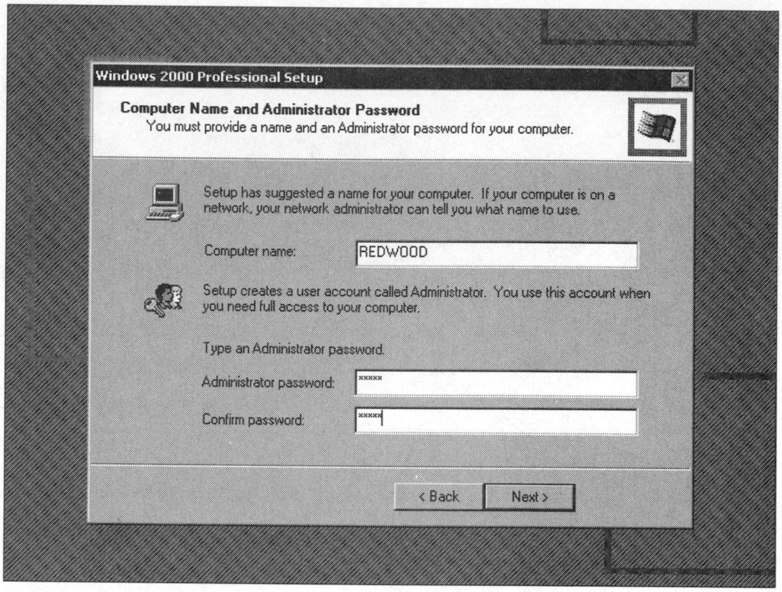

**FIGURE A-4.**
Type the computer name assigned by your network administrator.

## Specifying Networking Settings

**SEE ALSO**
For information about configuring network connections, see "Working on a LAN," page 272.

On the Networking Settings page, the Setup program offers two choices: Typical Settings and Custom Settings. The latter choice takes you to additional dialog boxes that let you set up network adapters, protocols, and services. Fortunately, in most cases you don't need to go there. If all the computers on your network run Windows 2000 or Windows NT, select Typical Settings. For other network configurations, consult your network administrator for the requirements of your particular setup. (If you don't have the information you need while you're running Setup, select Typical Settings. You can always change networking settings after you complete the installation.)

On the Workgroup Or Computer Domain page (see Figure A-5), you specify whether your computer is a member of a domain or a workgroup, and you specify the name of the domain or workgroup.

If your computer will be part of a domain with security managed by a domain controller running Windows 2000 Server or Windows NT Server, select Yes and enter the name of the domain, which your network administrator should provide. The network administrator must set up an account for your computer on the domain controller before you install Windows 2000. If Setup can't find a computer account on the domain controller, it offers you the opportunity to create a computer account. To do that, however, you'll need to provide the user name and password of an account that is a member of the Domain Admins group on the domain controller.

If your computer account hasn't been set up and you don't have a user account with sufficient privileges to set up the computer account yourself, return to the screen shown in Figure A-5 and select No. Join a workgroup for now, complete the installation, and then work with the network administrator to join the domain.

In all other cases (your computer is not connected to a network or the network is not set up as a domain), select No. Type the name of the workgroup used by other computers on your network; the default (WORKGROUP) is perfectly adequate for a small network with a single workgroup.

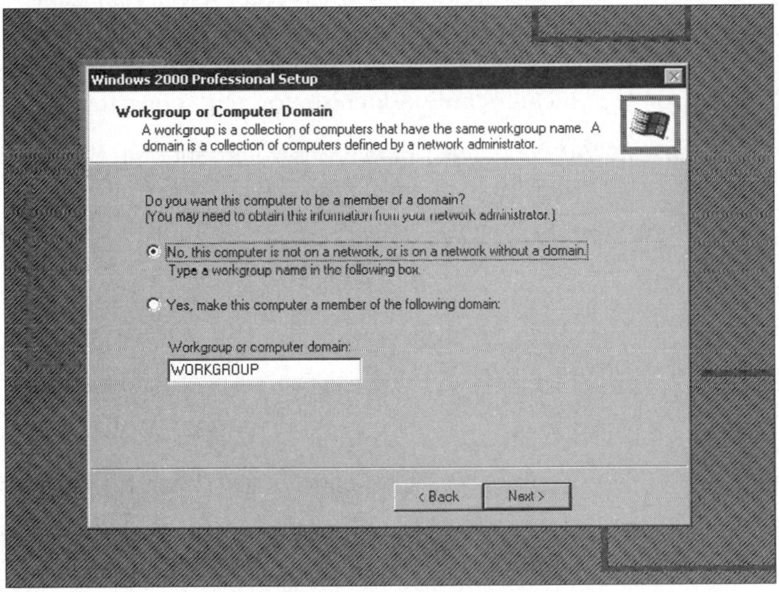

**FIGURE A-5.**

If you're unable to join a domain during setup, select No and then join a domain after you complete the installation.

**Configuring Logon Options**

After you see the Completing The Windows 2000 Setup Wizard page and click Finish, you might think you're done. In fact, after the computer restarts, the Network Identification Wizard leads you through one final task: setting up logon options. See Figure A-6, on the next page.

Unless your computer is not connected to a network (or the Internet) and it's in a secure location where others don't have physical access to it, we recommend that you select the first option: Users Must Enter A User Name And Password To Use This Computer. If you select this

**? SEE ALSO**

For information about logging on, see Appendix B, "Logging On and Logging Off." For information about creating user accounts, see "Working with Local User Accounts and Groups," page 564.

option, you'll need to log on by providing a user name and password each time you start your computer. The first time you log on after you complete the installation, use Administrator as the user name and the password you created earlier. Then immediately create a new user account for yourself and use that account ever after. (If your computer is part of a domain, you can log on using your domain user account and password; you don't need to log on as Administrator or set up a local user account.)

If you select the second option in the dialog box shown in Figure A-6, whenever you start your computer, Windows automatically enters the user name and password you specify here—in effect bypassing the entire logon process. Although this sounds convenient, it means that anyone who turns on your computer logs on using your credentials. If you decide to go this route, select your name in the User Name list. (If you joined a domain earlier in the setup process, the list includes all the domain user accounts. If you didn't join a domain, the list includes only Administrator and your name.)

If you have a domain user account, enter its password in the two password boxes; the domain controller requires its entry before you can log on to the domain. If you're not part of a domain, you can create a password by entering it here—but because you're eschewing security with this choice, there's little need to create a password.

After the Network Identification Wizard finishes, the installation is complete and you can log on to Windows 2000 Professional for the first time.

**FIGURE A-6.**

For best security, select the first option.

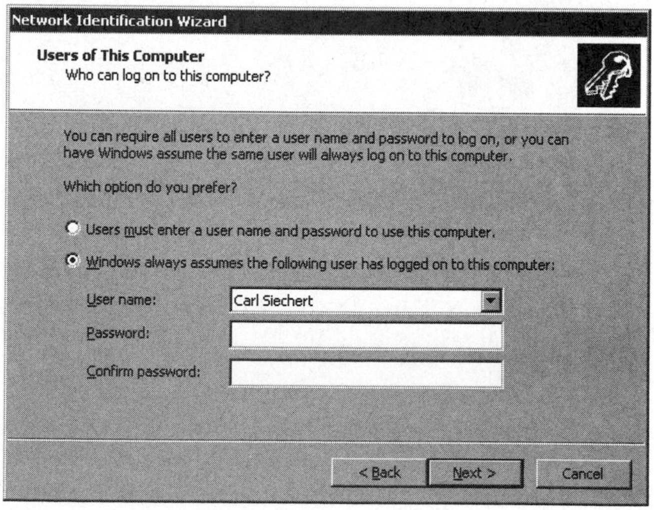

## APPENDIX B

# Logging On
# and Logging Off

Microsoft Windows 2000 is designed to be a secure operating system. One requirement of a secure operating system is that each person who uses the computer must have an existing user account, must log on, and must be authorized by the operating system before he or she can do anything useful with the computer. This is quite a departure from Microsoft Windows 98 and its predecessors, which allow anyone to log on—using an existing account name, by creating a new account, or by using no account at all. In fact, most computers running Windows 98 and earlier versions are set up so that users never need to log on at all, so this process might be new to you even if you're a long-time Windows user.

# Starting a Windows 2000 Session

To start a Windows 2000 session on a computer that's turned off, first be sure there's no disk in drive A, and then turn on the system. In a moment or three, you'll be in Windows 2000.

If your computer has been set up to run two or more different operating systems—Windows 2000 and Windows 98, for example—you'll arrive first at the multiple-boot screen. You'll see the names of the available operating systems and a countdown timer. If you do nothing, the default program will start once the countdown expires. The default program will be the one most recently installed, unless you've manually changed the setting. To avoid the countdown delay, be sure Microsoft Windows 2000 Professional is highlighted (move the highlight with the arrow keys if necessary), and then press Enter.

## Logging On

What you see next depends on whether your computer is part of a network and how it was set up. After Windows completes its startup tasks, you'll see one of the following:

- Welcome To Windows dialog box

- Log On To Windows dialog box

- The Windows desktop, taskbar, and (possibly) some open windows

These three possibilities actually represent the steps required to log on, which we describe in greater detail in the next section. The section after that explains how to change the logon options so that you can bypass the first or second step if you like.

Systems set up for the greatest security initially display a Welcome To Windows dialog box that invites you to log on by pressing Ctrl+Alt+Delete, as shown in Figure B-1.

You might recall that in early versions of Windows and MS-DOS, pressing Ctrl+Alt+Delete resets your computer. In Windows 2000, however, pressing this key combination invokes a component of the Windows 2000 security system, allowing you to do such things as log on or off.

When you press this key combination at startup, you arrive at the Log On To Windows dialog box, where you're asked to supply your user account name and password. (See Figure B-2.) Note that passwords in

Windows 2000 are case sensitive—that is, the system distinguishes uppercase letters from lowercase ones. If your password is gK47LnZ, for example, you must type it exactly that way every time you log on. Your user name, on the other hand, is not case sensitive.

**FIGURE B-1.**
If this dialog box appears, press Ctrl+Alt+Delete to initiate the logon process.

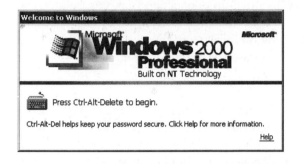

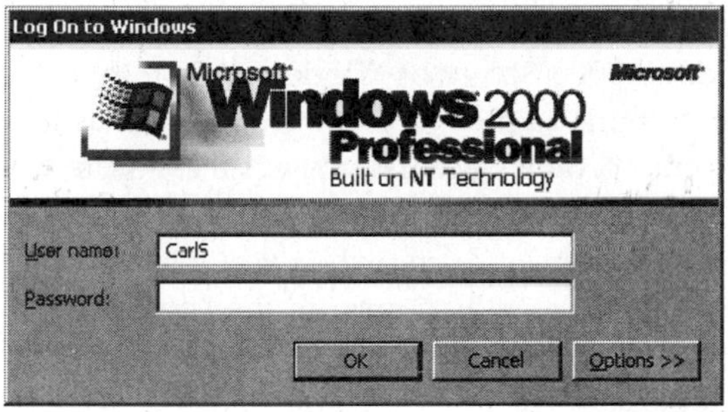

**FIGURE B-2.**
Ordinarily, the User Name box is filled in with the name of the last user who logged on.

**NOTE**

If you don't fill in the Log On To Windows dialog box within a certain amount of time, Windows redisplays the welcome message. Simply press Ctrl+Alt+Delete again to bring back the Log On To Windows dialog box.

## Setting Other Options

You can make your first forays into Windows 2000 Professional on your computer with just the User Name and Password entries. Clicking the Options button in the Log On To Windows dialog box enlarges the dialog box to display some additional options that you might find useful later:

- Log On Using Dial-Up Connection

- Log On To

- Shutdown

## Log On Using Dial-Up Connection

For information about dial-up connections, see "Using Dial-Up Connections," page 281.

Selecting the Log On Using Dial-Up Connection check box allows you to connect to a network via a modem and a dial-up connection. Depending on how your system is configured, you might be able to set up a dial-up connection from this point. (A wizard appears when you click OK.) More likely, your system is configured so that you must first log on locally and then set up a dial-up connection, which you can then use for future logon attempts.

## Log On To

For information about user accounts and access privileges, see Chapter 27, "Implementing Windows 2000 Security." For information about switching between domains and workgroups, see "Joining a Domain or Workgroup," page 276.

If your computer is part of a domain-based network, your Log On To Windows dialog box includes a Log On To box, from which you can select the name of your computer or the name of a domain. A *domain* is a collection of computers that, for security purposes, obtain user account and password authentication from one or more network servers known as *domain controllers*. (Domain controllers run Windows 2000 Server or Windows NT.) On a domain-based network, your account name and password, as well as the information concerning your account's access privileges, are stored on the domain controller rather than on your own computer. In that case, you'll need to supply the domain name when you log on. If the correct domain name doesn't already appear in the Log On To box, click the arrow at the right side of the box and select the domain name from the list that opens.

**NOTE**

> A network that doesn't use domain security is known as a *workgroup*. In a workgroup, each computer uses a local security database with its own list of user accounts, passwords, and access privileges. The Log On To box doesn't appear if your computer isn't configured for domain use because each person's user account and password are checked only against the local security database; no centralized security database exists, as in a domain.

Even if it participates in a domain, your computer also maintains the local security database with its own list of user accounts, passwords, and access privileges. If your computer is part of a domain, you can choose to log on using the local security database by selecting your computer's name in the Log On To box—but there's rarely any reason to do so. You might want to log on locally when you set up new hardware or software and your domain user account doesn't have local administrative privileges. In that case, log on using the local Administrator account (or another account that's a member of the local Administrators group).

## Shutdown

The third additional option revealed by clicking Options in the Log On To Windows dialog box—Shutdown—simply provides a way to shut the system down (or restart it or place it on standby) without first logging on. *For information about shutdown options, see "Ending a Windows Session," page 830.*

# Completing the Logon Process

Each time you log on to Windows, the User Name and Log On To portions of the logon dialog box are automatically filled out with the most recently used entries, so if you're the only one using your computer, all you need to do is type your password. In any case, once you've supplied all the required information, simply click OK to begin your session. Windows completes the logon process by restoring your personal working environment, including your Start menu setup, your choice of wallpaper and screen colors, your mouse and keyboard option settings, your home folder and local path, and any network-drive connections you've established.

If a logon script has been associated with your user account, the commands in that script are executed. A *logon script* is a program that runs automatically on startup. Your system administrator might have created one for you, or you can create one yourself. *For more information, see "Specifying a Logon Script," page 570.*

---

### Locking Your Computer

Locking your computer protects your privacy while you're away from your machine. It also prevents other users (except ones with administrative privileges) from taking over your computer while you're away. To lock your computer, press Ctrl+Alt+Delete and click the Lock Computer button. Windows hides whatever you were working on and displays a message indicating when and by whom the computer was locked.

While your computer is locked, programs keep on running. Screen savers save, for example, and macros go on executing. Locking simply shuts other users out, preventing them from seeing what's going on or otherwise interacting with Windows.

To unlock a locked computer, press Ctrl+Alt+Delete again and type your password.

# Changing Logon Options

As explained in the previous sections, you might see a Welcome To Windows dialog box and Log On To Windows dialog box before you're allowed to see the Windows desktop—or you might not. If your computer is in a secure location and you're not concerned that others might use it to access your data, you can bypass those dialog boxes.

Don't make the decision to bypass either of these dialog boxes lightly.

- Pressing Ctrl+Alt+Delete might be a little annoying, but it ensures that the Log On To Windows dialog box that appears is really the one that's part of Windows 2000 Professional—and not an impostor that looks just like it but actually has the dual purpose of logging you on *and* capturing your password for sinister reasons. Only Windows itself can respond to the Ctrl+Alt+Delete key combination.

- Bypassing the Log On To Windows dialog box means that the system effectively enters your user name and password when you turn on the power. Anyone who has physical access to your computer can then log on as "you" and have access to all computer resources that you normally have.

To bypass the Welcome To Windows dialog box (the one that asks you to press Ctrl+Alt+Delete):

**1** Open the Start menu and choose Settings, Control Panel. In Control Panel, open Users And Passwords.

**2** In the Users And Passwords dialog box, click the Advanced tab.

**3** Under Secure Boot Settings, clear the Require Users To Press Ctrl-Alt-Delete Before Logging On check box.

To bypass the Log On To Windows dialog box (the one that asks for your user name and password):

**1** Open the Start menu and choose Settings, Control Panel. In Control Panel, open Users And Passwords.

**2** On the Users tab, clear the Users Must Enter A User Name And Password To Use This Computer check box.

> **NOTE**
>
> This check box doesn't appear if your computer is part of a domain. Only computers that aren't connected to a network or are part of a workgroup can bypass this dialog box. Domain users must enter a user name and password, even to log on locally.

The Automatically Log On dialog box appears.

**3** Type the user name and password for the account that you want to be logged on each time you start your computer.

# Ending a Windows Session

When it's time to quit, *never simply turn off your computer*. Instead, open the Start menu and choose Shut Down. In the dialog box that appears (see Figure B-3), select Shut Down from the list and click OK. Windows closes any running programs, and in a moment or two, turns off the power to your computer. (On older computers that don't have power management capabilities, a message notifies you that it is safe to turn off your computer.)

**FIGURE B-3.**
Click the arrow to view your shut-down options.

 **NOTE**

Shutting down your computer makes all its shared resources unavailable to other users on your network. If any of your computer's resources—folders or printers, for example—are shared and you want to quit without disconnecting your colleagues, you can log off without shutting down your computer. *See "Logging Off Without Quitting," on the next page.*

**TIP**

You can also display the Shut Down Windows dialog box by pressing Ctrl+Alt+Delete and clicking the Shut Down button.

If for any reason your system isn't ready to be shut down, you will be advised. For example, if you have unsaved work in a program, that program displays a prompt, giving you the opportunity to save before quitting. A program might also display a "can't quit" message if it objects to being closed for any other reason. This can happen, for example, if the program is in the middle of a communications session or if it's displaying a dialog box and waiting for you to respond.

If you don't respond to the "can't quit" message within a certain period of time, Windows displays the message shown in Figure B-4. Your choices are spelled out in the text of the message. The safest thing to do is click Cancel, return to your program, and then either respond to its needs or wait until it has finished whatever it's doing.

The message shown in Figure B-4 also appears if a program has stopped responding to the operating system. You can use the End Now button to terminate such a hung program. Do not use this button capriciously, however. If a program isn't hung but is simply busy, terminating it without closing it normally might have adverse consequences—such as the loss of any work you've created since the last time you used the program's Save command.

**FIGURE B-4.**

This message appears if you don't respond to a program's "can't quit" message or if a program is hung.

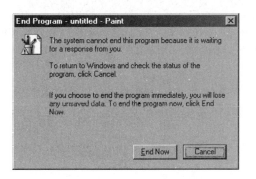

## Switching to Low Power States

**SEE ALSO**

For information about configuring standby and hibernate options and reawakening a slumbering computer, see Chapter 26, "Power Management."

The list of options in your Shut Down Windows dialog box might include one or two options that let you end a session by switching to a low power state. The Stand By option shuts off your display and hard disk and reduces your computer's other vital functions to a barely detectable pulse. Hibernate provides maximum power savings: selecting it saves the contents of your computer's memory to disk and then shuts off the power altogether.

## Logging Off Without Quitting

The Log Off option in the Shut Down Windows dialog box closes all running programs and logs you off your computer and network but doesn't shut down Windows. You might want to use this option at quitting time if someone else will be using your computer.

When you log off without quitting, any resources shared by your computer remain available to other users on the network. You might want to quit in this manner, for example, if others will be printing to a printer attached to your computer.

To log off, do either of the following:

- Open the Start menu and choose Shut Down. In the dialog box that appears, select Log Off and then click OK.

- Press Ctrl+Alt+Delete and then click Log Off. Windows asks you to confirm that you want to end your session.

After you log off, Windows presents the same Welcome To Windows dialog box that you saw at the beginning of your current session, allowing you or another user to log back on. (If you've elected to bypass the Ctrl+Alt+Delete requirement, the Log On To Windows dialog box appears instead.)

# APPENDIX C

# Learning the Basics

The following pages provide a brief orientation to the Microsoft Windows user interface, including the following topics:

- Touring the Windows 2000 Desktop
- Working with windows
- Working with menus and dialog boxes
- Using scroll bars

We begin with a brief tour of the Windows 2000 desktop.

# A Quick Tour

Figure C-1 shows some of the elements of a typical Windows 2000 desktop. Along the left edge of the screen are five *system icons*— My Documents, My Computer, My Network Places, Recycle Bin, and Internet Explorer. These are objects that Windows 2000 usually creates for you automatically when you install the operating system. Along the bottom edge is the *taskbar*. Within the taskbar are the *Start button*, the *Quick Launch toolbar*, two *taskbar buttons*, and the *status area*. The desktop shown in the figure also includes some program icons and some shortcuts to programs (the shortcut icons are the ones with the arrows in their lower left corners).

**? SEE ALSO**

For information about customizing your desktop, see Chapter 4, "Customizing the Desktop."

Your desktop might look similar to this figure, or it might look much different. Your taskbar might be taller than the one shown, it might lie against a different edge of your desktop, or it might be temporarily invisible. You might have a picture or a "wallpaper" pattern draped over your desktop, or your desktop might look like a Web page. Unlike the icons shown in the figure, yours might not be underscored. It's even possible that your desktop has no visible icons at all.

**FIGURE C-1.**

A typical Windows 2000 desktop includes these elements. Yours may have other kinds of objects as well.

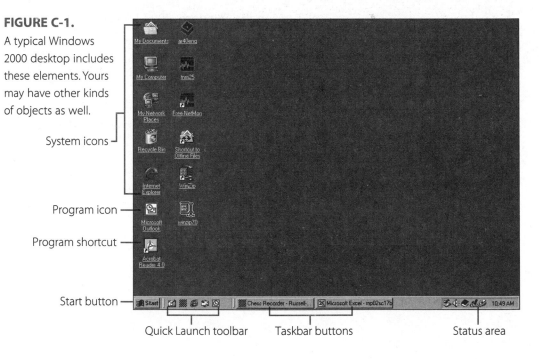

Windows 2000 gives you great flexibility regarding the layout, content, and display style of your desktop. You can personalize it to suit your tastes and moods, and you can switch from one visual mode to another at will. For now, we'll concentrate on the objects shown in Figure C-1, because these are important elements of the Windows user interface—elements that you're likely to see at one time or another as you work with the operating system.

## The Start Button and Start Menu

The Start button's function is to open the Start menu. Click it once, and a set of choices, similar to the one shown in Figure C-2, emerges.

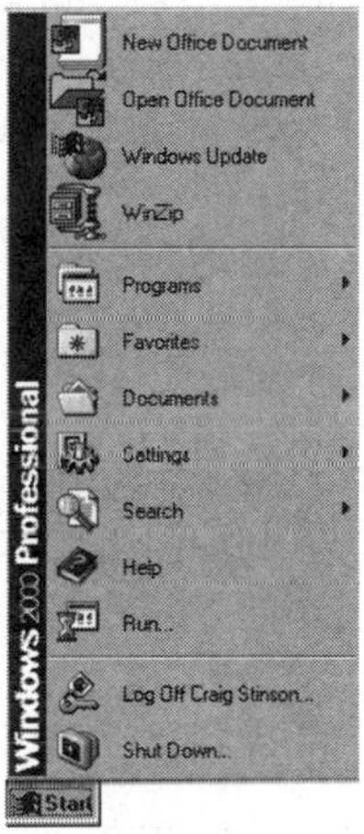

**FIGURE C-2.**

Clicking the Start button displays the Start menu's folder and programs.

New Office Document
Open Office Document
Windows Update
WinZip

Programs ▶
Favorites ▶
Documents ▶
Settings ▶
Search ▶
Help
Run...

Log Off Craig Stinson...
Shut Down...

Start

The Start menu makes most of your programs, the documents you've most recently used, and even your favorite Internet sites, available with a single mouse click. It's also one of the simplest ways to accomplish several other important tasks, such as finding documents and programs on your computer or on a network and accessing general Help topics. The Start menu is also a "quit" menu; you can use its Shut Down command whenever you need to end a Windows session.

**TIP**

You can always get to the Start menu by pressing Ctrl+Esc, even if the Start button isn't visible.

## Toolbars

Toolbars contain sets of related buttons for easy mouse activation of commonplace tasks, such as launching programs or opening documents. The Quick Launch toolbar, shown in Figure C-1 on page 834, provides icons for launching Microsoft Internet Explorer and Microsoft Outlook Express. It also includes the Show Desktop icon, which hides your applications and makes your desktop completely visible with a single click. A second click restores the application windows. You can add additional program icons to launch other applications.

**? SEE ALSO**

For information about using toolbars, see "Using Desktop Toolbars," page 50.

Windows provides several toolbars that you can use or ignore as you please. To see which ones are available, right-click a blank area of your taskbar. Then choose Toolbars from the shortcut menu that appears. You can add icons or remove icons from the standard toolbars, and you can create new toolbars of your own. Toolbars can remain on the taskbar, or they can be dragged away to "float" anywhere on the desktop.

## Taskbar Buttons

In the center portion of the taskbar, you will see a button for each program you've started and each folder you've opened. (If you use Microsoft Word 2000 with more than one document, you'll also see a button for each open Word document.) You can click these buttons to move from one open program or folder to another.

If you have a many programs or folders open, you may not be able to read all the text on the taskbar buttons. However, if you rest your mouse pointer for a moment on any button whose text is not completely visible, the full text will appear in a pop-up box, or *ScreenTip*.

## The Status Area

In the right corner of the taskbar (if the taskbar is displayed horizontally) or at the bottom (if it's displayed vertically), Windows provides information about the status of your system. When a printer is active, for example, a printer icon appears in this status area. When you're connected by modem to the Internet, an icon that looks like two connected computers appears. If you're running Windows on a portable computer, icons in this area let you know whether your computer is currently draining or recharging its battery. The icons that appear in the status area depend on how you use your system and what equipment and programs you have installed. If you're not sure what an icon represents, hover your mouse pointer over it and read the ScreenTip description. In many cases, you can get additional information about a status-area icon by double-clicking it. Some icons in the status area will open a menu that lets you open a program or configure a device's options when you double-click them or click them with the right mouse button.

The status area also includes, by default, a clock. You can set the clock by double-clicking it and setting the correct time in the dialog box that appears. The clock is also a calendar; hover the mouse pointer over the time, and the current date appears.

# Working with Windows

All Windows-based programs run within rectangular frames called windows. As shown in Figure C-3, on the next page, these features are common to nearly all windows.

**Borders.** The four edges that define the perimeter of a window are called borders. You can drag the borders of most windows to change their size. *Dragging* is accomplished by pressing your mouse button while you move the mouse.

**Title bar.** Directly below the top border is a region that includes the window's name. This is called the title bar. You can move a window by dragging its title bar.

**Menu bar.** Directly below the title bar is the menu bar. The menu bar provides access to most of a program's commands.

**Toolbar.** Many windows include a toolbar, which is a row of buttons that provide mouse-click shortcuts for a program's commonly used commands.

**Work area.** The inside of a window is called the work area or client area.

**Control-menu box.** At the left edge of the title bar is the control-menu box. You can click here to get a menu of basic commands for sizing and positioning the window. These commands all have mouse-action equivalents, so you might never need to click the control-menu box.

**FIGURE C-3.**

Nearly all Windows-based programs run in windows that include these elements.

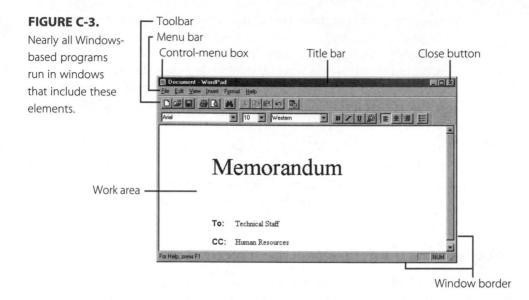

Toolbar
Menu bar
Control-menu box
Title bar
Close button
Work area
Window border

**Close button.** At the right edge of the title bar is a square containing an X. You can click here to close a document or folder, or to terminate a program.

TIP

Another way to close a program window, folder window, or dialog box is to press Alt+F4.

**Minimize, Restore, and Maximize buttons.** To the left of the Close button, you will find other buttons that look like these.

Minimize     Restore     Maximize

SEE ALSO

For information about using Alt+Tab to switch windows, see "Switching Between Windows," on the next page.

Clicking the Minimize button causes a window to collapse into its taskbar button. The window is still open, and the program inside it continues to run. But the window no longer takes up space on your desktop. You can reopen a minimized window by clicking its taskbar button or by using the Alt+Tab shortcut key.

Clicking the Maximize button causes a window to occupy all of the desktop. While you're using a program, you might want to keep its window maximized most of the time so that you have as much screen real estate as possible to work with.

Clicking the Restore button causes a window to assume an intermediate size—neither maximized nor minimized. With windows restored, you can keep two or more programs in view at the same time. You can adjust the size of a restored window by dragging its borders. *See "Sizing and Moving Windows," below.*

> **★ TIP**
>
> Another way to maximize a window is to double-click its title bar. If the window is already maximized, you can restore its intermediate size by double-clicking the title bar.

## Sizing and Moving Windows

To change a window's size, drag its borders. For example, to make the window wider, drag either the left or right border. To make a window both wider and taller, you can drag one of the corners.

To move a window, drag its title bar.

> **★ TIP**
>
> If your view is obstructed by another window or program, move it out of the way by dragging its title bar.

## Switching Between Windows

When two or more program windows are open at once, the one lying on top has what's called the *focus*. The window with the focus is the one that will respond to your next keystrokes. (The window that has the focus is sometimes also called the *foreground* or *active* window.) To switch the focus to another window, you can use any of the following techniques:

- Click anywhere on or in the window that you want to switch to.

- Click the taskbar button for the window you want to switch to.

- Press and hold the Alt key. Then press Tab to display an icon for each running program. A box surrounds the icon whose window currently has the focus. Continue holding Alt and pressing Tab until the window you want to switch to has the focus.

⭐ **TIP**

**Finding the Active Window**

If you're ever in doubt about which window has the focus, check your windows' title bars. The active window's title bar is normally displayed in one color, while the title bars of all inactive windows are displayed in another color. In addition, the taskbar button for the active window appears to be pressed in.

# Arranging Windows on the Screen

If you have several windows open at once, it might be hard to see what's going on. Windows provides some handy commands for making all your windows visible. To put all the windows in a neat stack, with each window's title bar visible, do the following:

**1** Right-click an unoccupied area of the taskbar. (Press Ctrl+Esc first if you can't see the taskbar.)

**2** Choose the Cascade Windows command.

With your windows in a cascade, you can easily switch focus by clicking any title bar.

If you want to see a portion of the contents of each open window, choose one of the tiling commands. Right-click the taskbar and choose either Tile Windows Horizontally or Tile Windows Vertically.

Show
Desktop

To minimize all open windows, right-click the taskbar and choose Minimize All Windows. Alternatively, if the Show Desktop button is visible, simply click it. *Show Desktop* is a standard element of the Quick Launch toolbar, one of several toolbars that can be displayed on the Windows 2000 taskbar. To select which toolbars display on your taskbar, right-click the taskbar, choose Toolbars, and then choose from the menu that appears. Those toolbars marked with a check mark are already turned on, and selecting them again will turn them off.

⭐ **TIP**

After you've minimized all windows by clicking Show Desktop, you can click it a second time to restore all windows to their former sizes and positions.

After cascading, tiling, or minimizing all windows, you can restore your windows to their previous positions by right-clicking the taskbar. The menu that appears includes a new command that reverses your previous action. For example, if you have just minimized all windows, the new command will read Undo Minimize All.

# Keeping Windows on Top

Some windows are designed to stay on top, even when they don't have the focus. Windows that contain help information, for example, often behave this way, allowing you to read their helpful text even while you're working in a maximized program.

Most programs that stay on top give you the option of disabling this behavior. If a stay-on-topper becomes a visual nuisance, look in its menu system for a command such as Always On Top or Stay On Top. Often you'll find it on the program's Control menu. *For information about the Control menu, see "Using the Control Menu and the Menu Bar," page 843.* These commands are usually *toggles*; you choose them once to turn the feature on and a second time to turn it off.

**TIP**

> The taskbar itself is a stay-on-top window. In its default display mode, it remains visible even when the foreground program is maximized. You can change this behavior by right-clicking an unoccupied part of the taskbar, choosing the Properties command, and clearing the check box labeled Always On Top by clicking the check box. (To get back to the taskbar when it's not visible, press Ctrl+Esc.)

# Adjusting Window Panes

Some programs use windows that are split vertically, horizontally, or even both vertically and horizontally. The resulting window divisions are called *panes*. Figure C-4 shows an example of a window divided vertically into panes.

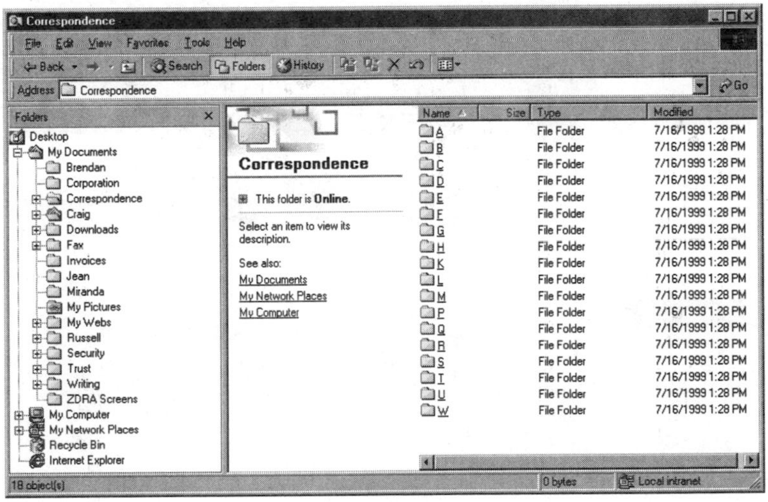

**FIGURE C-4.**
This window is divided into a left pane and a right pane. You can change the size of the panes by dragging the pane divider.

In most cases, when a window has been divided into panes, you can change the relative sizes of the panes by dragging the pane divider. In Figure C-4, for example, you could make the left pane wider by dragging the divider to the right.

## Working with Document Windows

*Document windows* are the windows you spend most of your time in, those that let you create or edit a document, whether it's text, a spreadsheet, or a work of art. Figure C-5 shows a program window containing three open document windows. Notice that each document window can be maximized, restored, minimized, moved, and sized. In most applications the documents must remain within the borders of the program window, in this case Finale 2000.

Notice that the title bar for one of the document windows (the one in the front of the cascade stack) is the same color as the title bar for the program window, indicating this document currently has the focus.

**FIGURE C-5.**

This program window shows three open document windows.

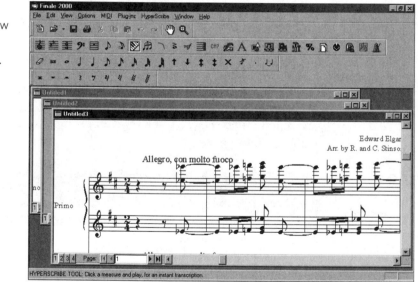

**TIP**

You can close the active document by pressing Ctrl+F4. The application and other documents remain open.

# Working with Menus and Dialog Boxes

In virtually all Windows-based programs, commands are chosen from *menus*—sets of options that appear when you click a menu title on a program's menu bar. When a program needs additional information from you before it can carry out your command, it presents a *dialog box*—a smaller window with places for you to fill in blanks or choose between preset options. Menus and dialog boxes behave in a consistent and predictable way in all Windows-based programs.

## Using the Control Menu and the Menu Bar

The two main elements of a Windows-based program's menu system are the Control menu and the menu bar. The *Control menu* opens when you click the icon at the left side of the title bar. The *menu bar* is the row of commands directly below the title bar.

The Control menu provides a set of window-management commands common to all programs, such as commands to move, resize, or close a window. With few exceptions, each program's Control menu includes the same commands.

The menu bar includes commands specific to the current program. Each word on the menu bar is the title of a menu that opens a set of related commands when you click the title. For example, a program's File menu includes commands for opening and saving files, the Edit menu has commands for changing the contents of a document, and so on.

## Choosing Commands with the Mouse

To open a menu with the mouse, click the desired menu title in the menu bar. To open the File menu, for example, click the word *File*. To open the Control menu, click the icon at the left edge of the title bar. To choose a command from an open menu, move the mouse pointer down until you reach the desired command, and then click.

To close the menu without choosing a command, click the mouse anywhere outside the open menu.

## Choosing Commands with the Keyboard

To choose any command with the keyboard, begin by pressing the Alt key. (You can also access the menu system by pressing F10.) When you do that, Windows highlights the first menu title on the menu bar. At this point, you can use the Left arrow and Right arrow keys to move around the menu bar. To open a particular menu, move to that menu and press the Down arrow or Up arrow key. To choose a command from an open menu, use the Up arrow and Down arrow keys to highlight the command you want, and then press Enter.

To leave the menu system without choosing a command, press the Alt key again, or click the mouse anywhere outside the menu system.

---

**Saving Time with Shortcut Keys**

Some menu commands have shortcut keys assigned to them. *Shortcut keys* are single keystrokes or simple keystroke combinations that execute a command directly. In many programs, for example, pressing Ctrl+S is equivalent to executing the File menu's Save command. When a shortcut key is available, it usually appears to the right of the command name on the menu.

A quick way to open a menu or select a command that doesn't have a shortcut key is to press Alt followed by the underlined letter in the menu, command, or dialog box option. *Dialog boxes are discussed in "Using Dialog Boxes," on the next page.* When possible, the underlined letter is usually the first letter of the menu name or command. In Microsoft Word, for example, you can open the File menu by pressing Alt+F, but to open the Format menu, you need to press Alt+O. Notice that once you open a menu, you can choose any of its commands by simply pressing the command's underlined letter.

---

# Using Shortcut Menus

In many parts of Windows 2000, as well as in many Windows-based programs, pressing the right mouse button opens a small menu appropriate to the currently selected object (or the one the mouse is pointing to). For example, if you right-click the taskbar, you get a menu of commands relating to only the taskbar. If you select a block of text in Microsoft Word and then right-click, you get a menu that includes commands for formatting, moving, and copying the selected text. These menus that appear when you right-click are called *shortcut menus*. Depending on how you set up your mouse or other pointing device, the right mouse button might act as the *secondary* button, as described here, or could be configured as the *primary* button. In this book we follow the conventional terminology, in which the primary button is referred to as the *left* button, and the secondary button described here is referred to as the *right* button.

**TIP**

When you right-click certain objects in Windows, the shortcut menu includes one command in boldface type. The boldface command is the one that would have been executed had you simply double-clicked the object instead of right-clicking it. *Double-clicking* is the art of tapping on the left mouse button twice in rapid succession.

# Dimmed Commands, Check Marks, and Submenus

Here are some other menu conventions observed by most Windows-based programs:

- A command that appears dimmed on a menu is one that's not available in the current context. In Microsoft Excel, for example, the Window menu's Unhide command appears dimmed until at least one window has been hidden.

- A check mark beside a command indicates that a certain condition has been turned on. Choosing such a command turns the condition off and removes the check mark.

- An arrowhead to the right of a command means that choosing this command opens a submenu. The Start menu on the taskbar, for example, has at least four such commands: Programs, Documents, Settings, and Search. Choose any one of these commands, and another menu unfurls.

# Using Dialog Boxes

An ellipsis (...) is a punctuation symbol signifying an incomplete sentence or quotation. In a Windows menu, an ellipsis following a command name indicates an incomplete command. Choosing such a command opens a dialog box.

Dialog boxes come in all sizes and shapes. Some are simple, others quite complex. But nearly all dialog boxes have the following components:

- One or more places for you to enter information or choose options

- One or more command buttons

Most dialog boxes have one command button that you click after you've filled in the dialog box to your satisfaction, and another that you click if you want to close the dialog box without making an entry. In many cases, these buttons are marked OK and Cancel, respectively. Many dialog boxes also have a button labeled Help or a button with a question mark on it; you can click this kind of button if you're not sure what some of the dialog box options mean.

**TIP**

> Pressing Esc or Alt+F4 in a dialog box is usually equivalent to clicking the Cancel button. It dismisses the dialog box without taking any further action. Still another way to dismiss a dialog box is to click the Close button on its title bar.

## Tabbed Dialog Boxes

The dialog box shown in Figure C-6 actually includes eight "pages" of options. You select the page you're interested in by clicking its tab at the top of the dialog box. For example, the View tab of the dialog box shown in the figure offers viewing options; to select editing options, click the Edit tab—and so on. Press Ctrl+Tab to flip through the pages with the keyboard.

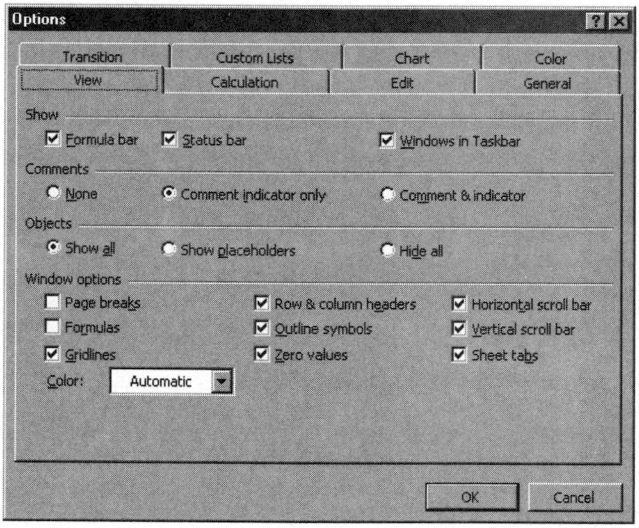

**FIGURE C-6.**

The tabs along the top of the dialog box let you shift from one set of options to another.

| Options | | | ? X |
|---|---|---|---|
| Transition | Custom Lists | Chart | Color |
| View | Calculation | Edit | General |

Show
☑ Formula bar   ☑ Status bar        ☑ Windows in Taskbar

Comments
○ None      ● Comment indicator only      ○ Comment & indicator

Objects
● Show all      ○ Show placeholders      ○ Hide all

Window options
☐ Page breaks        ☑ Row & column headers    ☑ Horizontal scroll bar
☐ Formulas           ☑ Outline symbols         ☑ Vertical scroll bar
☑ Gridlines          ☑ Zero values             ☑ Sheet tabs
Color:  [ Automatic ▼ ]

[ OK ]   [ Cancel ]

**TIP**

> If the current tab has a dotted marquee around it, as the View tab does in Figure C-6, you can also move between tabs by pressing the arrow keys.

# Using Scroll Bars

If a window isn't long enough to display its contents completely, Windows adds a *vertical scroll bar* to the right side of the window. If the window isn't wide enough, Windows adds a *horizontal scroll bar*. If it's neither long enough nor wide enough, Windows adds both kinds of scroll bars. Figure C-7 shows a window with vertical and horizontal scroll bars.

Scroll bars offer an easy way to navigate through a window with the mouse. They also provide useful information about the contents of the window.

In Figure C-7, notice the rectangular *scroll box* in each scroll bar. The position of this box within the scroll bar tells you where you are in the window itself. In the vertical scroll bar, for example, the scroll box is situated about 10 percent of the way down the bar. That means that roughly 10 percent of the window's contents lie above your current position in the window.

**FIGURE C-7.**

Scroll bars provide information about the contents of a window and allow you to move quickly from one part of the win- dow to another.

Now notice the size of the scroll boxes relative to the length of the scroll bars. The vertical box is about 5 percent of the length of the scroll bar itself. That means that about one twentieth of the window's vertical extent is currently visible within the window frame. The hori- zontal scroll bar works the same way.

For navigation purposes, you can use scroll bars in the following ways:

- To move up or down a line at a time, simply click the arrow at either end of the vertical scroll bar. To move side to side a character at a time (or by a small increment in a noncharacter display), click the arrow at either end of the horizontal bar.

- To move by approximately one windowful, click the mouse in the scroll bar itself, on either side of the scroll box.

- To continuously scroll a line at a time, click an arrow and hold down the mouse button. To continuously scroll a windowful at a time, click in the scroll bar itself and hold down the mouse button. When you arrive where you want to be, release the button.

- To move to a specific location, drag the scroll box. To move halfway down a long document, for example, you could move the vertical scroll box to about the midpoint of the vertical scroll bar.

## APPENDIX D

# Cutting, Pasting, Embedding, and Linking

T hree forms of data exchange are common in Microsoft Windows:

- Static moving and copying

- Embedding

- Linking

A "static" move or copy is a one-time transaction with a no-return policy. If you copy or cut a range of numbers from your spreadsheet and paste them statically into your word processor document, your word processor handles those numbers exactly as though you had typed them directly at the keyboard. You can format them, edit them, delete them, or stand them on their heads (if your word processor does that sort of thing), but they have no further relationship to the document and program in which they originated.

When you *embed* one document's data in a second document, the data remembers where it came from. If you want to edit that data, Windows lets you work in the data's original context. For example, suppose you copy a block of numbers from a spreadsheet and embed them in a word

**?** **SEE ALSO**

For more information about embedding, see "How to Embed," page 853. For more information about linking, see "How to Link," page 856.

processing document. When you want to edit those numbers, the original spreadsheet program reappears, allowing you to use its commands, instead of your word processor's, to do your editing.

When you *link* one document's data to a second document, the data you link isn't actually stored in the receiving document. Instead, the receiving program stores a visual representation of the data plus information about where the data came from. Continuing with our spreadsheet–word processor example, if you use a linking command to paste the spreadsheet numbers into your word processor document, the numbers look exactly as if you typed them in at the keyboard. But when you save that document to a disk file, the file doesn't include the numbers. Instead, it includes everything Windows needs to know to find those numbers again the next time you open the file. If you change the numbers in the spreadsheet, your changes also appear in your word processor document.

Embedding and linking also have one other important virtue: they allow you to incorporate material into your documents that your documents can't render directly. For example, you can embed or link a sound annotation or a video clip into documents created by most word processors, database managers, and spreadsheet programs. Those programs display an icon to indicate where the sound or video has been embedded or linked. When you want to hear the sound or see the video, you simply double-click the icon. Windows then renders the object, using the sound or video program in which the object originated.

**★** **TIP**

Many programs give you the option of displaying embedded or linked data as an icon, even if the program *can* render the data. For example, your word processor might permit you to embed a block of text but display it as an icon. The readers of your document can then skip over the embedded material if they're not interested in it. If they are interested, they can double-click the icon and read the embedded text.

# Using Cut, Copy, Paste, and Paste Special

As you probably know, the universal method for moving or copying an item from one place to another is as follows:

**1** Select whatever it is you want to move or copy—a block of text, a region within a graphical image, a range of spreadsheet cells, a file in a folder window, or whatever.

**2**   Choose the Cut command if you want to move the selected object. Choose the Copy command if you want to copy it. In virtually all Windows-based programs, these commands can be found on the Edit menu. In many programs, you can right-click and choose these commands from the shortcut menu.

**3**   Move to the place where you want the data transferred and choose Paste or Paste Special. Like Cut and Copy, these commands can be found on most programs' Edit menus. If you're pasting something onto the desktop or into a folder window, right-click and choose Paste from the shortcut menu.

Now that many programs support moving and copying via drag and drop, this cut-and-paste (or copy-and-paste) sequence is no longer the only way to relocate data in Windows documents. But it's probably still the most commonly used method, so let's take a look at what happens when you use these commands.

## The Clipboard: Windows' Invisible Transfer Agent

When you select data and use a program's Cut or Copy command, the selected data is stored on the Clipboard, an area of memory used to hold data in transit. When you use a program's Paste command, the Clipboard's data is copied into the program.

Data on the Clipboard usually remains there until new data arrives to replace it. That means that you can copy or cut something to the Clipboard, and then paste it as many times in as many places as you please. But as soon as you use another Cut or Copy command, the data you were previously pasting disappears from the Clipboard. (Some programs allow multiple Clipboard entries, but most do not.)

## Controlling the Outcome with Paste Special

When you cut or copy information from a program, the program supplies the information to the Clipboard in as many formats as it can. If you cut a paragraph in a Microsoft Word document, for example, Word transfers that paragraph to the Clipboard in both text and graphics formats. If you copy a spreadsheet range from Microsoft Excel, the Clipboard receives your selection in a large assortment of formats.

This multiple-format arrangement allows a program to receive Clipboard data in whichever format best suits it. For example, the fact that a Microsoft Word paragraph is stored on the Clipboard in both graphics and text formats means that you can paste it into Notepad, a program that accepts only text, as well as into other programs that accept only graphics.

The multiple-format arrangement also means that you often have choices about how to paste your data. When you use a program's Paste command, you get whatever format the program thinks you're most likely to want. But in many programs, you can use a Paste Special command and choose an alternative format. Figure D-1 shows an example of a Paste Special dialog box. In this example, the source data is a range of spreadsheet cells. If you want to paste an image of those cells, rather than the text contained in the cells, you can choose one of the available graphics formats: Picture, Bitmap, or Picture (Enhanced Metafile).

**FIGURE D-1.**
The Paste Special command lets you choose which format to paste, as well as whether to embed, link, or paste statically.

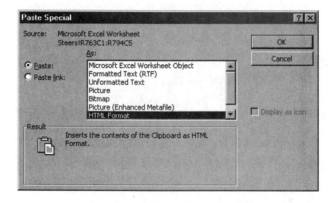

> **TIP**
>
> The Result section of the Paste Special dialog box often contains information about each available format. This information can help you decide which format to paste.

You can also use Paste Special to control whether Clipboard data is embedded, linked, or pasted statically.

# To Embed, to Link, or Merely to Paste?

Should you embed, should you link, or should you do neither? Here are a few guidelines.

Embedding's advantages are permanence and portability. Because the embedded object actually resides in the receiving program, you don't have to worry about what will happen if the source document becomes unavailable. Thus, for example, you'll want to choose embedding, not linking, if you plan to move the receiving document somewhere where it won't have access to the source document. (Of course, if changes are subsequently made to the source document, the version you embedded will no longer match the source.)

Linking has two advantages over embedding:

- The resulting compound document is smaller because it stores only a small amount of information describing the location and nature of the source object, not the object itself.

- Changes in the source data can be reflected automatically in the receiving document.

You should use linking when you want your compound document to stay current with its component sources over time.

What about plain old-fashioned static pasting? If the documents involved don't support OLE Linking and Embedding, of course, that is your only choice. For example, if you paste a paragraph from a Notepad document into your word processor, that paragraph arrives as static text because Notepad is a simple program that doesn't support OLE Linking and Embedding. Even with OLE-compatible source programs, though, a straightforward static paste might sometimes be more suitable than a fancy embedded object. You might know that a given bit of information won't need to be edited or updated in the future. Or you might find the convenience of editing an object in its source program is offset by the time required for Windows to launch that program. If that delay is vexing, don't embed. OLE Linking and Embedding is a service, not an obligation.

# How to Embed

In most cases, you can embed an object simply by selecting it in its source document and pasting it into its destination document. That's because when multiple formats are available on the Clipboard, the format that produces an embedded object is usually the default. It's not *always* the default, however. So if you want to be certain that you're embedding something and not simply pasting it statically, use the Paste Special command. In the list of available formats presented by the Paste Special dialog box, the one that does the embedding will typically have the word *object* somewhere in its name. When you select that option, the explanatory text at the bottom of the dialog box will probably include words such as *so that you can edit it using*, followed by the name of the source program.

For Newcomers to Windows

# Embedding a New Object

The previous paragraph assumes that the object you want to embed already exists somewhere in its source document. But what if it doesn't? Suppose, for example, that you're working in a Microsoft WordPad document and you want to embed a graphic that doesn't exist yet. In that case, you can go to the Start menu, launch your graphics program, create the object, copy it to the Clipboard, and so on. Alternatively, you can simply use the Object command on WordPad's Insert menu. Figure D-2 shows the dialog box you will see.

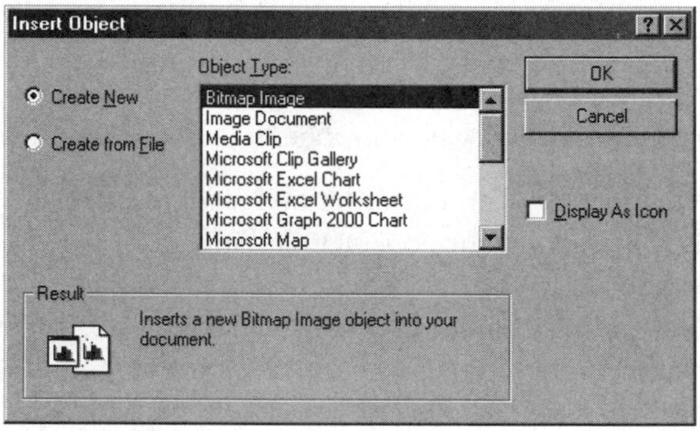

**FIGURE D-2.**

To embed an object that doesn't exist yet, you can use the Object command on the Insert menu.

The Object Type list in this dialog box enumerates all the embeddable data types known to the Windows registry. Select the type of object you want to embed, select the Display As Icon check box if you want the embedded object to appear as an icon, and click OK. Windows then either starts the program that's appropriate for the object type you selected or simply displays that program's menus and toolbars. At that point, you can create the object you want to embed. For example, if you are working in WordPad and select Bitmap Image as the object type, Windows replaces WordPad's menus with those of Microsoft Paint, the program with which the Bitmap Image object type is associated by default. Figure D-3 shows what you would see.

The menus and tools shown in Figure D-3 are those of Paint. The frame below the text is a Paint frame, embedded within a WordPad document. As long as the frame is selected, you can use Paint's menus and tools to create a bitmap image. When you finish, you can return to WordPad by simply selecting any part of the document outside the Paint frame.

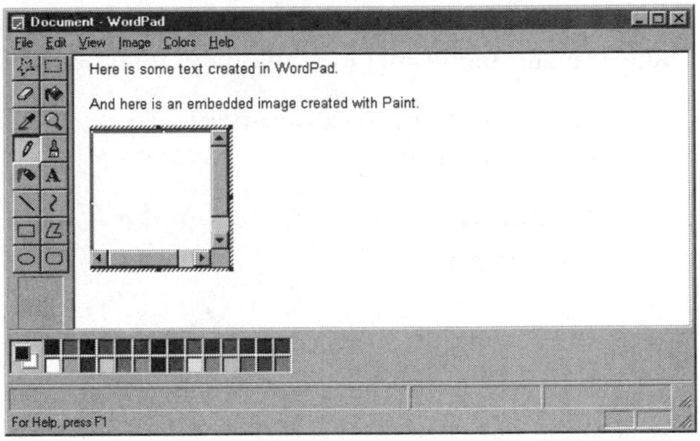

**FIGURE D-3.**

If you choose the Bitmap Image object type from WordPad's Object dialog box, Paint's menus and toolbars replace those of WordPad, allowing you to create a new bitmap object.

If you choose to have the embedded object displayed as an icon, or if the program you're working with doesn't support in-place editing, clicking OK in the Insert Object dialog box causes Windows to launch the program that creates the object, rather than simply displaying that program's menus and toolbars within the destination program. In that case, when you finish creating the object, you can embed it by choosing the Exit & Return To Document command, at the bottom of the File menu. Figure D-4 shows what you see if you choose the Insert Object command in WordPad, select Bitmap Image as the object type, and also select the Display As Icon check box.

**FIGURE D-4.**

If you choose to display a new embedded object as an icon, or if your program doesn't support in-place editing, Windows launches a full copy of the program with which the object type is associated.

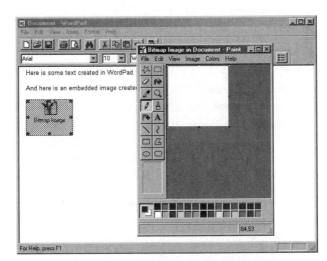

The copy of Paint shown in Figure D-4 is exactly like what you get by running Paint directly from your Start menu, except for its title bar and File menu. The title bar reveals the fact that this instance of Paint was launched for the purpose of creating (or editing) an embedded object, and the File menu includes two new commands:

- **Exit & Return To Document.** To quit Paint and update the containing document

- **Update Document.** To update the containing document without leaving Paint.

# How to Link

To link an object, follow these steps:

**1** Select the object in its source document and copy it to the Clipboard.

**2** Activate the destination document and place the insertion point where you want the linked object to go.

**3** Choose the Edit menu's Paste Link command. (If there is no Paste Link command, choose Paste Special, select the Object Type, and then choose the Paste Link option.)

This creates a link to the source document and displays the source object in the default format. If you prefer a different format, choose Paste Special instead of Paste Link. In the Paste Special dialog box, select the format you want and then choose Paste Link.

## Two Linking Hazards to Avoid

When you create a link, a visible change occurs in the destination document: new data arrives. At the same time, Windows makes a change in the source document, but this change isn't visible. The reason for the change in the source document is that the source document now has a new responsibility: it must notify the destination document whenever the linked object changes.

If you close the source document immediately after performing a paste link, you will be prompted to save your changes, even though you might not have done any editing in that document since your most recent save. Windows prompts you to save your changes because the document has assumed the responsibility of supplying a link. If you ignore the prompt, the data in the destination document will be correct (for the time being), but the link might be broken. To avoid this mishap, be sure to save the source document after performing a paste-link of an object into a destination document.

Another hazard arises when the source document is a spreadsheet. In a typical spreadsheet link, the source data is identified in the destination document by its cell coordinates. However, what happens to the link in this situation if someone working with the source document decides to add a few new rows or columns? Any such worksheet rearrangement can change the cell coordinates of the linked object and thereby invalidate the link—or worse, the link can remain valid as far as Windows is concerned, but it no longer contains the data you're interested in.

To avoid this trap, do the following:

**1** In the source document, name the cell or range you want to link.

**2** After you perform a paste-link into your destination document, use the Links command on the destination program's Edit menu to verify that the link is recorded by your worksheet range name, not by absolute cell coordinates.

**3** If the link isn't identified by the range name, edit the link, replacing the cell coordinates with the range name.

The exact procedure for editing the link depends on the destination program. In WordPad, for example, the Links dialog box includes a Change Source button. Clicking this button opens a dialog box, in which you can change the name of the source file or the description of the source object. As Figure D-5 shows, the source object is described in a box marked Item Name. To replace cell coordinates with a range name, simply type the range name into the Item Name box.

**FIGURE D-5.**

In WordPad, by choosing Links from the Edit menu and then clicking the Change Source button, you can change the description of the linked object.

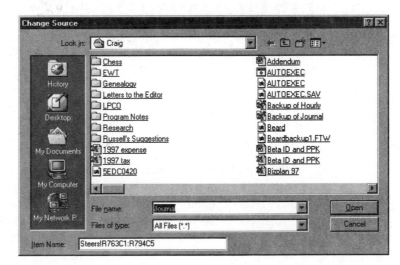

# Embedding or Linking a File

In all our examples so far, the source object to be linked or embedded has been a part of a file—for example, a range of spreadsheet cells, a paragraph in a word processing document, or a selection from a graphic image. You can also link or embed entire files. Depending on the type of file involved and your preferences, the destination document either displays the contents of the file or an icon representing the file.

To embed or link a file, choose the Object command (in many programs, it's called New Object) from the containing program's Insert menu, and then select the Create From File option. The object type list in the center of the dialog box is replaced by a File box and a Browse button, as shown in Figure D-6.

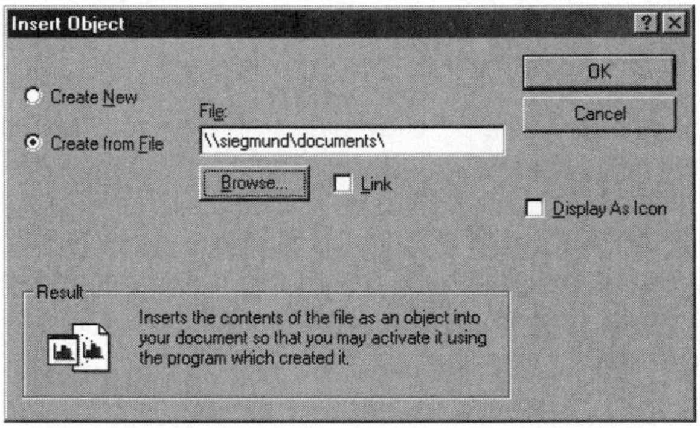

**FIGURE D-6.**

If you select the Create From File option, the Insert Object dialog box changes to let you type or browse for a filename to embed or link.

# Working with Embedded Objects

The simplest way to edit an embedded object is to double-click it. Depending on whether the object is fully visible or shown as an icon, and depending on the level of OLE Linking and Embedding support provided by your programs, the object either opens in the object's source program, or the source program's menus and toolbars appear in your current program. In either case, you edit the object using the facilities of the object's source program.

If you're editing from within the source program, choose the Exit & Return To Document command on that program's File menu when you're finished editing. This command closes the source program and returns you to the document in which the object is embedded.

If the menus and toolbars of the object's source program have replaced those of the destination program (that is, you are editing in place), simply select another part of the container document when you're finished editing the object. The original menus and toolbars then reappear.

Alternatively, you can edit an embedded object by selecting it and looking for an editing command at or near the bottom of the Edit menu. Figure D-7 shows what you see on WordPad's Edit menu when you select an embedded bitmap image.

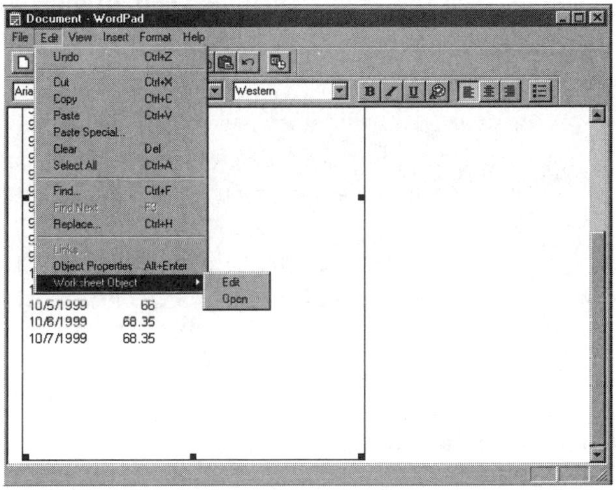

**FIGURE D-7.**

To edit an embedded object, simply double-click it. Or select it and look for an editing command on the Edit menu.

## Playing an Embedded Sound or Video Object

To play an embedded sound or video object, double-click it. Or, select the embedded object and choose the object command on your program's Edit menu. This command identifies the type of object you selected. If you select a sound clip created in Sound Recorder, for example, the command says *Sound Recorder Document Object*. When you choose this command, a submenu appears. Choose Play from the submenu to play the embedded object.

## Modifying the Properties of an Embedded Object

Like just about everything else in Windows 2000, embedded objects have properties that can be inspected and modified. To open the properties dialog box for an embedded object, you can do any of the following:

- Right-click the object and choose Object Properties from the shortcut menu.

- Select the object and press Alt+Enter.

- Select the object and choose Object Properties from the Edit menu (if you're working in a context where there is an Edit menu).

Depending on the type of object, its properties dialog box might let you do such things as switch between a rendered and an iconic display of the object or change the object's display size.

**TIP**
If the selected object is displayed as an icon, you can use the object's properties dialog box to change the icon, the icon's caption, or both. Even if you're content with the default icon, you might want to replace the default caption with something descriptive. *Picture of Mom*, for example, might serve your needs better than *Bitmap Image*. To do so, click the Change Icon button in the properties dialog box, and then modify the Label text.

# Working with Links

When a data object is linked to a document, changes to the object are reflected in the destination document. Whether they're reflected automatically or only on demand is up to you. Most (but not all) programs create automatic links by default. In any case, you can switch between automatic and manual linking by opening the properties dialog box for the link in question. Open the linked object's properties dialog box in one of the three ways just described for embedded objects. Figure D-8 shows an example of a linked object's properties dialog box.

**TIP**
If your destination program doesn't include an Object Properties command, look for a Links command on the Edit menu. That command displays a list of all links in the current document. By selecting an item in the list and choosing command buttons in the Links dialog box, you can switch between automatic and manual linking, update the link, open the source document for editing, break the link, or change the source document.

To switch between automatic and manual linking, go to the Link tab in the properties dialog box and choose the appropriate option under

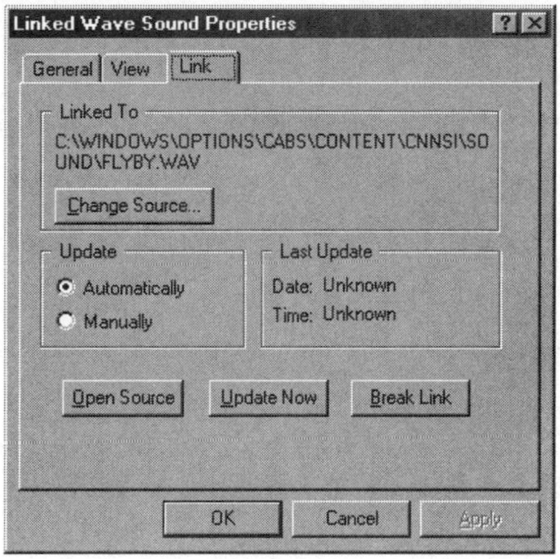

**FIGURE D-8.**

The Link tab lets you switch between automatic and manual linking, update the link, open the object's source document for editing, sever the object from its source document, or specify a different source document.

Update. If you choose Manually, you can refresh the containing document by clicking the Update Now button. If you choose Automatically, the containing document is refreshed any time the source document changes.

## Another Linking Hazard

Under certain circumstances, an automatic link might *not* reflect the current state of the source document. Here's how it can happen:

**1**  You double-click the linked object to edit it in its source program.

**2**  You change the object in the source program, and the link is updated appropriately.

**3**  You close the source program without saving changes.

After this sequence, the source document reverts to its former state (because you didn't save your changes in the source program), but the destination document does not. The two documents are now out of step with one another.

To be absolutely sure that all links in a destination document—both automatic and manual—are up-to-date, follow these steps:

**1**  In the destination document, choose the Links command from the Edit menu.

**2**  In the Links dialog box, select the first link listed. Then scroll to the bottom of the list and hold down the Shift key while selecting the last link listed. (This selects all links in the list.)

**3**  Click the Update Now button.

## Breaking a Link

If you no longer want a linked object to reflect changes in the object's source, visit the Link tab in the object's properties dialog box, and then click the Break Link button. If it can, Windows converts the item to an embedded object.

# Using Scrap Files to Save and Share OLE Objects

Windows Explorer is an OLE Linking and Embedding program. That means you can embed data objects in folders or on your desktop. So, for example, if you want to use a particular image repeatedly, you can drag it out of a Paint window to a Windows Explorer window or onto the desktop. To reuse it in your word processor, simply drag it again to the receiving document.

OLE objects in folders or on the desktop are called *scrap files*. When you create such an object, Windows gives it a default name based on its contents or source, such as "WordPad Document Scrap 'Now is the time...'" You can assign your own name by pressing F2 and typing the name.

A scrap file must originate in a program that supports OLE Linking and Embedding as a source. If the program also supports OLE drag and drop, you can create the scrap by simply dragging the object. If not, select the object in its source program, choose the Copy command, and then move to your folder or to the desktop and choose Paste.

By storing scrap files in a shared folder, you can make OLE objects on your system available to other network users. Similarly, by opening a shared folder on a server, you can access OLE objects stored on that server. To embed a server-based scrap file, for example, simply open the network folder in which the scrap resides, using My Network Places or a mapped folder. Then drag the object to wherever you want it to go. Alternatively, select the object in the network folder, and then paste it into an application or local folder.

To activate a network scrap object's parent application, either for editing purposes or to render an object that's embedded as an icon, you must have a local copy of the parent application.

# Index

Advanced Attributes dialog
box, *597*
Advanced Configuration and
Power Interface (ACPI),
7, 505
Advanced Download Options
dialog box, *348*
Advanced Power Management.
*See* APM
Advanced Scheduling Options
dialog box, *259*
Advanced Settings For
FilterKeys dialog box,
*132*
Airbrush tool, 726–27
aligning
objects on fax cover page, 442
text in WordPad, 703–4
All Users profile, *34*
Always On Top option
(Taskbar And Start Menu
Properties dialog box),
*49*
Analysis Report dialog box,
*656*
annotating images, 784–87, *786*
announcing Phone Dialer conferences, 477
APIPA (Automatic Private IP
Addressing), 275
APM (Advanced Power
Management)
enabling or disabling, 544–47,
*545*
standards for ACPI and, 543–44
support for on Windows 2000
server editions, 546
APM tab (Power Options Properties dialog box), *545*
appearance schemes
modifying, 64, *64*
saving, 68
toggling between, 121
Appearance tab (Display Properties dialog box), *64*
application log, 670
applications. *See also specific
Windows 2000 programs
listed by name*
adding or removing components
of, 264
changing file type association of,
170
checking Windows compatibility
of, 809

applications, *continued*
hanging up, 661, 831, *831*
importing Address Book data
from, 307–9, *308*
installing new, 262, *263*
launching with embedded icon
displayed, 854–55, *854,
855*
moving, 264
opening documents in different,
150–51, *150*
parent
changing for file type, 151
opening documents not having, 151
printing documents from Print
dialog box, 216–19, *217*
running, 149–51, 253–60
overview, 253
with Run command, 254
as scheduled tasks, 257–60,
*258, 259, 260*
at startup, 256, *257*
under different user account,
254–55, *255*
sending faxes from, 435–38,
*436, 437*
sharing with NetMeeting, 464–
65, *464*
uninstalling, 25, 263–64, 652
using My Network Places with,
178, *179*
Applications tab (Task Manager), *679*
Apply button, 101
Approved Sites tab (Content
Advisor dialog box), *367*
archive attribute, 167, 607
archiving logs, 677
arithmetic operations in scientific Calculator, 752–53
arrows, indicating Briefcase
updates, *202*
ASCII characters, 244
ASCII files, 495
ASCII Setup dialog box, 494,
*495*
assigning
permissions to shared folders,
186–88, *187*
rights to users and groups,
577–78, *577, 578–79*
shortcut keys, 27
asterisk (*), 209
attached files, 309, 397

attack bumpers, *791*
attributes
adding font, 701
archive, 167, 607
setting for folders, files, and
shortcuts, 167–68
Attributes dialog box, *719*
audio CDs. *See* CD Player
Audio tab (Options dialog
box), *456*
Audio/Video tab (Options
dialog box), *482*
audit events, 670
Authenticated Users group, 563
Auto Arrange feature, 88–90,
*89*
AutoComplete
clearing entries for, 375–76
entering Web addresses with,
329–30
setting options for, 375–76, *375*
AutoComplete Settings dialog
box, *375*
Auto Hide option (Taskbar And
Start Menu Properties
dialog box), *49*
Automatically Log On dialog
box, *829*
automatic backups, 625–28,
*626, 627, 628*
automatic e-mail replies, 407
automatic linking, 860–61, *861*
Automatic Private IP Addressing (APIPA), 275
automatic synchronization,
198–99, *199*
automatic synchronization
reminders, 196–97
avoiding broken links, 861

**B**

Back button, 146, *146*
Back command, *323,* 331
background color
choosing for Paint drawing, 718
in e-mail messages, 395
indicator for, *714*
background images
adding to folder, 92–93, *93, 94*
for folders, *93*
as pictures in e-mail messages,
395

First line header.

# About the Authors

**Craig Stinson** An industry journalist since 1981, Craig Stinson is a contributing editor of *PC Magazine* and was formerly editor of *Softalk for the IBM Personal Computer*. Craig is author of *Running Microsoft Windows 98* and coauthor of *Running Microsoft Excel 2000*, both published by Microsoft Press. Craig is an amateur musician and has reviewed classical music for various newspapers and trade publications, including *Billboard*, the *Boston Globe*, the *Christian Science Monitor*,  and *Musical America*. He lives with his wife and children in Littleton, Colorado.

Craig can be reached at **craigstinson@free-market.net**

**Carl Siechert** began his writing career at age 8 as editor of the Mesita Road News, a neighborhood newsletter that reached a peak worldwide circulation of 43 during its eight-year run. Following several years as an estimator and production manager in a commercial printing business, Carl returned to writing with the formation of Siechert & Wood Professional Documentation, a Pasadena, California firm that specializes in writing and producing books and product documentation for

the personal computer industry. Carl is a coauthor of *Field Guide to Microsoft Works for Windows 95* and *Running Microsoft Windows NT Workstation*, both published by Microsoft Press. Carl hiked the Pacific Crest Trail from Mexico to Canada in 1977 and would rather be hiking right now. He and his wife, Jan, live in southern California.

Carl can be reached at **carl@swdocs.com**

# Colophon

The manuscript for this book was prepared and submitted to Microsoft Press in electronic form. Text files were prepared using Microsoft Word 2000. Pages were composed using Adobe PageMaker 6.52 for Windows, with text in Garamond and display type in Myriad. Composed pages were sent to the printer as electronic prepress files.

**Cover Graphic Design**

Girvin | Strategic Branding & Design

**Interior Graphic Designer**

Amy Peppler Adams, designLab

**Production Management**

Publishing.com

**Copy Editor**

Chrisa Hotchkiss

**Technical Editor**

Curtis Philips

**Layout Artist**

Lisa Bravo

**Proofreader**

Andrea Fox

**Indexer**

Rebecca Plunkett

**OWNER REGISTRATION CARD**    *Register Today!*    1-57231-838-4

Return the bottom portion of this card to register today.

## *Running Microsoft® Windows® 2000 Professional*

_____    _____    _____

**FIRST NAME**          **MIDDLE INITIAL**       **LAST NAME**

_____

**INSTITUTION OR COMPANY NAME**

_____

**ADDRESS**

_____

_____    _____    _____

**CITY**                        **STATE**     **ZIP**

_____    ( )

**E-MAIL ADDRESS**          **PHONE NUMBER**

U.S. and Canada addresses only. Fill in information above and mail postage-free.
Please mail only the bottom half of this page.

*For information about Microsoft Press®*
*products, visit our Web site at*
**mspress.microsoft.com**

**Microsoft**®*Press*